ANNUAL DIGEST OF
PUBLIC INTERNATIONAL LAW CASES
1927–28

CAMBRIDGE
UNIVERSITY PRESS

University Printing House, Cambridge CB2 8BS, United Kingdom

Cambridge University Press is part of the University of Cambridge.

It furthers the University's mission by disseminating knowledge in the pursuit of education, learning and research at the highest international levels of excellence.

www.cambridge.org
Information on this title: www.cambridge.org/9780521463492

First published by Messrs. Longman, Green and Co. 1932
Reprinted by Grotius Publications Ltd 1981
Reprinted by Cambridge University Press 2004, 2006
3rd printing 2016

Printed in Singapore by Markono Print Media Pte Ltd

A catalogue record for this publication is available from the British Library

ISBN-13 978-0-521-46349-2 hardback
ISBN-10 0-521-46349-1 hardback

DEPARTMENT OF INTERNATIONAL STUDIES OF THE
LONDON SCHOOL OF ECONOMICS AND POLITICAL SCIENCE
(UNIVERSITY OF LONDON)

ANNUAL DIGEST OF PUBLIC INTERNATIONAL LAW CASES

Being a Selection from the Decisions of International and National Courts and Tribunals given during the

YEARS 1927 and 1928

EDITORS

ARNOLD D. McNAIR, C.B.E., LL.D.

FELLOW OF GONVILLE AND CAIUS COLLEGE; READER IN PUBLIC INTERNATIONAL LAW IN THE UNIVERSITY OF CAMBRIDGE; ASSOCIATE OF THE INSTITUTE OF INTERNATIONAL LAW

AND

H. LAUTERPACHT, LL.D., Dr. Jur., Dr. Sc. Pol.

LECTURER IN PUBLIC INTERNATIONAL LAW IN THE LONDON SCHOOL OF ECONOMICS AND POLITICAL SCIENCE

GROTIUS PUBLICATIONS
CAMBRIDGE
UNIVERSITY PRESS

CONTRIBUTORS

DECISIONS OF INTERNATIONAL COURTS AND TRIBUNALS:

Dr. H. Lauterpacht

(except those of the Mixed Claims Commission between France and Mexico which have been digested by Professor J. H. W. Verzijl, President of the Commission)

DECISIONS OF NATIONAL COURTS:

Dr. B. Akzin	Latvia.
Mr. Norman Bentwich	Egypt, Palestine and Syria.
Professor Arrigo Cavaglieri	Italy.
Dr. Georg Cohn	Denmark.
Professor A. Decencière-Ferrandière	France.
Professor Edwin DeWitt Dickinson	United States of America.
Professor Ludwik Ehrlich	Poland.
Professor Francis Faluhelyi	Hungary.
Mr. C. Kruse Jensen	Norway.
Professor E. Korovine	Russia.
Dr. Lauterpacht	Germany and Danzig.
Professor R. W. Lee	Union of South Africa.
Professor Barbosa de Magalhães	Portugal.
Dr. McNair	Great Britain and Northern Ireland.
Professor K. Mori	Japan.
Professor Mileta Novakovitch	Yugoslavia.
Professor Julius I. Puente	Central and South America.
Dr. E. Sandström	Sweden.
Professor Dietrich Schindler	Switzerland.
Dr. Jan Slmák	Czechoslovakia.
Professor H. A. Smith	British Dominions and Colonies (except the Union of South Africa).
Professor C. G. Ténékidès	Greece.
Professor Alfred Verdross	Austria.
Professor J. H. W. Verzijl	Holland.
Professor Fernand de Vischer	Belgium.

PREFACE

For the object and the scheme of this series we beg leave to refer to the Preface to the first volume, published in 1929 and covering the years 1925 and 1926.

The reception with which that volume met, and the evidence of the use which is being made of it by practitioners, by writers, and by students, have determined us to continue the series. The present volume, covering the years 1927 and 1928, consists of 389 digests, of which 172 come from the decisions of international courts and tribunals, and the remainder from those of national courts. (Of the total, 20 belong to the years 1925 and 1926.) As in the previous volume, most countries are represented, but in a few cases a search has yielded no decisions requiring to be digested.

To the contributors of digests of national decisions, whose names will be found on the page following the title-page, we must again express our sincere gratitude. In most cases the actual yield of relevant digests very inadequately reflects the amount of labour expended by our contributors in the examination of the law reports of their countries. In many cases we felt bound to take upon ourselves the responsibility of omitting digests submitted, on the ground that the international element contained in them was not of sufficiently general importance to justify their inclusion in a limited volume of this nature. We must again make it clear that our contributors must not be held responsible either for the selection of the decisions representing their respective countries or for the final form of the digests of those decisions. The notes appended to some of the digests are the work of the contributors except when they are followed by the letters : " Ed."

To the members of our Advisory Committee we are once more greatly indebted for the very practical interest which they have shown in our work by advice in planning the volume and in the selection of the digests, and by reading a very large number of the digests in proof. This help has in some cases involved them in heavy work and much personal inconvenience. They have left the final word to us, and, while we acknowledge the value of their help in the most emphatic manner, it must be clearly understood that they cannot be held responsible for the form or the substance of the volume, or for any views expressed in the notes.

From reviewers and users of the first volume we have received useful criticism and suggestions. Certain criticism indicates that a few further words of explanation of the objects of this series are desirable. In the first place, these volumes are not case-books but digests ; they are intended to stimulate and facilitate recourse to the actual decisions, and not to render that unnecessary. In the second place, it seems to us to follow from the conception of a digest that a decision in which several distinct points of law are discussed and decided usually requires to be dissected into a number of different entries, each appearing in its appropriate place in the classification ; the Island of Palmas Award is a case in point.

To the Governors and the Director of the London School of Economics and Political Science and to the publishers, Messrs. Longmans, Green and Co., we are again grateful for the public spirit which is necessary in the early stages of a series of volumes of this character. Both our publishers and our printers, Messrs. T. and A. Constable Limited, of the University Press, Edinburgh, have given us, patiently and ungrudgingly, the advice and care which we have learned to expect from them. We must also thank Mrs. Marjorie Candler (*née* Owen), Barrister-at-Law, and Mr. S. H. Bailey, M.A., both of the

London School of Economics and Political Science, for translating a number of the digests into English.

The next two volumes to appear will cover the six years 1919 to 1924 inclusive. They are being edited by Sir John Fischer Williams and Dr. Lauterpacht, and the contributors have already been at work in collecting the material for some months past. The undertaking of these two volumes has been made possible by the generosity of the Carnegie Endowment for International Peace (Division of International Law under the direction of Dr. James Brown Scott), of the Benchers of Gray's Inn, the Inner Temple, Lincoln's Inn and the Middle Temple, and, once more, of the Governors and the Director of the London School of Economics and Political Science. These two volumes will be published late in 1932 or early in 1933.

ARNOLD D. McNAIR.
H. LAUTERPACHT.

DEPARTMENT OF INTERNATIONAL STUDIES,
LONDON SCHOOL OF ECONOMICS AND POLITICAL SCIENCE,
ALDWYCH,
LONDON, W.C. 2.
1st October 1931.

The correct method of citation of cases in this volume is as follows:

Annual Digest, 1927-1928, Case No.

TABLE OF CONTENTS

(*See also* Classification)

PART VI

PART VII

PART VIII

PART IX

PART X

PART XI

TABLE OF CASES DIGESTED

(ALPHABETICAL)

[References are to pages.]

[References are to pages.]

[References are to pages.]

[References are to pages.]

[References are to pages.]

[References are to pages.]

TABLE OF CASES DIGESTED

I. DECISIONS OF INTERNATIONAL COURTS AND TRIBUNALS

Permanent Court of International Justice

Permanent Court of Arbitration

[References are to pages.]

France and Mexico : Mixed Claims Commission

Mixed Arbitral Tribunals

Rhineland Occupation Agreement Interpretation Committee

[References are to pages.]

Special Arbitral Tribunals

United States, Austria, and Hungary (Tripartite Claims Commission)

United States and Germany: Mixed Claims Commission

United States and Mexico: General Claims Commission

Upper Silesian Arbitral Tribunal

[References are to pages.]

II. DECISIONS OF NATIONAL COURTS[1]

[References are to pages.]

[1] As in some countries it is not the practice to state the names of the parties in reporting cases, we have ventured to invent titles for these cases in the interest of convenience of citation.

[References are to pages.]

[References are to pages.]

[References are to pages.]

[References are to pages.]

TABLE OF CASES CITED

LIST OF ABBREVIATIONS

OF TITLES OF COLLECTIONS OF DECISIONS, LAW REPORTS, TREATISES, PERIODICALS, ETC., QUOTED IN THE TEXT

A.C.	= British House of Lords and Judicial Committee of the Privy Council.
A.J.	= The American Journal of International Law.
Annuaire	= Annuaire de l'Institut de Droit International.
B. and C.P.C.	= British and Colonial Prize Cases.
Boh.	= Collection of the Decisions of the Czechoslovak Supreme Administrative Court (Sbírka nalezů nejvyššího spravniho soudu). Edited by Bohuslav. This Collection contains two series: decisions in administrative matters, abbreviated "adm.", and decisions in financial matters, abbreviated "fin."
B.Y.	= British Year Book of International Law.
Ch.	= Chancery Division of the English High Court of Justice.
Clunet	= Journal du droit international.
Dickinson, Cases	= Dickinson, Cases and Other Readings on the Law of Nations (1929).
Fauchille	= Fauchille, Traité de droit international public, 8th ed. of Bonfils' Manuel de droit international public, vol. i., part 1 (1922), part 2 (1925), part 3 (1926), vol. ii. (1921).
Fed.	= Federal Reporter (United States).
Hague Recueil	= Recueil des cours, Académie de Droit International de La Haye.
H.L.R.	= Harvard Law Review.
Hudson, Cases	= Hudson, Cases and Other Materials on International Law (1929).
Hyde	= Hyde, International Law chiefly as Interpreted and Applied by the United States, 2 vols. (1922).

J.C.L.	= Journal of Comparative Legislation and International Law.
K.B.	= King's Bench Division of the English High Court of Justice.
Lafontaine	= Lafontaine, Pasicrisie Internationale (1902).
Lapradelle-Politis	= Lapradelle-Politis, Recueil des arbitrages internationaux, vol. i. (1905), vol. ii. (1924).
L.J.	= Law Journal Reports.
L.Q.R.	= Law Quarterly Review.
L.T.	= Law Times Reports.
Martens, N.R.G.	= Martens, Recueil de Traités (Nouveau Recueil Général).
Moore	= Moore, History and Digest of International Arbitrations to which the United States has been a Party, 6 vols. (1898).
Moore, Digest	= Moore, A Digest of International Law, 8 vols. (1906).
Nielsen	= American and British Claims Arbitration (under the special agreement of August 18, 1910), Report by Nielsen (1926).
N.R.G.	= See Martens.
Opinions of Commissioners	= United States and Mexico General Claims Commission under the Convention of September 8, 1923 (1927).
Oppenheim	= Oppenheim, International Law, 4th ed. by McNair, vol. ii. (1926), vol. i. (1928).
O.S.P.	= Orzecznictwo Sądów Polskich (an unofficial collection of decisions of Polish Courts).
P.	= Probate, Divorce and Admiralty Division of the English High Court of Justice.
P.C.I.J.	= Permanent Court of International Justice. Series A—Judgments. B—Advisory Opinions. C—Acts and Documents relating to Judgments and Advisory Opinions given by the Court.[1] D—Collection of Texts Governing the Jurisdiction of the Court. E—Annual Reports. F—General Index.
P.P.A.	= Przegląd Prawa i Administracji.

[1] In particular, the attention of the reader is drawn to the records of the oral proceedings, the cases and counter-cases submitted by the Parties, and the legal opinions of writers on international law printed in this Series.

Ralston	=	Ralston, The Law and Procedure of International Tribunals, revised ed. (1926).
Ralston, Arbitrations	=	Ralston, Venezuelan Arbitrations of 1903 (1904).
Recueil	=	Recueil des décisions des tribunaux arbitraux mixtes.
R.G.	=	Revue générale de droit international public.
R.I.	=	Revue de droit international et de la législation comparée.
R.I. (Paris)	=	Revue de droit international.
Rivista	=	Rivista di diritto internazionale.
R.O.	=	Arrêts du Tribunal Fédéral Suisse, Recueil officiel.
R.P.E.S.	=	Ruch Prawniczy, Ekonomiczny i Społeczny.[1]
Sirey	=	Recueil général des lois et des arrêts (founded by Sirey).
T.L.R.	=	Times Law Reports.
U.S.	=	United States Reports (Supreme Court).
Váž.	=	Collection of the Decisions of the Czechoslovak Supreme Court of Justice (Sbírka rozhodnutí nejvyššího soudu). Edited by Vážný. The Collection contains two series: decisions in civil and commercial matters, abbreviated "civ.", and in criminal matters, abbreviated "cr."
Zb. O.S.N.	=	Zbiór Orzeczeń Sądu Najwyższego (Collection of the Decisions of the Polish Supreme Court).
Z.W.N.T.A.	=	Zbiór Wyroków Najwyższego Trybunału Administracyjnego (Collection of the Decisions of the Polish Supreme Administrative Court).
Z. für a. ö. R. und V.	=	Zeitschrift für ausländisches öffentliches Recht und Völkerrecht.
Z.I.	=	Zeitschrift für internationales Recht.
Z.V.	=	Zeitschrift für Völkerrecht.

[1] This periodical contains only brief digests and headnotes of decisions.

CLASSIFICATION

PART I

INTERNATIONAL LAW IN GENERAL

I. NATURE AND BINDING FORCE.

II. EXTENT.

III. SOURCES. *See also* PART X, ARBITRATION: The Law Applied by Arbitral Tribunals.

IV. SUBJECTS OF INTERNATIONAL LAW. *See* PART VI, THE INDIVIDUAL IN INTERNATIONAL LAW: In General; *and* PART VIII, TREATIES: Operation and Enforcement of Treaties.

V. RELATION TO MUNICIPAL LAW. *See also* PART VIII, TREATIES: Operation and Enforcement of Treaties.

VI. INTERNATIONAL COMITY.

VII. MISCELLANEOUS.

PART II

STATES AS INTERNATIONAL PERSONS

A. IN GENERAL

I. BEGINNING OF STATE EXISTENCE. (For RECOGNITION, *see below*, D.)

II. SOVEREIGNTY AND INDEPENDENCE—

i. In Foreign Relations. *See also below*, Recognition of Acts of Foreign States and Governments; PART IV, JURISDICTION; *and* PART VIII, TREATIES: Interpretation of Treaties—Restrictive Interpretation.

ii. In Matters of Domestic Jurisdiction.

iii. Acts of Sovereignty and Transactions of a Private Character. *See also* PART IV, JURISDICTION: Exemptions from.

III. EQUALITY OF STATES.

IV. RECOGNITION OF ACTS OF FOREIGN STATES AND GOVERNMENTS. *See also* PART IV, JURISDICTION: Territorial; *and below*, Recognition of States, Governments and Belligerency.

V. CONTINUITY OF STATES. *See also* STATE SUCCESSION.

VI. EXTINCTION OF STATES.

B. COMPOSITE AND DEPENDENT STATES AND TERRITORIES

I. UNIONS OF STATES—

i. Federal States and Confederations.
ii. Other Unions (including Customs Unions).

II. BRITISH COMMONWEALTH OF NATIONS.

III. PROTECTED AND VASSAL STATES AND PROTECTORATES.

IV. MANDATES—

i. Sovereignty over Mandated Territories. Status of the Mandated Territories.
ii. Rights and Duties of the Mandatories.
iii. Rights and Duties of the League.
iv. Equality of Opportunity.
v. Nationality in Mandated Territories.
vi. Other Matters.

V. TERRITORIES UNDER JOINT OR INTERNATIONAL GOVERNMENT.

C. NEUTRALISATION AND DEMILITARISATION

I. OF STATES.

II. OF PARTS OF STATE TERRITORY.

III. OF PARTS OF THE HIGH SEAS. *See also* PART III, CANALS.

D. RECOGNITION. *See also above,* Recognition of Acts of Foreign States and Governments; *and* PART IV, JURISDICTION: Territorial.

i. Of States.
ii. Of Governments.
iii. Of Insurgency.
iv. Of Belligerency.
v. Conditional Recognition.

E. STATE SUCCESSION

I. SUCCESSION IN RIGHTS.

II. SUCCESSION WITH REGARD TO CONTRACTUAL AND OTHER OBLIGATIONS, AND CONCESSIONS.

PART III

STATE TERRITORY

B. PARTS OF STATE TERRITORY

I. Boundaries—
- i. Land Boundaries.
- ii. Water Boundaries.

II. Rivers—
- i. National Rivers.
- ii. Multi-national Rivers.
- iii. International Rivers.
  - (*a*) The Principle of Freedom of Navigation on International Rivers.
  - (*b*) Functions and Competence of International Commissions on International Rivers.
- iv. The Utilisation of the Flow of Non-National and International Rivers.

III. Territorial Waters—
- i. Nature of the Maritime Belt.
- ii. Breadth of the Maritime Belt.
- iii. Jurisdiction in the Maritime Belt.
- iv. Coasting Trade and Fisheries. *See* Part IV, Jurisdiction : Territorial.

IV. National Waters.

V. Straits.

VI. Bays.

VII. Canals, International—
- i. In Time of Peace.
- ii. In Time of War.

VIII. Lakes and Land-Locked Seas.

IX. Islands.

X. State Servitudes.

C. MISCELLANEOUS

PART IV

JURISDICTION

A. JURISDICTION IN GENERAL. TERRITORIAL AND PERSONAL

I. Territorial—

(*a*) Over Territory in General and Persons and Property Situated therein. Expropriation of Alien Property ;
See also Part II, Recognition of Acts of Foreign States and Governments, *and* Recognition of Foreign States and Governments.

(*b*) Criminal Jurisdiction over Foreigners.
(*c*) Over Ports and National Waters. *See also* PART III, TERRITORIAL WATERS.
(*d*) At the Maritime Frontier. Hovering Laws. *See also* HIGH SEAS.
(*e*) Coasting Trade.
(*f*) Fisheries.
(*g*) Exemptions from and Restrictions upon Territorial Jurisdiction.
(i) Foreign States. *See also* PART II, SOVEREIGNTY AND INDEPENDENCE: Acts of Sovereignty and Transactions of a Private Character.
(ii) Heads of Foreign States.
(iii) Public Ships and other Property of Foreign States.
(iv) Foreign Armed Forces.
(v) Diplomatic Immunities. *See* PART VII.

II. PERSONAL—
(*a*) Over Subjects in Respect of Crimes Committed outside the Realm ;
(*b*) Over Subjects Abroad or on the High Seas and their Property Situated Abroad.

B. EXTRATERRITORIAL JURISDICTION

I. CONSULAR JURISDICTIONS. RÉGIME OF CAPITULATIONS. MIXED COURTS. JURISDICTION AND ORGANISATION.

C. HIGH SEAS

I. CONCEPTION OF THE HIGH SEAS AND OF THE FREEDOM OF THE SEA.

II. JURISDICTION ON THE HIGH SEAS. *See also* JURISDICTION.
i. For Ensuring the Safety of Traffic. Collisions. Salvage.
ii. For Enforcement of International Conventions.
iii. Visit, Search and Arrest by Men-of-War in Time of Peace.
iv. The Law Governing the Flag. Ship's Papers.
v. Right of Pursuit.
vi. Enforcement of Hovering, Revenue and other Municipal Laws.
vii. Piracy.

See also PART III, TERRITORIAL WATERS, BAYS *and* STRAITS.

III. SUBMARINE CABLES—
i. In Time of Peace.
ii. In Time of War.

D. MISCELLANEOUS

PART V

STATE RESPONSIBILITY

A. WHERE DOES RESPONSIBILITY REST IN FEDERAL AND OTHER COMPOSITE STATES?

B. NATURE AND KINDS OF STATE RESPONSIBILITY

I. In General. When does State Responsibility become Engaged? Absolute Responsibility and Responsibility based on Fault.

II. For Breaches of Treaty Obligations.

III. For Revocation of, or Interference with, Concessions or Concessionary Contracts.

IV. For Debts.

V. For Other Breaches of Contractual Obligations.

VI. For Wrongs Unconnected with Contractual Obligations—

(*a*) Acts and Omissions of State Organs and Officials.

i. Denial of Justice. Exhaustion of Legal Remedies.

ii. Executive Action or Inaction.

iii. Connected with Legislation.

iv. Connected with Use of Adjacent Land or Water. *See also* Part III, Rivers.

v. Plea of Non-Discrimination against Foreigners. *See also* Part IV, Territorial Jurisdiction: Expropriation.

(*b*) Acts of Insurgents, Rioters and Private Individuals in General.

VII. For Acts and Omissions of Revolutionary or *de facto* Governments.

C. CLAIMS

I. In General.

II. Nationality of Claims.

III. Assignment of Claims.

IV. State Control over Private Claims.

D. PRESCRIPTION (EXTINCTIVE PRESCRIPTION)

I. Before International Tribunals.

II. Effect of Municipal Statutes of Limitation.

III. Effect of War.

E. DAMAGES (MEASURE OF DAMAGES)

I. Award of Damages in General. Grounds for Awarding Damages.

II. Indirect Damages and Damages for Loss of Profits.

III. Punitive and Exemplary Damages.

F. INTEREST

I. In General.

II. Rate of Interest. Compound Interest.

III. The *Dies a Quo*. The *Dies ad Quem*.

G. MISCELLANEOUS

PART VI

THE INDIVIDUAL IN INTERNATIONAL LAW

A. IN GENERAL

I. Position of Individuals in International Law. *See also* Part I, International Law in General: Relation to Municipal Law; *and* Part VIII, Treaties: Operation and Enforcement of Treaties.

II. Before International Tribunals.

B. NATIONALITY

I. In General.

II. As Affected by Changes of Sovereignty.

III. As Determining the Right of Protection of Citizens Abroad.

IV. Protected Persons and *de facto* Subjects.

V. NATURALISATION.

VI. EXPATRIATION. LOSS OF NATIONALITY.

VII. DENATIONALISATION.

VIII. DOUBLE NATIONALITY.

IX. OPTION.

X. STATELESSNESS.

XI. NATIONALITY OF CORPORATIONS. *See also* PART XI, WAR AND NEUTRALITY: Enemy Character.

C. ALIENS

I. ADMISSION OF ALIENS.

II. POSITION OF ALIENS—

i. Subjection to Territorial Sovereignty of the Receiving State.
ii. Protection by the National State.
iii. Treatment by and Responsibilities of the Receiving State. *See also* PART V, STATE RESPONSIBILITY.
iv. Plea of Non-Discrimination. *See* PART V, STATE RESPONSIBILITY.
v. Respect for Property. Expropriation. *See* PART IV, JURISDICTION: Territorial.

III. EXPULSION OF ALIENS—

i. Rights of Expulsion.
ii. Procedure of Expulsion.
iii. Reception of Expelled Nationals.

D. EXTRADITION

I. EXTRADITION IN GENERAL.

II. EXTRADITABLE CRIMES.

III. EXTRADITION OF NATIONALS.

IV. CONDITIONS OF EXTRADITION.

V. PROCEDURE OF EXTRADITION.

VI. POLITICAL CRIMINALS.

E. MINORITIES (PROTECTION OF MINORITIES)

I. MINORITY TREATIES AND THEIR INTERPRETATION.

II. ENFORCEMENT OF MINORITY TREATIES THROUGH THE LEAGUE OF NATIONS AND PROCEDURE WITH REGARD TO PROTECTION OF MINORITIES.

PART VII

DIPLOMATIC AND CONSULAR INTERCOURSE AND PRIVILEGES

VI. Members of International Commissions, and Officials of International Unions and Similar Bodies.

D. CONSULS

I. Appointment and Exequatur.

II. Position and Function of Consuls.

III. Privileges and Immunities of Consuls.

E. MISCELLANEOUS

PART VIII

TREATIES

I. Conception of Treaties as International Contracts.

II. Forms of International Agreement and Methods by which they are Concluded—

i. Treaties. Conventions. Governmental Agreements. Exchanges of Notes.

ii. Signature. Accession and Adhesion.

III. Multilateral Treaties.

IV. Conditions of Validity of Treaties. Registration of Treaties.

V. Parties to Treaties. Right to Conclude Treaties. Composite and Dependent States and Territories.

VI. Constitutional Limitations.

VII. Reservations.

VIII. Ratification of Treaties. Entrance into Force.

IX. Operation and Enforcement of Treaties. Necessity of Municipal Legislation. *See also* Part I, International Law in General: Relation to Municipal Law; *and* Part VI, The Individual in International Law: In General.

X. Effect of Treaties on Third Parties.

XI. Termination of Treaties—

i. By Operation of Law.

(*a*) In General.

(*b*) Extinction and Dismemberment of Contracting Party.

(c) Outbreak of War. *See* PART XI, WAR AND NEUTRALITY.
(d) The *clausula rebus sic stantibus.* Reconsideration of Treaties under Article 19 of the Covenant.
(e) Merger in Subsequent Treaty.

ii. By Act of Party.
(a) In General.
(b) Mutual Consent.
(c) Unilateral Denunciation. Result of Non-Performance by the Other Party.

iii. Effect of Termination upon Acquired Rights.

XII. INTERPRETATION OF TREATIES—

i. Construction in Accordance with the Intention of the Parties.
ii. Restrictive Interpretation.
(a) Restrictions of Sovereignty.
(b) Interpretation against the Party Responsible for the Drafting.
iii. Bilingual Treaties.
iv. Consideration of Preparatory Work.
v. Various other Rules of Interpretation.

XIII. SPECIAL KINDS OF TREATIES—

(a) Commercial Treaties. Most-Favoured-Nation Clause.
(b) Peace Treaties. *See* PART XI, WAR AND NEUTRALITY.

XIV. MISCELLANEOUS.

PART IX

INTERNATIONAL ORGANISATION AND ADMINISTRATION

A. LEAGUE OF NATIONS

I. CHARACTER OF THE LEAGUE.
II. THE ASSEMBLY
III. THE COUNCIL.
IV. INTERPRETATION OF THE COVENANT OF THE LEAGUE.
V. THE LEAGUE AND NON-MEMBER STATES.

B. INTERNATIONAL LABOUR OFFICE

I. ORGANISATION AND CONSTITUTION.
II. CONCLUSION AND INTERPRETATION OF LABOUR CONVENTIONS.
III. ENFORCEMENT OF LABOUR CONVENTIONS.

C. OTHER ORGANS OF INTERNATIONAL ADMINISTRATION. *See also* PART II B (Territories under Joint or International Government), *and* PART III B (Functions and Competence of International Commissions on International Rivers).

D. MISCELLANEOUS

PART X

DISPUTES

A. ARBITRATION

I. ARBITRATION IN GENERAL—
- i. Conception and Function of Arbitration.
- ii. The Law Applied by Arbitral Tribunals. Arbitration and Judicial Settlement.
- iii. The Arbitration Treaty. Appointment and Withdrawal of Arbitrators.

II. PROCEDURE—
- i. Procedure before the Tribunal (Oral and Written Arguments).
- ii. Competence. Competence to Determine Jurisdiction.
- iii. Intervention.
- iv. Counter-Claim and Set-Off.
- v. Exceptions and Demurrers.
- vi. Costs.
- vii. Injunctions and Interlocutory Orders.
- viii. Experts.

III. RULES OF EVIDENCE. BURDEN OF PROOF. As to Consideration of Preparatory Work in the Interpretation of Treaties, *see* PART VIII, TREATIES: Interpretation of Treaties.

IV. ADMISSION OF LIABILITY. WAIVER. ESTOPPEL.

V. THE AWARD—
- i. Scope and Binding Force of the Award.
- ii. *Res Judicata.*
- iii. Appeal and Revision.

B. PERMANENT COURT OF INTERNATIONAL JUSTICE

I. ORGANISATION OF THE COURT.

II. RELATION OF THE COURT TO THE LEAGUE.

III. Contentious Jurisdiction—
i. Competence.
ii. Procedure.
iii. Law Applicable.
iv. Judgment.

IV. The Advisory Opinion—
i. Competence.
ii. Procedure.
iii. Law Applicable.
iv. Opinion.

C. CONCILIATION

I. By the Council of the League.

II. Under Special Treaties.

III. Negotiation.

D. UNILATERAL MEANS OF REDRESS SHORT OF WAR

i. Retorsion.
ii. Reprisals.
iii. Pacific Blockade. Blockade under the Covenant of the League.
iv. Intervention.

E. NEGOTIATION

F. MISCELLANEOUS

PART XI

WAR AND NEUTRALITY[1]

A. WAR IN GENERAL

I. Definition and Technical Meaning of War. Insurgency.

II. Commencement of War.

III. Region of War.

IV. Belligerent Forces.

V. Effects of Outbreak of War—
i. In General.
ii. On Treaties.
(*a*) During the War.
(*b*) After the War.

[1] As it is at present not intended to go back further than the beginning of the year 1919, and not to digest decisions of Prize Courts save in so far as they raise questions of general international law, War and Neutrality are only dealt with in this Classification in very general terms.

iii. On Private Contracts.
iv. On Enemy Subjects with regard to—
(*a*) Their Personal Status in the Territory of the Belligerent. *Persona standi in judicio.*
(*b*) Their Property and other Rights.
v. On Enemy Merchant Ships in Port.
vi. On Neutral Persons and Property. Embargo. The Right of Angary.
vii. Trading with the Enemy.

VI. ENEMY CHARACTER—
i. Of Individuals.
ii. Of Corporations.
iii. Of Vessels.
iv. Of Goods.

VII. THE BINDING FORCE OF THE LAWS OF WAR.

VIII. ENFORCEMENT OF THE LAWS OF WAR—
i. Reprisals.
ii. Punishment of War Crimes. Defence of Superior Orders.
iii. Compensation and Reparation.

IX. PRISONERS OF WAR.

X. NON-HOSTILE RELATIONS BETWEEN BELLIGERENTS, ESPECIALLY ARMISTICES.

XI. TERMINATION OF WAR.

XII. EFFECTS OF TREATIES OF PEACE—
i. In General.
ii. Amnesty.
iii. Revival of Treaties.
iv. Miscellaneous.

XIII. PERFORMANCE OF PEACE TREATIES.

B. WARFARE ON LAND

I. MEASURES AND INSTRUMENTS OF FORCE.

II. APPROPRIATION, UTILISATION AND DESTRUCTION OF ENEMY PROPERTY.

III. OCCUPATION OF ENEMY TERRITORY—
i. Nature and Effects of the Occupation.
ii. Legislative, Judicial and Administrative Functions of the Occupant.
iii. Respect of Private Property. The Public Property of the Enemy State. Requisitions and Contributions.
iv. Inhabitants. Services. Deportations. Hostages.

C. WARFARE AT SEA

I. Measures and Instruments of Force.

II. Visit, Search, Capture, and Destruction—

(*a*) Of Enemy Merchantmen.
(*b*) Of Neutral Merchantmen.

III. Restrictions on the Right of Capture (Hospital Ships, etc., Postal Correspondence, Property under Neutral Flag).

IV. Prize Law—

i. Nature and Extent of Jurisdiction in Prize Courts.
ii. Procedure.
iii. Indemnities and Damages.

D. AIR WARFARE

E. NEUTRALITY IN GENERAL

I. Nature of Duties of Neutrality.

II. Neutral and Military and Naval Operations and Preparations.

III. Neutral Asylum.

IV. Supplies, Loans and Services to Belligerents.

V. As Affected by the Covenant of the League.

F. CONTRABAND

I. Conception of Contraband. Absolute and Relative Contraband.

II. Carriage of Contraband and Doctrine of Continuous Voyage.

III. Penalty for Carriage of Contraband.

G. BLOCKADE

I. Establishment of Blockade, Conditions of Validity.

II. Breach and Penalty.

III. Blockade and the Doctrine of Continuous Voyage. For Neutralisation *see* Part II, *above*.

PART I

INTERNATIONAL LAW IN GENERAL

I.—Nature and Binding Force

International Law—In General—Extent of Application in Point of Time—So-called " Inter-temporal " Law—Appreciation of Juridical Facts in the Light of the Law Contemporary with Them—Continued Existence of Rights and the Evolution of International Law—Application to Questions of Occupation—Effectiveness of Inchoate Title. **Case No. 1**

ISLAND OF PALMAS ARBITRATION CASE.

United States and Holland : Permanent Court of Arbitration.
4 April, 1928.

(HUBER, Arbitrator.)

THE FACTS.—(See Cases Nos. 68, 70, 72, 75.) The claim of the United States to sovereignty over the Island of Palmas was based principally on the fact of the discovery of that island early in the sixteenth century by Spain, from whom the United States claimed to have acquired the title over the island by cession in the Treaty of Paris of 10 December, 1898. Both parties admitted that, as international law underwent profound changes between the Middle Ages and the end of the nineteenth century in the matter of the law relating to acquisition of title by discovery of uninhabited regions or regions inhabited by savage or semi-civilised peoples, the relevant juridical facts must be appreciated in the light of the law contemporary with them and not of the law in force at the time when the dispute arose or when it was submitted for settlement.

Held : (*a*) In conformity with the submissions of the parties, that the discovery by Spain is to be determined by the rules of international law in force in the first half of the sixteenth century ; but that (*b*) even if, as claimed by the United States, it could be admitted that in accordance with the law obtaining in the sixteenth century title was conferred by mere discovery, that is, by the mere fact of seeing land without any act even symbolical of taking possession, there would still remain the

Case No. 1 ***contd.***

question whether sovereignty still existed at the moment of the conclusion and coming into force of the Treaty of Paris of 10 December, 1898.

Thus (*c*) " as regards the question which of different legal " systems prevailing at successive periods is to be applied in a " particular case (the so-called 'inter-temporal' law), a dis- " tinction must be made between the creation of rights and the " existence of rights. The same principle which subjects the act " creative of a right to the law in force at the time the right arises, " demands that the existence of the right, in other words its " continued manifestation, shall follow the conditions required " by the evolution of law. International law in the nineteenth " century, having regard to the fact that most parts of the globe " were under the sovereignty of States members of the com- " munity of nations, and that territories without a master had " become relatively few, took account of a tendency already " existing and especially developed since the middle of the " eighteenth century, and laid down the principle that occupa- " tion, to constitute a claim to territorial sovereignty, must be " effective, that is, offer certain guarantees to other States and " their nationals. It seems therefore incompatible with this " rule of positive law that there should be regions which are " neither under the effective sovereignty of a State, nor without " a master, but which are reserved for the exclusive influence " of one State, in virtue solely of a title of acquisition which is " no longer recognised by existing law, even if such a title ever " conferred territorial sovereignty. For these reasons, dis- " covery alone, without any subsequent act, cannot at the " present time suffice to prove sovereignty over the Island of " Palmas (or Miangas). . . ."

(*d*) Throughout the nineteenth century there prevailed the principle that an inchoate title of discovery must, in order to be productive of definite title, be completed within a reasonable period by effective occupation. This principle must, in accordance with the rules governing the so-called " inter-temporal " law, be applied in the present case. No act of occupation nor any exercise of sovereignty by Spain at Palmas Island had been alleged. Even if it were possible to admit that the Spanish title still existed as an inchoate title in 1898 and as such passed over to the United States, such inchoate title could not prevail over the continuous and peaceful display of authority by Holland. [Reports : *Permanent Court of Arbitration, Arbitral Award rendered in conformity with the Special Agreement concluded on* 23 *January*, 1925, *between the United States of*

America and the Netherlands, pp. 26-28; *A.J.*, XXII (1928), pp. 883, 884.]

NOTE.—As to "inter-temporal" law, see Strupp in his analysis of the *Grisbadarna* case decided in 1909 by the Permanent Court of Arbitration and analysed in Schücking—*Das Werk von Haag*, vol. II, Part I (1917), pp. 113, 114. See also on the same question Lammasch, *Die Lehre von der Schiedsgerichtbarkeit in ihrem ganzen Umfange* (1914), pp. 178, 179, and see the case of *Pelletier and Lazare* between the United States and Haiti, in which the arbitrator was instructed to decide "according to rules of international law existing at the time of "the transaction complained of." (Moore, vol. II, p. 1750.)

International Law—Reference to as an Element of Interpretation of Treaties.

See Case No. 292 (*Georges Pinson Case*, § 50).

II.—Extent

International Law — Extent of — Applicability to Relations between Members of Federal States—Agreement creating a State Servitude between two Swiss Cantons—Application of *clausula rebus sic stantibus*.

See Case No. 289 (*Canton of Thurgau* v. *Canton of St. Gallen*).

International Law—In General—Applicability to Relations between Members of Federal States.

See Case No. 86 (*Württemberg and Prussia* v. *Baden*).

III.—Sources

[See also Part X, ARBITRATION: *The Law Applied by Arbitral Tribunals*, Cases Nos. 317, 318.]

International Law—Sources of—Opinions of Writers—International Conventions and Municipal Decisions as a Source of International Law—Value of Opinions of Writers—Stipulations of Conventions—Whether Expressing General Principles of International Law—Authority of Municipal Decisions—How far Constituting International Custom—Requirement of *Opinio Necessitatis*.

Case No. 2

PERMANENT COURT OF INTERNATIONAL JUSTICE. JUDGMENT No. 9.

TURKEY *v.* FRANCE.

THE CASE OF THE S.S. *LOTUS*.

7 September, 1927.

THE FACTS.—(See Case No. 98.) The French Government invoked the works of publicists,

Case No. 2 ***contd.***

precedents of municipal and international tribunals, and international conventions in support of the contention that there had grown up a rule of customary international law establishing the exclusive jurisdiction of the State whose flag is flown over everything which occurs on board a merchant vessel on the high seas, even in cases when the act committed on board the vessel produces effects on a vessel flying another flag, in particular in case of collisions.

Held: A. *In regard to the opinions of publicists:* "Apart from the question as to what their value may "be from the point of view of establishing the exist-"ence of a rule of customary law," although they adhered to the principle of exclusive jurisdiction of the State whose flag the ship flies, they did not attribute to that principle a scope larger than that of assimilating such jurisdiction to the State's jurisdiction over its territory. Many of them qualified that exclusive jurisdiction by the consideration of the locality of the effect of the act committed on board the foreign vessel.

B. *In regard to international conventions:* That it was not absolutely certain, in regard to conventions reserving jurisdiction exclusively to the State whose flag is flown, that "this stipulation is to be regarded "as expressing a general principle of law rather than "as corresponding to the extraordinary jurisdiction "which these conventions confer on the State-owned "ships of a particular country in respect of ships of "another country on the high seas. Apart from that, "it should be observed that these conventions relate "to matters of a particular kind, closely connected "with the policing of the seas, such as the slave trade, "damage to submarine cables, fisheries, etc., and not "to common-law offences. Above all, it should be "pointed out that the offences contemplated by the "conventions in question only concern a single ship; "it is impossible therefore to make any deduction "from them in regard to matters which concern two

" ships and consequently the jurisdiction of two " different States " [1] (at p. 27).

C. *In regard to municipal decisions:* The cases *Ortigia—Oncle-Joseph*, decided by the Court of Appeal of Aix, and *Franconia—Strathclyde*, decided by the English Court for Crown Cases Reserved (which the Permanent Court regarded as overruled on the question of the locality of the offence by *R.* v. *Nillins* [2] and *R.* v. *Godfrey* [3]), supported the French contention, while the cases *Ortigia—Oncle-Joseph*,[4] decided by Italian courts,[5] and *Ekbatana—West-Hinder*, decided by Belgian courts, militated against it. " Without pausing to consider the value " to be attributed to the judgments of municipal " courts in connection with the establishment of the " existence of a rule of international law, it will suffice " to observe that the decisions quoted sometimes " support one view and sometimes the other " (at p. 28). " As municipal jurisprudence is thus divided, it is " hardly possible to see in it an indication of the ex- " istence of the restrictive rule of international law " which alone could serve as a basis for the contention " of the French Government " (at p. 29).

D. *Rarity of municipal decisions as evidence of international custom:* That their rarity would only show " that States had often, in practice, abstained " from instituting criminal proceedings, and not that " they recognised themselves as being obliged to do so; " for only if such abstention were based on their being " conscious of having a duty to abstain would it be " possible to speak of an international custom " (at p. 28). The fact that there were only a few instances of exercise of jurisdiction was not, therefore, conclusive for establishing the contention of the French Government. [Report: Series A, No. 10, pp. 25-30.]

[1] The student will note the bearing of this passage on the general question as to how far it is permissible to draw deductions from specific treaty provisions: Are such provisions expressive of the principle of international law obtaining on the matter, or do they constitute an exception from the generally accepted principle?

[2] (1884) 53 L.J.M.C. 157.

[3] L.R. [1923] 1 K.B. 24.

[4] Both the Court of Aix and an Italian court gave decisions in this case.

[5] At Leghorn and Florence.

Case No. 3

International Law—Sources of—Customary International Law —Requirements of—Value of a Single Act.

LÜBECK *v.* MECKLENBURG-SCHWERIN.

German Staatsgerichtshof. 6 and 7 July, 1928.

THE FACTS.—(See Case No. 88.) It appeared that in 1874 Mecklenburg-Schwerin issued an ordinance concerning the preservation of the shores and dunes of part of the Bay of Lübeck and requested Lübeck to promulgate it in her territory.[1] Lübeck complied with that request. It was contended that that action of Lübeck amounted to a recognition of the rights of Mecklenburg-Schwerin in the disputed part of the Bay. The latter also invoked certain correspondence between Lübeck and Prussia.

Held : That the contention of Mecklenburg-Schwerin must be rejected. A single act of a Lübeck authority could not create international rights in favour of Mecklenburg-Schwerin if none had existed before. Conduct, if it is to be creative of international custom, must be regular and repeated ; it must emanate from the competent authorities of the State ; and it can create rights only as between States between which it took place. The fact that the Lübeck authorities on a single occasion acted in a certain manner or that they expressed certain views in their correspondence with Prussia cannot be regarded as decisive. [Reports : *Entscheidungen des Reichsgerichts in Zivilsachen*, vol. 122, Appendix, p. 1 ; *Z. für a. ö. R. und V.*, vol. I (2) (1929), p. 180.]

NOTE.—The Court discussed at some length the general question of the means of creating international law, in particular by reference to the doctrine of *Vereinbarung*, and referred to a number of German writers (Liszt, Hatschek, Heilborn, Triepel, Strupp and Holtzendorff).

International Law—Sources of—Persuasive Effect of Foreign Decisions *in pari materia.*

See Case No. 284 (*Robertson* v. *General Electric Co.*).

[1] The Ordinance issued on 10 October, 1874, by Mecklenburg-Schwerin prohibited the digging of sand, flint and clay, or the cutting of grass and other vegetation, or the removal of stones in the dune district and along the shore, as well as in the Ostsee four hundred metres from the shore, without the permission of the local authorities. The Ordinance is cited and discussed in Wenzel, *Die Hoheitsrechte in der Lübecker Bucht* (1926), p. 85.

International Law—Sources of—As Applied by Arbitral Tribunals.

See Case No. 369 (*Goldenberg and Sons* v. *Germany*).

International Law—Basis of—Consensus of States—Presumption of Freedom of Action.

See Case No. 98 (*The Case of the S.S. " Lotus "*).

IV.—Subjects of International Law

[See Part VI, The Individual in International Law : (*A*) *In General* ; and Part VIII, Treaties : IX. *Operation and Enforcement of Treaties.*]

Subjects of International Law—Native Chiefs and Princes—Treaties with.

See Cases Nos. 68, 70 (*Island of Palmas Arbitration Case*).

V.—Relation to Municipal Law

[See also Part VIII, Treaties : IX. *Operation and Enforcement of Treaties. Necessity of Municipal Legislation,* Cases Nos. 277-285 ; and Part VI, The Individual in International Law : (*A*) *In General,* Cases Nos. 187, 188.]

Relations between Municipal and International Law—Interpretation of the Former in accordance with the Latter—National Constitutions Subordinate to the Law of Nations. **Case No. 4**

Georges Pinson Case, §§ 31 and 32.

France and Mexico : Mixed Claims Commission.[1]
19 *October*, 1928.

(Verzijl, President.)

The Facts.—Article 30, section III, of the former Mexican Constitution of 1857 reads thus: " Son Mexi- " canos : . . . III. Los extranjeros que adquieran " bienes raíces en la República, . . . siempre que no " manifiesten la resolución de conservar su nacionali- " dad." [2] The umpires in the American-Mexican

[1] The two national commissioners were: for France, V. Ayguesparsse, and for Mexico, F. Gonzalez Roa.

[2] " The following are Mexicans . . . III. Aliens who acquire immovable " property in the Republic, . . . provided that they do not express the wish to " preserve their nationality."

Case No. 4 *contd.*

Claims Commission of 1868, Dr. Lieber and Thornton, had interpreted this provision in a liberal way (*in re Anderson and Thompson*, Moore, III, pp. 2480, 2482), viz.:

(Dr. Lieber) "There is a law of the Mexican re- " public converting every purchaser of land into a " citizen unless he declares, at the time, to the con- " trary. This law clearly means to confer a benefit " upon the foreign purchaser of land, and equity " would assuredly forbid us to force this benefit upon " claimants."

(Umpire Thornton) "The part of the Mexican " Constitution which says that those are citizens who " hold land is permissive and not obligatory."

With express reference to these awards the Mexican Government had afterwards proposed to Congress, and the latter unanimously decided, to insert accordingly in the new Nationality Law of 1886[1] a provision embodying the liberal interpretation. Notwithstanding these facts, the Mexican Government questioned the awards of the Commission of 1868, and contended that the Law of 1886 was in contradiction with the Constitution of 1857.

Held: That the Commission agreed absolutely with its predecessor of 1868 in the interpretation of the Constitution of 1857, particularly at the present time, in view of the fact that the Mexican Government and Congress had, in the meantime, unanimously adopted, in 1886, the decisions of the umpires; and that this interpretation was, indeed, in harmony with the general principle of interpretation pursuant to which municipal law must, in doubtful cases, always be read in the sense that ensures its conformity with international law.

Held further: That in any case the Commission was firmly opposed to the official Mexican contention (*La cuestión internacional mexicano-americana, durante el Gobierno del General Alvaro Obregón*, p. 56), according to which a municipal Constitution, being the supreme law of the land, ought to be respected above treaties, since the latter cannot have a greater force than the Constitution itself. This contention is in direct contradiction to the very axioms of international law and seems to be only capable of explanation by a double confusion: (*a*) between the points of view of the national courts and of international

[1] See Flournoy and Hudson, *Nationality Laws*, pp. 426-435.

tribunals respectively; (*b*) between the case of the pre-existence of constitutional provisions prohibiting the Government from concluding international treaties having certain effects, and the case of pre-existing treaties or (what comes to the same thing) customary law. (*a*) National courts of justice being an emanation of the sovereignty of each particular State *may* indeed be (not, must necessarily be) obliged to enforce or apply municipal law, even when they consider the latter to clash with international law; this depends upon the principles consecrated by the national public law of the State concerned. International tribunals, however, as organs of the law of nations, must neglect even the Constitution of a State in favour of international law. (*b*) In the former case it may be doubted whether a treaty concluded by the Government concerned with a foreign State in defiance of express prohibitive provisions of the Constitution may be considered as valid, since it is possible to argue that in such a case the Government has exceeded the limits of its constitutional power to represent its State in the act of concluding an international convention. In the latter case, however, every doubt is excluded since "the very fact of "existence of a previous treaty or of customary rules in the "international domain constitutes an absolute impediment to "the State to enact valid constitutional rules in defiance of the "rules of international law, the latter implying in themselves "a corresponding restriction on national sovereignty."

[Till now unreported.]

International Law—Relation to Municipal Law—German Law and the Treaty of Versailles—Article 4 of the German Constitution—Effect of Treaties upon Individuals—Alleged Violation of the Treaty of Versailles by Germany—Publication by German Subject—High Treason—The State's Right of Self-Defence—How far Limited by International Treaties. **Case No. 5**

HIGH TREASON (TREATY OF VERSAILLES IN GERMANY) CASE.

German Reichsgericht. 14 *March*, 1928.

THE FACTS.—This was a prosecution for attempted high treason. The accused was charged with publishing details as to certain alleged plans of the *Reichswehr* which, if true, would have constituted a violation of the Treaty of Versailles. The information published by the accused was not accurate, but the accused believed it to be

Case No. 5 ***contd.***

true. The prosecution was based on section 92 of the Criminal Code, which lays down, *inter alia*, that a person shall be liable to punishment who publishes information as to facts of which he knows that it is in the interest of Germany that they should not be revealed to a foreign Power. The accused contended that the Treaty of Versailles, which had become part of German law,[1] had rendered Article 92 of the Criminal Code inoperative also in respect of individual German subjects. He also relied on Article 4 of the German Constitution, which lays down that generally recognised rules of international law shall be regarded as binding constituent parts of German Federal law.

Held: That that contention must be rejected. It was true that according to Article 178 of the German Constitution the operation of such of its provisions as are inconsistent with the Treaty of Versailles shall be suspended so long as the Treaty is in force. But there was no provision of the Treaty of Versailles which was contrary to the continued validity of Article 92 of the Criminal Code. There was nothing in it to deprive Germany of the right to protect her State secrets. The natural right of defending such State interests cannot be renounced. The renunciation of such a right would be tantamount to renouncing the right of self-defence, a right expressly recognised in the Treaty of Locarno of 6 October, 1925. The *Reichsgericht* itself had in numerous judgments adopted the view that the Espionage Law of 3 June, 1914, had remained intact.

Neither could the *Reichsgericht* admit the relevance of Article 4 of the Constitution. There is no generally recognised rule of international law to the effect that a national is entitled to communicate to a foreign State the existence of facts which are contrary to the law but of which he knows that they ought to be kept secret in the interest of his own State.

The *Reichsgericht* must reject the view that the conviction of the accused would violate the rule of international law which lays down that treaties ought to be fulfilled in good faith. For this rule binds only the contracting parties, not individuals.

In general, the *Reichsgericht* must adhere to the legal principles which it had occasion to lay down in former judgments in similar cases. " The citizen has to keep faith with his own " State. It is his primary duty to promote the interests of his

[1] By a Law of 16 July, 1919, the Treaty of Versailles has become part of German Federal law.

" own State regardless of the interests of another country. He " has to look only to competent national authorities in order to " give effect to the existing law ; he must not seek to achieve " this end by bringing the alleged violation of the law to the " notice of the foreign Government. The Court declines to give " unqualified recognition, in particular in the sphere of foreign " relations, to the view that the revealing and bringing to " public notice of illegal conditions can never injure the State " but must always bring advantage to it seeing that the well- " being of the State is realised through its law. If the well- " being of the State is the supreme law and the guiding principle, " then it must be conscientiously and impartially examined in " order to decide which of two interests, in the event of any " conflict between them, has in an individual case the greater " need of protection." [Reports : *Entscheidungen des Reichsgerichts in Strafsachen*, vol. 62, p. 65 ; *Z. für a. ö. R. und V.*, vol. I (2) (1929), p. 708.]

International Law—Relation to Municipal Law—Primacy of International Law—Treaty of Versailles and Belgian Municipal Law. **Case No. 6**

DELPLANQUE ET AL. *v.* STATE OF BELGIUM.

Belgian Court of Cassation. 27 May, 1927.

THE FACTS.—Paragraphs 1 and 2 of Annex IV to Part VIII of the Treaty of Versailles oblige Germany to replace all material seized, used or destroyed by her as a direct consequence of military operations. The goods imported by the Belgian State under these provisions included certain apparatus protected by a Belgian patent in the possession of the claimants. These claimants brought an action against the State, basing their claim on a breach of the terms of Article 4 of the Patent Law of 24 May, 1854. They were unsuccessful both in the court of first instance and in the Brussels Court of Appeal (30 January, 1924). They appealed to the Court of Cassation.

Held : That the appeal must be dismissed. The abovementioned provisions of the Treaty of Versailles are intended to further " the material re-instatement of the invaded territories." Furthermore, " it follows from the discussion of the bases of " the Patent Law of the 24 May, 1854, that this statute was " designed to reconcile the interests of the inventor with those

Case No. 6 *contd.* " of society at large. Hence the draughtsman of the statute " cannot have intended that its provisions should be called into " play where they would tend to hinder or complicate executive " action under the terms of a treaty to restore economic pros-" perity in an invaded territory. . . . In any such conflict of " laws, public international law takes precedence over the " system of private municipal law ; if we were to accept the " view of the claimants, it would follow that the Belgian State " could not demand any reparations payments in kind from " Germany, in respect of material carried off from the war " victims, wherever a private individual should object to the " importation of these materials by virtue of any patent he " might have taken out. . . ." [Report : *Pasicrisie Belge,* 1927, I, p. 240.]

NOTE.—The concept of the " primacy " of international law seems to be introduced somewhat irrelevantly to secure the priority of a treaty provision inserted for the exclusive advantage of one State over the municipal laws of that State. A more logical basis for the decision might be found in the concept of the " primacy " of municipal legislation of general concern, such as the Law of 15 September, 1919, adopting the Treaty of Versailles, over legislation protecting the private rights of particular individuals.

Case No. 7 **International Law—Relation to Municipal Law—Treaties—Relation to Municipal Legislation—Abrogation of Statute by later Treaty.**

OGIJEWICZ *v.* GOVERNOR OF WILNO.

Supreme Administrative Court of Poland. 11 *May,* 1928.

THE FACTS.—A Polish statute of 20 January, 1920, provides, *inter alia,* that a person who is still liable to military service may not acquire foreign nationality except by permission of the Minister of War. The Polish-Russian Peace Treaty of Riga, concluded, ratified, and published in the Polish Journal of Laws, in 1921, provides, *inter alia,* that former Russian nationals who on the day of the ratification of the Treaty will be over 18 years of age and will sojourn in Russia or the Ukraine, can, if they were previously registered in the lists of the inhabitants of territories now belonging to Poland, opt for Polish nationality in the manner prescribed in the Treaty. Plaintiff was in Russia from 1916 until November 1921 (the Treaty having been ratified on 30 April, 1921). In 1925 he applied to be granted recognition of his Polish nationality on the basis of the Law of 1920, which attributes Polish nationality to every person born or resident in Poland who has no other nationality. The defendant having refused to grant the recognition, the present action was brought.

Held: (1) That the Treaty, by granting to certain persons the right of opting for Polish nationality, had by implication deprived them of such nationality if they had acquired it under the Law of 1920. Under the Treaty defendant was a Russian or Ukrainian, but not a Polish, national.

(2) That the provision of 1920 under which plaintiff, being of military age, could not acquire foreign nationality without permission from the Minister of War, was superseded with regard to the acquisition of Russian or Ukrainian nationality by the Peace Treaty of Riga, which constitutes a subsequent law. [Reports: Z.W.N.T.A., VI (1928), No. 1454; R.P.E.S., 1929, p. 237.]

International Law in General—Relation to Municipal Law—Treaties—Conflict of Operation and Enforcement. **Case No. 8**

HARDT *v.* GOVERNOR OF POZNAN.

Supreme Administrative Court of Poland. 21 *December*, 1927.

THE FACTS.—Plaintiff demanded from the local administrative authority and, upon refusal by the same, from the defendant as competent superior administrative authority, a recognition of plaintiff's Polish nationality. The defendant having refused the declaration demanded by the plaintiff, the latter brought the present action (to have defendant's decision quashed), claiming, *inter alia*, that his title was based on the Treaty of Versailles (Article 91) and on the treaty between the Principal Allied and Associated Powers and Poland, bearing the same date (the so-called Polish Minorities Treaty), which two Treaties could not be altered by the German-Polish Convention of Vienna of 30 August, 1924, to which the Principal Allied and Associated Powers were not parties.

Held: *Inter alia*, that the Court could not admit the argument that the Vienna Convention could not alter or supplement the Treaties signed previously at Versailles, "because the Vienna

Case No. 8 *contd.* "Convention, having been ratified by an act of the President "(of Poland) . . . which act mentioned that its basis was the "authorisation given by the statute of 28 January, 1925 . . . "and having been duly published in the Journal of Laws . . . "must be treated on a parity with a duly published law, and "the Supreme Administrative Court, under Article 1 of the "statute which organized it, has not the right to enquire "into the validity of duly published laws. . . ." [Reports: Z.W.N.T.A. (1927), No. 1345; P.P.A., 1928, pp. 383-395.]

Case No. 9 **International Law in General—Relation to Municipal Law—Treaties—Operation and Enforcement of Treaties—Applicability to Internal Relations of the State.**

(POLISH) STATE TREASURY *v.* WLODZIMIERZ (CITY OF).

Supreme Court of Poland, First Division. 14 *December*, 1928.

THE FACTS.—The Russian Government had confiscated certain real estate in Wlodzimierz belonging to a Catholic monastery and had, later, in 1881, presented it to the City of Wlodzimierz. After the restoration of Poland, the Treasury brought action against the City of Wlodzimierz to recover the property, and based its claim, *inter alia*, on Article XII of the Polish-Russian Peace Treaty of Riga (18 March, 1921) which recognised as the property of each contracting party all State property situated in its territory, including "all property and "property rights given away by the late Russian "Tsars." The action having failed in the District Court of Luck, an appeal was brought before the Court of Appeal of Lublin, which dismissed it on the ground, *inter alia*, that "Article XII of the Treaty of Riga does "not justify the claim, because it defines State property "as between the parties to the Treaty, and this definition is not applicable to internal relations in the "Polish State." On appeal by the Treasury to the Supreme Court,

Held (*inter alia*, while dismissing the appeal for other reasons): That "the view of the Court of Appeal according to "which the Treaty is not applicable to internal relations in "Poland is wrong, because the Treaty, having been ratified by "the legislature of the State, and having been duly published

" . . . has become a legislative act which has binding force in " internal relations within the State, as the Supreme Court has " had occasion to point out before. . . ." [Report: Z.O.S.N.C., 1928, No. 188.]

NOTE.—I. The case referred to by the Supreme Court is that of the *Procurator-General of the Republic* v. *Pawow and Pawow*, Z.O.S.N.C., 1922, No. 139, in which the Court based its decision, *inter alia*, on Article XII of the Treaty of Riga.

II. The problem of the "transformation" of treaty into municipal law is not stated in the decision of 1928 quite precisely. There is, in Polish law, no enacted rule corresponding to that of Article VI, s. 2, of the Constitution of the United States. Article 49 of the Polish Constitution provides that " The President concludes agreements with other States and " brings them to the notice of the House of Deputies." The Article goes on to enumerate certain types of treaties which " require the assent of the " House," while Article 50 enacts that " the President cannot declare war " or conclude peace except by the previous assent of the House." The Treaty of Riga was signed a day after the Constitution was voted, but it was ratified before the Constitution went into effect. The Constituent Assembly which voted the Constitution and assented to the ratification of the Treaty of Riga was considered " sovereign," while the Constitution as voted by it conferred upon both Houses of the Diet specific powers. Nevertheless, it is not correct to say that the legislature " ratified the Treaty " ; for ratification is a function of the representative of the State, *i.e.* the Chief of State (as his title ran before the Constitution) or the President (as his title is now). In fact, the statute which authorised ratification declares that the Assembly " approves (confirms) " the Treaty . . . (and) authorises the Chief of State to sign the ratifica- " tion of the said Treaty in the name of the Republic of Poland." The Chief of State, relying on this authorisation, ratified (" I ratify and " declare . . .") the Treaty on the day following the passing of the law.

At present the practice is for both Houses to pass a statute which (1) assents to the ratification of the treaty, and (2) entrusts the Foreign Minister with the execution of the statute and the Ministers concerned with the execution of the treaty itself. Ratification is then executed by the President (the act being countersigned by the Prime Minister and the Foreign Minister), whereupon the treaty itself is published (as has been, before ratification, the statute itself) in the Journal of Laws, together with a declaration that ratification has taken place.

Thus, at present, the " transformation " of the treaty into municipal law is the result of the clause which entrusts the execution of the treaty to the ministers concerned. This practice, while not perfect from the legal point of view (the " transformation clause " being in abeyance between the moment of its publication and that of the publication of the treaty after the latter has been ratified), is undoubtedly an improvement on the previous practice, under which the statute authorising ratification sometimes entrusted only the Foreign Minister with the execution of that statute itself, *i.e.* with bringing about the ratification. On the other hand, since the Constitution creates two Houses and requires the assent to peace treaties, etc., of one House only, the procedure of obtaining statutory authority instead of authority by resolution

Case No. 9 *contd.* is justified only by the fact that the clause entrusting individual ministers with the execution of the act is, in fact, a " transformation clause," which embodies the treaty in question, on condition of its ratification and publication, in the municipal law. See Ehrlich, *Prawo Narodów*, p. 17.

International Law—Relation to Municipal Law—Treaties—Necessity of Municipal Legislation.

The opinion expressed in the decision Boh. 5772 adm. (see *Annual Digest*, 1925-1926, Case No. 5, p. 6), *i.e.* that the stipulations of international treaties have no binding force upon individuals if not incorporated into the municipal law, was again expressed by the Supreme Administrative Court of Czechoslovakia in the decisions of 29 September, 1927, No. 19.898 (Boh. 3833 fin.); of 5 May, 1928, No. 11.876 (Boh. 7259 adm.); and of 19 December, 1928, No. 31.904 (Boh. 4535 fin.).

International Law and Municipal Law—Judgments of International Tribunals in relation to Judgments of Municipal Tribunals.

See Case No. 198 (*Ruinart Père & Sons* v. *Franzmann*).

International Law—Relation to Municipal Law—Relation of Judgments of International Courts to those of Municipal Courts.

See Case No. 356 (*Case concerning the Factory at Chorzów*).

International Law—Relation to Municipal Law—Examination of the Latter by International Tribunals.

See Case No. 324 (*Georges Pinson Case*, §§ 29, 30 ff., 34 ff.).

International Law—Relation to Municipal Law—Statutes Conflicting with Generally Recognised Rules of International Law—Article 4 of the German Constitution.

See Case No. 225 (*Reparations Levy* (*Aliens in Germany*) *Case*).

VI.—International Comity

International Comity—Respect for the Laws of a Foreign Country in relation to Acts Taking Place within its Jurisdiction—Partnership to Commit Acts in Foreign Country Illegal by Local Law—Illegal Association. **Case No. 10**

FOSTER (plaintiff) *v.* DRISCOLL AND OTHERS (defendants).
LINDSAY (plaintiff) *v.* ATTFIELD AND ANOTHER (defendants).
LINDSAY (plaintiff) *v.* DRISCOLL AND ANOTHER (defendants).

English Court of Appeal on appeal from the King's Bench Division of the High Court of Justice. 13 *December*, 1928.

THE FACTS (much simplified).—These three actions arose out of a project on the part of five persons for the purchase of a steamship and the shipment of a cargo of whisky for carriage across the Atlantic with a view to its sale in the United States of America, in violation of the laws of that country, either directly or ultimately after its sale in Canada or St. Pierre or on the high seas. The actions which were brought upon two contracts made between four of the said co-adventurers and upon two bills of exchange made in pursuance of the agreements raised, *inter alia*, the question of the legality of a contract the performance of which would or might involve the violation of the laws of a foreign State. It was contended (in reliance upon Dicey, *Conflict of Laws*, 4th ed., 1927, p. 620) that " an English contract . . . " will only be held invalid on account of illegality if it " actively necessitates the performance in a foreign and " friendly country of some act which is illegal by the " law of such country," and that a contract was not invalid if it was possible to carry it out without a violation of law. The view of the facts which was taken by the judge of first instance (Wright, J.) made it unnecessary for him to deal with the plea of illegality. On appeal,

Held: By the Court of Appeal (Lawrence and Sankey, L.JJ., *dissentiente* on this point Scrutton, L.J.) that the contracts were void on the ground of public policy because their enforcement would involve this country in a breach of international comity.

Per Lawrence, L.J. (at p. 510): " On principle however I

Case No. 10 ***contd.***

"am clearly of opinion that a partnership formed for the main "purpose of deriving profit from the commission of a criminal "offence in a foreign and friendly country is illegal, even "although the parties have not succeeded in carrying out their "enterprise, and no such criminal offence has in fact been com-"mitted. . . . The ground upon which I rest my judgment "that such a partnership is illegal is that its recognition by our "courts would furnish a just cause for complaint by the United "States Government against our Government (of which the "partners are subjects), and would be contrary to our obliga-"tions of international comity as now understood and recog-"nised, and therefore would offend against our notions of "public morality."

Per Sankey, L.J. (as he then was) (at p. 521): "An English "contract should and will be held invalid on account of "illegality if the real object and intention of the parties necessi-"tates their joining in an endeavour to perform in a foreign "and friendly country some act which is illegal by the law of "such country notwithstanding the fact that there may be, in "a certain event, alternative modes or places of performing "which permits the contract to be performed legally." He distinguished (at p. 518)[1] the principle governing contracts involving a breach of the revenue laws of a foreign State, of which Lord Mansfield said, "No country ever takes notice of "the revenue laws of another,"[2] on the ground that "the "American law which it was proposed to infringe in the present "case was no mere revenue law; it was intended to prevent a "*malum in se* rather than a *malum prohibitum*." [Report: L.R. [1929] 1 K.B. 470.]

EDITOR'S NOTES.—(*a*) This decision deals mainly with a question of Private International Law but deserves mention in this volume because it appears to indicate a development in the conception of international comity by including within it a positive duty of international co-operation in the observance of internal laws. As to the meaning of the term "international comity," see Oppenheim, *International Law*, 4th ed., 1928, p. 28, note 3. The statement by Lawrence, L.J. (on p. 510) that the recognition by an English court of the partnership in question "would "furnish a just cause for complaint by the United States Government "against our Government" must (it is submitted) be understood as referring to a charge of breach of comity and not of international law.

---

[1] While stating later that he considers this old distinction requires reconsideration.

[2] In *Holman* v. *Johnson* (1775), 1 Cowp. at p. 343. For a modern illustration see *In re Visser*, Case No. 18 in this volume, though there is a difference between the enforcement and the recognition of a revenue law of a foreign country.

(*b*) " International comity " is a term not free from ambiguity, so that it may be worth while noting here another recent instance of its use. In an important case, decided by the British House of Lords, *Bankers and Shippers Insurance Company of New York* v. *Liverpool Marine and General Insurance Company Limited*, 24 Lloyd's List Law Reports (1926) at p. 87, Lord Buckmaster, speaking of the effect which ought to be given in an English court to an interpretation of a New York statute by the Court of Appeals of the State of New York, said that " though technically no judgment of a foreign court . . . would " bind this House, yet, none the less, the comity of international " affairs would require special and unusual circumstances to lead this " House away from a clear decision of a final court upon such a matter " of construction."

PART II

STATES AS INTERNATIONAL PERSONS

A. IN GENERAL

I.—Beginning of State Existence

[For Recognition, see below, *D*, p. 58.]

Establishment of New States—Beginning of State Existence—Acquisition of Nationality in the New State—Beginning of Austrian Republic. **Case No. 11**

H. E. *v.* Federal Ministry of the Interior.

Austrian Administrative Court. 1925. *No.* 13,752 *A.*

The Facts.—The plaintiff had acquired rights of citizenship (*Heimatrecht*) in a community of the Austrian Republic on 4 December, 1918, having up to this date had his *Heimatrecht* in a commune of Galicia. The State Government in question (*Landesregierung*) and the Federal Ministry of the Interior decided in 1923 that the acquisition of the *Heimatrecht* in Austria on 4 December, 1918, was null and void, the plaintiff not being an Austrian national on that date, but a Polish national. The plaintiff appealed on the ground that, as the Treaty of St. Germain did not come into force until 16 July, 1920, he continued, in his capacity as a native of Galicia (which formed part of the Austrian Empire), to be an Austrian subject until that date, and that he was, therefore, an Austrian national on 4 December, 1918.

Held: That the appeal failed. The foundation of the Austrian Republic did not date from the ratification of the Treaty of St. Germain, but from the Resolution of the Austrian Constituent Assembly of 30 October, 1918. The plaintiff was a Polish national on 4 December, 1918, and could not acquire *Heimatrecht* in an Austrian commune. [Report: *Sammlung der Erkenntnisse des Verwaltungsgerichtshofes*, vol. XLIX (1925), pp. 61-63.]

Note.—See also a decision of the same court on 11 February, 1922, No. 13,021. See Kunz, *Die völkerrechtliche Option*, vol. II (1928), pp. 147, 148; and also, to the same effect, a decision of 17 April, 1925, No. 13,835 A.

Establishment of New State—Czechoslovak Territory—Establishment of Czechoslovak Territorial Sovereignty in Bohemia, Moravia and Silesia.

The same opinion as in the decisions Váž. 550 civ., Váž. 5592 civ. and Váž. 5593 civ. (see *Annual Digest*, 1925-1926, p. 14, footnote 1, and Case No. 8), *i.e.* that the " historical " countries "—Bohemia, Moravia and Silesia—as defined by their pre-war (historical) boundaries formed a part of Czechoslovak State territory since 28 October, 1918, was expressed by the Supreme Court of Justice of Czechoslovakia in the decision of 23 November, 1927, No. Zm. II 434 (Váž. 2978 tr.).

Establishment of New State—Establishment of Territorial Sovereignty by Establishment of Civil Administration—Czechoslovak Territory—Establishment of Czechoslovak Territorial Sovereignty in Slovakia and Subcarpathian Russia.

The same opinion as in the resolution of 14 April, 1919, No. 352 (Boh. VI, 1919), and in the subsequent decisions (see *Annual Digest*, 1925-1926, Case No. 9), *i.e.* that the Czechoslovak laws apply to Slovakia and Subcarpathian Russia from the day on which the *zupan* took over his duties in the various parts of those territories, was expressed by the Supreme Administrative Court of Czechoslovakia in the decision of 4 February, 1927, No. 22.456/25 (Boh. 3526 fin.).

States—Establishment of—Beginning of Czechoslovak State.

See Case No. 94 (*Czechoslovak Agrarian Reform* (*Swiss Subjects*) *Case*).

Effect of Establishment of New State upon Nationality of Subjects of Former State—Acquisition of Czechoslovak Nationality by Austrian Nationals.

See Case No. 220 (*Bohemian Union Bank* (*plaintiff*) v. *Administrator of Austrian Property* (*defendant*)).

Establishment of New State—Time of Coming into Existence of the Czechoslovak State—Effect of the Treaties of Peace.

See Case No. 220 (*Bohemian Union Bank* (*plaintiff*) v. *Administrator of Austrian Property* (*defendant*)).

II.—Sovereignty and Independence

i.—In Foreign Relations

[See also below: *Recognition of Acts of Foreign States and Governments;* Part IV, JURISDICTION; and Part VIII, TREATIES: *Interpretation of Treaties. Restrictive Interpretation.*]

Act of Sovereignty—Jurisdiction of Courts over Political Acts —State Responsibility—Action of Neutral Government to Prevent Traffic in Arms. **Case No. 12**

THE EGYPTIAN GOVERNMENT *v.* THE BRITISH INDIA S.S. NAVIGATION CO.

Mixed Court of Appeal of Egypt. 11 *May*, 1927.

THE FACTS.—A cargo of rifles and ammunition which was sold to the Hedjaz Government during the war between the King of Hedjaz and the Sultan of Nejd was trans-shipped in the port of Suez from a vessel belonging to the plaintiffs, the British India Steamship Co., to another ship bound for Djeddah, to which the arms and the ammunition were consigned. The Egyptian Government issued an order forbidding the loading of the cargo, which thereupon remained in the warehouses of the plaintiffs at Suez for four months, when the Government announced that it would no longer oppose the reshipping of the cargo to any port save Djeddah. In an action brought by the Company against the Egyptian Government for damages resulting from a wrongful governmental order, it was held by the Mixed Tribunal of Mansurah that the Court had jurisdiction to entertain a claim, although the Government demurred on the ground that the Mixed Courts had no power to consider acts of sovereignty. On appeal to the Mixed Court of Appeal,

Held: (1) The action of the Egyptian Government in prohibiting the trans-shipment of the cargo was a purely political act based on its judgment that it is wrong that its territory should serve as a base for the transport of arms destined for one of two Moslem peoples who were at war with each other.

(2) Acts of sovereignty are placed outside the competence of the Mixed Courts, although the courts may in certain cases allocate an indemnity to individuals who have suffered by them.

Case No. 12 *contd.* (3) The act of the Government in opposing the despatch of arms to a neighbouring place through its territorial waters does not constitute any infringement of the acquired right of the consignee of the cargo, since the traffic in arms, however legitimate it may be in itself, must be carried on at the risk and peril of those engaged in it, without regard to the question whether a state of war has been declared in accordance with the rules of international law or not, or whether the State which refuses the despatch of arms has made a formal declaration of neutrality or not. The same principle applies where there is internal trouble in a country. A Government is not infringing any acquired right in prohibiting foreigners, in the interests of its own security, from engaging and transporting arms over its territory to a neighbouring State. [Report: *Gazette des Tribunaux Mixtes d'Egypte*, 17th year, 1927, p. 248.]

Act of State—Jurisdiction of Mixed Courts in Egypt in regard to Acts of the British Occupying Forces during the Great War.

See Case No. 25 (*Heinrich Finck* v. *Egyptian Government*).

Conclusiveness of Declarations of the Executive upon National Courts as to Certain International Matters.

See *Annual Digest*, 1925-1926, Case No. 96 (Note (*d*)).

See also Case No. 20, *Erste Allgemeine, etc.*, v. *A. J. van Rijt*, on the conclusiveness of the statements of the executive on the validity of treaties.

iii.—Acts of Sovereignty and Transactions of a Private Character

[See also Part IV, JURISDICTION: *Exemptions from.*]

Case No. 13

States in their Sovereign and in their Private Capacities—Purchases made by German Army of Occupation in Russian Territory—Subjection of Germany to Polish Law.

GWIRZMANN *v.* GERMAN STATE.

Polish-German Mixed Arbitral Tribunal. 16 *July*, 1927.

(LACHENAL, SCHOLZ, VAN MEENEN, NAMITKIEWICZ, LEBINSKI.)

THE FACTS.—This was a claim for the value of a quantity of provisions which the claimant furnished to German provisioning authorities in Modlin (occupied Russian territory, now belonging to Poland). The claimant produced a receipt signed by the competent German officer and certifying the receipt of the goods in question. Germany contended before the Mixed Arbitral Tribunal that the goods delivered were obtained by requisition, and not by purchase. This contention the Tribunal rejected.

It was then contended by Germany that, even if the transaction amounted to a contract of sale, German, and not Polish, law was applicable, as Germany could be subjected only to its own legislation in view of the fact that it is a sovereign State and that it has no other domicile except its own territory.

Held : That that contention must be rejected. There had been in the present case no exercise of public power, but only a contract in private law. By concluding a contract of this nature, the State subjects itself to the relevant provisions of private law and assumes the position of an individual. In order to rebut this presumption it would be necessary to show that as the result of special provisions enacted at that time in the occupied territory the purchases made by the German authorities were withdrawn from the application of private law and placed under a special legal régime to which the vendor had been made subject. This was not so in the present case. [Report : *Recueil,* VII, p. 733.]

States and Governments in their Private and Public Capacities—States as " Nationals." **Case No. 14**

ROUMANIAN MINISTER OF WAR *v.* TURKISH GOVERNMENT.

Turkish-Roumanian Mixed Arbitral Tribunal. 26 *April,* 1928.

(BARON DE NORDENSKJOELD, AHMED RECHID, JONESCU, MOUZAFFER SABRI, LYCURG MANU.)

THE FACTS.—Article 65 of the Treaty of Lausanne provided for the restitution of certain categories of property taken away by one of the contracting parties from the territories of the other. It also laid down that the Mixed Arbitral Tribunal shall have jurisdiction in respect of claims put forward under this Article by the nationals of the contracting parties.

The present claim was put forward by the Roumanian Minister of War. It referred to a large quantity of machinery and material as well as certain pieces

Case No. 14 *contd.*

of artillery taken away by the Turkish military authorities during the occupation of Roumania in 1916-1918.

Held: That although Article 65 referred only to claims put forward by Allied or Turkish nationals, the Tribunal was competent. In claiming the restitution of the objects mentioned, the claimant was not performing an act of sovereignty; he acted in his capacity as the proprietor of the objects claimed. When acting in that capacity, he possessed the same rights and duties as any other party. Seeing that Governments could appear as defendants before the Mixed Arbitral Tribunal, there was no reason why they should not be able to appear as claimants.[1] [Report: *Recueil,* VII, p. 993.]

NOTE.—See *Annual Digest,* 1925-1926, Cases Nos. 12 and 13, as showing the extensive interpretation of the term "national" so as to cover Governments.

Case No. 15

States in their Sovereign and Private Capacity—Jurisdiction—Immunity of Foreign States from Jurisdiction—State Trading—Commercial Representation of the Soviet Government—Inscription on the Commercial Register.

IN RE COMMERCIAL REPRESENTATION IN FRANCE OF THE UNION OF SOCIALIST SOVIET REPUBLICS.

Commercial Tribunal of the Seine. 13 January, 1927.

THE FACTS.—Persons and corporations habitually engaging in commercial transactions are required in France to enter their names upon the commercial register, kept in the registry attached to the *tribunaux de commerce.* The obligation applies to foreign merchants (*commerçants*) if they have in France their principal establishment or a branch or an agency. In reply to a request addressed to the Commercial Representation of the Soviet Government to make the required entry upon the register, the latter refused to comply and, upon a further request being issued by the judge appointed to supervise the observance of the law, repeated the refusal.

Held: That the Commercial Representation in France of the Union of Socialist Soviet Republics was liable to a fine of 16 francs, and that it must complete the entry within fourteen

[1] The Tribunal also referred to Article 64 of the Treaty of Lausanne as showing that the term "*ressortissants*" included not only physical, but also juridical, persons.

days. The Commercial Representation was engaged in regular commercial transactions. It was irrelevant that its personnel enjoyed diplomatic immunity, or that foreign trade was a State monopoly in Russia. " The present proceedings have not been " taken against a sovereign State in its public capacity " ; comprehensive commercial activities have no connection with the principle of State sovereignty.[1] If the Commercial Representation cannot supply all the details which are required by law, it can at least furnish as many as possible. [Report : 54 *Clunet* (1927), p. 680.]

Heads of States—Distinction between Private Property of Monarch and Trust Property Administered by Him as Head of Royal Family—Position of the Royal Prussian Brandenburger Family Trust. **Case No. 16**

DAS KÖNIGLICH PREUSSISCH-BRANDENBURGISCHE HAUSFIDEIKOMMISS *v.* THE ADMINISTRATION OF SOUTH-WEST AFRICA AND THE REGISTRAR OF DEEDS.

High Court of South-West Africa. 7 September, 1928.

THE FACTS.—Article 257 of the Treaty of Versailles provided, *inter alia*, that " All property and possessions " belonging to the German Empire or to the German " States situated in such territories shall be trans- " ferred with the territories to the Mandatory Power " in its capacity as such and no payment shall be made " nor any credit given to those Governments in con- " sideration of this transfer. For the purposes of this " Article the property and possessions of the German " Empire and of the German States shall be deemed " to include all the property of the Crown, the Empire " or the States and the private property of the former " German Emperor and other Royal personages."

Acting under this Article the Governor-General-in-Council passed two resolutions in October, 1921, approving of the cancellation of the title of two farms " Dickdorn " and " Kosis " in the district of Gibeon, South-West Africa, registered in favour of " Das Königlich Preussisch-Brandenburgische Haus- " fideikommiss " and directing the Registrar of Deeds

[1] The Court referred here to the decision of the Court of Appeal of Paris, 19 November, 1926 : *Gazette du Palais*, 1927, I, 165.

Case No. 16 ***contd.***

to effect the necessary entries in his registries. The directions were carried out accordingly.

Application was made on behalf of the former title-holder to the High Court of South-West Africa for an order (1) declaring that the provisions of the Treaty do not apply to the said title-holder, (2) interdicting the Administration of South-West Africa from disposing of the farms, and (3) directing the Registrar of Deeds to rectify his deeds register by striking out the entry cancelling the registration of the properties in favour of the applicant. In support of this application it was alleged that the applicant was by German law a duly constituted *universitas personarum* or corporation entitled to sue and be sued, to make contracts, to hold immovable property, and generally to exercise all the rights, as well as being subject to all the obligations, of a legal *persona*. There was evidence to show that the Hausfideikommiss was constituted in 1733 by King Frederick William I of Prussia, and that the King, or, as the case may be, the Head of the family for the time being, had sole authority to administer the assets of the Hausfideikommiss without consulting the agnates, was under no obligation to account for his administration, alone represented the Hausfideikommiss as against third parties, and allotted to each member of his family in his free discretion so much as he was to receive as additional allowance towards his living expenses. In his capacity as Head of the Royal House and sole administrator of the Hausfideikommiss, the ex-Emperor purchased, in the year 1912, the aforesaid farms " Dickdorn " and " Kosis," out of funds belonging to the Hausfideikommiss which were then available, and the farms were accordingly registered in the name of the Hausfideikommiss aforesaid.

Held : (1) That the property of the Königlich Preussisch-Brandenburgische Hausfideikommiss had its origin in property owned by Frederick William I of Prussia in 1733 in his private capacity, and that nothing had happened to change the character of the property since that time ;

(2) That the farms " Dickdorn " and " Kosis " formed part of the property of the Hausfideikommiss aforesaid ;

(3) That this property was therefore not part of the property and possessions of the German Empire and of the German

States within the meaning of Article 257 of the Treaty of Versailles, inasmuch as it was not Crown or State property ;

(4) That the words " other Royal personages " in Article 257, read in connection with Articles 56, 120, 144, 153 and 256, mean " other German sovereigns," and do not extend to members of the family of the ex-Emperor who are not German sovereigns ;

(5) That if the ex-Emperor could be said to have any personal interest in the property in question, it would be at most an undivided interest of a usufructuary nature, and since the other beneficiaries are not German sovereigns, the Mandatory Power would not under any circumstances have the right to dispose of their interest in the subject of the Hausfidcikommiss ;

(6) That in fact the property in question did not belong to the ex-Emperor or to the members of his family but to the Hausfideikommiss itself, which is a separate legal *persona*. This legal *persona* was the private owner of the fideicommissary properties ; the individual member of the family was merely entitled to a life usufruct in the fideicommissum. This solution was adopted by the learned judge from an opinion rendered by the members of the Faculty of Law and Political Science of the Silesian Friedrich-Wilhelm University, which is referred to in the judgment as the " Breslau Opinion."

The Court made an Order in terms of the Petition. [Report: *South African Law Reports*, [1928] *South-West Africa*, p. 82. ([1928] S.W.A. 82.)]

Foreign Sovereign Plaintiff—Costs Awarded Against.

See Case No. 18 (*In re Visser : H.M. The Queen of Holland* (*Married Woman*) (*plaintiff*) v. *Drukker and Others* (*defendants*)).

IV.—Recognition of Acts of Foreign States and Governments

[The attention of the reader is drawn to the fact that questions involving Recognition of Acts of States and Governments in one form or another will also be found in Cases Nos. 35-47, dealing with *Recognition of States, Governments, Insurgency or Belligerency*, and in Cases Nos. 91, 92, dealing with *Territorial Jurisdiction* where the main point is the scope of a Government's jurisdiction and the question of its recognition is merely incidental.]

Case No. 17 **Recognition of Acts of Foreign States and Governments—Forces of Foreign State in Occupation of Foreign Territory—British Forces in Constantinople after the World War—Seizure of Goods by Command of the Occupying Military Authority—Jurisdiction of Foreign Court in regard to Acts of Sovereignty of a Recognised Power in Occupied Territory.**

S. Papadopoulos, of Péra (Constantinople) (appellant) *v.* (1) N. V. Koninklijke Nederlandsche Stoomboot-maatschappij, of Amsterdam (respondents); (2) J. W. Whittal & Co. Ltd., of Constantinople (interveners).

Court of Appeal, Amsterdam. 13 *March,* 1928.

(Appeal from judgment of District Court of Amsterdam, 17 April, 1925. See *Annual Digest,* 1925-1926, Case No. 19.)

The Facts.—See *Annual Digest,* 1925-1926, Case No. 19.

Held: (*a*) That the Court of Appeal dissents from the District Court in so far as the latter declined, without limitation, to question the acts of sovereignty of foreign Governments and to consider the legality of the acts committed by the G.O.C. of the Allied troops in Constantinople. These questions would by international law be withdrawn from the Dutch courts if any one of the Powers in occupation of Constantinople had itself been a party to the suit in which the legality of its sovereign acts was questioned, but not in the case under consideration where their legality is questioned in a suit between two private individuals. The District Court was wrong in holding that by pronouncing such acts illegal it would have negatived acts which had been done by the occupying Power; on the contrary, all those acts would remain in force, notwithstanding the decision of the Dutch court. So it is impossible to consider as a violation of foreign sovereignty the decision of a Dutch court that such acts of the occupying Power constituted acts of embezzlement under Turkish law. The Dutch tribunal being an independent organ of the State of the Netherlands, bound to render judgment in a dispute relating to proprietary rights, cannot be deemed to engage the international responsibility of that State by a judicial decision pronouncing illegal certain acts of a foreign Government.

(*b*) That, however, Article 137 [1] of the Peace Treaty of Lausanne must be construed as a waiver by the Turkish Re-

[1] See p. 414, n. 1.

public of the right to challenge the legality of all decisions and orders of the occupying Powers, and that, therefore, the appellant party, as a Turkish subject, is equally precluded from doing so.[1] (See Case No. 285.) [Report: *Weekblad van het Recht*, 31 May, 1928, No. 11816.]

Foreign Revenue Laws—Foreign Sovereign as Plaintiff—Action to Recover Duties under Revenue Laws—Non-Enforceability. **Case No. 18**

In re Visser: H.M. The Queen of Holland (Married Woman) (plaintiff) *v.* Drukker and Others (defendants).

Chancery Division of the English High Court of Justice—Mr. Justice Tomlin. 29 *June*, 1928.

The Facts.—David Visser died in Holland in December, 1926, a Dutch subject, domiciled in Holland, leaving assets in England. Drukker was the executor of his will, and he and another defendant, Zeegen, were the heirs of Visser. The third defendant, Bisschop, was resident in England and had obtained letters of administration of Visser's estate in England under a power of attorney from Drukker. The domicile and nationality of the three defendants are not stated. The net assets of Visser in England amounted to about £1150. The plaintiff alleged that according to Dutch law the estate of Visser was liable to succession duty, and she claimed, *inter alia*, a declaration that she was a creditor of the estate of Visser and an order for an account. It does not appear from the report whether the plaintiff's claim was made in respect of the whole of Visser's estate or only in respect of the English assets, nor does this point appear to have been taken in argument. Upon an application by the defendant Zeegen to strike out the plaintiff's statement of claim under the Rules of the Supreme Court, Order XXV, Rule 4, on the ground that it disclosed no reasonable cause of action,

Held: For the defendant Zeegen: (1) That the statement of claim must be struck out as disclosing no reasonable cause of action, and (2) that costs should be paid by the foreign

[1] For certain repercussions of the incident dealt with in this case in the English courts see *Sedgwick Collins & Co. Limited* v. *Highton and Others* (1929), 34 Lloyd's List Law Reports, 448.

Case No. 18 contd. sovereign, who had submitted to the jurisdiction by instituting proceedings.

Per Tomlin, J. (at p. 884): "There is a well recognised rule, "which has been enforced for at least 200 years or there-"abouts, under which these Courts will not collect the taxes of "foreign States for the benefit of those foreign States; and this "is one of those actions which these Courts will not entertain."

It appeared that there was no previous decision actually in point, but *Municipal Council of Sydney* v. *Bull*, L.R. [1909] 1 K.B. 7, afforded a strong analogy. See also *The Eva*, L.R. [1921] P. 454 (a Finnish law imposing a duty of 2½ per cent. on the sale of Finnish ships), and *King of the Hellenes* v. *Bostrom*, Law Journal Newspaper, 1923, p. 306, and Dicey, *Conflict of Laws*, 4th ed., 1927, p. 226. [Report: L.R. [1928] 1 Ch. 877.]

Case No. 19 **Recognition of Acts of Foreign Governments—Validity of Marriages Contracted in Russia under Soviet Régime.**

SOVIET MARRIAGES IN RUSSIA (HUNGARY) CASE.

Supreme Court of Hungary. 23 *February*, 1927.
(*No. P. III*, 1616/1926.)

THE FACTS.—The defendant, a Hungarian national, while in Russia as a prisoner of war in the town of Petropavlovsk, entered into a so-called Soviet marriage. The Public Prosecutor asks now for a declaration that that marriage is not valid.

Held by the Supreme Court of Hungary: That the marriage was null and void. At the time when the marriage was concluded, marriage law was regulated by the Decree of the Soviet Government of 27 September, 1921, and by the provisions of a law passed in 1918. According to these provisions a marriage is valid when it is registered with the office charged with keeping documents relating to personal status. The marriage is concluded by the fact of being entered in the registry book. Divorce takes place by way of judicial proceedings, but it can be demanded, and obtained, by one party even against the will of the other. The law does not recognise any grounds for divorce or principles of guilt.[1] In case of change of residence the other party is not bound to follow the spouse to the new place of residence. "According to generally recognised rules of inter-

[1] For an examination of the methods of marriage and divorce in Soviet Russia see *Nachimson* v. *Nachimson*, L.R. [1930] P. 85, 217.

"national law, such foreign laws and rules which conflict with the "principles of humanity and with the moral conceptions and laws "obtaining within the State need not be applied. A marriage "concluded in Soviet Russia before Soviet authorities cannot "be recognised as a marriage which corresponds to our laws "and our moral conceptions." [1] [Reports: *Magánjogi Döntvénytár*, XX, No. 26; *Magánjog Tára*, VIII, No. 22 (Note by L. Sömjén).]

NOTE.—See *Annual Digest*, 1925-1926, Case No. 22 (Note).

V.—Continuity of States

[See also STATE SUCCESSION.]

Continuity of States—Identity of the Former Austrian Monarchy and the Republic of Austria—Difference of Opinion between Austria and Holland concerning the Question of Identity—Attitude of Dutch Courts—Convention of 17 July, 1905, concerning the Conflicts of Laws relative to Procedure in Civil Cases—Continued Binding Force of the same between Holland and the Austrian Republic. **Case No. 20**

ERSTE ALLGEMEINE UNFALL- UND SCHADEN-VERSICHERUNGS-GESELLSCHAFT, OF VIENNA *v.* A. J. VAN RIJT.

District Court, Amsterdam. 29 *October*, 1926.

In a civil suit before the District Court the claimant, an Austrian joint stock company, was held to be exempted from

[1] But see *Church Marriages in Russia* (*Hungary*) case, decided by the Supreme Court of Hungary on 3 May, 1928 (No. P. III, 8803/1927). In this case the defendant, while in Russia as a prisoner of war, entered on 2 June, 1917, into a contract of marriage with a Russian subject before a priest of the Greek Orthodox Church. He then returned to Hungary, and there married again. The action was brought with a view to declaring the second marriage void. The plaintiff contended that he had not concluded a valid marriage in Russia. It was held (by the Supreme Court of Hungary) that the first marriage was valid: at the time when the defendant contracted the first marriage, the provisions of family law laid down in the Civil Code obtaining in Czarist Russia were still in force. The Decree issued in 1918 by the Revolutionary Government concerning personal status and marriage law states that Church marriages concluded prior to 20 December, 1917, in accordance with the rules and formalities laid down in the former Civil Code shall remain valid. The first marriage concluded by the defendant was in accordance with these rules and it must therefore be regarded as valid. Reports: *Magánjog Tára*, IX, No. 89; *Magánjogi Döntvénytár*, XXI, No. 92.

See also *Lewis T.* v. *Theodora A.*, decided by the Supreme Court of Hungary on 6 November, 1928 (No. P. III, 8411/1927). The plaintiff and the defendant woman were married in Soviet Russia in May, 1921, before the Soviet civil authorities. In August of the same year the same parties went through a religious ceremony of marriage in Russia. The plaintiff contended that there

Case No. 20 ***contd.*** depositing the *cautio judicatum solvi* on the grounds: that the Austro-Hungarian Monarchy had been a Party to the Convention of The Hague of 17 July, 1905, concerning the Conflicts of Laws relative to Procedure in Civil Cases; that the Court, at its request, had been informed by the Dutch Government that, according to a diplomatic correspondence between the new Austrian Government and itself, the two Governments were at variance as to the juridical identity between the former Austrian Monarchy and the new Austrian Republic, the Dutch Government having declared that it considered the latter as juridically identical with the former, but the new Austrian Government having denied the correctness of this opinion; that, however, the Austrian Government, notwithstanding this denial of the continued existence of the former State of Austria, had nevertheless declared to the Dutch Government that it would consider the Convention of 1905 as binding in future between Holland and the new Austrian Republic; that, on these conditions, "the Court had to respect the agreement "reached between the two Governments and that, therefore, "in the case under consideration, it was not for the Court to "enter into an examination of the question whether the "Austrian Republic has to be considered as continuing the "existence of the former Austrian Monarchy according to the "Law of Nations." [Report: *Weekblad van het Recht*, 30 May, 1927, No. 11659.]

Continuity of States—The Austrian Empire and the Austrian Republic—The Pre-War and Post-War Kingdoms of Hungary—Whether Differing Essentially.

See Case No. 54 (*Tripartite Claims Commission*).

was no valid marriage in existence between him and the defendant. It was held (by the Supreme Court of Hungary) that the marriage was valid. It was true that Soviet marriages concluded in Russia cannot in any way be regarded as valid in Hungary. "However, according to the law "of the Christian Church, be it the Roman Catholic Church or the Greek "Orthodox Church as predominant in Russia, marriages concluded before "these Churches have the same effect, that is to say, they create the same "rights and obligations, as marriages recognised by Hungarian private law. "Accordingly, there is no reason why a marriage concluded by the parties in "Russia before a Christian Church authority in accordance with Church law "which is still in force should not in every respect be regarded as a valid "marriage so long as it has not been legally annulled or declared void." Reports: *Magánjogi Döntvénytár*, XXII, No. 44; *Magánjog Tára*, X, No. 1 (Note by G. Tóth).

Upon the attitude of the English courts toward a Soviet marriage contracted in 1924 see *Nachimson* v. *Nachimson*, L.R. [1930] P. 217.

VI.—Extinction of States

End of State Existence—Termination of Diplomatic Representation—Extinction of the Kingdom of Montenegro.

See Case No. 106 (*In re Savini and Others*).

B. COMPOSITE AND DEPENDENT STATES AND TERRITORIES

I.—Unions of States

i.—Federal States and Confederations

[As to Responsibility of Federal States for Acts and Obligations of their Member States see Part V, A, Case No. 135.]

Federal State—State Member of a Federation—Absence of International Status—Loan in France—Competence of the French Courts. **Case No. 21**

STATE OF CEARA *v.* DORR.

Court of Appeal of Colmar (First Chamber). 27 *June*, 1928.

THE FACTS.—The State of Ceara (a Member State of the Federal State of Brazil) was summoned before the Court of First Instance of Metz by the plaintiff Dorr for the payment of the coupons and re-payment of the capital in respect of bonds of the 5 per cent. Loan, issued in 1910 in France by this State. Payment was demanded either in gold or in notes of the Bank of France calculated from the date on which the bonds fell due.

The Tribunal of Metz rejected the plea to the jurisdiction of the French courts raised by the State of Ceara. The State of Ceara appealed.

Held: That the judgment of the Tribunal of Metz must be upheld. "In virtue of a clear principle of international law, "based on a mutual respect for their sovereignty and inde-"pendence, foreign States cannot be summoned before the "courts of another State in connection with engagements con-"tracted by them with the subjects of that other State." But

Case No. 21 *contd.* immunity from jurisdiction presupposed the sovereignty of the State. " A State cannot be recognised in international law as " sovereign if, whatever the extent of its authority in domestic " matters, the Constitution to which it is subject recognises in " it no authority to exercise the rights of sovereignty in inter- " national relations." This was the position of the State of Ceara in accordance with Article 48 of the Constitution of Brazil, 24 February, 1891, and it was therefore unable to claim immunity from the jurisdiction of French courts. [Report: 56 *Clunet* (1929), p. 1040.]

Federal States—Legal Status of—Applicability of Rules of International Law in Relations between them.

See Case No. 86 (*Württemberg and Prussia* v. *Baden*).

Federal States—Nationality in—Direct and Indirect Nationality—Extinction of.

See Case No. 190 (*Alsace-Lorraine Nationality* (*Statelessness*) *Case*).

Federal States—How far Taking Over the Obligations of State Members.

See Case No. 56 (*Land Tax Immunities Case*).

Federal States—Nationality in Federal States—German and Prussian Nationality.

See Case No. 189 (*De Luck* v. *Germany*).

ii.—Other Unions (including Customs Unions)

Case No. 22 **Unions of States—How far do International Technical Conventions Apply as between them—Former Relations of Austria and Hungary—The Berne Convention of 1890 concerning Railway Transports and Freights.**

N. N. *v.* ADMINISTRATION OF HUNGARIAN STATE RAILWAYS.

Supreme Court of Hungary. 31 *August*, 1928.
(*No. P. IV*, 5731/1925.)

THE FACTS.—The plaintiff's goods were forwarded for transport to Vienna on one of the lines of the defendant State Railways on 18 October, 1918. The plaintiff claimed for loss and damage and contended that the defendant Railway Administration was liable under the terms of the Berne Convention of 1890 concerning Railway Transports and Freights.

Held by the Supreme Court of Hungary: That the claim must be dismissed. At the time of the said transport the Berne Convention was, in accordance with its first Article, to be applied to transports from the territory of one of the contracting States to the territory of another by virtue of a direct freight note. In regard to transport between Austria and Hungary, who, together with other contracting parties, had jointly signed the Convention, it had no application. There existed between Austria and Hungary a Convention of Commerce and Transport concluded in 1907, which applied to transport between those two countries, but under its terms the defendant was not liable in this case. [Report: *Hiteljog Tára*, X, No. 41.]

Unions of States—Status of—International Status of the Members of the Union—The Former Union between Austria and Hungary.

See Case No. 54 (*Tripartite Claims Commission*).

II.—British Commonwealth of Nations

British Commonwealth of Nations—Nationality in—Naturalisation in South Africa under Former Law—Effect in Great Britain—Meaning of the Words " One of the Contracting " Parties " in relation to Great Britain. **Case No. 23**

L. Hanau *v.* C. Hanau.

Anglo-German Mixed Arbitral Tribunal (*2nd Division*).
24 *November*, 1927.

(Van Heeckeren, Hart, Johannes.)

The Facts.—Article 296 of the Treaty of Versailles provided, *inter alia*, as follows:

" There shall be settled through the intervention " of clearing offices to be established by each of the " High Contracting Parties within three months of " the notification referred to in paragraph (*e*) here- " after the following classes of pecuniary obligations:

" 1. Debts payable before the war and due by a

Case No. 23 *contd.*

"national of one of the Contracting Powers, residing "within its territory, to a national of an Opposing "Power, residing within its territory. . . .

"4 (*b*) Each of the High Contracting Parties shall "be respectively responsible for the payment of such "debts due by its nationals, . . .

"(*c*) The sums due to the nationals of one of the "High Contracting Parties by the nationals of an "Opposing State will be debited to the clearing office "of the country of the debtor, and paid to the "creditor by the clearing office of the country of the "creditor;

"(*d*) Debts shall be paid or credited in the cur-"rency of such one of the Allied and Associated "Powers, their colonies or protectorates, or the "British Dominions or India, as may be con-"cerned. . . .

"(*e*) The provisions of this Article and of the "Annex hereto shall not apply as between Germany "on the one hand and any one of the Allied and "Associated Powers, their colonies or protectorates, "or any one of the British Dominions or India on the "other hand, unless within a period of one month "from the deposit of the ratifications of the present "Treaty by the Power in question, or of the ratifica-"tion on behalf of such Dominion or of India, notice "to that effect is given to Germany by the Govern-"ment of such Allied or Associated Power or of such "Dominion or of India as the case may be."

Carl Hanau, from whom the debt in respect of which the action was brought was alleged to be due, was born in Germany. In March, 1874, he obtained letters of naturalisation issued under the Aliens Naturalisation Act, 1883, of the Colony of the Cape of Good Hope, which later, and before the war of 1914-1918, was incorporated in the Union of South Africa. The letters of naturalisation certified as follows: "Carl Hanau "shall henceforth to all intents and purposes whatso-"ever be deemed, taken and assumed to be entitled to "all political and other rights and powers and privi-"leges and be subject to all obligations to which a "natural-born British subject is entitled or subject in "this colony."

In January, 1920, Hanau was resident in Great Britain. The Union had not adopted the above-mentioned provisions of the Treaty and had made its own arrangements directly with the German Government. It was contended on behalf of the trustee in bankruptcy of Carl Hanau that, as the latter was not a British subject in Great Britain, the alleged debt could not be recovered in the proceedings before the Mixed Arbitral Tribunal.

Held: That the Tribunal had no jurisdiction.

In accordance with the English decision in the case of *Markwald* v. *Attorney-General* (L.R. [1920] 1 Ch. 348), from the standpoint of English law the British nationality of Carl Hanau was limited to his political status in South Africa. In England he was an alien. He could not therefore be regarded as a British national for the purpose of the clearing proceedings between Great Britain and Germany. "The words 'one of the "'Contracting Powers' in Article 296 must be construed as "meaning, on the one hand, the German Government, and, on "the other hand, the Government of that part of the British "Empire—whether the United Kingdom, one of the four "Dominions or India, which in the event shall have given the "notice specified in clause (*e*) above"—and that the conditions precedent of the residence and nationality of the debtor must be determined with reference to that Government alone. Accordingly, "so far as British nationals are concerned, the "clearing system as between Great Britain and Germany does "not apply to those who, being resident in Great Britain, are "aliens according to the law prevailing there." [Report: *Recueil*, VII, p. 469.]

NOTE.—On the subject of Imperial Naturalisation see Oppenheim, vol. I (4th ed., 1928), § 307; Sargant in *J.C.L.*, XXXI, p. 327; and van Pittius, *Nationality within the British Commonwealth of Nations* (1930), p. 70. The Union of South Africa adopted Part II (Naturalisation) of the British Nationality and Status of Aliens Act, 1914, in 1926. See Flournoy and Hudson, *Nationality Laws* (1929), p. 116.

III.—Protected and Vassal States and Protectorates

Case No. 24

Protectorates—Status of Inhabitants of—Whether Included within the Conception of *Ressortissant*—Distinction between a National and a *Ressortissant*—Persons of Tunisian Nationality.

FALLA-NATAF AND BROTHERS *v.* GERMANY.

Franco-German Mixed Arbitral Tribunal. 30 *December*, 1927.

(ASSER, GANDOLPHE, FROELICH.)

THE FACTS.—The claimants were nationals of Tunis. It was contended on behalf of Germany that the Franco-German Mixed Arbitral Tribunal had no jurisdiction on the ground that being of Tunisian nationality they could not be considered as nationals of an Allied or Associated Power as provided in Article 297 of the Treaty of Versailles.

Held : That the Tribunal had jurisdiction. A Protectorate constituted a legal relationship. The term " *ressortissant* " used in Article 297 (*e*) was not limited to nationals of a State, but comprised all persons connected with a State by a juridical link other than nationality proper. Accordingly, Tunisian nationals were entitled to the benefits of the provisions of the Treaty of Versailles like other French *ressortissants*. [Report : *Recueil*, VII, p. 642.]

NOTE.—Cf. Case No. 205 (*Hrand Djevahirdjian* v. *Germany*). The English text of the Treaty refers to " nationals."

Case No. 25

Protectorates—Relations of Egypt and Great Britain during the Great War—Capitulations—Jurisdiction of the Courts over Acts of Sovereignty.

HEINRICH FINCK *v.* EGYPTIAN GOVERNMENT.

Mixed Court of Appeal of Egypt. 1 *March*, 1927.

THE FACTS.—The plaintiff was a German subject who conducted a bookselling business at Cairo. He left Egypt of his own accord with his family on the 15 October, 1914, entrusting the administration of his bookshop to two agents, one of German and the other of Austrian nationality. His agents were subsequently required by the Egyptian police, at the instance of the British military authorities, to be interned, and were removed to Malta. The British military authorities then appointed a sequestrator of the business, who liquidated it, but in such a manner that the proceeds of the sale only served to cover the expenses of the administration and liquidation. The plaintiff instituted a claim before the Mixed Courts against the Egyptian Government for damages for the loss caused to him by the action of the Government acting under the orders of the British military authorities. The Government pleaded (1) that the courts had no jurisdiction over an act of sovereignty which was taken for the defence of the country, in interning the subjects of the States which were at war with Great Britain and the Allied Powers; and (2) that the Bill of Indemnity (Law No. 25 of July, 1923) protected the Egyptian Government from liability for having failed to prevent the British authorities from doing acts for which no redress could be obtained in any Egyptian court. The Mixed Tribunal of Cairo dismissed the claim of the plaintiff on the ground, *inter alia*, that a German plaintiff was not entitled to bring his claim before the Mixed Courts. On appeal it was

Held: (1) The Egyptian authorities in giving their help to the British Army in Occupation in Egypt acted on account of the British military forces and, therefore, had no independent responsibility.

(2) The capitulations which regulated the relations between the Egyptian authorities and foreign subjects in no way regulated the relations of capitulatory Powers between each other, and therefore the court has no jurisdiction in a claim made by a German subject against the British Government on account of the action taken by the British Government.

(3) There was no declaration of war between Egypt and Germany, but the decision published in the Official Journal in 1914 "with a view to assure the defence of Egypt in the War "between Germany and Great Britain," by which the Government authorised the forces of His Britannic Majesty which were already in occupation of the country to exercise rights of war in the ports and territory of Egypt, was an "act of sovereignty"[1] which the court was not competent to enquire into.

[1] For a similar defence of "act of sovereignty" in Egyptian courts see *Annual Digest*, 1925-1926, Case No. 14.

Case No. 25 *contd.* (4) The Bill of Indemnity (Law No. 25 of 1923) declares that any demand based on acts done by the military authority under Martial Law is inadmissible in the Egyptian courts, and protects the Egyptian Government against any liability for having failed to prevent the military authorities from doing anything for which no redress can be obtained in the Egyptian courts. [Reports: *Gazette des Tribunaux Mixtes d'Egypte*, 17th year, 1927, p. 257; 55 *Clunet* (1928), p. 194. For the decision of the Cairo Court of First Instance see *B.Y.*, 1925, pp. 219-226.]

Case No. 26

Protectorates—French Protectorate of Tunis—Status of Tunisians in Egypt.

EGYPTIAN GOVERNMENT *v.* ABDUL LATIF ABDALLAH.

Mixed Court of Appeal of Egypt. 1 *May*, 1928.

THE FACTS.—A claim was brought by the plaintiff against the Egyptian Government for payment of an indemnity granted to retired officers who were subjects of a capitulatory Power. The plaintiff was born in Alexandria on the 14 April, 1885, to a Tunisian father registered in the French Consulate, and maintained his Tunisian nationality. He was, therefore, entitled to the treatment of a foreign subject. It was objected by the Egyptian Government that the law with regard to the position of foreign subjects did not apply to a Tunisian, on the ground that he was not a national, but only a protected subject, of a capitulatory Power, and that former Turkish subjects were excluded from the benefit of the law.

Held: While the Turkish Government refused to recognise the French Protectorate of Tunis, the Egyptian Government had granted recognition since 1884 and recognised Tunisians as persons under French protection. The benefit of the provisions of the law with regard to compensation of foreign officers of the Egyptian Government is to be extended to protected persons as well as foreign subjects; and the only ex-Turkish subjects who are excluded from the law are those who lost their Turkish nationality in consequence of the Great War, and not persons such as Cretans or Tunisians who had lost it previously to the war. [Report: *Gazette des Tribunaux Mixtes*, 18th year, p. 178.]

IV.—Mandates

i.—Sovereignty over Mandated Territories. Status of the Mandated Territories

Mandates—Status of Mandated Territories—Application of Extradition Treaties to Mandated Territories—Treaties Concluded by the Mandatory. **Case No. 27**

EXTRADITION OF CRIMINALS TO AND FROM MANDATED TERRITORIES.

Alta Corte de Justicia de Uruguay. 7 March, 1928.

THE FACTS.—It was suggested by the British Legation at Montevideo to the Government of Uruguay that the treaty of extradition between the British Government and the Uruguayan Government, dated 26 March, 1884, be construed to comprehend mandated territories held by Great Britain under the Covenant of the League of Nations.

Held : " That the said treaty of extradition of 1884 cannot " be applied to territories under the mandate mentioned . . . " because when it was concluded such territories did not exist " under mandate, and therefore could not be comprehended in " the stipulations of the said treaty. Article 1 of the treaty says " that its provisions shall apply to the crimes and offences " enumerated in Article 2, and which may be committed in the " territory of one of the parties ; and Article 10 adds that ' the " ' stipulations of the present treaty shall be applicable to the " ' foreign colonies and possessions of His Britannic Majesty.' " And, as the territories under mandate are not ' of one of the " ' parties,' nor colonies or possessions of His Britannic Majesty, " we are forced to reach the conclusion that the treaty of 1884 " does not embrace the persons residing in those territories over " which England exercises no more than a simple mandate. " And this is recognised by the British Legation when it says " . . . that its Government desires that demands for extradi- " tion may be made with regard to the territories under its " mandate ' in the same manner, as if these territories were " ' possessions of His Britannic Majesty and as if the natives " ' or aborigines of such territories were British subjects.' To

Case No. 27 *contd.*

"include, then, in the treaty of extradition the territories "under British mandate would be to do something which would "amount to a modification of the said treaty, and that there-"fore cannot be authorised by our authorities. The Attorney-"General understands, as does also the President of the Re-"public, that it would be convenient to extend to the territories "alluded to the stipulations of the treaty in question; but he "also understands that to do this it would be necessary to draw "up an additional protocol similar to the one drawn up on "20 March, 1891, to amplify Article 9 of the treaty of 1884, "and to submit it then to the approval of the Legislative "Power. Until this has been done, it will not be possible to "apply the treaty in question to the territories referred to. "Such is the opinion of the Attorney-General in this matter." [Report: 1 *Supplement* (1928) *Jurisprudencia de la Alta Corte de Justicia*, p. 36.]

NOTE.—The Opinion quoted *verbatim* and *in toto* above was that of the Attorney-General of the Nation to the Supreme Court, to whom that Court had referred the matter for an Opinion. The Court adopted that Opinion as the Resolution of the Court in this matter.

Case No. 28

Mandates—Territories Detached from Turkey—Recognition of States—Jurisdiction of Mixed Courts.

ANTOINE BEY SABBAGH *v.* MOHAMED PACHA AHMED AND OTHERS.

Mixed Court of Mansura, Egypt. 15 *November*, 1927.

THE FACTS.—In an action brought in the Mixed Tribunal of Mansura against the Ministry of Public Works in Egypt and the Minister, the plaintiff, who was of Lebanese nationality, had opted therefor in accordance with the provisions of the Treaty of Lausanne and had received a passport from the French Mandatory Government. Objection was raised to the jurisdiction by the defendants, on the ground that the plaintiff could not be deemed to be a foreign subject, and therefore the matter was within the jurisdiction of the native courts.

Held: Syria and the Lebanon, being countries placed under an "A" Mandate, are, in accordance with the Covenant of the League of Nations, to be deemed to be independent

States and persons of public international law, and the inhabitants have acquired the nationality of those States. Syrians and Lebanese must, therefore, be considered in Egypt as foreigners on the same basis as the subjects of countries which had been detached from the Turkish Empire prior to the Great War.

The recognition of a treaty of peace on the part of a State which has not been a direct party to it may be express or implied. The diplomatic relations between Egypt and the new States which have been created under the Treaty of Lausanne, and also the conclusion of a *modus vivendi* with regard to Syria and the Lebanon between Egypt and France as the Mandatory Power, served to establish the implied recognition by Egypt of the Treaty of Lausanne in virtue of which on the one hand Syria and the Lebanon were constituted as States detached from the Turkish Empire, and Turkey on the other definitely renounced all rights of suzerainty over Egypt.

The privileges of jurisdiction which the *modus vivendi* declared not to extend to the Syrians are concerned only with the French consular tribunals and not with the competence of the Mixed Courts; since the Egyptian and French Governments have no power to modify that competence which is prescribed by international treaty affecting all the Powers which drew up the organisation of the courts.

The previous decision of the Mixed Courts which treated Turkish subjects on the same footing as local subjects in Egypt, even after the Proclamation of December, 1914, declaring the British Protectorate in Egypt, cannot be maintained after the complete renunciation by Turkey of suzerainty over Egypt. Since Egypt and Turkey have become completely independent of one another, the Mixed jurisdiction, which in civil and commercial matters is the common jurisdiction between all persons of different nationalities, applies to Turks as to all other foreigners. [Report: *Gazette des Tribunaux Mixtes d'Egypte*, 18th year, 1927-1928, p. 13.]

NOTE.—The decision of the Tribunal is in direct conflict with the decision of the Mixed Court of Appeal in the case of *Rizgalla* v. *Zahar*, in the *Annual Digest*, 1925-1926, Case No. 138. It has been followed, however, by the Court of Cairo in the case of *Ismail El Ghonnama* v. *Saleh J. Ibrahim* in *Gazette des Tribunaux Mixtes*, December, 1928, p. 26, and 57 *Clunet* (1930), p. 212.

ii.—Rights and Duties of the Mandatories

Case No. 29

PERMANENT COURT OF INTERNATIONAL JUSTICE. JUDGMENT No. 10.

Mandates—Rights and Duties of the Mandatories—Interpretation of—Article 11 of the Mandate for Palestine—Conception of " Public Control."

GREECE *v.* GREAT BRITAIN.

CASE OF THE READAPTATION OF THE MAVROMMATIS JERUSALEM CONCESSIONS.

(JURISDICTION.)

10 *October*, 1927.

THE FACTS. — (See Case No. 148 in *Annual Digest*, 1925-1926.) In Judgment No. 2, the Court held that it had jurisdiction to entertain the claim put forward by the Greek Government in regard to certain concessionary rights in Jerusalem of M. Mavrommatis, a Greek subject, under Article 11 of the Mandate for Palestine which empowered the Mandatory " to " provide for public ownership or control of " any of the natural resources of the country " . . . " subject to any international obligations " accepted by the Mandatory." The Court came to this conclusion on the ground that the concessionary rights in question were covered by Protocol XII of Lausanne which constituted the " international obligations " for which provision was made in Article 11.

In Judgment No. 5, the Court held that the disregard by the Palestine Government of the concessionary rights of M. Mavrommatis was contrary to the international obligations of Great Britain, that the concessions were valid, and that they ought to be readapted to new conditions. Negotiations then followed between M. Mavrommatis and the Palestine Government which, however, produced no definite result.

The present claim was put forward by

Greece on behalf of M. Mavrommatis on the ground that during the negotiations for the readaptation of the concession the British and the Palestinian authorities had displayed towards M. Mavrommatis a hostility which was responsible for delays and which caused him irreparable injury by rendering it impossible for him to obtain the financial assistance indispensable to the formation of the company for the operation of his concession.

Great Britain objected to the jurisdiction of the Court mainly on the ground that under Article 11 the Court had jurisdiction only in cases of such alleged breaches of the international obligations of the Mandatory as resulted from the manner in which the Palestine Administration has exercised its full power to provide for public ownership or control of any of the national resources of the country, and any delays or hostility, even if they actually had taken place, could not be regarded as an exercise of the power of public control.

Held: That the Court had no jurisdiction. The question whether in a given case there had been an exercise of the full power to provide for public control was a question that could be decided only for each particular case as it arose. Accordingly "although the "present suit at first sight would seem to be a con-"tinuation of the case decided by Judgments Nos. 2 "and 5, it does not follow from this circumstance that "the jurisdiction accepted by the Court in Judgment "No. 2 also exists as regards the present case. For "this case concerns facts which have occurred since "these judgments were given, and the solution of the "question now before the Court depends upon the "nature of these facts in relation to the clauses govern-"ing the Court's jurisdiction in the present suit." Even if the attitude of the British and Palestine officials in this matter were not legally justifiable or even were of an arbitrary character, the non-approval of

Case No. 29 *contd.* the plans submitted by M. Mavrommatis within a certain time did not constitute a case of the exercise of the full power to provide for "public control." [Report: Series A, No. 11, pp. 14, 16, 20.[1]]

NOTE.—This case concerns only the interpretation of a single provision of a Mandate, but it has been thought useful to digest it here as throwing light upon the scope of the jurisdiction of the Permanent Court in regard to Mandates.

Case No. 30 **Mandates—Authority of Mandatory Power to make Treaties on behalf of Mandated State or its Citizens—Mandate of France over Syria and the Lebanon.**

PABLO NÁJERA (OF THE LEBANON) CASE.

France and Mexico: Mixed Claims Commission.
19 *October*, 1928.

(VERZIJL, President.)

THE FACTS.—The French-Mexican Claims Convention of 25th September, 1924, provided for the submission to a Mixed Claims Commission of all claims brought against the Mexican Government for losses or damages suffered during the revolutionary period from 1910 to 1920 by French subjects or protected persons. The Mexican Government opposed the jurisdiction of the Commission to hear and decide the claims brought before the latter by citizens of Syria and the Lebanon on the ground, *inter alia*, that the Convention had not been concluded expressly on behalf of those mandated States and could not be deemed, therefore, to be in force between Mexico, on the one side, and the said States on the other. Moreover, the Mexican Government asserted that the Convention should have been approved by the Council of the League of Nations, so far as citizens of Syria and the Lebanon were concerned.

Held: That the Commission had jurisdiction. (*a*) Every State needs an international title to be authorised to represent another State in its juridical intercourse with third States. However, the necessity of the existence of such a title does not involve the necessity of mentioning it *expressis verbis* in each

[1] See also Series E, No. 4, pp. 176-183. And see Michel de Grotte in *R.I.*, 3rd ser., vol. X (1929), pp. 394-399, and Bentwich in *L.Q.R.*, XLIV (1928), pp. 450-763.

particular convention concluded in virtue of the same. There are different international titles of that kind, of a special or general character, such as Customs Union conventions, treaties for the establishment of protectorates or other forms of international subordination, Mandates of the League of Nations. Article 3 of the Mandate for Syria and the Lebanon constitutes a fully sufficient title for France to make treaties on behalf of the mandated States, or on behalf of individual Syrians or citizens of the Lebanon, without any further authorisation either of these States or of the Council of the League of Nations.

(*b*) There is no ground whatever for holding that each particular treaty concluded by a Mandatory on behalf of a mandated State or its nationals must be approved by the Council of the League of Nations. Article 12 of the Mandate for Syria invoked by the Mexican Government does not require any such approval.

[Till now unreported.]

Mandated Territory—Position of Mandatory—British Dominions as Mandatories—Validity of Legislation of Dominion Parliament for Mandated Territory. **Case No. 31**

TAGALOA *v.* INSPECTOR OF POLICE.
FUATAGA *v.* INSPECTOR OF POLICE.

Supreme Court of New Zealand. 21 October, 1927.

THE FACTS.—The Administrator of Western Samoa, acting under an Ordinance made by the Legislative Council in 1922, issued an order banishing the two appellants from a certain district. The appellants disobeyed and were convicted by the Court of Western Samoa. From this sentence they appealed to the Supreme Court of New Zealand, challenging the constitutional validity of the chain of legislation by virtue of which the order of banishment was issued.

The Ordinance of 1922 issued by the Legislative Council of Western Samoa was made by virtue of the Samoa Act of 1921, passed by the Legislature of New Zealand. The appellants contended that this statute, on which the subsequent Samoan legislation and judicial proceedings depended, was *ultra vires* the Dominion Legislature. The Dominion Legislature derives its powers from the New Zealand Constitution Act of 1852, whereby it was given power to legislate for the "peace,

Case No. 31 *contd.*

"order, and good government" of New Zealand. The appellants argued that this Act did not enable the Parliament of New Zealand to legislate for territories not forming part of the Dominion.

Held (by Sim, Acting C.J., Herdman, Reed, Ostler and Adams, JJ.): The Constitution Act of 1852 of the Imperial Parliament neither confers nor limits the legislative jurisdiction of the Dominion Parliament in respect of the mandated territory. This jurisdiction depends upon the Order in Council of 11 March, 1920, made in accordance with the terms of the Treaty of Peace with Germany, and in exercise of powers conferred by the Foreign Jurisdiction Act, 1890.

". . . The Dominion had a representative at the negotia-" tion of the Treaty of Peace, who signed the Treaty on behalf of" New Zealand, which thus agreed as a separate nation to the" Covenant of the League of Nations and became a member of" the League. The Mandate for Samoa was conferred by the" Council of the League of Nations upon His Majesty the King" for and on behalf of the Government of the Dominion of New" Zealand. That means that it was conferred directly upon the" Dominion, and the Dominion is the sovereign Power re-" sponsible to the League of Nations. The Mandate provided" in Article 2 that

"'The Mandatory (*i.e.* the Dominion) shall have full" ' power of administration and legislation over the terri-" ' tory subject to the present Mandate as an integral part" ' of the Dominion of New Zealand, and may apply the laws" ' of New Zealand to the territory, subject to such local" ' modifications as circumstances may require. . . .'

" The authority is given by the League of Nations directly to" the Dominion as a member of the League. This is a matter" of history, of which, in my opinion, this Court must take" judicial notice. In my opinion it is ample authority for the" legislation now attacked, and it is entirely outside the pur-" view of the Constitution Act."

There was a division of opinion on the subsequent question whether the Ordinance of the Samoan Legislature, by virtue of which the order of banishment had been made, was not itself repugnant to the Samoa Act of 1921 of the Dominion Legislature.

Ostler, J., believed it to be repugnant; the majority of the Court, however (Sim, Acting C.J., Herdman, J., Reed, J., and Adams, J.), held the Ordinance valid, and dismissed the appeals. [Report: *New Zealand Law Reports*, 1927, p. 883.]

Mandates—Functions of Mandatory in Syria—Representative of the Mandatory Not Responsible for Administration in the Case of an " A " Mandate. **Case No. 32**

CASE OF THE DÉLÉGUÉ-ADJOINT OF THE HIGH COMMISSIONER IN THE SANDJAK OF ALEXANDRETTA.

Court of Appeal of Aleppo, Syria. 24 *October*, 1927.

THE FACTS.—The case concerned the raising of an attachment (*saisie-arrêt*) on the house of a foreign resident in the town of Antioch, which is the principal place of the district (Sandjak) of Alexandretta included in the mandated territory of Syria. The attachment had been made in the course of proceedings in a succession suit; and the attempt to obtain its release by administrative means had failed.

In an action brought against the Public Authority, a summons was served on the French Delegate as the representative of the High Commissioner for Syria to make him a party. He demurred to the jurisdiction on the ground that he was not responsible for the acts of the Administration of the Sandjak.

Held: Syria is subject to a Mandate of the " A " type, which confers on the Mandatory State certain powers in regard to diplomatic, military and commercial matters, but does not give it any right of direct administration. The Mandatory Power is indeed bound to abstain from all direct administration and to render advice and assistance to the local authorities. That is precisely the principal difference between the " A " Mandates on the one hand and the " B " and " C " Mandates on the other, because in the latter types of Mandate the Mandatory exercises direct administration. The representative of the High Commissioner for Syria, therefore, cannot be cited to represent the Administrative Service of the Sandjak. [Report: *Gazette des Tribunaux Libano-Syriens*, 3rd year, 1927, p. 1010.]

See *Annual Digest*, 1925-1926, Case No. 31.

Mandated Territory—Palestine Mandate—Discrimination on the Ground of Religion—Invalidity of Legislation Contrary to Mandate. **Case No. 33**

ATTORNEY-GENERAL *v.* ABRAHAM ALTSHULER.

Palestine Supreme Court. May, 1928.

THE FACTS.—The respondent in the appeal was charged before the Municipal Court of Tel-Aviv (a Jewish

Case No. 33 *contd.*

suburb of Jaffa) with the breach of a municipal bye-law passed by the Local Council of Tel-Aviv which prescribed that no establishment other than a restaurant shall be open on the Jewish Sabbath day within the area of the Local Council, provided that the prohibition shall not apply to a shop owned by a Moslem or Christian, and that restaurants, other than those owned by Moslem and Christians, may be open only at certain hours on the Jewish Sabbath day. The respondent was a Jew who opened his restaurant outside the prescribed hours, and was sentenced by the Court to pay a fine. On appeal, the District Court set aside the conviction, holding that the bye-law was invalid as being contrary to Article 15 of the Mandate for Palestine which lays down that " no discrimination " of any kind shall be made between the inhabitants " of Palestine on the ground of race, religion or lan- " guage." On further appeal to the Supreme Court,

Held: The bye-law limits the freedom of action on the Jewish Sabbath of shopkeepers if they are Jews. It is none the less discrimination against the Jews that the bye-law makes a discrimination in favour of the very small non-Jewish minority in the area of the Local Council. The bye-law is, therefore, invalid as contrary to the provisions of the Mandate and to Article 17 of the Palestine Order in Council, which prescribes that no legislation shall be promulgated which shall tend to discriminate in any way between the inhabitants of Palestine on the ground of race, religion or language.

[The case has not been reported in any Law Reports, but was published in the Palestine Press.]

NOTE.—One of the judges of the Supreme Court gave a dissenting judgment, holding that where a law is made to be binding on the general public, but a certain class is exempt from the operation of the law on the ground of religious belief, that is a privilege exceptionally granted on the ground of its religion, and is not a discrimination against the public at large. The bye-law granted a privilege to Moslems and Christians on the ground of their religion, so that they should not be compelled to close on the day of Sabbath in addition to their own day of rest. It cannot be regarded in any way as a discrimination against the Jewish inhabitants on the ground of their religion. Cf. *Annual Digest*, 1925-1926, Case No. 32.

Mandates—Mandate for Syria—Maintenance of Religious Jurisdiction—Religious Autonomy.

See Case No. 65 (*Succession of Rizcallah Gazalé Case*).

V.—Territories under Joint or International Government

Case No. 34

Condominium—Status of the Sudan—Anglo-Egyptian Convention of January, 1899—Jurisdiction over Foreign Subjects.

CARALLI *v.* SAOULLI.

Mixed Commercial Tribunal of Cairo. 18 *June*, 1927.

THE FACTS.—The plaintiff as syndic of a bankruptcy demanded the cancellation of a contract made between the bankrupt and the defendant. In the contract, which was for the sale of a bookshop belonging to the bankrupt in Khartoum in the Sudan, the defendant stated that she was domiciled in Alexandria, and that the bankrupt resided in Cairo. The defendant objected to the jurisdiction of the Mixed Courts of Egypt on the ground that she was now domiciled in the Sudan, that the subject-matter of the contract was property in the Sudan, and that by Article 8 of the Anglo-Egyptian Convention, 1899, it is prescribed that " the jurisdiction of the Mixed Tribunals shall not " extend nor be recognised for any purpose whatsoever " in any part of the Sudan."

Held: The effect of that Article was not to confer on persons domiciled in the Sudan any exceptional and privileged position in relation to the subjects of the capitulatory Powers who were domiciled in Egypt; but it does not exempt foreign subjects quitting Egypt and taking up residence in the Sudan from the general provisions of the Mixed Codes so far as concerns contracts which were made, or were to be executed, in Egypt. [Report: *Gazette des Tribunaux Mixtes d'Egypte*, 18th year, p. 56.]

D. RECOGNITION

[The attention of the reader is drawn to the fact that questions involving Recognition of States, Governments, Insurgency or Belligerency in one form or another will also be found in Cases Nos. 17-19, dealing with *Recognition of Acts of Foreign States and Governments*, and Cases Nos. 91, 92, dealing with *Territorial Jurisdiction*, where the main point is the scope of a Government's jurisdiction and the question of its recognition is merely incidental.]

i.—Of States

Case No. 35 **Refusal of Recognition of Government Distinguished from Refusal of Recognition of a State—Non-Recognition of the Soviet Government by the United States.**

LEHIGH VALLEY R. CO. *v.* STATE OF RUSSIA.

United States Circuit Court of Appeals, Second Circuit.
8 *August*, 1927.

THE FACTS.—This was a suit commenced by the Russian Government against the railroad company to recover for loss of explosives and ammunition destroyed by fire and explosion while in defendant's possession as carrier. The loss occurred on 30 July, 1916. The United States recognised Bakhemeteff as the representative of the Russian Government on 5 July, 1917. This suit was commenced by his authority on 23 July, 1918. Meanwhile, late in 1917, the Government which appointed Bakhemeteff had been overthrown and the Soviet Government established in its place. Bakhemeteff retired on 30 July, 1922, and custody of the property of the Russian Government for which he was responsible was recognised by the United States Department of State to vest at that time in Ughet, financial attaché of the Russian Embassy, who continued the action against the defendant railroad company. The United States did not recognise the Soviet Government. It was contended that the suit should be dismissed for want of a proper party as plaintiff. The District Court permitted the action to continue in the name of the State of Russia and gave judgment for plaintiff. On writ of error,

Held: That the judgment of the District Court should be affirmed. Delivering the opinion of the Court, Judge Manton said: "Abatement of the action or a dismissal could only be "sustained by reason of the non-existence of the State, or the "action of our government to no longer recognize the agency "once accredited and never revoked. The action was pro- "perly started by an unquestioned agency. The attorneys "and the agency thus employed were obliged to continue until "some other government was recognized. . . ." "The grant- "ing or refusal of recognition has nothing to do with the "recognition of the state itself. If a foreign state refuses "the recognition of a change in the form of government of an "old state, this latter does not thereby lose its recognition "as an international person. Oppenheim, *International Law*, "2nd ed., vol. I, p. 120; Moore, *Digest of International Law*, "vol. I, p. 298. The suit did not abate by the change in the "form of government in Russia; the state is perpetual, and "survives the form of its government. *The Sapphire*,[1] *supra*. "The recognized government may carry on the suit, at least "until the new government becomes accredited here by "recognition." (21 F. (2nd) 396, 400, 401.) [Reports: 293 Fed. 135; 21 F. (2nd) 396, 401; Dickinson, *Cases*, p. 905; and Hudson, *Cases*, p. 96.[2]]

Recognition of States—Implied Recognition—Recognition of Syria by Egypt.

See Case No. 28 (*Antoine Bey Sabbagh* v. *Mohamed Pacha Ahmed and Others*).

ii.—Of Governments

Recognition of Governments—Effects of Non-Recognition on Treaties—Convention of 17 July, 1905, concerning Conflicts of Laws relative to Procedure in Civil Cases—Continued Binding Force of the Same between Holland and Russia—Russian Citizens as Direct Subjects of Treaty Rights—Exemption from *Cautio Judicatum Solvi*. **Case No. 36**

E. L. WIRBELAUER, OF PARIS *v.* DE HANDELSVENNOOTSCHAP ONDER DE FIRMA LIPPMANN ROSENTHAL EN CO., OF AMSTERDAM.

District Court, Amsterdam. 16 *October*, 1925.

THE FACTS.—In a civil suit before the District Court, the claimant, a Russian citizen, opposed the demand of the defendant that the claimant should be compelled to deposit the *cautio judicatum solvi*. In support of this demand, the claimant invoked the Convention of The Hague of 17 July, 1905, concerning Conflicts of Laws relative to Procedure in Civil Cases, to which both Holland and Russia were parties. The Soviet

[1] Dickinson, *Cases*, p. 904; 78 U.S. (11 Wall.) 164.

[2] Where it is stated that certiorari was denied by the United States Supreme Court (1927), 275 U.S. 571, 48 Sup. Ct. 159.

Case No. 36 ***contd.***

Government had not yet been recognised by the Dutch Government. No regular withdrawal from the Convention seemed to have been notified by the Soviet Government, nor had the Dutch Government denounced it, as far as Russia was concerned.

Held: That the claimant was not obliged to deposit the *cautio judicatum solvi*; that the Convention of 1905 had conferred individual rights upon Russian subjects before Dutch courts; and that those rights of individuals continued to exist so long as the binding force of the treaty as between Holland and Russia had not duly terminated. [Report: *Weekblad van het Recht*, 6 January, 1926, No. 11441.]

NOTE.—This judgment has been analysed by Professor J. H. W. Verzijl in the *Weekblad van het Recht*, No. 11443, of 11 January, 1926: *Nederland, Rusland en het Rechtsvorderingstractaat.* He agrees with the Court's conclusion, but does not approve of its statement of reasons, particularly on the ground that the judgment lays undue and unnecessary stress upon the doctrine of independent rights of individuals under the treaty, in contradistinction to the rights of the States and Governments concerned. If Holland and Russia are no longer bound by the Convention, all rights of individuals are also annulled; if, on the contrary, the Convention is still in force between the two States, their courts are bound to apply its provisions, in order to fulfil the treaty obligations of their State, and independently of the question whether it is correct to say that international rights have accrued from the treaty to the citizens of the States concerned. In this connection the suspension of diplomatic intercourse between the Governments of the High Contracting Parties is immaterial. In case of non-fulfilment of Russia's treaty engagements by the Soviet Government, or by the Soviet courts, the Dutch Government would be entitled to denounce the Convention on that ground, so far as Russia is concerned, but even in that case the Dutch courts would not be entitled to refrain from applying the Convention, as long as their Government had not actually denounced it.

Case No. 37

Recognition of Governments—Effect of Legislative and Executive Acts of Unrecognised Government before Courts of a State which has not Recognised it—Russian Bank.

SOKOLOFF *v.* NATIONAL CITY BANK.

Court of Appeals of New York. 31 December, 1928.

THE FACTS.—This was an action on a contract for the purchase of Russian roubles. Plaintiff paid money to defendant at its New York office in June, 1917, for the purpose of opening an account at defendant's Petrograd branch. After plaintiff had withdrawn part of the amount deposited in the Petrograd branch, he directed the transfer of the balance to his credit in the Kharkoff Mutual Credit Society of Kharkoff, Russia. Later, learning that the transfer had not been completed, he directed the Petrograd branch to cancel the transfer and hold the money subject to his sister's disposal. The transfer was never completed, and the defendant's Petrograd branch was finally confiscated by the Soviet Government. The referee held that defendant remained liable for the deposit (130 Misc. (N.Y.) 66). The Appellate Division of the New York Supreme Court affirmed judgment for plaintiff entered upon the referee's report (223 App. Div. 754). On appeal,

Held: That judgment for the plaintiff should be affirmed. While the judgment appears to have been founded upon the duty to make restitution of a sum not in excess of the benefit received, the opinion included a dictum to the effect that seizure and nationalisation by an unrecognised Government would not justify a plea of impossibility of performance. Delivering the opinion of the Court, Judge Crane said: "The "bank did not wilfully breach its contract; all its property "was seized by the Soviet Government. Under certain con- "ditions, this also might have justified the defendants in "pleading impossibility of performance, the same as the fact "excuses the plaintiff from making a demand. The difficulty "is that the United States has not recognized the Soviet "Government, and in consequence, the seizure and nationaliza- "tion of the banks is not an act of government within the "recognized principles of international law. All this has been "fully explained in our previous decision and need not be "repeated here." (250 N.Y. 69, 81.) (See *Sokoloff* v. *National City Bank*, 239 N.Y. 158.) [Report: 250 N.Y. 69.]

NOTE.—See Dickinson in *A.J.*, XXV (1931), pp. 214-237. See also *Annual Digest*, 1925-1926, Cases Nos. 40, 41, 42, 101 and 102.—[Ed.]

Recognition—Of Governments—Effects of Non-Recognition—Whether Rendering Deportation of Aliens Impossible. **Case No. 38**

PESTEREFF *v.* REED.

District Court of Alaska, Second Division, Nome.
1 *October*, 1927.

THE FACTS.—This was a petition for habeas corpus. Petitioner was an alien and native of Russia. In 1927, with eight other aliens, he left East Cape, Siberia, in a

Case No. 38 ***contd.***

small skin boat, crossed to Cape Prince of Wales, Alaska, and landed with the intention of making the United States his future residence. Making his way down the coast to Nome, he was taken into custody by United States immigration authorities, and brought before a Board of Special Inquiry, where it was decided that he should be debarred for want of an immigration visa. While the case was still pending before the Department of Labour, he petitioned for habeas corpus, contending that since there were no diplomatic relations between the United States and Russia, he could not be deported to Russia and should, therefore, be set at liberty.

Held : That the writ should be denied. An order had not yet issued from the Department of Labour and the hearing was still pending.

Delivering the Opinion of the Court, Judge Lomen said: " To discharge the petitioner would be an unwarrantable inter- " ference with proceedings now pending in a political depart- " ment of the government. There is no presumption that the " Department of Labor will not do its duty, nor that deporta- " tion cannot be made, with or without diplomatic relations. " If that department cannot deport, its duty must be found in " some other direction. It is not for the court to instruct " it. We cannot admit that the United States is powerless." (7 Alaska 644, 653.) [Report : 7 Alaska 644.]

Case No. 39

Recognition of Governments—Effects of Non-Recognition—Legislation of Non-Recognised Government as a Mere Fact—Soviet Marriage Legislation in Swiss Courts.

TCHERNIAK *v.* TCHERNIAK.

Swiss Federal Court. 15 *June*, 1928.

THE FACTS.—The Russian national Rouvin Tcherniak and his wife each petitioned for a divorce. Tcherniak settled in Switzerland before the war of 1914-1918. The Geneva court of first instance declared itself incompetent to grant a divorce. This decision was confirmed in the Cantonal court of second instance on the ground that a declaration produced by the claimant to the effect that Russian law would grant a divorce on the grounds alleged in this case and would recognise the legal standing of the Swiss court, emanated from a Government which was not recognised by Switzerland. The Federal Court reversed the decision, and remitted the case to the lower court for a decision on the merits.

Held: On the question of the Russian nationality of the parties, that it is clear that the period of five years fixed by the Decree of the Pan-Russian Executive Committee, dated 15 December, 1921, governing registration of Russian nationality, in Article 1, section A, has not yet begun to run, since Russia has no representation in the Swiss Confederation.

It follows from the declaration of the Russian Soviet Consulate in Paris concerning the legislation in force in Russia at the present time that:

" The Soviet legislation permits divorce at the unilateral " request of one of the spouses: in granting a divorce, the " courts enjoy complete discretion, as the legislature has not " defined the grounds for divorce in a restrictive sense."

The Federal Court decided in the case of *Hausner* on 10 December, 1924, that:

" The non-recognition of the Soviet by Switzerland is opera- " tive in another sphere, but the Swiss judge will take cognisance " of the Russian rules of law so long as they do not offend " against the canons of public policy (R.O. 50, II, p. 512; see on " the last point, R.O. 51, II, p. 264, and 53, III, p. 58). More- " over, in the present case, it is unnecessary to afford explicit " recognition of the indirect effect of the revolutionary legis- " lation on Swiss soil, since in Switzerland divorces may be " granted to aliens without reference to the legislation of their " own State. The grounds for a decree of divorce, and the " effect of such a decree, are governed by the *lex fori*, but " federal legislation has voluntarily imposed two restrictions on " the competence of the courts; the validity of the grounds on " which the divorce is granted must be recognised by the " national courts of the parties, as also must the jurisdiction of " the Swiss courts. The fact that the acts and judgments of " the Bolshevist authorities have no executory force within " Swiss territory does not debar the parties from alleging and " the judges from finding as a *fact* that the Russian courts " would recognise a decree of divorce pronounced by the Swiss " courts."

Evidence tending to prove the existence of these conditions has been adduced by the parties. It is not necessary to enquire

Case No. 39 *contd.* whether the Commissariat of Justice was keeping within the bounds of its competence when it issued on 6 July, 1923, the decree in question. That is a matter of Russian internal law, into which it is outside the province of the Federal Court to enquire. [Report: *Entscheidungen des schweizerischen Bundesgerichts*, 54, II, 225.]

NOTE.—See *Annual Digest*, 1925-1926, Cases Nos. 20, 22 and 23, and Cases Nos. 17, 45 in this volume, and the English case of *Nachimson* v. *Nachimson*, L.R. [1930] P. 217.

Case No. 40 **Recognition of Governments—Non-Recognition of Soviet Government—Position of Russians in Egypt—Capitulations.**

HERGENSTEIN *v.* PUBLIC PROSECUTOR OF THE NATIVE COURTS.

Mixed Court of Appeal of Egypt. 15 *December*, 1926.

THE FACTS.—The question raised in the case was whether a Russian subject in Egypt was subject to the jurisdiction of the Egyptian courts. The accused, a Russian subject, was sentenced to a fine and the closing of his factory by a native court for a contravention, and made opposition to the execution of the judgment before the Mixed Courts on the ground that in virtue of his Russian nationality the native courts had no jurisdiction, and he could be tried only by the Mixed Courts. The Judge of the Mixed Court rejected the opposition on the ground that Russian capitulations were abrogated by the rupture of diplomatic relations between Egypt and the Soviet Government. On appeal to the Mixed Court of Appeal, it was

Held: That the opposition to the execution of the judgment was well founded. It was unnecessary for the Court to decide whether the Egyptian Government by breaking off diplomatic relations with Russia had definitely suppressed the Russian capitulations, since, even on the assumption that Russians in Egypt were deprived of their capitulatory rights, they nevertheless came within the jurisdiction of the Mixed Courts which cover foreign subjects of States that do not enjoy the benefit of the capitulations. [Report: 55 *Clunet* (1928), p. 199.]

Recognition of Governments—Non-Recognition of Soviet Government in Egypt—Change of the Russian Law—Effect on Contracts to Pay in Russian Currency in Egypt. **Case No. 41**

CHARALAMBOS PAPADOPOULOS *v.* MONASTERY OF MOUNT-SINAI.

Mixed Court of Appeal of Egypt. 23 *June*, 1927.

THE FACTS.—A Russian Archimandrite who was the representative in Kiev of the Monastery of Mount-Sinai made a declaration in August, 1919, that he had borrowed from the plaintiff for the needs of the Monastery the sum of 100,000 roubles, and that the Monastery undertook to pay the sum on demand by its representative at Kiev. By a second declaration, in January, 1920, the same Archimandrite declared that he had received from the plaintiff another sum payable by the Monastery after the termination of the Russian Revolution and the establishment of a regular Government. The plaintiff drew a bill at Cairo on the Monastery of Mount-Sinai for 100,000 roubles, which was protested for non-payment in 1926; after making a seizure of property belonging to the Monastery in the hands of third parties, he brought a claim against the Monastery before the Mixed Court of Cairo for payment of the sum of £8000, being the equivalent of 100,000 roubles, and for the enforcement of the seizure. He subsequently added a claim on account of a bill drawn upon the defendants in respect of the second sum.

The Mixed Court of Cairo gave judgment rejecting the claim and declaring the seizure null. On appeal, the question was raised as to whether the debt was payable at the value of gold or paper roubles. It was claimed by the appellant (the creditor) that the law of the Soviet Government introducing the paper currency was not applicable because the Soviet Government was not recognised by Egypt.

Held : That the judgment must be affirmed and the claim rejected. The Court then held (*obiter*) that the fact that Egypt has not recognised the Soviet Government does not derogate from the right of courts in Egypt to take account of the Russian law when that law is the *lex contractus* adopted by the parties. The demonetisation of the paper roubles of the Imperial dynasty is a fact which must be recognised by the courts. [Report : *Gazette des Tribunaux Mixtes d'Egypte*, 17th year, 1927, p. 293.]

See *Annual Digest*, 1925-1926, Case No. 40.

Case No. 42 **Recognition of Foreign Governments—Recognition of Soviet Government—Soviet Decrees of Nationalisation—Provisions Contrary to Public Order—Dissolution of Russian Companies by Soviet Legislation—Termination of Existence in France.**

CIE NORD DE MOSCOU *v.* PHENIX ESPAGNOL.

Court of Appeal of Paris (Third Chamber). 13 *June,* 1928.

THE FACTS.—By a series of decrees made in 1918, the Soviet Government nationalised a number of commercial companies without compensation. The French Government recognised the Soviet Government on 28 October, 1924. In the present action the question arose as to whether the French Court could recognise the right of the plaintiffs, a nationalised Russian company, to take legal proceedings in France.

Held : That the action brought by the Cie Nord de Moscou must be dismissed. " The recognition of the Soviet Government by the French Government cannot result in the application in France of legislation adopted in Russia since 1918, when it is incompatible with the general principles of French law and *ordre public* in France. To admit the principle of the Soviet Decree of 13 December, 1918, which abolished in the interest of the State the right of private property without compensation, would have the effect of recognising a right of expropriation opposed to the respect for private property embodied in French law and to the inviolability of the right of property. Such a principle could neither directly nor indirectly be accepted in France." However, " although the Decree of 13 December, 1918, providing for expropriation without previous compensation is incompatible with *ordre public* in France, and therefore inapplicable in France, yet it is not the concern of a foreign Government to interfere with legislation, validly adopted, in the territory of a Government invested with the right to legislate within that territory." The Cie du Nord de Moscou, as a Russian company, " is exclusively subject, so far as its existence is concerned, to the rules of Russian legislation." By the Decree of 13 December, 1918, the company ceased to exist in Russia and, under the circumstances, cannot be held to have continued to exist independently in Paris in such a way as to be subject not to Russian law but to *droit international.* [Reports: 56 *Clunet* (1929),

p. 119, with the observations of Advocate-General Sevestre on the case, and a note by MM. Picart and Tager; Sirey, 1928, Part II, p. 161, with a note by M. J. P. Niboyet.]

NOTE.—See also *ibid.*, to the same effect, the case of *Société Vairon et Cie* v. *Banque de Commerce de Sibérie*, and the decision of the Court of Cassation (Appeals Chamber) delivered on 29 July, 1929 (*Dalloz Hebdomadaire*, 1929, p. 457), confirming the decision of the court below.

Recognition—Effects of—Recognition of Legislation of Recognised Government—Soviet Government—Nationalisation of Property—Russian Commercial Fleet—Reasons of Public Policy of the Recognising State—Methods of Acquisition of Property Compatible with Public Order—Intervention of the Soviet Government. **Case No. 43**

UNION DES RÉPUBLIQUES SOCIALISTES SOVIÉTIQUES *v.* INTENDANT GÉNÉRAL BOURGEOIS ÈS-QUALITÉ ET SOCIÉTÉ LA ROPIT.

French Court of Cassation (Appeals Chamber). 5 *March*, 1928.

THE FACTS.—The Commercial Tribunal of Marseilles considered the joint application of the masters of several ships belonging to a Russian Navigation Company, known as "Ropit," and certain of its shareholders and creditors, and by its decision, on 10 April, 1923, recognised the authority of a Provisional Administrator who had been appointed to administer the ships of the company berthed at Marseilles and its property and interests in France.

The Government of the Union of Socialist Soviet Republics, intervening as a third party through its Ambassador in Paris, opposed the decision and requested that it should be quashed. The Soviet Government claimed ownership of the ships of the "Ropit" on the grounds that the Soviet Decree of 26 January, 1918, had nationalised the Russian mercantile marine. The Court of Appeal of Aix, on 23 December, 1925, rejected the appeal of the Soviet Government.

Held, by the Court of Cassation (Appeals Chamber), on the appeal of the Soviet Government: That the decision of the Court of Appeal of Aix must be upheld. The Soviet Government had claimed that the decision of the Court of Appeal of Aix wrongfully denied the rights of property vested in that

Case No. 43 *contd.*

Government by the terms of its own legislation and thus violated a generally recognised rule of international law.

The Court said that " although the principle that the " courts of a State faced with a juridical situation governed " by foreign legislation should apply the foreign law must be " admitted, this rule is only obligatory in so far as the appli- " cation of the foreign law and respect for the rights acquired " thereby are not incompatible with those principles and pro- " visions of their national law which are held essential for " *ordre public* " ; that the rule incorporated in Article 545 of the Civil Code providing that " no one in France can be forced " to give up his property except in the public interest and in " return for a fair and prepaid compensation," was one of the fundamental bases of French social institutions ; that it could not be waived in face of foreign legislation without a profound disturbance of the order established in French territory ; that the Soviet Decree of 26 January, 1918, nationalised the Russian mercantile marine without providing for the payment of fair compensation to the dispossessed owners ; that the Decree established a method for the acquisition of property repugnant to the French courts ; and that, therefore, the Soviet Government had no just grounds for its intervention as a third party. [Reports : 55 *Clunet* (1928), p. 674 ; Sirey, 1929, Part I, p. 217, with a note by M. Audinet.]

NOTE.—See the English case *The Jupiter* (*Annual Digest*, 1925-1926, Case No. 100, at p. 142), a ship belonging to the same company, in which the Court refused to recognise the property of the Soviet Government in the ship on the ground that *The Jupiter* had never been within the jurisdiction of the R.S.F.S.R., whose nationalisation decrees could not have extraterritorial effect.—[Ed.]

Case No. 44

Recognition of Foreign Governments — Recognition of the Soviet Government—Personal Status of Russian Subjects —Retroactivity.

DE MAYENNE *v.* JOUTEL ÈS-QUALITÉ.

Civil Tribunal of the Seine. 24 *December*, 1926.

THE FACTS.—De Mayenne, born in Moscow of Russian parents, and formerly a Russian military officer, had made a declaration of paternity on 19 August, 1919, in respect of an illegitimate daughter, born at Turin. He subsequently sought to repudiate this recognition before the French courts, claiming, *inter alia*, that it was incompatible with Russian law before the establishment of the Soviet Government ; and he contended that a Russian who was politically opposed to the Soviet Government and had been denationalised by it was subject to the pre-Soviet Russian law alone.

Held : That there were no grounds for the nullification of the recognition of paternity. De Mayenne was a Russian subject on 19 August, 1919. It was necessary to decide which Russian law was applicable. The *de jure* recognition of the Soviet Government by the French Government in October, 1924, " compels the French courts, in *questions d'état*,[1] to apply to " Russian subjects their personal status as determined by " Soviet legislation, except where the said legislation is con- " trary to *ordre public* in France. The *de jure* recognition of " the Government of the Union of Socialist Soviet Republics, " in so far as existing rights are not prejudiced, is retroactive " in effect and dates back to the commencement of the juridi- " cal existence of the new Government." [Report : 55 *Clunet* (1928), p. 710.]

Recognition of Acts of Foreign States and Governments—Refusal to Apply the Decrees of an Unrecognised Government Abrogating the Legislation in Force under its Predecessor—Validity of a Divorce Decreed in Accordance with this Legislation—Divorce Granted by the Russian Orthodox Church in Paris—Disregard of Legislation of Soviet Russia by Belgian Courts. **Case No. 45**

DIGMELOFF *v.* THE STATE CIVIL OFFICER OF ST.-JOSSE-TEN-NOODE.

Brussels Civil Court. 16 *June*, 1928.

THE FACTS.—The claimant petitioned the Civil Officer for a declaration that the former marriage which he had contracted at Tiflis, then and now in Russia, had been validly dissolved, in contemplation of Belgian law, by the divorce pronounced on 25 July, 1927, in Paris by the diocesan authority of the Orthodox Russian Churches in Western Europe. The former marriage had taken place on 1 April, 1912, and the claimant now contemplated a second marriage. The claimant contended that no weight should be given to the legislation of the Soviet régime, which confines legal effect to divorces pronounced by the civil authorities.

[1] Matters of status, *e.g.* birth, marriage, etc.

Case No. 45 *contd.*

Held for the claimant: "Belgium has not given either "*de jure* or *de facto* recognition to the Soviet Government; "hence, Belgian tribunals are not competent to recognise or "enforce any decrees of this Government. The personal status "of Russian refugees on Belgian soil is, therefore, governed by "the legislation last in force before the coming of the Soviet "régime." The legislation in question is that of the Provisional, or so-called Kerensky, Government, which "was recog-"nised by Belgium on 5 April, 1917, through the medium of "a declaration of the Belgian Minister at Petrograd." The Kerensky Government did not alter the purely religious character which the old Code of the Russian Empire gave to the institution of divorce. It effected, however, the following alteration:

"In future, all divorces pronounced by local consistories are "to be subject to confirmation not by the Holy Synod, but by "the Bishop of the Diocese."

Since the divorce of the claimant was pronounced by the diocesan authority for the Orthodox Russian Churches in Western Europe, in accordance with the foregoing provisions, this divorce is "good and valid in Belgian law, and will take "full legal effect in this country to permit of the claimant's "contracting the second marriage which he has in contempla-"tion." [Reports: 55 *Clunet* (1928), p. 1253 on; *Belgique judicaire*, 1928, col. 470.]

NOTE.—See to the same effect a decision of the same court, *Annual Digest*, 1925-1926, Case No. 20, and Editors' Note. But the 1925 case appears to ignore the recognition afforded to the Kerensky Government by the Government of Belgium. In the present case, the purely religious divorce of the claimant was upheld by virtue of the circumstance that it was pronounced in France. Both in France and in Belgium, the rules of public policy which would compel the tribunals to disallow any such ceremony which had been performed upon their own soil are strictly territorial in effect. This is perhaps more properly a question of Private International Law, but deserves mention as illustrating the attitude of the Belgian courts towards the Soviet régime.

Case No. 46

Recognition of Governments—Lack of Recognition—Factual Situation brought about by the Decrees of a Non-Recognised Government—Legislation of Soviet Russia—Effect in Belgium.

N. D'AIVASSOFF *v.* DE RAEDEMAEKER AND PARTNERS.

Brussels Civil Court. 28 February, 1927.

THE FACTS.—In 1899, at Tiflis, then and now in Russia, the plaintiff formed a partnership with one Tobie for the exploitation of certain lands in the neighbourhood. The defendants are the widow and another taking under the estate of the late Tobie. The action is brought to recover a sum due under the partnership agreement.

Held : That the claim must be dismissed. The obligation to pay the sum forming the basis of the plaintiff's claim " was " annulled by the decree of the 31 October of the Soviet " Government," together with any other obligations which might be alleged by the plaintiff to arise out of this agreement. The claimant cannot invoke the continuance of earlier legislation. " It appears to be impossible to ignore completely the " fact of the existence of the Soviet Government ; nor, in the " face of circumstances which show every prospect of con- " tinuing indefinitely, can the courts refuse absolutely all effect " to the only system of law in actual application in Russia " to-day without gross inequity.

" It is sufficient to consider the present action as based upon " a bilateral contract, and to conclude that the indivisibility of " the obligations created by such a contract will prevent its " enforcement in Belgium, so long as in Russia, the place of " execution, these same obligations have been destroyed." [Report : *Pasicrisie Belge*, 1927, III, p. 38.]

NOTE.—Compare the Court of Appeals of New York, *Annual Digest*, 1925-1926, Case No. 40 : " While the Soviet Government has not " been recognised . . . yet the factual situation cannot be overlooked " when 'justice and common sense' required it to 'give effect to the " 'conditions existing in Russia.' "

Recognition of Acts of Foreign States and Governments—Unrecognised Governments—Validity of Acts of Unrecognised Governments—Effect of Russian Soviet Decrees—Continued Existence of Joint Stock or Limited Liability Companies in Russia. **Case No. 47**

VSEOBTCHAIA STROITELNAIA KOMPANIA (General Construction Company), OF PETROGRAD (plaintiff) *v.* L. J. SMIT, OF KINDERDIJK (defendant).

District Court, Dordrecht. 12 *January*, 1927.

THE FACTS.—In an action brought by a Russian limited liability or joint stock company against a Dutch subject, the latter maintained that the former had lost its legal existence by virtue of Soviet legislation. Though the Soviet Government had not yet been recog-

Case No. 47 *contd.*

nised by the Dutch Government, the Tribunal did not refuse *in limine* to examine the legal effect of the Soviet legislation.

Held : That no concrete provision of the said legislation had put an end to the legal existence of Russian limited liability or joint stock companies, and that, though the socialisation of their properties had paralysed such companies in their normal activity, nevertheless their existence as juridical entities had remained unimpaired. [Report : *Weekblad van het Recht*, 11 March, 1927, No. 11625.]

NOTES.—For a criticism of this judgment, see van Royen, *De rechtspositie en de volkenrechtelijke erkenning van nieuwe staten en de facto-regeeringen*, p. 88 and note 2. In the author's opinion, the Court should have refused to enter into an examination of the true meaning of the Soviet legislation on the ground that it was promulgated by a Government not yet recognised by the Government of the Court's State.

The interpretation placed by the House of Lords in England upon the Soviet legislation affecting Russian banking and insurance companies is similar to that adopted by this Dutch court. See *Annual Digest*, 1925-1926, Cases Nos. 101 and 102.—[Ed.]

Recognition—Non-Recognition of Soviet Government—Effect on Jurisdiction over—Application of Reprisals.

See Case No. 110 (*The National Navigation Company of Egypt* v. *Tavoularidis*).

Recognition—Effect of Non-Recognition of Soviet Government —Succession to Estates of Russian Subjects in Countries where Soviet Government is not Recognised.

See Case No. 268 (*Dessouki Moustapha* v. *A. Petroff*).

Recognition of Governments—Effects of Non-Recognition— Distinguished from Non-Recognition of State.

See Case No. 35 (*Lehigh Valley R. Co.* v. *State of Russia*).

Recognition—Of New Government—Effect upon Respect due to Judgment of Extraterritorial Consular Court Continuing to Sit under Authority of Extinct Government.

See Case No. 125 (*Herzfeld* v. *Russian Volunteer Fleet*).

Recognition of Governments—Governments *de facto* and *de jure*—Whether Recognition by a Foreign State Relevant—Recognition *de jure* Distinguished from the *de jure* Character of a Government.

See Case No. 136 (*Georges Pinson Case,* § 51).

Recognition of Governments—Recognition *de facto*—Irrelevant to the Question as to the *de facto* Character of a Government.

See Case No. 164 (*Georges Pinson Case,* §§ 49, 51, 52, 54).

E. STATE SUCCESSION

I.—Succession in Rights

State Succession—Succession in Rights. **Case No. 48**

(POLISH) STATE TREASURY *v.* SKIBNIEWSKA.

Supreme Court of Poland, Third Division. 24 January, 1928.

THE FACTS.—The Austrian Governor of Lwów was supplying farmers during the World War with agricultural machinery on credit. The Polish State having taken over the territory formerly administered by that Governor, the Polish Treasury sued the defendant, who had been thus supplied, for the purchase price. Article 208 of the Treaty of St. Germain provides that States to which is transferred territory of the former Austro-Hungarian Monarchy acquire all property and possessions (" *biens et propriétés* ") situated within their territory belonging to the former or existing Austrian Government. The defendant pleaded, *inter alia,* that the right of the Austrian Government to repayment did not fall under Article 208, because it was not within the category of " *biens et propriétés* " and was not " situated " in that, or, indeed, in any territory, and that " *acquerront* " meant that some future legislation would determine the matter.

Held : On appeal :

(1) That the expression " *biens* " included all property and, therefore, also claims ;

Case No. 48 contd. (2) That claims were in a definite relationship to the territory of a State and were, therefore, situated in the territory of a State;

(3) That the word "*acquerront*" did not imply the necessity of further legislation which would bring the provision in question in force. [Report: P.P.A., 1928, p. 284.]

Case No. 49 **State Succession—Succession in Rights—Succession with regard to Contractual and other Obligations—Succession with Regard to Obligations for Delinquencies—Set-Off against Succession State of Claims of a Different Character against Previous State.**

(POLISH) STATE TREASURY *v.* PADUCHOWA AND OTHERS.

Supreme Court of Poland, Third Division. 20 *March*, 1927.

THE FACTS.—In 1915 and 1916 the father (now deceased) of the defendants had obtained from the Austrian State Treasury various loans for economic purposes, and had executed bonds for such loans. Poland having taken over the territory in which the debtor resided, the Polish Treasury brought an action against the heirs of the debtor. The defendants sought to set off claims which they alleged they possessed against the former Austrian State on account of war damage and requisitions.

Held: On appeal:

(1) That the claim presented by the Polish Treasury was no longer a claim of the former Austrian State, the Polish Treasury having acquired it, not under private law, as, for instance, by inheritance or cession, but by international treaty;

(2) That, therefore, the defendants could not set off against this claim certain claims which they alleged that they had against the former Austrian State, though of an entirely different character, viz. for war damage and requisitioned property;

(3) That Poland had not obtained Austrian State property under Article 208 of the Treaty of St. Germain as a free gift but that she undertook to pay its value on account of Austrian reparations (with the exception of the value of schools and forests which had been the property of Poland before her partition in the eighteenth century), and that, therefore, it would be contrary not only to the Treaty, but to the principles of most

elementary justice, if for property thus given over to her she were compelled to pay again to the creditors of the former Austrian State [1];

(4) That the law applicable to the case could not be changed by the argument that the private creditor would suffer a loss, since this was always the case whenever a debtor became insolvent. [Report: P.P.A., 1927, p. 310.]

State Succession—Succession in Rights—Alleged Exclusion of Loans by Previous State to Inhabitants of Ceded Territory. **Case No. 50**

DĘBICCY (THE DĘBICKI FAMILY) (appellants) *v.* (POLISH) TREASURY (respondent).

Supreme Court of Poland, Third Division. 4 *October*, 1927.

THE FACTS.—In 1917, *i.e.* while part of Poland remained part of the Austro-Hungarian Monarchy, the appellants obtained from the Austrian authorities acting on behalf of the Austrian Treasury a loan (in connection with war losses) repayable in instalments. After the recovery of Polish independence an agreement was

[1] See, to the same effect, the case of *Knoll* v. (*Polish*) *State Treasury*, decided by the Supreme Court of Poland, Third Division, on 25 January, 1927. In this case the plaintiff had concluded in 1917 with the Austrian Government an agreement by virtue of which he built for it, on land supplied by it, barracks for refugees, himself supplying building materials and labour. In 1919, during the Ukrainian rebellion, the plaintiff surrendered to the Ukrainians the unfinished buildings, which, later, on the re-establishment of the Polish Government, were taken over by the latter and, by virtue of Article 208 of the Treaty of St. Germain, became its property. The plaintiff sued the Polish Treasury for a sum said to represent either the amount of undue enrichment on the part of the Polish Government, or the value of the buildings alleged to be the plaintiff's property, or the sum due to the plaintiff by virtue of the agreement of 1917. It was held, on appeal (affirming the judgment of the Court of Appeal of Lwów, which had reversed the judgment of the District Court of Lwów rendered in favour of the plaintiff):

1. That the agreement of 1917 concluded by the plaintiff with the Austrian Government was not binding on the Polish Government;

2. That the Polish State had acquired the buildings by virtue of Article 208 of the Treaty of St. Germain as property of the Austrian State situated in Polish territory, and that this acquisition was original and not derivative;

3. That the Polish Treasury had acquired the property, not gratuitously, but as a consideration for the sum which Poland had undertaken to pay on account of Austrian war indemnities, on the basis of a valuation by the Reparations Commission, so that there was no undue enrichment on the part of the Treasury. [Report: P.P.A., 1927, p. 312.]

Other statements in this judgment refer to the untenability of the action from the point of view of the Austrian Civil Code still in force in that part of Poland. It is interesting to note in the judgment the statement that the acquisition of State property under Article 208 of the Treaty of St. Germain (cf. Article 256 of the Treaty of Versailles, etc.) is, from the point of view of civil (internal, private) law original and not derivative.

Case No 50 *contd.*

made by appellants with the Polish Treasury as to the sum to be paid to the latter in settlement of the balance of the debt. Appellants having, later, stopped paying the agreed instalments, action was brought by the Treasury. Appellants (defendants in the action) pleaded an agreement alleged by them to have been concluded by the Polish with the Austrian Government, under which the latter would not be entitled to recover loans granted in 1914-1918 in connection with war losses in the then Austrian and now Polish territories. If, therefore, the Polish Government were to recover the debts formerly due to Austria, it would thereby authorise the Austrian Government to recover from it those sums. The plea having been dismissed by the District Court of Lwów and the judgment confirmed, on appeal, by the Court of Appeal of Lwów, defendants appealed to the Supreme Court, contending, *inter alia*, that taking over rights must necessarily have for its corollary the taking over of duties, and since the Polish Government did not assume the duties of the Austrian Government it could not take advantage of the latter's rights.

Held: (1) That while there is no special Polish-Austrian agreement under which Poland is expressly exempted from any duty to return to Austria the sums paid by the latter to inhabitants of Austrian Poland on account of reparation of war damages, yet this follows from the Treaty of St. Germain which is binding law in Poland;

(2) That, nevertheless, the Polish Treasury cannot be said not to have the right to recover the sum in question, since the Polish Treasury, under Article 208, paragraph 1, of the Treaty of St. Germain, acquired all property of the former Austrian State in the territory which became Polish;

(3) That taking over said property had no connection with the reparation of war damages alleged to have been due from the Austrian Treasury to its then citizens. [Report: P.P.A., 1928, pp. 85-86.]

NOTES.—I. Article 208 of the Treaty of St. Germain, paragraph 1, stipulates:

" States to which territory of the former Austro-Hungarian Monarchy " is transferred and States arising from the dismemberment of that Mon- " archy shall acquire all property and possessions situated within their " territories belonging to the former or existing Austrian Government." (In the French text the expression used is " *tous biens et propriétés* ").

II. It seems that the Supreme Court derived, in this case, the rights of the Polish Treasury from the Treaty of St. Germain for the reason that the defendants pleaded an unnamed treaty between Poland and Austria and the Court desired apparently to lay it down that the only treaty in question could be the Treaty of St. Germain, which, however, did not justify the defendants' contention.

State Succession—Succession in Rights—Claims Arising out of Deeds. **Case No. 51**

(POLISH) TREASURY *v.* HEIRS OF DIETL.

Supreme Court of Poland, First Division. 2 *March*, 1928.

THE FACTS.—In 1889 one Dietl executed a deed by which he undertook to erect in Sosnowiec in Russia (now in Poland) a school for the children of his factory workmen and certain others. In 1924 the Polish Treasury, represented by the Attorney-General, sued the heirs of Dietl for the performance of the deed, namely, for the erection of a school building on their own land, and for making over the land and building to the Treasury, or, alternatively, for authority for the Treasury to have such building erected at the expense of the defendants. The District Court of Sosnowiec gave judgment for the plaintiff; the Court of Appeal in Warsaw allowed the defendants' appeal and dismissed the action, (*a*) because the Polish State had no title to present a claim based on a deed executed in favour of the Russian Government in 1889, and (*b*) because the gift contained in the deed had not been duly accepted by the properly authorised representative of the (Russian) school authorities of the time. The plaintiff appealed to the Supreme Court.

Held: That the appeal must be dismissed for the second reason (*b*) stated above. As regards the first reason (*a*), the Supreme Court dissented from the Court of Appeal and said that, as laid down by the Supreme Court in 1923 (*Graff* v. *Ministry of Agriculture* and *Procurator-General* v. *Tomecki*), "the "Polish State, the moment its independence had been restored, "had by virtue of its sovereignty become possessed of all "public law and private law property of the partitioning State "which was situated in the territories occupied by it" (Poland), and that there was no basis for making a distinction in this respect in order to exclude from such property incorporeal hereditaments, such as claims arising out of deeds. [Report: O.S.P., VIII, No. 120.]

Case No. 52

State Succession—Succession to Rights—Lease by Previous State.

CZARIO *v.* VALENTINIS.

Italian Court of Cassation. 15 *October*, 1927.

In this case it was *Held* that the Italian State, as successor in former Austrian territory, became a party to a contract of lease concluded between the Austrian authorities and a private party. "The Italian sovereignty having succeeded to the "Austrian in the annexed territories by force of arms, it is to "be assumed that the Italian State replaces the Austrian with "regard to juridical relations of private law existing between "the latter State and the private citizens." [Report: *Foro delle nuove provincie*, 1927, pp. 311-314.]

NOTE.—On this point the Court of Cassation upheld the principle sanctioned by the Trieste Court. The appeal bore in the main upon a question of Italian administrative law not connected with international law.

Case No. 53

State Succession—Cession of Territory—Succession in Rights—Continuity in the Collection of Taxes.

SUCCESSION IN TAXES (CZECHOSLOVAKIA) CASE NO. II.

Supreme Administrative Court of Czechoslovakia. No. 25.268. 30 *November*, 1927.

THE FACTS.—The territory of Hlučín, the cession of which was stipulated for by the Treaty of Peace of Versailles, was incorporated into the Czechoslovak State by the Czechoslovak Law of 30 January, 1920, No. 76.[1] In 1921, *i.e.* after the incorporation of the territory, the Czechoslovak authorities demanded from a certain owner of coal mines in that territory the payment of coal duty due for a certain period prior to the incorporation, but not yet paid. He lodged an objection against this demand.

[1] Law of 30 January, 1920, No. 76, regarding the incorporation of the territory of Hlučín:—*Par.* 1. By virtue of the stipulations of Article 83 of the Treaty of Peace which was signed on 28 June, 1919, at Versailles between the Allied and Associated Powers and the German Empire and which came into force in the international sphere on 10 January, 1920, the Czechoslovak State extends its sovereignty to that part of Upper Silesia the boundaries of which are to be finally settled by an international commission by virtue of the said Treaty of Peace and in accordance with its stipulations. *Par.* 2. The laws and decrees hitherto existing in the incorporated territory remain in force, so far as it is consistent with the change of the sovereignty and as long as they will not be repealed or modified by the laws and decrees of the Czechoslovak Republic. *Par.* 3. . . . etc.

Held, by the Supreme Administrative Court: "The "taxing authority based its assessment, against which the "objection is lodged, upon the opinion that the claim of the "Czechoslovak State to the duty was a consequence of the "extension of the sovereignty of that State to the territory "concerned by the law No. 76/1920. The Court finds this "opinion correct. . . . By paragraph 1 of the law No. 76/1920, "the Czechoslovak State extended its sovereignty to the terri- "tory of Hlučín, where the coal mines subjected to the duty "are situated. According to paragraph 2 of the law, the laws "and decrees hitherto existing in the incorporated territory "remained in force there, as far as was consistent with the "change of the sovereignty, and as long as they were not "repealed or modified by the laws and decrees of the Czecho- "slovak Republic. In accordance with that legal provision, "the German law regarding the coal duty also remained in "force in that territory. According to that law the objector "had to pay the duty for the period concerned. As, however, "a payment to the German Treasury would be inconsistent "with the change of sovereignty in the territory which took "place upon its incorporation, it was necessary for the objector "to make the payment to the Czechoslovak Treasury." [Report: Boh. 3965 fin.[1]]

II.—Succession with regard to Contractual and Other Obligations, and Concessions

State Succession—Succession in Obligations—Dissolution of Unions of States—Dissolution of the Austro-Hungarian Monarchy—Liability of the Republic of Austria and of the Kingdom of Hungary for the Acts of the Austro-Hungarian Monarchy—Whether Joint or Several—Legal Status of the Austro-Hungarian Monarchy. **Case No. 54**

TRIPARTITE CLAIMS COMMISSION (UNITED STATES, AUSTRIA, AND HUNGARY).

Administrative Decision No. 1 Announcing Definitions and General Governing Principles and Dealing with the Functions and Jurisdiction of the Commission. 25 May, 1927.

(PARKER, Commissioner.)

THE FACTS.—As to the jurisdiction of the Commission, see

[1] See, to the same effect, *Annual Digest*, 1925-1926, Case No. 48, and the decision of the Supreme Administrative Court of Czechoslovakia in the decisions of 25 May, 1927, No. 9.774 (Boh. 3730 fin.) and of 19 December, 1928, No. 31.904 (Boh. 4335 fin.).

Case No. 54 *contd.*

p. 262, n. 1, and p. 542, n. 1. In the Agreement establishing the Commission it was provided that the Commissioner shall determine the amounts to be paid to the United States by Austria and by Hungary.

Under the financial clauses (Part IX) of the Treaties of St. Germain and Trianon provision was made for the apportionment between the successor States, including the Austrian Republic and the Kingdom of Hungary, of the pre-war indebtedness of the former Austro-Hungarian Monarchy. Each successor State was made solely responsible for the proportion of the debt allocated to it. By Article 178 of the Treaty of St. Germain, Austria was to make compensation for certain specific damage to the civilian population of the United States and to their property by the aggression of Austro-Hungary and her allies. By Article 162 of the Treaty of Trianon, Hungary was to be subject to the same obligation. These provisions were incorporated in the Treaties of Vienna and Budapest establishing respectively friendly relations between Austria and the United States and Hungary and the United States.

The questions before the Commission were : (*a*) what existing Government or Governments are liable for the acts of the Austro-Hungarian Government or its agents resulting in damage to American nationals ? (*b*) is that liability joint or several ? (*c*) what is the extent of the liability ?

Held : That the compensation will be borne, as to 63·6 per cent. by Austria and as to 36·4 per cent. by Hungary, this being the proportion in which the joint expenditures were apportioned between the former Austrian Empire and the former Kingdom of Hungary by the Austro-Hungarian Law of 30 December, 1907. The nature of the pre-war relationship between the two States, the opinions of writers in regard to State succession, and the language of the Treaty, indicated that the liability was intended to be several and not joint.

(*a*) *The International Status of the former Austrian Empire and the former Kingdom of Hungary. The Question of their Identity with the new Austrian Republic and the new Kingdom of Hungary.* " The former Austrian Empire and the former " Kingdom of Hungary while existing as independent States " had no international status. It was against the Imperial and

" Royal Austro-Hungarian Government that the United States " waged war (see Resolutions of Congress effective December 7, " 1917, and July 2, 1921). Following the armistice that Govern- " ment ceased to exist (see recitations in preambles to the " Treaties of Vienna and of Budapest). In pursuance of the " terms of the several treaties entered into between the opposing " Powers after the armistice, not only was the Austro-Hungarian " Dual Monarchy dismembered but substantial parts of the " territories of the former Austrian Empire and of the former " Kingdom of Hungary were ceded some to new and some to " existing States. The Austria and the Hungary dealt with by " the United States in entering into the Treaties of Vienna and " of Budapest respectively not only bore little resemblance " either to the Government or the territory of the Dual Mon- " archy with which the United States had been at war but " differed essentially from the former Austrian Empire and the " former Kingdom of Hungary. Unlike the Treaty of Berlin " '*restoring* friendly relations' between the United States and " Germany, these treaties in terms '*establish*' for the first time " such relations between Austria and the United States and " between Hungary and the United States." [1]

(*b*) *State Succession.* Although there was a divergence of views among writers on the question whether the obligations of the old State pass to its successor or successors, neither group maintained that a *joint* liability rests upon two or more successor States where the territory of a dismembered State has been divided between them.

(*c*) *Interpretation of the Treaties.* It was clear from the treaty

[1] The Commissioner gave the following picture of the pre-war relations of the two States: " Prior to the war the former Austrian Empire and the former " Kingdom of Hungary were separate and distinct States. Each had its own " governmental machinery, including a parliament. The citizenship of each " was distinct from the other. Austro-Hungarian citizenship did not exist. " An Austrian citizen could abandon his Austrian citizenship and acquire " Hungarian citizenship and *vice versa*.

" In 1867 a *de facto* and constitutional union with limited powers was " formed whereby each of these States delegated to the Austro-Hungarian " Dual Monarchy the power to act for them in the common administration of " (1) foreign affairs, (2) the common army and navy (excluding the special " army of each State), and (3) matters of finance in so far as concerned joint " expenditures for State purposes. This union was expressed in the common " head who bore the title 'Emperor of Austria and Apostolic King of Hungary.' " These joint expenditures were apportioned between the former Austrian " Empire and the former Kingdom of Hungary by the Austro-Hungarian Law " of December 30, 1907 (B.L.I., No. 278), on the basis of 63·6 per cent. to be " borne by Austria and 36·4 per cent. to be borne by Hungary. This was the " basis upon which contributions were made by the former Austrian Empire " and the former Kingdom of Hungary to the Imperial and Royal Austro- " Hungarian Government enabling it to wage war against the United States."

Case No. 54 *contd.*

provisions mentioned above that the treaties intended neither double compensation nor a joint undertaking.[1] This was also clear from the notes exchanged between the United States and Austria during the negotiations preceding the agreement establishing the Commission. [Report: *A.J.*, XXI (1927), pp. 606-609.]

NOTE.—The Commissioner referred to the practice of the Reparation Commission which had provisionally adopted the same proportion in crediting Austria and Hungary with the value of the property which passed under the treaties to the Allied and Associated Powers.

Case No. 55

State Succession—Succession in Obligations—Enrichment of Succeeding State to the Detriment of an Individual.

ZILBERSZPIC *v.* (POLISH) TREASURY.

Supreme Court of Poland, First Division. 14 *December*, 1928.

THE FACTS.—A contractor had, before the World War, concluded an agreement with the Russian Orthodox Charitable Society of Kielce (in the part of Poland then under Russian rule) to build an apartment house for the Society on land belonging to it, and had duly executed his part of the agreement, but, the war having broken out and the Russians having soon withdrawn from that part of Poland, part of the money due to him remained unpaid. In November, 1918, he assigned his unpaid claim to the plaintiff in the present action, who had in fact been his partner and had financed the contract, and who in the same month brought an action before the court at Kielce against the said Society. Under Article XII of the Peace Treaty of Riga, of 18 March, 1921, Poland was recognised as the " indubit- " able " owner of all (formerly Russian) State property situated in her territory, the expression " State pro- " perty " including " all kinds of property and property " rights given up by the former Russian Tsars." The land in question, which had, after the Polish insurrection of 1863, been granted to the Society by the Russian Government in 1868, became the property of the Polish Treasury, which was in 1925 cited by the plaintiff as defendant in the action. The Treasury having pleaded that it had not assumed any obligations

[1] The Commissioner referred here to the case *Wapa* v. *République d'Autriche* decided by the Austro-Yugoslav Mixed Arbitral Tribunal, *Recueil*, III, p. 702.

in connection with the land in question, and the court of first instance having sentenced the Treasury to pay the plaintiff a certain sum, the Court of Appeal at Lublin allowed an appeal by the Treasury and dismissed the action on the ground that the building had, under the rule *superficies solo cedit*, acquired the same legal status as the land on which it was built, and had thus become the property of the Treasury by virtue of the recovery of independence by Poland and of Article XII of the Treaty of Riga. On appeal to the Supreme Court,

Held: (1) That the rule against unjustified enrichment at the expense of another, being one of the fundamental rules of law, though not expressed in so many words in the (French) Civil Code (still prevailing in that part of Poland), is, in fact, recognised by that code, and the action called *de in rem verso* is available to enforce that rule.

(2) That, as the land alone had been the object of the grant of 1868 and the building itself had never formed Russian State property, and as the plaintiff had spent his own money on the construction of the building without being in contractual relations with the Treasury, the plaintiff can claim from the Polish Treasury, whose property the building has now become, that part of his expenditure which would not exceed the increase in the value of the land due to the construction of the building, deduction being made of the sum already paid for the construction of the building. [Report: Zb. O.S.N.; 1928, No. 190.]

NOTES.—I. This case differs from that of *Niedzielskie* v. (*Polish*) *Treasury* (*Annual Digest*, 1925-1926, Case No. 53), in that:

(1) In the latter case there was a contractual debt on the part of the Austrian State to pay for work done on a building which belonged to the Treasury, and the Supreme Court held that such contractual debts do not pass to the State acquiring territory, unless it expressly takes over the debts of its predecessor.

(2) The Supreme Court also rejected the claim of Niedzielskie based on unjustified enrichment, on the ground that Poland had undertaken to pay for most of the former Austrian State property to the credit of the Austrian reparations account. In the present case there was no contractual debt on the part of the Russian Treasury, the building in question had never formed Russian State property, and it came to Poland through the operation of a rule of private law, following the declaration as State property of land originally granted away by the Russian Government. It was, therefore, right to apply the rule of private law concerning unjustified enrichment.

II. The Polish courts have consistently held that Russian State property was recovered by Poland by virtue of her regained freedom,

Case No. 55 *contd.* and that Article XII of the Treaty of Riga was only declaratory (this is borne out, *inter alia*, by its wording : " Both High Contracting Parties " recognise that State property . . . situated in the territory of either " of them . . . falls under its indubitable ownership . . ."), *e.g.* *Procurator-General* v. *Tomecki*, 1923, to be reported in another volume of this *Digest*.

III. In the case of Polish territories to which the Treaty of Riga has reference, it should be noted that Article XIX of that Treaty frees Poland " of all responsibility for the debts and other obligations of any " kind of the former Russian Empire, including . . . external and " internal debts . . . except guarantees granted to institutions and " businesses situated in the territory of Poland." That is why the Court emphasises the fact that there was no contractual debt.

IV. The present case has since been approved in a decision of 5 December, 1929, given in another case to be reported in another volume of this *Digest*.

Case No. 56

State Succession—Succession of a Federal State to the Obligations of the Member States—Succession of the German Reich to the Obligations of Prussia.

LAND TAX IMMUNITIES CASE.

German Reichsfinanzhof (*Federal Tribunal in Revenue Matters*). 9 *March*, 1927.

THE FACTS.—In this case the appellant maintained that his property could not be subjected to land tax in accordance with the German Property Tax Law of 1922 because in the Treaties of Vienna [1] and of Prague [1] Prussia undertook to exempt the properties in question from land taxation.

Held : That the appeal must be rejected. There was no rule of international law imposing upon Germany the duty to take over the obligations incurred by Prussia. [Report : *Steuer und Wirtschaft*, VI (1927), p. 170.]

NOTE.—(1) The Court pointed out that there were at least three opinions as to the duty of Germany to take over the obligations of Prussia. A number of writers maintained that the treaties concluded by Prussia before the establishment of the North German Confederation were automatically binding upon the *Reich*. Others denied that any such obligations devolved *ipso jure* upon Germany. The intermediate views were that these obligations passed to the *Reich* if they related to matters in regard to which the *Reich* alone was competent, or if, having regard to the purpose of the treaty, the passing of the obligation on to the *Reich* ought to be assumed.

---

[1] *Quære*, of 1864 or of 1866. It is not clear to the editors which are the two treaties referred to. The Treaty of Vienna of 1864 and the Treaty of Prague of 1866 do not appear to contain any provision of this character.

(2) The Court observed in the course of the judgment that even if the appellant's main contention could be sustained, there still remained the question whether international treaties may not be rendered obsolete as the result of a change of circumstances and thus abolished without any express rescission.

State Succession—Succession in Obligations—Treaty of Versailles, Article 67—Succession of the French State to Rights of the German State—Railway System in Alsace-Lorraine—Dispatch of Goods before Armistice—No French Responsibility for Loss. **Case No. 57**

ALSACE-LORRAINE RAILWAY *v.* DUCREUX ÈS-QUALITÉ.

French Court of Cassation, Civil Chamber. 30 *March*, 1927.

THE FACTS.—A grain truck, forwarded on 6 November, 1918, from Metz to St. Avold, failed to arrive at its destination. The receiver of the forwarding company brought an action against the French Administration of the Alsace-Lorraine railway system, which had taken over the system after the armistice, on 1 December, 1918. The receiver claimed that the French Administration was responsible for private contracts entered into by the former German Administration.

This contention involved the interpretation of Article 67 of the Treaty of Versailles which reads:

"The French Government is substituted in all "the rights of the German Empire over all the rail- "ways which were administered by the Imperial "railway administration and which are actually "working or under construction. . . . This substi- "tution shall not entail any payment on the part "of the French State."

The Court of Appeal of Colmar (Second Chamber) held the French Administration responsible. On appeal,

Held, by the Court of Cassation: That the sentence of the Court of Appeal of Colmar must be reversed, as being in derogation of the general principle of law that a person is not responsible for an act which he has not committed.[1] The Treaty of Versailles, both in the letter and spirit of the text, recognised that the stipulations made in favour of France were in the nature of reparation. Although Article 67 invested France

[1] "Puisqu'elle tend à rendre un tiers responsable de faits qui ne lui sont "pas imputés."

Case No. 57 *contd.* with the rights of the Empire over all the lines operated by the German Administration, the Article concluded by expressly exempting the French State from the payment of any indemnity connected therewith. [Reports: 55 *Clunet* (1928), p. 1034, with a note by M. Marcel Nast; Sirey, 1928, Part I, p. 300, with an unsigned note; *Gazette du Palais*, 1927, 2, 21, with a note; *Dalloz Hebdomadaire*, 1928, p. 512.]

NOTE.—The Franco-German Mixed Arbitral Tribunal in a series of decisions adopted the same view. (See decisions of 11 February, 1922, 8 June, 1923, and 10 July, 1924.) See also Court of Appeal of Colmar (First Chamber), 16 May, 1927, 56 *Clunet* (1929), p. 447.

Case No. 58

State Succession—Succession in Obligations—Money Paid to Former State for Duty not yet Payable.

SUCCESSION IN OBLIGATIONS (ADVANCE PAYMENT OF DUTY) CASE.

Supreme Administrative Court of Czechoslovakia.
23 *November*, 1928. *No.* 30.910.

THE FACTS.—The plaintiff paid to the authorities of the former Hungarian State a sum of money on account of duty for spirit which he intended to buy, but subsequently did not buy. He demanded reimbursement of this sum from the Czechoslovak authorities, but his demand was dismissed having regard to the Czechoslovak Law of 23 June, 1926, No. 156 (see Note below). The plaintiff appealed to the Supreme Administrative Court, contending that in consequence of the continuity of the legal system before and after the revolution, proclaimed by the Law of 28 October, 1918, No. 11, he was entitled to recover.

Held, against the plaintiff: "It is true that the Law No. 11 "(1918) proclaimed the principle of the continuity of the legal "system before and after the revolution by leaving in force all "legal provisions from the time before 28 October, 1918,[1] so "far as those provisions could be brought into accord with "the new legal system arisen from the revolution, particularly "as far as they could be brought into accord with the sovereignty of the Czechoslovak Republic. It could be, therefore, correctly maintained that the Czechoslovák State by "virtue of its sovereignty is entitled to collect, in accordance "with the legal provisions maintained in force, all rates and "taxes, fees and duties not yet paid, but that, on the other

[1] The date of the coming into existence of the Czechoslovak State.

"hand, it is a consequence of that sovereignty that the Czecho-"slovak State is also responsible to the taxpayers for claims "which had accrued to them, though in the period prior to "the revolution, in accordance with the legal provisions regu-"lating the tax or duty concerned. This state of law was, "however, substantially altered by the Law No. 156 of 1926, "by which it was provided that the Czechoslovak State is not "responsible for obligations arising from arrangements with the "former Hungarian Government or its organs (except for "obligations expressly stated in the Treaties of Peace), nor "for obligations accruing against the former Hungarian State "from other facts. By those legal provisions taxpayers are "deprived, as from the date of the promulgation of the Law "(14 August, 1926), of the possibility of making against the "Czechoslovak Treasury such financial claims as had accrued "to them against the Treasury of the former Hungarian State "in the period before the revolution in accordance with the "legal provision regarding the tax or duty concerned, except "in cases provided for by law, *i.e.* cases where such a claim "of the taxpayer has been recognised by a special act of "the Czechoslovak financial administration." [Report: Boh. 4501 fin.]

NOTE.—As to the previous decisions now overruled by the present decision, see *Annual Digest*, 1925-1926, Case No. 50.

The Czechoslovak Law of 23 June, 1926, No. 156, provides that the Czechoslovak State is not responsible for obligations arisen from arrangements with the Governments of the former Austria, of the former Hungary and of the former Austro-Hungarian Monarchy or with their organs, except obligations expressly stated in the Treaties of Peace. Similarly the Czechoslovak State is not responsible for obligations arising against those States from other facts. The same provisions apply also with regard to obligations of the German Empire and of the German States. The Law of 23 July, 1919, No. 440 (see *Annual Digest*, 1925-1926, p. 71), by which a *moratorium* was declared in respect of claims arising against the former Austro-Hungarian, Austrian and Hungarian Treasuries is repealed. The provisions of the Law of 9 October, 1924, No. 236 (see *Annual Digest*, 1925-1926, p. 72), remain in force, by which the Czechoslovak Government was authorised to take over the claims arising against the former Austro-Hungarian, Austrian and Hungarian Treasuries from deliveries made during the war. There also remain in force all laws and acts by which the Czechoslovak State specifically assumed the fulfilment of certain obligations which otherwise would fall within the scope of the general provisions of the Law No. 156 (1926).

[As to the details of the interpretation of the Law No. 156, 1926, see also decisions of the Supreme Court of Justice of 24 November, 1927, No. Rv. I, 838 (Váž. 7547 civ.), of 9 December, 1927, No. Rv. I, 331 (Váž. 7595 civ.), of 20 April, 1928, No. Rv. I, 1494/27 (Váž. 7984 civ.), and of 2 November, 1928, No. Rv. I, 278 (Váž. 8428 civ.).]

State Succession—Succession in Obligations—Austro-Hungarian " Unsecured Unified Public Debt "—Obligations of Austria and Hungary.

See Case No. 305 (*Henry Neugass* v. *Austria and Hungary*).

V.—Respect of Private Rights

Case No. 59 **State Succession—Respect of Private Rights—Roumanian Agrarian Reform—Measures of Liquidation and Expropriation—Whether Compatible with International Law —Article 250 of the Treaty of Trianon—*Prima facie* Jurisdiction of the Mixed Arbitral Tribunal—Future Consideration of the Merits.**

KULIN, EMERIC *v.* ROUMANIAN STATE.

Roumanian-Hungarian Mixed Arbitral Tribunal.
10 *January*, 1927.

(CEDERKRANTZ, SZEKACZ.)

THE FACTS.—(See also Case No. 321.)

The claimant was the owner of certain rural property situated in former Hungarian territory ceded to Roumania in the Treaty of Trianon. As the result of the application of Roumanian agrarian legislation, his property was taken away from him in return for an insignificant sum, promised, but not paid, and the Roumanian Government was substituted for the claimant in the land registry as the registered owner.

Before the Tribunal the claimant asked for a declaration that certain laws enacted by the Roumanian Government and restricting his rights of property were contrary to Article 250 of the Treaty of Trianon, and that the Roumanian Government was bound to restore to him his property, to reinstate it in its original position in the land registry, and to pay him compensation for damage suffered. Article 250 of the Treaty of Trianon provided as follows :

" Notwithstanding the provisions of Article 232 " and the Annex to Section IV, the property, rights " and interests of Hungarian nationals or companies " controlled by them situated in the territories which " formed part of the former Austro-Hungarian

"Monarchy shall not be subject to retention or "liquidation in accordance with these provisions.

"Such property, rights and interests shall be "restored to their owners freed from any measure "of this kind, or from any other measure of transfer, "compulsory administration, or sequestration, taken "since the 3rd November, 1918, until the coming "into force of the present Treaty, in the condition "in which they were before the application of the "measures in question.

"Claims made by Hungarian nationals under this "Article shall be submitted to the Mixed Arbitral "Tribunal provided for by Article 239.

"The property, rights and interests here referred "to do not include property which is the subject of "Article 191, Part IX (Financial Clauses).

"Nothing in this Article shall affect the provisions "laid down in Part VIII (Reparation), Section I, "Annex III as to property of Hungarian nationals "in ships and boats."

It was contended on behalf of Roumania that the measures complained of did not fall within Article 250 of the Treaty, which, it was argued, referred only to liquidation undertaken as a war measure for war purposes and affecting ex-enemy property as such, but not to expropriation arising out of peace legislation, undertaken in pursuance of a general agrarian reform and bearing no discriminatory character; and that the Tribunal, therefore, had no jurisdiction.

Held (by a majority of the Tribunal, the Roumanian judge refusing to sign the decision): That the Tribunal had jurisdiction.

Article 250, when compared with Article 232 and other Treaty provisions, referred both to war liquidation and post-war liquidation. It covered all cases of subjecting ex-enemy property or rights to a treatment contrary to the rules generally applied to aliens and to the principle of the respect of acquired rights. The question whether there had taken place discrimination or whether there were or were not reasons justifying any departure from the principle of international law relating to respect of private rights, was one to be decided in the subsequent stage of proceedings dealing with the substance of the claim as distinguished from the plea to the jurisdiction.

Case No. 59 *contd.*

The preparatory work relating to Article 250 of the Treaty of Trianon and Article 267 of the Treaty of St. Germain showed that the intention of the contracting parties was fully to protect the rights of Hungarian nationals situated within the territory of the former Austro-Hungarian Monarchy, and to place these rights under the régime of common international law. A measure as the result of which the property of an exenemy is taken away in its entirety from the owner constitutes, *prima facie*, a violation of the general principle of respect of acquired rights and oversteps the limits of common international law. As such it is covered by Article 250 of the Treaty. However, while there are sufficient elements to establish the jurisdiction of the Court, it is only after examining " the substance of the claim that the Tribunal will be in " the position to judge whether the circumstances of the case " are really of a nature to justify the application of Article 250." [Report: *Recueil*, VII, p. 138.]

NOTE.—(1) See *ibid.*, pp. 151-162, for the dissenting opinion of the Roumanian judge who refused to sign the decision.

(2) Twenty-two identical decisions were given by the Tribunal on the same day. The above case has been digested in some detail, as, in addition to illustrating certain questions in respect of State succession, treatment of aliens and the jurisdiction of the Mixed Arbitral Tribunal, it became the most important event in the protracted Hungarian-Roumanian Optants dispute which occupied jurists and statesmen during the years 1923 to 1929.

Case No. 60

State Succession—Respect of Private Rights.

E. THALHEIMER *v.* YUGOSLAV STATE.

See the above case decided on 6 September, 1928, by the Hungarian Yugoslav Mixed Arbitral Tribunal (at p. 582 of the *Recueil*, vol. VIII), in which Article 250 of the Treaty of Trianon [1] is referred to by the Tribunal as having (in contradistinction to Article 232 of that Treaty, which allowed certain measures of liquidation) reaffirmed in favour of Hungarian nationals and their property in transferred territory the rule of international law according to which a State acquiring foreign territory by way of cession or conquest is bound to respect existing private rights, and in particular is not authorised to deprive of their property the subjects of the State to which it has succeeded.[2]

[1] For the text see Case No. 59.

[2] The same reference is made in the case *Les Anciens Urbalistes de la Commune de Beremond* v. *Yugoslav State* (*Recueil*, VIII, p. 584).

Succession—Respect of Private Rights—Purchase of Property Confiscated as Punishment for Participation in an Insurrection.

See Case No. 375 (*Kulakowski and Others* (*appellants*) v. *Szumkowski* (*respondent*).

VII.—International Conventions

Succession of States—Annexation—Application of Existing Treaties to Annexed Territories—Application of Sardinian Treaties to the New Italian State. **Case No. 61**

GASTALDI *v.* LEPAGE HEMERY.

Italian Court of Cassation. 3 December, 1927.

THE FACTS.—This was a case concerning the execution of a judgment of a French court. The Italian Court of Appeal decided that certain investigations ordered by the French courts ought to have been carried out, not according to Article 941 of the Code of Procedure and to the Italian Decree of 1919, but on the basis of the Declaration signed on 11 September, 1860, by the French envoy and the Minister for Foreign Affairs of Sardinia, laying down rules for the interpretation of Article 22 of the Treaty of 24 March, 1760, relative to the execution of judgments given by the courts of the two States. The Court of Appeal pointed out that the international treaty enjoyed priority over the Code of Civil Procedure in regard to the rules to be observed in the matter of execution of foreign judgments as laid down in Article 10 of the preliminary provisions of the Civil Code. The plaintiff appealed against this decision on the ground that Article 10 was not applicable to the Sardinian-French Treaty of 1760 which did not bind the new Italian State.

Held by the Court of Cassation : That the appeal must be dismissed. An international treaty with a State takes effect also in regard to new territories added to the old State and forming with it the new national territory. The united Italian State arose by way of annexation, and that implied the automatic extension of the international treaties to the new territories. The international status of the contracting State does

Case No. 61 *contd.*

not undergo any change by reason of the growth of its territory. Consequently the Sardinian-French Treaty of 24 March, 1760, relative to the execution of judgments of the courts and confirmed by the subsequent Sardinian-French declaration of interpretation of 11 September, 1860, is valid as between Italy and France. [Report: *Rivista di diritto internazionale*, 1930, pp. 102-103.]

VIII.—In Matters of Administration. Officials

Case No. 62

State Succession—No General Obligation to Take Over Officials.

FRYSTATZKI *v.* POLISH STATE.

Upper Silesian Arbitral Tribunal. 27 January, 1928.

THE FACTS.—The plaintiff was appointed, in April, 1920, postman in Tarnowitz, in the part of Silesia which was subsequently ceded to Poland. To the appointment there was attached a right to pension. In October, 1921, he was further appointed "mail-conductor," subject to termination of his appointment by three months' notice. After the cession of that part of Silesia he received an appointment, in 1923, in the Polish Postal Service, but that appointment was terminated in 1927 on the ground that the claimant was of German nationality. It appeared that the dismissal was made subject to an old-age pension in accordance with the terms of his appointment in 1923.

The claimant contended that as he had been taken over from the German Postal Service, he was entitled to certain payments and to an old-age pension in accordance with the terms of his appointment in 1920 and 1921. Poland contended that he had not been taken over from the German Postal Service, and that the Decree of 1921 by which he was appointed to the Polish Postal Service was of constitutive character and created an altogether original right. The claim was brought on the basis of Article 4 of the Geneva Convention of 15 May, 1922, providing for the respect of private rights.

Held: That the claim must be rejected. There was no

legal basis for the view that the claimant's employment in Poland was a continuation of his employment in Germany. The claimant had no acquired right to be taken over by Poland. "There is no rule of international law to the effect that a State "which acquires territory is *ipso facto* bound to take over "officials employed by its predecessor. Accordingly, there is "no rule of international law which establishes the right of an "official to be taken over. Such taking over of officials can "take place only by virtue of treaties or special agreements." The Geneva Convention which provided for taking over the railway officials did not contain similar provisions in respect of other officials. Accordingly, the appointment of the claimant could not be regarded as a continuation of his former employment in Germany, but only as the commencement of a new legal relation. The question of any rights derived from that new relation was not within the jurisdiction of the Tribunal, which was competent only in respect of acquired rights existing at the time of the transfer of sovereignty. [Report: *Official Collection of Decisions of the Upper Silesian Arbitral Tribunal*, vol. I, Nos. 1-2 (in German and Polish), p. 46.]

State Succession—Succession in Matters of Administration—Continuance in Employment of Officials. **Case No. 63**

KOT *v.* (POLISH) MINISTRY OF PUBLIC WORKS.

Supreme Administrative Court of Poland. 2 March, 1928.

THE FACTS.—Plaintiff had been up to 1918 a petty official in the Austrian Roads Administration. Shortly after the Polish authorities took over the country he was told that he would be employed no longer. He applied to be either reinstated, or told why he would not be employed, or pensioned. This application having failed, he brought the present action to have the decision of the defendant quashed. Defendant pleaded that plaintiff had never been formally appointed by Polish authorities nor had he been sworn in, so that no public law relationship had arisen.

Held: (Following a previous decision) that "Polish authorities had the right to use their free discretion in accepting or "not accepting for Polish service employees of the States "responsible for the partitioning of Poland who were serving "in the territories which came to Poland." Consequently,

Case No. 63 *contd.* " the admission of such an employee to the Polish service " would require a distinct act on the part of the competent " authority. . . ." [Report: Z.W.N.T.A., VI (1928), No. 1399; P.P.A., 1928, p. 546.]

Case No. 64 **State Succession—In Matters of Administration—Continuance of Employment of Officials.**

HUTNIKIEWICZ *v.* (POLISH) STATE TREASURY.

Supreme Court of Poland, Third Division. 15 *November*, 1927.

THE FACTS.—Plaintiff was a State railway workman in Stryj until the downfall of the Austro-Hungarian Monarchy. Then, and until May, 1919, he continued to serve with the railway which was in the hands of the so-called Western Ukrainian Republic. The Polish Government, having taken over the railways, refused to employ him. He brought an action claiming an indemnity and a pension for life. The District Court of Stryj dismissed the action. The Court of Appeal of Lwów dismissed his appeal, adding that although " under general principles of international law the " Polish Railway Administration had the duty of admitting to its service former Austrian employees if " they had remained in Austrian employment until the " railways were taken over by the Polish railway administration," it was at least doubtful in the present case whether the facts warranted an application of this rule, because plaintiff had accepted employment with the Western Ukrainian Republic. On appeal,

Held, by the Supreme Court, dismissing the appeal: (1) that plaintiff's contention that Austrian sovereignty over the territory in question had lasted until May, 1919, and that the Austrian Emperor had, on 18 October, 1918, assigned that sovereignty to the Ukrainian National Council, was entirely baseless ;

(2) That Poland is bound by obligations of the former Austrian State only in so far as by international treaty she has taken them over ;

(3) That this is particularly the case with regard to railway employees ;

(4) That the above-quoted statement of the Court of Appeal as to general principles of international law is quite baseless, no

such obligation existing either on general principles or in the stipulations of the Treaty of St. Germain;

(5) That, this being the case with regard to Austrian employees, it was *a fortiori* true of employees of the Ukrainian National Council which was carrying on an armed contention against Poland. [Report: P.P.A., 1928, 373.]

IX.—Binding Force of Laws and Judgments of Courts

Succession of States—Maintenance of Religious Jurisdiction—Mandate for Syria—Religious Autonomy. **Case No. 65**

SUCCESSION OF RIZCALLAH GAZALÉ CASE.

Court of Appeal of Aleppo, Syria. 7 *May*, 1928.

THE FACTS.—Rizcallah Gazalé (an ex-Turkish subject belonging to the Greek Catholic Church) died on 15 April, 1926, without leaving issue, at Aleppo. His heirs were his widow on the one side, and the children of his brother and his sisters on the other. In an action concerning the succession to his movable property, it was claimed by the nephews and nieces that the succession should be regulated by the religious law of the Community of the deceased. The widow, on the other hand, claimed that the succession should be governed by the law of the Koran, which, in virtue of the last enactments of the Turkish legislation prior to the Allied Occupation, applied in Syria to Christians as well as to Moslems.

Held: In the Turkish Empire matters of personal status, including marriage and succession, were governed for Moslems by the law of the Koran administered by a Moslem court, but for Christians by their religious law administered by Ecclesiastical courts. The Sultan Abdul Majid, in a Decree issued in 1856, of which note was taken at the Congress of Paris in that year, confirmed the privileges and immunities granted by the earlier Sultans to all Christian Communities, and laid down that actions of succession between persons of the same Christian or non-Moslem Community might at their request be decided by the Councils of the Patriarchates or the Communities.

Case No. 65 *contd.* The Greek Catholic Community, which was separated from the Greek Orthodox Community, has the right of enjoying its own laws of personal status.

The disappearance of the Turkish Empire does not in any way derogate from the force of its legislation with regard to the jurisdiction of the religious Communities; and the application of the law of the Christian Communities in matters of succession has been recognised by numerous decisions of the French courts.

The Mandate for Syria and the Lebanon provides that the Mandatory shall introduce a judicial system which shall assure to natives as well as to foreigners a complete guarantee of their rights; and respect for the personal status of the various peoples and communities and their religious interests shall be fully guaranteed. Another Article of the Mandate provides that the Mandatory shall guarantee to every person complete liberty of conscience, and there shall be no discrimination between the inhabitants on the ground of race, religion or language. It follows from these provisions that the laws of personal status of the different populations must be maintained in their integrity, even though under the previous régime their application has been subject to infringements. The Christian populations of Syria are, therefore, entitled to regulate matters of personal status according to their own religious law in the same way as the Moslem population. [Report: 56 *Clunet* (1929), p. 165.]

NOTE.—The question of the jurisdiction of the Christian Ecclesiastical courts in Syria has been much discussed in the courts. In an earlier decision given by the Court of Appeal at Aleppo, dated 26 November, 1927, it was held that the succession of Christian subjects was to be governed by the Moslem Tribunal according to the Koran, unless all the parties concerned consented to the jurisdiction of the Patriarch. See *Gazette des Tribunaux Libano-Syriens*, November, 1927, p. 976.

F. SUCCESSION OF GOVERNMENTS

I.—In General

Succession of Governments—Action Instituted by Accredited Agent of Recognised Government—Non-Abatement of Action by Succession of Unrecognised Government.

See Case No. 35 (*Lehigh Valley R. Co.* v. *State of Russia*).

G. MISCELLANEOUS

The Holy See—Right to Sue—Portugal and the Holy See.

Case No. 66

THE HOLY SEE (represented by Mgr. Achilles Locatelli) *v.* ENGRÁCIO SUPARDO AND HIS WIFE.

Supreme Court of Justice, Portugal. 13 *January*, 1928.

THE FACTS.—The Holy See, represented by the Apostolic Nuncio in Portugal, brought an action before the Civil Tribunal of Lisbon against Engrácio Supardo and his wife in order to compel the defendants to remove a balcony and staircase erected contrary to Article 2325 of the *Code Civil* and adjoining certain premises belonging to the Holy See, or to erect a wall protecting those premises from being thus overlooked. The defendants contended that the plaintiff had no *locus standi* to sue.

Held by the Supreme Court of Justice, confirming the decisions of the courts of first and second instance: That the plaintiff had capacity to sue. According to the opinion of writers on international law and the decisions of national and foreign tribunals, the Holy See by virtue of the so-called Italian Law of Guarantees of 13 May, 1871, constitutes in its capacity of a foreign State (either under the régime of Concordats or under the régime of separation, which does not exclude political relations) a collective personality in private law which gives it a *locus standi* in courts through its diplomatic representative.[1] [Report: *Gazeta da Relação de Lisboa*, vol. 44, p. 170.]

[1] See also the case of *Apostolic Nuncio* v. *Perez*, decided by the National Supreme Court of Justice of Argentina, on 27 March, 1925. This was an ejectment suit originally filed in the National Supreme Court by the Apostolic Nuncio, as representative of the Holy See, against Martin Perez, who occupied certain premises located in Buenos Aires. [Report: 15 Jurisprudencia Argentina, 198.] In his Opinion on this case the Solicitor-General of the Nation, Dr. Larreta, said as follows: " The Apostolic Nuncio accredited to " this Republic, invoking the character inherent in him as representative of " the international entity, as he states at page 5, brings before Your Excellency " suit in ejectment against Martin Perez, occupant of the house at No. 629, " Chacabuco Street.

" The cause instituted concerns, then, the diplomatic agent mentioned, and " its original cognisance pertains to the Supreme Court in accordance with the " provisions of Articles 101 of the National Constitution, and 1, paragraph 3, " of Law No. 48, relative to the jurisdiction and competency of the federal " tribunals." Article 101 of the National Constitution of Argentina provides: " In these cases the Supreme Court shall exercise its jurisdiction by appeal,

Case No. 66 *contd.*

NOTE.—This decision, as well as that of the courts of first and second instance, are, it is believed, the first decisions in which Portuguese courts have recognised the juridical personality of the Holy See in private matters. In Portuguese public law the Holy See has always been considered as a foreign State and consequently as possessing juridical personality. This was the case not only under the régime of Concordats when the religion of the Portuguese State was the Catholic, Apostolic and Roman religion, but also under the régime of the separation of Church and State established by the Decree of 20 April, 1911, and confirmed in Article 3, No. 5, of the Political Constitution of the Portuguese Republic of 19 June, 1911 (Professor Marnoco e Sousa, *Comentario á Constituição da Republica Portugueza*, pp. 62, 63; Professor Carneiro Pacheco, *Codigo Civil Actualisado*, vol. I, p. 86). Thus, according to a Decree of 16 May, 1911 (Article 37), a Portuguese Legation was established at the Vatican. It is true that no diplomatic representative was actually appointed and that the representation itself was suppressed shortly afterwards by a Law of 10 July, 1913, but, as pointed out by Professor Machado Vilela, *Tratado elementar téorico e prático de direito internacional privado*, vol. I, p. 274, this fact shows merely that it was considered that it was not necessary to maintain regular diplomatic relations with the Holy See and not that the latter was incapable of maintaining such relations. This appears clearly from the fact that in 1918 the Legation was re-established at the Vatican, and that that position still continues. It ought to be added that by the Decree No. 15417 of 30 April, 1928, there was concluded, subject to the ratification of the Executive Power, a protocol signed in Rome and providing for the limitation of dioceses, the nomination of Bishops and the double jurisdiction regulated in the Concordat of 1886 in regard to the rights of Patronage of Portugal in the East. This agreement was ratified and published in the *Diário do Governo*, No. 102, Series 1, of 5 May, 1928.

There is therefore no doubt that, so far as Portuguese public and private law are concerned, the Holy See enjoys juridical personality in accordance with Articles 32 and following of the Civil Code. This is the opinion of Portuguese publicists (Professor Machado Vilela, *loc. cit.*; Dr. Adriano Antero, *O direito internacional*, p. 20; Antonio Batoque and Antonio Cesar Abranches, *Os principios geraes de direito internacional privado* (extrait des leçons du Professeur Mário de Figueiredo, pp. 76-78); Professor Carneiro Pacheco, *loc. cit.*

This situation continues since the conclusion of the recent Lateran agreements of 11 February, 1929.

"according to the rules and exceptions prescribed by Congress; but in all "matters concerning foreign ambassadors, ministers and consuls, and in those "in which a province shall be a party, it shall exercise it originally and ex-"clusively." Article 1, paragraph 3, Law No. 48, of 14 September, 1863, provides: "The National Supreme Court of Justice shall have cognisance, in "the first instance, of: All causes concerning foreign ambassadors or other "diplomatic ministers, the persons composing the legation, the members of "their families or domestic servants, in the manner in which a court of justice "can proceed in conformity with the law of nations."

The Holy See—Crimes Committed in the Basilica of St. Peter—Whether Committed in Italian Territory—Article 5 of the Italian Civil Code. **Case No. 67**

In re Stella and Others.

Italian Court of Cassation (Second Division). 1 *July,* 1927.

The Facts.—This was a prosecution for the crime of larceny committed in the Basilica of St. Peter.

Held: That the Italian Court has jurisdiction. In virtue of the Law of Guarantees of 13 May, 1871, a crime committed in the Basilica of St. Peter must be deemed to be committed on foreign territory. The provisions of Article 5 [1] of the Penal Code are consequently applicable in the case before the Court. The archpriest of the Basilica is qualified to prosecute the perpetrators of a theft in that church. [Report: *Monitore dei Tribunali*, 1927, p. 958.]

[1] Article 5 of the Italian Criminal Code provides, *inter alia*, that if an Italian subject commits abroad a crime which is punishable by imprisonment for a term not exceeding three years, no prosecution shall be issued except at the demand of the injured party or of a foreign Government.

PART III

STATE TERRITORY

A. STATE TERRITORY IN GENERAL

I.—Nature of Territorial Sovereignty

Territory—Nature of Territorial Sovereignty—Acquisition of —Discovery—Occupation—Effectiveness of Occupation—Prescription—Peaceful Display of Sovereignty. **Case No. 68**

ISLAND OF PALMAS ARBITRATION CASE.

United States and Holland: Permanent Court of Arbitration. 4 April, 1928.

(HUBER, Arbitrator.)

THE FACTS.—(See also Cases Nos. 1, 70, 72, 75.)

This was a dispute between the United States and Holland concerning the sovereignty over the Island of Palmas. The United States, who, by a treaty with Spain of 10 December, 1898, acquired the Philippines by way of cession, based its title to the Island of Palmas, as successor of Spain, mainly on discovery. It was also maintained on the part of the United States that, as the Island of Palmas formed a geographical part of the Philippines group of islands, it belonged by virtue of the principle of contiguity to the United States, who exercised sovereignty over the Philippines.

On the part of Holland it was contended that Holland, represented for this purpose in the seventeenth and eighteenth centuries by the Dutch East India Company, possessed and exercised rights of sovereignty over the island as far back as 1677, or even 1648. It was also contended that rights of sovereignty were granted to the Company and later to Holland in treaties concluded by the Company and by Holland with native princes, and that these treaties established the suzerainty of Holland over their territories.

On the basis of the evidence produced before him the Arbitrator found that Holland exercised certain acts of sovereignty over the disputed island at different

Case No. 68 ***contd.***

periods between the middle of the seventeenth century and 1898. For reasons stated elsewhere (see Case No. 72) he rejected the claim of the United States in so far as it was based on mere discovery or contiguity. In regard to the Dutch contention,

Held : That as Holland's title of sovereignty was proved by evidence of continuous and peaceful display of sovereignty for a long period of time, probably going back beyond the year 1700, the Island of Palmas must be adjudged to form part of Holland's territory. The decision of the Arbitrator was based on the following general considerations upon the nature and acquisition of territorial sovereignty :

Territorial Sovereignty.

In relation to a portion of the surface of the globe sovereignty is the legal condition necessary for the inclusion of that portion in the territory of a State. Sovereignty, which in relation to territory may be called territorial sovereignty, in the relation between States signifies independence. Independence in relation to territory is the right to exercise therein, to the exclusion of any other State, the functions of a State. International law has established this principle of the exclusive competence of the State in regard to its own territory as the point of departure in settling most questions that concern international relations. Subject to the reservation (more apparent than real) of composite States and of collective sovereignty, territorial sovereignty belongs always to one State, or in exceptional circumstances to several States, to the exclusion of all others.

Establishment and Continuance of Territorial Sovereignty.

In case of a dispute as to the sovereignty over a portion of territory, it is usual to examine which of the States claiming sovereignty possesses a title (by cession, conquest, occupation, etc.) superior to that of the other State. However, if the dispute is based on the fact that one State has actually displayed sovereignty, it is not sufficient to establish the title by which territorial sovereignty was validly acquired at a certain date ; it must also be shown that the territorial sovereignty has continued to exist and did exist at the moment which must be considered as critical for the decision of the dispute. This demonstration consists in the actual display of normal State activities. An element which is essential for the constitution of sovereignty must not be lacking in the maintenance of sovereignty. So true is this, that practice, as well as doctrine, recognises that the continuous and peaceful display of territorial sovereignty, in relation to other States, constitutes a good title. " The growing insistence with which international law, " ever since the middle of the eighteenth century, has demanded " that the occupation shall be effective, would be inconceivable, " if effectiveness were required only for the act of acquisition " and not equally for the maintenance of the right. If the " effectiveness has above all been insisted on in regard to occu- " pation, this is because the question rarely arises in connection " with territories in which there is already an established order " of things. Just as before the rise of international law " boundaries of lands were necessarily determined by the fact " that the power of a State was exercised within them, so too, " under the reign of international law, the fact of peaceful and " continuous display is still one of the most important considera- " tions in establishing boundaries between States."

Prescription and Protection of Peaceful Possession.

" Although municipal law, thanks to its complete judicial " system, is able to recognise abstract rights of property as " existing apart from any material display of them, it has none " the less limited their effect by the principles of prescription " and the protection of possession. International law, the " structure of which is not based on any super-State organisa- " tion, cannot be presumed to reduce a right such as territorial " sovereignty, with which almost all international relations are " bound up, to the category of an abstract right, without con- " crete manifestations."

The principle that continuous and peaceful display of State activities is a constituent element of territorial sovereignty is not only widely accepted in international jurisprudence and doctrine ; it has been recognised in several federal States in which there exist tribunals applying rules of international law for the settlement of disputes between States Members. This is the more significant as in federal States possessing a more complete judicial system than that obtaining in the domain of international relations it is natural that there should be applied to territorial questions the principle that a lawfully acquired *jus in re* shall prevail over *de facto* possession.[1]

Peaceful and Effective Possession as Presumption of Continuous Exercise of Territorial Sovereignty.

" Although continuous in principle, sovereignty cannot be

[1] *Indiana* v. *Kentucky* (1890), 136 U.S. 479 ; *Rhode Island* v. *Massachusetts*, 4 How, 591, 639.

Case No. 68 ***contd.***

" exercised in fact at every moment on every point of a territory. The intermittence and discontinuity compatible with the maintenance of the right necessarily differ according as inhabited or uninhabited regions are involved, or regions enclosed within territories in which sovereignty is uncontestably displayed, or again regions accessible from, for instance, the high seas. It is true that neighbouring States may by convention fix limits to their own sovereignty, even in regions such as the interior of scarcely explored continents where such sovereignty is hardly manifested, and in this way each may prevent the other from any penetration of its territory. The delimitation of hinterland may also be mentioned in this connection. If, however, no conventional line of sufficient topographical precision exists, or if there are gaps in the frontiers otherwise established, or if a conventional line leaves room for doubt, or if, as, for example, in the case of an island situated in the high seas, the question arises whether a title is valid *erga omnes*, the actual continuous and peaceful display of State functions is in case of dispute the sound and natural criterium of territorial sovereignty."

The Date of Effective Display of Sovereignty.

It is not necessary that the display of sovereignty should go back to a distant period. It is sufficient that it existed in 1898, and had existed before that date long enough to enable any other Power claiming sovereignty over the island to ascertain the existence of a state of things contrary to its real or alleged right. Neither is it necessary that it should be established as having begun at a precise epoch. It is sufficient that it had existed at the crucial period preceding the year 1898. " It is quite natural that the establishment of sovereignty may be the outcome of a slow evolution, of a progressive intensification of State control. This is particularly the case if sovereignty is acquired by the establishment of the suzerainty of a colonial power over a native State, and in regard to outlying possessions of such a vassal State." [Reports: *Permanent Court of Arbitration, Arbitral Award rendered in conformity with the Special Agreement concluded on* 23 *January,* 1925, *between the United States of America and the Netherlands,* pp. 14-19, 58; *A.J.*, XXII (1928), pp. 867-912.]

NOTE.—See also :—

(*a*) on prescription and its effect upon conventional rights, Case No. 75;

(*b*) on the application of so-called " inter-temporal international law" to questions of occupation and discovery, Case No. 1;

(*c*) on the duty of notification and applicability of the rules of the Berlin Conference of 1885, Case No. 71;
(*d*) on the principle of contiguity, Case No. 72;
(*e*) on acquisition of title by corporations, Case No. 70;

and see also Cases Nos. 74, 288, 332, 336, 340 for other questions of international law and arbitral procedure dealt with in this Award.

See on this award Jessup in *A.J.*, XXII (1928), pp. 735-752, and F. de Visscher in *R.I.*, 3rd ser., vol. X (1929), pp. 735-762.

State Territory—Extension of—Ships on the High Seas—Assimilation to State Territory. **Case No. 69**

AMBAS BAY TRADING CO. LTD. *v.* GERMAN GOVERNMENT.

Anglo-German Mixed Arbitral Tribunal. 24 *July*, 1928.

(SANDSTROEM, ROBINSON, ALBRECHT.)

THE FACTS.—Goods belonging to the claimant British company in a German ship were requisitioned on the high seas after the outbreak of war by the Commander of a German cruiser. Article 297 (*e*) of the Treaty of Versailles laid down, *inter alia*, that the nationals of Allied and Associated Powers shall be entitled to compensation for damage inflicted upon their property in German territory as it existed on 1 August, 1914, by the application of exceptional war measures.

Held: That as in accordance with a generally recognised conception of international law, ships on the high seas are in certain respects assimilated to the territory of the State to which they belong, requisitions of enemy property laden on board German ships must be considered as having taken place in German territory within the meaning of Article 297 (*e*). [Report: *Recueil*, VIII, p. 288.]

NOTE.—See, however, on the question of territoriality of ships, Cases Nos. 123, 192.

Territory—In General—Whether Territory under Régime of Capitulations Assimilated to National Territory.

See Case No. 124 (*In re Durante*).

II.—Acquisition of Territorial Sovereignty

ii.—Occupation. The Principle of Contiguity. Effect of Discovery

Case No. 70

Territory—Acquisition of—Title Acquired by Corporations—Contracts Made by the Dutch East India Company.

ISLAND OF PALMAS ARBITRATION CASE.

United States and Holland: Permanent Court of Arbitration. 4 *April*, 1928.

(HUBER, Arbitrator.)

THE FACTS.—(See Cases Nos. 1, 68, 72, 75.)

The claim of Holland to the Island of Palmas was based, *inter alia*, on the contention that the Dutch East India Company, acting on behalf of Holland, established Dutch sovereignty over the Island of Palmas as early as the seventeenth century by means of conventions with native princes and chieftains, and that sovereignty thus acquired was displayed during the eighteenth and nineteenth centuries. The text of these conventions concluded in 1677, 1697, 1720 and 1758 by the Company showed that they were based on the conception that the prince received his principality as a fief of the Company or the Dutch State which was the suzerain.

Their political character was emphasised by supplementary agreements concerning the obligation of the vassal in time of war. The dependence of the vassal was ensured by important powers being given to the representatives of the Dutch Government. The oldest of these contracts, concluded in 1677, contained clauses binding the vassal State of the Company to refuse to admit the nationals of other States, in particular of Spain, and to tolerate no religion other than Protestantism. The question having been raised by the United States whether the Company had power to act validly under international law for Holland, in particular by concluding so-called political treaties with native rulers,

Held: That Holland was entitled to rely in the international sphere on the rights acquired by the Dutch East India Company.

1. The acts of the Company must in international law be entirely assimilated to acts of the State of Holland itself. From the end of the sixteenth century to the nineteenth century companies formed by individuals and engaged in economic ventures (so-called Chartered Companies) were invested by their States with public powers for the acquisition and administration of colonies. It was essential for the assumption of continuous and peaceful display of actual power in a contested region that the disputed territory should be attached to the State by a legal relation which is recognised in international law as valid against a State contesting the claim. There had been in the present case a legal relation of that nature.

2. " As regard contracts between a State or a Company such " as the Dutch East India Company and native princes or " chiefs of peoples not recognised as members of the community " of nations, they are not, in the international law sense, " treaties or conventions capable of creating rights and obliga- " tions such as may, in international law, arise out of treaties. " But, on the other hand, contracts of this nature are not wholly " void of indirect effects on situations governed by inter- " national law ; if they do not constitute titles in international " law, they are none the less facts of which that law must in " certain circumstances take account. From the time of the " discoveries until recent times, colonial territory has very " often been acquired, especially in the East Indies, by means " of contracts with the native authorities, which contracts " leave the existing organisation more or less intact as regards " the native population, whilst granting to the colonising " Power, besides economic advantages such as monopolies or " navigation and commercial privileges, also the exclusive " direction of relations with other Powers, and the right to " exercise public authority in regard to their own nationals " and to foreigners. The form of the legal relations created " by such contracts is most generally that of suzerain and " vassal, or of the so-called colonial protectorate.

" In substance, it is not an agreement between equals ; it " is rather a form of internal organisation of a colonial terri- " tory, on the basis of autonomy for the natives. In order " to regularise the situation as regards other States, this " organisation requires to be completed by the establishment " of powers to ensure the fulfilment of the obligations im- " posed by international law on every State in regard to its

Case No. 70 *contd.*

" own territory. And thus suzerainty over the native State " becomes the basis of territorial sovereignty as towards other " members of the community of nations. It is the sum-total " of functions thus allotted either to the native authorities or " to those of the colonial Power which decides the question " whether at any certain period the conditions required for the " existence of sovereignty are fulfilled. It is a question to be " decided in each case whether such a régime is to be considered " as effective or whether it is essentially fictitious, either for " the whole or a part of the territory. There always remains " reserved the question whether the establishment of such a " system is not forbidden by the pre-existing rights of other " States." [1] [Reports: *Permanent Court of Arbitration, Arbitral Award rendered in conformity with the Special Agreement concluded on 23 January, 1925, between the United States of America and the Netherlands*, pp. 41-46; *A.J.*, XXII (1928), pp. 894-898.]

Case No. 71

Territory—Acquisition of—Occupation—Conditions of—Notification—Applicability of the Rules of the Berlin Conference of 1885 to other Regions and States.

ISLAND OF PALMAS ARBITRATION CASE.

United States and Holland: Permanent Court of Arbitration.
4 *April*, 1928.

(HUBER, Arbitrator.)

THE FACTS.—(See Cases Nos. 1, 68, 70, 72, 75.) It was contended by the United States that the establishment of suzerainty by Holland over the group of islands including the Island of Palmas and the display of sovereignty by the Netherlands in these territories could not be recognised, as no notification of these acts to other Powers had taken place.

Held: That no such notification was necessary. " Such " notification, like any other formal act, can only be the con- " dition of legality as a consequence of an explicit rule of law. " A rule of this kind adopted by the Powers in 1885 for the

[1] The Arbitrator referred here, as being in conformity with the view enunciated above, to the Note from the United States Secretary of State to Spain, dated 7 January, 1900, and relating to two small islands lying just outside the line drawn by the Treaty of Paris of 1898 but claimed by the United States under that Treaty.

" African continent does not apply *de plano* to other regions." (See also Case No. 75.) [Reports: *Permanent Court of Arbitration, Arbitral Award rendered in conformity with the Special Agreement concluded on 23 January, 1925, between the United States of America and the Netherlands*, pp. 58, 59; *A.J.*, XXII (1928), p. 909.]

Territory—Acquisition of—Principle of Contiguity—In General —In regard to Groups of Islands. **Case No. 72**

Island of Palmas Arbitration Case.

United States and Holland: Permanent Court of Arbitration.
4 *April*, 1928.

(Huber, Arbitrator.)

The Facts.—(See Cases Nos. 1, 68, 70, 75.) The United States contended, *inter alia*, that, as the Island of Palmas formed a geographical part of the group of the Philippine Islands, it ought by virtue of the principle of contiguity to belong to the United States, who exercised sovereignty over the Philippines.

Held: That the claim, in so far as it is based on the principle of contiguity, must be rejected:

(*a*) In general. " Although States have in certain circum-" stances maintained that islands relatively close to their " shores belonged to them in virtue of their geographical " situation, it is impossible to show the existence of a rule " of positive international law to the effect that islands situated " outside territorial waters should belong to a State from " the mere fact that its territory forms the *terra firma* (nearest " continent or island of considerable size). Not only would " it seem that there are no precedents sufficiently frequent " and sufficiently precise in their bearing to establish such " a rule of international law, but the alleged principle itself is " by its very nature so uncertain and contested that even " governments of the same State have on different occasions " maintained contradictory opinions as to its soundness. The " principle of contiguity, in regard to islands, may not be out of " place when it is a question of allotting them to one State " rather than another, either by agreement between the parties " or by a decision not necessarily based on law; but as a rule " establishing *ipso jure* the presumption of sovereignty in favour

Case No. 72 *contd.*

" of a particular State, this principle would be in conflict with " what has been said as to territorial sovereignty and as to the " necessary relation between the right to exclude other States " from a region and the duty to display therein the activities of " a State. Nor is this principle of contiguity admissible as a " legal method of deciding questions of territorial sovereignty; " for it is wholly lacking in precision and would in its applica-" tion lead to arbitrary results. This would be especially true " in a case such as that of the island in question, which is not " relatively close to one single continent, but forms part of a " large archipelago in which strict delimitations between the " different parts are not naturally obvious."

It was true that there may be gaps both in point of time and of space in the exercise of sovereignty and also that a break in continuity on the part of either of the parties responsible did not necessarily imply that sovereignty was non-existent. But international jurisprudence—for instance in the case between Italy and Switzerland concerning the Alpe Cravairola [1]—showed that more importance ought to be attached to acts of display of sovereignty than to contiguity of territory.

(*b*) In regard to islands "it is possible that a group may " under certain circumstances be regarded as in law a unit, and " that the fate of the principal part may involve the rest. " Here, however, we must distinguish between, on the one hand, " the act of first taking possession, which can hardly extend to " every portion of territory, and, on the other hand, the display " of sovereignty as a continuous and prolonged manifestation " which must make itself felt through the whole territory." The application of this rule to the Island of Palmas militated against the claim of the United States. The Island of Palmas is a somewhat isolated island, and ought therefore to be regarded as a clearly delimited territory. Moreover, it is an island which is permanently inhabited and occupied by a population sufficiently numerous to necessitate some kind of permanent administration. In these circumstances the fact that the United States were unable to indicate any acts of public administration in regard to the island makes it difficult to assume that there was any actual display of sovereignty at all. [Reports: *Permanent Court of Arbitration, Arbitral Award rendered in conformity with the Special Agreement concluded on* 23 *January,* 1925, *between the United States of America and the Netherlands,* pp. 39, 40; *A.J.*, XXII (1928), pp. 893, 894.]

[1] Award of 31 December, 1873, Lafontaine, pp. 201-209.

Acquisition of Territorial Title—Presumption of Existence of Sovereignty Arising from Display of Sovereignty. **Case No. 73**

ISLAND OF PALMAS ARBITRATION CASE.

United States and Holland: Permanent Court of Arbitration. 4 April, 1928.

(HUBER, Arbitrator.)

THE FACTS.—(See Cases Nos. 1, 68, 70, 72, 75.) It was contended by Holland that as the display of territorial sovereignty was proved early in the eighteenth century and throughout the nineteenth century, this fact, by analogy with French, Dutch and German civil law, created a rebuttable presumption of the existence of sovereignty in the meantime.

Held: That that contention must be rejected. No presumption of this nature can be applied in international arbitration except under express provisions of the arbitration treaty. It is in each case a matter for the tribunal to decide whether or not it is satisfied with the continued display of sovereignty. [Reports: *Permanent Court of Arbitration, Arbitral Award rendered in conformity with the Special Agreement concluded on* 23 *January*, 1925, *between the United States of America and the Netherlands*, p. 53; *A.J.*, XXII (1928), pp. 904, 905.]

iii.—Cession. Conditional Cession. Plebiscite

[See also Part VIII, TREATIES: VIII. *Ratification. Entrance into Force.*]

Territory—Cession of—The Rule "Nemo plus juris transferre "potest quam ipse habet." **Case No. 74**

ISLAND OF PALMAS ARBITRATION CASE.

United States and Holland: Permanent Court of Arbitration. 4 April, 1928.

(HUBER, Arbitrator.)

THE FACTS.—(See Cases Nos. 1, 68, 70, 72, 75.) The United States based its claim to sovereignty over the Island of Palmas on the fact of cession brought about by the Treaty of Paris of 1898 between the United States and Spain, which transferred to the United States all rights of sovereignty which Spain may have possessed in the

Case No. 74 *contd.*

region indicated in Article 3 of that Treaty, and said to include the Island of Palmas.

Held : That that Treaty could not be regarded as conclusive as to the title of the United States. " It is evident that Spain " could not transfer more rights than she herself possessed." [Reports : *Permanent Court of Arbitration, Arbitral Award rendered in conformity with the Special Agreement concluded on* 23 *January*, 1925, *between the United States of America and the Netherlands*, p. 22 ; *A.J.*, XXII (1928), p. 879.]

NOTE.—The Arbitrator pointed out that the above principle of law was expressly recognised in a letter, dated 7 April, 1900, from the Secretary of State of the United States concerning a divergence of opinion which arose about the question whether the islands claimed by Spain as Spanish territory and lying just outside the limits traced by the Treaty of Paris were to be considered as included in or excluded from the cession. In that letter the Secretary of State said : " This " Government must consequently hold that the only competent and " equitable test of facts by which the title to a disputed cession in that " quarter may be determined is simply this : ' Was it Spain's to give ? " ' If valid title belonged to Spain, it passed. If Spain had no valid " ' title, she could convey none.' "

Territory—Cession—Territories under Plebiscite—Effect on Nationality—Date of Transfer of Sovereignty.

See Case No. 201 (*Oedenburg* (*Change of Nationality*) *Case*).

Territory—Cession of—How far Affecting Nationality.

See Case No. 190 (*Alsace-Lorraine Nationality* (*Statelessness*) *Case*).

iv.—Prescription

Case No. 75

Prescription—Continuous and Peaceful Display of Sovereignty —Effect upon Conventional Rights—Conditions of Continuous and Peaceful Display of Sovereignty—The Duty of Notification.

ISLAND OF PALMAS ARBITRATION CASE.

United States and Holland : Permanent Court of Arbitration. 4 *April*, 1928.

(HUBER, Arbitrator.)

THE FACTS.—(See also Cases Nos. 1, 68, 70, 72.) In addition to the title based on discovery, the United States claimed, as the successor of Spain, sovereignty over the Palmas Island on the ground of the recognition of the Spanish title in the Treaty of Munster of 30 January, 1648, which established a state of peace between Spain and the Estates General of the United Provinces of the Netherlands. The Tribunal found that that Treaty did not in fact contain any reference to the Island of Palmas, in particular having regard to the circumstance that it was not proved that Spain was at the beginning of 1648 in possession of that island. It was also contended by the United States that certain requirements of acquisition of title by prescription did not exist, namely, that the Dutch exercise of sovereignty was not sufficiently manifested and not accompanied by the necessary notification.

Held : (*a*) Even if Spain had acquired a title by the Treaty of Munster, the question would still remain to be decided whether continuous and peaceful display of sovereignty by another Power at a later period might not have superseded any conventional rights thus acquired.

(*b*) That there was no obligation upon Holland to notify other States of the establishment of suzerainty over the group of islands to which Palmas Island belonged, or of the display of sovereignty in these territories. It was impossible to assume a clandestine exercise of sovereignty over an inhabited territory during a considerable length of time. As the display of sovereignty was open and public it must be held to have been in conformity with the usages relating to the exercise of sovereignty over colonial territories. (As to the duty of notification under the Berlin Treaty of 1885, see Case No. 71.) [Reports : *Permanent Court of Arbitration, Arbitral Award rendered in conformity with the Special Agreement concluded on 23 January*, 1925, *between the United States of America and the Netherlands*, pp. 28, 33, 59 ; *A.J.*, XXII (1928), pp. 907-912.]

Prescription—Acquisition of Territorial Rights. **Case No. 76**

LÜBECK *v.* MECKLENBURG-SCHWERIN.

German Staatsgerichtshof. 6 *and* 7 *July*, 1928.

THE FACTS.—See Cases Nos. 3 and 88.

On the basis of documentary and other evidence submitted to it, the Court found that Lübeck had for centuries possessed

Case No. 76 *contd.* exclusive rights of fishery in the disputed parts of the Bay of Lübeck. "This immemorial possession justifies the presumption of its legality as well as the attribution to Lübeck of these rights for the future." The same applied to the rights of navigation.

However, the Court found no such evidence of immemorial possession in other respects and, in accordance with the principle enunciated elsewhere (see Case No. 88), it proceeded to a division of the Bay between the two States in matters other than fisheries and navigation. [Reports: *Entscheidungen des Reichsgerichts in Zivilsachen*, vol. 122, Appendix, p. 1; *Z. für a. ö. R. und V.*, 1 (2) (1929), p. 180.]

IV.—Effects of Changes of Sovereignty

[See also Part II, E, SUCCESSION OF STATES.]

Case No. 77 **Effect of Change of Sovereignty on the Operation of a Law as to Prescription—Acts of Foreign Courts in Ceded Territory—Interruption of the Period of Limitation.**

CESSION (STATUTE OF LIMITATIONS) CASE.

Supreme Court of Hungary. 16 *May*, 1928.
(*No. II*, 956/1927.)

THE FACTS.—In the course of criminal proceedings instituted against the accused, the documents of the prosecution were forwarded by the Royal Court at Gyula (in Hungary) on 5 May, 1919, to the Royal Court of Appeal at Nagyvárad, in order to be sent from there to the Supreme Court at Budapest. However, Nagyvárad was in the meantime occupied by Roumania and then ceded to Roumania by virtue of the Treaty of Trianon. The convention between Hungary and Roumania concerning mutual assistance in criminal proceedings was only concluded in 1924. The documents in question were submitted in 1921 to the Roumanian Minister of Justice, who returned them to the Hungarian courts in 1927. The accused contends now that the criminal proceedings are barred by the law as to prescription, as those which had taken place were before foreign courts and are unable to interrupt the five years' period provided by the law as to prescription.

Held by the Supreme Court: That the law as to prescription did not apply so as to bar the proceedings. The Treaty of Trianon entered into force on 4 June, 1920. From that time the Court of Appeal at Nagyvárad became the court of a foreign State. It is true that the acts of a foreign State cannot be regarded as having legal relevance in regard to the law as to prescription. But, prior to the conclusion of the treaty of mutual assistance in criminal proceedings, there had taken place an interruption of the statutory period of prescription. That interruption had ceased at the time when the treaty of mutual assistance entered into force, that is to say, in 1924. [Report: *Jogi Hirlap*, 1928, No. 852.]

Cession—Effect on the Jurisdiction of Courts in respect of Immovable Property. **Case No. 78**

J. MADÁR & COMPANY *v.* P. STANNBERGER & COMPANY.

Supreme Court of Hungary. 1 *October*, 1925.
(*No. P.V.* 564/1925.)

THE FACTS.—The defendants, who are Hungarian nationals, sold to the plaintiffs certain immovable property in Hungary. This immovable property was situated in a part of Hungary which was subsequently separated from Hungary by virtue of the Treaty of Trianon. In an action brought to enforce the contract the defendants contended that the Hungarian courts had no jurisdiction in respect of this contract of purchase.

Held by the Supreme Court: That Hungarian courts had jurisdiction. "The action is one for the fulfilment of a con-"tractual obligation between Hungarian subjects. The fact "that the object of the purchase is in a part of Hungarian "territory which has subsequently been ceded to a foreign "State can have no influence on the mutual obligations of the "parties. This fact influences only the question of the exe-"cution of the judgment." [Report: *Perjogi Döntvénytár*, XII, No. 25.]

V.—Occupation of Foreign Territory in Time of Peace

Case No. 79

Military Occupation in Time of Peace—Allied Occupation of the Rhineland—The Paris Convention of 5 May, 1925, for the Interpretation of the Rhineland Agreement—General Principles and Special Provisions Governing Occupation.

RHINELAND OCCUPATION (Rhineland Agreement Interpretation) CASES.

Committee for the Interpretation of Articles 8-12 *of the Rhineland Agreement of* 28 *June*, 1919. 29 *May*, 1926–13 *July*, 1929.

NOTE.—In Part II of the Financial Regulations [1] of 5 May, 1925, relating to the contributions and services due under Articles 8 to 12 of the Rhineland Agreement [2] provision was made for the procedure for the assessment of contributions due by virtue of these Articles. The assessment of contributions was entrusted in the first instance to Local Commissions consisting of Allied and German members; and in the second instance to a Commission of Arbitration. In addition, Part II provided for the setting up of a Commission of Interpretation entrusted with the duty of settling all disputes on questions of interpretation of principle which might be submitted to it by the Commission of Arbitration, by the Governments, or by the Agent-General for Reparation Payments. The Commission was to consist of six members—three Allied subjects and three Germans—presided over by a Chairman appointed by agreement between the German Government and the Reparation Commission, or, failing such agreement, by the President of the Permanent Court of International Justice. It was laid down that the decisions of the Commission must be given in the form of reasoned judgments.[3]

---

[1] See League of Nations Treaty Series, LV, pp. 229-347.

[2] The following may be mentioned as examples:

Transport contributions and placing of means of transport at the disposal of the Allies; postal services, telegraphs and telephones; contributions in the form of furniture and fittings, and household effects; buildings and ground belonging to private individuals; hotel rooms, temporary occupation by troops on the march; heat, lighting and supply of water; supply of copies of newspapers and publications; upkeep of soldiers' graves and military cemeteries; office supplies; shooting and fishing rights, etc. It should be noted that in regard to shooting and fishing rights a Special Mixed Commission was set up to decide claims under this head. Some of the decisions of this Commission are printed in vol. I, pp. 160-175, of the publication referred to in the text.

[3] The Commission of Interpretation sat in Berlin between 1926 and 1929 and gave a large number of awards. One hundred of these decisions, given between 26 May, 1926, and 13 July, 1929, are printed in the French and German languages in a collection entitled *Die Entscheidungen des im Pariser Abkommen vom 5 Mai 1925 über die " Finanzielle Regelung der Leistungen aus " Artikel 8-12 des Rheinlandabkommens " vorgesehenen Auslegungsauschusses,"* vol. I (1928) and vol. II (1929), edited by Dr. Ronde; vol. III (1930) by F. Haaser. These decisions do not raise general points of international law, and it is therefore not thought necessary to digest them in detail. On the other hand, they are instructive as illustrating the law, and the contractual arrangements made between the parties, relating to the occupation of foreign territory in time of peace and to the legal status of the forces of occupation.

Occupation of Foreign Territory in Time of Peace—Operation of the Laws of the Sovereign Power—Occupation of the Rhineland by the Allied Powers—Binding Force of German Laws. **Case No. 80**

RHINELAND (GERMAN LEGISLATION) CASE.

Administrative Tribunal of Bavaria (Bayerischer Verwaltungsgerichtshof). 5 *December*, 1928.

THE FACTS.—In January, 1920, the Inter-Allied Rhineland Commission issued an ordinance in which it was laid down that any new German legislation must, before being put into operation in the occupied territory, be submitted to the Commission for examination.

In the present case the Bavarian Administrative Court had to decide what effect, so far as Bavaria was concerned, this ordinance had on the legal validity of Bavarian laws, and whether the latter required approval on the part of the Commission before entering into force in the occupied territory. The case arose out of a dispute between a municipality in the occupied Palatinate of Bavaria and a private firm concerning certain matters of taxation governed by a recently issued Bavarian Decree.

Held: That the Bavarian Decree was valid and did not require the previous approval of the Rhineland Commission. It was clear from Articles 42-44 of the Treaty of Versailles and from Articles 1 and 5 of the Rhineland Agreement of 28 June, 1919, that the occupied territories constitute, from the constitutional and international law point of view, part of German territory. The occupation by the Allied Powers, although of a military character, is nevertheless a contractual one, and the question before the Court must therefore be answered solely by reference to the relevant treaties. These treaties do not derogate from the authority of German legislation in the occupied territory; neither do they impose upon Germany the obligation to submit her laws to the occupation authorities for approval. According to Article 3 of the Rhineland Agreement the occupation authorities may protest against and prevent the putting into operation of German laws which threaten the security of or are against the interests of the army of occupation, but otherwise no limitation is imposed upon the validity of German legislation. This legal position is not affected by those ordinances of the occupation authorities which lay down that new

Case No. 80 *contd.* German legislation is to be registered with the Inter-Allied Commission, and that it can be put into operation only after ten days' registration, provided that the Commission does not veto them. In principle, German (or Bavarian) legislation enters into force in the occupied territory simultaneously with its entering into force in other parts of Germany (or Bavaria). [Report : *Reichsverwaltungsblatt und Preussisches Verwaltungsblatt*, vol. 50 (1929), p. 638.]

VI.—International Leases

Rights of the United States in the Panama Zone—Jurisdiction of Panama Courts over Members of the United States Army.

See Case No. 114 (*The Republic of Panama* v. *Wilbert L. Schwartzfiger*).

B. PARTS OF STATE TERRITORY

I.—Boundaries

i.—Land Boundaries

Case No. 81 **Boundaries—Land Boundaries—Doctrine of Occupation Extending back to Crest of Watershed—Meaning of Words " Coast," " Coasts "—Labrador Boundary.**

IN THE MATTER OF THE BOUNDARY BETWEEN THE DOMINION OF CANADA AND THE COLONY OF NEWFOUNDLAND IN THE LABRADOR PENINSULA.

Judicial Committee of the British Privy Council.
1 *March*, 1927.

The question referred to the Privy Council upon the joint petition of the Dominion of Canada and the Colony of Newfoundland was as follows : " What is the location and definition " of the boundary between Canada and Newfoundland in the " Labrador Peninsula under the Statutes, Orders in Council, " and Proclamations ? "

This Opinion, though given upon an inter-imperial and not an international question, deserves to be briefly mentioned. Their lordships (Lords Cave, L.C., Haldane, Finlay, Sumner and Warrington), in delivering their Opinion in favour of Newfoundland, were apparently influenced by the analogy of what they stated (at p. 194 of Law Times Report) to be " the doctrine " of international law by which the occupation of a sea coast " carries with it a right to the whole territory drained by the " rivers which empty their water into its line (see Hall's *International Law*, 5th ed., p. 104 ; Westlake's *International Law*, " Part I (1st ed.), p. 112 ; and Lawrence's *Principles of International Law*, 3rd ed., p. 151) ; and it is certainly difficult, in " the absence of any specified boundary or of any special " feature (such as a political frontier), which could be taken as a " boundary, to suggest any point between the sea-shore and the " watershed at which a line could be drawn."

The meaning of the words "coast," "coasts," which occurred in certain material documents, and the extent of territory comprised therein was considered at p. 192 of Law Times Report. Upon a consideration of the relevant Statutes, Orders and Proclamations, their lordships rejected the contention of Canada that the Labrador boundary must follow the sinuosities of the coast at a distance of one mile or thereabouts and upheld the contention of Newfoundland that it must be found at the crest of the watershed of the rivers falling into the sea on the shores of Labrador. More than 100,000 square miles of territory were involved in the opinion. [Reports: 137 L.T. at p. 187; 43 T.L.R. at p. 289.]

NOTE.—The oral and written proceedings, including the Cases, Counter-Cases, Documents, etc., before the Judicial Committee are printed in fourteen volumes and are available at some libraries, such as the British Museum, and the offices of the Judicial Committee. In vol. IX there is an Index to the written proceedings which contains numerous references to a number of boundary disputes to which Great Britain was a party. See in particular vol. V, pp. 2073-2260.

ii.—Water Boundaries

Boundaries—Boundary Rivers—The Doctrine of *Medium Filum* —*Medium Filum* and Boundary Line in Niagara Not Identical. **Case No. 82**

IN RE VILLAGE OF FORT ERIE AND BUFFALO AND FORT ERIE PUBLIC BRIDGE COMPANY.

Appellate Division of the Supreme Court of Ontario.
8 *and* 29 *December*, 1927.

(Appeal from an Order of the Ontario Railway and Municipal Board.)

THE FACTS.—The respondent company was incorporated in 1923 by a Dominion statute, for the purpose of constructing an international " Peace Bridge " over the

Case No. 82 *contd.*

Niagara river, from the Village of Fort Erie on the Canadian shore to a point in New York State. The bridge was so built, and the Village of Fort Erie assessed the bridge for taxation up to the international line. The company disputed the legality of the assessment before the Board, from whose decision the Village appealed. The Board found that the Village was entitled to assess the bridge for taxation, but not beyond the shoreline.

Held, dismissing the appeal of the Village: That the claim of the Village is based on the old common law doctrine that the rights of riparian landowners extend to the *medium filum* of the water. This doctrine has never been applied to international waters. The suggestion that the doctrine should be applied in the present case is further weakened by the fact that in the case of the Niagara river the *medium filum* and the international boundary do not coincide.

The judgment of the Court (Latchford, C.J., Riddell, Middleton, Maston, and Orde, JJ.) was delivered by Riddell, J., who observed:

" By the Treaty of Peace concluded on the 3rd September, " 1783, the boundary of that part was to 'the middle of the " 'communication into Lake Erie' from Lake Ontario; the " real boundary line was not established on the ground till " after the Treaty of Ghent, 1814, under the provisions of " which a commission was appointed to fix the international " boundary from the present Cornwall to Lake Superior. " It is known that there was much give and take by and " between the Commissioners[1]—it was strongly asserted at " the time, and official documents seem to bear out the con- " tention, that most of the 'give' was on one side and most of " the 'take' on the other. However that may be, the Com- " missioners did not take the middle of the stream as the " international line—in many cases the middle of the navigable " channel was taken, and in a few cases what was considered an " utterly inadmissible and unfounded claim was allowed for the " sake of peace. It cannot be said that at any point the inter- " national line, as declared in the Utica Award of 1822, is the " middle thread. But even assuming that this principle can " ever be applied to the Niagara river, it is wholly inapplicable " to this case." [Report: *Ontario Law Reports*, vol. LXI, p. 502.]

[1] That is, the Boundary Commissioners.

II.—Rivers

iii.—International Rivers

(*a*) THE PRINCIPLE OF FREEDOM OF NAVIGATION ON INTERNATIONAL RIVERS

International Rivers—Rhine—Convention of Mannheim, of 17 October, 1868—Article 354 of the Treaty of Versailles—Court for Navigation Rights on the Rhine—Exequatur of Judgments—Court Authorised to Grant the Exequatur. **Case No. 83**

BADISCHE A.G. FÜR RHEINSCHIFFART UND SEETRANSPORT *v.* CIE CENTRALE D'ASSURANCES MARITIMES, CIE MELUSINE ET UNION MARITIME.

Tribunal of Strasbourg. 20 *February*, 1927.

THE FACTS.—The Badische A.G. took proceedings against the defendant companies for the execution of a judgment rendered by the Court for Navigation Rights on the Rhine at Rüdesheim (Germany) which had ordered the defendants to pay the costs of a case brought before it by them against the plaintiff.

The plaintiff company invoked, first, Article 354 of the Treaty of Versailles which provides that " the Convention of Mannheim of 17 October, 1868, . . . shall " continue to regulate navigation on the Rhine," and, secondly, the provisions of the Convention relating to the execution of judgments. The defendants protested that certain of the items of costs which they had been ordered by the decision to pay to their opponent were contrary to the terms of this Convention, and moreover, that the decision had been communicated to them, not at their domicile in France, but at that of their counsel in Rüdesheim, which was contrary to the terms of the Convention.

Held for the claimant: The decision of the Court for Navigation Rights on the Rhine at Rüdesheim must be upheld.

(*a*) The principles established in the Convention of Mannheim and recently confirmed by the Treaty of Versailles had not been changed either generally or in the provisions for the execution of decisions rendered by the Rhine Navigation Courts. By Article 40 of the Convention of Mannheim the decisions of these Courts must be executed in all other States provided that the forms required by the law of the countries in which execu-

Case No. 83 *contd.* tion shall take place are observed. They are not subject to judicial review. Accordingly, the decision of the Court for Navigation Rights must be executed on French territory when the Civil Tribunal of Strasbourg had appended the necessary certificate. Under the terms of Article 8 of the Law of 25 July, 1923, on the judicial organisation in the recovered departments " the Court of First Instance of Strasbourg " acts as the Court of Appeal in France for Rhine Navigation " rights in accordance with Article 3 of the Law of 21 April, " 1832."

(*b*) The decision was communicated to the counsel of the defendant at Rüdesheim, which place must be regarded as the domicile voluntarily chosen for the purpose of the present action. [Reports: 55 *Clunet* (1928), p. 1043; Sirey, 1929, Part II, p. 81, with a note by M. J. P. Niboyet.]

Case No. 84 **International Rivers—Internationalisation of the Rhine—Liability to Insurance of the Crews of Foreign Ships Operating Exclusively in the German Section of the Rhine—How far Affected by the Provisions of the Treaty of Peace of Versailles.**

FOREIGN CREWS (RHINE) CASE.

First Senate of the Department for the Insurance of the Sick and Invalid in Germany. 25 *September*, 1927.

THE FACTS.—According to the provisions of the German Federal Insurance Code, persons performing work liable to insurance within German territory are subject to insurance against incapacity arising from accident or sickness regardless of their nationality and regardless of whether they are employed by alien employers. In pursuance of this provision the authorities of the *Reich* laid down in 1899 that the work of crews of foreign ships employed in navigating German navigable waters are to be regarded as subject to insurance in cases where the ships in question operate in Germany for a considerable period of time. In 1900 it was further laid down that ships which operate in Germany on an average of ten weeks in the year shall be regarded as operating for a considerable period of time within German territory.

The Swiss Tug Navigation Company contended that as the result of the internationalisation of the Rhine by the provisions of the Treaty of Versailles, the crews, composed of aliens, employed by them were not liable to insurance under the German Federal Insurance Code.

Held : That the crews of the craft of the Swiss Tug Navigation Company are subject to insurance when entering German territory. This duty is not affected by the fact that the Treaty of Versailles provided for the internationalisation of the Rhine. The internationalisation of a navigable waterway aims at the free international use of the river.

Such a waterway is only excluded from the territorial sovereignty of the riparian State in so far as this is required by the obligation to ensure freedom of navigation.

The internationalisation of the Rhine was provided for in the Rhine Navigation Act of 31 March, 1831, and in the revised Rhine Navigation Act of 17 October, 1868. The Treaty of Versailles expressly incorporated, in Article 354, the revised Rhine Navigation Convention. In addition, Articles 321-326, 327-339 and 354-362 lay down further provisions for the internationalisation of German navigable waterways. In particular, Article 332 lays down that the subjects, property and flag of all Powers shall enjoy full equality, that is to say, that there shall be no discrimination between the subjects, property and flag of any one of those Powers and the subjects, property and flag of the riparian State itself or of the most-favoured nation. Article 327 of the Treaty lays down that no other impediment in the transit and transport of persons and goods shall be introduced apart from those relating to customs, police, sanitation, emigration, immigration, and import and export of prohibited goods, and that these provisions must be appropriate and uniform and not constitute an undue obstacle to navigation. These provisions of the Treaty, like the analogous provisions of the Rhine Navigation Act, have merely the object of securing freedom of navigation and of preventing discrimination against the subjects of foreign States. The internationalisation of the Rhine cannot, therefore, prevent Germany from putting into effect the principles of social insurance in regard to foreign ships navigating the Rhine within Germany territory. [Report : *Amtliche Nachrichten des Reichsversicherungsamts*, 1927, p. 586.]

International Rivers—Freedom of Navigation on European International Rivers—The Danube.

See Permanent Court of International Justice Advisory Opinion No. 14, Series B, pp. 38 ff., for an exposition of the history of international regulation of the freedom of navigation on the Danube and other European international rivers from 1815 onwards.

(*b*) Functions and Competence of International Commissions on International Rivers

Case No. 85

PERMANENT COURT OF INTERNATIONAL JUSTICE.

ADVISORY OPINION No. 14.

International Rivers—Regulation of Navigation on—Powers of the European Danube Commission between Galatz and Braila—Nature of the Powers of the European Danube Commission.

Jurisdiction of the European Commission of the Danube between Galatz and Braila.

8 *December*, 1927.

The Facts.—(See Cases Nos. 295, 303.) One of the three questions put before the Court by the Council of the League of Nations was as follows :

" Should the European Commission of the " Danube possess either the same powers on " the Galatz-Braila sector as on the sector " below Galatz, or certain powers, do these " powers extend over one or more zones, " territorially defined and corresponding to " all or part of the navigable channel, to the " exclusion of the Roumanian authorities ? " If so, according to what criteria shall the " line of demarcation be fixed as between " territorial zones placed under the com- " petence of the European Commission and " zones placed under the competence of the " Roumanian authorities ? If the contrary " is the case, on what non-territorial basis " is the exact dividing line between the " respective competence of the European " Commission of the Danube and of the " Roumanian authorities to be fixed ? "

Held : That although the powers of regulation and jurisdiction belong to the territorial authorities, the right of supervision, with a view to ensuring freedom of navigation and equal treatment of all flags, belongs to the European Commission.[1]

The Court arrived at this view after having discarded the principle of territorially defined zones as, *inter alia,* not being recognised by international practice. In adopting the principle stated above, the Court made the following observations on the nature of the powers exercised by the European Danube Commission: "Although the European Commission "exercises its functions 'in complete independence "'of the territorial authorities,' and although it has "independent means of action and prerogatives and "privileges which are generally withheld from in- "ternational organisations, it is not an organisation "possessing exclusive territorial sovereignty. Rou- "mania exercises power as territorial sovereign over "the maritime Danube in all respects not incompatible "with the powers possessed by the European Com- "mission under the Definitive Statute. When in one "and the same area there are two independent "authorities, the only way in which it is possible to "differentiate between their respective jurisdictions is "by defining the functions allotted to them. As the "European Commission is not a State, but an inter- "national institution with a special purpose, it only "has the functions bestowed upon it by the Definitive "Statute with a view to the fulfilment of that purpose, "but it has power to exercise these functions to their

[1] The relevant part of the Opinion is as follows (p. 69):

". . . the powers of the European Commission of the Danube extend over "the whole of the maritime Danube, and are not excluded from zones terri- "torially defined and corresponding to harbour zones;

". . . the dividing line between the respective competences of the European "Commission of the Danube and of the Roumanian authorities in the ports "of Galatz and Braila is to be fixed according to the criteria

"(i) of navigation, in the sense of the movement of ships as part of their "voyage, the European Commission of the Danube being also competent in "regard to navigation in ports, whether the ships are passing through or "coming to or leaving their moorings, as far as navigation so understood is "concerned; and

"(ii) of the obligation to ensure freedom of navigation and equal treatment "of all flags, the European Commission of the Danube being competent, also "as concerns the ports, to exercise the supervision inherent in this obligation."

Case No. 85 *contd.* "full extent, in so far as the Statute does not impose "restrictions upon it." [Report: Series B, No. 14, pp. 59-69.[1]]

International Rivers—Danube Commission—Power to Abandon Functions Entrusted by Treaties.

See Case No. 295 (*Jurisdiction of the European Commission of the Danube between Galatz and Braila*).

iv.—The Utilisation of the Flow of Non-National and International Rivers

Case No. 86 **Rivers—Rights and Duties of States which are Members of Federal States—Analogy with International Rivers—Interference with Natural Flow of—Duty to Maintain the Bed of the River in Proper Condition—Applicability of International Law—Relations between Member States—Article 4 of the German Constitution.**

WÜRTTEMBERG AND PRUSSIA *v.* BADEN.

(The *Donauversinkung* Case.)

German Staatsgerichtshof. 18 *June*, 1927.

THE FACTS.—When coming from the Black Forest, in the upper part of its course, the Danube passes the (Swabian) Jura mountains. In passing them between Braunlingen and Hufingen (Baden) and Fridingen (Württemberg), it loses during certain periods of the year a considerable part of its water in consequence of the water sinking under the bed of the river and flowing to the lower levels of the Lake of Constance and of the Rhine. The reason for this loss of water—which is usually referred to as the sinking of the Danube (*Donauversinkung*)—is the geological composition of the banks and of the bed of the river. They are composed of chalk through the cracks and pores of which the water of the Danube in this section flows south in subterranean passages in order to emerge eventually as the source of the river Aach in Baden. This source is one of the most powerful in Germany. As the result, the river Aach, in the course of its short course through Baden terminating in the Lake of Constance,

[1] See also Series E, No. 4, pp. 201-212.

is very rich in water which is extensively utilised for industrial purposes. The effect of the change upon Württemberg is that, in a portion of the river extending from 10 to 12 kilometres, there occurs, for varying periods of time, a so-called total sinking of the Danube, that is, a complete drying up of the river. The number of days on which the river was thus dried up was 309 in 1921, 29 in 1922, 148 in 1923.

In the present action, Württemberg asked for an injunction restraining Baden from constructing and maintaining certain dams and water-power plant near Immendingen calculated to intensify the "sinking of "the Danube" by forcing the stream of the water in the direction of the Aach, as well as for an order instructing Baden to render possible, by removing the natural obstacles which accumulate in the bed and on the banks of the river near Möhringen, an unimpeded flow of water.

Baden, on the other hand, asked for an injunction restraining Württemberg from constructing and maintaining certain works near Fridingen erected and operated with a view to preventing the natural flow of the waters of the Danube to the Aach.

After leaving the territories of Baden and Württemberg the Danube flows through Prussian territory, which is also injuriously affected by the escape of the waters of the Danube. For this reason Prussia intervened in the suit on the side of Württemberg and supported her application.

Held: That Baden must refrain from causing such increase in the natural sinking of the waters of the Danube as is due (*a*) to the artificially erected dams and works in Immendingen and (*b*) to the accumulation of sand and gravel in the bed of the Danube near Möhringen, but that it is not bound to undertake the responsibility for the permanent improvement of the bed of the river;

That Württemberg must refrain from causing such decrease of the natural sinking of the waters of the Danube as is due (*a*) to certain works in Fridingen, and (*b*) to the artificial damming of avenues of sinking in so far as the damming exceeds the limits of the right to maintain a natural flow of the water.

A. *The Nature of the Dispute.*—The present suit was brought

Case No. 86 ***contd.*** by virtue of Article 19 of the Constitution, which provides that the *Staatsgerichtshof* shall have jurisdiction in disputes of a public character between German States. The Court is of the opinion that the action comes within that provision. The parties do not ask for recognition of private rights, either of their own or of their subjects. The object of the dispute is the manner of exercise of public authority over the waters of the Danube in the " *Versinkung* " sector. Both parties assert the existence of obligations in the field of public law.

B. *The Law Applicable. International Law in the Relations of Members of Federal States : Legal Position of Member States.*—As the dispute was one of public law between States it was impossible to apply the municipal law of a single State. There were in the Constitution no provisions bearing upon the dispute. In view of this the Court was bound to apply rules of international law the applicability of which, as between members of the German Federation, must be recognised, though to a limited extent. The members of the Federation have, subject to considerable limitations, preserved their position as independent States. This appears clearly from the fact that the Constitution has in principle reserved to States the power of legislation : Article 6 of the Constitution assigns only certain well-defined, although extensive, fields of legislation to the *Reich* as a whole. That the members have remained States may be seen, *inter alia,* from paragraph 2 of Article 78 of the Constitution, which lays down that in matters subject to State legislation they may, subject to the confirmation of the *Reich,* conclude treaties with foreign Powers. In so far, therefore, as these States act as independent communities, *i.e.* in matters reserved for their exclusive competence, their relations are governed by international law which in Article 4 of the Constitution has been recognised as forming part of German Federal law. It is possible that that Article was originally intended to apply to relations of Germany with foreign States, but there is nothing in the Constitution to prevent its application to the relations of German States *inter se.*[1]

The recent development of international law has gone in the direction of restricting the territorial sovereignty of individual States in consequence of their forming part of the family of nations. This fact gives rise to the duty of reciprocal respect and consideration, that is to say, the duty not to injure one another. The community embracing the German States is

[1] The Court referred here to its decision in the case of *Bremen* v. *Prussia, Annual Digest,* 1925-1926, Case No. 266.

closer than the international community of nations, and the duty of reciprocal consideration of interests is, therefore, more intensive than in the relations of other States.

C. *The Rule of International Law as to the Utilisation of the Flow of International Rivers. The Duty to Abstain from Injurious Interference.*—International law contains no express rules relating to a situation such as that with which the Court is confronted in the present case. A natural phenomenon of this kind takes place so seldom that no special rules of international law have evolved in this matter. Accordingly, one has to fall back upon the general principles of international law concerning the flow of international rivers as distinguished from boundary rivers. The exercise of sovereign rights by every State in regard to international rivers traversing its territory is limited by the duty not to injure the interests of other members of the international community. Due consideration must be given to one another by States through whose territories there flows an international river. No State may substantially impair the natural use of the flow of such a river by its neighbour. This principle has gained increased recognition in international relations, in particular in modern times when the increased exploitation of the natural power of flowing water has led to a contractual regulation of the interests of States connected by international rivers. The application of this principle is governed by the circumstances of each particular case. The interests of the States in question must be weighed in an equitable manner against one another. One must consider not only the absolute injury caused to the neighbouring State, but also the relation of the advantage gained by one to the injury caused to the other.

D. *The Duty to Perform Positive Acts.*—The above principle merely prohibits artificial alterations in the flow of the river. It follows that every State must submit to the natural flow of the water in spite of its consequences. Barring an express contractual undertaking, no State is under a duty to interfere, in favour of another State, with the natural flow of the water. It need not, for the benefit of another State, counteract the effects of natural changes in the flow of the water. The sinking of the Danube is a natural, though rare, phenomenon, and Württemberg and Prussia must submit to it. They cannot demand from Baden that it should close the cracks which suck away the water of the Danube. Neither is Baden bound to counteract such diminution in the waters of the Danube as is due to the natural enlargement of and accretion to the banks. It is only

Case No. 86 ***contd.*** within certain closely defined limits that Baden is bound to act in a positive manner.

The principle that a State is under no duty to regulate, in the interest of another State, the natural phenomena affecting an international river, is subject to one limitation grounded in the modern practice of States in regard to rivers. Rivers, including those which are non-navigable, are to-day no longer merely the product of natural forces. Their banks are inhabited, and it is in the interest of the inhabitants, both in the upper and lower parts of the rivers, that the banks be strengthened and that the flow of the water be subject to regulation, not only on account of possible inundation, but as a matter of normal policy. Thus, while a State is under a duty to abstain from altering the flow of the river to the detriment of its neighbours, it must not fail to do what civilised States nowadays do in regard to their rivers. If a Government fails to undertake, or even prohibits, measures which it must be expected to undertake in accordance with generally recognised rules of law and economic policy—with the intention or with the result that the interests of persons outside its territory are thereby injuriously affected—then such an attitude cannot be regarded as being in accordance with the nature of a community of nations. This ceases to be a mere passive attitude, and becomes an unlawful furthering, through acts of omission, of certain natural events. This duty to perform positive acts has been clearly recognised in regard to the requirements of navigation on international rivers. There is no reason why it should not apply to questions relating to the utilisation of the flow of rivers for industrial purposes. [Report : *Entscheidungen des Reichsgerichts in Zivilsachen*, vol. 116, Appendix, pp. 18-45.]

NOTE.—It will be noted that the present judgment of the *Staatsgerichtshof* is in the nature of an interlocutory decision laying down the relevant principles of law. The Court refrained from making an order for the production of detailed and technical evidence. In view of its possible more general application the following concluding passage of the judgment may be usefully quoted :

" . . . It is doubtful whether a decision of the *Staatsgerichtshof*, " even if based on detailed evidence, would in fact definitely settle the " controversy. For even this subsequent decision would necessarily " be limited to laying down some guiding principles. The questions " brought about by the *Donauversinkung* are so complicated, their " scientific and technical aspects so controversial, and the interests of " the States in dispute so interdependent, that only a settlement by " agreement will be able to produce a final settlement of the contro- " versy. The ascertainment in the present judgment of important " preliminary questions, in particular in the legal sphere, should provide

" the necessary basis for such an agreement. This is in fact the object " of the interlocutory judgment of the *Staatsgerichtshof*. The *Staatsgerichtshof* expects that the parties will now enter into new negotiations " and try to arrive at an agreement giving effect to the principles laid " down in the interlocutory judgment."

III.—Territorial Waters

ii.—Breadth of the Maritime Belt

Extent of Territorial Waters—Norway—Criminal Jurisdiction in respect of Unlawful Importation of Spirits, etc. **Case No. 87**

THE PUBLIC PROSECUTOR *v.* P. F. WEBER AND OTHERS.

Supreme Court of Norway. 30 *June*, 1927.

THE FACTS.—By a judgment pronounced by the District Court of Hitra a German citizen, Paul Frantz Weber, and others were convicted of unlawful importation of spirits, the Court having found it to be proved that they had sold from the S.S. *Deutschland*, whilst she was lying between Halten and Kya, a considerable quantity of spirits which had been shipped at Danzig for the purpose of sale off the Norwegian coast. In the judgment the Court stated that " it has been proved that " the sale took place within a limit of four miles from a " line drawn from Utgrunnskjaer to Kya " (two small rocks off the west coast of Norway). The accused appealed to the Supreme Court on the ground that the decision of the District Court as regards fixing the boundary of the territorial waters was based on an erroneous interpretation of the law.

Held by the Supreme Court: That the judgment of the District Court must be reversed. Considering the evidence given during the hearing of the case, the Court below was not justified in taking the above-mentioned line as the basis for fixing the boundary of the territorial waters when examining the question of the unlawfulness of the action of the accused. It was a matter of fact that the Norwegian authorities concerned had not made known their claims as regards the extent of the maritime belt on this section of the coast of the kingdom, and it would be unreasonable therefore if the Court in giving judgment in a criminal action such as the one under consideration were to fix a boundary of Norwegian territorial waters on

Case No. 87 *contd.* the basis of a line as disputable as the one adopted by the Court. [Report: *Norsk Rettstidende* (Norwegian Judicial Journal—Law Reports), 1927, pp. 513-526.]

NOTE.—The President of the Supreme Court dissented and voted for the dismissal of the appeal, stating that he considered that the interpretation on which the District Court had based its decision as to where the boundary line should be drawn was in conformity with the rules always maintained by the Norwegian authorities whenever the question of the actual extent of the territorial waters had been raised with regard to other sections of the coast.

[See on the subject of the claims of Norway in respect of her territorial waters *The Principal Facts Concerning Norwegian Territorial Waters*, a Memorandum prepared by the Royal Norwegian Committee of 7 November, 1924. See in particular pp. 49, 50, on which reference is made to the General Regulations respecting the extent of territorial waters issued in a Royal Decree of 22 February, 1812. In this Decree it was "established to be a rule in all cases, where there is a question "of the defining of the territorial limit of our sovereignty at sea, that "this shall be taken to extend for a distance of one ordinary geographical "league from the outermost isles or rocks which are not submerged by "the sea."

VI.—Bays

Case No. 88

Bays and Gulfs—Sovereignty Over—The Bay of Lübeck—Bays Enclosed by Territory of more than one State—Conception of National Waters.

LÜBECK *v.* MECKLENBURG-SCHWERIN.

German Staatsgerichtshof. 6 *and* 7 *July*, 1928.

THE FACTS.—This was a dispute between Lübeck and Mecklenburg-Schwerin concerning the sovereignty in general and the rights of fishery in particular in regard to the Bay of Lübeck. It was maintained by Mecklenburg-Schwerin that according to international law [1] the sovereignty over bays enclosed by the territory of more than one State is divided territorially between these States.

Held: That that contention must be rejected. There are no clear rules of international law on the subject, and a considerable number of writers admit that the question is a contro-

[1] It will be noted that in disputes between Member States of the German *Reich* the *Staatsgerichtshof* applies, in the absence of rules of German law, rules of international law. See *Annual Digest*, 1925-1926, Case No. 266, and 1927-1928, Cases Nos. 86 and 289.

versial one. There are many who deny altogether the territorial character of such bays and who maintain that they form part of the open sea. On the whole, the question must be decided on the merits of each particular case, having regard to the historical development and to the needs of the States in question. These considerations may result in attributing to each State sovereignty over a portion of the bay; or they may lead to a joint and indivisible exercise of sovereignty over the whole bay; it is also possible that the bay, without falling under the full sovereignty of either State, partakes of the nature of the maritime belt; finally, it is not impossible that one of the States may possess full sovereignty over the whole bay. However, the correct view is that the historical development and the actual needs of the interested States are of decisive importance. According to this view the sovereignty over the same part of the bay may be divided functionally, *i.e.* one State may exercise sovereignty in regard to some matters and the other State in regard to others.[1] (See Case No. 76.) [Reports: *Entscheidungen des Reichsgerichts in Zivilsachen*, vol. 122, Appendix, p. 1; *Z. für a. ö. R. und V.*, I (2) (1929), p. 180.]

NOTE.—At the same time the Court refused to accede to the request of Lübeck that the disputed part of the bay be declared as part of the national waters (*Eigengewässer*) of Lübeck. The Court's refusal was based, *inter alia*, on the ground that "the conception of national "waters is not in international law sufficiently clear for the purpose "of a judicial decision." See on this matter Hurst in *B.Y.*, 1922-1923, pp. 52-54. The Bay of Lübeck is about 13 kilometres in width at the narrowest part.

Bays—Measurement of—The Monterey Bay of California. **Case No. 89**

OCEAN INDUSTRIES, INC., *v.* SUPERIOR COURT.

Supreme Court of California. 11 *January*, 1927.

THE FACTS.—This was an application for prohibition to prevent the Superior Court of Santa Cruz County from proceeding in a suit for injunction. Plaintiff was a Nevada corporation engaged in operating a fishing vessel in Monterey Bay three and a half miles from shore. The question presented was whether Monterey Bay was within the boundaries of California and so subject to the legislation which was sought to be enforced in the injunction suit. In the language of the

[1] The Court referred here to the fact that, for instance, the breadth of the maritime belt is often differently determined in regard to different functions and uses made of it.

Case No. 89 *contd.*

Opinion, " The bay of Monterey, thus designated from " its first discovery as a ' bay,' is a body of water having " headlands approximately eighteen miles apart, with " receding shores, giving a total width of twenty-two " miles inside the headlands, with a total depth of " approximately nine miles. It thus satisfies the de- " finition of a ' bay ' given by the lexicographers as a " body of water around which the land forms a curve ; " or a recess or inlet between capes or headlands." (200 Calif. 235, 241.) The Constitution of California included within the State " all the islands, harbors " and bays " along the coast.

Held : That the application should be denied. The Court concluded that " the bay of Monterey between its headlands " and the ocean adjacent to a line drawn between these head- " lands for a distance of three nautical miles is within the " boundaries of the state of California." (200 Calif. 235, 246.) The Court referred to the successful assertion of territorial claims to such bays as Conception, Cancale, Delaware, Chesapeake, and Bristol Channel. [Report : 200 Calif. 235.]

Note.—As regards, however, the Bristol Channel, see the English case of *The Fagernes*, L.R. [1926] P. 185 ; [1927] P. 311, *Annual Digest*, 1925-1926, Case No. 96.—[Ed.]

X.—State Servitudes

Case No. 90

State Servitudes—Rights in Foreign Territory—German Railway Establishment at Basle—Nature of the Rights Ceded to Germany—Competence of German Courts and German Law in regard to the Railway Establishments of the Federal Railways in Swiss Territory—Extraterritorial Operation of the Public and Private Law of the State.

German Railway Station at Basle Case.

District Labour Court of Karlsruhe. 22 June, 1928.

The Facts.—The Administration of the German section of the railway station at Basle, a branch of the German Federal Railway Company, gave notice of dismissal to one of its workers. The worker in question lodged a complaint against the notice with the Works Council of the railway station at Basle. After abortive negotiations with the Administration of the railway at Basle, the Works Council invoked the Labour Court at Karlsruhe asking for a declaration that the worker's complaint against the notice was justified and that the Federal Railway Administration was bound either to continue the employment or to compensate the worker.[1]

The defendant Administration pleaded to the jurisdiction of the Court on the ground that the provisions relating to the establishment of Works Councils, and, generally, to the legislation affecting protection of labour, belonged to public law, which had no validity abroad, *i.e.* in Basle. It contended that the territorial frontier was the necessary limit of the exercise of rights of sovereignty so far as public law was concerned, and that the present case did not therefore fall within the competence of German courts.

Held : That the Court had jurisdiction.

A. *Extraterritorial Operation of Public and Private Law.*—The legal position of the Works Councils was based on public law. Their rights in connection with the dismissal of workers were given to them for the purpose of protecting the employee by way of action based on public law ; in general the Works Councils have been endowed with functions of a public law character. The question of the nature of the legal rules to be applied by a court, namely, whether they are of a private law or a public law nature, is as a rule of decisive importance for the purpose of answering the question of jurisdiction. Jurisdiction in the domain of private law, in particular in so far as it consists merely of the declaration of rights, that is, without aiming at their enforcement, is not bound up with territorial frontiers. The situation is different in regard to rules of a public law nature. They are the product of State sovereignty as such, and are accordingly limited to the frontiers of the State so far as the competence of its courts is concerned. The competence of courts is a manifestation of State sovereignty and is, as such, limited to the territory of the State. However, the District Labour Court had nevertheless jurisdiction in the present case in view of the fact that Switzerland, as the result of having granted to Germany the right to maintain certain railway establishments in Basle, had surrendered to Germany part of her judicial supremacy.

B. *Legal Nature of the German Railway Establishment at Basle.*—Although the State cannot part with its people or with

[1] The right to invoke the intervention of the Works Council and, if necessary, of the Labour Court against dismissal is one of the principal features of the German Works Councils Law.

Case No. 90 *contd.* its territory, it is, according to the predominant doctrine, at liberty to give up part of its sovereignty so long as it retains a certain residuum of it. The grant of the rights connected with the railway establishment at Basle constitutes such a partial cession of sovereignty, for the building and maintenance of railways within the State belong to the exercise of sovereignty. By having granted the right to these establishments, Switzerland has parted with her rights of sovereignty in regard to railways in respect of the areas placed at the disposal of Germany. It follows that as the result of this grant Switzerland has parted with her judicial supremacy in regard to the area in question. For the grant of such rights cannot be separated from the rights of sovereignty directly and necessarily connected with this right. A State which hands over rights of sovereignty connected with railways at the same time also hands over the rights of sovereignty in respect of judicial supremacy in so far as they are directly connected with the undertaking. Not every grant of the exercise of the rights of sovereignty on foreign territory has the same result. First, it is necessary that these rights should be permanently exercised; it is not sufficient if they are exercised on a single occasion. Secondly, it is necessary that these rights should be exercised within a self-contained area. If these requirements are present, there is in existence the judicial supremacy directly connected with the undertaking.

It is immaterial that the State to which the exercise of this right of sovereignty has been ceded does not itself and by its own officials exercise them. States may exercise their rights of sovereignty through other legal persons, for instance, the German Federal Railways Company. That Company, being the legal successor of the German *Reich*, exercises the sovereign rights connected with railways to the extent to which the Swiss Confederation ceded them to the German *Reich* and thus acquires for the German *Reich* the judicial supremacy normally connected with the State's sovereign rights in respect of railways. [Report: *Arbeitsrechtssprechung*, 1928, No. 238, p. 369.]

State Servitudes—*Clausula rebus sic stantibus* as Applied to State Servitudes—State Servitudes between Swiss Cantons.

See Case No. 289 (*Canton of Thurgau* v. *Canton of St. Gallen*).

PART IV

JURISDICTION

A. JURISDICTION IN GENERAL TERRITORIAL AND PERSONAL

I.—Territorial

(a) Over Territory in General and Persons and Property Situated therein. Expropriation of Alien Property

[See also Part II, RECOGNITION OF ACTS OF FOREIGN STATES AND GOVERNMENTS, and RECOGNITION OF FOREIGN STATES AND GOVERNMENTS.]

[The attention of the reader is drawn to the fact that questions involving the scope of a Government's jurisdiction will also be found in Cases No. 17-19 dealing with *Recognition of Acts of Foreign States and Governments*, and in Cases Nos. 35-47 dealing with *Recognition of Foreign States and Governments.*]

EDITORS' NOTE.—The editors are aware that the appearance of Cases Nos. 91-92 in this *Digest* is open to criticism on the ground that they involve mainly questions of Private International Law, but their topical importance and the uncertainty of the frontier between Public and Private International Law justifies, in the opinion of the editors, their inclusion.

Jurisdiction—Territorial—(1) Effect of Decrees of Foreign Governments Nationalising Assets of Corporations Incorporated under Laws of that State—Effect Limited to Assets within Territory of that State—(2) Effect of Decrees of Foreign Government Cancelling Shares and Monopolising Business—Effect upon Bearer Shares Held by Persons outside Territory of that State. **Case No. 91**

THE MANUFACTURING COMPANY I. A. WORMIN LUETCHG AND CHESHIRE LIMITED AND CHESHIRE (plaintiffs) *v.* FREDERICK HUTH & COMPANY (defendants).

English High Court of Justice (King's Bench Division).
2 May, 1928.

(MR. JUSTICE WRIGHT.)

THE FACTS.—The plaintiff company was incorporated in Russia before the Great War and owned a cotton mill

Case No. 91 ***contd.***

in Petrograd. It had no branch or agency in England. The defendants were the plaintiff company's bankers and correspondents in England. The shares in the plaintiff company, with the exception of the directors' qualification shares, were bearer shares, and the statutes of the company provided that the holders of receipts for the deposit of share warrants at banks were entitled to vote at meetings. At some date in the year 1917 the defendants held nearly £82,000 of the moneys of the plaintiff company.

In November, 1917, the Soviet Government established itself in Russia by means of a revolution, and on 28 June, 1918, it issued a Decree purporting to nationalise all the property of joint stock companies engaged in the cotton industry and having a capital exceeding one million roubles. The capital of the plaintiff company was six million roubles divided into 6000 shares. A Decree of October, 1918, required the owners of shares in textile companies to produce their shares for registration, and Decrees of November, 1918, and March, 1919, established a National Textile Board, provided for the financing of State enterprises, and purported to cancel the shares of all companies whose enterprises had been confiscated or nationalised.

In March, 1917, the directors of the plaintiff company were or included the plaintiff Cheshire and three other persons, W. and B. and S. In August, 1918, at a meeting held or purporting to be held in Petrograd, V. W. and B. C. and L. M. were elected directors. During 1918 and 1919 W. and B. and S. died, the plaintiff Cheshire and V. W. and B. C. came to England, and the remaining director L. M. went to Paris. The four surviving directors held or purported to hold meetings in England in the years 1920 to 1924 and passed resolutions authorising certain payments by the defendants to shareholders of the plaintiff company, but in 1926 the defendants, acting upon legal advice, declined to make further payments. In May, 1926, the four surviving directors held an alleged board meeting and authorised the issue of a writ to recover the balance in the hands of the defendants standing to the credit of the plaintiff company and a sum of War Loan in which part of the moneys of the plaintiff company had been invested.

In March, 1927, an alleged general meeting of shareholders was held in England at which 4000 shares, the holders of which were all outside Russia, were represented. The rights of these shareholders were evidenced by the production of receipts for the deposit of share warrants in Russian banks. (Whether the banks or branches of banks with whom the share warrants had been deposited were all located in Russia or not does not appear, but it seems probable that some of them at least were in Russia.) Of the remaining 2000 shares, the owners of some could not be traced and the owners of others were or had been in Russia and had presumably produced their shares for registration and cancellation in accordance with the Decrees of October, 1918, and March, 1919. The action was commenced in the name of the plaintiff company or alternatively in the name of the plaintiff Cheshire on behalf of himself and all the other directors of and shareholders in the plaintiff company. (Cheshire Limited appears to be part of the name of the plaintiff company.)

Held: (1) Following *Russian Commercial and Industrial Bank* v. *Comptoir d'Escompte de Mulhouse, Banque Internationale de Commerce de Petrograd* v. *Goukassow*, L.R. [1925] A.C. 112, 150; *Employers' Liability Assurance Corporation* v. *Sedgwick, Collins & Co.*, L.R. [1927] A.C. 95; and *The Jupiter* (No. 3), L.R. [1927] P. 122, 250 (*Annual Digest*, 1925-1926, Cases Nos. 100, 101 and 102), that although the effect of the Soviet Decrees might be to terminate the practical existence of the plaintiff company in Russia, to take away its property and deprive its statute of working effect, its existence as a legal entity was not thereby extinguished but still continued;

(2) As to the authorising of the present action in the name of the plaintiff company, that the Soviet Decrees did not purport to invalidate the statutes of the company, which therefore remained in force so far as their effect outside Russia was concerned, and must be interpreted in accordance with the law of Imperial Russia; that the Decrees did not purport to put the company into liquidation or to appoint a liquidator, and did not supersede the powers of the directors outside Russia; that upon evidence of the law of Imperial Russia the directors had authority to protect the company's property by instituting the present action; that the Decree of March, 1919,

Case No. 91 *contd.* for the cancellation of shares had no effect outside Russia and did not operate upon bearer shares held by persons outside Russia, such shares being choses in action with their own local situation which need not be that of the actual scrip or the original location of the share register; and that the circumstances described above gave the company a residence in England and the shares a local situation in England;

(3) That the Soviet Decrees purporting to nationalise the property of the company could not operate upon property which was in the hands of the defendants and outside Russia; and

(4) That the plaintiff company was entitled to recover the War Loan and moneys standing to its credit in the hands of the defendants. [Report: *British Year Book of International Law*, 1930, pp. 235-237, which is believed to be the only report, and of which the above is a close reproduction. See also comment on page 230 of the *Year Book*.]

Case No. 92

Jurisdiction—Territorial—Effect of Legislation of Foreign Government Dissolving Corporations.

FIRST RUSSIAN INSURANCE COMPANY (in Liquidation) (plaintiffs) *v.* LONDON AND LANCASHIRE INSURANCE COMPANY LIMITED (defendants).

English High Court of Justice (*Chancery Division*).
23 *May*, 1928.

(MR. JUSTICE ROMER.)

THE FACTS (much simplified).—The Russian Company (plaintiffs) and the London Company (defendants) had entered into an arrangement for the sharing of insurance risks underwritten by each of them by means of reinsuring a part of the risks with the other of the two parties. This arrangement was embodied in contracts of which that relating to the cession by the London company of insurance risks and a proportionate part of the premiums to the Russian company was concluded in 1907, and was known as the "Outward "Treaties," and that providing for a reciprocal cession of risks and premiums was concluded in 1892 and was known as the "Inward Treaty." A Decree of the Russian Soviet Government, entitled "On the organisa-"tion of Insurance Business in the Russian Republic," was made on 1 December, 1918, and it was acknowledged on behalf of both parties that the effect of this Decree was at least to constitute a monopoly of insurance business transacted in Russia in the Soviet Government, and that after that Decree no person or company could carry on insurance business in any part of Russia then subject to the Soviet Government. No transactions under the Inward Treaty took place after the date of the Decree, but transactions under the Outward Treaties continued until 31 December, 1919, at which date the London company terminated those Treaties. At that date there was a balance due to the Russian company of £42,000 odd, but it does not appear how much of that sum was due in respect of business transacted between 1 December, 1918, and 31 December, 1919. On 18 May, 1926, the Chancery Division of the English High Court of Justice made an order for the winding-up of the Russian company and the appointment of a liquidator, who thereupon instituted proceedings against the London company to recover the above-mentioned balance alleged to be due. The London company, *inter alia*, contended that as the result of the action and the legislation of the Soviet Government the Russian company ceased to function on 1 December, 1918; that accordingly the Outward Treaties came to an end on the same date in accordance with the principles governing "frustration of "contract"; and therefore that the accounts between the parties should be taken as at 1 December, 1918. They also claimed the right to set off sums due to them under the Inward Treaty.

Held: (1) (at p. 936) that "the effect of the Decree was to "deprive" the Russian company "of the power of carrying on "an insurance business within Soviet territory, but that it did "not affect their power of carrying on that business abroad"; and

(2) That transactions under the Outward Treaties were carried into effect in London through the Russian company's agents there, and therefore were not prohibited by the above-mentioned Decree;

(3) That accordingly the Russian company was entitled to recover the sum due under the Outward Treaties;

(4) On the London company's counterclaim the Court held that there was a sum due to the London company from the

Case No. 92 *contd.* Russian company under the Inward Treaty, and that the Soviet Decree of 4 March, 1919, relieving State enterprises of the obligation to pay to private persons debts incurred prior to their nationalisation did not have the effect of extinguishing the debts nor relieve such enterprises of the obligation to pay them out of assets situated outside Russia. The Court directed that an account should be taken and that the sum found to be due to the London company should be set off against the sum due to the Russian company under the Outward Treaties. [Report: L.R. [1928] Ch. 922.]

NOTE.—Having regard to the decision of the British House of Lords in *Employers' Liability Assurance Corporation* v. *Sedgwick, Collins & Co.*, L.R. [1927] A.C. 95 (*Annual Digest*, 1925-1926, Case No. 102), it was not contended that the effect of the Decree of 1 December, 1918, was to dissolve the Russian company; nor in the light of the decision in *The Jupiter* (No. 3), L.R. [1927] P. 122, 250 (*Annual Digest*, 1925-1926, Case No. 100), was it contended that the Decree had or could have any extraterritorial effect.

Case No. 93

Jurisdiction—Territorial—Attachment of Debts Owing Outside the Jurisdiction—Refusal of Attachment.

RICHARDSON (Judgment Creditor) *v.* RICHARDSON (Judgment Debtor): NATIONAL BANK OF INDIA, LIMITED (Garnishees).

English High Court of Justice (Probate, Divorce and Admiralty Division). 12 *May*, 1927.

THE FACTS.—The judgment creditor had obtained a garnishee order attaching the account of the judgment debtor with the National Bank of India at the head office of the Bank in London. The question in dispute was whether the attachment could and, if so, should be extended to cover any balances that might be due to him at the branches of the Bank at Mombasa in Kenya Colony and at Dar-es-Salaam in Tanganyika Mandated Territory.

Held: That the balances, if any, standing to the debtor's credit at the branches named could not be covered by an order of attachment made by the Court. "The debt must be "properly recoverable within the jurisdiction. In principle, "attachment of debts is a form of execution, and the general "power of execution extends only to property within the "jurisdiction of the court which orders it. A debt is not pro-"perty within the jurisdiction if it cannot be recovered here."

(*Martin* v. *Nadel*, [1906] 2 K.B. 26; *Swiss Bank Corporation* v. *Boehmische Industrial Bank*, [1923] 1 K.B. 673, 681, 682.) The Court added that, even if it had power to extend the order to cover these balances, it ought not, as a matter of discretion, to do so, "if payment under it will not be a good "discharge in the Courts of Kenya Colony and Tanganyika." There was evidence to this effect. [Report: L.R. [1927] P. 228.]

NOTE.—This case is interesting as being complementary to the decisions digested in *Annual Digest*, 1925-1926 (Cases Nos. 100, 101, 102), upon the effect in England of decrees of the Russian Soviet Government. See also *B.Y.*, 1928, pp. 169 and 179.

Jurisdiction—Territorial—Over Property Situated Therein—Expropriation of Alien Property—Expropriation, Confiscation and Liquidation—Judgment No. 7 of the Permanent Court of International Justice—Effect of the Judgments of the Permanent Court—Establishment of the Czechoslovak State. **Case No. 94**

CZECHOSLOVAK AGRARIAN REFORM (SWISS SUBJECTS) CASE.

Supreme Court of Justice of Czechoslovakia.
8 *April*, 1927. *No. RI* 120.

THE FACTS.—The plaintiffs (Swiss subjects) appealed against measures taken by the lower courts in connection with the agrarian reform. They based their claim to exemption from the operation of that measure on the ground that, according to international law, aliens were not liable to expropriation in the same way as nationals. They contended that, the inviolability of private property and the protection of acquired rights being amongst the main principles of international law, the expropriation of the property of aliens except upon payment of full compensation was illegal.

Held: By the Supreme Court of Justice, that the appeal failed:

(i) Although so-called "private international law" is only regulated in the Czechoslovak law (paragraphs 1, 4, 33-38 and 300 of the Civil Code) in a fragmentary manner, the provisions with regard to expropriation are very exhaustive and precise. Paragraph 300 contains the principle recognised by all legal systems *immobilia obnoxia sunt territoriis*. The principle that immovables are subjected *legi rei sitae* is so evident and so conformable to the nature of things that it is not necessary to give reasons

Case No. 94 *contd.* for it (Walker, *Internationales Privatrecht*, Wien, 1921, p. 279). It seems, however, useful to indicate the legislative basis (*ratio legis*) of the principle in order to show its rigid and absolute character. Immovables situated inside the boundaries represent in their totality the territory of a State; they are portions of which the territory is composed or, inversely, into which it is divided. Since territory is one of the vital conditions of a State, it is only natural that the State should wish to see it subjected exclusively to its own will, and should not admit any disposition of a foreign State in respect of it, for thus its own existence would be endangered. But, if the State desires to subject the territory and any of its parts, *i.e.* any immovable, only to its own will and to exclude any foreign will and disposition, it means that the State subjects it exclusively to its own law and excludes any foreign law in respect of it. The principle *legis rei sitae* is based upon the vital interest of the State: its *ratio* is of a public law character and the principle itself constitutes a binding rule, the application of which in no case can be eliminated by an agreement between the parties. In other words, the principle *immobilia obnoxia sunt territoriis* involves the territorial sovereignty which no State can renounce, as it is an attribute of its independence. But the State not only does not allow a foreign law to be applied to the immovables in its territory, but also it does not admit, for the same reason of sovereignty, a foreign court or a foreign authority to adjudicate upon them, even if they should belong to a foreigner, and even if that foreigner should enjoy the rights of exterritoriality (Article IX, paragraph 2, of the Law No. 110/1895). Since territorial sovereignty is involved, only the immovables themselves are considered: the person of the owner recedes into the background and is irrelevant; the law makes no distinction between the case of a national and the case of a foreigner, as with regard to the *ratio legis* this fact does not matter.

(ii) The Court rejects the opinion that the Czechoslovak State was created by the Treaties of Peace, that the mere fact of taking possession of the former Austrian territory without international recognition granted by the Treaties was not sufficient for this purpose, and that by the Treaties of Peace the obligation was imposed upon the Czechoslovak State not to expropriate alien property without full compensation, an obligation resulting from the principles of international law as they appear both in the Peace Treaties and in the decisions of the Permanent Court of International Justice.

The Czechoslovak State was not created by the Treaties of Peace. There is no stipulation in the Treaties which could admit such a contention. The Treaties regard the Czechoslovak State as already in existence as one of the Allied and Associated Powers and as one of the contracting parties. The Czechoslovak State was created by the Czechoslovak Nation, which has re-established it by reassumption of the ancient and imprescriptible historical rights, by its own Law of 28 October, 1918, No. 11. The fact that the Czechoslovak State had established itself as an independent State and that it already existed, was expressly stated in the preamble of the Treaty of St. Germain between the Principal Allied and Associated Powers and Czechoslovakia of 10 September, 1919 (Minorities Treaty).[1]

(iii) A provision of international law which prohibits expropriation of alien property without full compensation cannot be traced in any of the sources of that law. There is no general or particular international convention containing such a stipulation. The stipulations of the Treaties of Peace which are chiefly referred to by the plaintiffs as illustrating the principles of international law relevant to the matter before the Court concern retention and liquidation of enemy property and not expropriation, which is a matter of peace-time legislation. There are also no concrete data which could be adduced in support of the existence of a relevant international custom, for before the war expropriation was carried through on such a small scale that there was no reason for a State to pay attention to similar measures of other States, and, as regards the post-war measures, which are of a far greater extent, that question is at issue. As regards the general principles of law recognised by civilised nations, it appears that the legislation of all countries recognises the permissibility of expropriation with an express or at least tacit reservation that, should it be prescribed by law for reasons of public welfare, the expropriation is admissible even with a partial compensation only or without any compensation at all.

(iv) The decisions of the Permanent Court of International Justice Nos. 6 and 7, referred to by the plaintiffs, do not contain anything which would go beyond the limits of the German-Polish case. They are based upon the Geneva Convention of 15 May, 1922, which forms a particular law between Germany

[1] See to the same effect: decision of the Supreme Administrative Court of Czechoslovakia of 29 May, 1925, No. 11.224 (Boh. 4752 adm.), *Annual Digest*, 1925-1926, Case No. 8.

Case No. 94 *contd.* and Poland, a law which in no way could be applied in respect of a third State. Also Article 59 of the Statute of the Permanent Court provides that the decisions of the Court have no binding force except between the parties and in respect of that particular case. In the conclusions of the Permanent Court themselves there is nothing which could be considered as prejudging the legality of the Czechoslovak agrarian reform.

Until the Treaties of Peace only two forms of deprivation of property were known in law: expropriation and confiscation. The Peace Treaties added a third form: liquidation. Expropriation means deprivation of property for reasons of public welfare. It takes place, as a rule, subject to full compensation; however, it may take place with partial compensation only or without any compensation at all, if the public welfare makes it necessary. "Retention and liquidation," or "liquidation," differs from expropriation by being based not on the public welfare, but on the war right of the victor against the vanquished; it is in some respects a fine and it has that mark in common with confiscation; but it differs from the latter in that, in accordance with the Treaties, compensation must be paid for the liquidated property. Confiscation means deprivation of property as a punishment and, therefore, without compensation.

In Judgment No. 7, the Permanent Court held that "any "measure affecting the property, rights and interests of German "subjects covered by Head No. III of the Convention, which is "not justified on special grounds taking precedence over the "Convention, and which oversteps the limits set by the generally accepted principles of international law, is, therefore, "incompatible with the régime established under the Convention," and that "the only measures prohibited are those "which generally accepted international law does not sanction "in respect of foreigners; expropriation for reasons of public "utility, judicial liquidation and similar measures are not "affected by the Convention." [1] By those conclusions it was recognised that expropriation would be admitted in so far as allowed by general international law, and that by that law expropriation for reasons of public welfare is allowed. As, however, expropriation for reasons of public welfare is the only expropriation in the genuine meaning of the term, it appears that in the decisions of the Permanent Court it was recognised that this expropriation was not affected by the Convention; in

[1] Judgment No. 7, p. 22.

other words that the Convention is concerned only with liquidation. [Report: Váž. 6976 civ.[1]]

Previous decisions: Decision of 28 April, 1925, No. RI 354 (Váž. 4977 civ.), *Annual Digest*, 1925-1926, Case No. 98, p. 133, and decision of 7 December, 1926, No. RI 1008 (Váž. 6543 civ.), *Annual Digest*, 1925-1926, Case No. 99, p. 135.

NOTE.—Also discussed: (*a*) International treaties and municipal law (the Court held that the Treaties of Peace came into force as regards the Czechoslovak municipal sphere by publication in the Collection of Laws, see *Annual Digest*, 1925-1926, p. 7, note 2).

(*b*) Effect of the Peace Treaties on Third States.

(*c*) Treaty of 29 June, 1920, between Czechoslovakia and Germany regarding the execution of Article 297 of the Treaty of Versailles.

See, however, the decision of the Hungarian-Czechoslovak Mixed Arbitral Tribunal of 31 January, 1929, in the case *Alexandre Pallavicini* v. *The Czechoslovak State*, *A.J.*, XXIII (1929), p. 851 (to be digested in a later volume of the *Annual Digest*).

Jurisdiction—Territorial—Taxation of Aliens—" Due Process of Law." **Case No. 95**

COMPAÑÍA GENERAL DE TABACOS DE FILIPINAS *v.* COLLECTOR OF INTERNAL REVENUE.

United States Supreme Court. 21 November, 1927.

THE FACTS.—This was an action to recover taxes paid under protest. Plaintiff was a Spanish company licensed to do business in the Philippines. Plaintiff had merchandise in its warehouses in the Philippines and had insured it with a London insurance company which was licensed to do insurance business in the Philippines through its agent there, and with a Paris insurance company which was not licensed to do business in the Philippines. The contracts were made and the losses were payable outside the Philippines. A Philippine statute taxed the premiums paid on such insurance. The taxes were paid under protest, and this suit com-

[1] See also the decision of the Supreme Court of Justice of 16 August, 1927, No. RI 739 (Váž. 7246 civ.), in which, with regard to the contention of the plaintiff (a German subject) that the measures taken in connection with the agrarian reform should be postponed until his action brought in the Mixed Arbitral Tribunal was decided, it was held that the Mixed Arbitral Tribunals are not competent to deal with matters concerning the Czechoslovak agrarian reform, so that, if the plaintiff brought an action with the Mixed Arbitral Tribunal, he brought it in a court not competent in the matter, and such a step, not based on the law, cannot have any influence on proceedings before the competent courts.

Case No. 95 *contd.*

menced. The validity of the tax was sustained. The Supreme Court of the Philippines affirmed the judgment. On certiorari,

Held: That the judgment of the Supreme Court of the Philippines should be reversed as to the tax on premiums paid to the Paris company. Since the company was not doing business in the Philippines, and since neither the insurance contract nor the premiums paid under it were within the jurisdiction of the Philippine Government, this tax deprived plaintiff of property without due process of law contrary to the Philippine Organic Act, § 3 (39 U.S. Stat. L. 545, 546). Delivering the Opinion of the Court, Chief Justice Taft said: "Even though it "is only equal to the tax upon normal premiums paid in the "Philippine Islands, it is imposed for the purpose of dis-"couraging insurance in companies that do not pay tribute to "the State because out of its taxing or penalizing jurisdiction." (275 U.S. 87, 95.)

The judgment was affirmed as to the tax on premiums paid to the London company. It was assumed that the tax would fall ultimately upon the London company. While conceding that the case was "a close one," the Court thought that making and carrying out the policy involved an exercise of the London company's right to "do business in the Philippine Islands under "its license, because the policy covers fire risks on property "within the Philippine Islands which may require adjustment, "and the activities of agents in the Philippine Islands with re-"spect to settlement of losses arising thereunder." (275 U.S. 87, 98.)

Justices Holmes and Brandeis dissented as to the tax on premiums paid to the Paris company on the ground that both plaintiff and the property insured were within the jurisdiction of the Philippines and the tax was just. [Report: 275 U.S. 87.]

Case No. 96

Jurisdiction—Territorial—Extraterritorial Effect of National Laws.

THE CHIQUITA.

United States Circuit Court of Appeals, Fifth Circuit.
6 *June*, 1927.

THE FACTS.—This was a libel to forfeit a vessel flying the Honduranean flag for violation of United States statutes prohibiting the sale of an American vessel to an alien without the consent of the United States Shipping

Board, for changing the vessel's name without official sanction, and for engaging in commerce for which she was not licensed. The vessel was built in the United States, and licensed for the coasting trade. She was seized at Nassau to enforce a maritime lien, sold under process issuing from the Supreme Court of the Bahamas, and purchased by a British subject who later sold her to a subject of Honduras. She was seized with a cargo of liquor about thirty-five miles off the Louisiana coast. Forfeiture was decreed. On appeal,

Held: That the decree of forfeiture should be reversed. The vessel was completely divested of American nationality by sale under process of the Supreme Court of the Bahamas. Citing *Williams* v. *Armroyd*, 7 Cr. (U.S.) 423. The United States statutes relied upon in proceeding against the vessel have no extraterritorial force. [Report: 19 F. (2nd) 417.]

Jurisdiction—Territorial—Effect of Foreign Legislation—Expropriation by Agrarian Law—Latvia. **Case No. 97**

KURSELL *v.* TIMBER OPERATORS AND CONTRACTORS LIMITED.

The English Court of Appeal. 10 *March*, 1926.

In this case, which does not require further mention, some discussion will be found as to the effect of a Latvian Agrarian Law in producing the frustration of an English contract for the sale of timber in a Latvian forest. [Report: L.R. [1927] 1 K.B. 298.]

(b) Criminal Jurisdiction over Foreigners

Criminal Jurisdiction over Foreigners—For Crimes Committed Abroad—Collision on the High Seas—Locality of the Offence—Question of Jurisdiction in General—Burden of Proof—The Rule of Freedom of Action in International Law. **Case No. 98**

PERMANENT COURT OF INTERNATIONAL JUSTICE.

JUDGMENT No. 9.

FRANCE *v.* TURKEY.

THE CASE OF THE S.S. *LOTUS*.

7 *September*, 1927.

THE FACTS.—On 2 August, 1926, a collision occurred on the high seas between the French mail steamer *Lotus*, proceeding to Constantinople, and the Turkish collier *Boz-Kourt*.

Case No. 98 *contd.*

The latter vessel was cut in two, and sank. Eight Turkish nationals who were on board of the *Boz-Kourt* were drowned. On 3 August, the *Lotus* arrived in Constantinople, where the Turkish authorities proceeded to hold an enquiry into the collision. On 5 August, Lieutenant Demons, a French subject, who was the officer of the watch on board the *Lotus* at the time when the collision occurred, was arrested, together with the captain of the *Boz-Kourt*, and criminal proceedings were instituted against both him and the captain of the *Boz-Kourt* on a charge of manslaughter. The case was first heard on 28 August before the Criminal Court of Stamboul. Lieutenant Demons' objection to the jurisdiction of the Court was overruled. On 15 September, the Court delivered judgment sentencing Lieutenant Demons to eighty days' imprisonment and a fine of twenty-two pounds. The other accused was sentenced to a slightly higher penalty.

The proceedings in the Turkish Court were instituted by virtue of Article 6 of the Turkish Penal Code, which provided, *inter alia*, as follows :

" Any foreigner who, apart from the cases " contemplated by Article 4, commits an " offence abroad to the prejudice of Turkey " or of a Turkish subject, for which offence " Turkish law prescribes a penalty involving " loss of freedom for a minimum period of " not less than one year, shall be punished in " accordance with the Turkish Penal Code " provided that he is arrested in Turkey."

The French Government protested against the arrest of Lieutenant Demons, and against the assumption of jurisdiction by the Turkish Court. On 12 October, 1926, France and Turkey signed a special agreement asking the

Permanent Court of International Justice to decide the question whether, by instituting proceedings against Lieutenant Demons, Turkey acted contrary to Article 15 of the Convention of Lausanne of 24 July, 1923, respecting conditions of Residence and Business and Jurisdiction, which provided as follows:

" Subject to the provisions of Article 16, " all questions of jurisdiction shall, as between Turkey and the other contracting " Powers, be decided in accordance with the " principles of international law."

Held: That Turkey had not acted contrary to the principles of international law by instituting criminal proceedings against Lieutenant Demons.

A. *As to the Question of Jurisdiction in General and the Burden of Proof.*

It was contended on behalf of the French Government that Turkey, in order to have jurisdiction, should be able to point to some title of jurisdiction recognised by international law. Turkey contended that she had jurisdiction whenever such jurisdiction was not excluded by some principle of international law.

Held: That the French contention must be rejected.

" International law governs relations between independent States. The rules of law binding upon " States therefore emanate from their own free will as " expressed in conventions or by usages generally " accepted as expressing principles of law and established in order to regulate the relations between these " co-existing independent communities or with a view " to the achievement of common aims. Restrictions " upon the independence of States cannot therefore be " presumed" (at p. 18).

According to international law, the jurisdiction of States was territorial in the sense that, failing the existence of a permissive rule to the contrary, a State

Case No. 98 *contd.*

must not exercise its power in any form in the territory of another State. But from that it does not follow that international law prohibits a State from exercising jurisdiction in its territory in regard to acts committed abroad. " Such a view would only be tenable if " international law contained a general prohibition to " States to extend the application of their laws and the " jurisdiction of their courts to persons, property and " acts outside their territory, and if, as an exception to " this general prohibition, it allowed States to do so in " certain specific cases. But this is certainly not the " case under international law as it stands at present. " Far from laying down a general prohibition to the " effect that States may not extend the application of " their laws and the jurisdiction of their courts to " persons, property and acts outside their territory, " it leaves them in this respect a wide measure of dis- " cretion which is only limited in certain cases by " prohibitive rules ; as regards other cases, every State " remains free to adopt the principles which it regards " as best and most suitable " (at p. 19).

B. *Criminal Jurisdiction.*

Held : That the general principle stated above applies also to criminal jurisdiction. This is so notwithstanding the close connection which for a long time existed between the conception of the State and the conception of supreme criminal jurisdiction and also notwithstanding the special importance of criminal jurisdiction from the point of view of the individual.

" Though it is true that in all systems of law the " principle of the territorial character of criminal law is " fundamental, it is equally true that all or nearly all " these systems of law extend their action to offences " committed outside the territory of the State which " adopts them, and they do so in ways which vary from " State to State. The territoriality of criminal law, " therefore, is not an absolute principle of international " law and by no means coincides with territorial " sovereignty " (at p. 20).

C. *Locality of the Offence.*

It was contended on behalf of France that international law does not permit States to assume jurisdiction over offences committed abroad merely because of the nationality of the victim of the offence, and that this was the situation in the present case, seeing that the offence was committed on board the French vessel.

Held : That apart from the question whether international law prohibited a State to punish crimes committed by foreigners abroad for the sole reason of the nationality of the victim—a question on which the Court reserved its opinion—in the present case the offence produced its effects on the Turkish vessel and, consequently, in a place assimilated to Turkish territory in regard to which Turkey was entitled to apply her own law. " No argument has come to the knowledge of the Court from which it could be deduced that States recognise themselves to be under an obligation towards each other only to have regard to the place where the author of the offence happens to be at the time of the offence. On the contrary, it is certain that the courts of many countries, even of countries which have given their criminal legislation a strictly territorial character, interpret criminal law in the sense that offences, the authors of which at the moment of commission are in the territory of another State, are nevertheless to be regarded as having been committed in the national territory, if one of the constituent elements of the offence, and more especially its effects, have taken place there " [1] (at p. 23).

D. *Question of Exclusive Jurisdiction of the Law of the Flag.*

It was contended by France that the assumption of

[1] It was on this ground that Judge Moore, in his dissenting Opinion, expressed his agreement with the final judgment of the Court, although he disagreed with the majority on the more general question of jurisdiction over foreigners for crimes committed abroad. See pp. 76-83 and the cases there cited. And see also the judgment of the majority at pp. 29, 30 in regard to the question of the localisation of the offence in the Franconia case (*R.* v. *Keyn* (1877), L.R. 2 Ex. Div. 63) and the subsequent abandonment of the view taken therein in *R.* v. *Nillins* (1884), 53 L.J.M.C. 157 ; *R.* v. *Godfrey*, L.R. [1923] 1 K.B. 24.

Case No. 98 ***contd.***

jurisdiction by Turkey was contrary to international law, as the latter recognised the exclusive jurisdiction of the State whose flag is flown as regards everything which occurs on board a ship on the high seas.

Held : That that contention must be rejected. It is true that as a rule vessels on the high seas are subject to no authority except that of the State whose flag they fly, but that does not mean that a State can never in its own territory exercise jurisdiction over acts which have occurred on board a foreign ship on the high seas. If by virtue of the principle of the freedom of the seas a ship is placed in the same position as national territory, then the rights of the State under whose flag the vessel sails do not go further than the rights which it exercises within its territory. " It follows that what " occurs on board a vessel on the high seas must be " regarded as if it occurred on the territory of the " State whose flag the ship flies. If, therefore, a " guilty act committed on the high seas produces its " effects on a vessel flying another flag or in foreign " territory, the same principles must be applied as if " the territories of two different States were con- " cerned, and the conclusion must therefore be drawn " that there is no rule of international law prohibiting " the State to which the ship on which the effects of " the offence have taken place belongs, from regarding " the offence as having been committed in its territory " and prosecuting, accordingly, the delinquent " (at p. 25).

E. *The Law in regard to Cases of Collision.*

It was contended by France that the principle of exclusive jurisdiction of the law of the flag applied with special force to cases of collision.

Held : That there was no evidence to support this contention of the French Government. The fact that there were only a few instances of criminal prosecutions of this nature in cases of collisions shows merely that States have abstained from exercising such jurisdiction. But it does not show that their abstention was the result of their being conscious of a duty to abstain from exercising jurisdiction. Only then would it be possible to speak of an international custom. Neither decisions of municipal courts (see Case No. 2) nor the attitude of States whose vessels have been submitted to the jurisdiction of foreign States (see Case No. 354) militated in favour of the French contention.

F. *Concurrent Jurisdiction.*

" The offence for which Lieutenant Demons appears " to have been prosecuted was an act—of negligence " or imprudence—having its origin on board the *Lotus*, " whilst its effects made themselves felt on board the " *Boz-Kourt*. These two elements are, legally, en- " tirely inseparable, so much so that their separation " renders [1] the offence non-existent. Neither the " exclusive jurisdiction of either State, nor the limita- " tions of the jurisdiction of each to the occurrences " which took place on the respective ships, would " appear calculated to satisfy the requirements of " justice and effectively to protect the interests of the " two States. It is only natural that each should be " able to exercise jurisdiction and to do so in respect " of the incident as a whole. It is, therefore, a case " of concurrent jurisdiction " (at p. 30). [Report: Series A, No. 10, pp. 18-32.[2]]

NOTE.—There were six dissenting Opinions appended to this judgment. However, as in other decisions given by the Court, the digest is confined to the decision of the majority.

---

[1] That is " would render." (The French text is authoritative.)

[2] See also Series E, No. 4, pp. 166-175.

On the *Lotus* case see, in addition to the bibliography compiled in Oppenheim, 4th ed., vol. I, p. 284, n. 3: Portail, *L'affaire du " Lotus "* (1928); Walther, *L'affaire du " Lotus " ou de l'abordage hauturier en droit pénal international* (1928); Canonne, *Essai de droit pénal international. L'affaire du " Lotus "* (1929); Hamacher, *Der Ständige Internationale Gerichtshof und der Fall " Lotus "* (1929); Fischer Williams in *R.G.*, XXXV (1928), pp. 367-376; Travers in *R.I.*, 3rd ser., vol. IX (1928), pp. 400-421; Michel de Grotte, *ibid.*, vol. X (1929), pp. 387-394; Niboyet in *Revue critique de législation et de jurisprudence*, XLVIII (1928), pp. 453-474.

(c) Over Ports and National Waters

[See also Part III, TERRITORIAL WATERS.]

Case No. 99

Jurisdiction—Over Ports and National Waters—Crimes Committed on Board Foreign Vessels in Port.

THE STATE *v.* DAVE JOHNSON PLAZEN.

Court of Cassation, Costa Rica. 1928.

THE FACTS.—Plazen, a citizen of the United States and a member of the crew of the British steamer *Coppename*, killed one Melvin Goff Yorke, a British subject and one of the crew of the same vessel, on board the vessel in the Port of Limon, Costa Rica, on 14 October, 1927. The defendant alleged the incompetence of the local courts to try him in view of the provisions of Article 219, paragraph 4, of the Penal Code of Costa Rica.

Held: "That neither Article 219 [1] of the Penal Code nor "Article 117 of the Organic Law of the Courts has been in-"fringed because, even though the deceased as well as the "offender were foreigners and members of the crew of a merchant "vessel also of foreign nationality. The vessel was moored "to one of the piers in the port of Limon, and the deceased was "transferred to the hospital of that city, and for this reason the "public authorities had to take cognisance of the act, and the "police authorities were compelled to take the customary "measures. Paragraph 4 of Article 219 gave the tribunals of "the country jurisdiction to take cognisance of the case." [Report: *Sentencias de la Corte de Casacion* (Segundo Semestre, 1928), p. 711.]

NOTE.—On the difference between the so-called French rule and the British and American practice in this matter, see Oppenheim, vol. I, 4th ed., 1928, §190 (*c*) and note 3 on p. 404.

---

[1] Article 219 of the Penal Code, mentioned above, provides:

"The following offences are subject to prosecution in Costa Rica, and to "punishment in accordance with its laws, whatever the nationality of the "offender may be: . . .

"(4) Those taking place on board a foreign merchant vessel lying in the "waters of Costa Rica, when the offender, the victim or both do not belong "to the personnel of the crew, or when, both being members of it, the offence "has affected the port or littoral."

Jurisdiction—Territorial—Foreign Ship in United States Port —Effect of Advance Payment of Wages to Foreign Seaman in Foreign Port on behalf of Foreign Ship. **Case No. 100**

JACKSON *v.* S.S. *ARCHIMEDES.*

United States Supreme Court. 3 *January*, 1928.

THE FACTS.—This was a libel *in rem* by a British seaman against a British vessel to collect full wages without deduction of advances made in England. The Dingley Act of 1884, § 10 (23 U.S. Stat. L. 53), as amended by the Seamen's Act of 1915, § 11 (38 U.S. Stat. L. 1164), made it " unlawful in any case to pay any seaman wages " in advance of the time when he has actually earned " the same " and provided that payment of such advance wages should not absolve the vessel or the master from " the full payment of wages after the same shall " have been actually earned." It was stipulated further " that this section shall apply as well to foreign vessels " while in waters of the United States, as to vessels of " the United States." The Merchant Marine Act of 1920, § 32 (41 U.S. Stat. L. 988), further amended § 10 of the Dingley Act to make the section applicable to advance payments " whether made within or without " the United States or territory subject to the jurisdic- " tion thereof." The District Court dismissed the libel. The Circuit Court of Appeals affirmed the decree. On certiorari,

Held: That the decree of the Circuit Court of Appeals should be affirmed. The Merchant Marine Act, § 32, was not intended to extend the provisions of the statute to advance payments made by foreign vessels while in foreign ports. *Sandberg* v. *McDonald*, 248 U.S. 185, followed. [Report: 275 U.S. 463.]

Jurisdiction—Territorial—In Ports and Territorial Waters— Foreign Merchant Ship in United States Port—Wages Dispute between Foreign Seaman and Foreign Shipowner. **Case No. 101**

THE SNELAND I.

United States District Court, E.D. Louisiana. 12 *May*, 1927.

THE FACTS.—This was a suit in admiralty brought by a Norwegian seaman against a Norwegian ship to recover

Case No. 101 *contd.*

wages. Libellant was hired in Norway but joined the ship at Philadelphia. He became ill on the voyage and was operated upon at New Orleans. He was discharged at New Orleans. There was an objection to the jurisdiction. The Norwegian consul also protested against the exercise of jurisdiction.

Held : That the plea to the jurisdiction should be dismissed. Delivering the Opinion of the Court, Judge Burns said : " Since " the alleged discharge and failure of payment of wages due " occurred at this port, and since the alleged failure of the " master to give the seaman necessary medical attention necessi- " tated the subsequent surgical operation at this port, where all " the witnesses reside, the case should be considered as coming " within the exception to the rule that jurisdiction will not " ordinarily be exercised of such cases between foreign seamen " and foreign owners, under foreign shipping articles, because a " hardship might otherwise be unjustly imposed on the sea- " man." (19 F. (2nd) 528, 529.) [Report : 19 F. (2nd) 528.]

Case No. 102

Jurisdiction—Territorial—In Ports and Territorial Waters—Foreign Ship—Dispute between Shipmaster of one Foreign Nationality and Charterers of Another Foreign Nationality.

DANIELSEN *v.* ENTRE RIOS RAILWAYS COMPANY.

United States District Court, D. Maryland.
21 *October*, 1927.

THE FACTS.—This was a libel *in personam*, with clause of foreign attachment, by the master of a Norwegian vessel against South American charterers. It was objected that all the parties being foreigners they were not entitled as matter of right to be heard by this Court.

Held : That the objection should be overruled. Delivering the Opinion of the Court, Judge Coleman said : " It is clear that " whether an admiralty court will take jurisdiction of suits be- " tween foreigners is a matter entirely within its discretion, and " such suits will be entertained, unless some special reason is " shown why the court should deny its aid." (22 F. (2nd) 326, 327.) [Report : 22 F. (2nd) 326.]

(g) Exemptions from and Restrictions upon Territorial Jurisdiction

(i) Foreign States

[See also Part II, Sovereignty and Independence : III. *Acts of Sovereignty and Transactions of a Private Character.*

Foreign States—Immunity from Jurisdiction—Cross-Suit—Implied Submission to Cross-Suit—Express Refusal to Submit to Jurisdiction. **Case No. 103**

French Shares (Cross-Suit) Case.

Prussian Tribunal for Conflicts of Jurisdiction (Kompetenzkonflikts-Gerichtshof). 10 *March*, 1928.

The Facts.—The French Republic, which owned a number of shares of a former mining company in Lorraine, brought an action, as against the successors of the company, for a declaratory judgment to the effect that it was entitled to the rights which the Valorisation Law (a German law enacted with a view to adjusting certain economic problems arising out of the depreciation of currency) granted to the owners of original shares in respect of the rate of valorisation. The defendant then brought a cross-suit for a declaratory judgment to the effect that the plaintiff's shares were not entitled to valorisation at all.

Held : That the German courts had no jurisdiction to entertain the cross-suit. A foreign State is not subject to the jurisdiction of German courts except when it has voluntarily submitted itself to their jurisdiction. There has been no such submission in the present case. It is not true that by bringing an action before German courts a foreign State necessarily submits itself to their jurisdiction in regard to all the means of defence, including a cross-suit, which the defendant may put forward. It is in each case for the court to decide how far a submission to jurisdiction may be implied from the fact of an action having been brought.[1] As a rule the court will be competent to decide all incidental questions arising out of the principal action. Thus in the present case it would appear that if

[1] The Court referred here to the *Chinese Embassy (Immunities)* case, decided on 23 June, 1925, and reported in *Annual Digest*, 1925-1926, Case No. 243.

Case No. 103 *contd.*

the court is asked to decide that certain shares are entitled to valorisation as original shares, it thereby acquires jurisdiction to decide in a cross-suit the question whether the shares are entitled to valorisation at all. However, submission cannot be implied in one case, namely, if, when or before bringing the action, the foreign State has expressly made it known that it does not intend to submit to the jurisdiction of German courts in regard to certain specific questions connected with the principal action.

The Court then examined in detail certain acts and declarations of the plaintiff State before and at the time when the action was brought, and found that the French Republic expressly declined to submit to the jurisdiction of German courts in regard to the question forming the subject-matter of the cross-suit. [Reports: *Z. für a. ö. R. und V.*, II (2) (1930), p. 96; *Juristische Wochenschrift*, 1930, p. 213.]

Case No. 104

Jurisdiction over Foreign States—Exemption from Jurisdiction—Foreign State as Tenant—Exemption from Jurisdiction in respect of Immovable Property—Jurisdiction in regard to Exercise of Act of Sovereignty.

HALIG LIMITED *v.* POLISH STATE.

Prussian Tribunal for Conflicts of Jurisdiction (Kompetenzkonflikts-Gerichtshof). 10 *March*, 1928.

THE FACTS.—The plaintiffs let certain offices to a firm in Stettin which sublet part of them to the Polish State for the accommodation of its vice-consul at Stettin. The plaintiffs reserved a certain space on the right and left of the main entrance to the building for any signs or notices which the tenants might wish to put up. In the contract with the principal tenant they stipulated that signs and notices should not be put up in places other than those reserved for that purpose by the landlords. Subsequently the Polish vice-consul had a round plaque with the insignia of the Polish State put up above the entrance; he refused to comply with the request of the plaintiffs to remove the plaque and to repair the damage done to the wall.

The plaintiffs thereupon brought an action for trespass and injury to their property. The writ was not served upon the Polish State, as the Ministry for Foreign Affairs refused to transmit it. The writ was then served upon the Polish vice-consul in Stettin.

However, before oral proceedings had taken place the Prussian Prime Minister lodged with the Court at Stettin a declaration questioning the jurisdiction of the Court on the ground that the action was contrary to a recognised principle of international law.

It was pointed out in the declaration that the Polish State could not be made defendant without its consent; that it was not admissible to make the property rights of a foreign State the object of an action or execution; that the object of the present action was the exercise of an act of sovereignty by the Polish State; and that the conclusion of the contract of lease could not be regarded as implying submission to the jurisdiction of German courts. The matter then came before the Tribunal in Matters of Conflicts of Jurisdiction.

Held: That German courts had no jurisdiction in the matter. It is a well-established principle of international law that a State is not, as a rule, subject to the jurisdiction of foreign courts in disputes concerning private law except in cases of voluntary submission or in disputes relating to immovable property.[1] The same principle applies to Poland, whose independence Germany recognised in Article 87 of the Treaty of Versailles.

The fact that the present action could be construed as one of disturbance of possession (Section 862 of the Civil Code) or of invasion of ownership (Section 1004 of the Civil Code) was immaterial. Even if such actions were regarded as relating to immovable property, a German court could not have jurisdiction in cases like the present one in which the plaintiff asks for the removal of the insignia of sovereignty of the Polish State. The putting up of a sign with the insignia of a foreign State is an act of sovereignty which in no case can be subject to the jurisdiction of the courts. The principle of independence and equality of sovereign States does not permit of the exercise of jurisdiction in such matters.

Even if it could be assumed that there was a contract of lease between the plaintiffs and the Polish State, the existence of such a contract would not imply a voluntary submission of the Polish State to the jurisdiction of German courts in matters arising out of the contract. [Reports: *Z.V.*, XV (1930), pp. 271-276; *Z. für. a. ö. R. und V.*, vol. II (2) (1930), p. 101.]

[1] The Court referred here to its previous decisions reported in *R.G.Z.*, XXII, p. 29; LXII, p. 165; CIII, p. 277; CX, p. 315.

Case No. 105 **Jurisdiction—Contract between a Private Person and a Foreign Sovereign State—Applicability of Foreign Law instead of Local Law.**

FRENCH STATE *v.* CARATHEODORY.

Court of Appeal of Paris. 5 *January*, 1928.

THE FACTS.—See *Annual Digest*, 1925-1926, Case No. 124.

Held by the Court of Appeal: That the decision of the Court of First Instance must be upheld. "A private person, "by the very fact of entering into transactions with a sovereign "State, becomes subject to its laws and jurisdiction; the "juridical effects, therefore, of the contract of lease [of a house "in Turkey by a Turkish subject to the French military "authorities] must be determined by reference to French law; "by Article 1733 of the French Civil Code the tenant is, in "principle, responsible for fire, unless he can prove the exist-"ence of any one of the facts entitling him to exemption from "responsibility." The French State had neither proved nor attempted to prove the existence of any one of these facts, and was therefore required to indemnify the lessor. [Report: 55 *Clunet* (1928), p. 964.]

Case No. 106 **Jurisdiction over Foreign States—Acts of Governments Enjoying the Hospitality of Foreign States—The Government of Montenegro in Italy in 1922—End of the Kingdom of Montenegro.**

IN RE SAVINI AND OTHERS.

Court of Appeal of Rome. 20 *October*, 1927.

THE FACTS.—In May, 1925, the Minister of the Interior informed the judicial authorities in Rome that Dino Savini, of the same place, had applied, in accordance with the Royal Decree of 22 March, 1923, for authorisation to practise dentistry, and had in support of his application produced a dentist's diploma signed in 1922 by Planematz, who was at that time Minister of the Interior of Montenegro. Savini was then charged with having fraudulently, with the connivance of Planematz, obtained that document. He maintained that he had passed the necessary examination in 1913, that he was only able to get the diploma some years later, and that he had made use of the same in the full conviction that it was authentic. The Court of Appeal, however, convinced of the forgery of the document, found Savini and others guilty, and condemned them each to three years' imprisonment. Savini appealed against this sentence on the ground, *inter alia*, that the Italian courts had no jurisdiction in the matter. He maintained that the acts of Planematz, who in October, 1922, had signed the diploma now held forged by the Court, and who at that time was on Italian soil as head and member of the Montenegrin Government at a time when Montenegro was occupied by Yugoslav troops, ought to be deemed to be covered by the principle of extraterritoriality; further, that the Italian courts could not dispute the legality of these acts since they had no jurisdiction over the political and administrative acts of a foreign Government.

Held: That the appeal must be dismissed. It is true that in certain historical circumstances and in the course of events of an international character, especially if these result from war, a State may exist outside its natural boundaries and still preserve the character of a person in public international law in its relations with other States and particularly in its relations with the State whose hospitality it enjoys. The Government of such a State, however, in order to be able to exercise the rights of sovereignty derived from the principle of extraterritoriality with regard to its political and administrative functions, free from interference on the part of the judicial authorities of the foreign State, must be enjoying full and formal recognition. Such recognition of the Government of Montenegro had not taken place. No legislative or administrative act can be produced establishing the fact that that Government had been allowed to transfer its residence to Italian soil with the express consent of the Italian Government and to exercise there all governmental functions on exactly the same footing as if it were still within the boundaries of the territory of Montenegro. Consequently, as the document which is the object of the present proceedings had been signed in October, 1922, there is no question of the operation of the principle of extraterritoriality or even of the juridical existence of the State of Montenegro itself. That State ceased to exist, so far as concerns the Italian Government, in September, 1921, when the Italian diplomatic representation in Montenegro was abolished. [Report: *Giustizia penale*, 1928, 1848 ff.]

Case No. 107 **Jurisdiction—Non-Amenability of Foreign State in Civil Actions—Exceptions—Informal Waiver not Effective—Effect of Waiver Contained in Agreement between Foreign State and a Private Individual.**

MATSUYAMA AND SANO *v.* THE REPUBLIC OF CHINA.

Supreme Court of Japan. 1928.

THE FACTS.—The plaintiffs, holders of two notes drawn by the then Chinese Chargé d'Affaires in Tokyo, applied to the District Court of Tokyo for a decree against the defendant, the Republic of China, represented by Wang Jung-pao, Minister Plenipotentiary and Envoy Extraordinary, for the payment of the notes with six per cent. interest as from 5 March, 1924, up to the execution of the decree. It was alleged that on their maturity the notes, each dated 5 December, 1923, and payable, on 4 March, 1924, at the Tokyo branch office of the Yokohama Specie Bank, to Y, who had subsequently endorsed and assigned them to the plaintiffs, were dishonoured by the Bank at the instance of the defendant State: the plaintiffs in due form protested against the non-payment on 6 March, 1924, and thereafter presented them repeatedly at the Chinese Legation; and yet were forced, by the defendant State's persistent refusal to meet its liabilities, to have recourse to legal proceedings. It was alleged, in addition, that the Chinese Minister had intimated his intention to acquiesce in the local jurisdiction in this case, and to contest the propriety of the claim.

The District Court, however, being satisfied by an enquiry *ex officio*, through the Minister for Foreign Affairs, that the defendant's representative had no intention either to defend the action or to abandon his diplomatic privilege *ad hoc*, quashed the proceedings for the reason that the writ of summons could not be served. An appeal was then made by the plaintiffs to the Court of Appeal, Tokyo, which overruled it and affirmed the original judgment.

Held, on further appeal: That " inasmuch as no State " acknowledges the authority of another except as an act of " voluntary submission, a foreign State, in principle, is not

" amenable to our law in a civil process unless some peculiar " ground, such as the fact of the proceedings being *in rem*, " exists. That there may be an exception is undoubted under " international law when, and in so far as, such State deliber- " ately accepts our jurisdiction ; and this may comprise occa- " sions provided for by a treaty or those in which it has ex- " pressed its willingness to abide by the decision of our courts " in the particular instance, or in contemplation of certain " specific cases. But concessions of that nature must always " and necessarily be made between the States concerned. Thus, " although an agreement might be concluded between a foreign " State and an individual Japanese subject in which the former, " on its part, agreed to recognise the competence of our Civil " Code, the agreement would not operate *per se* to bring that " State under our jurisdiction.

" That being so, a suit against a foreign State cannot be " entertained in the courts of this country save in special cir- " cumstances of the kind just mentioned, where its jurisdiction " has been formally acquiesced in ; which sufficiently shows " that the present action is not maintainable. In consequence, " the argument at the bar that the drawing of the notes in " question implied, as between the parties, the Republic of " China's assent to be bound by our law in respect of them, " must fail, since the implied undertaking is, of itself, incapable " of producing that result. It is true that the view that upon " the institution of any litigation against a foreign State it is " still the duty of the court, quite apart from the exceptional " cases alluded to, to issue a writ of summons and cite the " parties to appear at an appointed date, so that an opportunity " may be afforded of ascertaining the intention of the defendant " (in this case the Republic of China), is a plausible one. It " must nevertheless be pointed out that such issue of the writ " and citation *ex officio*, under Articles 193 and 161 of the Law " of Procedure, is in itself an exercise of our authority and " cannot be effected against a State which does not submit to " our jurisdiction. Accordingly, neither of the appellants' pro- " positions can be accepted. The decree of the second court, " while not fully explicit, is, therefore, upheld on the point of " the dismissal of the action, and the appeal is rejected." [Report : 7 Supreme Court Decisions, 1128.]

Case No. 108 **Jurisdiction—Sovereignty and Independence—Right of Foreign States to Sue—Consequential Submission to Ordinary Incidents of Procedure Available against an Ordinary Plaintiff.**

TRADE DELEGATION AT WARSAW OF U.S.S.R. *v.* MAURYCY FAJANS (COMMERCIAL AND INDUSTRIAL JOINT STOCK CO.).

Supreme Court of Poland, First Division (Plenary Session). 10 *February*, 1928.

THE FACTS.—The plaintiff, the Trade Delegation of the Union of Soviet Socialist Republics, was the holder of certain bills of exchange upon which the defendant was liable, and which had been duly protested. The plaintiff applied to the District Court of Warsaw for leave to put in force the " execution clause " (which resembles an order *nisi*) against the defendant. The Court, on appeal from the Judge in chambers, and without hearing the parties, refused to entertain the application on the ground that it was made by an organ of a foreign State which could not be sued, without its express consent, before a Polish court, so that the debtor could not bring, under the code of civil procedure, an action against the plaintiff to call upon him to show cause why the order *nisi* for execution should be withdrawn ; for in these conditions the principle of equality of both parties to each action would be impaired by the endorsement of the executory clause. On appeal,

Held : (1) That the District Court was wrong in applying a stipulation of the code of civil procedure which referred to actions against members of foreign diplomatic missions, because in the case now before the Court the subject of the right and party to the action was a State as a legal entity acting through its organ.

(2) That the question of *locus standi* in cases of a foreign State could be decided by positive stipulations of a treaty, if any, and that, there being no such treaty, it had to be settled by applying " the general principles of the so-called law of " nations, based on customs which are accepted in the relations " between States."

(3) That, " according to universal opinion, a foreign State " is entitled to enforce its civil rights, if it is recognised by the

" State in which it brings action, and of course only if the claim " is not contrary to the law of that State or to public order. " The very fact of political recognition of a foreign State im- " plies, subject to contrary reservation, the recognition of its " personality at civil law. Hence results for the foreign State " in question the right of concluding contracts with the citizens " of the recognising State and of acquiring property (subject to " certain reservations notably with regard to real estate). It " is a further consequence of the same principle that the foreign " State cannot be deprived of the possibility of enforcing its " civil claims by actions at law, within the limits of the local " laws, and without excluding simplified proceedings such as, " under our law, the endorsement of the executory clause."

(4) That, " although both in the theory and the judicial " practice of certain States it is an accepted view that a State, " as an entity which is sovereign and the equal of other States, " may not be sued before a foreign court unless it resigns that " immunity, yet that problem does not arise in the present pro- " ceedings, for apart from the question whether the U.S.S.R. " had not, by the very fact of taking up commercial activities in " Poland, submitted altogether to the jurisdiction of Polish " courts in all disputes arising in Poland from those activities, " . . . the Union, by having started judicial proceedings against " a local citizen in the matter of a claim, had by that very act " recognised the jurisdiction of the Polish Court in this case " and, having thus submitted to all the legal consequences of " the proceedings which it had started, cannot plead its im- " munity, and in particular cannot use that plea to hinder or " weaken the means of defence which are at the disposal of " the debtor."

(5) That, since the debtor can in the proceedings in question bring an action against the creditor in order to refute his claim, such action being in its nature and owing to its special form not an ordinary action but a means of defence against the claim of a creditor, the action is admissible against a foreign State whether the latter does or does not ordinarily enjoy immunity from suits. Refusal of leave to put in force the " execution clause " held to be wrong. [Reports : Zb. O.S.N., I, 1928/1, No. 28 ; R.P.E.S., 1928, p. 764.]

Case No. 109 **Jurisdiction—Exemptions from—Foreign States in their Public and Private Capacities—Union of Socialist Soviet Republics—Contract with a Greek National—Jurisdiction of Greek Courts.**

SOVIET REPUBLIC (IMMUNITY IN GREECE) CASE.

Court of Athens. 1928. *No.* 1681.

THE FACTS.—The Union of Socialist Soviet Republics sold to a Greek national 3500 oxen, cows and calves, by a contract containing a clause fixing penalties for non-performance or defective performance. The cattle were delivered in bad condition. The purchaser distrained in satisfaction upon property of the vendor within the jurisdiction, and now asked for a declaration that the distress was valid. In regard to the question of jurisdiction,

Held by the majority of the Court: That the Court had jurisdiction. The Union of Socialist Soviet Republics possesses in common with all other States all the indicia of a sovereign State. There is no reason to enquire into the details of its internal structure and organisation. The Union possesses all the attributes of sovereignty within the international field, such as the right of representation, both in the active and in the passive sense, inviolability, and immunity from jurisdiction for all the organs which represent it abroad.

However, when the Union chooses to act as the vendor of goods, it assumes the character of an *entrepreneur*, undertakes an ordinary piece of civil business and enters into a contract at municipal law. Its relations become then cognisable by the Greek courts, since the claimant is a Greek national invoking this jurisdiction to settle the question at issue. It must also be noted that by virtue of the contract the Union has voluntarily submitted to Greek jurisdiction. [Report: Themis, vol. 40, p. 486.]

NOTE.—This decision was upheld by the Areopagus on appeal: Areopagus, No. 29, Themis, vol. 40, p. 842.

Jurisdiction over a Foreign State—Act of Sovereignty of a Foreign State—Non-Recognition of State—Reprisals. **Case No. 110**

THE NATIONAL NAVIGATION COMPANY OF EGYPT *v.* TAVOULARIDIS.

Mixed Court of Alexandria. 9 *November*, 1927.

THE FACTS.—The plaintiffs demanded the seizure of two vessels of the Soviet Government, which were anchored in the port of Alexandria, as security for a claim which they had against the Soviet Government. A vessel of the plaintiffs flying the Egyptian flag had been seized on the high seas by members of the crew and conducted to Odessa, and there by decision of the Soviet Court of Odessa had been confiscated on the ground of its identity with a vessel which had belonged to the Soviet Commercial Fleet and which had been removed. An objection to the jurisdiction of the Mixed Courts was raised by the agent of the Soviet Government Fleet on the ground that there was no right to seize a vessel belonging to a foreign State, and that the Mixed Courts had no competence to consider the act which was alleged by the plaintiffs against the Soviet Government or the claim alleged to arise from that act.

Held: (1) However illegal may have been the act of the Soviet Government in employing force to seize the vessel of the plaintiff company, it was nevertheless a manifestation of the sovereign authority of the State.

(2) The legality of an act done by a foreign State cannot be tried by the courts of another State; and although this rule is subject to exceptions in a case where a State has acted as an individual or as a civil person, no exception can be raised when the basis of the action against the State is the exercise of the State's sovereign powers.

(3) The objection that the Soviet Government has not been recognised by the Egyptian State does not impair the prerogatives of the Soviet State which it exercises in fact, particularly when the courts are invited to give a decision against the Soviet Government acting as the representative of the Soviet State. Moreover, the agreement of the Soviet and Egyptian Governments by which the vessels of the Soviet Fleet were authorised to anchor in the port of Alexandria involves the

Case No. 110 *contd.*

application of the principles of international law with regard to jurisdiction over States in all transactions in which the vessels are concerned.

(4) The plaintiffs' claim, as justification for the seizure, was that a State which has been injured by the abusive exercise of the sovereign powers of another State may act in a similar way against that State by way of reprisals or retorsion. The right, however, to take measures in self-defence depends on the sovereign and exclusive authority of the Government, and must be applied by an act of the public power towards the property or the territory of the offending Government. The courts would be straying outside the limits of their powers if they should order for political reasons a measure not authorised by any provision in the civil law which they are required to administer. [Reports: *Gazette des Tribunaux Mixtes*, 19th year, 1929, p. 251. See also 57 *Clunet* (1930), p. 203.]

See *Annual Digest*, 1925-1926, Case No. 152.

Case No. 111

Jurisdiction—Exemption from—Foreign States—No Exemption as to Immovable Property—Execution of Awards of Mixed Arbitral Tribunals against Hungary before Czechoslovak Courts.

ENFORCEMENT OF INTERNATIONAL AWARDS (CZECHOSLOVAKIA) CASE.

Supreme Court of Justice of Czechoslovakia.
26 *April*, 1928.[1] *No. RI* 305.

THE FACTS.—The stipulations of the Treaties of Peace regarding the Mixed Arbitral Tribunals (Article 304 of the Treaty of Versailles, Article 256 of the Treaty of St. Germain, Article 239 of the Treaty of Trianon, Article 188 of the Treaty of Neuilly) were put into force as regards the Czechoslovak municipal sphere by the Czechoslovak Law of 28 April, 1922, No. 146, by which in respect of execution of the decisions of the Mixed Arbitral Tribunals it was provided (i) that those decisions shall have the same effect as final judgments, and (ii) that as regards their execution the provisions of the Czechoslovak law concerning the execution of judgments of the Czechoslovak courts shall apply to them.

The plaintiff before the Czechoslovak-Hungarian Mixed Arbitral Tribunal (a Czechoslovak national),

[1] The decision has been also quoted under the date of 8 May, 1928.

whose claim against the Hungarian State was recognised by the decisions of that Tribunal (of November 11, 1927, Nos. 5 and 9), ceded his claim to a bank. The bank applied to the Czechoslovak courts for execution [1] of the decisions of the Mixed Arbitral Tribunal by means of compulsory sale of certain immovable property of the Hungarian State situated in Czechoslovak territory.[2] The lower courts dismissed the application on formal grounds (in particular, on the ground that it was not proved that the claimant had taken appropriate steps with the competent Hungarian authorities to obtain payment). On appeal,

Held by the Supreme Court of Justice: That the decision of the lower courts must be quashed and the matter must be remitted to them for a new decision. According to Article 239 (*g*) of the Treaty of Trianon, the contracting parties agree to regard the decisions of the Mixed Arbitral Tribunal as final and conclusive, and to render them binding upon their nationals. The Law No. 146/1922, by which the stipulations of that Article are being put into force, is, in accordance with that Article, to be interpreted as regulating the execution of the decisions of the Mixed Arbitral Tribunal only against private individuals, and not against the contracting parties, as in international law there is up to the present no sort of judicial execution. Accordingly it would seem that it is not possible to admit execution against a foreign State. However, this is not so. The question turns on the object in regard to which the execution should be applied. In the decision of 8 April, 1927, No. RI 120 (Váž. 6976 civ.)[3] the principle of international law *immobilia obnoxia sunt territoriis* was elucidated in detail, and it was shown there that this principle applies without distinction, whether the immovable property belongs to a national or to a foreigner, and in that latter case, whether this foreigner is a private individual or a foreign sovereign or a foreign State, and that this principle governs both the rules of

[1] It might be noted that the question, hitherto controversial, of the modalities of payments to be made by the Hungarian State to the nationals of the Allied and Associated Powers by virtue of the decisions of the Mixed Arbitral Tribunals has now been regulated by the Accord (No. 1), signed at Paris, 28 April, 1930 (Eastern Reparations).

[2] The immovable property in question was identical with the building of the Hungarian Legation. This fact, however, was not raised either before the lower courts or before the Supreme Court of Justice in the present case. See Case No. 251.

[3] See Case No. 94.

Case No. 111 *contd.* competence of the courts and the rules of procedure. In respect of immovables, it is irrelevant whether their proprietor is a national or a foreigner, and in that latter case whether it is a foreigner enjoying the rights of exterritoriality, for instance, a foreign State. Consequently, Article IX, paragraph 2, of the Law of 1 August, 1895, No. 110, provides that the municipal jurisdiction applies to the immovable property of exterritorial persons.[1] Jurisdiction includes, however, both procedure and execution. Thus it appears that, as regards immovable property situated in the country, a foreign State is also to be considered as a private individual, and paragraph 33 of the Civil Code, which must be regarded as complementary to the provisions of Article 239 (*g*), provides that foreigners have the same civil obligations (*i.e.* obligations of private law) as nationals. All that leads to the conclusion that the immovable property of a foreign State situated in the country is subjected to execution in the same way as the immovable property of nationals. If it were a question of the property of a foreign State other than immovable property, the courts could not permit or order execution, as, in that case, the foreign State would not be placed on an equal footing with nationals. [Report: Váž. 8000 civ.]

NOTE.—In dealing with the question of the enforcement of the awards of the Mixed Arbitral Tribunals, the Court discussed the question whether these awards can be enforced before Czechoslovak courts against the Czechoslovak State. The Court denied the possibility of such an enforcement. It said:

" Both law and commonsense are opposed to such a solution. Why " should the State undertake the execution against itself of these " arbitral awards? Why should it not simply pay its debt? Surely " it would be the duty of the Government to fulfil the obligations arising " out of a decision recognised by it and not the duty of the courts to " compel their own State to fulfil these obligations. Further, it is " possible that the Government of a State does not recognise the award, " as may be seen for instance from Part I of the Peace Treaties, in " particular from the last paragraph of Article 13. It is laid down in this " paragraph that in cases in which the decision of the arbitral tribunal is " not given effect to by the parties, the Council of the League of Nations " shall recommend measures calculated to put the decision into effect. " Such a recommendation does not of course partake of the nature of a " judicial execution; it is rather tantamount to the exercise of pressure

[1] Article IX, paragraph 2, of the Law No. 110/1895 reads as follows (translation): " The municipal jurisdiction applies to persons who, in accordance " with the principles of international law, enjoy exterritoriality, if and in so " far as they voluntarily submit to the municipal courts, and if and in so far " as the matter concerns their immovables situated in the country or their " real rights upon immovables of other persons situated in the country."

" on the part of the Great Powers represented on the Council of the " League of Nations."

See on this case an article by Deák in *A.J.*, XXII (1929), pp. 582-594, criticising the decision of the Supreme Court of Justice, and by Bosco in *Rivista di diritto internazionale*, XXI (1929), p. 48. However, it should be noted that the judgment of the Supreme Court does not refer to the question of immunity of legation buildings. See below, Case No. 251.

Exemption of a Foreign State from Jurisdiction—Transactions Concluded as a Private Person—Breach of Contract Unconnected with Public Policy—Claim for Compensation from French State for Non-Payment for Goods—Jurisdiction of National Courts. **Case No. 112**

SOCIÉTÉ MONNOYER ET BERNARD *v.* FRANCE.

Charleroi Civil Court, Belgium. 8 April, 1927.

THE FACTS.—The plaintiff company claims damages, together with compensation for an adverse movement of the rate of exchange, against the State of France for alleged delay in payment for goods delivered to the Office of Industrial Reconstruction at Valenciennes. In reply, the defendant State denies the competence of the Court, maintaining that the agents of the Valenciennes Office had acted " in their character of public servants " of the French State, a public organ acting on behalf " of the public interest, and not in the character of " mandatories of the French State considered as a " private individual, acting for commercial advantage ; " hence, the principle of the sovereignty of States " renders the Court incompetent to hear the case."

Held : That the Court was competent.[1] " Even if it were " true that the French Government acted as a public organ " when it assumed by the Act of 6 August, 1917, the initiative " towards industrial reconstruction in the invaded regions " . . . " nevertheless, in seeking to accomplish this end after the " war, the French State was compelled to make purchases of " raw materials, machinery, etc.," . . . In transactions of this kind there can be no question of the power of a public organ, and the State can only act " in the capacity of a private individual." "And when, in this capacity, the State, after treating " the other contracting party on an equal footing, wishes to have

[1] The action was dismissed on other grounds.

Case No. 112 *contd.* " a dispute determined, or has itself been guilty of a breach of " the contract, not coming within the head of public policy, a " case exists raising questions of municipal law and solely " cognisable by the courts in accordance with Article 92 of the " Constitution." The Court, in taking cognisance of the present case, " does no injury to the sovereignty of France, but renders " judgment exactly as if the case concerned a French Citizen." [Reports: *Pasicrisie Belge*, 1927, III, p. 129 on; 55 *Clunet* (1928), p. 480, with note by L. Loewenthal.]

NOTE.—This decision is in line with a principle generally followed by the Belgian courts. See *Annual Digest*, 1925-1926, Case No. 120. It illustrates the principle which derives the competence of the courts to pass on cases affecting foreign States, not from the objects inspiring the enterprises undertaken by these States, but from the actual nature of the transactions and legal relations into which they have entered.

Case No. 113 **Jurisdiction Over Foreign States—Effect of Ownership of Immovable Property—Binding Force of International Law as a Subsidiary Source.**

FOREIGN STATES (LEGATION BUILDINGS) IMMUNITIES CASE.

Austrian Supreme Court in Civil Matters.
11 *September*, 1928.

THE FACTS.—The plaintiff met with an accident in the Czechoslovak Legation in Vienna. He brought an action for damages against the Czechoslovak Republic.

Held (*a*) By the court of first instance (the District Court of Hitzing): That the plea to the jurisdiction must be rejected as the defendant State owns immovable property in the district, and that therefore, according to paragraph 99 of the Regulations Concerning the Jurisdiction of Courts, the Court had jurisdiction.

(*b*) By the Court of Appeal (the Land Court for Civil Matters, Vienna): That the Austrian courts had no jurisdiction for the following reasons: The court of first instance had disregarded the fact that the applicability of paragraph 99 is dependent upon a decision of the preliminary question whether the defendant Republic is liable to the jurisdiction of Austrian courts in general. The Court of Appeal was of the opinion that " at present at least there are no reasons, in the absence of an " express submission of the foreign State to the jurisdiction, to " subject it to the jurisdiction of Austrian courts."

(*c*) By the Supreme Court: That the decision of the Court of Appeal must be upheld: "The Court is not prepared to "accept the more extreme view that, having regard to the "indivisibility of State sovereignty, a State can never be sub-"jected to the jurisdiction of the foreign court, regardless of "the fact whether the dispute arises out of the exercise of its "sovereign rights or of its activity as the subject of private law, "or whether it subjects itself expressly to the jurisdiction of "the foreign court. However, in regard to the building in "which the plaintiff met with an accident, the defendant State "is subject to Austrian jurisdiction only in so far as the case "affects the immovable property itself or any contract relating "thereto. Claims like the present one—in which it cannot be "said that the foreign State has availed itself of the legal pro-"visions of Austrian law and has therefore subjected itself to "its jurisdiction—do not come within the competence of the "Austrian courts. It is pointed out on the part of the appel-"lants that there is no express provision in Austrian law to the "effect that a foreign State is not subject to the jurisdiction of "Austrian courts. However, this is one of the fundamental "rules of international law which has a validity equal to that of "any other legal provision." [Report: *Decisions of the Austrian Supreme Court in Civil and Administrative Matters*, vol. 10, 1928, No. 177, pp. 427-429.]

Jurisdiction—Exemptions from—Foreign States—Contract by Ambassador for Purchase of Building for Embassy.

See Case No. 247 (*Perrucchetti* v. *Puig y Cassauro*).

States — Jurisdictional Immunities — States Members of Federal States.

See Case No. 21 (*State of Ceara* v. *Dorr*).

Jurisdiction—Exemption from—Foreign States—Exemption from Jurisdiction in respect of Immovable Property.

See Case No. 251 (*Immunity of Legation Buildings (Czechoslovakia) Case*) (which was decided upon its final hearing before the Supreme Court of Justice of Czechoslovakia without reference to the fact that the buildings formed the Legation of a foreign State).

(iv) Foreign Armed Forces

Case No. 114 **Jurisdiction—Exemptions from—Foreign Armed Forces—The Forces of the United States in the Panama Canal Zone.**

The Republic of Panama *v.* Wilbert L. Schwartzfiger.

Supreme Court of Justice of Panama. 11 *August*, 1925.

The Facts.—On 5 December, 1924, the American military authorities at France Field, Panama Canal Zone, ordered Wilbert L. Schwartzfiger, an American soldier, to convey to hospital in a motor ambulance a workman who had fallen from a scaffolding and sustained serious injuries. While carrying out the order, Schwartzfiger crossed the Panama city of Colon. In crossing the city, his car, driven at a speed in excess of that permitted by the regulations, struck a pillar and caused the death of a person. Schwartzfiger was indicted for involuntary manslaughter. The lower court, without quashing the process, ordered the termination of the proceedings on the ground that it had no jurisdiction.

By Articles 2, 3, 7, 9 and 23 of the Treaty between Panama and the United States of 18 November, 1903, Panama granted to the United States, among other rights and privileges, the use, occupation and control of waters and lands outside of the five miles on each side of the centre of the Canal for its operation, sanitation and protection (Article 2). In Article 23 the United States were given the right to use their military and naval forces for these purposes. On appeal,

Held by the Supreme Court: That the courts of Panama had no jurisdiction. The Court said: " In accordance with " the text of that Treaty, the Canal Zone authorities may " employ their forces, assigned for the protection of the Canal, " to assure the security, operation and sanitation of the same, " and in such case those forces, when acting in the name or on " behalf of the Government of the United States, are subject to " the authority and jurisdiction to which they belong, and not " to our national authorities; nor to both simultaneously, be- " cause such a double jurisdiction is contrary to law.

" It is a principle of international law that the armed forces " of one State, when crossing the territory of another friendly " country, with the acquiescence of the latter, are subject, not " to the jurisdiction of the territorial sovereign, but to that of " the officers and superior authorities of its own command.

" In such case the government to which the army belongs " is responsible for any damage that may be caused by the " passage of the force, and for any violations of local law which " it may commit. But individually its members remain sub- " ject to the jurisdiction of their own officers, and to the laws of " the country to which they belong.

" This exemption from the local jurisdiction is recognised by " all civilised nations ; and is not considered a diminution of " their sovereignty or independence." [Reports : *Official Judicial Register*, Republic of Panama, 18 August, 1926, vol. XXIV, pp. 772-775 ; *A.J.*, XXI (1927), p. 182.]

Foreign Army—Status of—Allied Armies in France during the War 1914-1918—Supplies for the Belgian Army—Tax upon Purveyor's Licence. **Case No. 115**

In re Pfister.

French Council of State. 20 *January*, 1928.

The Facts.—The applicant appealed against a decree of the Council of the Prefecture of a Department ordering him to pay a tax on his licence as purveyor to *administrations publiques* and *établissements publics.* The question concerned supplies furnished by him to the Belgian army in 1917, when it was in France.

Held : That the application must be rejected. " During " the war the allied armies stationed on French territory were " assimilated in matters of taxation to the national army . . . " and must be regarded as an *administration publique.*" [Report : 55 *Clunet* (1928), p. 1188.]

II.—Personal

(a) Over Subjects in Respect of Crimes Committed outside the Realm

Jurisdiction—Territorial—Crimes Originating Abroad and Consummated in the National Territory. **Case No. 116**

Claramont *v.* United States.

United States Circuit Court of Appeals, Fifth Circuit. 15 *June*, 1928.

The Facts.—This was a prosecution for unlawfully counselling and procuring the bringing into and landing in

Case No. 116 *contd.*

the United States from Cuba of an alien not entitled to enter. The defendant participated in the transactions in Cuba. He was convicted. On writ of error,

Held: That the conviction should be affirmed. " For such " participation in the criminal offence charged in . . . the " indictment, amounting to the counselling and procuring " alleged, Claramont was criminally liable, though he was not " physically present in the United States when the alleged " unlawful transaction was begun and consummated. By so " procuring the commission by other accused of the offence " charged, Claramont became amenable to the criminal laws " of the United States, though at the time he was beyond its " jurisdiction." [Report: 26 F. (2nd) 797.]

NOTE.—Whether Claramont was an American citizen or not does not appear and (it is submitted) does not matter, see *Ford* v. *United States*: *Annual Digest*, 1925-1926, Case No. 110.

On the question of jurisdiction in regard to crimes originating abroad and consummated in the national territory, see Dickinson, *Cases*, pp. 656 (n.), 670 (n.), *Adams* v. *The People*, 1 Comstock (N.Y.) 173, *Reg.* v. *Nillins* (1884), 53 L.J.M.C. 157, and others referred to by Judge Moore in his Dissenting Opinion in the *Lotus* case, P.C.I.J., Series A, No. 10, pp. 77-80. And see the Judgment of the Court, *ibid.*, pp. 29, 30.—[Ed.]

Case No. 117

Jurisdiction—Territorial—Illegal Acts within the Jurisdiction Combined with Foreign Governmental Action.

UNITED STATES *v.* SISAL SALES CORPORATION.

United States Supreme Court. 16 *May*, 1927.

THE FACTS.—This was a suit by the United States to enjoin an alleged combination and conspiracy to monopolise the importation and sale of sisal in the United States. The suit was brought under the Sherman Anti-trust Act and the Wilson Tariff Act as amended. Sisal is produced almost exclusively in Yucatan, a province of Mexico. The defendants were United States and Mexican corporations and their officers and agents and other individuals. The Governments of Mexico and Yucatan aided the combination by passing discriminatory legislation. The trial court dismissed the bill in reliance on *American Banana Co.* v. *United Fruit Co.*, 213 U.S. 347. On appeal,

Held: That the judgment dismissing the suit should be

reversed. Delivering the Opinion of the Court, Mr. Justice McReynolds said : " The circumstances of the present contro- " versy are radically different from those presented in *American* " *Banana Co.* v. *United Fruit Co., supra,* and the doctrine there " approved is not controlling here. The Banana Company " sued for treble damages under the Sherman Act, basing its " claim upon acts done outside the United States and not " unlawful by the law of the place. . . . Here we have a con- " tract, combination and conspiracy entered into by parties " within the United States and made effective by acts done " therein. The fundamental object was control of both impor- " tation and sale of sisal and complete monopoly of both internal " and external trade and commerce therein. The United States " complain of a violation of their laws within their own terri- " tory by parties subject to their jurisdiction, not merely of " something done by another government at the instigation of " private parties. True, the conspirators were aided by dis- " criminating legislation, but by their own deliberate acts, here " and elsewhere, they brought about forbidden results within " the United States. They are within the jurisdiction of our " courts and may be punished for offences against our laws." (274 U.S. 268, 275, 276.) [Report : 274 U.S. 268.]

(b) Over Subjects Abroad or on the High Seas and their Property Situated Abroad

Jurisdiction—Injunction to Restrain Party within the Jurisdiction from Enforcing Judgment Obtained in Foreign State. **Case No. 118**

ELLERMAN LINES LIMITED (plaintiffs) *v.* READ AND OTHERS (defendants).

English Court of Appeal on appeal from the King's Bench Division of the High Court of Justice. 31 *January,* 1928.

THE FACTS.—The main facts were that the defendants had rendered salvage services to a British steamer ashore on the coast of Roumania and had floated her and taken her to Constantinople, and that one of them, in breach of an agreement to permit the vessel to leave Constantinople after security had been given for the payment of salvage remuneration in the form of a guarantee deposited with the Committee of Lloyd's, had caused the vessel to be arrested under a

Case No. 118 *contd.*

process of the Turkish Court at Constantinople, and had obtained judgment for an excessive sum by means of fraud.

Held: That an injunction must issue to restrain the defendants from taking steps to enforce the judgment of the Turkish Court.

Although an English court would not seek to assume jurisdiction over the courts of a foreign State, it does not consider itself to be precluded from granting an injunction to restrain a party to proceedings in a foreign court from enforcing a judgment which he has obtained there and which in the opinion of the English court it would be unconscientious and inequitable on his part to seek to enforce. (Scrutton and Atkin, L.JJ. and Eve, J.)

Per Atkin, L.J. (at p. 155): "The principle on which the "English court acts in granting injunctions is not that it seeks "to assume jurisdiction over the foreign court, or that it arrogates to itself some superiority which entitles it to dictate to "the foreign court, or that it seeks to criticise the foreign "court or its procedure; the English court has regard to the "personal attitude of the person who has obtained the foreign "judgment." [Report: L.R. [1928] 2 K.B. 144.]

Editors' Note.—This decision deals mainly with a question of Private International Law, but deserves a brief mention in this volume by reason of its connection with the question of Jurisdiction. Stress is laid upon the fact that the defendant who had fraudulently obtained the judgment of a foreign court was a British subject, but the essential requirement appears to be that the person enjoined should be a person "subject to the English jurisdiction," see p. 152.

Case No. 119

Jurisdiction—Personal—Crimes Committed upon National Ships in Foreign Ports.

United States *v.* Mathues.

United States District Court, E.D. Pennsylvania. United States Circuit Court of Appeals, Third Circuit. 10 September, 1927. 27 June, 1928.

The Facts.—This was a petition for habeas corpus. Relator was indicted for an offence arising out of homicide committed on board a United States vessel tied by cables to the wharf in an Italian port. Relator was a seaman on the vessel.

Held: That relator should be discharged. United States Criminal Code, § 272, providing for the punishment of homicides " committed upon the high seas, or . . . within the admiralty and maritime jurisdiction of the United States and " out of the jurisdiction of any particular state, . . . on board " any vessel belonging in whole or in part to the United States " or any citizen thereof " did not apply where the offence was committed on a United States vessel moored to a wharf in a foreign port. On appeal,

Held by the Circuit Court of Appeals: That the judgment of the District Court should be affirmed. [Reports: 21 F. (2nd) 533; 27 F. (2nd) 518.]

NOTE.—The nationality of the seaman does not appear from the report.—[Ed.]

Jurisdiction—Jurisdiction of National Courts over Nationals in regard to Actions Concerning Immovable Property Abroad. **Case No. 120**

JURISDICTION OVER IMMOVABLE PROPERTY (AUSTRIA) CASE.

Austrian Supreme Court in Civil Cases. 22 February, 1927. Ob. II, 129/27.

THE FACTS.—The plaintiff had immovable property in Italy. There was in the Italian Land Registry a notice in favour of the defendant to the effect that the plaintiff owed him a sum of money. The plaintiff contended that this sum had been paid, and brought an action with a view to procuring in Austria the deletion of the entry in the Italian Registry. The defendant resided in Austria.

Held by the court of first instance: That the court had no jurisdiction. The competent court was the one in which the immovable property was situated.

Held by the Court of Appeal and the Supreme Court: That Austrian courts had jurisdiction. " There is no legal provision " or principle of international law which says that the defendant " who is resident in Austria is not subject to Austrian jurisdiction on the ground that the object of the suit is immovable " property situated abroad." [Report: *Entscheidungen des Obersten Gerichtshofes in Zivil- und Justizverwaltungssachen,* vol. IX (1927), No. 53, pp. 134, 135.]

Jurisdiction—Territorial—In respect of Legation Buildings Abroad.

See Case No. 252 (*In re Zoltán Sz.*).

Jurisdiction—In respect of Contract as to Immovable Property Abroad—Effect of Cession Subsequent to Contract.

See Case No. 78 (*J. Madár & Company* v. *P. Stannberger & Company*).

Case No. 121 **Jurisdiction—High Seas—National Ships—Operation of the National Law on National Ships—Exterritorial Operation of Municipal Statute.**

UNITED STATES SHIPPING BOARD EMERGENCY FLEET CORPORATION *v.* GREENWALD.

United States Circuit Court of Appeals, Second Circuit.
10 *January*, 1927.

THE FACTS.—This was an action by an administratrix to recover compensation for death resulting from the defendant's wrongful act. The intestate was a seaman on a United States Shipping Board vessel. He was made ill by bad food while the vessel was on the high seas and died in the British dependency of Gold Coast, Africa. Judgment for plaintiff. On writ of error,

Held: That the judgment for plaintiff should be affirmed. The case was governed by a statute of the District of Columbia permitting an action in case of death by wrongful act. Delivering the Opinion of the Court, Judge Manton said: "But this "merchant ship on the high seas is of the country of the flag she "flies, and the law of the flag applies to the right of action which "arose on the high seas." "The statute of the District of "Columbia says: 'Whenever by an injury done or happen- "'ing within the limits of the District of Columbia the death "'of a person shall be caused by the wrongful act, neglect, "'or default of any person or corporation, . . .' suit may "be maintained and the recovery is limited to $10,000. "31 Stat. 1394, c. 854, §§ 1301, 1302, 1303. Jurisdiction and the "laws of the nation accompany the ship, not only over the "high seas, but also in the ports and harbors, and every- "where else they may be water-borne. *United States* v. "*Rodgers*, 150 U.S. 249, 14 S. Ct. 109, 37 L. Ed. 1071. This

" ship was within the district as contemplated by the statute " when on the high seas, since she was a vessel of the District " of Columbia, resident and registry. This seaman was under " the protection of that flag, and his administratrix is entitled " to the benefits of that statute." (16 F. (2nd) 948, 950, 951.) [Report: 16 F. (2nd) 948.]

NOTE.—The exterritorial operation of a municipal statute must depend mainly upon its wording. There is no doubt that a British statute can be made to operate so far as British subjects are concerned outside the United Kingdom and its territorial waters; whether it does or not is a question of construction, see Craies on *Statute Law*, 3rd ed., 1923, pp. 373-407.

Jurisdiction—High Seas—National Ships—Seizure of a United States Vessel by United States Coastguard. **Case No. 122**

MAUL *v.* UNITED STATES.

United States Supreme Court. 31 May, 1927.

THE FACTS.—This was a proceeding commenced in the United States District Court to forfeit a United States vessel seized by the coastguard 34 miles from the coast for violation of provisions of the United States Revised Statutes governing vessels licensed for the coasting trade. An exception to the jurisdiction was sustained in the District Court on the theory that the coastguard was without authority to seize the vessel at sea more than 12 miles from the coast. The decree was reversed by the Circuit Court of Appeals. On certiorari,

Held: That the decree of the Circuit Court of Appeals should be affirmed. The Court reviewed United States statutes defining the powers of the coastguard and concluded that there was authority to make the seizure. Delivering the Opinion of the Court, Mr. Justice Van Devanter said: " If Congress were " without power to provide for the seizure of such vessels on the " high sea, a restrictive construction might be justified. But " there is no want of power in this regard. The high sea is " common to all nations and foreign to none; and every nation " having vessels there has power to regulate them and also to " seize them for a violation of its laws."[1] (274 U.S. 501, 511.) [Report: 274 U.S. 501.]

[1] Followed in *United States* v. *Lee*, in the United States Supreme Court (31 May, 1927). This was a prosecution for conspiracy to violate the United

Case No. 122 *contd.*

NOTE.—While dissenting from the construction of the statute on which the majority Opinion was based, Justices Brandeis and Holmes concurred in the decision on the ground that the coastguard's authority should be implied as an incident of " the police duties of ocean patrol " imposed by Congress. The concurring Opinion contains a valuable review of United States legislation with respect to police duties of ocean patrol.

Case No. 123

Jurisdiction—High Seas—National Ships—Territorial Character of Ships.

WONG OCK JEE *v.* WEEDIN.

United States Circuit Court of Appeals, Ninth Circuit.
19 *March*, 1928.

THE FACTS.—This was a petition for habeas corpus. Petitioner was born in China of Chinese parents. His father was a Chinese merchant domiciled in the United States. He received a visa as minor son of a resident merchant from the United States consul at Hong-Kong, and sailed on the first vessel leaving Hong-Kong for Seattle. The vessel reached Seattle the day after he became twenty-one years of age. He claimed the right to admission as minor son of a resident merchant. He was excluded by the immigration authorities. Judgment for defendant (the immigration officer). On appeal,

Held: That the judgment denying the writ should be affirmed. Delivering the Opinion of the Court, Judge Dietrich said: " Appellant's case falls within neither the letter of the " rule nor the reasoning of the decisions defining the rights of " the members of a merchant's family. Nor do we find in the " fact that, while he was still a minor, he obtained a visa and " boarded a ship of American registry, any reason for enlarging " the rule. The American consul was without authority to " admit him to the United States or to determine his right to " admission. The visa only operated to enable him to make

States Tariff and Prohibition Acts. Defendant was an American citizen. He was arrested on the high seas outside the 12-mile limit, and convicted on evidence found on the vessel seized. On writ of error the Circuit Court of Appeals vacated the judgment on the ground that evidence had been admitted which was obtained by illegal search and seizure. On certiorari it was held that the judgment of the Circuit Court of Appeals should be reversed. " Officers of the Coastguard are authorized, by virtue of Revised Statutes, " § 3072, to seize on the high seas beyond the twelve-mile limit an American " vessel subject to forfeiture for violation of any law respecting the revenue." (274 U.S. 559, 562.) Citing *Maul* v. *United States*, 274 U.S. 501. [Report: 274 U.S. 559.]

" application for admission, at a port of entry, to officers em-
" powered to determine his right. In a metaphorical sense a
" vessel upon the high seas is sometimes spoken of as consti-
" tuting a part of the territory of the country whose flag she
" flies; but this is only for restricted purposes. . . . And
" neither any treaty nor statute suggests the notion that, upon
" boarding an American vessel, either in foreign waters or upon
" the high seas, an alien is deemed to have entered the United
" States." (24 F. (2nd) 962, 963.) [Report: 24 F. (2nd) 962.]

Jurisdiction—High Seas—Law Governing the Flag—Territoriality of Ships.

See Case No. 98 (*The Case of the S.S. Lotus*) (*B-D*).

High Seas—Territorial Character of Ships.

See Case No. 192 (*In re Lam Mow*).

B. EXTRATERRITORIAL JURISDICTION

I.—Consular Jurisdictions. Régime of Capitulations. Mixed Courts. Jurisdiction and Organisation

Consular Jurisdiction—Crime Committed by an Italian Subject in a Country under the Régime of Capitulations—Assimilation to a Crime Committed on National Territory. **Case No. 124**

In re Durante.

Italian Criminal Court of Cassation (*Second Division*).
21 *October*, 1927.

The Facts.—The Italian Consular Tribunal of Cairo, Egypt, on 6 August, 1926, found the Italian subject, Amedeo Durante, guilty of bigamy and sentenced him to eighteen months' imprisonment. The Court of Appeal of Ancona upheld this sentence on 18 February, 1927. Durante appealed on the ground that the conviction was contrary to Article 5 of the Penal Code, the crime having been committed by an Italian subject on foreign territory.

Case No. 124 *contd.*

Held : That the appeal failed. The Court once more confirms the principle which it applied many times before (see *Annual Digest*, 1925-1926, Cases Nos. 142, 143) and which is based not on the justly repudiated legal fiction that the territory subjected to the régime of capitulations has to be considered as part of the national territory, but on the substantial ground that Italian law is applied therein by the effective exercise of the function of sovereignty. Justice being administered in the territory where the crime has been committed by means of national magistrates and in accordance with national law, it would be absurd to maintain that the crime has been committed in a foreign country : Article 5 cannot, therefore, be invoked. It seems impossible to agree with the appellant that the consular judge, who is an Italian judge, ought to consider a crime as perpetrated abroad, while in truth it had been committed in his own jurisdiction, and that he should also overlook the social disturbance resulting from it by treating it as if the place of the crime had been far away, whereas it had been perpetrated in the very environment and among the very citizens for whom and in the interest of whom he has to administer the law. It seems only fair and reasonable that an accused person who is not subjected either to a foreign judge or to a foreign law should not have his responsibility lessened on this account ; and that he should not, with regard to the prosecution of the crime, be subject to treatment different from that prescribed for any other citizen committing an offence at home. [Reports : *Rivista di diritto internazionale*, 1928, pp. 408-409; *Foro italiano*, 1928, II, p. 86 ; *Monitore dei Tribunali*, 1928, p. 118.]

Note.—This view of the Italian Court of Cassation according to which, for penal purposes, territories subjected to the régime of capitulations are to be considered Italian territories will no longer be possible on the coming into force of the new Penal Code whose Article 4 provides that " State territory is the territory of the Kingdom, the territory of " the colonies and any other territory subjected to the sovereignty of " the State." It follows that the countries under the régime of capitulations will have to be considered for every purpose with regard to their relations to the Italian State as " alien territories." This will be in accordance with the fact that the jurisdictional activity of the consuls is exercised *ratione personae* and not *ratione loci*. See also, to the same effect : *Sampo* (appellant), Italian Criminal Court of Cassation (Second Division), 12 November, 1928. [Report : *Foro italiano*, 1929, II, p. 127.]

On the British attitude towards consular jurisdiction exercised in non-British territory see Hall, *Foreign Jurisdiction of the British Crown* (1894), and Jenkyns, *British Rule and Jurisdiction Beyond the Seas* (1902).

Jurisdiction—Extraterritorial—Consular Court Purporting to sit under Authority of Extinct Government—Effect of its Judgments in Foreign Court. **Case No. 125**

HERZFELD (plaintiff) *v.* RUSSIAN VOLUNTEER FLEET (defendants).

English High Court of Justice (*King's Bench Division*). 28 *May*, 1928.

(MR. JUSTICE MACKINNON.)

THE FACTS.—The plaintiff Herzfeld, whose address was in Paris, sued the defendants, whose address was in London, to recover the sum of £9000 upon what was alleged to be a judgment of the Russian Consular Court at Constantinople dated 24 June, 1921, given in an action brought by the plaintiff against the defendants. The debt was alleged to have been due in respect of certain arrangements for chartering the defendants' steamers.

Held: That there was not enough evidence on which the learned judge could hold that the so-called Russian Consular Court was " a Court of competent jurisdiction, the judgment of " which he ought to enforce here," and that this ground of the plaintiff's action must fail.

" It was quite clear " (said the learned judge at p. 167) " that that Court in appearance and in pretence was a con- " tinuing operation of the old Russian Consular Court that had " existed under the Imperial régime. They used the seal and " referred to the Court as the Russian Consular Court. There " was no seal and no Consulate opened by the Soviet Govern- " ment, and in fact the judges who were sitting in that Con- " sular Court were refugees of General Wrangel's party. " Counsel for the plaintiff relied strongly on the fact that in " some circumstances the decrees of the pseudo-Russian " Consular Court were at this time sometimes enforced by the " Allied police acting under the orders of General Harington " and the French and Italian commanders. That, counsel " for the plaintiff said, was a recognition that the Court had " proper jurisdiction. His lordship did not think that was " a proper inference."

Great Britain had recognised the Soviet Government as the Government of Russia on 16 March, 1921, but the learned judge while mentioning this fact does not, at any rate expressly, rest his judgment upon it.

Case No. 125 *contd.* Upon the plaintiff's alternative claim on the merits, and apart from any question of enforcing the foreign judgment, the Court gave judgment in favour of the plaintiff. The case is mentioned again in 22 Lloyd's List Law Reports, at p. 479, upon a question of security of costs on appeal, but the appeal seems to have been abandoned. [Report: 22 Lloyd's List Law Reports, at p. 166.]

Case No. 126 **Capitulations—Denunciation during the War by the Ottoman Government—Effect of the Treaty of Lausanne.**

SYRIAN CAPITULATIONS (DENUNCIATION BY TURKEY) CASE.

Court of Appeal, Beirut, Syria. 16 *June*, 1926.

THE FACTS.—In this case a question arose as to the effect of a judgment given by the Commercial Tribunal of Constantinople, on 11 June, 1918, against a Greek subject. This Tribunal had declared the bankruptcy which had been pronounced at Alexandria on 20 November, 1911, against a person domiciled there to be of no effect in regard to creditors in Constantinople who had attached the current account of the bankrupt in Constantinople. It was now argued that the judgment of the Turkish Tribunal, which was given by a bench composed entirely of Turkish judges, was null and void because the composition of the Court was contrary to the provisions of the Capitulations; and the denunciation of the Capitulations by the Turkish Government at the outbreak of the Great War was contrary to international law and of no effect.

Held: The judgment of the Turkish Court must be treated by the Syrian courts as non-existent on account of the violation of international treaties. One State which is a party to a treaty cannot, by a unilateral declaration, denounce the treaty which is a contract made with other Powers. It cannot be maintained that the legislative acts which followed on the conclusion of the Treaty of Lausanne could give any retrospective effect to the abrogation of the Capitulations. The law cannot retroactively affect any acquired right; and the syndic of the bankruptcy pronounced at Alexandria had an acquired right to treat as non-existent the judgment of the Turkish Tribunal relating to the bankruptcy of a Greek subject with which it was incompetent to deal: [Report: *Gazette des Tribunaux Libano-Syriens*, Third year, 1928, p. 121.]

NOTE.—The Court of Appeal rejected the argument of the appellants that Article 28 of the Treaty of Lausanne, which provides for the complete abrogation of the Capitulations, has a retroactive effect. The Court pointed out that whenever that Treaty intended a retroactive effect for its provisions, it said so expressly, *e.g.* in Article 69. The Court drew attention to the fact that the Mandatory Power of Syria expressly recognised that the Turkish Capitulations should remain in force in the mandated territory until 1 November, 1923.—[Ed].

Jurisdiction—In respect of Crimes Committed in Territories under Consular Jurisdiction.

See Case No. 124 (*In re Durante*).

Capitulations—Jurisdiction of Mixed Tribunals in Egypt over Egyptian State in Matter of Taxation.

See Case No. 227 (*Egyptian Government* v. *Nicolas Zintzos*).

Capitulations—Position of Russians in Egypt—Non-Recognition of Soviet Government.

See Case No. 40 (*Hergenstein* v. *Public Prosecutor of the Native Courts*).

C. HIGH SEAS

II.—Jurisdiction on the High Seas

[See also JURISDICTION.]

iii.—Visit, Search and Arrest by Men-of-War in Time of Peace

Jurisdiction—High Seas—Foreign Ships—Search and Seizure Contrary to International Law. **Case No. 127**

UNITED STATES *v.* FERRIS.

United States District Court, N.D. California, S.D.
20 April, 1927.

THE FACTS.—These were indictments for conspiracy to violate the United States Tariff and Prohibition Acts. The defendants were taken from a British-owned ship of Panama registry 270 miles off the west coast of the United States. On pleas to the jurisdiction,

Case No. 127 *contd.*

Held: That the pleas should be sustained. Search and seizure on the high seas are governed by international law. Between Panama and the United States they are governed by the Treaty of 1924 (43 U.S. Stat. L. 1875). Delivering the Opinion of the Court, Judge Bourquin said: " As the instant " seizure was far outside the limit, it is sheer aggression and " trespass (like those which contributed to the War of 1812), " contrary to the treaty, not to be sanctioned by any court, " and cannot be the basis of any proceeding adverse to de- " fendants." (19 F. (2nd) 925, 926.) One illegally before the court in violation of a treaty cannot be subjected to trial. [Report: 19 F. (2nd) 925.]

v.—Right of Pursuit

Case No. 128

Jurisdiction—High Seas—Foreign Ships—Hot Pursuit—Conditions of.

THE VINCES.

United States District Court, E.D. South Carolina. United States Circuit Court of Appeals, Fourth Circuit. 13 *June*, 1927. 12 *June*, 1928.

THE FACTS.—This was a suit to assess penalties against the British vessel *Vinces* and to forfeit her cargo of liquor for violation of the United States Tariff Act of 1922. The vessel cleared from Halifax ostensibly for Nassau. She was intercepted by the United States coastguard when headed for the Carolina coast at a point approximately $7\frac{1}{2}$ miles from shore, and was captured after pursuit at a point approximately $12\frac{3}{4}$ miles from shore. She carried no manifest of cargo.

Held: That penalties should be assessed and forfeiture decreed. Delivering the Opinion of the Court, Judge Cochran said: " Every nation has the inherent right to protect itself and " to provide for the enforcement of its laws and the security " of its territorial jurisdiction. For the purpose of self- " protection and the due execution of its laws, and for the pre- " vention of frauds on its revenue, it may exercise an authority " on the high seas beyond the 3-mile limit " (20 F. (2nd) 164, 172), citing *Church* v. *Hubbart*, 2 Cr. (U.S.) 187, and other cases. The exercise of this right in the United States is determined by the executive and legislative departments of government. These departments have provided by legislation for searches and seizures under certain limitations within a 12-mile limit. The legislation thus provided was not abrogated by the liquor smuggling treaty with Great Britain. The principle of "hot pursuit" is applicable to seizures outside the 12-mile limit for violations of such legislation after pursuit commenced inside the 12-mile limit. It was suggested that "hot pursuit" might be applicable also where pursuit is commenced within the one-hour sailing zone under the liquor smuggling treaties and the seizure is made outside the zone. On appeal,

Held by the Circuit Court of Appeals: That the decree of the District Court should be affirmed. Delivering the Opinion of the Court, Judge Parker said: "We think it is clear, under "the 'hot pursuit' doctrine, that if the right of seizure existed "at the time the vessel was signalled, the right was not lost "because she had succeeded in getting farther from shore in "her attempt to run away. . . .

"While it is true, as contended, that the vessel never came "within the 3-mile limit of the territorial waters of the United "States, we think that, as she was bound for the United States "with an unmanifested cargo and came within 12 miles, or "4 marine leagues, of the coast, her seizure was justified under "the revenue statutes of the United States, and that these "statutes constitute a valid exercise of the sovereign power of "the government. . . .

"We think it equally clear that these statutes are valid, "notwithstanding the fact that the territorial boundaries of "the United States extend only to the 3-mile limit. Such pro- "visions have been a part of every tariff act passed by Congress "beginning with the statute of 1790 (1 Stat. 145) which intro- "duced the 4-league limit (section 31) of the British hovering "statutes. While in effect an assertion of extraterritorial "jurisdiction, they are justified on the ground that they are "necessary to territorial security and the proper enforcement "of the laws of the country." (27 F. (2nd) 296, 299.) [Reports: 20 F. (2nd) 164; 27 F. (2nd) 296.]

NOTE.—For comment on this case, see Masterson, *Jurisdiction in Marginal Seas* (1929), *passim*. The question of "hot pursuit" also arose in the sinking of the *I'm Alone* on 22 March, 1929, which is still the subject of negotiation between the United States of America and Canada.—[Ed.]

Case No. 129

Jurisdiction—High Seas—Foreign Ships—Hot Pursuit.

The Newton Bay.

United States District Court, E.D. New York.
16 *November*, 1928.

The Facts.—This was a libel to forfeit a British vessel under the United States Tariff Act of 1922, § 584. The vessel was found at anchor about 8½ miles from shore with a cargo of liquor. After pursuit she was captured about 13 miles from shore. The Court was satisfied that she was bound for the United States with her cargo.

Held: That forfeiture should be decreed. Delivering the Opinion of the Court, Judge Inch said: "If the right to seize "the *Newton Bay*, because of an absence of a manifest, under "the circumstances, existed, this right was not lost because "she had succeeded in getting further than 12 miles from shore "in her continuous attempt to escape before she was over-"taken. *Gillam* v. *U.S.* (C.C.A.) 27 F. (2nd) 296." (30 F. (2nd) 444, 445.) [Report: 30 F. (2nd) 444.]

Note.—See *The Vinces* (1927), 20 F. (2nd) 164; Case No. 128 in this volume.—[Ed.]

vi.—Enforcement of Hovering, Revenue and other Municipal Laws

Case No. 130

Jurisdiction—High Seas—Foreign Ships.

The Sylvia II.

United States District Court, D. Massachusetts.
6 *August*, 1928.

The Facts.—These were libels to forfeit a cargo of liquor and impose penalties upon a British vessel for violation of the United States revenue laws. The vessel was seized a little outside the 12-mile limit. She did not intend to discharge her cargo inside the 12-mile limit.

Held: That the libels should be dismissed. The vessel was not bound for the United States within the meaning of the Tariff Act of 1922. The Act does not apply to a vessel whose cargo is destined to the United States by trans-shipment on the high seas outside the 12-mile limit. *United States* v. *Bengochea*, 279 Fed. 537, and *United States* v. 63 *Kegs of Malt*, 27 F. (2nd) 741, distinguished. [Report: 28 F. (2nd) 215.]

Jurisdiction—High Seas—Foreign Ships—Jurisdiction, under the Tariff Act of 1922, over a Cargo Destined to the United States by Discharge into Contact Boats. **Case No. 131**

UNITED STATES *v.* 63 KEGS OF MALT.

United States Circuit Court of Appeals, Second Circuit.
2 *July*, 1928.

THE FACTS.—This was a libel to forfeit the unmanifested cargo of liquor of a British vessel for violation of United States revenue laws. The vessel was seized about 11 miles from the United States coast. The District Court dismissed the libel. On appeal,

Held: That the decree of the District Court should be reversed. A foreign vessel carrying liquor destined for the United States by discharge into contact boats, and intercepted within the 12-mile limit, is bound for the United States within the meaning of the provisions of the Tariff Act of 1922, §§ 581-584, providing for the forfeiture of unmanifested cargo. [Report: 27 F. (2nd) 741.]

Jurisdiction—High Seas—Foreign Ships. **Case No. 132**

THE GEORGE AND EARL.

United States District Court, E.D. New York.
16 *November*, 1928.

THE FACTS.—This was a libel to forfeit a British ship and her cargo of liquor under the United States Tariff Act of 1922, § 584. The ship was intercepted outside the 3-mile limit when headed away from shore, though, as it was alleged, still within the 12-mile limit.

Held: That the libel should be dismissed. Since there was nothing to show that the vessel was bound for the United States, there was no right to seize her for failure to produce a manifest. [Report: 30 F. (2nd) 441.]

D. MISCELLANEOUS

Case No. 133 **Jurisdiction—Miscellaneous—Collision between Foreign Ships of Different Nationalities in Foreign Waters.**

ROYAL MAIL STEAM PACKET CO. *v.* COMPANHIA DE NAVEGACAO LLOYD BRASILEIRO.

United States District Court, E.D. New York. 15 *May*, 1928.

THE FACTS.—This was a suit by a British corporation against a Brazilian corporation in a case of collision between their respective vessels occurring in Belgian waters. Jurisdiction in the United States was acquired by attachment of another of respondent's vessels. The Belgian pre-war law permitting respondent to limit liability to 200 francs per gross ton was still in force and had not been revised to accord with the depreciation of the franc. The respondent wished to have the case adjudicated in Belgium. Motions were made to vacate the attachment and dismiss the libel.

Held : That the motions should be denied and jurisdiction retained. In order that full justice might be done, the case should be retained and tried in the United States Court. See also 31 F. (2nd) 757. [Report : 27 F. (2nd) 1002.]

NOTE.—As to the jurisdiction of the English Admiralty Court in cases of collision in foreign waters, see Dicey, *Conflict of Laws*, 4th ed., 1927, Appendix, note 11, p. 869.—[Ed.]

Case No. 134 **Jurisdiction—Miscellaneous—Jurisdiction over a Non-Resident Foreigner by Reason of Submission.**

NEPTUN *v.* J. H. JONGMAN.

Supreme Court of Sweden. 15 *March*, 1928.

THE FACTS.—A Swedish salvage company rescued a Dutch steamer which had run ashore in the Gulf of Bothnia outside Swedish territorial waters, and the vessel was thereupon brought into a Finnish harbour. Before the salvage, the captain had entered into a contract with the company which contained a stipulation that if the salvage money could not be settled by amicable agreement, the case was to be decided by the Court of Stockholm.

Later the company brought a suit in the aforesaid Swedish Court against the captain for the salvage money.

It was admitted that the captain, who was Dutch, had never resided in Sweden, that the writ had been served on him in Amsterdam, and that after the salvage the vessel had never been in Sweden, but the captain declared that he had no objection to the case being dealt with and decided by the Court.

The Court, quoting several provisions of Swedish municipal law, held that it had no jurisdiction.

Held : " As the captain had appeared before the Court and " made no objection to its jurisdiction, and it was not a case " where the Court ought to decline jurisdiction *ex officio*, the " case must be remitted to the Court of Stockholm for re- " hearing." [Report : *Nytt juridiskt Arkiv*, 1928, p. 149.]

NOTE.—The decision of the Supreme Court of Sweden implied a recognition of the general rule in international law that, in addition to the compulsory jurisdiction which is independent of the consent of the defendant, the courts of the country can assume jurisdiction even over a non-resident foreigner by his submission to the courts.

PART V

STATE RESPONSIBILITY

A. WHERE DOES RESPONSIBILITY REST IN FEDERAL AND OTHER COMPOSITE STATES?

State Responsibility—Responsibility of a Federal State for the Contracts of a Member State. **Case No. 135**

ROSENSTEIN *v.* GERMANY.

Roumanian-German Mixed Arbitral Tribunal.

17 *January*, 1927.

(FAZY, FROELICH, ANTONIADE.)

THE FACTS.—This was a claim for damages arising out of the cancellation of a contract concluded by the claimant, a Roumanian subject, with the State of Hamburg.

Held: That the claim, so far as it is directed against Germany, must be rejected. The State of Hamburg, which alone is a party to the contract, possesses a juridical personality distinct from that of the German State, which, in this case, has declined to accept responsibility for the cancellation of the contract. [Report: *Recueil*, VII, p. 121.]

NOTE.—Time was granted to the claimant to amend the claim so as to make the State of Hamburg the direct defendant.

B. NATURE AND KINDS OF STATE RESPONSIBILITY

I.—In General. When does State Responsibility become Engaged? Absolute Responsibility and Responsibility based on Fault.

State Responsibility for Acts of a Government *de jure*—Criterion for Existence of Government *de jure*—Relevance of Recognition *de jure* by Foreign Powers—Form and Substance of Legality. **Case No. 136**

GEORGES PINSON CASE, § 51.

France and Mexico: Mixed Claims Commission.

19 *October*, 1928.

(VERZIJL, President.)

THE FACTS.—In virtue of the French-Mexican Claims Convention of 1924 Mexico was liable to award damages

Case No. 136 *contd.*

for losses caused to French subjects and protected persons by, *inter alia*, the forces of a Government *de jure*. Before the Commission the French Agent asserted that the Government of Victoriano Huerta of 1913 and 1914 was a Government *de jure*, since the transmission of the supreme power in the State from President Madero to Huerta had taken place in a constitutional form, and the French Government had afterwards recognised the Government of Huerta as *de jure*. The Mexican Government, on the contrary, described Huerta as a mere usurper, and did not recognise his Government as a Government either *de jure* or *de facto* (see Case No. 164), or even as a revolutionary Government (see Case No. 159).

Held: That the *de jure* character of a Government depends exclusively upon the constitutional law of the State concerned at the time of the change in the Government. Neither the fact of recognition *de jure* by foreign Governments nor the refusal for political reasons only of a subsequent Government to recognise its predecessor as a regular Government, may be taken into account. The only doubtful question concerns the point whether it is sufficient that the formal provisions of the Constitution have been complied with, or whether incidental circumstances (such as compulsion, restraint upon the freedom of election, etc.) must also be taken into consideration. However, it is not necessary to decide this point. For the rest, a Government of illegal origin may afterwards obtain legal, *de jure*, character by express or tacit consent of the country concerned.

[Till now unreported.]

Responsibility of States—In General—Requirements of Responsibility—Questions of Fault.

See Case No. 154 (*H. G. Venable Case, under* (*a*)).

Responsibility of States—In General—International and Municipal Law—Nature of the Law to be Applied by International Tribunals.

See Case No. 174 (*George W. Cook* (*No.* 2) *Case*).

Responsibility of States—In General—Non-Fulfilment of the Obligation by one Party in Consequence of an Illegal Act of the Other.

See Case No. 346 (*Case concerning the Factory at Chorzów*).

V.—For Other Breaches of Contractual Obligations

State Responsibility—Contractual Obligations—Rate of Exchange in Awards. **Case No. 137**

GEORGE W. COOK (NO. 2) CASE.

United States and Mexico: General Claims Commission.

3 *June*, 1927.

(VAN VOLLENHOVEN, NIELSEN, MACGREGOR.)

THE FACTS.—(See Case No. 174.) After a consideration of the various methods applied by national courts in translating into the currency of their own country monetary judgments in satisfaction of obligations fixed in the terms of the currency of some other country,[1] it was

Held by Nielsen, the American Commissioner, for the Commission: That in the instant case the par value of the Mexican peso should be adopted in determining the amount to be awarded in the currency of the United States. There were several considerations justifying this conclusion. Mexico withheld payment of the money orders, and the claimant should be reimbursed to the full value of the orders. The date upon which payment of each order was refused was uncertain, and it was natural that the claimant should not be in the position to furnish precise information in each case. In addition there was not before the Commission the proper kind of evidence on which it could determine the rate of exchange on each of those dates or an average rate of exchange during the period within which the money orders were dishonoured.[2] [Reports: *Opinions of Commissioners*, 1927, p. 318; *A.J.*, XXII (1928), p. 189.]

[1] *E.g.* the par value: *Birge-Forbes Company* v. *Haye*, 251 U.S. 317; rate of exchange on the date of the breach of the contractual obligation; rate of exchange on the date of the judgment; rate of exchange at the time the suit is brought: *Die Deutsche Bank Filiale Nürnberg* v. *Humphrey*, 272 U.S. 517.

[2] The Commission subsequently adopted the same method in the *John A. M'Pherson* case, *Opinions of Commissioners*, 1927, p. 325.

Case No. 138

Responsibility of States—Responsibility for Contractual Obligations of Provinces—Responsibility of Turkey for the Contractual Obligations of the Vilayet of Adrianople.

RANSOMES, SIM AND JEFFERRIES *v.* TURKISH GOVERNMENT.

Anglo-Turkish Mixed Arbitral Tribunal. 7 *March*, 1928.

(HAMMERICH, MEMDOUH, GRIMSTON.)

THE FACTS.—This was an action to recover a certain sum said to be owing to the plaintiffs under a contract of sale of agricultural machines made with the Governor-General of the Vilayet of Adrianople.

Held: That the claim must be rejected. According to Turkish law Vilayets are distinct juristic persons with their own property and their own budgets composed partly of their own revenue. Although subject to the administrative supervision of the State, they possess both a personality distinct from the latter and the juristic capacity to contract obligations. The remedy open to the creditors is one based on the assets of the Vilayet, for whose contractual obligations the Turkish Government cannot be held responsible. [Report: *Recueil*, VIII, p. 203.]

Case No. 139

Responsibility of States—State as Carrier—Responsibility for Damage done during Revolutionary Disturbances.

BLANCK *v.* GERMANY.

Franco-German Mixed Arbitral Tribunal. 29 *October*, 1928.

(ASSER, GANDOLPHE, FROCHIL.)

THE FACTS.—The plaintiff asked for the value of a wagon of wine confiscated by a Council of Workers and Soldiers during the revolutionary disturbances in November, 1918.

Held: That this act of confiscation by a revolutionary agency constituted a case of *vis major* for which the German State in its capacity as carrier was not responsible. [Report: *Recueil*, VIII, p. 489.]

Schleimer v. *Germany* (*Recueil*, V, p. 848) followed.

Responsibility of States—Contracts made by Officials outside the Scope of their Competence—Contracts Conditional upon the Acceptance of the Next Administration.

Case No. 140

JOSEPH E. DAVIES CASE.

United States and Mexico : General Claims Commission.
23 *March*, 1927.

(VAN VOLLENHOVEN, NIELSEN, MACGREGOR.)

THE FACTS.—This was a claim to obtain payment of $170,000 alleged to be due for legal services rendered by the claimant under a contract concluded in October, 1920, between him and the Government of Mexico, acting through Roberto V. Pesqueira, Financial Agent of the Mexican Government in the United States. The contract was accompanied by a communication addressed by Pesqueira to Davies in the following terms :

"As I have explained to you, this contract is "limited by one reservation. My authorisation pro-"ceeds from President de la Huerta, and I have no "present power to bind the incoming administration "of President Obregon."

The contract provided, *inter alia*, for the immediate payment of $50,000 as the salary for the first year of employment. Of this sum the plaintiff actually received $30,000. The Mexican Agent denied that Davies entered into any contract with the Mexican Government, represented by Roberto V. Pesqueira, and asserted that the Government of Mexico never entrusted any legal matters to the claimant.

Held : That the claim must be dismissed except in so far as it referred to the unpaid balance of the first year's salary which was payable immediately on the conclusion of the contract.

Relevant international precedents did not fully accept the rule of the municipal law in many countries that a State is responsible for and is bound by acts of its agents within the scope of their competence as defined by municipal law. Thus in the *Hemming* case [1] the United States was held liable to make compensation for legal services rendered by the claimant at the request of the American consul at Bombay, but only on the ground that, irrespective of what was the consul's authority to employ an attorney at the expense of the United States, the

[1] Nielsen's *Report*, p. 61.

Case No. 140 *contd.*

Government, after having become aware of Hemming's employment, did not object to it, and approved the action taken by the consul. In the *Trumbull* case [1] the Tribunal overruled the contentions advanced by the United States with respect to non-liability for unauthorised acts of an American minister to Chile in employing a Chilean citizen in 1889 in connection with an extradition case. The Commission held that there was " a " promise in the name of his Government which, according to " the rules of the responsibility of governments for acts per- " formed by their agents in foreign countries, can not be repudiated."

However, the case before the Commission must be distinguished from the above-mentioned cases. There was in this case an explicit notice to the claimant with regard to the limitations on the authority of the Mexican representative with whom the contract was made. Pesqueira, by giving explicit notice of the limitations of his authority, took precaution to protect the interests of his Government and to define his position. The communication of October, 1920, left no doubt that Pesqueira was without authority to bind the coming administration ; that he therefore bound solely the provisional Huerta administration ; and that therefore whatever he undertook to do after the termination of the latter's administration must be considered as merely a personal undertaking. [Report : *Opinions of Commissioners*, 1927, p. 197.]

VI.—For Wrongs Unconnected with Contractual Obligations

(a) Acts and Omissions of State Organs and Officials

(i) Denial of Justice : Exhaustion of Legal Remedies

Case No. 141

Responsibility of States—Denial of Justice—Reduction of Sentence—Review of Decisions of Courts—Non-Execution of the Sentence.

Ida Robinson Smith Putnam Case.

United States and Mexico : General Claims Commission.

15 *April*, 1927.

(Van Vollenhoven, Nielsen, MacGregor.)

The Facts.—This was a claim on account of the murder, perpetrated in June, 1909, by a certain Uriarte, a

[1] Moore, p. 3569.

Mexican policeman, on the person of George B. Putnam, an American citizen. The lower court rejected the plea of self-defence and found Uriarte guilty of homicide perpetrated without provocation and with treachery, for which it sentenced him to death. The higher court considered that the homicide had been committed during an encounter and that the treachery had not been proved, and reduced the death sentence to eight years' imprisonment and hard labour. In 1913 Uriarte was released from prison by the military commander of the city.

It was alleged by the United States that Mexico was responsible for a denial of justice by imposing a light sentence on the accused, and, secondly, by not making him serve the whole sentence thus imposed.

Held by MacGregor, Mexican Commissioner, for the Commission: (*a*) That Mexico was not responsible for denial of justice in respect of the charge of having violated its international duty by imposing on the man responsible for the death of Putnam a penalty out of proportion to his crime. "A question which has been passed on in courts of different jurisdiction by the local judges, subject to protective [1] proceedings, must be presumed to have been fairly determined. Only a clear and notorious injustice visible, to put it thus, at a mere glance, could furnish ground for an international arbitral tribunal of the character of the present to put aside a national decision presented before it and to scrutinise its grounds of fact and law." [2] The Commission had before it the judgment rendered by the highest court of a Mexican State. There was no evidence to show that the proceedings leading to that decision were dilatory or inadequate. The question whether there was premeditation or not, or whether there was self-defence or not, were matters for the highest Mexican Court. Neither was the charge justified that the Supreme Court reduced the sentence without receiving new evidence, seeing that courts of appeal in Mexico do not as a rule receive new evidence as to facts. Neither was the commutation of the death penalty sufficient to establish a denial of justice. "The penalty is notoriously unjust only when there is imposed for a crime a penalty which does not correspond to the classification of the said crime or when an unusual penalty is imposed for it. But

[1] The meaning of this term is not clear to the editors.

[2] The Commission referred here to its views expressed on this subject in the *Roper* case (Case No. 150).

Case No. 141 *contd.*

"to impose, for example, on a voluntary homicide one of the "various penalties that are imposed for its different grades, "aside from the death penalty, where there are doubtful circum-"stances concerning its perpetration, can never mean *prima* "*facie* a wide deviation from justice." . . . The sentence of the highest court in question was not subject to further review by the Commission.

(*b*) However, Mexico was responsible for denial of justice by reason of the fact that the culprit was liberated before having fully served his sentence. No satisfactory explanation was offered why he served only thirty months of imprisonment. It could not therefore be said that Mexico entirely fulfilled its international obligation to punish the murderer. Mexico is responsible for the denial of justice resulting from such conduct. [Reports: *Opinions of Commissioners*, 1927, p. 222; *A.J.*, XXI (1927), p. 798.]

NOTE.—See a useful analysis of the case law on denial of justice in the volume entitled *Research in International Law: Draft Conventions on Nationality, Responsibility of States, and Territorial Waters*, published by the Harvard Law School, 1930, pp. 173-187.

Case No. 142

Responsibility of States—Denial of Justice—Void and Irregular Warrant Issued by a Judicial Officer—Killing of the Person Arrested—Responsibility for Acts of Judicial Officers.

WILLIAM T. WAY CASE.

United States and Mexico: General Claims Commission. 18 *October*, 1928.

(SINDBALLE, NIELSEN, MACGREGOR.)

THE FACTS.—Clarence Way, an American citizen, was killed in July, 1904, at Aguacaliente de Baca, State of Sinaloa, Mexico, by police officers who under the warrant issued by H. Torres, a magistrate (Alcalde), were effecting the arrest of Way. It appeared that the warrant was issued without sufficient justification, on the ground of alleged lack of respect to the person of the magistrate, and that the killing was wanton and unprovoked. Torres and the officers were subsequently arrested and tried. Torres was eventually sentenced to one year and fifteen days' imprisonment for abuse of power, one officer was sentenced to ten years' imprisonment for murder, and the other was sentenced to death. The claim was based on an assertion of a denial of justice growing out of the failure of Mexican authorities adequately to punish the magistrate said to have been responsible for the murder of Way. It was also contended that Mexico was responsible for the officials whose acts caused the death of Way.

It was contended on behalf of the United States that the sentence passed on Hermolao Torres, who planned the murder, was inadequate; that it was rendered under circumstances indicating that there had been a distinct denial of justice for the reason that the sentence of the Court with respect to Torres was not in accordance with the facts; and that it bore unmistakable evidence of intentional leniency towards him.

It was pointed out that Torres was the instigator of the crime; that there was sufficient evidence to establish that before issuing the warrant Torres had given expression to his feelings of enmity against Torres, and that he gave instructions to the officers to kill Way; that he must be considered to be responsible for the act of the police officers acting under his orders; and that he should therefore have been punished for the crime of murder, either as perpetrator or as accomplice, in accordance with the provisions of the applicable Penal Code.

The Mexican contention was that it was immaterial whether Torres had actually had in mind the desire or intention to cause the death of Way, which he possibly had, that on the evidence before the courts, in accordance with Mexican law and procedure, Torres could not have been found guilty of any offence other than that for which he was finally sentenced; and that Mexico's international obligations were fully complied with by the arrest and trial of Torres and the sentence passed upon him.

Held by Nielsen, American Commissioner, for the Commission: That Mexico was responsible. " It is believed to be a " sound principle that, when misconduct on the part of persons " concerned with the discharge of governmental functions, " whatever their precise status may be under domestic law, " results in a failure of a nation to live up to its obligations " under international law, the delinquency on the part of such " persons is a misfortune for which the nation must bear the " responsibility."

Case No. 142 *contd.*

Torres exercised certain judicial functions. Under international law a nation was responsible for the conduct of judicial officers. In addition, there were certain other broad principles with respect to personal rights and recognised by the laws of Mexico, the laws of the United States, and under the laws of civilised countries generally, and also under international law. " There must be some ground for depriving a person of his " liberty. He is entitled to be informed of the charge against " him if he is arrested on a warrant. Gross mistreatment in " connection with arrest and imprisonment is not tolerated, and " it has been condemned by international tribunals." The guarantees of this nature were violated when Torres, who had authority to issue proper warrants, issued a void warrant stating no charge, and directed the execution of that so-called warrant by armed men who killed a cultured and inoffensive man. All this constituted a " tragic violation of personal rights secured by " Mexican law and by international law," for which Mexico was responsible. [Reports: *Opinions of Commissioners*, 1929, p. 94; *A.J.*, XXIII (1929), p. 466.]

NOTE.—The Commissioner referred to and discussed the *Massey* case, decided by the same Commission in 1927, see Case No. 166, in connection with the question of the responsibility of the State for acts of minor officials.

Case No. 143

Responsibility of States—Executive Action—Denial of Justice through the Granting of an Amnesty.

F. R. WEST CASE.

United States and Mexico: General Claims Commission.
21 *July*, 1927.

(VAN VOLLENHOVEN, NIELSEN, MACGREGOR.)

THE FACTS.—In this case the United States claimed for damages on account of the murder, in 1922, of Edgar G. West, an American oil-well driller, by Mexican bandits who thereafter were granted amnesty by Mexico. It appeared that the murder was an ordinary case of wanton killing and robbery void of any political background. Article 1 of the amnesty decree of 30 December, 1922, provided as follows: " Amnesty is hereby " granted to those guilty of rebellion and sedition and " any act committed in connection therewith up to the " date of the publication of the present act and begin-

"ning with the year 1920." The Mexican authorities were of the opinion that the crime in question came within the scope of the amnesty decree.

Held by Van Vollenhoven, the Presiding Commissioner for the Commission: That Mexico was responsible.

It was not for the Commission to interpret the amnesty decree; the relevant point was how Mexico construed it. She had voluntarily deprived herself of the possibility of punishing and prosecuting an ordinary crime. The granting of amnesty for a crime has the same effect, under international law, as not punishing such a crime, not executing the penalty, or pardoning the offence. It fastens upon Mexico an indirect liability for the murder. [Reports: *Opinions of Commissioners*, 1927, p. 404; *A.J.*, XXII (1928), p. 452.]

Responsibility of States—Responsibility for Acts of Officials—Acts in Private and in Official Capacity—Lack of Adequate Protection—Denial of Justice by Inadequate Punishment—Denial of Justice by Actual Remission of the Sentence—Special Protection of Consuls—Measure of Damages. **Case No. 144**

FRANCISCO MALLÉN CASE.

United States and Mexico: General Claims Commission.
27 April, 1927.

(VAN VOLLENHOVEN, NIELSEN, MACGREGOR.)

THE FACTS.—This was a claim put forward by Mexico on behalf of Francisco Mallén, a Mexican national. The claim was based on two assaults made on Mallén at El Paso, Texas, U.S.A., where he had been consul of Mexico since 1895, by one Juan Franco, a deputy-constable of Mexican origin. On the occasion of the first assault Franco addressed the consul in uncouth language, telling the standers-by that he would kill Mallén. He then walked up to him and either slapped him in the face or knocked his hat off. Franco was prosecuted before the County Court, and fined $5 the next day on account of disturbing the peace.

The second assault took place about two months later. Franco boarded the car in which the consul was sitting, struck him violently and repeatedly on the head with his fist, and then took Mallén, whose face was covered with blood, to the county jail. For this

Case No. 144 ***contd.***

assault he was fined $100, but it did not appear that the whole fine was paid. Franco's appointment was cancelled. In 1908, however, he was appointed deputy-sheriff.

Mexico alleged that the United States was responsible for illegal acts of an American official, including an unwarranted arrest, for lack of adequate protection for the person of the consul, and for denial of justice in both trials relating to the assaults, and claimed on behalf of Mallén damages for compensation and satisfaction in the amount of $200,000 with interest.

Held by Van Vollenhoven, the Presiding Commissioner, Nielsen, the American Commissioner, concurring in his conclusions: That, with the exception of the charge of lack of protection and denial of justice on the ground of the leniency of the fine on the occasion of the first assault, the United States of America was responsible. Indemnity of $18,000 awarded.

(*a*) *Denial of Justice on Account of the Leniency of Punishment.*—It cannot be admitted that there has taken place denial of justice on the ground that, in regard to the first assault, the court treated an attempt to kill Mallén as a mere disturbance of the peace. As Mallén refrained from submitting evidence to the police court, the court could not have deemed the occurrence to be a dangerous attack of importance. As to the second assault, the evidence before the American court was of such a nature that it did not warrant a conviction for aggravated assault. Accordingly, the fine of $100, being within the limits of the penal law, could not be regarded, merely because of its moderate amount, as a denial of justice.

(*b*) *Subsequent Lack of Protection.*—On the other hand, it would seem quite unsatisfactory that a deputy-constable, after disturbing the peace he was appointed to protect, was neither punished nor warned in any disciplinary way. It was imprudent and improper on the part of the authorities to maintain in office a man of this type, without taking any precautions, in a position in which he might easily cause great harm to peaceful residents. There was a further lack of protection in the fact that in 1908 the culprit was appointed deputy-sheriff. "This re-appointment means lack of protection in so serious "a form that it amounts to a challenge; it is exactly the "reverse from that protection due to all peaceful citizens "whether aliens or nationals." This attitude was particularly grave as the safety of a consular representative was involved.

The impropriety of this attitude was amply shown by the second assault.

(*c*) As to the special protection to be afforded to consuls, see Case No. 254.

(*d*) *As to the Official Character of the Culprit.*—There was no doubt that Franco's acts were acts of an official on duty. He showed his badge pointing to his official capacity, and he could not have arrested the consul if he had not been acting as a police officer. " Though his act would seem to have been " a private act of revenge which was disguised, once the first " thirst of revenge had been satisfied, as an official act of arrest, " the act as a whole can only be considered as the act of an " official."

(*e*) *Denial of Justice on Account of Non-Payment of the Fine.*—There was no record on the part of the county auditor to show that the fine had actually been paid. The sentence read that if the fine was not fully paid, Franco should be committed to prison. " It was for the United States to show that " he has been committed to jail. Punishment without execution of the penalty constitutes a basis for assuming a denial " of justice."

(*f*) As to the measure of damages, see Case No. 176.

[Reports: *Opinions of Commissioners*, 1927, p. 254; *A.J.*, XXI (1927), p. 803.]

Responsibility of States—Denial of Justice—Failure to Apprehend Criminals—Murder Committed during Occupation by Revolutionary Force—Duties of the Lawful Government. **Case No. 145**

LOUISE O. CANAHL CASE.

United States and Mexico: General Claims Commission.
15 *October*, 1928.

(SINDBALLE, NIELSEN, MACGREGOR.)

THE FACTS.—On the night of 16 June, 1915, Gilbert T. Canahl, an American citizen, attended a dance in the course of which several Mexicans engaged in a quarrel, and before long the participants were attacking one another with knives. Canahl interfered as a peacemaker, and thereupon the infuriated persons turned upon him and brutally murdered him.

The United States claimed damages on the ground that the Mexican authorities failed to take proper steps

Case No. 145 ***contd.***

to apprehend persons responsible for the death of Canahl, and that the negligence of the authorities constituted a denial of justice.

The Mexican defence was that at the time Canahl was killed the locality in question was in the control of the revolutionary forces of Francisco Villa, who was in arms against the Carranza Government, and that the Mexican Government cannot be held responsible for the acts of the revolutionary forces in this matter. It was further contended for the defence that the authorities of the Federal Government had no knowledge of the matter until it was brought to their attention in a communication addressed to them by the local American consul in 1922.

The forces of Villa were driven from the locality in question by the Carranza governmental authorities three weeks after the murder took place.

Held by Nielsen, the American Commissioner, for the Commission: That Mexico was responsible. The contention that there is no continuity between a mere revolutionary faction and the Government of a country cannot be sustained with respect to matters like that before the Commission. The change of authority due to internecine disturbances may seriously interfere with the discharge of governmental functions, and account should be taken of a situation of this kind in considering a complaint against lax administration of justice. But authorities responsible for law and order could not properly ignore a murder just because it had been committed three weeks before rebel forces were driven from the locality in which it took place. The lawful authorities took possession of the town in question approximately three weeks after they drove out the Villa authorities. The situation would be different if rebel forces had been in possession of a territory for years after a murder had been committed and if the relevant records had in the meantime been destroyed.

In fixing the amount of this award account must be taken of the difficulties attending the administration of justice owing to the revolutionary disturbances. The Commission awarded the sum of $5000.00 as an appropriate indemnity. $50,000.00 were claimed. [Report: *Opinions of Commissioners*, 1929, p. 90.]

Responsibility of States—Denial of Justice—Release on Bond—Failure to Bring Accused to Trial.

Case No. 146

JOHN D. CHASE CASE.

United States and Mexico: General Claims Commission. 26 *September*, 1928.

(SINDBALLE, NIELSEN, MACGREGOR.)

THE FACTS.—This was a claim presented by the United States of America on behalf of John D. Chase, who, in the course of a scuffle, was seriously wounded by a Mexican, a certain Jacinto Flores. They were both arrested, as in the course of the struggle Chase fired a shot which wounded a Mexican woman. Subsequently Chase was released on bond, and a few months later Flores was similarly released. It was contended on behalf of the United States that Mexico was responsible for failure to take adequate measures to apprehend and punish the assailant after he had fled while under release on bond.

It appeared from the record that prior to the release on bond the Mexican authorities took the necessary steps to elucidate the facts; they arrested Flores, decreed his formal commitment, examined eye-witnesses, confronted them with each other, employed experts to examine the wounds, and so forth.

Held by MacGregor, the Mexican Commissioner, for the Commission: (*a*) That in view of this record Mexico could not be held guilty of a denial of justice as regards failure to apprehend the culprit, but (*b*) she was responsible for denial of justice by not bringing Flores to trial after his release. International justice is not satisfied if a Government limits itself to instituting and prosecuting a trial without reaching the point of defining the defendant's guilt and meting out the proper penalty. It is possible that in certain cases the police or judicial authorities might declare the innocence of a defendant without bringing him to formal trial. But if the circumstances indicate the possible guilt of a defendant, even in the slightest degree, there is a duty to determine the responsibility of the accused. The present case fell within that category.

In view of the attendant circumstances, the Commission did not consider that this denial of justice constituted an extreme

Case No. 146 *contd.*

case. It awarded 5000 dollars to the United States on behalf of Chase, who was permanently disabled from work as the result of the wounds received. [Report: *Opinions of Commissioners*, 1929, p. 17.]

Case No. 147

Responsibility of States—Executive Inaction—Failure to Apprehend Criminals—Denial of Justice.

IRMA EITELMAN MILLER, LILLIAN EITELMAN AND B. B. EITELMAN CASE.

United States and Mexico: General Claims Commission. 26 *September*, 1928.

(SINDBALLE, NIELSEN, MACGREGOR.)

THE FACTS in this case were not unlike those in the case of *L. F. Neer* and *Pauline E. Neer* (*Annual Digest*, 1925-1926, Case No. 154).

Held: Following the principles underlying the decision in that case, that Mexico was not responsible. [Report: *Opinions of Commissioners*, 1929, p. 15.]

Case No. 148

Responsibility of States—Denial of Justice—Undue Delay in the Prosecution of a Crime.

SALOMÉ LERMA VDA. DE GALVÁN CASE.

United States and Mexico: General Claims Commission. 21 *July*, 1927.

(VAN VOLLENHOVEN, NIELSEN, MACGREGOR.)

THE FACTS.—This was a claim for compensation in satisfaction for a denial of justice on account of undue delay in the prosecution by the courts of Texas of an American subject responsible for the killing of a Mexican citizen in the course of a quarrel. The killing took place in August, 1921. The accused was immediately taken into custody by the local authorities and charged with murder. Several days later he was given a preliminary hearing before a justice of the peace, at which several eye-witnesses of the shooting were examined. He was then released on bail. In March, 1922, an indictment was found against him, charging him with murder. The trial was set for April, 1922. The accused was again admitted to bail. The trial was then repeatedly postponed " because of defaulting witnesses." It was not terminated by April, 1927.

Held by Nielsen, the American Commissioner, for the Commission : That the United States were responsible. There was a failure on the part of the authorities of the State of Texas to comply with the general principle of international law requiring authorities to take proper measures to apprehend and punish a person who appears to be guilty of a crime against an alien. The explanation given by the United States that a certain eyewitness had not been located could not be admitted. There was no reason to suppose that the legal machinery of the State of Texas was so defective that in a case in which a preliminary trial reveals that there were at least five eye-witnesses to the shooting of the murdered man, the authorities during a period of six years after the shooting found themselves unable to conduct a proper prosecution. Any such defect would not be an adequate defence to the claim. If witnesses actually disappeared during the course of the delay in the trial, then that in itself would constitute evidence of negligent delay in the prosecution. [Reports : *Opinions of Commissioners*, 1927, p. 408 ; *A.J.*, XXII (1928), p. 455.]

Denial of Justice—Equality of Treatment of Citizens and Aliens—Grounds of Impugning Judgments of National Courts. **Case No. 149**

CANTERO HERRERA *v.* CANEVARO & COMPANY.

Supreme Court of Peru. 25 *May*, 1927.

THE FACTS.—Cantero Herrera, a Cuban national residing in Lima, Peru, filed suit, on 22 July, 1913, as agent for certain non-resident Cuban citizens, against a Peruvian national named Cesar Saco y Flores, in the Civil Court of Lima, for the partition and distribution of an inheritance in the estate known as " Huayto." Later, on 29 September, 1913, the Sociedad Canevaro & Cia, also of Lima, was made a co-defendant as the purchaser of the estate from Saco y Flores, and the Court was asked to declare the sale to it void.

The court of first instance, on 10 January, 1919, decided against Cantero Herrera and his co-plaintiffs on three grounds : (*a*) That they had shown no right to the

Case No. 149 ***contd.***

distribution prayed for; (*b*) that the sale by Saco y Flores to Canevaro & Cia was a valid one; and (*c*) that the action was barred by the statute of limitations. This judgment was affirmed by the Superior Court on 23 September, 1920, and by the Supreme Court on 21 August, 1921.

Nothing further was done by the plaintiffs, but on 28 January, 1927, the Cuban Envoy Extraordinary and Minister Plenipotentiary at Lima addressed a Note to the Foreign Minister of Peru, which impugned generally the above-mentioned judgments, laid particular stress on alleged errors of law on the question of the "prescription" of the action, and concluded by alleging that the judgments were tantamount to a denial of justice to the plaintiffs on the ground that they were contrary to Peruvian law; wherefore he called upon the Government of Peru to acknowledge that there had been a denial of justice and to make due reparation. The matter was referred by the Executive to the Supreme Court.

Held: That the claim, in so far as it is based on denial of justice, must fail.

"Between Peru and Cuba there is no treaty regarding "foreigners; but the tenor of our laws and the principles "generally accepted, especially those proclaimed in American "international law, are sufficient to make the question raised by "the diplomatic representative of Cuba doctrinally simple.

"The condition of foreigners in Peru, from the point of "view of private rights, is not left entirely to the provisions of "international convenience, nor subordinated to the simple fact "of reciprocity, since Articles 32 and 33 of our Civil Code pro-"vide that 'civil rights are independent of the status of the "'citizen,' and that 'foreigners enjoy in Peru all rights con-"'cerning the security of their persons and property and the free "'administration of the same.'

"Equality between natives and foreigners before the Civil "Law implies their equality as to judicial competency and form "of proceeding in the same subject-matter; hence, foreigners "enjoy in Peru the same rights, means, recourses and guaran-"tees as nationals to sue for and defend their rights; the *cautio* "*judicatum solvi* (which, as a dilatory objection against the "alien plaintiff, transient or without known assets, was allowed "under the Code abrogated in 1912) is no longer in force, not-

" withstanding that it is still sanctioned by a legislation of some
" countries, including that of Cuba. . . .

" The diplomatic representative of Cuba agrees, as must be
" true, that the ordinary suit commenced by Cantero Herrera
" against Saco and Canevaro came to a close with the judgment
" of the Supreme Court, dated 11 August, 1921. As a result,
" that judgment has placed a final, absolute and definitive seal
" upon all questions of a legal and juridical character ventilated
" in the litigation between the said parties, in conformity with
" the precepts of the Constitution and the laws of Peru, from
" whose sovereignty the foreigner litigating in the national
" jurisdiction cannot abstract himself, and which merely give
" positive expression to the old classic adage *res judicata pro*
" *veritate habetur*. . . .

" There is no doubt that nations reciprocally owe one
" another justice, and are bound to extend it to foreigners
" having recourse to their tribunals and to give them the
" opportunity to obtain it in the like measure with nationals;
" but the good understanding among them, harmonising all
" interests, has raised to the category of an international law
" the authority of the thing adjudged, and no self-respecting
" country will countenance that any other country should
" impeach the force and legality of an executed judgment,
" rendered regularly by its authorities, as an emanation of
" sovereignty.

" It is on this account that, in keeping with our political
" Constitution, it belongs to the President of the Republic, who
" represents abroad the national sovereignty, 'to enforce,
" 'obligatorily, the judgments and resolutions of the tribunals
" 'and courts' (Article 121, par. 10); and Article 39 of the
" same Constitution contains this important provision, which
" it is timely to mention with respect to a claim growing out of
" litigation over territorial property: 'foreigners are, as to
" 'their property, in the same condition as Peruvians, and
" 'cannot in any case invoke with regard thereto an exceptional
" 'situation, nor have recourse to diplomatic claims. . . .

" It is erroneous to suppose that the conclusion of a proceed-
" ing in which a foreigner has failed, marks the occasion for the
" transference of the issue to the diplomatic plane. If it were
" so, the passions accumulated around matters of an entirely
" private nature would constantly poison the best cemented
" international relations.

" In the relations of nation to nation, the rule is respect for
" the sovereignty of friendly powers, typified in the authority

Case No. 149 ***contd.***

" of its judges and of its decisions. The exception is the claim " based on the motive of denial of justice; but to make such " claim conformably with the principles and usages of inter- " national law, it is necessary that the case be one of the utmost " seriousness, that the denial of justice be *manifest* or *notorious*, " that is, that the hearing which the foreigner claims, or the " recourse which he interposes, has been denied him, and in " general that the exercise of his rights and rights of action is " interfered with contrary to law, or is subjected to unwarranted " delays; because all this involves and constitutes an odious " exception, a legal infringement which can be established " objectively, without offending the jurisdiction of the country, " and which compromises the responsibility of the State.[1]

" Cantero Herrera has not been denied a hearing by our " tribunals, nor the interposition of any recourse or means of " defence permitted by the law, nor has he been subjected to " any objectionable treatment. Neither can he aver, as has " been alleged in other cases, that he has been cited before a " court lacking jurisdiction, or has been judged without being " summoned; being the plaintiff, he has selected the court " and the proceeding, and with the most absolute freedom has " pleaded at every stage, by word of mouth and in writing, " everything he has deemed necessary in support of his right. " Of what, then, does he complain? Of not having won the " action? It is not on that condition, nor on any other, that " the portals of justice are thrown open to the public author- " ities, to foreigners, or to any one else." [Report: 23 *Anales Judiciales* (Peru), 493.]

NOTE.—This is the latest and perhaps the fullest and best reasoned case in Latin America on the question of diplomatic intervention on the ground of *denial of justice*.

---

[1] The Court referred here to the Pan-American Conferences held in 1889 at Washington, and in 1901 in Mexico, respectively, although without the attendance of Cuba, whose autonomy had not been as yet established, and to the recommendations approved by them with regard to the status of foreigners.

The Court also referred to Article 5 of a treaty between Peru and the Argentine Republic, of 9 March, 1874, and to Article 6 of a treaty between Spain and Peru, of 18 June, 1898: " Spaniards in Peru, and Peruvians in " Spain, shall have no right to diplomatic intervention except in the event of " *manifest denial of justice*, that is, refusal to administer it or negligence in its " administration."

(ii) Executive Action or Inaction

State Responsibility—Responsibility for Acts of Police Officers and Minor Officials—Indiscriminate Use of Firearms—Insufficient Investigation and Prosecution—Distinction between the Findings of an Investigating Judge and the Judgment of a Tribunal. **Case No. 150**

Margaret Roper Case.

United States and Mexico: General Claims Commission.
4 *April*, 1927.

(Van Vollenhoven, Nielsen, MacGregor.)

The Facts.—This was a claim for damages on account of the death of William Roper, an American seaman, who was drowned in the Pánuco river as a result, it was alleged, of an assault upon him and three fellow-seamen, committed by Mexican policemen and Mexican private citizens. It was stated in the Memorial that the seamen, while returning from shore leave on a boat, were assaulted, that they jumped into the water to escape by swimming to their ship, the American merchant vessel *Saxon*, and that Roper was wounded by a pistol-shot and sank immediately. It appeared from a subsequent investigation that the shots were fired by Mexican policemen for the purpose of intimidating certain persons, in whose pursuit they were engaged, believed to have committed an act of robbery. In September, 1922, about eighteen months after the death of the seamen had taken place, the investigating judge reached the conclusion that there was no reason to institute a prosecution in connection with the death of the seamen. The United States contended that Mexico was responsible for the unlawful acts of Mexican policemen, who fired the shots, for the failure of Mexican authorities to afford proper protection to the American citizens, and for a denial of justice growing out of the failure of Mexican authorities to prosecute the persons implicated in the death of the seamen.

Held: That Mexico was responsible.

(*a*) *Indiscriminate Use of Firearms.*—The record showed that had it not been for the unlawful acts of the police in firing the shots, the seamen would not have met their death. Even

Case No. 150 ***contd.***

though the police had fired simply to "intimidate" the seamen, such action must be regarded as improper. The Commission referred here to the principles underlying the Commission's decisions in the *Swinney* case,[1] the *Falcon* case,[2] and the *Garcia* case,[3] in regard to the reckless and unnecessary use of firearms by persons engaged in the enforcement of law.

(*b*) *Responsibility for Acts of Policemen.*—The Commission was unable to agree with the contention that the Mexican Government was not responsible under international law for the acts of such minor officials as policemen. The Commission referred here to the *Quintanilla* case,[4] in which the Mexican Government contended that the Government of the United States was responsible for the acts of a deputy-sheriff in Texas, and in which an award was rendered by the Commission in favour of the claimant. In addition, it was the duty of the Commission to give effect to Article 1 of the Convention of 8 September, 1923, in which the jurisdiction of the Commission was described as covering "all claims for losses or damages "originating from acts of officials or others acting for either "government and resulting in injustice."

(*c*) *Insufficient Investigation and Prosecution. Conclusions of the Investigating Judge and Judgment of a Tribunal.*—The Commission considered that the occurrences pointing clearly to the commission of crime were not adequately met by this investigation. These occurrences were of such a character that the persons directly concerned with them should have been prosecuted and brought to trial to determine their innocence or guilt with respect to the death of the Americans.

Mexico invoked the frequent declarations of international tribunals and of authorities on international law with regard to the respect due to the judiciary of a State. The Commission was not of the opinion that these arguments were relevant in regard to the question of enquiring into the propriety of the findings of the judge responsible for the investigation. "We "do not consider the functions exercised by a judge in making "an investigation whether there should be a prosecution as "judicial functions in the sense in which the term judicial is "generally used in opinions of tribunals or in writings dealing "with denial of justice growing out of judicial proceedings. It "may readily be conceded that actions of the judge should not "be characterised by this Commission as improper in the

[1] *Annual Digest*, 1925-1926, Case No. 155.
[2] *Ibid.*, Case No. 160.
[3] *Ibid.*, Case No. 157.
[4] *Ibid.*, Case No. 163.

" absence of clear evidence of their impropriety . . . to " undertake to pick flaws in the solemn judgments of a nation's " highest tribunal is something very different from passing " upon the merits of an investigation conducted by an official " —whether he be a judge or a police magistrate—having for " its purpose the apprehension or possible prosecution of " persons who may appear to be guilty of crime." [Reports: *Opinions of Commissioners*, 1927, p. 205; *A.J.*, XXI (1927), p. 776.]

Responsibility of States—Lack of Protection—Failure to Prosecute. **Case No. 151**

GEORGE DAVID RICHARDS CASE.

United States and Mexico: General Claims Commission.
23 *July*, 1927.

(VAN VOLLENHOVEN, NIELSEN, MACGREGOR.)

THE FACTS.—G. D. Richards, an American citizen, who was engaged in superintending the construction of a road in the State of Oaxaca, Mexico, was ambushed by a number of men and mortally wounded. Difficulties seem to have existed at that time between certain occupants of the land in that region and its owners, on account of certain taxes which the latter were endeavouring to collect from the former. The Mexican authorities, upon request, had granted an escort of three soldiers for the protection of Richards, two of whom were accompanying him on horseback at the time of the events. The United States alleged that Mexico was responsible for the failure to afford adequate protection to Richards notwithstanding its knowledge of the conditions of insecurity which prevailed in that region, and for the failure to apprehend and punish the perpetrators of the crime.

Held by MacGregor, Mexican Commissioner, for the Commission: That Mexico was not responsible for lack of protection. The Mexican authorities had endeavoured to protect the life of Richards by placing at his disposal a special guard. It was also proved that the military authorities had detachments in that region with the object of keeping order. Attacks on the lives and property of individuals cannot always be prevented even by using the most efficacious preventive measures. The fact, relied upon by the United States, that other foreigners had

Case No. 151 *contd.*

been killed there two years before, does not sufficiently prove a state of disorder which would require special measures. But Mexico was responsible for laxity and delay in the prosecution of the claim. The murder was committed in August, 1921. In March, 1922, a decree was issued releasing the persons accused of having committed the crime. The Prosecuting Attorney appealed from this decree in the same month. However, that appeal was admitted only almost three years afterwards (2 March, 1925). And although the Court of Appeal revoked the decree of release and ordered the re-apprehension of the accused on 1 August, 1925, no evidence was presented by Mexico showing the continuation of the prosecution, or of their having been finally judged. More than six years, then, have elapsed without the parties presumably responsible for Richards' death having been brought to judgment.[1] [Reports : *Opinions of Commissioners*, 1927, p. 412 ; *A.J.*, XXII (1928), p. 660.]

Case No. 152

State Responsibility—Prolonged Detention—Responsibility for the Death of the Prisoner during Illegal Detention.

MARY ANN TURNER CASE.

United States and Mexico : General Claims Commission.
23 *July*, 1927.

(VON VOLLENHOVEN, NIELSEN, MACGREGOR.)

THE FACTS.—Edward Turner, a naturalised American national, who was a locomotive engineer in Mexico, became involved in a train collision on 20 March,

[1] See also the case of *A. L. Harkrader*, decided by the United States and Mexico General Claims Commission (Sindballe, Nielsen, MacGregor) on 3 October, 1928. This was a claim for damages for failure on the part of the Mexican authorities to take appropriate steps to apprehend and punish the murderers of an American subject killed by unknown persons who enticed him, together with a companion, into their motor-car, promising to show them the sights of the town, and there committed the murder after robbing the two Americans. It was argued by counsel for the United States that, apart from other errors in the conduct of the investigation, M'Kinnon, the murdered man's companion, who escaped after being wounded, was not questioned as to what persons he and Harkrader met with during their drive in the car, and that no testimony was obtained from the man at the gasoline station who sold oil and gasoline to the car in question. It appeared from the record before the Commission that immediate steps were taken by the police authorities to apprehend the murderers. Thus a squad of policemen was sent out on 19 November, 1922—the day on which the Chief of Police was informed of the murder—and another squad on the next day. In a dispatch from the local American consul to the American Department of State it was stated that the Mexican authorities were doing their best in the matter. It was held (by Sindballe, the Presiding Commissioner, for the Commission) that Mexico was not responsible as no negligence was proven in the conduct of the investigation as a whole. The "conclusion whether the investigation that took

1899, which caused the death of the fireman serving on the other colliding engine. Turner was arrested about 1 April, 1899, then released on bail, and then again imprisoned until 28 January, 1900, on which day he died, without having had a trial. The United States alleged direct responsibility of Mexico for an illegal arrest, undue and illegal delay of proceedings, and inhuman treatment in prison, all of which contributed to causing Turner's death. Damages were claimed on behalf of the widow of the deceased.

Held by Van Vollenhoven, Presiding Commissioner, for the Commission: That Mexico was responsible. According to the Mexican Code of Criminal Procedure, the preliminary investigations should have ended within five months after the date on which the accused came at the disposal of the judge. This period had been exceeded. Though there was no convincing proof that his death was caused by his treatment in prison, it was clear that, if at liberty, he would have been able to take better measures for restoring his health than he could do either in prison or in a prison hospital. " If having a man in custody " obligates a government to account for him, having a man in " *illegal* custody doubtless renders a government liable for " dangers and disasters which would not have been his share, " or in a less degree, if he had been at liberty." Mexico could not be held responsible for Turner's death. But it should be held responsible for the bad effects of the illegal and careless custody on Turner's health.[1] [Reports: *Opinions of Commissioners*, 1927, p. 416; *A.J.*, XXII (1928), p. 663.]

" place was below the minimum standard required by international law must " be based on a broad and general view of the steps taken rather than on a " criticism of some particular point." [Report: *Opinions of Commissioners*, 1929, p. 66.]

[1] See also, for a case on State responsibility in connection with illegal imprisonment and injury inflicted upon the prisoner by a cell inmate, the case of *I. R. Clark*, decided by the United States and Mexico General Claims Commission (Sindballe, Nielsen and MacGregor), on 18 October, 1928. This was a claim for $25,000.00 grounded on alleged illegal arrest and imprisonment by Mexican authorities, and maltreatment in prison. In addition to these charges it was alleged (and, in the opinion of the Commissioners, there seemed to be evidence corroborating the charge) that when the claimant was in jail a drunken Mexican, who was placed in the cell with him, without provocation, and under encouragement of Mexican soldiers, dealt the claimant a severe blow on the head which resulted in a permanent condition of deafness in both ears. Medical evidence was produced to the effect that the claimant's hearing had been impaired as the result of a blow. It was held (by Nielsen, the American Commissioner, for the Commission) that there was not before the Commission evidence upon which to base a definite conclusion with respect to this particular item of damage. An award of $200.00 was rendered on other counts. [Report: *Opinions of Commissioners*, 1929, p. 131.]

Case No. 153

State Responsibility for Wrongs Unconnected with Contractual Obligations—Acts and Omissions of State Organs and Officials—Negligence on the Part of Administrative Authorities—Negligence of Customs Authorities in Keeping Goods.

TOBERMAN, MACKEY & COMPANY CASE.

United States and Mexico: General Claims Commission.
20 *May*, 1927.

(VAN VOLLENHOVEN, NIELSEN, MACGREGOR.)

THE FACTS.—This was a claim presented by the United States of America in behalf of Toberman, Mackey & Company, an American corporation, demanding from the United Mexican States the sum of $1845.57, with interest, the value of 376 bales of hay, property of the corporation, which was damaged in the Mexican Custom House of Progreso, Yucatan, Mexico, between the beginning of June, 1919, and 23 July, 1920. It was alleged that the hay was spoiled by exposure to the weather, on account of the negligence or lack of care of the authorities of the Mexican Custom House, and that the Mexican Government was responsible according to general principles of law, as well as under special provisions of its General Customs Regulations. The Mexican Government contended that the loss of the hay was due to the negligence of the consignees, of the shipping company or of the claimant corporation, who did not comply with the Customs Regulations.

The terms of the Arbitration Convention of 8 September, 1923, conferred upon the Commission jurisdiction in respect of acts of authorities resulting in injustice to the citizens of either party.

Held by MacGregor, Mexican Commissioner, for the Commission, Van Vollenhoven, the Presiding Commissioner, concurring: That the claim must be dismissed. There is no clear principle of international law " which obliges a government to " take special care, as if it were a private storage concern, of " merchandise which comes in through its Custom Houses, for " the mere purpose of exercising the sovereign right of collecting " import and export duties." The decisive consideration is whether the law of the State imposes on its Custom Houses the obligation of guarding, at all times and without limit, like a good *paterfamilias*, goods and merchandise which pass through its ports of entry. In the present case the damage to the goods was due to the delay by the parties incurred on account of their failure to comply with the clear provisions of Mexican law in respect of the dispatch of the goods. It was their negligence which threw on the Mexican Custom House authorities the care of the merchandise, which care the Mexican authorities did not assume and which their regulations implicitly declined to undertake. [Reports: *Opinions of Commissioners*, 1927, p. 306; *A.J.*, XXII (1928), p. 182.]

NOTE.—Nielsen, American Commissioner, while concurring in the above opinion, was not prepared to say that under the terms of the Convention of 8 September, 1923, liability might not be fastened upon a Government for the acts of its Customs authorities in a case revealing negligence with respect to protection of imported commodities. In the present case there was not, however, convincing evidence of negligence on the part of the Custom House officials.

Responsibility of States—Executive Action—Detention and Destruction of Locomotives—Acts of Railway Officials—Requirement of Fault—Indirect Damages—Responsibility for Irregularities in Bankruptcy Proceedings—Responsibility for Acts of Appointed Bankruptcy Trustees—Executive Action and Action of Persons Appointed in the Course of Judicial Proceedings. **Case No. 154**

H. G. VENABLE CASE.

United States and Mexico: General Claims Commission.
8 *July*, 1927.

(VAN VOLLENHOVEN, NIELSEN, MACGREGOR.)

THE FACTS.—In April, 1921, a company of which the claimant was president had, together with a company of which one E. S. Burrowes was president, entered into a contract with the Illinois Central Railroad Company at Chicago for the rental of some locomotives to them for use in Mexico. A few days before, Burrowes in his personal capacity had entered into another contract with the Mexican National Railways allowing him to use the Mexican tracks with these locomotives. In May the company under the contract requested the return of the engines. When Venable tried to arrange for the engines to leave Mexico, a Mexican railway superintendent by name of C. C. Rochin sent, at Burrowes' request, a telegram which forbade his railway personnel to allow these engines to leave Mexican territory. The locomotives were then attached for liquidated debts of

Case No. 154 ***contd.***

Burrowes' company, which was subsequently declared bankrupt. Venable made unsuccessful efforts to effect the release of the engines. They were retained in a railway yard, where, after a few months, three of them appeared to have been deprived of so many essential parts as to have become practically useless. Even before these occurrences, one of the four engines had been wrecked in a railway collision. The United States claimed on behalf of Venable that Mexico was liable to him in the amount of $184,334.84, on account of (*a*) direct responsibility for the act of the railway superintendent; (*b*) direct or indirect responsibility for the action of the Court in delaying the release of the engines; (*c*) direct responsibility for the destruction of three engines; and (*d*) direct responsibility for the destruction of one engine in a collision.

Held by Van Vollenhoven, the Presiding Commissioner, for the Commission: (*a*) That Mexico was responsible for the unauthorised act of the superintendent in preventing the locomotives from leaving Mexico.[1] This act violated the contract rights of the claimant. It was immaterial that the superintendent was unaware of their existence. His act was illegal and outside the contract. Direct responsibility for acts of executive officials does not depend upon the existence on their part of aggravating circumstances such as an outrage, wilful neglect of duty, etc.

As to the damage caused by the act of the superintendent, it was possible that his telegram may have been the cause of the subsequent damage to and destruction of the engines. However, the Commission could consider only those losses or damages caused by the superintendent which were the immediate and direct results of his telegram.[2] As such losses the Commission could only consider the payments due to the Illinois Central Railroad Company under the contract in case of non-fulfilment of the duty to return the engines in good condition and in time. However, as the Illinois Central Railroad Company never claimed any amount under this head until after all the events subsequent to the superintendent's action had occurred, it was difficult to make the money value of the damage thus caused the object of a precise calculation.

[1] The Mexican Commissioner dissented on this point.

[2] The Commissioner referred here to the award in the *Lacaze* case between Argentine and France under the decree of 17 December, 1860 (Lapradelle et Politis, II, 298), and the *Mallén* case (Case No. 176).

(*b*) *As to the Irregularities of the Bankruptcy Proceedings.*—In the opinion of the Commission there were certain irregular features in the proceedings. Thus, when the claimant instituted a suit against the trustee in bankruptcy, the Court, in disregard of the periods fixed by the rules of procedure, accepted an answer filed by the trustee fifteen days late. Secondly, the judge had private conversations on the case in the court room with the claimant, his lawyer, and the trustee, in which he made a kind of informal ruling as to the party authorised to claim release of the engines, but in which he never told the claimant that his action was not in conformity with the forms of Mexican law. However, these and other similar facts did not show a defective administration of justice such as might give ground for their being made the reason of a condemnatory award.

(*c*) *Delay in Bankruptcy Proceedings.*—Mexico was responsible, in particular for the reasons stated under (*d*), for failing to take appropriate steps to bring the bankruptcy proceedings to an end, by allowing them to remain at a standstill and by not directing the trustee to account for his acts or for the custody of the goods entrusted to his care.

(*d*) *Damages to and Destruction of the Engines.*—Mexico was indirectly responsible for the losses under this head. It was established by the record that the engines during the times in which they were in the custody of the trustee were left in an unprotected position, exposed to the weather, and that subsequently so many parts had been removed or injured that the engines had been reduced to a practically worthless condition.

If the goods had been taken into custody by Mexican officials or other persons acting on behalf of Mexico, then the direct responsibility of the Government would have been involved.[1] However, in the present case the situation was different. A trustee in bankruptcy, such as the one appointed in Mexico, cannot be considered as an official, or as one "acting "for" the Government; he acts "as representative of the "creditors." When a court places a bankrupt estate in the

[1] The Commission referred here to the *Nick Cibich* case (*Annual Digest*, 1925-1926, Case No. 159), where it was held that Mexican police officers having taken a man's money into custody must account for it; to the *Quintanilla* case (*ibid.*, Case No. 163), in which it was held that, once a Government has taken into its custody war prisoners, hostages, interned soldiers or ordinary delinquents, it is obliged to account for them; to the *Lord Nelson* case, in which the United States were held responsible for the embezzlement of funds in custody of the clerk of a Federal Court (Nielsen's *Report*, p. 433); to the *Toberman, Mackey & Company* case (Case No. 153), distinguished as having no bearing on the present problem, since a real custody of imported goods in the hands of Custom House officials was held not to have existed.

Case No. 154 ***contd.***

custody of some kind of trustee (in Mexico a *sindico* and an *interventor*), in many countries, including Mexico, it does the same thing for an estate as it does for a debtor's specific goods when allowing a plaintiff to attach them in order to preserve for his benefit the property of the debtor. Such goods are not taken into custody by the courts themselves; a private citizen is appointed trustee, acting for the benefit of the plaintiff.[1] However, though the direct responsibility for the attached goods does not rest with the courts and the Government of their country, they remain nevertheless indirectly responsible. The Government obligates owners and other persons interested in certain goods to leave the care of these goods entirely to the custodian. It cannot exculpate itself by merely stating that it placed the goods in some one's custody. In the present case, "even if there was not wilful neglect of duty there doubtless "was an insufficiency of governmental action so far short of "international standards that every reasonable and impartial "man would readily recognise its insufficiency" (at p. 345). It was immaterial whether this insufficiency proceeded from the law or from deficient execution of the law. The court in question "having constrained private individuals to leave "their property in the hands of others, having allowed unknown "men to spoil and destroy this property, and not having taken "any action whatsoever to punish the culprits, to obtain in-"demnification, to have the custodians removed and replaced, "or to bring the bankruptcy to an end, it rendered Mexico "indirectly liable for what occurred." [Reports: *Opinions of Commissioners*, 1927, p. 331; *A.J.*, XXII (1928), p. 433.]

NOTE.—The two national Commissioners, while agreeing that an award should be made in favour of the United States, and while agreeing substantially as to the amount to be awarded, delivered separate opinions on a number of points, in particular in regard to the question dealt with under (*a*). In his Opinion, Nielsen, the American Commissioner, emphasised the view that the action of the superintendent must be regarded as illegal, irrespective of what may be the information or motive that prompted it. "Mistaken action can not properly be "asserted as a legal defense against liability." He referred to the case of the *Costa Rica Packet*, Martens, *N.R.G.*, 2nd ser., XXIII (1898),

[1] The Commission referred here to the resolution of the *Institut de droit international* on bankruptcy law adopted in 1902, in which persons like this Mexican bankruptcy trustee were referred to as "the representatives of the "estate" ("*les représentants de la masse*"), and to the draft convention on bankruptcy law inserted in the final protocol of The Hague Conference on private international law of October–November, 1925, which laid down in its Article 4 that the syndic can take all conservatory measures or administrative measures and execute all actions "as representatives of the bankrupt or of the estate" ("*comme représentant du failli ou de la masse*").

pp. 48, 715 and 808; case of the *Union Bridge Company* under the Special Agreement of 18 August, 1910, between the United States and Great Britain, Nielsen's *Report*, p. 376; cases of the *Jessie, Thomas F. Bayard* and *Pescawha, ibid.*, p. 479.

He dissented in regard to the responsibility of Mexico for the acts of the trustee. He pointed out that under the law of the United States the receiver and trustee and other persons connected with bankruptcy proceedings are officers of the court, and that under international law a nation has responsibility for the conduct of judicial officers. He expressed the opinion that the Government of Mexico cannot be without responsibility for persons performing the same kind of duties in Mexico on the possible ground that such persons are not designated or considered as officers under Mexican law.

State Responsibility—Acts of Soldiers—Soldiers and Auxiliary Forces—Unjustified Shooting—Failure to Prosecute—Denial of Justice. **Case No. 155**

CHARLES S. STEPHENS AND BOWMAN STEPHENS CASE.

United States and Mexico: General Claims Commission.
15 *July*, 1927.

(VAN VOLLENHOVEN, NIELSEN, MACGREGOR.)

THE FACTS.—This was a claim arising out of the death, in 1924, of an American national killed by a shot fired by a member of some Mexican guards or auxiliary forces. This auxiliary force was a sort of informal municipal guards organisation—at first called "*defensas sociales*"—which had sprung up, partly to defend peaceful citizens, partly to fight the rebellion if necessary. The car in which Stephens was travelling was ordered to halt by the sentry. As the car did not stop, the soldier in question, without adding any warning, fired the shot with a fatal result. The soldier who caused his death was arrested by the civil authorities, and then handed over to the military authorities at their request. He was subsequently released by Colonel Hermógenes Ortega, who, when ordering the discharge of the auxiliary forces (or guards) under his command, discharged also this military prisoner. Ortega was then prosecuted as responsible for the escape and sentenced by the court of first instance to three years' imprisonment; but he was acquitted on appeal by the Supreme Court of Justice of the State of Chihuahua. The United States alleged that Mexico was liable for (*a*) the unlawful killing of Stephens; (*b*) for not prosecuting the soldier responsible for the death; and (*c*) for

Case No. 155 contd.

not punishing Ortega. It claimed an indemnity of $50,000.00 in favour of the deceased's two brothers.

Held by Van Vollenhoven, the Presiding Commissioner, for the Commission: That Mexico was responsible.

(*a*) *Responsibility for the Auxiliary Forces.*—Although it may be difficult to determine with precision the status of these guards as an irregular auxiliary of the army, in particular as they lacked both uniforms and insignia, it was clear that they were under the orders of a superior, that they were assimilated to soldiers, that they were "acting for" Mexico or for its political subdivisions, and that Mexico must be held responsible for their acts.

(*b*) *Responsibility for the Shooting.*—Although, when trying to halt the car, the soldier in question acted in the line of duty, the use he made of his firearm was utterly reckless. The absence of uniforms rendered it difficult to recognise the guards as persons entitled to halt others, in particular as some had the appearances of peasants, or even bandits. The excuse proffered by the soldier that he merely intended to "intimidate" Stephens deserved no attention.[1]

To hold that Mexico was internationally responsible for the shooting does not necessarily mean that the act was punishable under Mexican law.

(*c*) *Failure to Prosecute.*—Mexico was responsible on the ground of denial of justice. The soldier responsible was allowed to escape and the man who released him was never punished. Both facts reveal a failure on the part of Mexico to employ adequate measures to punish wrongdoers. [Reports: *Opinions of Commissioners*, 1927, p. 397; *A.J.*, XXII (1928), p. 448.]

Case No. 156

Responsibility of States—Executive Action—Responsibility for Acts of Military Authorities in the Conduct of Military Operations—Requisition of a Boat Chartered to Convey a Wounded Person—Absence of Imperative Necessity.

BOND COLEMAN CASE.

United States and Mexico: General Claims Commission.
3 *October*, 1928.

(SINDBALLE, NIELSEN, MACGREGOR.,

THE FACTS.—The claimant was employed by a Mexican company as a geologist. During the first few days of

[1] The Commission referred here to the *Swinney* case, the *Falcon* case and the *Teodoro García* case—all in *Annual Digest*, 1925-1926.

the month of June, 1924, the claimant and three other men in his charge were travelling, in the conduct of their work of survey and investigation, on horseback in Tabasco, Mexico. On 4 June, 1924, while engaged in the performance of their work, they were unexpectedly attacked by armed supporters of de la Huerta. The attack was apparently made on the assumption that claimant and his associates were members of Federal forces. During the attack, a bullet lodged in the claimant's wrist, fracturing the bone and inflicting a painful wound. The claimant and his party were then robbed of their equipment and mules, and subsequently were permitted to continue on their way to Villa Hermosa, where the claimant was given medical treatment. In view of the seriousness of the claimant's injury his employers had chartered a boat and sent it to Villa Hermosa for the purpose of taking the claimant to Galveston, Texas, for medical treatment. However, General Gonzales, Federal Commander in charge at Villa Hermosa and vicinity, detained the boat for a period of three days for the purpose of transporting his troops and equipment. As a consequence of that delay, the wound in the claimant's wrist became infected, causing serious pain, the loss of the full use of the hand, and a diminution of the earning capacity.

The United States claimed an indemnity for the claimant on two grounds: (1) for the failure of Mexican authorities to apprehend and punish the culprits; (2) for the action of Mexican military authorities in depriving the claimant of the means of conveyance urgently needed for medical treatment.

Held by Nielsen, the American Commissioner, for the Commission: That while no indemnity could be awarded owing to the absence of proof of negligence in the apprehension and punishment of the persons who injured the claimant, Mexico was responsible for the wrongful act of General Gonzales in seizing the boat which was sent to enable the wounded man to obtain medical assistance. "It is unnecessary to consider any "legal questions with respect to the right of military authori-"ties to requisition, conformably to law and on the payment "of proper compensation, a vessel that may be needed for "public purposes. This ship was seized without compensa-"tion, and at a time when the dictates of humanity should

Case No. 156 *contd.*

" have prompted assistance to the claimant, measures taken " for his relief were frustrated. No imperative necessity for " taking the boat has been shown." [Report: *Opinions of Commissioners*, 1929, p. 56.]

NOTE.—The case is digested here as illustrating the principle that the large measure of freedom from responsibility for acts of military authorities in the conduct of military operations—see, for instance, the *Luzon Sugar Refining Co. Ltd.* case (*Annual Digest*, 1925-1926, Case No. 164)—is subject to the general requirement of reasonableness and necessity of such action.

Case No. 157

Responsibility of States—Executive Action—Maltreatment in Prison—Detention "*incomunicado*"—Rules of Evidence —Admissibility of Sworn Statements by Interested Parties.

DANIEL DILLON CASE.

United States and Mexico: General Claims Commission. 3 *October*, 1928.

(SINDBALLE, NIELSEN, MACGREGOR.)

THE FACTS.—This was a claim for damages for alleged unlawful detention for a period of about fifteen days and for alleged maltreatment during that time.

The claimant, who had a position as representative of the International News Service in Mexico City, was, in June, 1916, arrested by two Mexican Federal officers, He was subsequently taken to the prison on the outskirts of Mexico City, and he alleges that there he was placed in a small cell with scant light, bad ventilation and unsatisfactory sanitary installations. Eventually he was handed over to the American " Special Repre- " sentative " in Mexico and left the country.

During all the time of his detention he was not allowed to communicate with anybody. Neither was information given him concerning the reason of his arrest and detention.

Held by Sindballe, Presiding Commissioner, for the Commission: (*a*) In regard to the charge of maltreatment, that there was not sufficient evidence to show that the prison in which the claimant was detained was below such a minimum standard as is required by international law.

(*b*) In regard to the long period of detention and the keeping of the claimant "*incomunicado*" and uninformed about the reason of his detention, that the conduct of Mexican authorities constitute a maltreatment and a hardship unwarranted by the purpose of the arrest to a degree which rendered Mexico responsible under international law. [Report: *Opinions of Commissioners*, 1929, p. 61.]

NOTE.—Commissioner Nielsen, while concurring in the decision, added a number of observations on the question of the right of expulsion and the admissibility of sworn statements of a claimant supported solely by his own testimony. In regard to the latter, he said: "Unimpeached testimony of a person who may be the best informed "person regarding transactions and occurrences under consideration "cannot properly be disregarded because such a person is interested in "the case. No principle of domestic or international law would "sanction such an arbitrary disregard of evidence." He added that although few concrete rules of international law have been developed in this respect in international practice, it was proper "to give effect to "certain elementary principles applied by domestic courts."

State Responsibility—Executive Action—Brutal Treatment by Customs Officials—Illegal Arrest—Prolonged Detention—Object of Maximum Period of Detention Prescribed by National Law. **Case No. 158**

PETER KOCH CASE.

United States and Mexico: General Claims Commission. 18 *October*, 1928.

(SINDBALLE, NIELSEN, MACGREGOR.)

THE FACTS.—On 10 July, 1912, after dark, the power-boat *Ella*, on board of which was the owner, Peter Koch, a naturalised American citizen, was boarded by Mexican Customs officials. The Mexicans wore no uniform, and Koch—believing they were robbers (it is alleged)—resisted them, trying to start the engine of the boat. As the result the Mexicans treated Koch brutally, inflicting upon him physical injuries. On board the *Ella* the Mexicans found a small quantity of guano. Koch was then charged with having resisted the authorities and with having stolen guano from Todos Santos Islands. He was detained under arrest until 1 February, 1913, when he was released on account of insufficient evidence.

The United States of America claimed on behalf of Koch damages in the sum of $10,000 U.S. currency. The claim was based upon the allegations of (1) brutal treatment of the claimant when his boat was searched by the Customs officials; (2) the illegal refusal of bail;

Case No. 158 ***contd.***

and (3) failure to grant to Koch the rights guaranteed to an accused by Mexican law in respect of the period of detention.

Held by Sindballe, Presiding Commissioner, for the Commission: (1) As there was no doubt that Koch was brutally treated by the Customs officials, that treatment amounted to a delinquency for which Mexico must be responsible under international law.

(2) As in view of the evidence it was somewhat doubtful whether there was probable cause for the arrest of the claimant, the Commission would not feel justified in basing an award on the supposition that the arrest itself was illegal.

(3) The refusal to release Koch under bond pending trial was ratified by the Third Circuit Court, and this refusal can hardly be said to constitute an international delinquency.

(4) With regard to the long period of the detention, the Commission is of opinion that a wrong had been inflicted upon the claimant for which Mexico was responsible. It was immaterial that the time limit fixed by Mexican law had not been exceeded. The object of provisions fixing a time limit for the duration of a detention is to establish a guarantee for the accused, but not to authorise detention up to the maximum period of time. The present case was not very complicated and the defendant Government produced no evidence to show what kind of investigations had been carried on during the detention of the claimant. [Report: *Opinions of Commissioners*, 1929, p. 118.]

(v) Plea of Non-Discrimination against Foreigners

[See also Part IV, Territorial Jurisdiction: (*a*) *Expropriation*.]

Responsibility of States—Plea of Non-Discrimination.

For an *obiter dictum* to the effect that "in countries where "the treatment accorded to citizens by their own authorities is "somewhat lax, a 'special protection' should be extended to "foreigners on the ground that their governments will not be "satisfied with the excuse that they have been treated as "nationals would have been," see Opinion of Van Vollenhoven, the Presiding Commissioner, in the *Mallén* case (Case No. 144), *Opinions of Commissioners*, 1927, p. 254; *Roberts* case and *Hopkins* case, *Annual Digest*, 1925-1926, Cases Nos. 160 and 170, referred to.

Responsibility of States—Exhaustion of Legal Remedies—Relation to Subsequent Recourse to International Tribunals.

See Case No. 321 (*Kulin, Emeric* v. *Roumanian State*).

Responsibility of States—Expropriation of Alien Property—Question of Non-Discrimination.

See Case No. 94 (*Czechoslovak Agrarian Reform* (*Swiss Subjects*) *Case*).

(b) Acts of Insurgents, Rioters and Private Individuals in General

State Responsibility—Limits of State Responsibility for Damages Suffered by Foreigners in Times of Revolution, Rebellion, Civil War, Insurrection, etc.—Meaning of the Conception of Revolution as Distinct from Rebellion, etc.—Determination of Persons or Groups of Persons whose Wrongful Acts Give Rise to Responsibility of the State. **Case No. 159**

GEORGES PINSON CASE, §§ 11, 48-66, 70.

France and Mexico : Mixed Claims Commission.
19 *October*, 1928.
(VERZIJL, President.)

THE FACTS.—(*a*) The French-Mexican Claims Convention of 25 September, 1924, arranged on an equitable basis (set out in Articles II and III) the settlement of all *bona fide* claims of French citizens and protected persons for damages which they might have suffered from acts of definite military forces, etc., since the Mexican revolution of 1910 to 1920. Thus the question of the limits of State responsibility in these circumstances under general principles of international law did not arise directly, but only incidentally, viz. in connection with (i) the Mexican contention that the Convention itself, as well as international law, rejected absolutely the idea of the responsibility of the State for damage to foreigners incidental either to rebellion or revolution, or to the suppression of the same, and that therefore the Convention was *strictissimae interpretationis* ; (ii) the necessity for the Commission to separate the cases in which interest ought to be awarded from those in which it ought not. (See also Cases Nos. 181 and 318.)

Case No. 159 ***contd.***

(*b*) Among the categories of military forces whose acts gave rise to indemnification, Article III of the Convention enumerated (i) forces of a Government *de jure* or *de facto* ; (ii) revolutionary forces which, in consequence of their success, have established Governments *de jure* or *de facto*, or revolutionary forces opposed to them ; (iii) forces arising from the disbanding of those mentioned under (ii) up to the time when a Government *de jure* established itself as a result of a particular revolution, etc. As for the Governments *de jure* and *de facto*, see Cases Nos. 136 and 164. In regard to the categories under (ii) and (iii) the Mexican Agent asserted that as " revolutionary " could be recognised only those forces which took part in a movement which, according to the view of Mexican officials, deserved the honorific denomination of " Revolution," that is to say, *inter alia*, the revolution of Francisco Madero against the Government of Porfirio Díaz (1910), the revolution of Venustiano Carranza against the Government of Victoriano Huerta (1913), and the revolution of Alvaro Obregón against the Government of Venustiano Carranza (1920) ; but that, on the contrary, the revolt of Victoriano Huerta against the Government of Francisco Madero (1913) and the rebellion of the Conventionist generals against Carranza as First Commander-in-Chief of the Constitutionalist Army in 1914 could not be described as revolutions. This purely political argument was supported by the contention that international law recognises as revolutions those revolts only which have succeeded in overthrowing the existing Government, all other subversive movements being no more than rebellions, mutinies, insurrections, etc.

Held by the President : (*a*) That he was prepared to agree so far with the Mexican Agent that positive international law now prevailing does not, or does not yet, recognise in a general way the obligation of a State to award to foreigners indemnification for damages which they may have suffered in consequence of insurrections, rebellions, revolutions, civil wars, etc. ; that, however, the Mexican contention, in its far more absolute form, was inadmissible ; that, indeed, there are many cases in which a State may be bound to award to foreigners adequate indemnity on account of damages incidental to rebellion, etc., for instance when the losses have been inflicted upon them by regular military requisitions (analogous to Article 52 of the Regulations annexed to Hague Convention IV of 1907), by wrongful acts of the Government itself, or of regular governmental forces exceeding the limits of military necessity, or by wrongful acts committed during a civil war by a revolutionary party that has gained the final victory (see for this point Case No. 161 also), or by mutinies or mobs provided the appropriate authorities omitted to take reasonable measures to suppress them. Consequently Mexico was, independently of the Claims Convention, responsible according to international law, *inter alia*, for pillage by its military forces or by successful revolutionary parties, for confiscations, bombardments of undefended towns, and other analogous delinquencies, formally declared to be prohibited acts by the Hague Regulations of 1907 above mentioned.

(*b*) That the Mexican contention was unfounded. The term " revolution " has no exactly defined meaning in international law, in contradistinction to rebellion, insurrection, civil war, etc. In particular, the ultimate success of a revolt has never been considered as the true criterion of a revolution ; were it so, the juridical character of an insurrectional movement would often remain in suspense for months or years. Neither can the criterion be found in the sublimity of its political or social ideals, nor in its local extent, nor in the recognition of the insurgents as belligerents by either the regular or foreign Governments. Unless there are indications to the contrary, every armed and more or less organised movement which, inspired by a definite social or political programme, under the impulse of general discontent, or under the influence of prominent leaders, strives for the overthrow of a particular Government or for a fundamental change in the system of government, may be styled a revolution. Thus the *coup d'état* of Huerta against Madero (1913) was no less a revolutionary movement than the other revolutions officially described as such. The insurrection of the so-called " Convention " of Aguascalientes against Carranza (1914) is even clearly and expressly alluded to in the second item of Article III (*supra*). This is the more unquestionable as President Obregón afterwards by his Decree of 19 July, 1924, expressly recognised the Conventionists as revolutionary forces, in the application of the national Mexican Claims Law. Consequently the Zapatists, Villists and other allied forces are also to be considered as revolutionary forces under the Claims Convention.

[Till now unreported.]

Case No. 159 *contd.*

NOTE.—(*a*) The President quoted in this respect: Dionisio Anzilotti, *La responsabilité internationale des Etats à raison des dommages soufferts par des étrangers* in *Revue générale de droit international public*, vol. XIII, pp. 305 ff.; Dr. K. Strupp, *Das völkerrechtliche Delikt* in *Handbuch des Völkerrechts* (Stier Somlo), pp. 97 ff., 103 ff.; V. Pennetti, *Responsabilità internazionale in caso di revolte o di guerre civili*, pp. 24 ff.; Baty, *International Law*, pp. 80, 136 ff.; P. Schön, *Die völkerrechtliche Haftung der Staaten aus unerlaubten Handlungen*, pp. 95 ff.; Borchard, *Diplomatic Protection of Citizens Abroad*, pp. 228 ff.; A. Rougier, *Les guerres civiles et le droit des gens*, pp. 473 ff.

In particular he rejected (*a*) the theory of State risk ("*risque étatif*"), propounded by Paul Fauchille (*Annuaire de l'Institut de droit international*, vol. XVIII, pp. 233 ff.); (*b*) the theory of presumption of fault on the part of the State, giving rise to a responsibility *quasi ex delicto*, propounded by C. Wiesse (*Reglas de derecho internacional aplicables a las guerras civiles*); and (*c*) the theory of Brusa (quoted above, *Annuaire*, vol. XVII, pp. 96 ff.) tending to establish an analogy between the case under consideration and the duty of a State under national public law to indemnify private owners for compulsory expropriation.

(*b*) In the paragraphs 57-65 and the Annexes I, II and III of his award, the President gave a complete survey of the evolution of the Mexican promise to indemnify the victims of the revolutions, from the Decree of Monclova (1913) to the conclusion of the Claims Conventions (1923 ff.), of the analogies and differences between the National Claims Laws and the Claims Conventions and between the successive draft conventions, and of the classification of the military forces in the revolutionary period from 1910 to 1920 according to the contentions of the French and the Mexican Agents.

Case No. 160

Responsibility of States—Responsibility for Acts of Insurgents —Responsibility for Acts of Soldiers.

G. L. SOLIS CASE.

United States and Mexico: General Claims Commission.
3 October, 1928.

(SINDBALLE, NIELSEN, MACGREGOR.)

THE FACTS.—(See Case No. 334.) It was contended by Mexico that a Government is not responsible for the acts of revolutionary forces or for malicious acts of soldiers committed in their private capacity.

Held by Nielsen, the American Commissioner, for the Commission: (*a*) In respect of responsibility for acts of insurgents that, following upon the principles enunciated by the British-American Mixed Arbitral Tribunal in the *Home Missionary Society* case under the Convention of 18 August, 1910,[1] and by Plumley, Umpire in the British-Venezuelan arbitration of

[1] Nielsen, *Report*, p. 423.

1903,[1] in the absence of convincing evidence of negligence on the part of the Mexican authorities, the claim must be rejected. In dealing with the question of responsibility for acts of insurgents two points must be considered, namely, " the capacity " to give protection, and the disposition of authorities to employ " proper, available measures to do so. Irrespective of the facts " of any given case, the character and extent of an insurrec- " tionary movement must be an important factor in relation " to the question of power to give protection."

(*b*) As to the item for the value of cattle said to have been taken by Federal forces, the claim must succeed. There was clear evidence that about one hundred soldiers were camped on the ranch for about a month. It must be taken for granted that some officer was charged with responsibility for their acts. It cannot therefore be reasonably assumed that the soldiers were stragglers for whom no one was responsible.

Thomas Y. Youmans case, *Annual Digest*, 1925-1926, Case No. 162, and the *Zafiro* case, *ibid.*, Case No. 161, referred to.

[Reports: *Opinions of Commissioners*, 1929, p. 48; *A.J.*, XXIII (1929), p. 454.]

State Responsibility for Wrongful Acts of Revolutionaries—Successful and Unsuccessful Revolts Contrasted—Retroactive Liability in regard to Acts Committed Before the Final Success of the Revolution. **Case No. 161**

GEORGES PINSON CASE, §§ 11, 55, 70.

France and Mexico: Mixed Claims Commission.
19 *October*, 1928.

(VERZIJL, President.)

THE FACTS.—In connection with the question of indebtedness for interest on the sums awarded by the Commission as indemnification, the President, in the face of a fundamental difference of opinion between his fellow

[1] In this case the Umpire referred to the following provision, as declaratory of international law, found in a treaty concluded in 1892 between Germany and Colombia:

" It is also stipulated between the contracting parties that the German " Government will not attempt to hold the Colombian Government " responsible, unless there be due want of diligence on the part of the " Colombian authorities or their agents, for the injuries, oppressions, or " extortions occasioned in time of insurrection or civil war to German " subjects in the territory of Colombia, through rebels, or caused by " savage tribes beyond the control of the Government."
(Ralston, *Venezuelan Arbitrations of* 1903, p. 384.)

Case No. 161 ***contd.***

Commissioners, had to decide the question in what circumstances a State is bound, under general principles of international law, to award damages to foreigners for losses and injuries suffered by them from wrongful acts of revolutionary forces. This question was particularly important on account of the extent of the damages caused by the so-called Conventionist forces, who in the autumn of 1914 rose in revolt against the supreme authority of Venustiano Carranza as First Commander-in-Chief of the Constitutionalist Army under the Plan of Guadalupe of 26 March, 1913, and who, under the command of the generals Villa, Zapata and others, persevered in their armed resistance for a considerable time until their ultimate subjection or dispersion. Although Mexico, on the basis of the Claims Convention, was declared to be liable for the award of damages for the losses caused by these Conventionist forces (see Case No. 159),

Held : " That, as a rule, a State which has endured the trial " of a revolutionary movement cannot be held bound by, or " liable for, the juridical acts or international delinquencies of " the revolutionists unless the movement has ended in their " ultimate victory and the conquest of the supreme power in " the State." In that event the State is, according to international law, responsible for the wrongful acts of the revolutionaries committed from the moment when the revolution broke out until the moment of its success, on exactly the same footing as it is responsible for the wrongful acts of a regular Government. Reference was made, *inter alia*, to Ralston and Sherman Doyle, *Venezuelan Arbitrations of* 1903 (Senate Document 316, 58th Congress, 2nd session, Washington, 1904), pp. 7, 17, 145, 458, 489, 810 ; §§ 4 and 5 of the award of the General Claims Commission, United States–Mexico (1923) *in re United Dredging Company* (*Opinions of Commissioners*, 4 February, 1926, to 23 July, 1927, pp. 395 and 396) ; Borchard, *The Diplomatic Protection of Citizens Abroad*, p. 241 ; Strupp, *Das völkerrechtliche Delikt*, p. 92 ; Kunz, in *Wörterbuch des Völkerrechts und der Diplomatie*, vol. II, pp. 605 ff.

In the application of this principle Mexico was held liable, under general principles of international law, for the wrongful acts committed by the Constitutionalist Army from the outbreak of the Carranzist revolution (February, 1913) to the definitive establishment of a new Government *de jure* (1 May,

1917), but held not liable, under the same law, for those committed by the Villists, Zapatists and other Conventionist forces from the time of their rebellion against Carranza to their final submission and dispersion.

[Till now unreported.]

Responsibility of States—Responsibility for Damage in the Course of Riots Directed against Foreigners as Such—Riots against Greek Subjects in Bulgaria in 1906. **Case No. 162**

SARROPOULOS *v.* BULGARIAN STATE.

Greco-Bulgarian Mixed Arbitral Tribunal.
14 *February*, 1927.

(DE LA BARRA, YOUPIS, PAPAZOFF.)

THE FACTS.—(See Case No. 173.) It appeared that the damage suffered by the claimant, a Greek subject resident in Bulgaria, was caused in the course of riots directed particularly against Greek subjects. Although it was not proved that the Bulgarian Government was directly implicated in the riots, the evidence before the Tribunal showed that they were organised and emanated from a common centre, and that the Bulgarian authorities had failed to take the necessary precautions to prevent them.

Held : That Bulgaria was in principle responsible.

The question of responsibility of States for damage suffered by foreigners in the course of riots was one of the most controversial questions in international law. In particular, the principle of absolute responsibility was hotly contested, and could not be accepted without serious qualifications. However, there were certain principles which even in the present state of the law could be accepted as non-controversial. One of these principles was that the State was responsible when the riots were directed against the foreigners as such, or when the damage caused was the result of negligence or fault of the local authorities. This was a principle recognised by the great majority of writers, by relevant conventions and by international jurisprudence. [Report : *Recueil*, VII, p. 46.]

VII.—For Acts and Omissions of Revolutionary or *de facto* Governments

Case No. 163

Contractual Obligations of *de facto* Governments—Automobile Ambulances Bought by Revolutionary Government—Actions done in the Ordinary Routine of Government Business.

THE PEERLESS MOTOR CAR COMPANY CASE.

United States and Mexico: General Claims Commission. 13 *May*, 1927.

(VAN VOLLENHOVEN, NIELSEN, MACGREGOR.)

THE FACTS.—This was a claim made by the United States of America on behalf of the Peerless Motor Car Company, an American corporation, to obtain payment of 23,000 Mexican pesos, alleged to be due as the purchase price of two automobile ambulances, under a contract entered into on 25 July, 1913, between the Mexican Government and the claimant.

In the arguments advanced before the Commission both Governments relied upon the decision rendered by the Commission in the *George W. Hopkins* case (*Annual Digest*, 1925-1926, Case No. 170). The Government of Mexico, while not disputing that the automobiles were delivered in accordance with the terms of the contract, contended that the Mexican Government was not responsible on the ground that the claim was for war material ordered by, and sold and delivered to, an illegitimate Administration, that is, the Administration of General Huerta.

Held by Nielsen, American Commissioner, for the Commission: That in accordance with the contention of the United States the purchase of the motor ambulances was an impersonal act covered by the principles laid down in the *Hopkins* case, and that the Government of Mexico was liable for the purchase price of the ambulances. [Report: *Opinions of Commissioners*, 1926, 1927, p. 303.]

NOTE.—The other two Commissioners, while concurring in the conclusions with respect to the liability of Mexico, expressed the opinion that the purchase of ambulances was not part of the ordinary routine of government business. But it was more akin to a transaction of government routine than to any kind of voluntary undertaking " having for its object the support of an individual or group of " individuals seeking to maintain themselves in office." For the distinction between the two kinds of acts see the *George W. Hopkins* case, paragraphs 5 and 6 of the original decision.

As to the Responsibility of States for Money Orders Issued by Revolutionary Governments, see the case of *Singer Sewing Machine Company*, decided by the United States and Mexico General Claims Commission (Sindballe, Nielsen and MacGregor) on 18 October, 1928. This was a claim for the non-payment of postal money orders for an aggregate sum of $31,273.39, Mexican currency, purchased by the claimant company or issued to it during the time from 18 March, 1913, to 30 September, 1914, by various post offices of the Mexican Government, all of them payable at sight. The Commission applied the principle adopted in the *George W. Hopkins* case.

State Responsibility for Wrongful Acts of Governments *de facto*—Criterion for Existence of (General *de facto* Government—Irrelevance of Illegal Origin. **Case No. 164**

GEORGES PINSON CASE, §§ 49, 51, 52, 54.

France and Mexico: Mixed Claims Commission.

19 *October*, 1928.

(VERZIJL, President.)

THE FACTS.—In virtue of the French-Mexican Claims Convention of 1924, Mexico was liable to compensate French subjects and protected persons for damages caused, *inter alia*, by the forces of a Government *de facto*. The question of the criterion of the existence of such a Government arose particularly in view of the struggling revolutionary Governments of Victoriano Huerta and Venustiano Carranza in 1913 and 1914. Huerta had upset by a *coup d'état* in February, 1913, the regular Government of Francisco Madero and established a new Government in Mexico City which governed a large part of the Federation with the aid of the Federal army. Carranza had proclaimed against Huerta a revolutionary movement, which at first still lacked an orderly governmental machinery.

Held: That the existence of a Government *de facto* is exclusively a question of fact, which by no means depends upon the constitutional law of the country nor upon the simple fact of recognition or want of recognition of its existence either by subsequent Governments or by foreign States, since the question of the recognition or the refusal of recognition of a definite group of leaders as a *de facto* Government is too often determined upon purely political considerations, and a refusal of recognition may be a pretext in order to escape responsibility for its acts. At best, recognition may be admitted as one of

Case No. 164 *contd.*

many elements of evidence. From the very nature of things the circumstances in which the question may arise differ considerably: thus a group of revolutionists who usurp power in the very centre of the Government and are immediately able to dispose of the whole governmental machinery, the army and navy, and the financial resources of the country (Huerta), will more readily be held to be a Government *de facto* than the leaders of a revolutionary movement who, operating in an outlying district, are under the necessity of gradually strengthening their authority and establishing a new Government.

[Till now unreported.]

C. CLAIMS

I.—In General

Case No. 165

Responsibility of States—Claims—Espousal of Claims of Fugitives from Justice—Denial of Justice—Faulty Judicial Procedure—Disregard of International Standards—Maltreatment in Prison.

B. E. Chattin Case.

United States and Mexico: General Claims Commission.
23 *July*, 1927.

(Van Vollenhoven, Nielsen, MacGregor.)

The Facts.—Chattin, who since 1908 was a railway employee, was arrested, in July, 1910, on a charge of embezzlement. He was accused, on the information of several other persons arrested in connection with the charge, of being the principal in a conspiracy for the fraudulent sale of railway tickets. In February, 1911, he was tried, convicted and sentenced to two years' imprisonment. In June, 1911, he was released from the jail by the population of the town, which threw open the gates of the prison in the course of the disturbances caused by the Madero revolution. He then returned to the United States. It was alleged by the United States that the arrest, the trial and the sentence amounted to a denial of justice and that the treatment in jail was inhuman. Mexico denied responsibility. She also contended that Chattin, being a fugitive from justice, lost the right to invoke the protection of the United States, and that the latter was not on that ground at liberty to espouse his claim.

Held by Van Vollenhoven, the Presiding Commissioner, with the concurrence of Nielsen, the American Commissioner, in his final conclusion : That Mexico was responsible.

(*a*) *The Alleged Loss of the Right to Protection.*—Quite apart from the question whether a person released from prison in the course of a revolution may be regarded as a fugitive from justice, it could not be agreed that a Government espousing a claim makes itself a party to the improper act of its national. International awards, far from establishing either the duty or the right of international tribunals to reject claims of fugitives from justice, have adopted a different practice. Thus in the *Pelletier* case [1] the award did not attach any importance to the fact that Pelletier had escaped from a Haytian jail. In the *Roberts* case [2] the Commission virtually held that protection of a fugitive from justice should be left to the discretion of the claimant Government, and it did so more explicitly in the *Massey* case.[3] A similar attitude was taken in cases in which forfeiture of the right to protection was alleged for other reasons. Thus in the *García* case [4] the Commission held that the American claimant's participation in Mexican politics was immaterial for the question of the right of the United States to intervene in his behalf. In international cases the question has frequently been raised whether a fugitive from justice loses his right to invoke protection—but that is a different question from whether his Government as well loses its right to protect him in its discretion.

(*b*) *The Charge of Denial of Justice.*—While expressing grave doubts as to the propriety of basing the charge on the conception of denial of justice, the Commissioner held that in this respect Mexico was responsible on several grounds.

The accused was not duly informed regarding the charge brought against him. The proceedings disclosed " a most " astonishing lack of seriousness on the part of the Court." There was no effort to have the two most important pieces of evidence investigated. There was no effort to find the principal persons able to throw light on the case. Neither during the investigations nor during the hearings in open court was there a serious attempt at oral examination or cross-examination of any importance. The accused was not given a real opportunity during the hearings in open court freely to speak for himself. " The Commission would render a bad service

[1] Moore, pp. 1779, 1794, 1800.
[2] *Annual Digest*, 1925-1926, Case No. 166.
[3] *Ibid.*, 1927-1928, Case No. 166.
[4] *Ibid.*, 1925-1926, Case No. 157.

Case No. 165 *contd.*

" to the Government of Mexico if it failed to place the stamp " of its disapproval and even indignation on a criminal pro- " cedure so far below international standards of civilisation " as the present one. If the wholesome rule of international " law as to respect for the judiciary of another country . . . shall " stand, it would seem of the utmost necessity that appellate " tribunals when, in exceptional cases, discovering proceedings " of this type, should take against them the strongest measures " possible under constitution and laws, in order to safeguard " their country's reputation."

Bringing the proceedings of the Mexican authorities in this case to the test of international standards, there could be no doubt of their being highly insufficient. The treatment of Chattin amounted to an outrage, to bad faith, to wilful neglect of duty, or to an insufficiency of governmental action recognisable by every unbiased man.

(*c*) *As to Maltreatment in Prison.*—Mexico could not be held responsible. The allegation of the claimant regarding insanitary conditions, bad food, and frequent compulsion to witness the shooting of prisoners, were not substantiated by other evidence than his own statements.[1] There was not, as in the *Faulkner* case (*Annual Digest*, 1925-1926, Case No. 219), evidence of any complaint of this kind made either by Chattin and his fellow prisoners, or by the American vice-consul, while the men were in prison. Neither was there, as in the *Roberts* case (*ibid.*, Case No. 166), a contemporary statement presented by either Government and emanating from a reliable authority who visited the prison at that time. [Reports: *Opinions of Commissioners*, 1927, p. 422; *A.J.*, XXII (1928), p. 667.]

Case No. 166

Responsibility of States—Right to Espouse Claim in regard to Claimants of Alleged Immoral Character—Responsibility for Acts of Minor Officials—Failure to Prosecute.

GERTRUDE PARKER MASSEY CASE.

United States and Mexico: General Claims Commission.
15 *April*, 1927.

(VAN VOLLENHOVEN, NIELSEN, MACGREGOR.)

THE FACTS.—In October, 1924, William B. Massey, an American subject and the terminal superintendent of

[1] The Presiding Commissioner referred here to the award in the *White* case (Moore, p. 4971) as showing the necessity of considerable caution in regard to uncorroborated statements of claimants regarding their treatment in prison.

a petroleum company, was killed by a Mexican citizen, named Joaquin R. Saenz, who fired six shots into Massey's body. It was alleged that the murder was committed as an act of vengeance for attempted rape on the wife of Saenz. After the killing Saenz fled. He was captured and confined in prison at Tuxpan, Vera Cruz, from which he escaped on 26 December, 1924, with the help of the assistant jail-keeper, and he was not apprehended. The jail-keeper was then arrested and action taken against him. The United States asked for damages on account of denial of justice growing out of the failure of the Mexican authorities to take adequate measures to punish the slayer.

Mexico objected to the claim on two grounds:

(*a*) In view of the charge of immoral and illegal conduct made against Massey, Mexico contended that "International law, justice and equity preclude a "claim from being set up, on the general maxim *ex* "*dolo malo non oritur actio*, when the alien from whose "death the claim arises by his own immoral, negligent, "or unlawful conduct caused or contributed to cause "his own death."

(*b*) *Responsibility for Minor Officials.*—Mexico advanced the contention that a State is not responsible for a denial of justice when a prisoner accused of killing an alien is allowed to escape by a minor municipal officer in violation of law and of his own duty, if the State arrests and punishes the officer responsible, and measures are taken for the apprehension of the fugitive.

Held by Nielsen, the American Commissioner, for the Commission: That both contentions must be rejected and that Mexico was liable.

(*a*) *Right to Espouse the Claim.*—The character and morality of the killed man were irrelevant to the issue. "The United "States invoked the rule of international law which requires a "government to take proper measures to apprehend and "punish nationals who have committed wrongs against aliens. "The legal issue presented to the Commission is whether or not "the obligations of that rule were properly discharged with "respect to the apprehension and punishment of the person "who killed Massey. Neither the character nor the conduct "of Massey can affect the rights of the United States to invoke

Case No. 166 ***contd.***

" that rule, nor can they have any bearing on the obligations " of Mexico to meet the requirements of the rule or on the " question whether proper steps were taken to that end."

(*b*) *Responsibility for Acts of Minor Officials.*—Any uncertainty with respect to responsibility for acts of minor officials was largely eliminated by the Convention of 8 September, 1923, which stipulated that the Commission should pass upon " all claims for losses or damages originating from " acts of officials or others acting for either Government and " resulting in injustice." However, apart from the provisions of the Convention, it was " a sound general principle that, " whenever misconduct on the part of any such persons, " whatever may be their particular status or rank under " domestic law, results in the failure of a nation to perform its " obligations under international law, the nation must bear the " responsibility for the wrongful acts of its servants."

Whether or not prison officials may properly be designated as minor officials, they are entrusted with important duties. This point is more important than the amount or character of their official emoluments or their status or designation of their position under the domestic law of their country. The fact that the assistant prison official in question was subsequently arrested was not a point of material importance, in particular when coupled with the fact that there was no evidence to show that he was prosecuted and punished (although there is evidence that he was arrested and spent some time in jail), and that certain circumstances surrounding the imprisonment of the murderer reveal a situation of a more serious nature than an unexpected breach of trust on the part of a single minor official.

(*c*) In regard to the responsibility of Mexico for the failure to apprehend the murderer, there was no evidence to show that any effective action had been taken by the appropriate authorities to apprehend him. Letters written by the Mexican Secretary of the Interior to the Governor of the State of Vera Cruz, requesting that all necessary measures be taken to apprehend the accused, or by the Governor of the State of Vera Cruz to the American consul at Tampico pointing to certain steps taken by the authorities, could not be regarded as sufficient. There was no specific evidence that the police authorities took any steps to apprehend him. Neither was it shown that difficulties were experienced by the authorities in locating this well-known fugitive. [Reports: *Opinions of Commissioners*, 1927, p. 228; *A.J.*, XXI (1927), p. 783.]

Claims—Undisclosed Principal as Claimant—Real Party in Interest.

Case No. 167

JOHN A. MCPHERSON CASE.

United States and Mexico: General Claims Commission.
3 *June*, 1927.

(VAN VOLLENHOVEN, NIELSEN, MACGREGOR.)

THE FACTS.—This was a claim to recover a sum due on eight postal money orders, which were alleged to be the property of the claimant and which were not paid upon presentation to Mexican postal authorities. The orders were issued during the month of June, 1914.

The decision on the merits was given as in the case George W. Cook (No. 1 and No. 2 [1]). But it was contended by Mexico that no claim could be maintained before the Commission on behalf of the claimant, since, as shown by the evidence, the money orders in question were not the property of the claimant, and, further, they were issued in the name of John Davidson, whose nationality was not established in the Memorial. With reference to this point the United States contended that Davidson was a duly authorised agent and banker for McPherson, and that the former bought the money orders with money belonging to the latter, who may be regarded as an undisclosed principal.[2] Reference was made to the rule of the law of the United States in respect of the right of an undisclosed principal to sue in his own name on a non-negotiable instrument made in his behalf in the name of an agent.

Held by Nielsen, the American Commissioner, with the concurrence of the other two Commissioners: For the claimant. Under principles of international law and of domestic law—at least Anglo-Saxon law—the Commission should look to the real party in interest. [Report: *Opinions of Commissioners*, 1927, p. 325.]

NOTE.—The Commissioner referred on this point to the *Henry* case before the American-Venezuelan Commission of 1903, Ralston's *Report*, p. 14; *Ford* v. *Williams*, 62 U.S. 287.

---

[1] See Case No. 174.

[2] Counsel for the United States cited the *Henry* case before the American-Venezuelan Commission of 1903, Ralston's *Report*, p. 14, and the claim of *Charles Watson, Executor of Henry Meigs*, before the United States and Chilean Claims Commission under the Convention of 7 August, 1892, *Report of Agent of the United States*, p. 80.

Claims—In General—Right to Espouse Claims of Claimants of Alleged Immoral Character.

See Case No. 166 (*Massey Case*).

II.—Nationality of Claims

Case No. 168

Claims—Nationality of—Expatriation by Presumption of the Law—Retroactive Effect of Subsequent Rebuttal of Presumption.

H. Rothmann *v.* Austria and Hungary.

Tripartite Claims Commission. (*United States, Austria and Hungary.*) 11 *July*, 1928.

(Parker, Commissioner.)

The Facts.—Section 2 of the Act of the Congress of the United States of 2 March, 1907, entitled "An Act in "reference to the expatriation of citizens and their "protection abroad," provides as follows:

"That any American citizen shall be deemed to "have expatriated himself when he has been "naturalised in any foreign State in conformity "with its laws, or when he has taken an oath of "allegiance to any foreign State.

"When any naturalised citizen shall have "resided for two years in the foreign State from "which he came, or for five years in any other "foreign State, it shall be presumed that he has "ceased to be an American citizen, and the place "of his general abode shall be deemed his place of "residence during said years: *Provided, however,* "That such presumption may be overcome on the "presentation of satisfactory evidence to a diplo-"matic or consular officer of the United States, under "such rules and regulations as the Department of "State may prescribe: *And provided also,* That no "American citizen shall be allowed to expatriate "himself when this country is at war."

The claimant was a naturalised American citizen. He was formerly an Austrian subject. Before the war he returned to Austria, and resided there for some time. During the war he was conscripted into the Austrian army—wrongfully according to his contention. In 1917, prior to the breaking off of relations between the United States and the Central Powers, he applied to the United States Embassy in Vienna for an emergency passport for immediate return to the United States. In applying for the passport he suppressed the fact that he was then and had for some six months been serving in the Austro-Hungarian army. When the facts became known to the American authorities, they cancelled the passport and refused to recognise him as an American citizen or to assist him to obtain release from military service. Subsequently, the American Department of State held that the statutory presumption of expatriation had arisen against the claimant. In 1919 the claimant returned to the United States.

Before the Commission it was contended on behalf of the claimant that by his return to the United States, where he had since continued to reside, he had retroactively overcome the legal presumption of the statute and that the presumption must therefore be treated as if it had never arisen.

The claim was for compensation on account of damages alleged to have been sustained by the claimant on account of enforced service in the Austro-Hungarian army, on account of confiscation of property, and other reasons.

Held : That the claim was not one which from its inception was impressed with American nationality, and that it did not therefore fall within the terms of the treaty conferring jurisdiction upon the Commission. The subsequent overcoming of the presumption against American nationality could not affect the nationality of the claim at the time when it arose, at which time the claimant was not entitled to, and was expressly denied, recognition and protection as an American citizen. As the United States themselves refused at the material period to recognise the claimant as an American citizen, they could not now complain that the Austrian authorities pursued a like course at that time. The Commissioner said : " While the " presumption of law is not conclusive and residence abroad " for the period prescribed by the statute does not of itself " terminate permanently American citizenship, nevertheless " when the statutory period has run and the legal presumption " has arisen against the individual, he has for the time being " forfeited all right to be recognised as an American citizen and

Case No. 168 *contd.*

" protected as such. . . . The purpose of the statute is to deny " the protection due an American citizen to one against whom " an unrebutted presumption of expatriation has arisen. That " purpose would be defeated if claimant could, subsequent to " the events forming the basis of a claim, overcome the pre- " sumption, and then as an American citizen demand and " receive compensation as damages resulting from acts against " which he was not entitled to protection." [Report: *A.J.*, XXIII (1929), p. 182.]

Case No. 169

Nationality of Claims—Nationality of the Claim at the Moment of the Damage and at the Moment of the Presentation of the Claim—Exceptional Conditions—Evolution of the French Protection over Syrians.

PABLO NÁJERA (OF THE LEBANON) CASE.

France and Mexico: Mixed Claims Commission.
19 *October*, 1928.

(VERZIJL, President.)

THE FACTS.—During the Mexican revolutions between 1910 and 1920, various Turkish subjects of Syrian and Lebanese origin, who were domiciled in Mexico and enjoyed before the World War the traditional *de facto* protection of France, suffered loss and damage. In 1923 and 1924 diplomatic negotiations between France and Mexico led to the conclusion of a convention whereby a Mixed Claims Commission was set up in order to examine all claims brought against the Mexican Government for losses suffered by French nationals and protected persons. At the time of the negotiation and conclusion of the said convention, Syria and the Lebanon were developing into mandated States in accordance with Article 22 of the Covenant of the League of Nations. When the claims were submitted to the Commission, the clauses of the Treaty of Lausanne, of 24 July, 1923, concerning the right of Turkish subjects of Syrian origin to opt for the new Syrian nationality, had not yet been finally put into operation. In these circumstances the Mexican Government claimed that the Claims Convention of 1924 could not apply to losses suffered by Syrians before 1920.

Held: That the Commission had jurisdiction.

(*a*) The general rule of customary law, according to which a State is authorised to put forward claims only on behalf of persons who possess its nationality (or stand under its protection) at the moment of the loss cr damage as well as at the moment of the coming into force of the Claims Convention or of the presentation of the claim or of the award, does not apply when the circumstances of the case prove a contrary intention of the High Contracting Parties.

(*b*) In the case under consideration the damage was suffered at a moment when the traditional protection of France, though suspended by the war, had not yet been abolished. The Convention was negotiated and concluded at a moment when the Mandate over Syria had already been conferred upon France, and the Treaty of Lausanne, 1923, provided for the option of Turkish subjects of Syrian origin abroad for Syrian nationality, under the conditions set forth in Article 34 of the said Treaty. The claim was submitted to the Commission at a moment when the claimant had already opted for the new nationality, but his option had not yet taken definite effect.

(*c*) Accordingly, the quality of French protected person of the claimant has itself undergone gradual changes in juridical character. However, the actual diplomatic protection exercised by France over the nationals of Syria in virtue of the Mandate is only a historically and politically more developed form of the traditional protection of former times, and, in these circumstances and in the light of the negotiations, Mexico is not entitled to invoke the general rule formulated under (*a*) against the application of the Convention of 1924 to Syrians as French protected persons.

(*d*) The claimant would have been no longer entitled to avail himself of the Convention, if he had not, in due time, taken the necessary steps to acquire the new nationality according to the Treaty of Lausanne—the traditional French protection of the Syrians having come to an end and having been replaced by the protection in virtue of the Mandate, after the establishment of autonomous Syrian States and a regular Syrian (Lebanese) nationality.

(*e*) In any case, the Commission would not be entitled to examine the regularity of an option for the new nationality, officially accepted by the competent French authorities according to Article 34 of the Peace Treaty of Lausanne, nor in particular to examine *a posteriori* the original Turkish nationality of the claimant and his racial affinity.[1]

[Till now unreported.]

[1] See an article on the " Nationality of Claims " by Sir Cecil Hurst, in *B.Y.*, 1926, pp. 163-182. See also Cases Nos. 196 and 206.

Nationality of Claims—Basis of Jurisdiction of International Commissions—Burden of Proof.

See Case No. 335 (*Edgar A. Hatton Case*).

Treatment of Aliens—Requisitions—Duty of Compensation—Evidential Value of Requisition Receipts.

See Case No. 335 (*Edgar A. Hatton Case*).

Nationality of Claims—Proof of Value of Affidavits in International Arbitration.

See Case No. 334 (*G. L. Solis Case*).

Double Nationality—Possible Effect on Nationality of Claims and Jurisdiction of International Tribunals.

See Case No. 334 (*G. L. Solis Case*).

Claims—Nationality of—Question of Evidence.

See Case No. 335 (*Edgar A. Hatton Case*).

IV.—State Control over Private Claims

Case No. 170
PERMANENT COURT OF INTERNATIONAL JUSTICE.
JUDGMENT No. 13.

Claims—State Control over Claims—Nature of Claims Arising out of an Injury to Private Persons and Put Forward by States—Is Compensation Due to the Individual or the State?

GERMANY v. POLAND.

CASE CONCERNING THE FACTORY AT CHORZÓW.

(CLAIM FOR INDEMNITY. MERITS.)

13 *September*, 1928.

THE FACTS.—(See Case No. 177.) In the Application Germany asked the Court to declare that the Polish Government was, in consequence of the measures of liquidation adopted by it in regard to the two Upper Silesian companies and declared by the Court in a previous judgment not to be in accordance with its international obligations, bound to make good the damage suffered by the companies; to award compensation for the damage suffered; to fix the method of payments; and, *inter alia*, to order the payments to be made to the account of the two companies with the Deutsche Bank at Berlin. In this connection there arose in the course of the proceedings a difference of opinion between the parties.

Germany contended that reparation need not necessarily consist in compensation to the companies concerned, and that the claimant Government may content itself with any form of reparation it deems proper. It was pointed out on her behalf that the suit before the Court was a suit between two Governments acting in their own name, that Germany did not appear as the representative of the individuals who suffered the injury, and that, as one of the consequences of this legal position, she was entitled to claim the payment at any *locus solutionis* which she may think proper.

On the part of Poland, it was contended that the above submission amounted to a modification of the subject of the dispute and, in some respects, of the nature of the application, which, it was alleged, was originally concerned only with compensation to the companies affected. It was contended that at that stage of the proceedings Germany was not entitled to modify the application by asking for compensation, not for the companies, but for herself.

Held: That Germany has not altered the subject-matter of the dispute in the course of the proceedings.

"It is a principle of international law that the "reparation of a wrong may consist in an indemnity "corresponding to the damage which the nationals "of the injured State have suffered as a result of the "act which is contrary to international law. This is "even the most usual form of reparation; it is the

Case No. 170 ***contd.***

"form selected by Germany in this case, and the "admissibility of it has not been disputed. The "reparation due by one State to another does not, "however, change its character by reason of the fact "that it takes the form of an indemnity for the calcula-"tion of which the damage suffered by a private person "is taken as the measure. The rules of law governing "the reparation are the rules of international law in "force between the two States concerned, and not the "law governing relations between the State which has "committed a wrongful act and the individual who has "suffered damage. Rights or interests of an individual "the violation of which rights causes damage are "always in a different plane to rights belonging to a "State, which rights may also be infringed by the "same act. The damage suffered by an individual is "never therefore identical in kind with that which "will be suffered by a State; it can only afford a "convenient scale for the calculation of the reparation "due to the State" (at p. 27).

It was true that there was nothing in international law to prevent one State from granting to another the right of recourse to international tribunals with the view to obtaining direct compensation for its nationals injured by the acts of that other State, but the Convention under which the Court exercised jurisdiction in the present case was not of that nature. [Report: Series A, No. 17, pp. 25-29.]

NOTE.—The Court also referred at some length to its previous judgments dealing with the same case and showing that it had always regarded the dispute as one between the two Governments (pp. 26, 27). While pointing to the "general character of an international tribunal "which, in principle, has cognisance only of inter-state relations," it referred to the fact that the Geneva Convention establishing the jurisdiction of the Court created at the same time special tribunals of an international character for certain categories of private rights. The purely inter-state character of the present dispute was also the reason why the Court in Judgment No. 7 reserved the case for judgment on the merits, although actions brought by the two companies *in pari materia* were pending at the same time before one of the special tribunals referred to above.

Cf. here also Series A, No. 2, p. 11, and *Annual Digest*, 1925-1926, Cases Nos. 178 and 179.

Claims—State Control over Private Claims—How far Affecting the Private Nature of the Claim—Requisition by Germany of Property in Germany of Roumanian Company—Subsequent Seizure by Roumania—Liability of Germany.

Case No. 171

SOCIÉTÉ PETROL BLOCK *v.* GERMANY.

Germano-Roumanian Mixed Arbitral Tribunal. 30 *July*, 1928.

(FAZY, FROELICH, MUNTEANU.)

THE FACTS.—Certain railway oil tanks belonging to the plaintiff, a Roumanian company, were requisitioned in Germany during the war. They were then brought by the German army to Roumania, where they were seized, apparently as war booty, in 1918 and 1919 by the Roumanian troops in the course of the German retreat. The Roumanian authorities refused to restore the tanks to the company, which thereupon brought an action against Germany by virtue of Article 297 (*e*) of the Treaty of Versailles.[1]

Held : That Germany was bound to compensate the owners. The subsequent seizure of the tanks by the Roumanian army was an act of sovereignty of the Roumanian State which was a matter between the belligerents and outside the cognisance of the Tribunal. [Report : *Z. für a. ö. R. und V.*, I (2) (1929), p. 97.]

NOTE.—This at first sight somewhat startling decision is apparently due to the fact that the Tribunal attached decisive importance to the purely private nature of the claim. Had the claim been in the nature of a State claim, then it might have been difficult for Roumania to ask for compensation for requisitioned property which she subsequently seized and which she refused to restore. The decision is digested here as illustrating the disputed question as to the legal nature of claims under Article 297 (*e*) of the Treaty of Versailles. See on this point Schmid, *ibid.*, pp. 102-104, who inclines to the view that these claims are State claims—a view which, in his opinion, is substantiated by the fact of the large degree of State control over the claims not only in regard to procedure before the Tribunal but also in regard to the right to dispose of the claim altogether in subsequent treaties without the consent of the interested parties. However, see *William A. Parker* case, *Annual Digest*, 1925-1926, Case No. 178, where it was held that " although the " claim becomes a national one in the sense that it is subject to the " absolute control of the State espousing it, its private nature inheres " in it and it is not made the property of the State." And see, to the same effect, the *North American Dredging Company of Texas* case, *ibid.*, Case No. 179.

---

[1] For the text of this paragraph see p. 543.

Case No. 172

Claims—State Control over—Effect upon the Character of Claims.

CLAIMS (NATIONAL CONTROL) CASE.

See statement by Edwin B. Parker, Commissioner, in Tripartite Claims Commission (United States, Austria and Hungary) Administrative Decision No. 1 Announcing Definitions and General Governing Principles and Dealing with the Functions and Jurisdiction of the Commission (25 May, 1927), to the effect that " all claims presented to this Commission shall be asserted " and controlled by the United States as claimant either on its " own behalf or on behalf of one or more of its nationals. With " respect to espousing or not the claim of its national at the " latter's request, and if espoused in determining when and how " the claim will be presented and pressed or withdrawn or com-" promised, the United States will exercise an untrammeled " discretion and the private owner will be bound by the action " taken. While the nation's absolute right to control a private " claim espoused by it is necessarily exclusive, because of the " national interest that may be or become involved, neverthe-" less the private nature of such claim continues to inhere in it " and the claim only in a very restricted sense becomes a " national claim. The act of espousal does not vest in the " nation the title to the claim. For the purpose of ascertaining " the nationality of a claim as determined by its being im-" pressed with the nationality of the private claimant, or for " any other purpose pertinent to the proper exercise of its " jurisdiction, the Commission will at any stage of a proceeding " require a full disclosure of the private interest therein." [Report: *A.J.*, XXI (1927), p. 605.[1]]

[1] It will be observed that the Tripartite Agreement between the United States and Austria and Hungary which became effective on 12 December, 1925, conferred upon the Commission jurisdiction in regard, *inter alia*, to the following categories of claims:

(1) Claims of American citizens arising since July 31, 1914, in respect of damage to or seizure of their property, rights and interests, including any company or association in which they are interested, within the territories of either the former Austrian Empire or the former Kingdom of Hungary as they respectively existed on August 1, 1914;

(2) Other claims for loss or damage to which the United States or its nationals have been subjected with respect to injuries to or death of persons, or with respect to property, rights and interests, including any company or association in which American nationals are interested, since July 31, 1914, as a consequence of the war;

(3) Debts owing to American citizens by the Austrian and/or the Hungarian Governments or by their nationals.

D. PRESCRIPTION (EXTINCTIVE PRESCRIPTION)

I.—Before International Tribunals

Prescription — Extinctive Prescription — Prescription as a General Principle of International Law—Duration of the Period Constituting Prescription. **Case No. 173**

SARROPOULOS *v.* BULGARIAN STATE.

Greco-Bulgarian Mixed Arbitral Tribunal. 14 *February,* 1927.

(DE LA BARRA, YOUPIS, PAPAZOFF.)

THE FACTS.—This was a claim, based on Article 179 of the Peace Treaty of Neuilly, for compensation for damage suffered by the claimant, a Greek subject, during the riots and revolutionary troubles which occurred in Bulgaria in 1906. Article 179 of the Treaty of Neuilly provides as follows:

" Diplomatic or consular claims made before the " war by the Representatives or Agents of the Allied " and Associated Powers with regard to the private " property, rights or interests of nationals of those " Powers shall, on the application of the Power con- " cerned, be submitted to the Mixed Arbitral Tribunal " provided for in Section VI."

Although the incidents in question formed the subject of a diplomatic note presented in 1906, it appeared that no claim had been put forward before 1921. The Bulgarian Government having invoked the plea of prescription,

Held: That the plea of prescription must be recognised.

" Positive international law has not so far established any " precise and generally adopted rule either as to the principle of " prescription as such or as to its duration. Neither do arbitral " decisions or opinions of writers yield any agreed solution.

" However, prescription appears to constitute a positive " legal rule in almost all systems of law. It is an expression of a " great principle of peace which is at the basis of the common " law and of all civilised systems of jurisprudence. Stability " and security in human affairs require that a delay should be " fixed outside which it should be impossible to invoke rights or " obligations. The difficulty of producing evidence after the

Case No. 173 *contd.*

" expiration of a certain period of time must frequently make " uncertain or impossible the recognition of a right.

" Prescription being an integral and necessary part of every " system of law must be admitted in international law.

" As to the period of prescription, there was no detailed rule " on the subject ; certain treaties, concluded in regard to cases " analogous to that before the Tribunal, limited this period to " twenty years.

" It was the duty of an arbitral tribunal, set up for the pur-" pose of deciding cases without restriction, to consider the " principles of international law in regard to prescription and " to apply it to the specific case submitted to it." [Report : *Recueil*, VII, p. 51.]

Case No. 174

Responsibility of States—Extinctive Prescription—National Statutes of Limitations.

George W. Cook (No. 2) Case.

United States and Mexico : General Claims Commission. 3 *June*, 1927.

(Van Vollenhoven, Nielsen, MacGregor.)

The Facts.—This was a claim to recover the aggregate amount of numerous postal money orders, which were owned by the claimant, and which it was alleged were not paid upon presentation to Mexican postal authorities. The orders were issued in the years 1913 and 1914.

It was contended by Mexico that the right to collect a postal money order is subject to a statute of limitations of two years after the date of issue, and that a recovery on the orders in question is now barred by that statute.

Held by Nielsen, the American Commissioner, the two other Commissioners concurring on this point : That the plea of the statute of limitations must be rejected. The Commissioner said (at p. 319) : " It has sometimes been said that " statutes of limitation are not a bar to international reclama-" tions. General statements of this kind have perhaps at times " led to some confusion of domestic law with a well-recognised " principle of international practice. There is, of course, no " rule of international law putting a limitation of time on

"diplomatic action or upon the presentation of an inter-
"national claim to an international tribunal. Domestic
"statutes of limitation take away at the end of prescribed
"periods the remedy which a litigant has to enforce rights
"before domestic courts. It is satisfactorily established by
"evidence that the claimant in the instant case presented his
"money orders and requested payment within the period
"during which payment could be made under Mexican law,
"and that payment was refused by Mexican postal authorities.
"The United States is not now debarred by any Mexican
"statute of limitations from recovering money wrongfully
"withheld from the claimant. The Mexican Government
"could not by withholding payment for a period prescribed
"by a domestic statute of limitation relieve itself from an
"obligation under international law to make restitution of the
"value of the orders. From a conclusion to this effect it does
"not follow that international tribunals must always dis-
"regard all statutes of limitation prescribing reasonable
"periods within which remedies may be enforced before
"domestic tribunals. And it may be further observed that
"in view of the stipulations of Article V of the Convention of
"8 September, 1923, no question can arise in this case with
"respect to the exhaustion of local remedies." [Reports: *Opinions of Commissioners*, 1927, p. 318; *A.J.*, XXII (1928), p. 189.]

NOTE.—It has been thought necessary to give a verbatim extract of this part of the decision, as it appears to the editors that the decision is liable to be misunderstood. So-called extinctive prescription has long been recognised by a series of international awards, *e.g.* the *Williams* case,[1] the *Butterfield* case,[2] the *Gentini* case [3]—and by writers, *e.g.* Oppenheim, vol. I (4th ed., 1928), § 155 (*c*). See also the emphatic resolution of the Institute of International Law in 1925.[4] What seems to be generally admitted is that national statutes of limitations do not in themselves constitute a bar to international action. This was the true import of the decision in the *Pious Fund* arbitration before the Permanent Court of Arbitration at The Hague in 1902. This qualification of the rule of extinctive prescription would, it is submitted, have been sufficient for the purpose of the decision in the present case.

---

[1] Moore, pp. 4181-4199.
[2] *Ibid.*, p. 1205.
[3] Ralston, *Venezuelan Arbitrations*, pp. 724-730.
[4] *Annuaire*, XXXII (1925), p. 558.

E. DAMAGES (MEASURE OF DAMAGES)

I.—Award of Damages in General. Grounds for Awarding Damages

Case No. 175

Damages—Distinction between Damages as a Solatium and Damages as Compensation for Material Losses.

CHARLES S. STEPHENS AND BOWMAN STEPHENS CASE.

United States and Mexico: General Claims Commission. 15 *July*, 1927.

(VAN VOLLENHOVEN, NIELSEN, MACGREGOR.)

THE FACTS.—(See Case No. 155.) As to the interests involved in the claim, the eldest brother of the deceased suffered a remote pecuniary loss by his death, in that the deceased together with this brother supported an aged aunt, and that the burden of supporting her fell subsequently upon the surviving brother alone. The youngest brother, who appeared to be suffering from melancholy or some mental disorder, did not seem to have sustained any financial damage.

Held by Van Vollenhoven, the Presiding Commissioner, for the Commission: That damages can properly be awarded. A distinction must be drawn between damages allowed in satisfaction for a moral wrong and those allowed as reparation for material losses. " When international tribunals thus far " allowed *satisfaction* for indignity suffered, grief sustained and " other similar wrongs, it usually was done *in addition to* re- " paration (compensation) for material losses." There were examples of awards for indignity and grief not combined with direct material losses, but in these cases the indignity or grief was suffered by the claimant himself, as in the *Davy* and *Maal* cases (Ralston, *Venezuelan Arbitrations of* 1903, pp. 412, 916). But there were instances of such damages being granted to persons other than the injured individual. Thus the American-German Mixed Claims Commission, in the *Vergne* case, awarded damages to a mother of a bachelor son, but not to his half-brother and half-sister, though " the evidence of pecuniary " losses suffered by this claimant cognisable under the law is " somewhat meagre and unsatisfactory " (*Consolidated Edition*, 1926, at p. 653). " It would seem, therefore, that, if in the " present case injustice for which Mexico is liable is proven,

" the claimants shall be entitled to an award in the character " of satisfaction, even when the direct pecuniary damages " suffered by them are not proven or too remote to form a " basis for allowing damages in the character of reparation " (compensation)." [Reports: *Opinions of Commissioners*, 1927, p. 397; *A.J.*, XXII (1928), p. 448.]

Measure of Damages—Question of Proof—Indirect Damages —Special Damages in Cases of Injuries Done to Consuls. **Case No. 176**

FRANCISCO MALLÉN CASE.

United States and Mexico: General Claims Commission.
27 April, 1927.

(VAN VOLLENHOVEN, NIELSEN, MACGREGOR.)

THE FACTS.—(See Case No. 144.) The claim for damages was largely based on the allegation that as the result of blows received by the claimant there ensued a series of illnesses and wounds, including a purulent discharge from the ear. The claimant produced certificates from private doctors from whom, some time after the occurrence, he received treatment.

Held by Van Vollenhoven, the Presiding Commissioner, for the Commission, with the concurrence of Nielsen, American Commissioner: (*a*) In respect of compensatory damages for injuries to health and earning capacity, that it was not certain whether there was a link between, on the one hand, Mallén's ailments of 1908 and subsequent years, together with their financial consequences, and, on the other hand, the events of October, 1907. The claimant should have furnished some conclusive medical testimony about the development of his illness between these periods, or at least an expert statement by some high medical authority of the present day establishing the value of the doctors' certificates. When accepting as the basis for an award the physical injuries inflicted upon Mallén in 1907, only those damages can be considered which are the direct result of the occurrence.

(*b*) In respect of damages claimed as satisfaction for indignity suffered, for lack of protection, and for denial of justice, that such damages must in principle be awarded. However, any award on account of the circumstances that the claimant was a consul must be influenced by the fact that high sums claimed or paid in order to vindicate the consular dignity

Case No. 176 *contd.*

related either to cases in which the nation's honour was involved, or to consuls in backward countries where their position approaches that of the diplomat. This may be seen from the award of the Permanent Court of Arbitration of 22 May, 1909, in the *Casablanca* case, where the Court mentioned " the " prestige of the consular authority " or " the consular prestige," but especially with reference to conditions in Morocco as they were before France established its protectorate. [Reports: *Opinions of Commissioners*, 1927, p. 254; *A.J.*, XXI (1927), p. 803.]

NOTE.—On the question of damages under the latter head, the following passage from the observations of Nielsen, the American Commissioner, may be quoted: " I think that international law undoubtedly secures to a consular officer the right to perform his " functions without improper interference. And it would seem that, " in a case in which his personal safety is threatened, authorities of the " country of his residence may well be expected to take especial pre- " caution to afford him protection. It is of course their duty to take " proper steps for the protection of all aliens. But when indemnity is " claimed before an international tribunal solely as personal compensa- " tion to a consular officer who has been injured, I do not believe that a " sum so large that it must properly be regarded as punitive damages " or as redress for indignity to a nation can properly be awarded on the " ground that the injured person is such an official." (*Opinions of Commissioners*, 1927, at p. 264.)

II.—Indirect Damages and Damages for Loss of Profits

Case No. 177 PERMANENT COURT OF INTERNATIONAL JUSTICE. JUDGMENT No. 13.

Damages—Measure of Damages—Damages for Loss of Profits —Distinction between Expropriation and Unlawful Deprivation of Property—Measure of Damages in Consequence of an Unlawful Act—Cumulative Damage of Interdependent Undertakings—Whether the Court can Rely on the Data Supplied by the Parties—Changes in the Value of the Property Taken Away—Offers of Compensation Made during Abortive Negotiations—Appointment of Experts—Indeterminate and Contingent Damages.

GERMANY *v.* POLAND.

CASE CONCERNING THE FACTORY AT CHORZÓW.

(CLAIM FOR INDEMNITY. MERITS.)

13 *September*, 1928.

THE FACTS.—In March, 1915, a contract was concluded between a German company styled the Bayerische Stickstoffwerke and the German *Reich*, according to which that company undertook, *inter alia*, to establish for the *Reich* a nitrate factory in Chorzów, Upper Silesia. The necessary lands were to be acquired on behalf of the German Government and entered in the name of Germany in the land registry. The *Reich* was given powers to terminate, as from March, 1926, the contract of management of the factory by Germany.

On 19 December, 1919, a new company, the Oberschlesische Stickstoffwerke, was formed and a number of documents were signed in which the *Reich* sold to that company the factory at Chorzów, including the land and the accessories. The management of the factory was to remain in the hands of the Bayerische. On 24 December, 1919, in a contract between the *Reich* and the Oberschlesische yet another company was formed, known as the Stickstoff Treuhand Gesellschaft, which, under the contract, took over in the place of the Oberschlesische all the obligations imposed by the contract upon the latter in regard to the *Reich* in consideration of receiving shares in the Oberschlesische to the nominal value of 109,750.000 marks out of the 110,000.000 of the total capital. Later the Treuhand became the sole shareholder of the Oberschlesische. However, as guarantee for the sum due to the *Reich* under the contract, the *Reich* acquired the right to obtain a lien on all the shares of the company, and it was authorised to exercise all the rights resulting from the possession of the shares. The company also undertook not to alienate, even after the expiration of the lien, any shares without the authorisation of the *Reich*. It was provided that, as a guarantee for the fulfilment of this obligation, the *Reich* would, even after the expiration of the

Case No. 177 *contd.*

lien, retain the possession of the shares and the exercise of all the rights resulting therefrom.

In July, 1922, a Polish court gave a decision to the effect that the registration of the Oberschlesische as the owner of the factory was null and void, and that the name of the Polish Treasury should be entered in the registry. The decision was based, *inter alia*, on Article 256 of the Treaty of Versailles and certain Polish laws of 1920 and 1922. In July, 1922, the Polish Government took possession of the factory.[1]

In July, 1926, the Permanent Court of International Justice gave judgment to the effect that the dispossession of the companies was contrary to the international obligations of Poland contracted in the Geneva Convention of 15 May, 1922, with Germany concerning Upper Silesia. In July, 1928, the Court gave another judgment to the effect that it was competent, under the Geneva Convention, to deal with the question of compensation due to Germany as the result of the breach by Poland of her international obligations. (See Case No. 345.)

In the present case, the Court was concerned with the question whether damages were in fact due to Germany, and what was to be the amount and the method of the payment of the compensation, if any. Before the Court, Poland recognised that damage was suffered by the Bayerische; her contention that no damage was suffered by the Oberschlesische was rejected by the Court. (See Case No. 356.)

Held: On the general question of damages:

(*a*) "In estimating the damage caused by an un-"lawful act, only the value of property, rights and "interests which have been affected and the owner of

[1] See *Annual Digest*, 1925-1926, Case No. 46.

"which is the person on whose behalf compensation "is claimed, or the damage done to whom is to serve "as a means of gauging the reparation claimed, must "be taken into account. This principle, which is "accepted in the jurisprudence of arbitral tribunals, "has the effect, on the one hand, of excluding from "the damage to be estimated injury resulting for "third parties from the unlawful acts and, on the other "hand, of not excluding from the damage the amount "of debts and other obligations for which the injured "party is responsible. The damage suffered by the "Oberschlesische in respect of the Chorzów under-"taking is therefore equivalent to the total value—"but to that total only—of the property, rights and "interests of this company in that undertaking, with-"out deducting liabilities" (at p. 31).

(*b*) The action of Poland was not an act of expropriation, which could be rendered lawful by the payment of fair compensation, but amounted to a seizure of property, rights and interests, which could not be expropriated even on payment of compensation; it was for this reason that it was contrary to her international obligations. Accordingly, the compensation due to Germany was not necessarily limited to the value of the undertaking at the moment of dispossession plus interest to the day of payment. Unlawful dispossession must not be made indistinguishable from lawful liquidation so far as their financial results are concerned. The object of the Geneva Convention was to provide for the maintenance of the economic life in Upper Silesia on the basis of respect for the *status quo*. This obligation was unlawfully disregarded by Poland.

"The essential principle contained in the actual "notion of an illegal act—a principle which seems to "be established by international practice and in "particular by the decisions of arbitral tribunals—is "that reparation must, as far as possible, wipe out all "the consequences of the illegal act and re-establish "the situation which would, in all probability, have

Case No. 177 ***contd.***

" existed if that act had not been committed. Restitution in kind, or, if this is not possible, payment of a " sum corresponding to the value which a restitution " in kind would bear; the award, if need be, of " damages for loss sustained which would not be " covered by restitution in kind or payment in place " of it—such are the principles which should serve to " determine the amount of compensation due for an " act contrary to international law " [1] (at p. 47).

Accordingly, the dispossession of the companies in question " involves the obligation to restore the under-" taking and, if this be not possible, to pay its value " at the time of the indemnification, which value is " designed to take the place of restitution which has " become impossible. To this obligation, in virtue of " the general principles of international law, must be " added that of compensating loss sustained as the " result of the seizure " (at p. 48).

The fact that the parties agreed that the actual restitution of the factory was no longer practicable could not have any influence on the assessment of the damage.

For certain specific questions connected with the present case see Note below. [Report: Series A, No. 17, pp. 31, 46-48.[2]]

NOTE.—See also: (*a*) *Ibid.*, pp. 48, 49: *Cumulative Damage of Interdependent Undertakings.* This is a statement that the Court could not in the present case be satisfied with merely adding together the damage suffered by the two companies seeing that their interests in the undertaking were interdependent and complementary. It followed that " they cannot simply be added together without running the risk of " the same damage being compensated twice over."

(*b*) *Ibid.*, p. 49: *Whether the Court can Rely on the Data Supplied by the Parties.* In awarding damages with the view to restoring, as far as possible, the dispossessed companies to the economic position which they would probably have enjoyed but for the unlawful dispossession, the Court cannot be satisfied with the data supplied by the parties.

(*c*) *Ibid.*, p. 50: *Changes in the Value of the Property Taken Away.* In considering the method of determining the amount of damage to be

---

[1] But see on the subject of damages the dissenting opinion of Lord Finlay, pp. 71, 72.

[2] See also Series E, No. 5, pp. 183-202. And see for an account and analysis of the various stages of the case Michel de Grotte in *R.I.*, 3rd ser., vol. X (1929), pp. 229-265.

awarded, the Court observed that the cost of construction of a factory may not necessarily correspond to the value which that factory will have when built. This will be especially the case when the factory was built under the exceptional circumstances of war time.

(*d*) *Ibid.*, p. 51 : *Offers of Compensation Made in the Course of Abortive Negotiations.* The Court stated that it could not take into account declarations, admissions, or proposals which the parties had made during the direct negotiations between them following upon Judgment No. 7, when such negotiations had not led to a complete agreement.

(*e*) *Ibid.*, pp. 51-54: *Appointment of Experts.* Accordingly, in conformity with Article 50 of the Statute, the Court announced the setting up in a special Order (see Case No. 357) of an expert inquiry to determine the value of the undertakings in question at the time of dispossession, the probable financial results (profits or losses) between the dispossession and the judgment, and the value of the undertaking at the time of the judgment had it remained in the hands of the companies in question. The Court gave certain general instructions, in accordance with the judgment given above, to guide the experts.

(*f*) *Indeterminate and Contingent Damages*: see Case No. 178.

Damages—Indeterminate and Contingent Damages.

Case No. 178

PERMANENT COURT OF INTERNATIONAL JUSTICE.

JUDGMENT No. 13.

GERMANY *v* POLAND.

CASE CONCERNING THE FACTORY AT CHORZÓW.

(CLAIM FOR INDEMNITY. MERITS.)

13 *September*, 1928.

THE FACTS.—(See Case No. 177, both Facts and Judgment under (*a*) and (*b*).) It will be noted that in that case, in view of the illegality of the dispossession, the Court held that damages or loss of profits ought to be awarded. In addition, however, Germany claimed damages for losses alleged to have been suffered by the Bayerische Stickstoffwerke as the result of the Polish management of the Chorzów factory having unlawfully become acquainted with and having obtained means of reproducing the company's processes.

Held: That the claim must be rejected. No evidence has been produced which could enable the Court to decide as to the existence and extent of damage resulting from the alleged competition of the Chorzów

Case No. 178 contd.

factory with the factories of the Bayerische. Neither has evidence been produced to show whether the methods of the Bayerische have been or are still being employed at Chorzów. The alleged damage must, accordingly, be regarded as not sufficiently proved. In addition, "it would come under the heading of "possible but contingent and indeterminate damage "which, in accordance with the jurisprudence of "arbitral tribunals, cannot be taken into account." [Report: Series A, No. 17, pp. 56, 57.]

NOTE.—It has been deemed expedient to give a separate digest of this aspect of the question of damages decided by the Court, in order to draw attention to the practical distinction, frequently disregarded, between damages for loss of profits (which the Court admitted) and contingent and indeterminate damages (which the Court refused to award).

Case No. 179

Measure of Damages—Indirect Damages.

PORTUGAL *v.* GERMANY.

(The *Naulilaa* Case.)

Special Arbitral Tribunal.[1] 31 *July*, 1928.

(MEURON, FAZY, GUEX.)

THE FACTS.—(See Case No. 360.) There were two categories of damage claimed by Portugal. One related to the direct consequences of the German invasion of Portuguese territory, like the killing or wounding of soldiers or of civilian population, and the destruction of property. The other related to the damage caused by the uprising of the natives in the territory evacuated by Portugal which became the scene of inter-tribal fighting, pillage and destruction, and for the pacification of which it was necessary to send a costly expedition.

After investigating the Portuguese contention that Germany was liable in damages on the additional ground that the uprising was fomented by German agents—a contention which the Tribunal rejected as unfounded—the Tribunal considered the question whether and how far Germany was responsible for the indirect damage caused by the invasion.

[1] For the constitution of this Tribunal see Case No. 317.

Held: That Germany was responsible for such damage as the German authorities ought to have regarded as the probable consequence of their action. It was natural that the German invasion should produce unrest among the native population and increase the opportunities for revolt, and Germany was, in so far, responsible. It would not be just to limit German responsibility to damage caused directly by the German troops themselves. But she was not responsible for the extension of the revolt and the inter-tribal strife, which was due to quite specific circumstances connected with the territory. Also it was not immaterial that the Portuguese commanding officer who ordered the retreat evacuated a rich area, although there was no pressure on the part of the German detachment, which after the engagement retired into German territory. Without criticising his decision from the military point of view, the Tribunal was of the opinion that Germany cannot be saddled with exclusive responsibility for the consequences of the Portuguese general's decision.

On the general question of damages the Tribunal referred to the fact that the decision in the *Alabama* case, denying compensation for other than direct damage, was subjected to criticism, and that international tribunals frequently awarded damages for indirect losses. " It would not be equitable to " allow the victim to suffer from losses which the author of the " first illicit act foresaw and, perhaps, willed, for the mere " reason that there were intermediate links in the chain con- " necting that act with the damage sustained." On the other hand, the Tribunal held that it was impossible to charge a State with the responsibility for damage connected with the initial act by a chain of exceptional circumstances which could not be foreseen. The Tribunal referred here to the decisions of the American-German Mixed Claims Commission set up by the Treaty of Berlin, of 25 August, 1921, which refused to award damages for losses which, although causally connected with the initial event, were at the same time due also to other causes. The Commission adopted that attitude although the Treaty provided for compensation for losses caused " directly or in- " directly " to American citizens. [Report: *Recueil*, VIII, p. 409, and pp. 425-429.]

NOTE.—See also the same decision, at pp. 413-416, for an application of the same principle to damages claimed by Portugal in connection with the *Maziua* incident—a surprise attack in August, 1914, upon a Portuguese frontier post by a German officer acting under the mistaken impression that Portugal was at war with Germany.

Case No. 180

Damages—Prospective Damages—Depreciation of Value of Securities.

ROSA VOLLWEILER *v.* GERMANY.

United States and Germany : Mixed Claims Commission.
23 July, 1927.

(PARKER, ANDERSON, KIESSELBACH.)

THE FACTS.—This was a claim for compensation from Germany, under the Treaty of Berlin of 11 November, 1921, for damage alleged to have been suffered as the result of certain German Government Bonds, bought by the claimant in 1915 and 1916, having been subjected by Germany to " exceptional war measures " which prevented her from withdrawing these bonds from Germany for the purpose of sale or exchange before their value depreciated.

The Commission found that " a German exceptional " war measure prevented the delivery of the bonds in " question during the time intervening between the first " unqualified request for their delivery made on 23 July, " 1919, and the date of their actual delivery, 25 Sep- " tember, 1919." But there was no evidence before the Commission that the claimant had suffered loss as a result of this delay in delivery.

Held : That no compensation can be awarded. The claimant had failed to establish that she would have sold or exchanged her bonds had she had possession of them at the period during which the delivery of the bonds was prevented by German exceptional war measures. " In order to establish a right to re- " cover compensation on account of depreciation in the value of " securities subjected to exceptional war measures, it is not " sufficient to prove depreciation during the period of such sub- " jection, but the claimant must go further and prove by com- " petent evidence that he would have disposed of such securities " by sale or exchange had he not been prevented from so doing " by such war measures."[1] [Report : *A.J.*, XXII (1928), p. 685.]

NOTE.—Decisions of the Anglo-German Mixed Arbitral Tribunal in *Hammer* v. *German Government, Recueil,* II, 526, and *Green* v. *German Government, ibid.*, III, 522, followed.

[1] The Commission said : " The ultimate issue of any war is necessarily " uncertain. The varying fortunes of the belligerents as variously viewed by

Damages—Direct and Indirect Damages.

See Case No. 154 (*H. G. Venable Case, under* (*a*)).

Damages—Consequential Damages—Injury Inflicted by a Cell Inmate.

See p. 227, n. 1 (*I. R. Clark Case*).

F. INTEREST

I.—In General

Interest—Whether, and under What Conditions, to be Awarded in the Absence of Express Treaty Provisions—Cases of Obligatory and Voluntary Indemnifications for Losses and Damages Contrasted—Limited Award of Interest in the Former Case, Refusal in the Latter. **Case No. 181**

GEORGES PINSON CASE, §§ 69-71.

France and Mexico: Mixed Claims Commission.
19 *October*, 1928.

(VERZIJL, President.)

THE FACTS.—By the Claims Convention of 25 September, 1924, Mexico had undertaken to indemnify *ex gratia* French subjects and protected persons for the losses and damages which they would prove they had suffered during and since the revolution of 1910 to 1920 from the acts of definite classes of military forces, etc., enumerated in Article 3. The Convention stipulated *expressis verbis* that the examination of the claims ought not to be carried on in the light of the general principles of international law relating to State responsibility but exclusively on the basis of the rules formulated in the Convention. (See for the interpretation of this clause Case No. 318.) The Convention was silent as to the question of interest on the damages awarded. The

" different individuals necessarily influenced the market value of their respec-
" tive securities. The fact that different investors at different times held
" different views with respect to the ultimate result of the war contributed
" to supplying both buyers and sellers, which made a market for these
" securities. Obviously this Commission can indulge no presumption with
" respect to the intention of a particular claimant to buy or sell at a particular
" time, but must require this fact to be established as any other fact."

Case No. 181 ***contd.***

French Agent claimed interest in practically all cases (except those of personal injury) as from the date of the presentation of the claim to the Mexican Government; the Mexican Agent, on the contrary, was hardly prepared to admit the payment of interest in any cases.

Held by the President: That among the claims for damages some did engage the international responsibility of Mexico, apart from any particular treaty promise, but others did not. As for the latter, no obligation whatsoever to pay interest beyond the principal sum could, as a rule, be admitted in the absence of express treaty stipulations, so that, at all events, the award of interest ought to be confined, on principle, to claims relating to the former group of damage. But even with respect to indemnification which is obligatory under the general principles of international law, payment of interest is not yet clearly recognised by customary international law as generally obligatory either from the date of the injurious or detrimental act or from the date of the presentation of the claim to the Government of the State responsible for the same. Thus, unless the amount due is fixed from the outset, payment of interest does not as a rule become obligatory until the date of the award. (See also Case No. 184.)

Held consequently: (*a*) That, as a rule, no interest whatever would be awarded in the case of damage for which Mexico was not responsible under the general principles of international law, such as acts committed by regular forces of the Mexican Government in the course of the suppression of a revolt within the limits of military necessity, or analogous acts committed by a revolutionary army during its successful struggle for the overthrow of the existing Government, or wrongful acts committed by revolutionaries or rebels who did not succeed in conquering the supreme authority in the State. This finding did not, however, discount in any way the obligation of Mexico to pay within a reasonable time the damages awarded;

(*b*) that interest should be awarded, from the date of the presentation of the claim to the Mexican Government or to the National Claims Commission, in the case of compulsory loans or contributions exacted by governmental or successful revolutionary forces, and amounting to a fixed sum of money;

(*c*) that in all other cases of obligatory indemnification (such as wrongful acts of governmental or victorious revolutionary forces, requisitions of cattle, clothes, victuals, etc.) interest would run from the date of the award only, that being the moment when the amount of the indemnity was fixed.

[Till now unreported.]

NOTE.—Reference was made to the award of the Permanent Court of International Justice in the *Wimbledon* case (Publications of the Permanent Court of International Justice, Series A, No. 1, p. 32) and to Van Vollenhoven, President of the General Claims Convention United States–Mexico (1923), *La jurisprudence de la Commission générale de réclamations entre les Etats-Unis d'Amérique et le Méxique*, in *Bulletin de l'Institut Intermédiaire International*, vol. XVII, p. 263.

Interest. **Case No. 182**

H. G. VENABLE CASE.

United States and Mexico : General Claims Commission. 8 July, 1927.

(VAN VOLLENHOVEN, NIELSEN, MACGREGOR.)

THE FACTS.—(See Case No. 154.) The Commission awarded $100,000 for the destruction of the locomotives in question. As to interest on that sum,

Held : That it was a lump sum for injustice inflicted and should bear no interest. [Reports : *Opinions of Commissioners*, 1927, p. 331 ; *A.J.*, XXII (1928), p. 433.]

NOTE.—Nielsen, the American Commissioner, dissented. He was of the opinion that interest should clearly be included in the award. The claimant had been deprived of property and subjected to large financial loss, and the amount of damages was a sum of money fixed with absolute precision. He quoted the following extract from the opinion of the Tribunal of the *Lord Nelson* case :

" In international law, and according to a generally recognised " principle, in case of wrongful possession and use, the amount of " indemnity awarded must represent both the value of the property " taken and the value of its use (Rutherforth's *Institutes*, Bk. 1, " ch. xvii, sec. v ; VI Moore's *International Law Digest*, p. 1029 ; " *Indian Choctaw's* case, Law of Claims against Governments, " Report 134, 43 Cong., 2nd sess., House of Representatives, " Washington, 1875, p. 220 *et seq.*)." (Nielsen's *Report*, p. 434.)

He referred to the *Illinois Central Railroad Company* case (*Annual Digest*, 1925-1926, Case No. 2) as discussing the practice of international tribunals with respect to the inclusion of interest in pecuniary awards.

Case No. 183

Interest—Invocation of Rules of Civil Law in International Procedure—Interest in International Law—Positive Rules of Private Law Irrelevant.

GEORGES PINSON CASE, § 69.

France and Mexico : Mixed Claims Commission.
19 *October*, 1928.

(VERZIJL, President.)

The positive rules of existing Civil Codes concerning interest on private pecuniary debts having been invoked in the Commission,

Held : That those rules have no direct relevance on the question of interest in international law, since the question has been developed in the international domain in independent conditions entirely different from those prevailing in the sphere of private debts.

[Till now unreported.]

II.—Rate of Interest. Compound Interest

Case No. 184

Rate of Interest.

(*a*) GEORGES PINSON CASE, § 70.
(*b*) HÉLÈNE BIMAR CASE.

France and Mexico : Mixed Claims Commission.
19 *October*, 1928.

(VERZIJL, President.)

In the leading test case, (*a*) above, the three Commissioners preferred to maintain to the last and to define exactly their personal points of view with regard to interest. Thus, the Mexican Commissioner was opposed to any award of interest ; the French Commissioner declined to lay down any general rule, either on the question of award or on the question of rate, but voted in this case for interest at the rate of 3 per cent. from the date of conclusion of the work of the Commission ; the President declined to act in an arbitrary way from case to case without any definite rule, laid down a set of principles upon which he proposed to act (see Case No. 181), and was of the opinion that, in view of the standard of rents in Mexico, a rate of 6 per cent., as was claimed by the French Agent, was not excessive; that, on principle, the date of the award ought to be decisive as *dies a quo*, but that, for practical reasons, it was preferable to fix one single date as *dies a quo* for all indemnities, which date he fixed as 1 May, 1929, approximately the middle date in the work of the Commission. In virtue of Article 4 of the Claims Convention, the opinion of the President prevailed in this case.

In the next case, however, (*b*) above, the Mexican Commissioner for practical reasons joined his French colleague, thus establishing, on the question of rate as well as of *dies a quo*, a majority in the Commission against the President, who thereupon adopted the view of the Commissioners. The interest allowed was 3 per cent. from the date of the conclusion of the business of the Commission.

[Till now unreported.]

III.—The *Dies a Quo*. The *Dies ad Quem*

Interest—*Dies a quo*.

See Case No. 184 ((*a*) *Georges Pinson Case*; (*b*) *Hélène Bimar Case*).

G. MISCELLANEOUS

***Ex injuria jus non oritur*—A State cannot Plead the Non-Fulfilment of its Obligations.**

Case No. 185
PERMANENT COURT OF INTERNATIONAL JUSTICE.
ADVISORY OPINION No. 15.

JURISDICTION OF THE COURTS OF DANZIG.

3 *March*, 1928.

THE FACTS.—(See Case No. 187.) In answer to the Polish contention that Danzig courts could not apply the provisions of the *Beamtenabkommen* (a valid international agreement relating to the rights of Danzig officials taken over by the Polish Railways Administration) because they had not been incorporated into Polish municipal law,

Case No. 185 *contd.*

The Court *observed* that Poland at any rate could not avail herself of an objection which would amount to relying upon the non-fulfilment of an obligation imposed upon her by an international engagement. [Report: Series B, No. 15, pp. 26, 27.]

Case No. 186

Responsibility of a Government Representing a Foreign Government in Time of War—Danish Protection of Interests of Austrian Subjects.

DANISH FOREIGN OFFICE *v.* EMIG.

Supreme Court of Denmark. 23 *December*, 1927.

THE FACTS.—In the year 1917 the Danish Ministry of Foreign Affairs appointed a travelling inspector of the Austro-Hungarian camps for prisoners of war in Russia, whose mission was under the protection of the Danish Legation at Petrograd. On account of difficult postal communication the inspector was left for a time without sufficient means, and he borrowed an amount of 5000 roubles from a Russian interpreter, named Emig, in order to meet the expenses incumbent upon him as representative of the Danish State. With this sum the inspector bought provisions for the prisoners of war. Emig then advanced a further 1600 roubles. Shortly afterwards the inspector and the interpreter were by mistake taken prisoners by the British authorities in Turkestan and brought through Persia and India, and not until five months afterwards was the mistake cleared up. In 1919 they arrived in Denmark, and Emig brought a claim against the Danish State for the 6600 roubles advanced by him and a further claim for 10,000 Danish kroner as compensation for the treatment to which he had been exposed. With regard to the latter amount, the Ministry of Foreign Affairs asserted that they could not be held responsible for the consequences of the treatment to which a Russian citizen had been exposed on the part of British authorities. This view was acceded to by the Court.

As to the loan, the Ministry of Foreign Affairs maintained that the inspector, in borrowing this sum, imposed no obligation upon the Danish State, but only upon Austria-Hungary.

Held by the *Ostre Landsret*, 29 December, 1926: That the Ministry of Foreign Affairs was bound to repay Emig the loan, as it had never been intimated to the inspector that he was acting on behalf of the Austro-Hungarian State and on its account. He had reason to believe that funds from neutral sources had been placed at the disposal of the Danish Legation.

Held by the Supreme Court: That that part of the judgment must be affirmed. [Report: *Ugeskrift for Retsvæsen*, 1928, pp. 84 *et seq.*]

NOTE.—A question was also raised and decided as to the rate of exchange at which the roubles should be converted.

PART VI

THE INDIVIDUAL IN INTERNATIONAL LAW

A. IN GENERAL

I.—Position of Individuals in International Law

[See also Part I, INTERNATIONAL LAW IN GENERAL: IV. *Relation to Municipal Law*; and Part VIII, TREATIES: IX. *Operation and Enforcement of Treaties. Necessity of Municipal Legislation.*]

Individuals—Position of—How far Acquiring Rights under International Treaties.

Case No. 187
PERMANENT COURT OF INTERNATIONAL JUSTICE.
ADVISORY OPINION No. 15.

JURISDICTION OF THE COURTS OF DANZIG.

3 *March*, 1928.

THE FACTS.—On 9 November, 1920, a Convention was concluded between Poland and the Free City of Danzig which, *inter alia*, contained provisions relating to the taking over by Poland of the major part of the Danzig railways. In pursuance of Article 22 of that Convention, which provided for the conclusion of supplementary agreements regulating questions relating to the retention of officials, employees and workmen hitherto employed on the Danzig railways, and to the maintenance of the rights acquired by them, two agreements were subsequently concluded between Danzig and Poland. One, concluded on 20 July, 1921, was a " Provisional Agreement in regard to " Officials " (*provisorisches Beamtenabkommen*); the other, concluded on 22 October, 1921, was a " Definitive Agreement in regard to Officials " (*endgültiges Beamtenabkommen*).

Subsequently, from the year 1925 onwards, certain Danzig railway officials who passed into the service of the Polish Railways Administration brought against it actions before the courts of the Free City for pecuniary claims. The actions were based on the provisions of the Agreement

Case No. 187 ***contd.***

of 22 October, 1921. The Polish Treasury raised objections against the jurisdiction of the Danzig courts, which, however, rejected the plea to the jurisdiction. Poland thereupon informed the High Commissioner of Danzig that in the future she would take no notice of the actions brought against her by virtue of the Agreement of 22 October, 1921, and that she would not comply with any judgment given by Danzig courts in such cases.

By virtue of Article 39 of the Agreement of 9 November, 1920, the High Commissioner gave, at the request of Danzig, on 8 April, 1927, a decision, in which he laid down that the clauses of the *Beamtenabkommen* are not to be regarded as provisions which constitute the contract of service of the Danzig railway officials, and that they cannot therefore give ground for a personal action to be brought in the courts.[1] Danzig appealed against this decision to the Council of the League of Nations, which then asked the Court for an Advisory Opinion as to whether the decision of the High Commissioner was legally well founded.[2]

Before the Court Poland contended that the Danzig courts had no jurisdiction, on the ground that the *Beamtenabkommen*, being an international treaty, created rights and obligations only between Poland and Danzig; that as it was not incorporated into Polish municipal law it could not create direct rights and obligations for the individuals concerned; and that

[1] The decision of the High Commissioner is printed in Series B, No. 15, pp. 28-36.

[2] Article 39 of the Convention of 9 November, 1920 (the so-called Paris Convention), provided as follows:

"Any differences arising between Poland and the Free City of Danzig in "regard to the present treaty or to any other subsequent agreements, "arrangements or conventions, or to any matter affecting the relations "between Poland and the Free City, shall be submitted by one or the other "party to the decision of the High Commissioner, who shall, if he deems it "necessary, refer the matter to the Council of the League of Nations.

"The two parties retain the right of appeal to the Council of the League "of Nations."

Poland was therefore responsible to Danzig alone if she had not carried out her international obligations.

Held: That, in the intention of the contracting parties, the *Beamtenabkommen* did govern directly the relations between the Polish Railways Administration and the Danzig officials. The provisions of the *Beamtenabkommen* constitute therefore part of the contract of service, and the officials have a right of action against the Polish Railways Administration for the recovery of the pecuniary claims based on the *Beamtenabkommen*. The Court said (at p. 17): "It "may be readily admitted that, according to a well-"established principle of international law, the *Beam-*"*tenabkommen*, being an international agreement, "cannot, as such, create direct rights and obligations "for private individuals. But it cannot be disputed "that the very object of an international agreement, "according to the intention of the contracting Parties, "may be the adoption by the Parties of some definite "rules creating individual rights and obligations and "enforceable by the national courts. That there is "such an intention in the present case can be established "by reference to the terms of the *Beamtenabkommen*. "The fact that the various provisions were put in the "form of an *Abkommen* is corroborative, but not con-"clusive, evidence as to the character and legal effects "of the instrument. The intention of the Parties, "which is to be ascertained from the contents of the "Agreement, taking into consideration the manner in "which the Agreement has been applied, is decisive. "This principle of interpretation should be applied by "the Court in the present case." The Court then proceeded to point out in detail that the wording and the general tenor of the *Beamtenabkommen* showed that its provisions were directly applicable as between the officials and the Administration. [Report: Series B, No. 15, pp. 17-21.[1]]

[1] See also Series E, No. 4, pp. 213-219. And see Michel de Grotte in *R.I.*, 3rd ser., vol. X (1929), pp. 408-414.

Individuals—Position in International Law—Conflict between Municipal Law and International Obligation.

See Case No. 5 (*High Treason* (*Treaty of Versailles in Germany*) *Case*).

Individuals—Position of—Rights Conferred by Treaties upon Individuals against their own State.

See Case No. 280 (*German Railways* (*Most-Favoured Treatment*) *Case*).

Individuals—Position of—How far Acquiring Direct Rights under Treaties—Self-Executory and Other Treaties—Right of German Subjects to Compensation by Germany for Property Liquidated in France—Articles 74 and 297 (*i*) of the Treaty of Versailles.

See Case No. 281 (*Liquidation of German Property* (*Treaty of Versailles*) *Case*).

Individuals—Position of—How far Directly Affected by Treaty.

See Case No. 285 (*S. Papadopoulos, of Péra,* v. *N. V. Koninklijke Nederlandsche Stoombootmaatschappij, of Amsterdam*).

Individuals—Position of—In respect of Treaties—Rights Conferred Directly upon Individuals.

See Case No. 36 (*E. L. Wirbelauer, of Paris,* v. *de Handelsvennootschap onder de firma Lippmann Rosenthal en Co., of Amsterdam*).

Individuals—Position of—Rights Acquired under Treaty—Termination as the Result of War.

See Case No. 363 (*McCandless* v. *United States*).

Individuals—Position in International Law—Corporations—Dutch East India Company—Acquisition of Territorial Title by.

See Case No. 70 (*Island of Palmas Arbitration Case*).

American Indians—Position of—Rights Acquired under Jay Treaty.

See Case No. 363 (*McCandless* v. *United States*).

II.—Before International Tribunals

Jurisdiction of International Tribunals in respect of Claims of Individuals against their own State. **Case No. 188**

STEINER AND GROSS *v.* POLISH STATE.

Upper Silesian Arbitral Tribunal. 30 *March*, 1928.

THE FACTS.—This was a claim for compensation for damage caused to the plaintiffs, the owners of a tobacco factory, as the result of the introduction of the tobacco monopoly in Poland. The claim was put forward on the basis of Article 4, § 2, Section 3, of the German-Polish Convention concerning Upper Silesia of 15 May, 1922, the provision in question relating to respect of private rights. The plaintiffs contended that, as the result of the monopoly law, rights which they possessed under German law were, on the occasion of the transfer of sovereignty, injuriously affected by Polish legislation. One of the plaintiffs, Cross, was of Polish nationality, the other, Steiner, of Czechoslovak nationality.

In § 1 of Article 4 of the Convention the contracting parties undertook to recognise and to respect rights of every kind, and in particular concessions and privileges enjoyed prior to the transfer of sovereignty. § 5 provided as follows: " La question de savoir si et " dans quelle mesure une indemnité pour la suppres- " sion ou la diminution de droits acquis doit être payée " par l'Etat, sera directement tranchée par le Tribunal " arbitral sur plainte de l'ayant droit."

Poland contended that the expression " l'ayant " droit " could not be interpreted as meaning that a right of action against the Polish State has been accorded to Polish nationals; that it was a general principle of international law that an individual could not invoke an international authority against his own State; that this principle ought to be applied in regard to the interpretation of the Convention; that any interpretation to the contrary would place the State against which such right was accorded in a position worse than that of States under the régime of capitulations [1] and that the Tribunal therefore had no jurisdiction.

[1] The relevance of the reference to capitulations appears from the following extract from the Polish argument, as summarised by the Tribunal:

" In some non-European countries like Turkey and China, which, owing

Case No. 188 *contd.*

Held: That the Polish contention must be rejected and that the Tribunal had jurisdiction. The Convention conferred in unequivocal terms [1] jurisdiction upon the Tribunal irrespective of the nationality of the claimants, and, the terms of the Convention being clear, it was unnecessary to add to it a limitation which did not appear from its wording. There was an additional reason for not introducing any such limitation seeing that the guiding principle of this part of the Convention was the respect of private rights and the preservation of the economic unity of Upper Silesia, and that no one of these considerations was compatible with the exclusion of any category of claims for the sole reason of the nationality of the claimant. [Report: *Decisions of the Upper Silesian Arbitral Tribunal*, vol. I, Nos. 1-2 (in German and Polish), pp. 1-36.]

Individuals—Position in International Law—Direct Access to International Tribunals—Rights Conferred in a Treaty upon Subjects of a State not Party to the Treaty.

See Case No. 188 (*Steiner and Gross* v. *Polish State*).

B. NATIONALITY

I.—In General

Case No. 189

Nationality in Federal States—Whether Prussian Nationality Identical with German Nationality.

De Luck *v.* Germany.

Franco-German Mixed Arbitral Tribunal. 31 *March*, 1928.

(Asser, Gandolphe, Freolich.)

The Facts.—This was a claim on account of certain measures of confiscation during the war. According to Annex 1 following Article 79 of the Treaty of Ver-

" to the low level of their administration and judiciary, were only recently " admitted to the international community, mixed courts were for a time " introduced in order to settle disputes in which Europeans were involved. " But these capitulation courts have never been granted jurisdiction in actions " of the nationals of those States against their own State. Accordingly, how " is it possible to assume such a restriction in relation to European States " whose administration and judiciary cannot be compared with those of " non-European States?"

[1] The Tribunal rejected the Polish contention that this expression of the Treaty was not sufficiently clear. It is not considered necessary to digest this part of the judgment (pp. 22-27 of the Report), based on a logical interpretation of the Treaty.

sailles the following persons, *inter alios*, are *ipso facto* reinstated in French nationality: "(1) Persons who lost "French nationality by the application of the Franco-"German Treaty of 10 May, 1871, and who have not "since that date acquired any nationality other than "German." The claimant, who was born in 1862 of French parents, lost his French nationality as the result of the latter treaty. He then became a Prussian subject by naturalisation. The German Government contended that the Tribunal had no jurisdiction in view of the fact that the claimant was not of French nationality.

Held: That the Tribunal had no jurisdiction. Prussian nationality was not identical with German nationality. Accordingly, as the claimant had acquired, after 10 May, 1871, a nationality other than German nationality, he was not reinstated in French nationality by the Treaty of Versailles. [Report: *Recueil*, VIII, p. 142.]

Nationality in Federal States—Extinction of—In Cases of Cession of Territory—Alsace-Lorraine Nationality—Direct German Nationality—Statelessness of Former Alsace-Lorraine Nationals. **Case No. 190**

ALSACE-LORRAINE NATIONALITY (STATELESSNESS) CASE.

German Reichsgericht. 22 *February*, 1928.

THE FACTS.—The present suit arose out of an action brought by the respondent as owner of certain immovable property. According to the law of Hesse aliens require a special authorisation by the State for the acquisition of land. It was contended that the respondent could not lawfully have acquired the property in question.

Article 1 of the German Federal Law of 22 July, 1913, provided that German nationality was acquired through the acquisition of nationality in one of the Member States, and that Alsace-Lorraine was to be regarded as a Member State. The respondent was before her marriage a national of Hesse (a Member State of the German Federal State). In 1906 she married her present husband, a national of Alsace-Lorraine, and according to German law lost her Hesse nationality and acquired that of Alsace-Lorraine.

Case No. 190 *contd.*

According to the Peace Treaty of Versailles the husband acquired French nationality automatically, whereas the wife acquired the right to claim French nationality within the period of one year. She had not availed herself of that right.

The *Oberlandesgericht* (Upper State Court) held that, although in view of the cession of Alsace-Lorraine to France the wife lost her Alsace-Lorraine nationality, this did not result in her losing her German nationality. The *Oberlandesgericht* was of the opinion that section 17 of the Law of 1913 relating to loss of nationality contained no provisions bearing upon the cession of the territory of a Member State to a foreign Power, and that there was no reason to interpret it extensively by adding yet another reason for loss of nationality. German subjects who had not become foreign subjects as the result of the Peace Treaty ought not to be penalised on account of the extinction of the Member State whose subjects they were. Accordingly, it was incumbent upon the Court to fill the gap and to assume that the German nationality of the wife, which was formerly an indirect German nationality, continued to subsist as direct German nationality.

Held by the *Reichsgericht*: That the decision of the Court below must be reversed and that the appellant was a stateless person. The law did not recognise direct German nationality except in certain specific cases which had no application in the present case. If the appellant suffered hardship as the result of the loss of nationality following upon the extinction of the Member State, the remedy lay in legislative or administrative measures calculated to remove the inconvenience and hardship arising therefrom. It was not for the Court to create a new category of direct German nationality. [Reports: *Entscheidungen des Reichsgerichts in Zivilsachen*, vol. 120, p. 198; *Z.V.*, XV (1930), p. 264; *Z. für a. ö. R. u. V.*, I (2) (1929), p. 702.]

NOTE.—See *ibid.*, p. 706, for a note by von Schwartzkoppen, who criticises the judgment. He points out that even if the Court's interpretation of Article 1 of the Law of 1913 was correct, the situation had been changed as the result of the Treaty of Versailles. As a rule, in case of cession the inhabitants of the ceded territory acquire the nationality of the new State (see Oppenheim, vol. I (4th ed., 1928), pp. 445, 446). However, if the Treaty provides that only certain categories of inhabitants acquire the new nationality, then the remaining categories retain their old nationality. It is contrary, he says, to the practice of States and to the requirements of international intercourse to create entire categories of stateless persons. See also, to the same effect, Schätzel, *Die elsass-lothringische Staatsangehörigkeitsregelung und das Völkerrecht* (1928), pp. 80 ff.; Strupp, in *Z.V.*, XV (1930), p. 270; Kunz, *Die völkerrechtliche Option*, vol. I (1925), p. 227, and vol. II (1928), p. 43; Weck, *Juristische Wochenschrift* (1922), p. 1459. But see Schwalb in *Z.V.*, XIV (1929), p. 57.

Nationality in the British Commonwealth of Nations—Naturalisation in South Africa—Effect in Great Britain.

See Case No. 23 (*L. Hanau* v. *C. Hanau*).

Nationality—By Birth—Persons Born Abroad of United States Citizens who have not Resided in the United States. **Case No. 191**

WEEDIN, COMMISSIONER OF IMMIGRATION, *v.* CHIN BOW.

United States Supreme Court. 6 June, 1927.

THE FACTS.—This was a petition for habeas corpus. Chin Bow was born in China in 1914. His father was a citizen of the United States under United States Revised Statutes, § 1993, but was never in the United States until 1922. Chin Bow was held for deportation by the immigration authorities. The District Court discharged him from custody. The Circuit Court of Appeals affirmed the order. On certiorari,

Held: That the judgment discharging Chin Bow from custody should be reversed. The proviso of § 1993 that "the "rights of citizenship shall not descend to persons whose fathers "never resided in the United States" must be construed to mean that persons born abroad of fathers who are United States citizens become United States citizens by birth only if the father has resided in the United States before such persons are born. [Report: 274 U.S. 657.]

Nationality—By Birth—Birth on the High Seas on Board a United States Vessel—Ships as National Territory—Territoriality of Vessels. **Case No. 192**

IN RE LAM MOW.

United States District Court, N.D. California, S.D. United States Circuit Court of Appeals, Ninth Circuit. 13 June, 1927; 20 February, 1928.

THE FACTS.—This was a petition for habeas corpus. Lam Mow applied for admission to the United States as a

Case No. 192 *contd.*

citizen thereof. He was born of Chinese parents on an American vessel on the high seas. The parents were domiciled in and returning to the United States at the time of his birth.

Held: That the writ should be denied. Birth on the high seas aboard an American vessel does not confer citizenship upon the child of alien parents residing in the United States. Delivering the Opinion of the Court, Judge Kerrigan said: "Modern "international law regards the fiction of territoriality of vessels "on the high seas as untenable" (19 F. (2nd) 951, 952). "Although born in a place where the United States had juris-"diction, namely, aboard the steamship *Korea*, on the high "seas, Lam Mow was not born 'in the United States,' and is "not a citizen of the United States" (19 F. (2nd) 951, 952). On appeal,

Held by the Circuit Court of Appeals: That the judgment of the District Court should be affirmed. Delivering the Opinion of the Court, Judge Dietrich said: "The general statement, or "its equivalent, that a vessel upon the high seas is deemed to be "a part of the territory of the nation whose flag she flies, must "be understood as having a qualified or figurative meaning" (24 F. (2nd) 316, 317). [Reports: 19 F. (2nd) 951; 24 F. (2nd) 316.]

NOTE.—It appears that only a small number of countries have express provisions to the effect that persons born on national ships shall be regarded as born on national territory. See, for instance, in Great Britain, the British Nationality and Status of Aliens Act, 1914 (as amended in 1918 and 1922), s. I (1) (*c*), and the nationality laws of the British Dominions, and of Argentina, Spain, Guatemala, Honduras, Mexico and Salvador.—[Ed.]

Case No. 193

Nationality—By Birth—Persons Born of United States Citizens Abroad—Offspring of Polygamous Marriage.

NG SUEY HI *v.* WEEDIN.

United States Circuit Court of Appeals, Ninth Circuit.
10 *October*, 1927.

THE FACTS.—This was a petition for habeas corpus. Petitioner was born in China, the offspring of a polygamous marriage. Her father was a citizen of the United States. She claimed admission to the United States as a citizen, was excluded, and filed this petition. The writ was denied. On appeal,

Held: That the judgment denying the writ should be affirmed. The child of a citizen of the United States born in China of a polygamous marriage is not a citizen of the United States under U.S. Rev. Stat., § 1993, in the absence of subsequent legitimation. As to the effect of subsequent legitimation, query? [Report: 21 F. (2nd) 801.]

Proof of Nationality—Relevance of the Municipal Law of the Claimant or of the Defendant State as to this Proof—Conclusive Force of Certificates of Birth and of Consular Certificates—Different Systems of Proof. **Case No. 194**

GEORGES PINSON CASE, §§ 13-22.

France and Mexico: Mixed Claims Commission.
19 *October*, 1928.

(VERZIJL, President.)

THE FACTS.—This was a claim put forward by France on behalf of Georges Pinson, born in Mexico in 1875, the son of Auguste Pinson, a French citizen who was born in France in 1835 but had established himself in Mexico as a merchant in 1864. At first the French Agent had confined himself to supporting the French nationality of the claimant by a certificate of matriculation, drawn up by a French consul in Mexico and dated 7 March, 1911. The Mexican Agent, however, challenged, as a matter of principle, the conclusive force of such consular certificate and urged the French Agent to forward to the Commission a duly certified copy of the registration of birth of the claimant, such copy being the only evidence of nationality he was prepared to admit. In view of this fact the French Agent had subsequently presented to the Commission a copy of the registration of birth not only of the claimant but also of his father, but without waiving his contention that, as a rule, it was sufficient to produce a consular certificate. In his turn the Mexican Agent, on the very basis of the newly presented documents, attacked the French nationality of the claimant. In the face of differences of opinion between his fellow Commissioners, and of two recent contradictory awards of the General Claims Commission, United States and Mexico (*William A. Parker* case, 31 March, 1926: see *Annual Digest*, 1925-1926, Case No. 176), and of the Special Claims Commission, Ger-

Case No. 194 ***contd.***

many and Mexico (*Karl Klemp* case, 11 April, 1927, interlocutory award of the Presiding Commissioner, Cruchaga Tocornal[1]), the President felt obliged to examine the whole controversy in detail.

Held : That, especially in the relations between France and Mexico, a consular certificate of matriculation may be admitted as *prima facie* proof of nationality, but that the defendant State is permitted to adduce evidence to the contrary. In a detailed award the President gave the following explanation :

The Claims Convention, as well as the Rules of Procedure, are silent with regard to the point at issue. On the other hand, the National Claims Regulations of Mexico of 24 December, 1917, had already mentioned consular certificates as the only admissible documents suitable to establish the nationality of foreigners. A critical analysis of the interlocutory award in the *Karl Klemp* case, 1927, shows that its reasoning is quite insufficient to support its conclusions that a person's nationality may only be proved decisively by a certificate of birth. Generally speaking, three different systems of proof of nationality have been propounded in the history of international arbitration, viz. : (1) in strict conformity with the law of the claimant State ; (2) in strict conformity with the law of the defendant State ; (3) according to the common sense of the tribunal, independently of national rules of evidence. In consequence of an exhaustive criticism of these systems and of a review of arbitral jurisprudence, the President rejected the first and the second systems, and admitted the third. In this last system the certificates of birth are neither conclusive of nor indispensable to the proof of nationality. Consular certificates may just as well be regarded as decisive, especially in the case under consideration, where both the French and the Mexican legislation have long since established the system of registration of nationals in the registers of their consular officers abroad. The French consular certificates are based upon previous detailed examination, and the special Mexican Claims laws recognise such certificates as sufficient evidence. The Mexican Government in particular cannot profit by a purely negative attitude in the face of regular French consular certificates of matriculation without offering any counterproof ; they are, however, permitted to establish that the real legal situation is contrary to the *prima facie* evidence.

[Till now unreported.]

[1] Printed in *A.J.*, XXIV (1930), p. 610.

NOTE.—The President quoted and criticised the following precedents of arbitral tribunals: *Medina contra Costa Rica* (umpire Bertinatti: Moore, *International Arbitrations*, III, p. 2588); *Brockway* case (umpire Thornton: *ibid.*, III, p. 2534); *Ramón Garay* case (umpire Thornton: *ibid.*, III, p. 2532); *Gilmore* case (umpire Bertinatti: *ibid.*, III, p. 2539; Lapradelle-Politis, *Recueil des arbitrages internationaux*, II, p. 164); *Miguel Esteves* case (umpire Gutiérrez-Otero: *Venezuelan Arbitrations of* 1903, Washington, 1904, pp. 922-923); decision of the umpire in the Italo-Peruvian Mixed Claims Commission of 1899 (Borchard, *Diplomatic Protection of Citizens Abroad*, p. 667, note 3); awards of the Permanent Court of Arbitration in the matter of the confiscation of properties of French, British and Spanish citizens by the Portuguese Republic in 1913 (awards of 4 September, 1920, especially those concerning the claims of Doña Tómasa Rocatallada y Escartín and of Doña Magdalena Rodríguez y Laplana: *Protocoles des séances et sentences*, La Haye, 1920, pp. 68, 75, 76); *Thomas Thompson* and *John Barker* cases (*Reclamaciones presentadas al Tribunal anglo-chileno*, 1894-1896, Santiago de Chile, 1896, I, pp. 578 and 658).

Nationality—Proof of Nationality—Counterproof against *Prima Facie* Evidence—Doubtful Case of Double Nationality—Necessity to Establish Separately Either of the Two Nationalities Involved—Analysis of French and Mexican Laws on Citizenship—Legal Consequences of Double Nationality, if Established. **Case No. 195**

GEORGES PINSON CASE, §§ 13, 23-42.

France and Mexico: Mixed Claims Commission.
19 *October*, 1928.

(VERZIJL, President.)

THE FACTS.—(See for the facts Case No. 194.) The French nationality of the claimant having been admitted *prima facie* on the evidence furnished by the certificate of consular registration, the President had further to examine in detail the numerous objections raised against that *prima facie* evidence by the Mexican Government on the strength of a double contention:

1. The claimant had never acquired French nationality, since his father (*a*) had already lost his own French nationality by leaving France in 1864 "sans esprit de "retour" (Article 17, sub. 3, of the French Civil Code in its original wording of 1804); (*b*) had afterwards acquired Mexican nationality in consequence of the birth of his children (Article 30, s. III, of the former Mexican Constitution of 1857: "Son Mexicanos: . . . III. Los "extranjeros que . . . tengan hijos mexicanos, siempre

Case No. 195 ***contd.***

" que no manifiesten la resolución de conservar su " nacionalidad.") ;

2. The claimant was on various grounds to be considered as a Mexican citizen, namely, (*a*) by reason of his birth to a father who had acquired Mexican nationality by virtue of the above-mentioned Article 30, s. III ; (*b*) by reason of his neglect to comply with the prescription of Article 2, s. II, of the Mexican law on citizenship of 1886, according to which the son of a foreigner who is born in Mexico acquires Mexican citizenship on attaining his majority unless he notifies the political Mexican authority in the place of his residence, within a year after reaching that age, of his desire to preserve his original nationality ; (*c*) by reason of his subsequent fatherhood of children born to him in Mexico (Article 30, s. III, above-mentioned) ;

And further, it was contended that he had never lost that Mexican citizenship, notwithstanding his service in the French army during the Great War.

Even if the contentions under (1) should be incorrect, the claimant would, it was argued, under (2), be precluded from invoking the French-Mexican Claims Convention in his favour.

Held : That the continual confusion in the Mexican argument, particularly under (1) (*b*), of the two quite different legal questions relating respectively to the French and to the Mexican nationality of the claimant and his father, necessitated a strictly separate treatment of each of them ; that neither the contentions under (1) nor those under (2) were correct ; and that, even if the case were recognised as one of double nationality from the strictly legal point of view, it would be very doubtful if the claimant could not have invoked the Convention notwithstanding, owing to the fact that the Mexican Government itself had always considered him, officially and exclusively, as a French subject.

Amongst the different points of public law dealt with by the President in his award were several which concerned the mutual relation between various contradictory provisions of Mexican laws (of 1854 and 1886) and constitutions (of 1857 and 1917), and the alleged anti-constitutional character of the law of 1886 on citizenship invoked by the Mexican Government itself. With regard to these questions, the President followed the precedents of the Mexican-American Mixed Claims Commission of 1868 (awards of the arbitrators, Dr. Lieber and Thornton *in re Anderson and Thompson*, Moore, III, 2480, 2482). For the rest, he decided the questions in the light of the broad principles according to which: (*a*) in case of ambiguity a legal or constitutional provision has to be interpreted in the sense that keeps it in harmony with international law; (*b*) in case of irreconcilable contradiction between municipal and international law, the former must be considered as null and void in the international sphere.

[Till now unreported.]

NOTE.—See also Cases Nos. 4 and 324.

Proof of Nationality—Citizenship of the State of the Lebanon—Conditions of the Right of Option—Article 34 of the Treaty of Peace of Lausanne of 24 July, 1923—Authority of an International Tribunal to Control Incidentally the Decisions of the Competent Authorities of a Sovereign State—Legal Presumption in Favour of the Regularity of Public State Acts. **Case No. 196**

PABLO NÁJERA (OF THE LEBANON) CASE.

France and Mexico: Mixed Claims Commission.
19 *October*, 1928.

(VERZIJL, President.)

THE FACTS.—This was a claim of a person originating from Bekfaya (Lebanon), acting as a French protected person under the French-Mexican Claims Convention of 1924 (see also Case No. 206). The claimant invoked his quality of citizen of the State of the Lebanon by virtue of his exercise of the right of option, defined by Article 34 of the Treaty of Lausanne, of 24 July, 1923. The Mexican Government opposed this claim on the ground, *inter alia*, that the claimant had failed to prove that he was formerly a Turkish subject and that, therefore, his right under Article 34 of the Treaty to opt for the Lebanese nationality was not established.

Held: That the conditions on which depends the right of option for the Syrian or Lebanese nationalities according to Article 34 of the Treaty of Lausanne are seven in number, viz. (1) Turkish nationality; (2) age of at least eighteen years; (3) being a native of Syria or of the Lebanon;

Case No. 196 *contd.*

(4) habitual residence in a foreign country at the date of the coming into force of the Treaty; (5) race affinity with the majority of the Syrian or Lebanese population ; (6) consent of the Government exercising authority in Syria or the Lebanon ; (7) exercise of the option within a term of two years from the coming into force of the Treaty ; that, as appeared from the documents, the conditions under (2), (3), (4), (6) and (7) were fulfilled, and that, therefore, all possible doubts were confined to the points under (1) and (5) ; that, the attitude of the Mexican Government being illogical in so far as they urged the Commission only to enquire into the condition under (1) and not equally into that under (5), and being, moreover, purely negative, since they adduced no evidence whatever against the former Turkish nationality of the claimant, the Commission decided to act upon the general rule that " a legal presumption militates in favour of " the regularity of all official acts of public officers," and that, therefore, " an international tribunal, in face of declarations of " option accepted by the Government concerned, is fully justi- " fied in considering those declarations as regular options and " in refraining from entering into an independent examination " of the conditions on which their validity depends."

[Till now unreported.]

Case No. 197

Nationality—Proof of Nationality—Holding of Office as Evidence of Nationality.

D. R. ARCHULETA CASE.

United States and Mexico : General Claims Commission. 10 *October*, 1928.

(SINDBALLE, NIELSEN, MACGREGOR.)

See the above case for a statement describing as pertinent evidence of nationality the fact that the claimant occupied important legislative offices in the State espousing the claim, which obviously he could not have held had he been an alien ; *Robert Eakin* case, under the Convention of 8 May, 1871, between Great Britain and the United States, *Hale's Report*, p. 15 ; the *Canevaro* case of 1910 before the Permanent Court of Arbitration ; *Boyd* v. *Thayer*, 143 U.S. 135—referred to. [Report : *Opinions of Commissioners*, 1929, p. 73.]

Nationality—Proof of—Burden of Proof—Decisions of Municipal Courts on Question of Nationality—How far Binding upon International Tribunals. **Case No. 198**

RUINART PÈRE & SONS *v.* FRANZMANN.

Franco-German Mixed Arbitral Tribunal. 27 *May*, 1927.

(BOTELLA, DE VALLES, HOENE.)

THE FACTS.—The defendant, who was born in 1886 in Germany and was resident before the outbreak of the war of 1914-1918 in Belgium, objected to the jurisdiction of the Tribunal on the ground that he was not a German national. He produced a document, dated 1892, emanating from the competent German authorities and releasing him from German nationality. He also produced an Argentine passport testifying that he was an Argentine national.

The claimant, on the other hand, submitted a copy of a judgment given by a Belgian Court of Appeal in 1923 and holding that the defendant was a German national and that his goods were subject to sequestration by virtue of Article 297 of the Treaty of Versailles. It appeared that that judgment was given under a Belgian law of 1921 according to which all persons who had at any time possessed German nationality, and who did not prove to the satisfaction of the Court that they lost it, shall be regarded as German nationals.

Held : That the Tribunal had no jurisdiction. The Tribunal was not bound by the decision of a Belgian court acting under a special law. The burden of proof was upon the claimant to show that the defendant possessed German nationality and that he had never lost it. As the defendant produced documents showing that he did not possess the German nationality attributed to him, the presumption was that he was no longer a German national.

It could not be said that the decision of the Tribunal was contrary to that of the Belgian Court of Appeal. According to a particular provision of the Belgian law, the burden of proof was upon the present defendant ; according to the law applied by the Mixed Arbitral Tribunal, it was upon the plaintiff. The question of the existence of a right ought not to be confused with the question of the proof of that right. [Report : *Recueil*, VII, p. 599.]

Case No. 199 **Presumption of Nationality—Presumed Nationality of Inhabitants of the Territories Annexed to the Successor-States of Hungary.**

PRESUMPTIVE NATIONALITY (YUGOSLAVIA) CASE.

Supreme Court of Hungary. 20 *January*, 1928.
(*No. P.V.* 8938/1926.)

THE FACTS.—The plaintiff and his family took up residence in Yugoslavian territory, as from 18 August, 1918, in a district which before the Treaty of Trianon belonged to Hungary. The plaintiff objects to the request of the defendant that he, the plaintiff, should be asked to deposit security for costs which, according to Hungarian law, aliens are bound to give.

Held by the Supreme Court: That security must be given. "The fact that the plaintiff together with his family had been "resident since 18 August, 1918, in a district which is situated "in the territory of Yugoslavia . . . and that since that date "he had not returned to Hungarian territory with the intention "of assuming permanent residence justified the court below "in presuming that the plaintiff was at that time already a "Yugoslav subject. . . . The plaintiff could have rebutted "this presumption by showing that he has not been admitted "to Yugoslav citizenship. No such proof, however, has been "adduced." [Report: *Perjogi Döntvénytár*, XIV, No. 20.]

II.—As Affected by Changes of Sovereignty

Case No. 200 **Nationality—Change of Sovereignty—Effect of Provisions of Treaty of Peace between Allied and Associated Powers and Hungary—Meaning of Expression "Nationals of the "former Kingdom of Hungary" in British Treaty of Peace (Hungary) Order.**

GROEDEL (plaintiff) *v.* ADMINISTRATOR OF HUNGARIAN PROPERTY (defendant).

English High Court of Justice (Chancery Division).
10 *November*, 1927.

(MR. JUSTICE ROMER.)

THE FACTS AND CONTENTIONS.—The Treaty of Peace between the Allied and Associated Powers and Hungary (hereinafter called the Treaty of Trianon) came into force on 26 July, 1921. Article 1 (ix) of the Treaty of Peace (Hungary) Order, 1921 (made under the Treaty of Peace (Hungary) Act, 1921, to give effect to Article 232 and the Annex to Section IV of Part X of the Treaty of Trianon), provided that " all property, " rights and interests within His Majesty's Dominions,[1] " or Protectorates belonging to nationals of the former " Kingdom of Hungary at the date when the Treaty " came into force " should be charged with certain payments. On 26 July, 1921, the plaintiff, Baron Albert Groedel, owned certain property situate in His Majesty's dominions and valued at £22,204. That property had been transferred to the Administrator of Hungarian Property, who claimed that it was subject to the above-mentioned charge.

The plaintiff admitted that in August, 1914, he was of Hungarian nationality, but alleged that on 26 July, 1921, or at some date between November, 1918, and 26 July, 1921, he had ceased to be a " national " of the former Kingdom of Hungary " and had become Polish. He based this claim upon (*a*) Article 3 of the " Minorities Treaty " between the Allied and Associated Powers and Poland, which came into force on 10 January, 1920 ; (*b*) the fact that he was habitually resident at Skole in Galicia, which on 10 January, 1920, was, he alleged, recognised as forming part of Poland, so that he had become a Polish national ; and (*c*) Article 213 of the Treaty of Trianon whereby Hungary undertook to recognise the loss of Hungarian nationality by her nationals who had acquired or might acquire any new nationality under the laws of the Allied and Associated Powers. Alternatively, he claimed that as from November, 1918, the independent State of Poland had exercised sovereign rights over the Galician territory in which Skole was situated, with the result that he thereby became a Polish national before 26 July, 1921, when the Treaty of Trianon came into force.

Held : (*a*) That the expression " nationals of the former " Kingdom of Hungary " meant persons who were Hungarian

[1] " Dominions " (with capital D) would ordinarily mean the " Self-Governing Dominions." It is thus in the Order in Council, but it clearly must mean the whole of His Majesty's dominions : see Section 3 of the Order.

Case No. 200 *contd.* nationals on 28 October, 1918, when the Austro-Hungarian Empire ceased to exist by the deposition of the Emperor. (The learned judge herein followed Eve, J., in *Rothschild* v. *Administrator of Austrian Property*, L.R. [1923] 2 Ch. 542, and stated that, but for that decision and the practice of the respective Administrators of Austrian and Hungarian Property founded upon it, he would have been disposed to hold that the expression meant "nationals of Hungary, treating Hungary as though "it were still the former Kingdom of Hungary," a meaning which would have included persons who became Hungarian nationals between 28 October, 1918, and 26 July, 1921.)

(*b*) That the plaintiff, being thus *prima facie* within the scope of the expression "nationals of the former Kingdom of "Hungary" in Article 1 (ix), must (if he was to succeed) establish his exclusion under Article 2 of the Treaty of Peace Order,[1] and under that Article it was necessary for him within six months from the coming into force of the Treaty to show to the satisfaction of the Administrator that he had acquired *ipso facto* in accordance with its provisions the nationality of an Allied or Associated Power. (See *Baron Reitzes de Marienvert* v. *Administrator of Austrian Property*, L.R. [1924] 2 Ch. 282.) This he had failed to do, and there was no suggestion that the Administrator in arriving at his conclusion had acted in bad faith. Accordingly the plaintiff's property must remain subject to the charge. [Report: 44 T.L.R., p. 65.]

Case No. 201

Nationality—Change of Nationality in Cases of Territorial Changes—Option—Beginning of the Period of.

OEDENBURG (CHANGE OF NATIONALITY) CASE.

Austrian Administrative Court. 2 *September*, 1927.
A. 317/26.

THE FACTS.—The appellant was resident in Oedenburg (Burgenland). He asked the Austrian Minister of the Interior for a declaration that he was an Austrian subject on the ground that Oedenburg had been assigned to the Austrian Republic by the Treaty of St. Germain. This application was refused on the ground that the town of Oedenburg had remained with Hungary as the result of the plebiscite which had taken place in pursuance of the Protocol of Venice of 13 October, 1921.

[1] Article 2 of the Order in Council corresponds with Article 232, 1 (*b*), subparagraph 3, of the Treaty of Trianon.

Held: That the appeal must be rejected. The acquisition of new nationality was conditioned by the actual exercise of sovereignty by Austria. In accordance with the opinions generally held on the subject and the unanimous practice of States it is, except when treaties provide otherwise, the change of territorial sovereignty which brings about the change of nationality in ceded territory. That change is brought about not as the result of the treaty of cession alone, but only as the result of the treaty of cession in conjunction with the actual taking possession of the territory. This is the reason why the periods for option laid down in the Treaties of Versailles and St. Germain begin only with the moment of the definitive transfer of sovereignty. In the case of plebiscitary territories this date coincides with the attribution of territory as the result of the plebiscite. (See Articles 91, 112, 113 of the Treaty of Versailles and Article 79 of the Treaty of St. Germain.) The view that as the result of cession a State loses its citizens at a time other than at the time of the actual transference of sovereignty would lead to impossible results. Thus, for instance, it would have to treat them for a time as aliens, and it could actually deport them before the transfer of territory has taken place. Oedenburg had never been ceded to Austria. Hungary, whose existence as an independent State had not been affected either as the result of the revolution or of the Peace Treaties, has continued to exercise sovereignty over this territory. Accordingly, Austria is bound by virtue of Article 17 of the Treaty of St. Germain to regard the residents of Oedenburg as Hungarian subjects. [Report: *Sammlung der Erkenntnisse des Verwaltungsgerichtshofes*, vol. LI (1927), administrative part, *Österreichische Staatsdruckerei*, No. 14,649 (A), pp. 134 ff.]

Nationality—How far Affected by Peace Treaties—Change of Nationality before the Entrance into Force of the Treaty—Sequestration in War Time—Enemy Nationality of Owner at Time of Sequestration—Meaning and Extent of Article 297 (*b*) and (*d*) of the Treaty of Versailles. **Case No. 202**

CHANGE OF NATIONALITY (GREEK SEQUESTRATION) CASE.

Areopagus. 1928. *No.* 170.

THE FACTS.—A German national, F., the owner of immovable property in Greece, assumed Greek nationality on March 26, 1920, four days before the provisions of the Treaty of Versailles affecting Greece came into

Case No. 202 *contd.*

effect (30 March, 1920), but some time after the sequestration of his Greek property. The Court was called upon to decide whether it was necessary, as a prerequisite to the liquidation of property, that the owner should be of German nationality (under the provisions of Article 297 (*b*) of the Treaty) at the date of liquidation, or whether this was necessary only at the date of sequestration (in the present case on 18 November, 1917). If the latter alternative were to be accepted, it would follow that no acquisition of an Allied nationality during the interval separating the actual sequestration and the coming into force of the Treaty could operate to hinder the sequestration or liquidation.

Held: The property was sequestrated by virtue of Statute No. 1073 of 1917, and rendered subject to liquidation by Statute No. 2023 of 15 February, 1920, so that a change of nationality after the sequestration does not affect the question. Article 297 of the Treaty of Versailles, as ratified by Statute No. 2084, renders all exceptional war measures, all dispositions and actions carried through or to be carried through in the future as a result of such war measures, as these are defined in paragraphs 1 and 3 of the Annex to Article 297, final and valid against all claimants, in so far as they may be called into question in the relations between the Allied and Associated Powers and their nationals on the one hand, and Germany and her nationals on the other. The sequestration is such an exceptional war measure as that contemplated in the Treaty. [Report: Themis, vol. 39, p. 642.]

Case No. 203 **Acquisition of Nationality as the Result of Cession—Nationality of a Wife Not Living in Transferred Territory—Articles 61 and 66 of the Treaty of Trianon.**

JULIANNA M. *v.* JOSEF SCH.

Supreme Court of Hungary. 14 December, 1927.

THE FACTS.—The plaintiff had been separated from her husband, the defendant, for the last thirty-four years. She was employed, with his consent, in a kindergarten school managed by the State in Nagyszalonta (Hungary). After the armistice Nagyszalonta was occupied by Roumanian troops and subsequently ceded in the Treaty of Trianon to Roumania. The Treaty entered into force on 26 July, 1921. On 15 June of that year the plaintiff settled in Szeged, which remained part of Hungarian territory. She assumed permanent residence there, and was in receipt of a pension from the Hungarian State. Her husband, who was resident in a commune ceded to Roumania, acquired Roumanian nationality as a result of the Treaty of Trianon. In 1925 the plaintiff instituted divorce proceedings against the defendant in a Hungarian court. The defendant contended that the plaintiff was not a Hungarian national, and that Hungarian courts had, therefore, no jurisdiction.

Held by the Supreme Court of Hungary: That the plaintiff was a Hungarian national, and that Hungarian courts had jurisdiction. The change in a husband's nationality as a result of cession only affects the nationality of his wife if she lives with him ; it has no effect on a wife who has been separated from him for a long time. As, prior to the entrance into force of the Treaty of Trianon, the wife returned to Hungarian territory and took up permanent residence there, she must be regarded as a Hungarian national. [Report : No. P. III, 2013/1927.]

IV.—Protected Persons and *de facto* Subjects

Protected Persons—British Protected Persons in Palestine—Question of Proof of the Quality of Protected Person. **Case No. 204**

N. N. BEROUTI *v.* TURKISH GOVERNMENT.

Anglo-Turkish Mixed Arbitral Tribunal. 14 *December*, 1927.

(HAMMERICH, MEMDOUH, GRIMSTON.)

THE FACTS.—This was a claim on account of requisitions and other measures adopted in regard to the claimant by Turkish authorities in Jaffa during the war. The claimant claimed to be a British protected person, and invoked Article 64 of the Treaty of Lausanne, which provided that the provisions of Part III of the Treaty relating to "Allied nationals"

"shall benefit persons who, without having the "nationality of one of the Allied Powers, have, in "consequence of the protection which they in fact "enjoyed at the hands of these Powers, received "from Ottoman authorities the same treatment as

Case No. 204 *contd.*

" Allied nationals and have, on this account, been " prejudiced."

In support of his claim to be a British protected person, the claimant produced a *laisser-passer*, dated 16 March, 1920, and issued by the British military authorities in occupation of Egypt, which described him as " sujet palestinien, protégé britannique." He also produced a declaration, dated 31 March, 1919, by a religious official of the " Latin nation " in Jaffa to the effect that as a British protected person he had been deported by the Turkish authorities between April, 1916, and October, 1918.

Held : That the claimant had not proved that he was a British protected person, and that the Tribunal therefore had no jurisdiction. The documents in question were not issued with a view to certifying as to the status of the claimant; they were issued by authorities which were not competent to pronounce upon the matter; and they contained no data showing that protection was actually exercised within the meaning of the Treaty, not only between 1916 and 1919, but as early as 29 August, 1914, when the war began. [Report : *Recueil*, VIII, p. 186.]

Case No. 205

Protected Persons—Status of—Whether Acquiring the Status of National in regard to Claims before International Tribunals—Armenians as French Protected Persons.

HRAND DJEVAHIRDJIAN *v.* GERMANY.

Franco-German Mixed Arbitral Tribunal. 27 *May*, 1927.

(BOTELLA, DE VALLES, HOENE.)

THE FACTS.—The claimant, an Armenian, had been granted by the French Government the status of " protégé " special." He contended that in that capacity he was entitled as a French national (*ressortissant français*) to invoke the jurisdiction of the Tribunal in accordance with Article 296 of the Treaty.

Held : That that contention must be rejected, and that the Tribunal had no jurisdiction. The French Government never possessed any general right of sovereignty over Armenian subjects. Armenia had never been a French colony or protectorate, or a French mandated territory. For this reason alone, the claimant could not be regarded as a French national in the meaning of the Treaty.

The position of "protégé special" constituted not so much an official status as a position arising from an act of grace and courtesy. It was restricted to non-Christian countries, and its general effects were more of a moral, than of a juridical, nature. In any case, this relation could not produce any effects outside the territories in which France exercised the function of protection over religious communities in the Islamic countries. [Report: *Recueil*, VII, p. 603.]

NOTE.—See also Case No. 24 (*Falla-Nataf and Brothers* v. *Germany*).

Protected Persons and *de facto* Subjects—Meaning of the Term "Protégés" in a Treaty—Different Titles of International Protection. **Case No. 206**

PABLO NÁJERA (OF THE LEBANON) CASE.

France and Mexico: Mixed Claims Commission.
19 *October*, 1928.

(VERZIJL, President.)

THE FACTS.—The French-Mexican Claims Convention of 25 September, 1924, provided for the submission to a Mixed Claims Commission of all claims brought against the Mexican Government for loss or damage suffered during the revolutionary period from 1910 to 1920 by French subjects or protected persons. The Mexican Government opposed the jurisdiction of the Commission to hear and decide the claims brought before the latter by citizens of Syria and the Lebanon on the ground, *inter alia*, that the term "protégés" has in international law the technical meaning of "subjects of an international "protectorate," and did not apply, therefore, to nationals of Syria and the Lebanon.

Held: That the Mexican contention was unfounded. The term "protégé" has generally a wider sense, for instance, *inter alia*, in the Convention of Madrid of July 3, 1880 (regarding the Right of Protection in Morocco), Article 32 of the General Act of the Brussels Anti-Slavery Conference of 1890, and the Award of the Permanent Court of Arbitration of 1905 in the matter of the *Muscat Dhows*. What the meaning of the term is in a particular case depends to a large extent on the intentions of the parties concerned; thus it may, for instance, mean all those who in virtue of an international title enjoy the diplomatic protection of a (foreign) State, as is the case of the nationals of

Case No. 206 *contd.*

Syria and the Lebanon in virtue of Article 3 of the Mandate. In general, this quality of "protégé" may be based either on the fact of citizenship of a State which is itself placed in a position of subordination to another State (protectorate, vassal State, mandated State, Danzig), or on a direct personal relation between the person concerned and a foreign State. In the case under consideration the context of the treaty provisions, the intentions of the parties as revealed by the diplomatic correspondence, the debate in the Mexican Senate, and the total absence in Mexico of persons under the protection of France other than the natives of Syria and the Lebanon, prove that the term must be construed as extending to these categories of protected persons, the more so as historically they have always stood under the diplomatic protection of France.

[Till now unreported.]

Protected Persons—Consuls as Protected Persons.

See Case No. 253 (*Simantov* v. *Bulgarian State*).

V.—Naturalisation

Case No. 207

Naturalisation—Duty of States to Recognise Naturalisation Granted by other States—Restrictions on the Right of Naturalisation—Whether Binding upon Tribunals of other States and upon International Tribunals.

APOSTOLIDIS *v.* TURKISH GOVERNMENT.

Franco-Turkish Mixed Arbitral Tribunal. 23 *May*, 1928.

(ASSER, MEHMED ALI, GANDOLPHE.)

THE FACTS.—The claimant, who was originally a Turkish subject, subsequently acquired French nationality by naturalisation. Article 5 of the Turkish Law of 19 January, 1869, relating to naturalisation laid down that the naturalisation of a Turkish subject abroad should be considered null and void if it had taken place without the previous authorisation of the Imperial Turkish Government. As in the present case no such authorisation had been given, Turkey contended that the claimant was still of Turkish nationality, and that the Tribunal had no jurisdiction.

Held: That that contention must be rejected, and that the Tribunal had jurisdiction. According to the principles of international law, the effects of naturalisation granted by one State ought to be recognised not only by the authorities of that State, but also by the judicial and administrative authorities of all other States. In the exceptional case where the laws of a State require previous authorisation for the naturalisation of their subjects abroad, it is only the authorities of that State who are bound by any effects of the failure by its national to comply with the requirement of such authorisation. In the present case the Turkish authorities were entitled to refuse to recognise the French naturalisation of the claimant. But all other judicial authorities, including the international tribunals, far from being bound in this matter by Turkish municipal legislation, were according to public international law under a duty to recognise the validity of the naturalisation and to treat the claimant as a French subject. [Report : *Recueil*, VIII, p. 373.]

Naturalisation—How far British Nationality Conferred by Naturalisation outside Great Britain.

See Case No. 23 (*L. Hanau* v. *C. Hanau*).

VI.—Expatriation. Loss of Nationality

Nationality—Loss of Nationality by Residence Abroad—Burden of Proof. **Case No. 208**

INDIA AND FAR EAST COMPANY *v.* SCHAEFER AND GERMAN OFFICE.

Franco-German Mixed Arbitral Tribunal. 25 *June*, 1928.

(BOTELLA, DE VALLES, HOENE.)

THE FACTS.—In this case the German Government denied that the defendant was a German national. It adduced a document issued on 15 February, 1913, by the Prussian authorities and stating that Schaefer lost his Prussian and consequently[1] his German nationality by uninterrupted residence abroad for a period of over ten years. There was no other proof pointing to the uninterrupted residence of the defendant for over ten years outside Germany.

Held : That the defendant must be regarded as a German national, and that the Tribunal, therefore, had jurisdiction.

[1] See, however, on this point, Case No. 189 (*De Luck* v. *Germany*).

Case No. 208 *contd.* The party alleging loss of nationality as the result of absence abroad is under a duty to prove both actual residence abroad and absence of return to the country of origin for the period required by national law. The said document signed by the President of the Prussian Administration did not contain any definite proof to this effect. [Report: *Recueil,* VIII, p. 155.]

Expatriation—Presumptive Expatriation as the Result of Stay Abroad—Question of Retroactive Effect of Rebuttal of Presumption—Effect on Diplomatic Protection and Nationality of Claims.

See Case No. 168 (*H. Rothmann* v. *Austria and Hungary*).

VII.—Denationalisation

Case No. 209 **Loss of Nationality—Denationalisation—Effect in Foreign States—Status of Russian *Émigrés* Denationalised by Soviet Government.**

RAJDBERG *v.* LEWI.

Supreme Court of Poland, First Division. 31 *October,* 1927.

THE FACTS.—Article XVII of the Polish-Russian Peace Treaty of Riga of 18 March, 1921, provides, *inter alia,* that private law questions between nationals of the contracting parties, in so far as they arise out of relations which have come into existence before the date of the Treaty, shall be decided by a Mixed Claims (Clearing) Commission, unless such questions are decided by the Treaty itself.

The plaintiff instituted proceedings in a Polish municipal court in respect of a partnership between himself and the defendant in the years 1918-1920. The Court of Appeal of Warsaw on appeal struck out all the proceedings in the case, on the grounds that, since the recognition of the Soviet Union by Poland, all persons domiciled in Soviet territory were, from the point of view of the Polish State, Russian nationals, and that the fact that through his residence abroad the plaintiff, under Soviet law, had lost Soviet nationality without acquiring any other was immaterial: consequently, jurisdiction in this case rested with the Mixed Claims (Clearing) Commission and not with the Polish municipal courts. On appeal,

Held: (1) That Article XVII of the Treaty refers to claims arising out of private law, and that such claims, if they had arisen before the date of the Treaty as between nationals of the two contracting parties, would belong to the jurisdiction of the Mixed Claims (Clearing) Commission, " and, consequently, are excluded from the jurisdiction of the (municipal) " courts " [1];

(2) That, consequently, the refusal of the Court of Appeal to entertain the action does not constitute denial of justice to a foreigner contrary to the Civil Code (the Napoleonic Code in force in that part of Poland);

(3) That, however, the plaintiff, who had been deprived under Soviet law of Soviet nationality, could not be considered a Soviet national by other States, least of all by States (such as Poland) which had recognised *de jure* the Soviet Republic;

(4) That the plaintiff's plea that he is a stateless person, living in Berlin under the protection of the League of Nations, could not be disregarded; for, even assuming that formally he was still a Soviet national, the Court would be justified in concluding from the circumstances pleaded by him that he was a political *émigré* and could not be considered a Soviet national, but must be looked upon as a person having for the present no nationality.

Accordingly (5) the Treaty of Riga did not apply, and the plaintiff was entitled to sue in a Polish municipal court. [Reports: Zb. O.S.N., 1927, No. 107; O.S.P., VII, No. 61.]

NOTE.—The grounds of the decision of the Supreme Court are not very clear to the editors, but in the dearth of authority bearing upon denationalisation by the Soviet Government the decision is interesting.—[Ed.]

VIII.—Double Nationality

Double Nationality—Proof of Effective Nationality —Nationality of Married Woman. **Case No. 210**

OLIVEIRA MACHADO *v.* NERI PINTO.

Portuguese Court of Cassation. 1 *July*, 1927.

THE FACTS.—The plaintiff, a Portuguese national, married in Brazil the defendant woman, who was a Brazilian national and retained that nationality according to Article 69 of the Brazilian Federal Constitution of

[1] Here an unreported judgment of the same year was referred to.

Case No. 210 ***contd.***

24 February, 1891, which provides that a woman does not lose her nationality by marriage with a foreigner. By her marriage with a Portuguese national she acquired Portuguese nationality by the terms of Article 18, paragraph 6, of the Portuguese Civil Code. The plaintiff, while domiciled in Brazil, brought an action for divorce in Portugal.

Held by the Supreme Court of Justice, on appeal from the judgment of the Court of Appeal of Lisbon: That the Court had jurisdiction. It was established in the documents produced before the Court that the defendant, although absent and without known residence at the time when the action was brought, had during the preceding year a domicile in Portugal, where she was still considered a Portuguese subject. Whatever may be the personal status of the parties to the contract of marriage concluded in Brazil, that is to say, of the Portuguese husband and the Brazilian wife, the Tribunal is not called upon to examine or to discuss their status, seeing that it was not contended that there exists a foreign law conflicting with the Portuguese law (see Article 2406 of the Civil Code). [Report: *Gazeta da Relação de Lisboa*, vol. 41, No. 11.]

NOTE.—This decision reverses that given by the Court of Appeal of Portugal on 9 February, 1926, reported in *Annual Digest*, 1925-1926, Case No. 207. As pointed out in a note to that judgment in the *Gazeta da Relação de Lisboa*, vol. 41, No. 11, pp. 175, 176, no reference was made to the provision of Article 2 of the Decree of 2 December, 1910, which was relevant to the question before the Court, although the judgment says that, as no foreign law contrary to Portuguese law had been invoked, there was no necessity to consider the personal status of the husband and the wife, seeing that, notwithstanding the provision of Article 2406 of the Portuguese Civil Code, the view was adopted, not without some divergencies in the literature and decisions of courts, that Portuguese tribunals ought to apply foreign law when the express or implied provisions of Portuguese law consider that other law as relevant for the decision of the legal relation in question. (See Professor Machado Vilela, *Tratado elementar téorico e prático de direito internacional privado*, vol. 2, pp. 256 ff.; *Estudo sôbre as Convenções da Haïa de direito internacional privado*, p. 555; Judgment of the Judge President of Beira of 17 October, 1914; and Decisions of the Supreme Court of Justice of 30 June, 1922, and 23 November, 1923, *Gazeta da Relação de Lisboa*, vol. 29, No. 22, p. 381, and vol. 37, No. 16, pp. 249 and 251.)

It appeared that the defendant wife was originally of Brazilian nationality. It was for the Tribunal to decide what her nationality was after marriage both according to Portuguese and to Brazilian laws, and, after having stated that she possessed two nationalities, to apply the provision of Article 2 of the Decree of 2 December, 1910, according to which " A Portuguese citizen, in case he is considered also as a national " of another State, cannot so long as he resides within the territory of "that other State invoke his Portuguese citizenship." The decision, without mentioning that provision, seems nevertheless to have taken it into consideration, seeing that it bases itself, in order to apply Portuguese law, on the fact that the defendant wife had resided in Portugal in 1922 and that her residence at the moment when the action was instituted was unknown, so that it was not proved that she was in Brazil, the country of her other nationality.

Double Nationality—Treatment of, by International Tribunals.

See Case No. 195 (*Georges Pinson Case*, §§ 13, 23-42).

IX.—Option

Option—Requirement of Racial Affinity—Meaning of "Race" —Article 80 of the Treaty of St. Germain. **Case No. 211**

A. H. *v.* Federal Ministry of the Interior.

Austrian Administrative Court. 29 *December*, 1925. *No.* 14,072 *A.*

The Facts.—The Federal Ministry of the Interior refused to recognise the option made by the plaintiff under Article 80 of the Treaty of St. Germain [1] on the ground that the plaintiff had given no proof of his belonging to the race of the majority of the Austrian population. He appealed.

Held: That the appeal must be dismissed as unfounded. It is true that the plaintiff had given proof of his belonging to the majority of the Austrian population as regards language. But option, under Article 80 of the Treaty of St. Germain, presupposes the proof of affinity both as to language and as to race. The proof of the existence of only one condition is not sufficient. The plaintiff had, therefore, to prove that he belongs to the majority of the Austrian population as regards race also, proof to be given, according to the Ordinance of 20 August, 1920, by

[1] Article 80 provides as follows: "Persons possessing rights of citizenship "in territory forming part of the former Austro-Hungarian Monarchy, and "differing in race and language from the majority of the population of such "territory, shall within six months from the coming into force of the present "Treaty severally be entitled to opt for Austria, Italy, Poland, Roumania, "the Serb-Croat-Slovene State, or the Czecho-Slovak State, if the majority "of the population of the State selected is of the same race and language as "the person exercising the right to opt. The provisions of Article 78 as to "the exercise of the right of option shall apply to the right of option given "by this Article."

Case No. 211 *contd.* the production of evidence of the " conclusive characteristics " ("*fassbare Merkmale*") showing his membership of the German race. [Report: *Sammlung der Erkenntnisse des Verwaltungsgerichtshofes*, vol. XLIX (1925), pp. 586-588.]

NOTE.—This is one of a long series of decisions to the same effect. The term " race " in Article 80 of the Treaty of St. Germain is a very vague one; the administrative authorities of Austria have always decided in the sense that " race " does not mean membership of the nation in the cultural sense (a meaning which would make the term dependent on the will of the optant), but that race means a permanent quality, acquired by a person by birth, and determined by anatomical characteristics independently of the individual will. The leading decision of the Court in this respect was given on 9 June, 1921, No. 2973. (See Kunz, *Die völkerrechtliche Option*, vol. II, pp. 226-228.)

Case No. 212

Option—Right of the Divorced Wife to Opt Individually and Separately from her Former Husband.

A. P. *v.* FEDERAL MINISTRY OF THE INTERIOR.

Austrian Administrative Court. 6 *October*, 1925.
No. 13,980 *A.*

THE FACTS.—On 4 January, 1921, Mrs. A. P. was divorced. Three days later she exercised a right of option under Part III, Section VI, of the Treaty of St. Germain individually and separately from her husband. The Federal Ministry of the Interior declined to recognise the option on the ground that, being married at the date of the coming into force of the Treaty of St. Germain, that is, 16 July, 1920, she had at this date no right of separate and individual option apart from her husband. She appealed.

Held: That the decision of the Federal Ministry of the Interior must be quashed as unfounded in law. The effect of Articles 78 and 80 of the Treaty of St. Germain is that a divorced woman may opt separately and individually if she was divorced after 16 July, 1920, but before the expiration of the period fixed for the option by the Treaty. [Report: *Sammlung der Erkenntnisse des Verwaltungsgerichtshofes*, vol. XLIX (1925), pp. 453-454.]

NOTE.—The only provision in Articles 78 and 80 of the Treaty of St. Germain specifically referring to married women is that option by a husband will cover his wife.

Option—Withdrawal of Declaration of Option. **Case No. 213**

J. E. *v.* Federal Ministry of the Army.

Austrian Administrative Court. 6 *October*, 1925.
No. 13,981 *A.*

The Facts.—J. E. had opted in 1921 for Austria, according to Article 80 of the Treaty of St. Germain. Later on, he withdrew his option, and the option was declared void by administrative decision. In 1924 the plaintiff asked for the recognition of the validity of his option. This demand was dismissed, and he appealed.

Held : That the administrative decision declaring the option void must be annulled as being unfounded in law. According to the Treaty of St. Germain, it is for the person having the right to opt to decide whether he will make use of this right or not ; but having made use of it, the right to opt is exhausted. A declaration of option, legally made within the legal period, cannot be withdrawn. The plaintiff had therefore definitively acquired Austrian nationality. [Report : *Sammlung der Erkenntnisse des Verwaltungsgerichtshofes*, vol. XLIX (1925), pp. 455, 456.]

Option—Declaration of Option for a Person who is not *sui juris*. **Case No. 214**

E. W. *v.* Federal Ministry of the Interior.

Austrian Administrative Court. 6 *March*, 1925. *No.* 13,783 *A.*

The Facts.—E. W. had acquired Austrian nationality by a declaration of option, made personally in 1921. In 1923 the Federal Ministry of the Interior annulled this declaration of nationality on the ground that he had, since 1914, been under guardianship on account of insanity. He appealed.

Held : That the appeal must be dismissed. The declaration of option for a person not *sui juris* must be made by his legal representative and within the legal period. This period having expired, the administrative authorities can no longer accept a declaration of option. [Report : *Sammlung der Erkenntnisse des Verwaltungsgerichtshofes*, vol. XLIX (1925).]

Case No. 215 **Option—Cretans Opting for Greek Nationality—Treaty of Athens, November, 1913.**

DAMIANOS *v.* EGYPTIAN GOVERNMENT.

Egyptian Mixed Court of Appeal. 21 *June*, 1927.

THE FACTS.—Damianos was engaged as a constable in the Egyptian Police in January, 1910. In his attestation paper he declared himself of Cretan nationality (being of Cretan origin), and he was informed that he would not be entitled to any pension or indemnity on the termination of his services, because he was treated in Egypt as a Turkish or local subject. After the conclusion of the Treaty of Athens in November, 1913, he exercised his right of option for Greek nationality. He remained in the Egyptian service till 1924, and on his retirement claimed to be entitled to the benefit of the Law of 1923, which dealt with the retirement of Government officers who were foreign subjects, but to the exclusion of former subjects of the Turkish Empire. The Government contested the claim on the ground that he had entered the service as of Turkish nationality, before the date of the Treaty of Athens in 1913, and, therefore, was not to be treated as a foreign subject. The Mixed Tribunal of Cairo gave judgment in favour of the Government, but on appeal

Held: The exclusion from the benefit of the Egyptian Law of 1923 does not apply to those who, though of Turkish origin, had obtained a foreign nationality and ceased to be subject to the native jurisdiction before the Great War. The tie between Turkey and Crete was severed at the end of the Balkan War by the Treaty of London of 30 May, 1913, when Crete was annexed to Greece. [Report: *Gazette des Tribunaux Mixtes*, 17th year, p. 253.]

Acquisition of Nationality—Right of an Arbitral Commission to Question the Acquisition of a New Nationality by Option.

See Case No. 196 (*Pablo Nájera (of the Lebanon) Case*).

Option—Beginning of Period of—Territories under Plebiscite.

See Case No. 201 (*Oedenburg (Change of Nationality) Case*).

X.—Statelessness

Statelessness—Position of Stateless Persons—Right to Poor Persons' Facilities before Courts—Admission to Unemployment Benefit. **Case No. 216**

STATELESS PERSONS (LEGAL AID) CASE.

German Kammergericht. 9 *February*, 1928.

THE FACTS.—This was an appeal against the decision of a district court refusing to the appellant, a stateless person, the benefit of the facilities provided by the law to poor persons appearing as parties before courts. While paragraph 1 of Article 114 of the German Code of Civil Procedure lays down the principle of legal aid for poor persons, paragraph 2 excludes from the operation of the Article foreign subjects unless their own State grants the same rights to German subjects. The court below held that, as in the case of stateless persons there could be no question of reciprocity, they could not be admitted to the benefits of Article 114.

Held: That the appellant was entitled to the benefits of Article 114. Paragraph 2 of that Article should be applied only in those cases in which it was possible to investigate whether reciprocity was granted or not. Such an investigation was impossible in the case of stateless persons. In their case there could, by the very nature of the thing, be no question of reciprocity. There would be no justification for putting a stateless person on the same footing as an alien whose State refuses reciprocity. Paragraph 2 was only a means of preventing the subjects of a foreign State from enjoying more favourable treatment than that accorded to German nationals abroad. It could not be regarded as directed against stateless persons. [Report: *Z.I.*, XL (1929), p. 313.]

NOTE.—(*a*) There is a conflict of views in the judicial practice in Germany on the matter dealt with in this decision. Thus, in a decision of 11 July, 1924, of the Upper District Court of Münich (*Juristische Wochenschrift*, 1925, p. 76) it was held that stateless persons are not entitled to the benefits of Article 114. This view was reaffirmed by the same Court on 2 May, 1928 (*Z.I.*, XL (1929), p. 315), on the ground, *inter alia*, that the intention of the law was in principle to confer that benefit only upon German subjects, and that Article 114 could not therefore be interpreted extensively. One of the reasons given by the Court was that an interpretation of Article 114 extending its benefits to

Case No. 216 contd.

stateless persons might act as an inducement to subjects of States refusing reciprocity to Germany to expatriate themselves and thus, by becoming stateless, achieve the benefits of Article 114. . . .

(*b*) The problem of statelessness has arisen in Germany also in connection with the admission to unemployment benefit. According to Section 6 of the Unemployment Benefits Order of 16 February, 1924, admission of aliens to unemployment benefit is made dependent upon reciprocal treatment of German subjects abroad. This provision was for a time interpreted as precluding stateless persons from participating in unemployment benefits. But see Communication of the Federal Minister of Labour of 17 February, 1927 (*International Survey of Legal Decisions on Labour Law*, 1927, Germany, Case No. 48), reversing the former practice and laying down that in the future stateless persons shall receive unemployment benefit provided that they fulfil the conditions of the insurance legislation : " In reconsidering the question, I " was specially impressed by the fact that the expense of the unemploy- " ment benefit is made up to a considerable extent of contributions " paid both by persons without nationality and by persons of German " nationality." However, stateless persons are not admitted to the benefits of the so-called " crisis " assistance, the expense of which is covered exclusively by public funds. (*Ibid.*) And see *ibid.*, Cases Nos. 49, 50, 51, on the admission of foreign subjects to " crisis " assistance and on the requirement of reciprocity.

Case No. 217

Statelessness—Claim of Stateless Persons to Privileges Dependent on Reciprocity.

Stateless Persons (Danzig) Case.

First Civil Senate of Danzig. 18 *October*, 1928.

The Facts.—This was a complaint by a woman against the decision of the court of first instance refusing to grant to her, in a divorce action instituted by her, the facilities provided for poor persons. The complainant was a stateless person, having lost her former Russian nationality, apparently as the result of denationalisation. Paragraph 114 of the Danzig Civil Procedure Code provides that aliens have the right to poor persons' facilities only subject to reciprocity.

Held : That paragraph 114 of the Code is not to be interpreted as meaning that stateless persons appearing before courts cannot be admitted to the benefits of the poor persons' provisions. That paragraph means merely that stateless persons have no legal right to such facilities. But it is within the discretion of the court to grant them, and the present case is one in which discretion ought to be exercised in favour of the complainant. [Report: *Danziger Juristische Wochenschrift*, 1929, p. 12.]

NOTE.—Cf. on this subject Schwartz in *Juristische Wochenschrift*, 1926, p. 394; Weck, *ibid.*, 1928, p. 1240; Magnus, *Tabellen zum internationalen Recht*, No. 1, p. 97.

Statelessness—As Result of Cession of Territory.

See Case No. 190 (*Alsace-Lorraine Nationality* (*Statelessness*) *Case*).

XI.—Nationality of Corporations

[See also Part XI, WAR AND NEUTRALITY: VI. *Enemy Character*.]

Nationality of Corporations—Theory of Control—Nationality of the Ottoman Bank. **Case No. 218**

BARON DE NEUFLIZE *v.* GERMANY AND THE DEUTSCHE BANK.

Franco-German Mixed Arbitral Tribunal. 25 *June*, 1928.

(BOTELLA, DE VALLES, HOENE.)

THE FACTS.—This was an action instituted by the claimant on behalf of a number of companies and individuals having certain interests in the Baghdad Railway. Amongst the groups on behalf of which the claimant appeared was the Ottoman Bank.

Held: That the Tribunal had no jurisdiction in respect of the Ottoman Bank as the latter was not of French nationality. In accordance with the principle laid down in the case of *Damas-Hamah* v. *Baghdad Railway*,[1] in order to fix the nationality of a corporation on the basis of the theory of control the Tribunal will consider not only the nationality of the persons possessing the majority of shares but also all factors of a financial, administrative and other character likely to secure for the subjects of one State the actual control of the affairs of the corporation. This being so, it could not be said that the Ottoman Bank was under French control. Its *siège social* was in Constantinople; it fulfilled the functions of the Turkish State Bank; it was directed by an Administrative Council composed of four directors and three administrators, the latter being permanently resident in Turkey and nominated by agreement with the

[1] *Recueil*, I, p. 401.

Case No. 218 *contd.*

Turkish Government; it was controlled by a "High Commissioner of the Turkish Government" who had absolute power to veto any measures deemed by him to be in violation of the Bank's *firman* of concession, of its statute or of the special *règlement* between the Turkish Government and the Bank; the special committee appointed to direct and to supervise its financial operations was composed of ten French, ten English and ten Austrian subjects; the amount of shares owned by French subjects did not exceed two-fifths of the total amount. It could not, therefore, be held that the Bank was under French control.[1] [Report: *Recueil*, VIII, p. 158.]

Case No. 219

Corporations—Nationality of Corporations—Theory of Control —Article 249 (*b*) of the Treaty of St. Germain.

OESTERREICHISCHE CREDIT ANSTALT *v.* YUGOSLAVIA.
(*Deutsche Industrie Gesellschaft* as intervening party.)

Austro-Yugoslavian Mixed Arbitral Tribunal.
8 *September*, 1927.

(LOGOZ, ZWIEDINECK, ARANGELOWITCH.)

THE FACTS.—The intervening party, a German company registered in Germany, claimed that as two-thirds of its shares were in the hands of Austrian banks, it should, by virtue of the previous decisions of the Mixed Arbitral Tribunal recognising the doctrine of control and of the provisions of Article 249 (*b*) of the Treaty of St. Germain, be regarded as an Austrian company and permitted to intervene.

Held: That the Court could not accede to that view. The practice of the Mixed Arbitral Tribunal in the matter of the doctrine of control was not uniform. While some judgments accepted the doctrine,[2] others refused to follow it.[3] As to Article 249 (*b*) of the Treaty of St. Germain, that Article permitted the liquidation of companies controlled by nationals of

[1] See the case *Crédit Foncier franco-bulgare* v. *Bulgaria*, decided on 23 April, 1928, by the French-Bulgarian Mixed Arbitral Tribunal (*Recueil*, VIII, p. 516), for another application of the theory of control; and for the English view see *Daimler Co.* v. *Continental Tyre and Rubber Co.*, L.R. [1916] 2 A.C. 307.

[2] The Tribunal referred here to *Société du Chemin de Fer de Damas-Hamah* v. *Compagnie du Chemin de Fer de Bagdad*, *Recueil*, I, p. 401, and *Elmores Metall A.G.* v. *Grimberg*, *ibid.*, V, p. 777.

[3] The Tribunal referred here to *Dawson & Son* v. *Balkanische Handels und Industrie, A.G.*, *ibid.*, III, p. 534.

the former Austrian Empire, whatever might be the nationality of the company. But that did not mean that it considered that merely because a company was controlled by Austrian nationals it therefore possessed Austrian nationality. [Report: *Recueil*, VII, p. 794.]

NOTE.—See also to the same effect the case *Société Anonyme du Chemin de Fer Vicinal, etc.* v. *Roumanian State* before the Hungarian-Roumanian Mixed Arbitral Tribunal, decided on 27 July, 1927 (Cederkrantz, Szekacz), *ibid.*, p. 839, in which the Tribunal, while rejecting the theory of control, adopted the test of *siège social* as one "for a long "time universally accepted both by writers and by judicial practice."

And see also the case of *Société Ottomane du Chemin de Fer de Damas-Hamah* v. *Turkey*, decided by the French-Turkish Mixed Arbitral Tribunal on 13 December, 1927 (*ibid.*, p. 950), in which the Tribunal equally refused to apply the doctrine of control to joint-stock companies under Article 64 (2) of the Treaty of Lausanne.

Nationality of Corporations—Change of Sovereignty—Provisions of Treaty of Peace between Allied and Associated Powers and Austria—Inclusion within the Term "Nationals of "former Austrian Empire." **Case No. 220**

BOHEMIAN UNION BANK (plaintiff) *v.* ADMINISTRATOR OF AUSTRIAN PROPERTY (defendant).

English High Court of Justice, Chancery Division.
24 *March*, 1927.

(MR. JUSTICE CLAUSON.)

THE FACTS.—The plaintiff company, the Bohemian Union Bank, was incorporated in 1872 under the laws of the Austrian Empire and had its seat and place of registration at Prague in Bohemia, which formed part of the Austrian Empire. In August, 1918, the Allied Governments recognised a certain *de facto* change in the status of that portion of the Austrian Empire which comprised Prague, as a result of which a new State under the name of the Czechoslovak State was established. Within the territory of Czechoslovakia it is customary to regard October 28, 1918, as the day on which the new State came into existence (see *Annual Digest*, 1925-1926, Case No. 8). It was admitted on behalf of the defendant, the Administrator of Austrian Property, that as from that date the Bank became, according to Czechoslovakian law, a Czechoslovakian company. By Article 249 (*b*) of the Treaty of St.

Case No. 220 *contd.*

Germain, the Allied and Associated Powers reserved the right to " retain and liquidate all property, rights " and interests which belong at the date of coming " into force of the present Treaty to nationals of the " former Austrian Empire, or companies controlled " by them, and are within the territories, colonies, " possessions and protectorates of such Powers (in- " cluding territories added to them by the present " Treaty) or are under the control of those Powers. . . . " Persons who within six months of the coming into " force of the present Treaty show that they have " acquired *ipso facto* in accordance with its provisions " the nationality of an Allied or Associated Power " (including those who obtain such nationality under Article 74 or 77) " will not be considered as nationals " of the former Austrian Empire within the meaning " of this paragraph."

Article 53 of the Treaty provides that:

" Austria, in conformity with the action already " taken by the Allied and Associated Powers, " recognises the complete independence of the " Czechoslavak State. . . ."

Article 70 of the Treaty provides that:

" Every person possessing rights of citizenship " (*pertinenza*) in territory which formed part of " the territories of the former Austro-Hungarian " Monarchy shall obtain *ipso facto* to the exclusion " of Austrian nationality the nationality of the State " exercising sovereignty over such territory."

The Treaty was signed on 10 September, 1919, and entered into force on 16 July, 1920.

The defendant, purporting to act under Article 249, had retained certain money and securities of the plaintiff to the value of £50,000, and the plaintiff now sought to recover this property.

It was contended on behalf of the plaintiff—

(1) That the expression " nationals of the former " Austrian Empire " could not be held to include persons, either physical or juridical, who at the date of the signature of the Treaty, namely, 10 September, 1919, were Czechoslovakian nationals;

(2) That a company may " by a figure of speech " be said to have a nationality;

(3) That juridical persons were included within the scope of Article 70 of the Treaty;

(4) That, whether or not Article 70 applied to juridical persons, the plaintiff company fell within the description of persons who acquired *ipso facto* in accordance with the provisions of the Treaty the nationality of an Allied or Associated Power in view of the fact that the Treaty contained provisions which recognised Czechoslovakia as an independent nation, for the plaintiff company being a *de facto* national at the date of the signature of the Treaty became one *de jure* or *de plein droit* by force of the Treaty.

Held by Clauson, J.: That the plaintiff company was entitled to recover its property, since Czechoslovakian corporations were entitled to the benefit of exemption from the powers to retain and liquidate conferred by Article 249 of the Treaty. The decision was based upon Article 70 of the Treaty (quoted above) or, in the alternative, upon Article 53 (quoted above) and the rest of the Treaty. The learned judge was also of the opinion that it would have been open to him to base his decision—had not either of the above-mentioned grounds been adequate—upon the general principles (at p. 195) "that a corporate body which owes its very existence to the laws of a particular country and which has its principal place of business in that particular country must be treated as a national of that country," and "that *ipso facto*, without any further formality, by reason of the formation of the Czechoslovakian State, by reason of that State having become recognised by the European community of nations—a recognition sealed by the Treaty—the corporate body here in question has become a Czechoslovakian, there being nothing in the Treaty to prevent it so becoming."

The decision of Eve, J., in *Rothschild* v. *Administrator of Austrian Property*, L.R. [1923] 2 Ch. 542, to the effect that the expression "nationals of the former Austrian Empire" was not confined to nationals of the new Austrian Republic, was followed.

The remark of Lord Parker in *Daimler Co.* v. *Continental Tyre and Rubber Co.*, L.R. [1916] 2 A.C., at p. 339, to the effect that "it is only by a figure of speech that a company can be said to have a nationality or residence at all," was referred to. [Report: L.R. [1927] 2 Ch. 175.[1]]

[1] See also *B.Y.*, 1928, pp. 175, 176.

Corporations—Position in International Law—Dutch East India Company—Acquisition of Territorial Title by.

See Case No. 70 (*Island of Palmas Arbitration Case*).

Companies—Nationality of—*Siège Social.*

See Case No. 225 (*Reparations Levy* (*Aliens in Germany*) *Case*).

C. ALIENS

I.—Admission of Aliens

Case No. 221

Admission of Aliens—Absence of Duty to Admit.

SOLTANOW *v.* (POLISH) MINISTRY OF FOREIGN AFFAIRS.

Supreme Administrative Court of Poland. 6 April, 1927.

THE FACTS.—Plaintiff, who was not a Polish citizen and was resident in Berlin, applied for permission to come to Poland. The permission was refused and no grounds for the refusal were given. Plaintiff brought an action to reverse the decision of the Ministry.

Held: That at the moment of the decision there was no rule which would give every foreigner the right to come to Poland. It was true that, under Article 95 of the Polish Constitution of 1921, " The Polish Republic guarantees within its " territory full protection for life, liberty and property to all its " inhabitants without distinction of origin, nationality, language, " race or religion," and that, under the same Article, " subject " to reciprocity, aliens enjoy the same rights as Polish subjects " and have the same duties, except in matters in which the " law expressly stipulates for Polish nationality."[1] [Report: Z.W.N.T.A., V (1927), No. 1183.]

NOTE.—This Article, as appears from its first paragraph, referred only to legal conditions within Polish territory, and did not grant to foreigners who are outside Poland a right to enter Poland. Hence no foreigner, unless there be special rules establishing in his favour an exceptional situation, had the right to claim admission to Poland. The Supreme Administrative Court established under a Law of 1922 has jurisdiction in all actions brought by "any one who claims that his

[1] Translation from *Select Constitutions of the World*, p. 75, published by the Irish Free State, 1922.

"right has been infringed or that he has without legal basis been subjected "to a charge." In these actions the Court decides upon the legality or otherwise of orders and decisions made by administrative authorities. The Court decides, as a rule, upon the legality of such orders and decisions if and after the question has formed the subject of decision of the highest administrative authority having jurisdiction in the matter. This case probably came before the Court by way of an appeal against the decision of the Polish Consulate of Berlin.

For the English law see *Attorney-General for Canada* v. *Cain*, L.R. [1906] A.C. 542.

Aliens—Admission of—Consular Visa—Nature of—Whether Entitling to Admission.

See Case No. 123 (*Wong Ock Jee* v. *Weedin*).

II.—Position of Aliens

iii.—Treatment by and Responsibilities of the Receiving State

[See also Part V, State Responsibility.]

Aliens—Right to Acquire Land. **Case No. 222**

Applegate *v.* Luke.

Supreme Court of Arkansas. 14 March, 1927.

The Facts.—This was a suit to enjoin enforcement of the Arkansas Alien Land Act of 1925. The Act allowed aliens eligible to naturalisation and those protected by treaty to acquire, use and transfer real estate, and prevented other aliens from doing so under penalty that the lands should escheat to the State and the violators become guilty of felony. Article 2, § 20, of the Arkansas Constitution provided that "No distinction "shall ever be made by law between resident aliens and "citizens in regard to the possession, enjoyment or "descent of property." A decree was granted declaring the act unconstitutional and enjoining enforcement.

Held: That the decree should be affirmed. Delivering the Opinion of the Court, Judge Humphreys said with reference to the Article of the Arkansas Constitution quoted above: "The "manifest and only intent which can be extracted from the "language is that all resident aliens in Arkansas, whether "eligible to naturalisation and citizenship under the laws of

Case No. 222 *contd.* " the United States [or not], have the same right to acquire " and enjoy the possession of property in this State, either by " purchase or descent, that any natural citizen has." (173 Ark. 93, 95.) [Report: 173 Ark. 93.]

Case No. 223 **Aliens—Alien's Right to Impart Instruction in his own Language—Fifth Amendment to the Constitution of the United States.**

FARRINGTON *v.* TOKUSHIGE.

United States Supreme Court. 21 *February*, 1927.

THE FACTS.—This was a suit to enjoin enforcement of the Hawaiian Foreign Language School Law. The Law required that all foreign language schools secure a permit from the Department of Public Instruction, pay a fee of one dollar per pupil, and submit to regulations to be prescribed governing entrance requirements, teachers, courses, text-books, equipment, etc. No foreign language school was permitted to hold sessions in the morning before the school hours of public schools nor during the hours that public schools were in session. Attendance at foreign language schools was limited to one hour per day, six hours per week, and thirty-eight weeks per year. Violation was made a misdemeanour with appropriate penalties.

There were in the Territory 163 foreign language schools (9 Korean, 7 Chinese, 147 Japanese), representing a substantial investment, and providing instruction for approximately 20,000 pupils. The petitioners (Tokushige and others) were " members of numerous " voluntary associations conducting foreign language " schools for instruction of Japanese children." It was contended that enforcement of the Act would deprive petitioners of " liberty or property without due pro- " cess of law," contrary to the Fifth Amendment to the United States Constitution. The District Court granted a temporary injunction. The Circuit Court of Appeals affirmed the decree. On certiorari,

Held: That the decree should be affirmed. Delivering the Opinion of the Court, Mr. Justice McReynolds said: "The School " Act and the measures adopted thereunder go far beyond mere "regulation of privately-supported schools where children "obtain instruction deemed valuable by their parents and "which is not obviously in conflict with any public interest. "They give affirmative direction concerning the intimate and "essential details of such schools, intrust their control to public "officers, and deny both owners and patrons reasonable choice "and discretion in respect of teachers, curriculum and text-"books. Enforcement of the Act probably would destroy most, "if not all, of them; and, certainly, it would deprive parents "of fair opportunity to procure for their children instruction "which they think important and we cannot say is harmful. "The Japanese parent has the right to direct the education of "his own child without unreasonable restrictions; the Consti-"tution protects him as well as those who speak another "tongue." (273 U.S. 284, 298.) [Report: 273 U.S. 284.]

Aliens—Admission to Ordinary Schools—Assignment to Coloured School. **Case No. 224**

BOND *v.* TIJ FUNG.

Supreme Court of Mississippi. 10 *October*, 1927.

THE FACTS.—This was a petition for mandamus to compel the Mississippi Superintendent of Education to admit the petitioner, a boy of Chinese nationality, to the school for white children. Judgment for petitioner. On appeal,

Held: That the judgment for petitioner should be reversed. His assignment to the coloured school was no violation of the Treaty of 1868 with China, Article 7, providing that "Citizens "of the United States shall enjoy all of the privileges of the "public educational institutions under the control of the "government of China, and, reciprocally, Chinese subjects shall "enjoy all . . . of the public educational institutions under the "government of the United States, which are enjoyed in the "respective countries by the citizens or subjects of the most "favoured nation." (16 U.S. Stat. L. 739, 740.) Nor was he deprived of a property right under the Fourteenth Amendment of the United States Constitution. [Report: 148 Miss. 462.]

NOTE.—See also Case No. 242, *Gong Lum* v. *Rice*.

Case No. 225 **Aliens—Liability to Taxation—Taxation for War Purposes—Distinguished from Taxation for Defraying a War Indemnity—Relation of International Law to Municipal Law—Article 4 of the German Constitution—Nationality of Companies—Interpretation of Commercial Treaties.**

REPARATIONS LEVY (ALIENS IN GERMANY) CASE.

German Federal Court for Revenue Matters (*Reichsfinanzhof*).
8 *August*, 1928.

THE FACTS.—Article 5 of the German-Italian Treaty of Commerce of 31 October, 1925, provided that the nationals of the contracting parties shall, when in the territory of the other contracting party, be exempted from " compulsory loans and contributions." The appellant company had its *siège social*, and conducted its business, in Germany. It was called upon to make certain advance payments in accordance with the *Aufbringungsgesetz* of 1927—a German Federal law imposing an extraordinary tax in connection with putting into effect the so-called Dawes Plan.

The appellant company contended that the capital of the company belonged to Italian subjects resident in Italy, and that as the company was, therefore, of Italian nationality the imposition of the tax was contrary to the Treaty. It was also contended on behalf of the company that there existed, apart from the Treaty, a rule of international law to the effect that, as aliens did not enjoy political rights, they were not subject to political duties like military service or to special contributions for military or war purposes. That rule of international law was, it was contended, binding upon courts by virtue of Article 4 of the German Constitution according to which generally recognised rules of international law are to be regarded as integral parts of German Federal law.

Held: That the appeal must be rejected.

(*a*) *Nationality of the Company.*—In principle the conception of nationality extends only to natural persons. In so far as it can be extended at all to juridical persons, it is determined exclusively by the seat of the latter. A company with its seat in Germany and registered in Germany can possess no other nationality than German.

(*b*) *The Nature of the Tax under the " Aufbringungsgesetz " and the Interpretation of the Treaty of Commerce.* The tax in question could not be regarded as a compulsory loan seeing that it was not intended to repay it. Neither is it a contribution, *i.e.* compulsory levy for the requirements of the army in occupied territory. The levy complained of was a tax analogous to other taxes levied in Germany. It was true that a former Treaty of Commerce concluded with Italy in 1891 and amended in 1904 exempted the subjects of the two countries from " compulsory loans " and other impositions levied on account of war or other exceptional circumstances. However, that Treaty, abrogated as it had been by the war and by Article 289 of the Treaty of Versailles, was now replaced by the Treaty of 1925. The Court had to consider the text of that latter Treaty and not the possible intention of the parties.

(*c*) *Aliens and War Taxation.*—It could not be admitted that the levy in question was a tax for war purposes, and that it fell therefore within strictly political duties to which aliens were not subject. It was not a tax connected with the conduct of war ; it was a tax imposed in order to enable Germany to pay her war indemnity. There was no rule of international law exempting aliens from taxes of this description.

(*d*) *International Law and Conflicting Municipal Legislation.*—However, even assuming that the *Aufbringungsgesetz* were from this point of view not in accordance with international law, it would still have to be applied by the Courts notwithstanding Article 4 of the Constitution. It was a special law, and would, in conformity with the rule *lex posterior derogat priori*, derogate from any general rule of international law, or indeed from any other Federal law, with which it might conflict. [Report : *Z. für a. ö. R. und V.*, II (1930), p. 88.]

Aliens—Non-Discrimination—Reciprocity, Formal and Substantial. **Case No. 226**

IN THE ESTATE OF JACOB HOROWITZ, DECEASED. ATTORNEY-GENERAL (INTERVENING) APPELLANT.

Supreme Court of Poland, Third Division. 11 *April*, 1928.

THE FACTS.—Article 33 of the Austrian Civil Code of 1811, still in force in certain parts of Poland, provides that " aliens enjoy, in general, civil rights equal to those of " natives and have equal civil duties, unless to enjoy " those rights citizenship be expressly required. In

Case No. 226 *contd.*

"cases of doubt aliens desiring to enjoy rights equal "to those of natives must prove that in the country "of which they are nationals rights such as those in "question are enjoyed by nationals of this country on "a parity with natives."

Horowitz died in Vienna in 1924, leaving real property in Poland. His heirs applied for probate to the District Court of Tarnopol. The latter first directed the heirs and legatees to present evidence to the effect that in Russia (of which both the deceased and his heirs and legatees were suspected of being subjects) Polish citizens can inherit real property; subsequently the Court withdrew the order, whereupon the Attorney-General intervened and appealed to the Court of Appeal of Lwów.

Held: That the appeal must be dismissed, because section 33 of the Civil Code required only "formal reciprocity," *i.e.* treatment on a parity with nationals, and not "substantial "reciprocity," *i.e.* the right of Polish nationals to enjoy in Russia such rights as were demanded for Russian nationals in Poland; if therefore Soviet nationals may not inherit in Russia real estate and the same rule be applied there to Polish citizens, the requirement of reciprocity under section 33 is satisfied.

On appeal to the Supreme Court, the latter

Held, setting aside the decrees of the Courts below:

(1) That the heirs and legatees must be directed to prove (*a*) the nationality of the deceased at the date of the will and at that of his death; (*b*) the nationality of the applicants at the date of the death of the testator; (*c*) in the event of the nationality of the applicants at that date being Russian, that at the same date they had had the legal capacity of inheriting real property in Russia, and (*d*) that at the same date it was by law guaranteed in Russia that in the matter of inheriting real estate Polish citizens had the same rights as Russian nationals;

(2) That, owing to the great changes which have occurred in Russia since the war, it was the duty of the Courts below to establish whether the testator could dispose of his real property situate in Poland and whether his family could, on the principle of reciprocity, inherit that real estate;

(3) That, should the heirs have lost their Russian nationality, they would have to prove what other nationality they had acquired at the date of the death of testator, since section 33

of the Civil Code does not deal with aliens without nationality and does not grant them the same rights as natives. [Report: P.P.A., 1928, pp. 257-259.]

Treatment of Aliens—Discrimination in Taxation against Foreign Subjects—Jurisdiction of the Mixed Courts of Egypt. **Case No. 227**

EGYPTIAN GOVERNMENT *v.* NICOLAS ZINTZOS.

Egyptian Mixed Court of Appeal. 3 *May*, 1928.

THE FACTS.—A claim was brought before the Mixed Tribunal of Alexandria by the plaintiff, who was a foreign subject, against the Egyptian Government, claiming damages on account of an alleged illegal demand for land tax on his property in Egypt. The Mixed Court appointed an expert to examine the land and ascertain if the taxation in question was in conformity with the principle of the uniform application of the land tax to all the inhabitants of the country. The Tribunal, in view of the report of the expert, gave judgment against the Government for the recovery of an amount representing the excess over the limits of the taxation imposed on lands of the same quality belonging to native proprietors. The Egyptian Government appealed on the grounds (*a*) that the Tribunal had no jurisdiction, and (*b*) that the claim was not well founded as to merits.

Held: (*a*) The Egyptian Government is subject to the jurisdiction of the Mixed Courts with regard to any claim brought by a foreign subject in respect of any infringement of an acquired right recognised by treaty, law or covenant. The Turkish Law of 1867, which accorded to foreign subjects the right of holding immovable property in the Turkish Empire on the same terms as native subjects, constitutes an acquired right for a foreign subject, so that any derogation of the rule of equality of treatment may give rise to a claim before the Mixed Courts.

(*b*) The Turkish Law, however, which was approved by the Powers, reserved to the Government the right of freely regulating the land tax with regard to foreigners as well as native subjects; and with regard to the rate of the tax, and also the method of assessment or collection of the tax, all the laws or regulations of the Egyptian Government are binding on foreign

Case No. 227 *contd.*

subjects. Hence a provision giving the administration exclusive authority to decide any dispute arising is valid. While foreign subjects, therefore, can have recourse to the courts to establish an inequality between them and native taxpayers, and may establish that inequality whether in the application of the laws and regulations, or in the failure to collect the rate of tax which has been fixed, or in the failure to grant to a foreign subject any right with regard to the provisional assessment which is accorded to native subjects, the Mixed Courts are not entitled to appoint an expert to enquire into an inequality when the explanations given by the Government sufficiently establish that the Government has acted in a manner which excluded all idea of discrimination between native and foreign taxpayers. Accordingly the appeal was dismissed on ground (*b*). [Report: *Gazette des Tribunaux Mixtes d'Egypte*, 18th year, p. 177.]

Case No. 228

Non-Discrimination in Regard to Taxes—Article 211 (*c*) of the Treaty of Trianon—Equality of Taxation—Restriction to Matters of an Economic Character.

IN RE SILVIA G.

Administrative Court of Hungary. (*No.* 18510/1927. *P.*)

THE FACTS.—The plaintiff, who is an Italian subject, contends that a contract of adoption made by her is liable to a stamp duty according to a rate provided for Hungarian subjects and not according to the higher rate obtaining in regard to aliens. According to Article 211 (*c*) of the Peace Treaty of Trianon, Hungary undertook not to subject nationals of the Allied and Associated Powers to any charge, tax or impost other or higher than those which are or may be imposed on her own nationals or their property, rights and interests.

Held by the Administrative Court: That the action must be dismissed. "The application of the provisions of the "Treaty of Trianon according to which citizens of the Allied "and Associated Powers, their property, rights and interests "must not be subjected to taxation higher than that obtaining "in regard to Hungarian nationals has reference only to matters "of an economic nature but not to matters in the domain "of family law which may result in obtaining Hungarian "nationality." [Report: *Közigazgatási és Pénzügyi Jogi Döntvénytár*, XX, No. 108.]

NOTE.—According to Hungarian law the adoption of a foreigner by a Hungarian subject has the effect of facilitating his naturalisation.

Aliens—Rights of Foreign Corporations—The Methodist Church in Italy. **Case No. 229**

TURBA *v.* FERRERO AND METHODIST COMMUNITY.

Court of Appeal at Milan. 17 *January*, 1928.

Held on appeal: That the appellant's contention that the Methodist Church cannot appear as plaintiff must be rejected. The Methodist Church, an American religious organisation, is a body which as such can exercise civil rights, including the right to sue. In accordance with the principle of international law which grants to foreigners the personal status of Italian citizens, corporations legally recognised abroad are subject, within the Italian territory, to the same limitation of activity as are all corporations recognised by the Italian law. Likewise, they are put on the same footing as national corporations with regard to the exercise of rights provided that their purpose is not contrary to the law of the kingdom or to the public order and morals. The objects of the non-Roman Catholic communities—in this particular case of the Methodist Church—are not at all inconsistent with the ethical and juridical conceptions of the Italian State. [Report: *Rivista di diritto internazionale*, 1928, pp. 527-528.]

Treatment of Aliens by the Receiving State—Taxation of Insurance Premiums—" Due Process of Law."

See Case No. 95 (*Compañía General de Tabacos de Filipinas* v. *Collector of Internal Revenue*).

iv.—Plea of Non-Discrimination

[See Part V, STATE RESPONSIBILITY. See also Cases Nos. 226, 227, 230.]

Treatment of Aliens—Expropriation—Plea of Non-Discrimination—Roumanian Agrarian Reform.

See Case No. 59 (*Kulin, Emeric* v. *Roumanian State*), in particular the dissenting opinion of the Roumanian national judge, *Recueil*, VII, p. 159.

v.—Respect for Property. Expropriation

[See Part IV, JURISDICTION: *In General. Territorial* (Case No. 94), and also *Plea of Non-Discrimination*, above.]

Case No. 230 **Aliens—Treatment of—Respect of Property—Right to Valorisation—The Rule of International Law—Most-Favoured-Nation Clause.**

VALORISATION IN GERMANY CASE.

German Reichsgericht. 6 June, 1928.

THE FACTS.—The appellant, an Italian subject, was the assignee of a Swiss bank, which, in January, 1920, deposited with the defendant, a German bank, two million paper marks for a period of three months, renewable for further periods of three months. The deposit was renewed until August, 1923, when it became worthless. According to section 66 of the German Valorisation Law, these monies were not subject to valorisation. It was contended on behalf of the appellant that section 66 could not be applied to an alien as, according to international law, which by virtue of Article 4 of the Constitution formed part of German law, it was impossible to deny the benefits of valorisation to an alien.

It was also contended that that Article was contrary to the Germano-Italian Treaty of Commerce of 31 October, 1925, which provided that the subjects of the contracting parties shall, when in the territory of the other contracting party, have full liberty to acquire and own property to the extent to which such right is enjoyed by the subjects of any other State. This Article, it was argued, constituted a most-favoured-nation clause, and the appellant claimed the benefit of the Treaty of Commerce between the United States and Germany of 1925, which laid down that the subjects of the contracting parties shall enjoy the protection of the rules of international law, and that they shall not be deprived of their property without due process of law and adequate compensation.

Held: That the appeal must be rejected.

(*a*) *The Right to Valorisation.* There was no rule of international law which gave to aliens the right to demand the repayment of their loans in gold. Section 66 could not therefore be regarded as contrary to international law.

(*b*) *The Most-Favoured-Nation Clause.* The clause was not relevant in the present case. Section 66 could not be regarded as constituting expropriation. The plaintiff had renewed the deposit from time to time, and he had to bear the consequences of the ensuing depreciation. He could not complain if the law, in section 66, refused to him certain advantages which it conferred upon creditors in other cases. [Report: *N.Z.*, XL (1929), p. 277.]

Treatment of Aliens—Plea of Non-Discrimination—Application of So-called Valorisation to Aliens—Question of Reciprocity. **Case No. 231**

VALORISATION (HUNGARY) CASE.

Supreme Court of Hungary. 12 *May*, 1927.
(*No. P. VI*, 8347/1926.)

THE FACTS.—The plaintiffs bought from the defendant certain immovable property. The transaction was subsequently annulled, and the plaintiffs therefore asked for restitution of the gold equivalent of the purchase money. The defendant contends that the plaintiffs have no right to ask for the so-called valorisation of the sum involved as they have opted for Yugoslavia and are therefore to be regarded as aliens, in whose favour the law establishing valorisation does not apply. On appeal,

Held by the Supreme Court: for the plaintiffs. Valorisation of debts is to be admitted in favour of aliens if their own State admits valorisation in favour of Hungarian subjects. [Report: *Jogi Hirlap*, 1927, No. 932.]

Treatment of Aliens—Distinction between Expropriation and Unlawful Dispossession.

See Case No. 177 (*Case concerning the Factory at Chorzów*).

Position of Aliens—Protection of Property of—Military Requisitions.

See Case No. 335 (*Edgar A. Hatton Case*).

III.—Expulsion of Aliens

ii.—Procedure of Expulsion

[In substitution for Case No. 221 in *Annual Digest*, 1925-1926.]

Case No. 232 **Aliens—Deportation of Subjects of State whose Government is not Recognised—Non-Recognition of Russian Soviet Government by the United States.**

PETITION OF BROOKS.

United States District Court, D. Massachusetts. 28 *April*, 1925.

THE FACTS.—This was a petition for habeas corpus by a person held for deportation. Petitioner was a Russian. The immigration authorities admitted their inability to deport him to Russia while the Soviet Government had not been recognised, but suggested that the United States would shortly resume diplomatic relations and that petitioner should be kept imprisoned pending recognition.

Held: That the writ must be granted. Delivering the Opinion of the Court, Judge Anderson said: "The right to "arrest and hold or imprison an alien is nothing but a neces-"sary incident of the right to exclude or deport. There is no "power in this court or in any other tribunal in this country "to hold indefinitely any sane citizen or alien in imprisonment, "except as a punishment for crime. Slavery was abolished by "the Thirteenth Amendment. It is elementary that de-"portation or exclusion proceedings are not punishment for "crime." (5 F. (2nd) 238, 239.) [Report: 5 F. (2nd) 238.]

NOTE.—*Ex parte Kazan*, which by a slip appears as the title of Case No. 221 in *Annual Digest*, 1925-1926, is reported in 5 Federal Reporter (2nd) 243, and refers to the proposed deportation of aliens who had been admitted to the United States in error. The case does not call for a digest in this series of volumes.—[Ed.]

Aliens—Deportation—Whether Impossible as the Result of Absence of Diplomatic Relations.

See Case No. 38 (*Pestereff* v. *Reed*).

D. EXTRADITION

I.—Extradition in General

Extradition—From Canada to Saar Basin—Application by France under Extradition Treaty with Great Britain. **Case No. 233**

IN RE INCAMPE.

Supreme Court of Nova Scotia. 2 *April*, 1928.

THE FACTS.—Application was made on behalf of the French Government for the extradition of a prisoner to the territory of the Saar Basin in Germany on account of an offence committed there. The prisoner was arrested in Halifax. The status of the Saar Basin is described in the judgment.

Held by Carroll, J.: " Several objections have been taken " by counsel for Incampe against the application for committal, " and I shall deal with only one, namely, the right of the French " Republic to have a person extradited, when the offence " charged was committed in German territory and against the " German criminal law. The purpose of the Treaty between " France and Great Britain, of course, is to deliver up fugitive " offenders, who have committed offences in either of the " countries, to the other, and the offence must be an infraction " of the criminal law in the applying country."

" In this case the circumstances are novel. By para- " graph 16 of the Annex [1] to Section 4 (Part III) of the Treaty " of Versailles:

" ' The Government of the territory of the Saar Basin shall " ' be entrusted to a Commission representing the League of " ' Nations. The Commission shall sit in the territory of the " ' Saar Basin ' ; and by paragraph 21 of the same Annex:

" ' It will be the duty of the Governing Commission to " ' ensure, by such means and under such conditions as it may " ' deem suitable, the protection abroad of the interests of the " ' inhabitants of the territory of the Saar Basin.'

" I am strongly of the opinion that paragraph 21 does not " confer upon the Governing Commission any rights or privi- " leges regarding the extradition from Great Britain or Canada " of fugitive offenders from the Saar region. The right of " extradition is founded on solemn treaty between nations

[1] Following Article 50 of the Treaty.

Case No. 233 *contd.*

"wherein are clearly set out the rights and duties of the contracting nations, and I can find nothing in the language of "paragraph 21 conferring such right on the Governing Commission of the Saar District. . . ."

Further, the applicants submitted copies of certain documents, including a decree purporting to have been passed by the Governing Commission, in which the protection abroad of the interests of inhabitants of the Saar District is entrusted to the French Republic. The Court held that even if this decree were operative for the present case, a copy of it is not receivable in evidence, but it must be proved as a fact.

Application dismissed. [Report: *Canadian Criminal Cases* (1927-1928), XLIX, p. 386.]

Extradition—Extradition Treaties in respect of Mandated Territories.

See Case No. 27 (*Extradition of Criminals to and from Mandated Territories*).

II.—Extraditable Crimes

Case No. 234

Extradition—Extraditable Crimes—Acts Declared to be Crimes after the Conclusion of the Extradition Treaty.

UNITED STATES *v.* HECHT.

United States Circuit Court of Appeals, Second Circuit.
10 *January*, 1927.

THE FACTS.—This was a petition for habeas corpus. The accused was a citizen of the United States, resident and engaged in business in Scotland. He filed a voluntary petition in bankruptcy in Scotland in 1924, and a little later went to the United States. He was indicted in Scotland for "making false entries in his ledger and "cashbook" in contemplation of bankruptcy. There was no statute in force in the United States at the time making such an act criminal. But an amendment of the United States Bankruptcy Act, which took effect in 1926, made such an act a crime. After this amendment took effect, proceedings were begun to procure his extradition from the United States to Scotland. The Treaty of 1842, Article 10, required surrender only "upon such evidence of criminality as, according to the

" laws of the place where the fugitive or person so " charged shall be found, would justify his apprehension " and commitment for trial, if the crime or offence had " there been committed." (8 U.S. Stat. L. 572, 576.) The Treaty of 1905 added to the list of extraditable crimes " offences, if made criminal by the laws of both " countries, against bankruptcy law." (34 U.S. Stat. L. 2903.) The writ was denied. On appeal,

Held : That judgment denying the writ should be affirmed, so that the extradition should proceed. Extradition treaties, unless stipulating to the contrary, cover offences committed prior to their conclusion. *In re De Giacomo*, 12 Blatchf. 391. " If asylum is thus destroyed by the making of a treaty, *a for-* " *tiori* is it taken away when one of the high contracting " parties somewhat belatedly recognizes as criminal a well- " known act of commercial immorality." (16 F. (2nd) 955, 957.) [Report : 16 F. (2nd) 955.]

Extradition—Identity of Crime under Laws of Requesting and Extraditing State.

See Case No. 240 (*Noblot Case*).

V.—Procedure of Extradition

Extradition—Handing over of Objects found with the Extradited Person—Their Connection with the Crime—Superiority of the Demand of the Requesting State over Attachment by Individual Creditors—Extradition for Crimes having Effect outside the Territory of the Requesting State. **Case No. 235**

B. AND M. FELLER AND E. SCHWARZ CASE.

Swiss Federal Court. 5 *November*, 1927.

THE FACTS.—The Italian Government claims the extradition of the brothers Bruno and Marco Feller, and of Ernesto Schwarz, who were arrested in Zurich on the ground of suspicious conduct and of being in wrongful possession of certain sums of money. The accused were the directors of a certain cloth exporting firm in Italy, the S.A.C.T.A., which was in a state of liquidation. They had obtained large deliveries of stock from other firms by means of producing false documents, and, after squandering the assets of the S.A.C.T.A., they

Case No. 235 ***contd.***

fled abroad. At the time of their arrest, the accused had in their possession large sums in English pounds, American dollars, gold marks, lire, and Swiss francs. These sums were seized, and the seizure was held good, although the money had been attached by the Swiss and German creditors of the S.A.C.T.A. The accused protested against the Italian demand for their extradition, and the Swiss creditors lodged a protest before the Federal Department of Justice and Police against any transfer of the money to Italy.

Held : The Federal Court grants the extradition of Benno Feller, as also of Ernesto Schwarz. In the last case, however, the grant of extradition is to be confined to the charges brought against him on account of his fraudulent bankruptcy. The extradition of Marco Feller is denied. There will be no delivery of the money found on Marco Feller and Ernesto Schwarz, but the money found on Benno Feller will be handed over to Italy.

In spite of the somewhat general provisions of Article 11 of the Italian-Swiss Extradition Treaty, objects found in the possession of the extraditable individual are not universally subject to delivery to the claimant State, but only those of them which have an immediate, or at least an indirect, connection with the offence in question. The sums of money found on Marco Feller are not subject to delivery, since the holder himself is exempt from extradition. There is no reason to connect this money with the trading capital of the S.A.C.T.A.

It may be pointed out in considering the fate of the money found on Benno Feller, which is the subject of a third-party claim, that, according to the practice of the Federal Court, such third-party claims are admissible in evidence when they emanate from persons having a legitimate interest in the denial of delivery. The circumstance that the money found on Benno Feller had been attached by various creditors of the S.A.C.T.A. would not prevent delivery being decreed, since attachment for private law purposes must yield before public law. Nor is the judgment of the Federal Court affected by the fact that the attaching creditors are Swiss firms. The only material question is this : Do the objects in question bear an immediate, or at least a remote, connection with the offence for which extradition is claimed ? The fact that this money is derived from payments made to the cashier of the S.A.C.T.A. by German purchasers residing in Germany and not in Italy, would not in itself justify a refusal of delivery sought by the latter State. The Italian courts may call Benno Feller to account for all his fraudulent business dealings, even for those whose effects extended from Italian soil into this country. The money found upon him has an evident connection with his fraud and fraudulent bankruptcy in the winding-up of the Italian business. The Swiss creditors suffer no injustice through the delivery of this money to Italy. The Treaty of Commerce and Settlement between Italy and Switzerland of 1868 ensures that the claims of Swiss nationals will be treated in Italy on an equal footing with those of her own citizens. [Report: *Entscheidungen des schweizerischen Bundesgerichts*, vol. 53, I, 320.]

Extradition—Procedure of Extradition—Surrender without Formal Extradition—The So-Called Principle of Speciality —Extension of the Extradition to Crimes other than those for which Extradition had been granted. **Case No. 236**

IN RE KÁROLY R.

Royal Hungarian Criminal Court at Budapest and Hungarian Ministry of Justice. 26 January, 1928.

THE FACTS.—The Criminal Court at Budapest issued a warrant of arrest of the accused on the ground of embezzlement. The accused left for Egypt, and the Ministry of Justice lodged a request for extradition with the Egyptian Government. Before the formal extradition proceedings had begun, the Egyptian police, acting at the request of the Hungarian consul, brought the accused from Alexandria to Trieste. Italy permitted the transport of the accused on the ground of an Extradition Convention concluded in 1869. Subsequently the Public Prosecutor asked that the application for extradition be extended so as to cover the crime of fraud. There was no extradition treaty between Hungary and Egypt.

The Criminal Court at Budapest thereupon asked the Hungarian Minister of Justice to issue a new request for extradition from Egypt and Italy.

Held by the Hungarian Minister of Justice: that the request cannot be granted.

(1) " There is no rule of public international law according " to which courts of a State have no right to conduct criminal " proceedings against an accused who returned from abroad

Case No. 236 *contd.*

"by any means other than extradition. The fact that the "accused had been brought home otherwise than in the course "of regular extradition proceedings can have no influence on "the prosecution of the crime."

(2) "It is true that Article 3 of the Extradition Treaty con-"cluded with Italy contains the so-called Speciality Clause. "However, this clause has been interpreted in practice to the "effect that it is not necessary to request the foreign State to "agree to a subsequent extension of the extradition, but that "it is sufficient to notify the foreign State to the effect that an "extension of the scope of the prosecution is taking place." [Reports: Criminal Court at Budapest, No. B. XXX, 2138/1925. Ministry of Justice, No. 3900/1928, I.M. VII.]

Case No. 237

Extradition—Documents Accompanying Demand for Extradition—Authentic Character of.

LEONARDO COSTANZO ET ALIA CASE.

National Supreme Court of Justice, Argentina. 1927.

THE FACTS.—This was a demand for extradition by the Italian Government through its diplomatic agent at Buenos Aires.

Held: That the fixed jurisprudence of this Court has settled that when the documents comprising a demand for extradition through diplomatic channels are presented through the medium of the Minister for Foreign Affairs and transmitted by the latter to the proper tribunal, the tribunal must regard them as authentic without further requirements, because they are under the protection of the faith doubly imposed upon them by the foreign Government soliciting the extradition and the Minister for Foreign Affairs transmitting it. [Reports: 150 Fallos, p. 80 (also in 26 Jurisprudencia Argentina, p. 865).]

NOTE.—This case restates the doctrine of the same Court in its following previous decisions:

Andres Zonco (1890), 10 Fallos, 3*a* series, 213;
Moises Ferris (1907), 108 Fallos, 151;
Juan Nappi (1919), 130 Fallos, 377.

Extradition—Nature of Extradition Proceedings—Waiver by the Person Surrendered. **Case No. 238**

DOMINGO SOAPA CASE.

National Supreme Court of Justice, Argentina. *March*, 1928.

Upon a petition for extradition,

Held: "That extradition not being, in reality, a cause in "which the culpability of the person is enquired into, but "merely a judicial proceeding to establish his identity and "compliance with the requirements of the law and of the "respective treaties, the affected party could validly waive, "for his personal advantage, as he has done, the requirements "of that proceeding, as such waiver does not affect the public "order nor infringe upon the rights of third parties." [Report: 150 Fallos, 316.]

NOTE.—See also the case *R.* v. *Corrigan*, L.R. [1931] 1 K.B. 527.

Extradition—Miscellaneous—Transport of the Accused from the Territory of one State through that of Another.

See Case No. 236 (*In re Károly R.*).

VI.—Political Criminals

Extradition—Political Crime—Requirements of the Political Character of a Crime—Direct Connection between the Crime and the Desired Political Object—Murder of an Alleged Fascist Spy by an Italian in France—French Request for Extradition. **Case No. 239**

PAVAN CASE.

Swiss Federal Court. 15 *June*, 1928.

THE FACTS.—On the 14th of March, 1928, the Italian fascist Angelo Savorelli was shot and killed in Paris by Alviso Pavan, an anti-fascist journalist from Treviso. The culprit was arrested on March 20, 1928, at Birsfelden in the Canton of Basle. Pavan admitted that he was the person whom the police authorities of the Seine Department were seeking on account of the murder. He was finally induced to confess that he was actually guilty of the crime. On the ground that the

Case No. 239 ***contd.***

crime was a political one he objected to be extradited. He maintained that Savorelli's murder had taken place from political motives, and that it was only one among the numerous episodes of the civil war which Fascismo had kindled at home and abroad. The murder had been intended to prepare and hasten the end of Fascismo.

Held: There can be no doubt that the act which the accused is alleged to have committed is not a political crime, in the usual sense of the word. That is to say, it is not a direct attack on the State or on its fundamental political institutions (as, for example, an act of high treason, cf. the case of *Vogt*, R.O. 50, I, p. 257, and the case of *Camporini*, 50, I, p. 304).

Homicide involves always, primarily, an attempt on the life of an individual, and is, therefore, in itself a crime at common law. " But it may also be a political crime in a relative sense " if it is an act which, while presenting all the *indicia* of a " common law crime, nevertheless assumes a political character " through its motive, its object, or the circumstances in which it " is committed. (Article 10 of the Federal Law of 22 January, " 1892, governing extradition to States abroad; cf. Martitz, " *Internationale Rechtshilfe in Strafsachen*, p. 527; Schwar- " zenbach, *Das materielle Auslieferungsrecht der Schweiz*, p. " 174.) In accordance with the consistent precedents of the " Federal Court, a political act of this nature would result in " the refusal of the extradition. (R.O. 17, p. 455; 27, I, p. 64; " 32, I, pp. 539 and 541; 33, I, p. 186; 34, I, p. 568; 49, I, p. " 266; 50, I, pp. 256 and 304; Corbaz, *Le crime politique et la* " *jurisprudence du Tribunal fédéral en matière d'extradition*, " p. 140 *et seq.*")

It is unnecessary to determine whether Pavan killed Savorelli for political reasons and with a political object in view, *i.e.* the reversal of the present political system in Italy and the substitution of some other system preferred by the accused (cf. R.O. 34, I, p. 570; 50, I, p. 258; Lammasch, *Auslieferungsrecht und Asylpflicht*, p. 294). For even if these subjective conditions were fulfilled, the objection to the competence of the Court to order extradition would not prevail in the absence of other objective conditions necessary to impress a common law crime with a political colour.

" According to precedents in the Federal Court, the crime " is invested with a predominantly political character only " where the criminal action is immediately connected with its "political object (R.O. 33, I, pp. 194 and 406; 34, I, pp. 571 and "577; 49, I, p. 275; 50, I, p. 504; von Bar, *Gerichtssaal*, 1882, "p. 500). Such a connection can only be predicated where "the act is in itself an effective means of attaining this object "(R.O. 32, I, p. 542), or where at least it forms an integral part "of acts leading to the end desired (R.O. 49, I, p. 275; Corbaz, "*op. cit.*, p. 156), or where it is an incident in a general political "struggle in which similar means are used by each side. (R.O. "33, I, p. 194, and the cases of *Ragni* and *Camporini*, R.O. 49, I, "p. 266 on, and 50, I, p. 303.)" In the present case such a direct connection is lacking. The relation between the murder of Savorelli and the reversal of political system in Italy is a distant one; nor can the death of the murdered spy or fascist *agent-provocateur*, if he really was such, be considered an appropriate means of attaining this end. Nor is this an incident in a wider anti-fascist campaign conducted in Italy, but rather a single act of personal terrorism, performed in a foreign country and directed only towards its immediate result (R.O. 27, I, pp. 68 and 87). Pavan's intention, as he admitted in his statement of April 12, 1928, was to disorganise the fascist spy system in Belgium and France, by removing the chief of this system.

According to precedent, also, if the political character of the crime is to carry weight, the damages involved must not be out of proportion to the desired result, so that "although the viola- "tion of private rights is, strictly speaking, illegal, it need not "be considered inexcusable" (R.O. 50, I, p. 259; 34, I, p. 572/3). Homicide—assassination and murder—is one of the most heinous crimes. It can only be justified where no other method exists of protecting the final rights of humanity. (See Message of the Federal Council dated June 9, 1890, in *Feuille officielle fédérale*, 1890, vol. III, p. 215 on; Walker, *Über politische Verbrechen und das Asylrecht*, in *Zeitschrift für öffentliches Recht*, vol. IV, p. 343 on; R.O. 27, I, pp. 67/86; 34, I, pp. 548 and 573.) But Pavan's action cannot be construed as the sole remaining means of protecting Italian political refugees and their families from the fascist spy service. In the present case, moreover, since the extradition is sought, not by Italy, where the anti-fascist views of Pavan would be weighed against him, but by France, where the courts afford a guarantee of impartiality and will be able to balance the disinterestedness of the political motives which, Pavan asserts, lead to the crime, this application should not be refused. [Report: *Entscheidungen des schweizerischen Bundesgerichts*, vol. 54, I, 207.]

Case No. 240

Extradition—Political Crime—Forgery of Documents with Political Object in View.

NOBLOT CASE.

Swiss Federal Court. 23 *November*, 1928.

THE FACTS.—Georges Noblot, a French national, was arrested in Ragaz (Canton of St. Gallen, Switzerland), at the request of the German authorities. Noblot had forged in Düsseldorf a private document (a bill of lading) for the carriage of 1172 tons of sugar from Hamburg to Le Havre, by adding "eleven" at the beginning of the words "thousand, hundred and "seventy-two" and by adding a figure nought at the end of the figures 1172. He made use of this forged document before the State Commissariat for Reparations Deliveries, with the intent to secure pecuniary profit to himself or to a third person by substituting in favour of France a cash transfer for a transfer in kind. Upon a request for Noblot's extradition being made by Germany, he disputed the validity of an extradition order on the ground that he had not forged the bill of lading from any motives of pecuniary profit, but, as he alleged, solely from political motives, in a desire to damage the working of the Dawes Plan. Article I, paragraph 17, of the Extradition Treaty between Switzerland and Germany specifies as extraditable offences the forgery of documents, and the use of such documents in the knowledge that they are forged, "with intent to deceive or defraud." The offence here in question is made criminal both by Articles 267 and 268 of the German Penal Code, and by Article 72 of the Penal Code of the Canton of St. Gallen. The prosecution proposed to permit the extradition of Noblot with the reservation that he should be prosecuted only for an offence against Article 267 of the German Penal Code. This Article is concerned with the simple forgery of a document.

Held: (*a*) That the request for extradition must be granted. The principle that extradition is granted only where the act in question is criminal both in the extraditing State and in the State which makes the request, does not mean that in the municipal law of each country precisely the same elements must be held to constitute the offence, for in many important cases such an interpretation of the so-called identity norm would render extradition illusory. Thus extradition should be granted where the act in question amounts only to a special offence [1] in the State seeking the extradition, while in the extraditing State it falls within a general criminal category. In the present case, the forging of a document with intent to defraud another, or to benefit oneself, is treated in the Canton of St. Gallen as a case of simple forgery ; in Germany, on the other hand, this intent places the offence within a special category. For this reason extradition must be granted unconditionally.

(*b*) The question whether the crime of Noblot should be treated as political in character must be answered by reference to the events in connection with which it had been committed. Even if an affirmative answer were given to this question, this could only mean that Noblot's action does not constitute a political offence in the absolute sense of this term, but rather in the relative sense, namely, that it presents all the elements of a crime in municipal law but is invested with the character of a political offence from certain additional reasons, such as its motive and the circumstances of its commission. However, in accordance with the former decision of the Federal Court on this matter, in order to recognise the political character of a crime of this description, it is necessary that the act in question should have been directed against the political régime of the State, either as an effort to secure power in the State, or as an isolated incident in such a struggle. The forgery would have in fact done an injury to the German economic system, since, on the one hand, the increased transfer of cash would have threatened the German rate of exchange, while, on the other, the change in the sum of payments in kind due on Reparations account would have involved a corresponding loss of goods to the German economic system. But Noblot has completely failed to show how such an economic injury to Germany could be expected to have as its natural result a change in the German political system, or how far such a change could be construed as the object of his actions.

Moreover, one would have to infer from the political motives which Noblot has invoked that the forgery was carried out at least with the tacit assent of the competent political organs in France. But he can point to no positive fact supporting such an assumption, which in addition is rebutted by the punishment of Noblot and his associate by a French court on account of this very forgery. [Report : *Entscheidungen des schweizerischen Bundesgerichts*, vol. 54, I, 338.]

[1] By which is meant an offence involving some particular intent or other additional element.

E. MINORITIES (PROTECTION OF MINORITIES)

I.—Minority Treaties and their Interpretation

Case No. 241
PERMANENT COURT OF INTERNATIONAL JUSTICE.
JUDGMENT No. 12.

Protection of Minorities—Minority Schools—Language of Instruction—Declaration by Parents—Right to Choose the School and the Language of Instruction—Minority Schools in Polish Upper Silesia.

GERMANY *v.* POLAND

RIGHTS OF MINORITIES IN UPPER SILESIA CASE.
(Minority Schools.)

26 *April*, 1928.

THE FACTS.—Article 72, par. 3, of the Geneva Convention of 15 May, 1922, between Poland and Germany provided as follows:

> "Poland further agrees that any difference of opinion as to questions of law or "fact arising out of these articles between "the Polish Government and any one of the "Principal Allied and Associated Powers or "any other Power, a Member of the Council "of the League of Nations, shall be held to "be a dispute of an international character "under Article 14 of the Covenant of the "League of Nations. The Polish Government hereby consents that any such "dispute shall, if the other Party thereto "demands, be referred to the Permanent "Court of International Justice. The decision of the Permanent Court shall be "final and shall have the same force and "effect as an award under Article 13 of the "Covenant."

Relying on that paragraph, Germany brought an action against Poland asking the Court to declare, *inter alia*, that, contrary to the attitude adopted by Poland, Articles 74, 106 and 131 of the Geneva Convention establish the unfettered liberty of any person to declare, according to his own conscience and on his own personal responsibility, that he does or does not belong to a racial, linguistic or religious minority, subject to no verification, dispute, pressure or hindrance in any form whatsoever on the part of the authorities, and that the above-mentioned Articles also establish the unfettered liberty of any person to choose the language of instruction and the corresponding school for the pupil or child for whose education he is responsible—likewise subject to no verification, dispute, pressure or hindrance in any form whatsoever on the part of the authorities.

In the Counter-case the Polish Government asked the Court either to dismiss the action or, alternatively, to declare, *inter alia*, that the Articles in question conferred upon the person responsible for the child the liberty to declare, in accordance with his conscience and on his personal responsibility, what is the language of the pupil or child ; but Poland did not admit that these Articles conferred upon him the unfettered liberty to choose the language of instruction and the corresponding school for the pupil or child for whose education he is legally responsible. Poland also refused to accept in its entirety the German contention regarding the exercise of these rights free from any " verification, dispute, pressure or " hindrance in any form whatsoever on the " part of the authorities." Article 74 of the Convention provided as follows :

> " The question whether a person does or " does not belong to a racial, linguistic or " religious minority may not be verified or " disputed by the authorities."

Article 106 provided as follows :

> " § 1.
>
> " 1. A minority school shall be established

Case No. 241 ***contd.***

"on the application of a national, supported "by the persons legally responsible for the "education of at least forty children belong- "ing to a linguistic minority, provided that "these children are nationals of the State, "that they belong to the same school dis- "trict (*Schulverband—związek szkolny*), that "they are of the age at which education is "compulsory, and that the intention is that "they should attend the said schools.

"2. If at least forty such children belong "to the same denomination or religion, a "minority school of the denominational or "religious character desired shall be estab- "lished on application.

"3. Should the establishment of a "minority school be inexpedient for special "reasons, minority classes shall be formed."

Article 131 provided as follows:

"1. In order to determine the language "of a pupil or child, account shall be taken "of the verbal or written statement of the "person legally responsible for the education "of the pupil or child. This statement may "not be verified or disputed by the educa- "tional authorities.

"2. Similarly, the educational author- "ities must abstain from exercising any "pressure, however slight, with a view to "obtaining the withdrawal of requests for "the establishment of minority educational "institutions."

Held: "That Articles 74, 106 and 131 of the German- "Polish Convention of 15 May, 1922, concerning Upper "Silesia, bestow upon every national the right freely to "declare according to his conscience and on his personal "responsibility that he does or does not belong to a "racial, linguistic or religious minority, and to declare "what is the language of a pupil or child for whose "education he is legally responsible;

" That these declarations must set out what their " author regards as the true position in regard to the " point in question, and that the right freely to declare " what is the language of a pupil or child, though com- " prising, when necessary, the exercise of some dis- " cretion in the appreciation of circumstances, does not " constitute an unrestricted right to choose the language " in which instruction is to be imparted or the corre- " sponding school ;

" That, nevertheless, the declaration contemplated " by Article 131 of the Convention, and also the ques- " tion whether a person does or does not belong to a " racial, linguistic or religious minority, are subject to " no verification, dispute, pressure or hindrance what- " ever on the part of the authorities " (at p. 46). [Report : Series A, No. 15, *passim*.[1]]

NOTE.—The above judgment, although not illustrating—apart from the question of jurisdiction (see Case No. 343)—any general problem of international law or of the protection of minorities, has nevertheless been digested as throwing light on a particular, and not unimportant, aspect of the law of minorities. However, it has not been thought necessary to trace in detail the reasons given by the Court for its judgment. Four dissenting Opinions were delivered.

V.—Treatment of Minorities Apart from Treaty

Minorities Apart from Treaty—Citizens of United States of America of Chinese Race—Separate Schools for Children of White and Coloured Races Respectively. **Case No. 242**

GONG LUM *v.* RICE.

United States Supreme Court. 21 *November*, 1927.

THE FACTS.—This was a petition for mandamus in behalf of Martha Lum, a child born of Chinese parents in the United States,[2] to compel high school trustees and the

[1] See also Series E, No. 4, pp. 191-199.

[2] Martha Lum was also an American citizen : see *United States* v. *Wong Kim Ark*, (1898) 169 U.S. 649 ; Dickinson, *Cases*, p. 190. She was probably also a Chinese subject by Chinese law. The United States Constitution guarantees equal protection to aliens as well as citizens : see *Truax and Another* v. *Raich*, (1915) 239 U.S. 33 : Dickinson, p. 850, and cases there cited. See also Case No. 224, *Bond* v. *Tij Fung*.

Gong Lum v. *Rice* does not turn upon any question of international law and is difficult to classify. It has been included by reason of the important part which the question of schools is playing in the matter of Minorities. It will be noticed that here the minority is claiming, not a separate school, but access to the ordinary school.—[Ed.]

Case No. 242 *contd.*

State Superintendent of Education to admit her to a public school in Mississippi assigned exclusively to white children. The Mississippi Constitution required that separate schools be maintained for children of the white and coloured races. There was no school in the district for children of the Chinese race, but it appeared that there were schools available for coloured children generally. The defendants demurred. The trial court overruled the demurrer. The State Supreme Court reversed the trial court. On writ of error,

Held: That the judgment of the State Supreme Court should be affirmed. A child born of Chinese parents in the United States is afforded equal protection of the laws if given the opportunity for a common school education in a school which receives only coloured children of the brown, yellow or black races. [Report: 275 U.S. 78.]

Minorities—Miscellaneous—Separate Schools for White and Coloured Races.

See Case No. 242 (*Gong Lum* v. *Rice*) and Case No. 224 (*Bond* v. *Tij Fung*).

PART VII

DIPLOMATIC AND CONSULAR INTERCOURSE AND PRIVILEGES

A. PERMANENT DIPLOMATIC ENVOYS

II.—Position and Functions of Diplomatic Envoys

Diplomatic Envoys—Position of—Special Protection Granted to—Loss of Privileged Position as the Result of Acts of the Envoy—Plea of Self-Defence. **Case No. 243**

THE STATE *v.* ACUNA ARAYA.

Court of Cassation, Costa Rica. 1927.

THE FACTS.—Acuna Araya, a native of Costa Rica, was indicted and tried for violating the diplomatic immunities of the Peruvian Chargé d'Affaires *ad interim*,[1] Horacio S. Garcia Albitres. The violation consisted in having assaulted the Chargé d'Affaires on the public street, and calling him " miserable, coward, and a " discredit to your country." It appeared, however, that the Chargé d'Affaires had a moment previously called the defendant a " miserable character and a " drunkard," and made a gesture as though to strike the defendant with his umbrella. The defendant pleaded self-defence.

Held by the Court of First Instance (at p. 672) :

" (i) That Article 450 of the Penal Code punishes with the " penalty of imprisonment in the first degree any one ' violat- " ' ing the immunities of the diplomatic representative of a " ' Power,' when the act does not, in its consequences, con- " stitute an offence punished more severely.

" (ii) That among the immunities which international law " recognises in favour of diplomatic agents is that of the in- " violability of the person of the Minister, which is a prero- " gative in virtue of which the person clothed with that privi- " lege is safeguarded against every outrage, aggression or " persecution.

[1] Perhaps better called, when *ad interim*, Chargé des Affaires: *see* Oppenheim (4th ed., 1928), vol. I, § 368.

Case No. 243 ***contd.***

" (iii) That, from what has been stated, any act of violence " committed by an individual against the person of a foreign " diplomatic agent has always been regarded as an offence " against the State. It should be understood likewise that the " act which has occasioned the proceeding under consideration " comes in a way within the sanction provided by the legal " text cited.

" (iv) That it is fitting, nevertheless, to enquire in " advance whether the aggression which gives rise to this " proceeding involves—in view of the special circumstances " under which it was committed—the violation of the personal " immunity which the victim enjoys in his character of Chargé " d'Affaires *ad interim* of Peru.

" (v) That it is a principle of public international law that " offences by word or deed perpetrated to the injury of a " diplomatic agent do not constitute an attempt against in- " violability if the agent offended ' through conduct indiscreet, " ' blameworthy or incompatible with his public character ' " has exposed himself to the insult or to the offence. (Bello, " *Derecho Internacional*, pte. 3ª, cap. I. Calvo, *Le Droit Inter-* " *national*, t. III, sec. 1492. Pradier-Fodéré, *Droit Inter-* " *national Public*, t. III, p. 1393. Rivier, *Principes du Droit* " *des Gens*, t. I, p. 479. Moore, *Digest of International Law*, " § 657. Fiore, *Droit International Public*, t. II, sec. 1132.)

" (vi) That to decide the questions of fact submitted to " judicial enquiry, the probative elements appearing in the " proceeding must be weighed in strict subjection to the pro- " cedural rules in force in the Republic (Articles 42 and 47 of " the Political Constitution, and 180, 181 and 421 of the Code " of Penal Procedure). The sworn declaration of the honour- " able Chargé d'Affaires, in itself—notwithstanding the cré- " dence reposed upon it by the undersigned—does not con- " stitute true and irrefutable proof, since the laws of the country " do not accord it that privileged character. In a matter so " delicate as the determination of the criminal guilt of a person, " the local law governs in its entirety. In the United States " of America it has been so recognised and maintained on " repeated occasions by the Secretary of State and the courts " of that Republic. (See Moore, *op cit.*, p. 657: case of Baron " von Gerolt, Minister of Prussia; of Mr. Mantilla, Minister " of Spain; and of Mr. Preston, Minister of Haiti.)

" (vii) . . . Under these conditions, the acts of violence " committed subsequently and immediately thereafter by the " accused against the person of the Chargé d'Affaires, being

" the logical and natural consequence of the situation brought " about by the offended person himself, cannot be considered— " in the judgment of the undersigned judge—as a violation of " the diplomatic immunity, since the attitude freely and " knowingly assumed by Mr. Garcia justified the reaction of " the accused Acuna." [Report: *Sentencias de la Corte de Casacion* (1927, Primer Semestre), p. 670.]

Diplomatic Intercourse — Protection of Foreign Interests Abroad — Protection of Interests of Austria-Hungary in Russia by Denmark.

See Case No. 186 (*Danish Foreign Office* v. *Emig*).

III.—Privileges and Immunities of

i.—Diplomatic Envoys and their Staff

Permanent Envoys—Immunities—Waiver of Immunities—Consent of the Accrediting State in respect of Wife, Family and Domestic Servants. **Case No. 244**

HERMAN *v.* APETZ.

Supreme Court of New York, New York County.
15 *October*, 1927.

THE FACTS.—This was an action to set aside a conveyance of real property on the ground of fraud on creditors. One defendant, after entering a general appearance and pleading to the merits, pleaded immunity from process as the wife of the Secretary of Legation of Costa Rica. Plaintiff moved to strike out the defence of immunity.

Held: That the motion to strike out should be granted. The defendant had waived her privilege by appearing and pleading to the merits. Delivering the opinion of the Court, Judge Frankenthaler said: " There is no doubt that an envoy " may not waive his diplomatic immunity without consent of " the sending state. Whether this inability to waive also " applies to his wife, family and domestic servants is a matter " of conflict among text-writers. The better view seems to be " that waiver on the part of such persons does not require the " consent of the home state and is, therefore, effective." (130 Misc. (N.Y.) 618, 619.) [Report: 130 Misc. (N.Y.) 618.]

Case No. 245 **Privileges and Immunities of Diplomatic Envoys—Members of the Diplomatic Staff of a Foreign Envoy—Status of a "Consular Secretary"—Manner in which Status is to be Proved to the Court—Conclusiveness of Statements Made by or on behalf of the Executive.**

ENGELKE (appellant) *v.* MUSMANN (respondent).

House of Lords on appeal from the English Court of Appeal. 18 *July*, 1928.

THE FACTS.—The defendant (appellant) was a member of the staff of the German Embassy in London under the style of "Consular Secretary," and his name appeared on the Diplomatic List issued by the British Foreign Office. In July, 1926, the plaintiff (respondent) issued a writ against the defendant in the King's Bench Division to recover rent alleged to be due under a lease dated 18 August, 1924. The defendant entered a conditional appearance and issued a summons asking that the writ should be set aside on the ground that he was a Consular Secretary on the staff of the German Embassy, and that his name appeared on the aforesaid Diplomatic List. The judge of first instance (Shearman, J.) made an order for the defendant to attend and be cross-examined on his affidavit so that the precise nature of the functions discharged by him might be ascertained, in order to enable the court to decide whether or not he was a person enjoying diplomatic immunity. On appeal to the Court of Appeal, the Attorney-General appeared at the request and on behalf of the British Foreign Office, and made a statement to the Court from which it appeared that the defendant's name had been submitted by the German Ambassador to the Foreign Office in the usual way; that he had been recognised without reservation as a member of the Embassy since December, 1920; that he performed "some service on the right side of the "line between consular service and ambassadorial "service," Germany having in 1919 amalgamated her diplomatic and consular services; and that in the view of His Majesty's Government the fact that a member of the diplomatic staff and performing diplomatic functions also performs some consular duties does not deprive him of the immunity which he possesses by reason of his diplomatic character.

The Court of Appeal by a majority (Scrutton and Sargant, L.JJ., Lord Hanworth, M.R., dissenting) declined to accept the Attorney-General's statement as to the result of the investigation of the facts by the Foreign Office as conclusive, and confirmed the order for the attendance of the defendant for cross-examination.

Held on appeal to the House of Lords (Lord Buckmaster, Viscount Dunedin, Lords Phillimore, Warrington of Clyffe, and Blanesburgh): That the Attorney-General's statement as to the defendant's diplomatic status was conclusive as to the fact of that status, and that the order for his attendance for the purpose of cross-examination must be discharged. The House arrived at this conclusion both as a matter of principle and upon a consideration of previous decisions which were passed under review.

These grounds of principle may be summarised as follows:

(*a*) Diplomatic status is created by the appointment of a person by a foreign State to a diplomatic post and his acceptance and recognition in that capacity by His Majesty's Government (at pp. 443, 445, 451 and 485);

(*b*) If a person possesses diplomatic immunity, it would not be consistent with such immunity to compel him to "litigate to establish his exemption" from the jurisdiction (at p. 449);

(*c*) The court must take judicial cognisance of a person's diplomatic status, and therefore is entitled to have recourse to the proper source of information (at p. 457);

(*d*) The proper source of information as to whether a person has or has not been appointed or received in a diplomatic capacity is a statement made by or on behalf of the Secretary of State for Foreign Affairs, the minister responsible for the reception of diplomatic persons (at pp. 443, 451, 457). [Reports: [1928] 1 K.B. 90; [1928] A.C. 433.]

NOTE.—For other illustrations of the practice of consulting the Executive upon matters affecting the prerogative and treating its reply as binding upon the courts, see *Mighell* v. *Sultan of Johore*, L.R. [1894] 1 Q.B. 149 (status of head of an independent foreign State); *Duff Development Co.* v. *Kelantan Government*, L.R. [1924] A.C. 797 (status of the Government of a foreign independent State); *Luther* v. *James Sagor & Co.*, L.R. [1921] 3 K.B. 532 (recognition of a new Government of an existing State); and *The Fagernes*, L.R. [1927] P. 311, *Annual Digest*, 1927-1928, Case No. 96; *In re Suarez*, L.R. [1918] 1 Ch. 176 (removal of a name from the Diplomatic List); *The Gagara*, L.R. [1919] P. 95. See also *B.Y.*, 1929, pp. 1 and 244.

Case No. 246

Diplomatic Immunities—Distinction between the Exercise of Official Functions and Acts Relating to Private Affairs—Privileges of the Subordinate Members of the Diplomatic Staff.

HARRIE LURIE *v.* STEINMANN.

Court of Rome. 26 *January*, 1927.

THE FACTS.—Harrie Lurie, engineer, claimed from Monsignor Steinmann, ecclesiastical counsellor to the German Embassy accredited to the Holy See, a commission for having purchased certain property on his behalf. Monsignor Steinmann pleaded to the jurisdiction of the Italian courts, and relied on Article 11 of the Law of Guarantee of 13 May, 1871, which provided for diplomatic immunities for the representatives of foreign States accredited to the Holy See. The claimant opposed the plea to the jurisdiction on the ground that Article 11 was meant to cover exclusively acts of the diplomatic agents executed in the exercise of their diplomatic functions, but not acts relating to their private affairs. He further maintained that the immunity protected only the head of the diplomatic mission, whereas Monsignor Steinmann was merely an ecclesiastical counsellor to the Embassy, and not an official representative of the German State.

Held: That the Court had no jurisdiction. It is quite obvious that when questions of privileges and immunity of diplomatic agents arise, as in the above-mentioned Law of Guarantee, such immunity can only refer to the persons of the diplomatic agents with regard to their private affairs. For one could hardly speak of immunity of diplomatic agents in cases where they act as the agents of their States. In such cases the immunity is the direct consequence of the right of autonomy and equality of the States which does not admit any jurisdiction of one State over another (*par in parem non habet imperium*). It is exactly in this way that the principle of immunity or extraterritoriality of the diplomatic agents had taken shape and grown up. This principle, which has been strengthened by the laws and customs of most civilised States, plainly implies the fact that diplomatic agents are to be considered outside the jurisdiction of the country in which they are officially recognised with regard also to their private affairs. Similarly, it is universally recognised by international customs that the immunity comprises the whole of the official staff of the Embassy or Legation. [Report: *Rivista di diritto internazionale*, 1928, pp. 528-530, with a note by Giacintho Bosco.]

NOTE.—By this judgment the Court of Rome reversed the rule formerly adopted by the Court of Cassation of Rome, which, in judgments of 20 April, 1915, and 31 January, 1922, had decided that the diplomatic agents are subject to the jurisdiction of the local courts, in accordance with the rules of the Italian common law, for acts done and obligations undertaken not as representatives of their own Governments, but as private persons. Moreover, in the first of these judgments the rule was laid down that only persons who are truly representatives of the sovereign Power and who fulfil diplomatic functions proper are entitled to the privilege of immunity, and not persons assisting them who can claim immunity only while they are exercising the functions of their chiefs. Anzilotti in the *Rivista di diritto internazionale* of 1915, pp. 215 ff., and of 1924, p. 173; and Cavaglieri in the *Foro Italiano*, 1922, p. 343, criticised these judgments. See also Case No. 247, *Perrucchetti* v. *Puig y Cassauro*.

Diplomatic Immunities—In respect of Private Law Contracts Concluded by Diplomatic Agents on behalf of their States —Foreign States in their Private and Public Capacity. **Case No. 247**

PERRUCCHETTI *v.* PUIG Y CASSAURO.

Court of Rome. 6 *June*, 1928.

THE FACTS.—Puig, acting as ambassador of Mexico and in the name of his Government, purchased from Perrucchetti certain property to be used as the Embassy building. A dispute then arose as to the interpretation and application of the contract, and, an action having been brought, Puig pleaded to the jurisdiction of the Court. He maintained that, as he was the representative of a foreign State, he could not be submitted to the jurisdiction of another State, and that the exercise of his diplomatic mission implied immunity from any local jurisdiction.

Held: That the Court had jurisdiction. Jurisdictional immunity, which was part of the privileges granted to the diplomatic representatives of sovereign States by other States in virtue of old international customs, aims principally at securing for diplomatic agents the fullest possible freedom in the exercise of their functions, and as such, it implies important

Case No. 247 *contd.* juridical consequences fully recognised by the Court. The Court, however, has to bear in mind the reasons for which the jurisdictional immunity had been created and kept alive. The privilege of jurisdictional immunity granted to the physical persons of a diplomatic mission cannot be extended to these agents beyond the sphere of their activity relating to the fulfilment of their main functions, *i.e.* for the exercise of their diplomatic functions. As a rule this privilege cannot be claimed by foreign States considered as foreign juridical corporations (*persone giuridiche*) in favour of the manifold and various activities which they may display in the territory of other States. Broadly speaking, the principle of immunity seems inadmissible with regard to economic and juridical relations quite unconnected with and foreign to political relations with foreign Governments. The care of political relations constitutes the real scope of a diplomatic mission.

It seems quite arbitrary to derive a claim of jurisdictional immunity in favour of foreign States for all their activities in foreign territories from the fact that, to a certain extent, there exists a privilege of immunity in favour of their ambassadors or ministers plenipotentiary. For if it is true that the foreign States having a mission abroad can avail themselves of the privilege of exemption from the local jurisdiction with regard to matters of international relations of public law, it is similarly true that a foreign State cannot claim immunity from jurisdiction in another State when juridical relations have been created in the territory of that State which are in no way connected with the above-mentioned international relations in the domain of public law. Neither can immunity be claimed on account of the fact that the legal relations in respect of which immunity is claimed have been entered into by a person who at that time was exercising functions of a diplomatic character. [Reports: *Foro Italiano*, 1929, I, pp. 112 ff., with a critical note by A. Cavaglieri; *Rivista di diritto internazionale*, 1928, pp. 521-527, with a critical note by G. Bosco.]

NOTE.—This case adopts the principle that the foreign State as a subject of private law relations, such as acquisition of property to be used as an Embassy, is subject to the jurisdiction of the Italian judicial authorities, and that the fact that the disputed contract had been concluded with a foreign State by means of its diplomatic representative in Italy, and that the foreign State had been summoned in the person of its representative, is irrelevant. Distinguish Case No. 246, *Harrie Lurie* v. *Steinmann*.

Diplomatic Privileges and Immunities—Immunity from Civil Jurisdiction—Imposition of a Fine on the Attorney of the Diplomatic Envoy—Extent of the Exemption of Diplomatic Persons from Taxation — Admissibility of Execution against the Property of the Envoy. **Case No. 248**

DIPLOMATIC ENVOYS. EXEMPTION FROM TAXATION (GERMANY) CASE.

German Reichsfinanzhof. 28 *May*, 1927.

THE FACTS.—The appellant, who acted as the attorney of a diplomatic envoy in Berlin, was served with a notice requesting him to make a declaration concerning the various classes of taxes to which his principal was liable. According to sections 84 and 89 of the Tax Decree it is the duty of the attorney to submit the tax declarations of his principal. The attorney is warned at the same time that a fine will be imposed should he fail to make the declaration. The attorney appealed against the decision of the tax authority by virtue of which he was served with the notice and threatened with a fine. His appeal was rejected.

Held, by the Reichsfinanzhof (Federal Tribunal in Revenue Matters): That the decision of the tax authorities must be set aside. The attorney's principal possessed the privileges of extraterritoriality. According to generally recognised rules of international law, which by virtue of Article 4 of the German Constitution formed part of German law, it was inadmissible to impose administrative penalties upon persons enjoying diplomatic privileges or to threaten them with such penalties. The attorney was right in maintaining that to threaten him, in his capacity of attorney of the envoy, with or to impose upon him these penalties would amount indirectly to constraining the envoy.

However, the Court pointed out that, should the attorney persist in his attitude, it was open to the tax authorities to fix the amount of the tax and to leave it to the attorney to appeal against the amount thus fixed; that the envoy's general immunity from taxation did not cover any income or property which might for special reasons be subject to taxation [1]; that in such cases the collection of the tax by way of execution was

[1] The judgment does not specify in which cases such limited taxation is admissible.

Case No. 248 *contd.* inadmissible only in so far as it interfered with the fulfilment of the normal functions of the envoy; and that, therefore, execution was inadmissible only against the person of the envoy and against such property as was necessary for the proper fulfilment of his diplomatic function, but not against other property. [Report: *Z. für a. ö. R. und V.*, I (2) (1929), p. 202.]

Case No. 249 **Diplomatic Agents—Counsellor and Chancellor of a Foreign Legation in Paris—Institution of Proceedings by a Diplomatic Agent in French Courts—Withdrawal of Proceedings—Cross-Suit—Absence of Definite Acceptance of the Competence of the French Courts by the Diplomatic Agent.**

DEMOISELLE B. *v.* D.

Civil Tribunal of the Seine. 20 *June*, 1927.

THE FACTS.—B. sued D. for the payment of 6425 francs for rent. She also asked for a declaration that a distress for rent levied by her was valid. D. pleaded his diplomatic immunity, and produced a letter from the French Minister of Foreign Affairs to the *Procureur-Général* of the Court of Appeal of Paris stating that since 1922 D. had been employed as chancellor in a foreign legation in Paris. Previously, however, D. had instituted proceedings against B. for the reduction of rent and had submitted to a cross-suit (under the law as to rented premises) brought by B. against him.

Held: That the action of B. must be dismissed. "Diplo-" matic agents enjoy an absolute immunity from jurisdiction in "civil and commercial matters; their voluntary submission "to the territorial jurisdiction of the country to which they "are accredited must be authorised by their government." Although D. had instituted certain proceedings of a kind specially provided for disputes as to rents, he had subsequently withdrawn his action. The case, so far as it concerned the question of cross-suit, had been the subject of an appeal to the Court of Cassation and had been referred back to the Tribunal of Versailles. B. had not pursued the matter further and those proceedings could therefore be considered as at an end. This was not so in the case of the action now brought by B. against her tenant. So far as this action was concerned, the courts "can only proceed when definite and formal acceptance of "their competence, duly authorised by the accrediting govern-

"ment, has been received from the diplomatic agent, an "assumption which, so far from being true, is formally con-"tradicted by the action taken by the diplomatic agent." [Report: 55 *Clunet* (1928), p. 637.]

NOTE.—See *Annual Digest*, 1925-1926, Case No. 242.

Diplomatic Envoys—Secretaries of Legation—Prosecution for Fraud. **Case No. 250**

PACEY *v.* BARROSO.

Court of Appeal of Santiago, Chile. 24 *September*, 1926.

THE FACTS.—One Barroso, the secretary of the Brazilian Embassy at Santiago, Chile, was prosecuted for fraud.

Held: "That, as a general rule, all persons residing within "the jurisdiction of a country, be they nationals or foreigners, "are subject to the laws enacted by it save the exceptions "recognised by international law, and, consequently, the courts "of each country are chargeable with taking notice of and "judging all acts brought under their jurisdiction by its Consti-"tution or its laws, and of lending the aid of the public authority "for the defence and vindication of all those rights created by "its laws which might be disregarded;

"That the exceptions recognised by international law and "accepted by all civilised countries are: (1) the person of a "Sovereign, when he comes upon the territory of a friendly "power; (2) diplomatic agents, comprising as such Ambas-"sadors, Diplomatic Ministers and Chargés d'Affaires, who re-"present the Sovereign or the Government of friendly nations; "(3) vessels of war sailing or lying in territorial waters; (4) the "armies or troops of other Powers visiting or passing through "the national territory;

"That the consular corps and the secretaries and employees "of embassies and legations are not comprised within the "exceptions recognised by the laws and the treaties of all "countries, and are therefore subject to all the obligations "established by the laws of the country wherein they reside "and render their services (Grotius, Bynkershoeck, Wheaton, "Vattel, Achmaz, *Droit de Gens*)." [Reports: 25 *Revista de Derecho, Jurisprudencia y Ciencias Sociales*, Part II, p. 49.]

NOTE.—This decision reflects a tendency in certain quarters of Latin America (case of *Phillippe Bonny* (1889), 9 *Semanario Judicial de la Federacion*, Mexico, 2ª Epoca, p. 225, "Considerando 3ro";

Case No. 250 *contd.*

1 Machado (1898), *Exposicion y Comentario del Codigo Civil Argentino,* p. 2), to restrict, so far as consistent with the discharge of the duties of diplomatic representation, the indiscriminate application of the fiction of extraterritoriality to every member of the diplomatic mission. The decision, although not of the court of last resort of Chile, but only of the Court of Appeal which, under section 15 of the Code of Criminal Procedure, acts as a court of first instance in criminal matters involving diplomatic ministers, stands as the first judicial approval, and hence as a precedent, of this new doctrine. The doctrine of this case is, however, at variance with the weight of judicial and textual opinion in Latin America. (See *Marquez'* case (1883), 21 *El Foro* (Mexico), 89, involving the servant of a legation; *Wamsen's* case (1907), 107 *Fallos* (Arg.), 395, involving a servant of the legation; *Cenzi's* case (1927), 66 *Gaceta del Foro* (Arg.), 349, involving a military attaché; 3 Antokoletz, *Tratado de Derecho Internacional Publico,* sec. 533, p. 278; 1 Borja, *Estudios sobre el Codigo Civil Chileno* (1901), paragraph 213, p. 251.)

iv.—The Official House of a Diplomatic Envoy.

Case No. 251

Legation Buildings—Immunities of—Whether Subject to Measures of Execution.

IMMUNITY OF LEGATION BUILDINGS (CZECHOSLOVAKIA) CASE.

Supreme Court of Justice of Czechoslovakia. 28 December, 1929. *No. RI* 979.[1]

THE FACTS.—In the course of the proceeding which followed the decision of the Supreme Court of Justice of 26 April, 1928 (see Case No. 111), the Court of First Instance, by a decision of 8 June, 1928 (not reported), admitted the execution. Subsequently, however, it was brought to the notice of the Court that the immovable property of the Hungarian State, against which property the execution had been applied for, was identical with the premises of the Legation of that State. The Court, being in doubt whether an execution would be admissible in that case, asked, in accordance with the provisions of paragraph 31, section 1, of the Law of 27 May, 1896, No. 79, concerning execution (as amended by the Law of 19 January, 1928, No. 23 [2]), for a declaration

[1] Although given in 1929, this decision is being reported in the present volume of the *Digest* as it is a continuation of Case No. 111 reported in the present volume.

[2] Paragraph 31, section 1, of the Law No. 79/1896—as amended by the Law No. 23/1928, which came into force on 1 May, 1928, *i.e.* after the decision of the Supreme Court of Justice of 26 April, 1928, No. RI 305 (Váž. 8000 civ.)—reads as follows (translation):

"Against a person who in the Czechoslovak Republic enjoys the "right of exterritoriality, and in exterritorial buildings and rooms, acts

of the Ministry of Justice. This Ministry, in agreement with the Ministry for Foreign Affairs, gave a decision on 22 April, 1929, No. 14.228 (not reported), to the effect that "execution by means of forced sale of premises of "a foreign Legation was according to international "law not admissible." Accordingly the Court of First Instance cancelled the execution, and referred to the provisions of paragraph 39, No. 5, of the Law No. 79/1896. The Court of Appeal confirmed the decision of the lower court, pointing out, however, that the execution had to be cancelled according to No. 2 of paragraph 39 of the Law No. 79/1896, and not according to No. 5.[1]

Held, on a second appeal (by the Supreme Court of Justice): That the opinion of the courts below was correct, and that the appeal must be dismissed. The appellant cannot adduce in his support the previous decision of the Court of 26 April, 1928, No. RI 305 (Váž. 8000 civ.), for in that decision the question which is at present at issue was not before the Court at all. In the documents submitted to the courts at the time there was no mention of the fact that the Hungarian Legation was situated in the building against which the execution had been applied for. This fact had not been indicated either in the application for execution or in the other documents submitted to the courts, nor was it known to the Court in any other way. The lower courts dismissed the application for execution on certain grounds, with which alone the decision of the Supreme Court of 26 April, 1928, dealt. That decision did not admit the execution; it reserved the decision on the merits to the lower courts, so that they were in a position to dismiss the application for execution upon any grounds except those which had been finally dealt with by the said decision of the Supreme Court.

"of execution may take place only in so far as international law permits. "In doubtful cases, the court has to apply for a declaration of the Minister "of Justice, who shall give it in agreement with the Minister for Foreign "Affairs; such a declaration shall be binding upon the courts. . . ."

[1] Paragraph 39 of the Law No. 79/1896 reads as follows (translation):

"Besides the cases mentioned in paragraphs 35, 36 and 37, the execu- "tion, with a simultaneous annulment of all acts of execution hitherto "carried out, is to be cancelled:

"1. . . . .

"2. if the execution is being conducted against objects, rights or "claims which in accordance with any existing provision of the law are "not subjected to execution; . . . . .

"3. . . . . 4. . . . .

"5. if the execution for other reasons has been declared inadmissible "by a final decision; . . . ."

Case No. 251 *contd.*

The question at issue is now whether the present dismissal of the application on the ground that the execution was directed against a Legation building was correct. The Court is of the opinion that it was. The Court of Appeal which—in opposition to the Court of First Instance which saw here a question arising out of paragraph 39, No. 5—was rightly of the opinion that the case was covered by paragraph 39, No. 2, which is intended for cases in which during the initial stage of the procedure of execution there was no clear reason known to the courts excluding the execution, and in which such reason appeared only in the subsequent stages of the proceedings—as happened in the present case. It is therefore not necessary to deal with the question whether the declaration of the Ministry of Justice of 22 April, 1929, No. 14.228, given in accordance with paragraph 31, section 1, of the Law No. 79/1896 (as amended), was a decision mentioned by paragraph 39, No. 5. It may merely be observed that, in accordance with paragraph 31, the court has to apply for such a declaration only in doubtful cases; in the present case, however, there was according to international law no such doubt. "According to international "law objects which directly or indirectly serve the purposes of "the diplomatic service are exempt from the operation of "municipal law. Consequently, as far as a building—as in the "present case—is concerned, immunity extends not only to the "building in which the diplomatic office is placed, but also to "the dwellings of all diplomatic persons. The law speaks "therefore not only of exterritorial buildings but also of exterritorial premises, *i.e.* of exterritorial premises in buildings "otherwise subject to territorial jurisdiction. On the other "hand, when a diplomatic person possesses in the country a "house or an agricultural estate or a factory, etc., for his own "private purposes, such immovable property does not enjoy "any exemption." [Report: Váž. 9491 civ.]

Case No. 252

Diplomatic Intercourse—Status of Legation Buildings—Extraterritoriality—Jurisdiction in Offences Committed in Legation Buildings.

IN RE ZOLTÁN SZ.

Supreme Court of Hungary. 1 *December,* 1928.
(*No. B. I,* 5368/1928.)

THE FACTS.—The accused took part in inducing the passport authorities at the Hungarian Legation in Vienna to issue a passport as the result of false information and a false photograph. The question arose as to where the offence was committed.

Held by the Supreme Court: "The offence was committed "not abroad but on the territory of the Hungarian State. The "premises of the Royal Hungarian Legation which enjoyed the "privileges of extraterritoriality must be regarded as Hun-"garian territory. Accordingly, all acts committed therein must "be judged according to the rules of Hungarian criminal law." [Report: *Büntetöjogi Döntvénytár*, XXII, No. 4.]

D. CONSULS

II.—Position and Function of Consuls

Consuls—Nationality of—Italian Consul of Turkish Nationality in Turkey as an Italian "*Ressortissant*"—Consuls as Protected Persons.

Case No. 253

SIMANTOV *v.* BULGARIAN STATE.

Italian-Bulgarian Mixed Arbitral Tribunal. 9 January, 1928.

(SOLDATI, RADULOVA, FAGGELLA.)

THE FACTS.—Article 179 of the Treaty of Neuilly provided as follows:

> "Diplomatic or consular claims made before the "war by the Representatives or Agents of the "Allied and Associated Powers with regard to the "private property, rights or interests of nationals of "those Powers shall, on the application of the Power "concerned, be submitted to the Mixed Arbitral "Tribunal provided for in Section VI."

The claimant, who claimed compensation for certain damage done to his property in the years 1912 and 1913 during the Balkan War, was a Turkish subject, and contended that as Italian consular agent in Turkey he enjoyed immunities which gave him the position of a person under Italian protection and that he therefore came within the definition of "*ressortissant*" as used in the Treaty.

Held: That the claimant could not be regarded as an Italian "*ressortissant*," and that the Tribunal therefore had no

Case No. 253 *contd.*

jurisdiction. It was impossible to admit that an alien was an Italian "*ressortissant*" by virtue of the simple fact that as a consular agent he enjoyed in Turkey special privileges and immunities. The very provision of the Turkish law in question—a Decree of 9 August, 1863—was to the effect that Turkish subjects acting as consular agents of foreign Powers in Turkey did not "for one moment" cease to be Turkish nationals subject to Turkish jurisdiction in their private and personal capacity. [Report: *Recueil*, VIII, p. 686.]

Case No. 254

Consuls—Duty of Special Protection of the Person of Consuls.

FRANCISCO MALLÉN CASE.

United States and Mexico: General Claims Commission.
27 *April*, 1927.

(VAN VOLLENHOVEN, NIELSEN, MACGREGOR.)

THE FACTS.—(See Case No. 144.)

Held, in answer to the question whether consuls are entitled to a "special protection" for their persons: That, if these words indicate that, apart from privileges extended to consuls either by treaty or by unwritten law, the State of their residence is bound to grant them other privileges not enjoyed by other residents, then the answer is in the negative. "But "if 'special protection' means that in executing the laws of the "country, especially those concerning police and penal law, the "Government should realise that foreign Governments are "sensitive regarding the treatment accorded their representa-"tives, and that therefore the Government of the consul's "residence should exercise greater vigilance in respect to their "security and safety, the answer as evidently shall be in the "affirmative." [Reports: *Opinions of Commissioners*, 1927, p. 254; *A.J.*, XXI (1927), p. 803.]

NOTE.—Annual Message of President Fillmore, of 2 December, 1851, Moore, *Digest*, VI, p. 813; the Report of the Committee of Jurists appointed by the Council of the League of Nations in connection with the Corfu affair in 1924, *A.J.*, XVIII (1924), p. 543; and Eagleton, *ibid.*, XIX (1925), pp. 303, 308 referred to.

Consuls—Duty of Receiving State to Protect—Serious Character of Offences of Violence upon State Representatives. **Case No. 255**

IN RE DOBROWOLSKY AND GOUKOVITCH.

District Court of Odessa of the Socialist Soviet Ukrainian Republic. 12 *February*, 1928.

THE FACTS.—On 28 December, 1927, there was found the dead body of the Italian vice-consul, Silvio Coccio. The body was naked, and it was subsequently established by medical experts that the cause of death was the breaking of the skull and haemorrhage of the brain as the result of blows on the head inflicted with a heavy stone which was found beside the dead man. Several days afterwards the police arrested Georges Goukovitch, resident of Poltava (Ukraine), aged 25, at the moment when he was attempting to sell the cloak belonging to the deceased. Goukovitch stated that he bought the cloak from a certain Woldemar Dobrowolsky, aged 24, resident of the district of Kouzsk, in whose possession were subsequently found the shoes of the murdered vice-consul.

Interrogated by the magistrate, Dobrowolsky said that on the evening of the murder he intended to commit robbery, and that with this object in view he tried unsuccessfully to force several doors. When thus engaged he met in one of the streets an unknown person who threatened him with a revolver. Dobrowolsky, thinking that the approaching person intended to arrest him, dealt him a blow, thereby unintentionally killing him. It was only after having read the newspapers that he learned that his victim was the Italian vice-consul.

Held (by reference to Articles 174 and 175 of the Criminal Code of the Ukrainian Republic): That the act of the accused must be regarded as " very dangerous from the social point of " view." " The assassination and the robbing of the Italian " vice-consul have provoked the indignation of the workers of " Odessa in view of the fact that the person murdered and " robbed was a representative of a friendly State, and also in " view of the cruelty of the murder and of the premeditated " robbery."

The tribunal condemned Goukovitch to three years' detention and confiscation of his property and expulsion from the

Case No. 255 *contd.* territory of the Ukrainian Republic for five years, and Dobrowolsky to capital punishment and confiscation of his property.

NOTE.—It will be observed that the Criminal Code of the Soviet Republics does not impose capital punishment except for crimes dangerous to the State as such. Cases of homicide are otherwise punished by ten years' detention. In punishing the murder of the Italian vice-consul with death the Tribunal assimilated this crime to a crime against the State.

Case No. 256 **Consuls—Functions of—Rights Conferred upon Consuls by International Conventions—Whether Imposing Duty upon the Consul to Exercise those Rights and Conferring Right upon the Subjects of the Consul's State to such Exercise.**

BELSITO *v.* MINISTRY FOR FOREIGN AFFAIRS.

Italian Court of Cassation (*Combined Divisions*).
17 *November*, 1927.

THE FACTS.—This was an action for compensation brought against the Ministry for Foreign Affairs by the heirs Belsito, whose father had died at Macao, Portuguese China. They alleged that the local authorities of Macao had ordered the sale of the property of the deceased at a ridiculous price and before news of the death had reached the plaintiffs. They maintained that the Italian consul and in the last resort the Ministry for Foreign Affairs were responsible for the said sale on the ground that in accordance with Article 9 of the Consular Convention between Italy and Portugal of 30 September, 1868, it was one of the duties of the Italian consular authority to take care of the property of the deceased and to confine the sale to objects which were liable to deterioration. Consequently, they contended, the Italian consul at Hong-Kong had committed a breach of the Convention in directing the Portuguese authorities to sell the property in question, or at any rate in concurring in the sale instead of preventing it. The Court of Appeal dismissed the action, and the heirs appealed to the Court of Cassation.

Held: That the appeal must be dismissed. The Consular Convention only recognises and sanctions the right of the Italian consul on Portuguese territory and of the Portuguese consul on Italian territory to substitute themselves at any time for the local authority for the exercise of certain functions relating to the protection of the interests of incapable or absent heirs, which functions, in the ordinary way, ought to be exercised by the local authority in virtue of the territorial sovereignty of the State. The Convention, however, does not and could not impose on the consul an obligation to act in these matters.

" Neither can it be maintained that what is merely an " optional power or a right of the Italian State in its relations " with another State should be changed into a juridical obli- " gation when relations of the Italian State with its subjects " are at issue, and this solely on the ground that from the " exercise of such functions the individual may derive some " benefit. . . . Such a juridical obligation would be both " juridically and politically inconceivable. The right of the " State in exercising the necessary functions for the protection " of the interests of its subjects abroad cannot be transformed " into a legal bond whenever interests of the private citizen " are concerned. . . . Where the State or on its behalf the " consular authorities representing it abroad do not choose to " avail themselves of the rights conferred by the Convention, " the citizen must accept as lawful, in his relations with the " authority of the foreign State in the territory in which he " has taken up residence and concentrated his interests, the " situation thus created." [Report: *Rivista di diritto internazionale*, 1928, pp. 381-384, with a note by G. Morelli.]

Consuls—Position of—Jurisdiction over—Action on account of Excess of Power against Foreign Consul Acting in his Official Capacity. **Case No. 257**

LUIS SANITAGE, VICE-CONSUL OF FRANCE, CASE.

Chamber of Appeals, South-Eastern Department, Argentina. 1927.

THE FACTS.—Luis Sanitage, French vice-consul, exceeding the powers given him as a consular officer by Article 3, Law No. 163, of 14 September, 1863, of the Argentine Republic, relative to the measures of conservation that consuls may take with reference to the estates of deceased nationals, took possession of the assets of the estate of one Juan Maria Bertrex, a Frenchman, and had caused negotiable instruments to be issued to himself by the debtors of the estate, without the sanction of the tribunal in charge of the administration. Upon his arrest on a charge of having

Case No. 257 contd.

exceeded his powers under the law above mentioned, he sued for his discharge on a writ of habeas corpus.

Held: That the consul of a foreign nation who exceeds the powers expressly mentioned in Article 3 of the Federal Law No. 163 relative to simple measures of conservation taken without the knowledge of the testamentary judge, does not commit an offence if there is no proof of damage to third parties, or of the perpetration of fraudulent acts for the purpose of withholding any assets from entry in the inventory.

The ordinary courts have no jurisdiction to take cognisance of a case against a foreign consular officer who, in his official capacity, takes possession of the assets of the estate, in excess of the powers given by Article 3 of Law No. 163. [Report: 26 Jurisprudencia Argentina, 1426.]

Case No. 258

Consuls—Function of—Evidence as to Law and Legal Effects of an Act Done in their own Country.

ESTATE OF VIDAL Y MAS.

Second Civil Chamber de la Capital, Argentina. 19 *April*, 1926.

Held: Consuls have no right to give evidence as to the legal effect of an act done in the country they represent; but can only certify the text of the foreign law applicable to the case, and leave it to the local judiciary to pass upon the question of the legal effect. [Report: 19 Jurisprudencia Argentina, 840.]

NOTE.—As to the practice in the United States of America, see *Church* v. *Hubbart*, (1804) 2 Cranch (U.S.) 187, and Hyde, *International Law*, vol. I, § 487. As to England, see cases cited by Westlake, *Private International Law*, 7th ed., § 357.

Consuls—Protection of Estates of Deceased Fellow-Nationals.

See Case No. 310 (*Estate of Clausen*).

III.—Privileges and Immunities of Consuls

Case No. 259

Consuls—Courts having Jurisdiction of Suits against—Suits for Divorce and Alimony.

POPOVICI *v.* POPOVICI.

United States District Court, N.D. Ohio. 15 *July*, 1927.

THE FACTS.—This was a suit for divorce and alimony brought against the Roumanian vice-consul stationed at Cleveland. Plaintiff claimed the right to bring her suit in the Federal district court of the United States under the United States Constitution, Article III, § 2, and the United States Judicial Code, § 24 and § 256. The section of the Constitution invoked by plaintiff provided that the judicial power of the United States shall extend to all cases affecting ambassadors, other public ministers, and consuls. Section 24 of the Judicial Code invested United States district courts with original jurisdiction of all suits against consuls and vice-consuls. Section 256 provided that the jurisdiction of the district courts of " all suits and proceedings " against ambassadors, or other public ministers, or their " domestics, or domestic servants, or against consuls or " vice-consuls " should be exclusive of the courts of the several States. Defendant moved to dismiss the suit.

Held : That defendant's motion should be granted. The Federal courts of the United States have no jurisdiction whatever in suits for divorce or alimony. Their jurisdiction of suits against consuls does not include divorce actions. [Report : 30 F. (2nd) 185.]

NOTE.—See later decision of Supreme Court of the United States in *Popovici* v. *Agler* (1930), 280 U.S. 379, Case No. 260 in this volume.

Consuls—Courts having Jurisdiction of Suits against—Divorce Proceedings against Consuls. **Case No. 260**

POPOVICI *v.* AGLER.

Supreme Court of Ohio. Supreme Court of the United States.
26 *December*, 1928. 20 *January*, 1930.

THE FACTS.—After the decision in *Popovici* v. *Popovici,*[1] 30 F. (2nd) 185, the plaintiff brought her divorce action in one of the inferior courts of the State of Ohio. The defendant applied to the Supreme Court of Ohio for a writ of prohibition.

Held : That the writ should be denied. The State courts of the United States are not excluded from jurisdiction by the Judicial Code, § 256, in cases in which the United States Federal courts disclaim any jurisdiction of the subject-matter. On certiorari to the Supreme Court of the United States,

[1] Case No. 259 in this volume.

Case No. 260 *contd.*

Held: That the decision of the Supreme Court of Ohio should be affirmed. Delivering the Opinion of the Court, Mr. Justice Holmes said: "The statutes do not purport to exclude "the State Courts from jurisdiction except where they grant "it to Courts of the United States. Therefore they do not "affect the present case if it be true as has been unquestioned "for three-quarters of a century that the Courts of the United "States have no jurisdiction over divorce. If when the Con-"stitution was adopted the common understanding was that "the domestic relations of husband and wife and parent and "child were matters reserved to the States, there is no diffi-"culty in construing the instrument accordingly and not much "in dealing with the statutes. 'Suits against consuls and vice-"'consuls' must be taken to refer to ordinary civil proceed-"ings and not to include what formerly would have belonged "to the ecclesiastical courts." (280 U.S. 379, 383.) [Reports: 119 Ohio St. 484; 280 U.S. 379.[1]]

Case No. 261

Consuls—Position of—Subjection to the Laws of the Receiving Country—Question of Domicile.

G. de N. R. *v.* N. R.

Camara Federal de Rosario, Argentina. 1926.

The Facts.—Upon a petition by the wife of a foreign consul against the consul for support and maintenance, it was objected that the Argentine courts had no jurisdiction by reason of the Uruguayan domicile attributed to the consul by the law of Uruguay.

Held by the Court of First Instance: That the Court has jurisdiction. The fact that the Uruguayan law may consider a consul here as domiciled in Montevideo and as merely residing in Rosario is not enough to exclude him from the Argentine Federal law or jurisdiction when he sues or is sued here on private business. It is an entirely inadmissible exaggeration of the principle of the extraterritoriality of foreign agents, even from the point of view of the public character they possess. In particular with respect to consuls international law has settled that they are amenable to the laws and to the jurisdiction of the country where they reside with regard to all acts not relating to the exercise of their functions. (See F. Fiore, *Der. Int. Pub.*, vol. 2, p. 460.) [Report: 23 Jurisprudencia Argentina, 90.]

[1] See comment in 28 Mich. Law Rev. 591.

Consular Privileges—Jurisdiction of National Courts in respect of Contracts Concluded by Consuls in their Official Capacity. **Case No. 262**

CALVARUSO *v.* BAYNGTON.

Court of Appeal of Naples. 20 *January*, 1928.

THE FACTS.—The Italian citizen Calvaruso, appointed to the post of inspector of the luggage of emigrants by the Consul-General of the United States of America, had been dismissed without any previous notice. He claimed damages.

Held : That the Court had no jurisdiction. The contract of employment having been concluded with the defendant in his capacity of Consul-General of a foreign State while engaged in the exercise of his official function, the matter could not be decided upon by the Italian judicial authorities. The legal tie created between the Consul-General of the United States of America and an Italian citizen whose duty it was to inspect the luggage of the emigrants embarking from an Italian port for the United States enters into the realm of public law. [Report : *Monitore dei Tribunali*, 1928, p. 672.]

Consuls—Immunities from Jurisdiction—Subjection of Consulate to Administrative Measures. **Case No. 263**

ATTACHMENT OF SALARY OF EMPLOYEE OF CONSULATE.

Administrative Commission of the Superior Court of the Canton of Zurich. 14 *January*, 1927.

THE FACTS.—An order for the attachment of the salary of the secretary of a foreign Consulate was notified by the appropriate Cantonal authority, the Collecting Office, to the Consulate in the usual form. The Embassy of the foreign State in question addressed a complaint to the appropriate Swiss political department, which requested the judicial authorities of the Canton of Zurich to put an end to the attachment. This request was referred to the Superior Court as the organ responsible for the control of the Collecting Office.

Held : The Consulate employee in question does not enjoy extraterritoriality, and the Canton of Zurich has therefore full jurisdiction over her as the debtor. All forms of execution may be put into force against her, including attachment of salary. It is immaterial whether she is employed in a public or private

Case No. 263 *contd.*

capacity. The mere fact that her salary is derived from an employment of a public law nature cannot result in ending the attachment.

On the other hand, the notification of the Collecting Office to the Consulate appears to the Superior Court to be inadmissible both in form and substance, and must be annulled. The Office has clearly overlooked the fact that the Consulate, by virtue of its character as the official organ of a foreign State, is not subject to the administrative authority of the Canton of Zurich, and in consequence is exempt from the sphere of application of the usual official procedure, as this is appropriate only to persons subject to the Cantonal administration. The utmost that could have been done was to apply to the Consulate for assistance in the execution of the attachment.

The annulment of the notification to the Consulate does not mean the end of the attachment itself. For the notification to the debtor is not in itself a condition of the validity of the attachment. The attachment is legally completed by the notification to the debtor. The Consulate is under no duty to hand over the amount in question to the Collecting Office. This is the duty of the debtor, who otherwise makes herself liable to penalties for frustrating the attachment. [Report: *Blätter für zürcherische Rechtsprechung*, XXVII, No. 198.]

Case No. 264

Position of Consuls—Local Taxation—Employees of Consulates.

THE TOWN OF ZURICH *v.* FINANCE DEPARTMENT OF THE CANTON OF ZURICH.

Upper Commission of Appeal in Taxation Questions of the Canton of Zurich. 10 *June*, 1927.

THE FACTS.—The Finance Department of the Canton of Zurich in application of paragraph 3, section 7 of the Finance Law, absolved an employee of the American General Consulate from liability to taxes, on the ground that he was the only such employee of an American Consulate in Switzerland who did not enjoy this immunity. The taxation authority of the town of Zurich appealed against this decision to the Upper Commission of Appeal of the Canton on the ground that paragraph 3, section 7, gives immunity only to "representatives of foreign States, in accordance with "the provisions of international law and of Federal "legislation," and that this provision does not include consular employees. The Finance Department contended that the decision here challenged rested on political grounds, and denied the competence of the Upper Commission of Appeal to question the legal validity of this decision.

Held: The Upper Commission of Appeal affirmed its competence. and upheld the appeal of the town of Zurich.

The Finance Law contemplates no political authorities which may grant immunity in individual cases. Neither the statutes nor the Constitution of Zurich permit the Finance Department or the Government Board to excuse individuals from payment where the necessary conditions of liability are present, with the exception of the case provided for in section 3 of the final clause of the statute, which is here inapplicable. The Upper Commission of Appeal, which is the highest administrative tribunal in taxation questions, decides as a court of final appeal upon the liability of individuals to the taxing power of Zurich, and its decisions cannot be influenced by political considerations. Employees of American Consulates are not entitled to plead extraterritoriality since they are not the representatives of a foreign State. Federal legislation contains no provisions absolving foreign consular employees from liability to be taxed. No such principle is to be found in international law. The Treaty of 25 November, 1850, between the Swiss Federation and the United States of America provides that consuls and vice-consuls of either State shall be treated on an equal footing, in matters of law and of usage, in their private and business dealings as the citizens of the place where they may be living. The Treaty contains no clause dealing specifically with consular employees. The case of such functionaries is covered by Article II of the Treaty, which provides that the nationals of one party in the land of the other must not be subjected to a higher tax than is paid by other residents, but that it is permissible to tax foreigners at the same rate as nationals. [Report: *Blätter für zürcherische Rechtsprechung*, XXVII, No. 79.]

Consular Immunities—Exemption from Jurisdiction—Meaning of the Term "Personal Immunity." **Case No. 265**

CONSULAR IMMUNITIES (MOTOR CAR ACCIDENT) CASE.

Oberlandesgericht (*Upper District Court*) *of Frankfort-on-the-Main.* 26 *October*, 1928.

THE FACTS.—This was a civil action against a Spanish consul arising out of a motor-car accident. The de-

Case No. 265 ***contd.***

fendant pleaded to the jurisdiction of the Court and invoked the provisions of the Consular Treaty with Spain of 12 January, 1872. That Treaty incorporated the Treaty of 28 February, 1870, between the Northern German Confederation and Spain, which, in Article 4, provided that consuls shall enjoy "personal immunity." The same Article laid down that consuls who are subjects of the State issuing the exequatur or who engage in commercial ventures shall enjoy personal immunity only in respect of such civil obligations as do not arise out of commercial transactions. The defendant invoked this provision in support of the contention that, as he belonged to neither of these categories, he was entitled to immunity from the jurisdiction of the Court in the present action.

Held: That the Court had jurisdiction. The expression "personal immunity" applied only to immunity from arrest. The fact that Article 4 also referred to personal immunity in connection with civil matters was not decisive, because according to the German Code of Civil Procedure (paragraphs 888, 890, 901, 933) arrest could also take place in civil actions. [Report: *Blätter für Internationales Privatrecht*, IV (1929), No. 6, p. 174.]

Case No. 266

Consular Privileges—Operation and Enforcement of Treaties —Personal Immunity of Consuls—Diplomatic Treaties— Interpretation before French Courts—Franco-American Consular Convention of 23 February, 1853.

PRINCESS ZIZIANOFF *v.* KAHN AND BIGELOW.

Tribunal Correctionnel of the Seine (*Twelfth Chamber*). 5 *April*, 1927.

Court of Appeal of Paris (*Tenth Chamber*). 28 *January*, 1928.

Court of Cassation (*Criminal Chamber*). 15 *December*, 1928.

THE FACTS.—Princess Zizianoff applied for a passport-visa valid for the United States. The request was refused by the American Consulate in Paris. The director of the Passport Section, Mr. Bigelow, then issued to certain journalists information reflecting unfavourably upon Princess Zizianoff, in explanation of the decision of his Government. This information was published in an American paper, sold in Paris, the *Boston Sunday Post*, the Paris representative of which was Mr. Alexander Kahn.

Thereupon Princess Zizianoff brought an action for libel and defamation of character against Mr. Kahn, Mr. Bigelow, as an accomplice, and two other defendants, in accordance with the Press Law of 29 July, 1881.

Mr. Bigelow, in demurring to the competence of the French courts, maintained that he could not be legally cited before them by reason of his "personal "immunity" established by the terms of the Consular Convention of 23 February, 1853, and as being immune, in international law, from any proceedings before the local courts, arising from acts performed in the course of his official duties.

Held by the *Tribunal Correctionnel*: That the Court has jurisdiction.

(*a*) In regard to the Convention of 23 February, 1853: "In "principle the courts can only interpret diplomatic treaties, "insufficiently clear in their terms, when private interests are "concerned: on the other hand, where it is required to deter-"mine their meaning and intention in international public law, "the interpretation can only be made by the governments, "parties to the treaties." (Cassation, Criminal Chamber, 23 February, 1912, *In re King*, 40 *Clunet* (1913), p. 182.) "The "question of the personal immunity enjoyed by consuls, by "the vagueness of the expression itself, is essentially one for "governmental interpretation." The Court then pointed out that the American and French Governments had considered the interpretation to be given to the Consular Convention of 23 February, 1853, in regard to personal immunity, and that although they had not reached agreement upon the special case of exemption from arrest or imprisonment in connection with a judgment, nevertheless they had agreed to recognise the competence of their respective courts, civil, *correctionnels*, and criminal, so far as concerns the acts, other than official, of their consuls.

(*b*) The subsidiary plea, made by Bigelow, that, in accordance with international law, proceedings arising from the performance of their official duties, or even from offences committed in their performance, can never be brought against consuls in the courts of the country in which their duties are performed, could not be accepted as valid. Bigelow was not sued for his refusal to grant a passport-visa. He had been an accomplice in the offence of defamation by providing, through an interview with the journalists, the means of its commission: "He could not have been unaware that his views would be

Case No. 266 ***contd.*** " published in the press and might give rise therefore to con-" duct repugnant to French law ; therefore he acted not as a " consul, but in his private capacity under his own responsi-" bility." [Reports : 55 *Clunet* (1928), p. 142 ; *Gazette du Palais*, 1927, II, p. 18.]

Held by the Court of Appeal (on the appeal of Bigelow) : That the judgment declaring the competence of the Court must be upheld.

(*a*) As regards the Consular Convention of 1853 : " The " Government, which alone is qualified to interpret diplomatic " treaties, had previously expressed its opinion upon the sense " to be attributed to the provisions of the Convention of " 23 February, 1853, and particularly to the phrase ' personal " ' immunity.' " This interpretation is embodied in the decision of the Court of Cassation of 23 February, 1912, and repeated in a letter of the Minister of Foreign Affairs dated 26 October, 1926, and produced in the course of the case. In accordance with this interpretation, the clause relating to personal immunity " provides for immunity not from juris-" diction, but from arrest and imprisonment." This view the courts must accept by virtue of the principle of separation of powers.

(*b*) The subsidiary plea of Bigelow that as his actions were part of his official functions the French courts had no competence could not be accepted, since the conduct complained of could in no way be associated with the performance of his official duties. The comments made by Bigelow to the representatives of the press of his country were in no way necessary for that performance. " These comments, " whether considered apart from or in association with the " official function itself, constitute a grave offence calculated " to prejudice private interest, and are personal in character. " This offence can be clearly separated from the official function " performed by Bigelow and in no way involves an examination " of the said function." [Report : *Gazette du Palais*, 1928, I, p. 727, with the opinion of the Advocate-General Reynaud.[1]]

[1] The Court of Appeal, unlike the *Tribunal Correctionnel*, made no attempt to establish the existence of an agreement, or at least a measure of agreement, between the French and American Governments upon the interpretation of the Consular Convention of 1853. The Court of Appeal confined itself to stating the view, expressed in the opinion of the Advocate-General, that the French Government alone is qualified to give an interpretation and is in no way bound by the conflicting opinion of another contracting State ; for the latter can always denounce a treaty whose application does not conform to its own view.

The Court of Appeal, in considering the connection between the conduct

Held by the Court of Cassation (on appeal by Bigelow): That the appeal must be dismissed.

(*a*) " Diplomatic treaties, published in a regular form in " France, have the force of law and therefore should be applied " by the judicial authorities. But the courts have only the " power of interpretation when interpretation is connected " with questions of private interest and not of international " public order. In the latter event, the courts are bound to " conform to the official interpretation as rendered by the " French Government."

(*b*) The act of Bigelow which formed the object of the action could not be considered as part of his official functions and excluded as such from the consideration of French courts. [Reports: *Dalloz hebdomadaire*, 1929, p. 69; *Gazette du Palais*, 1929, I, p. 194.]

Consular Immunities—Duration of—Termination of Consular Office—Distinction between Immunity from Jurisdiction and Immunity from Arrest. **Case No. 267**

CONSULAR IMMUNITIES (AUSTRIA) CASE.

Austrian Supreme Court acting as Court of Cassation.
29 *October*, 1928. 5 Os. 767/28.

THE FACTS.—This was an action for libel brought against the Italian Consul-General. It appears that there existed between Austria and Italy a treaty conferring jurisdictional immunities upon consuls.

Held by the District Court of Graz: That the Court had jurisdiction. It was true that Consuls-General, in so far as they are subjects of the State which appoints them, enjoy personal immunity. That does not mean, however, that they are not subject to Austrian jurisdiction. Their immunity merely means that they may not be arrested except when they commit a crime.

Held by the Court of Second Instance: That the sentence must be quashed. The defendant enjoyed personal immunity. No writ could be issued, no proceedings taken, and no sentence pronounced, against him. However, as the defendant had

complained of and the consular functions of Mr. Bigelow, seems to have had in mind the theory of French administrative law concerning the responsibility of officials and the distinction between acts done in a personal capacity and acts performed in the course of official duties. The Advocate-General in dealing with this question before the Court cited several writers on Public Law, especially MM. Laferrière, Jèze, Duguit and Barthélemy.

Case No. 267 *contd.*

ceased to be consul since judgment had been given, he no longer enjoyed jurisdictional immunity, and new proceedings could therefore begin.

Held by the Supreme Court acting as Court of Cassation: That the case should be returned to the Court of First Instance for judgment. Consular officials of foreign Powers have no diplomatic character. Subject to special treaty provisions, they are amenable to the laws and the jurisdiction of the place where they have been permitted to reside (Decree of 23 September, 1817). There are in fact some exceptions to this rule in several treaties, as, for instance, in the present case in the Consular Convention with Italy of 15 May, 1874. Accordingly the defendant had the right to personal immunity. "However, personal immunity from jurisdiction is not identical "with the total exclusion of the jurisdiction of national courts. "It consists only in the exclusion of execution and arrest "against the person of the consular official." Thus, with the exception of the case mentioned in Article 4 of the said Treaty, namely, the case of the commission of a crime, he may not be arrested. But there is nothing to prevent an Austrian court from instituting criminal proceedings and from convicting the accused. The immunity of the consular agent is merely a personal right which he enjoys in his official capacity. It lapses when his official function ceases. [Report: *Entscheidungen des Obersten Gerichtshofes in Strafsachen und Disziplinarangelegenheiten*, vol. VIII (1928), No. 133, pp. 266-269.]

Case No. 268

Privileges and Immunities of Consuls—Continuance after Retirement—Succession to Estates of Russian Subjects in Country where Soviet Government Not Recognised.

DESSOUKI MOUSTAPHA *v.* A. PETROFF.

Egyptian Mixed Court of Appeal. 10 *February*, 1927.

THE FACTS.—A Russian subject died at Mansura in Egypt in 1912. The Russian vice-consul in the town, claiming the deceased as a Russian subject, took steps to administer the estate with the consent of the officers of the Egyptian Government. The deceased left a single heir in Russia and a daughter in Egypt, and the Russian authorities conferred the guardianship of the daughter on the grandmother in Egypt.

In February, 1913, the plaintiff, the uncle of the daughter, addressed a petition to the Russian consul for the liquidation of the succession in his favour. The liquidation had not been completed in 1923, when the Egyptian Government put an end to the recognition of the Russian diplomatic and consular officers previously established in Egypt. Petroff, the late Russian consul at Alexandria, subsequently delivered to the Egyptian authorities the estate of the deceased which was in his charge. The plaintiff then obtained a decree of the local Egyptian court nominating him as guardian of the daughter of the deceased, and declaring the daughter the sole heir of the deceased; and he instituted an action before the Mixed Court against the late Russian consul, Petroff, and the Bank in which the property of the estate was deposited, claiming a declaration that the daughter was the sole heir of the deceased and that the late consul should be ordered to deliver to him all the property and the assets of the succession and pay interest on the value of the estate as from 1912. The Tribunal declared itself incompetent as regards the claim against the defendant Petroff in respect of acts done by him in the exercise of his functions as Russian consul. On appeal by the plaintiff,

Held: That, in accordance with the provisions of international law, diplomatic and consular officers are not subject to the jurisdiction of the courts for acts done in the execution of their functions. The late Russian consul is, therefore, not liable to the control of the courts for anything done by him in his official capacity, and he cannot be deprived of that immunity after he has retired from the office. The order made by the Egyptian Court in regard to the succession of the deceased Russian subject cannot be accepted; but the Mixed Courts themselves have no competence in matters of succession and cannot therefore take the place of the judge of personal status and make a declaration as to the heirs of a foreign subject. [Report: *Gazette des Tribunaux Mixtes d'Egypte*, 18th year, 1928, p. 35.]

Consular Immunities—Honorary Consuls—Immunities in Egypt—Penal Action against such Consuls. **Case No. 269**

DE GERBER *v.* MUNICIPALITY OF ALEXANDRIA.

Egyptian Mixed Court of Appeal. 22 *November*, 1926.

THE FACTS.—The appellant, who was Swedish consul at Alexandria, applied to the Court of Cassation to quash

Case No. 269 *contd.*

a judgment given by the Mixed Tribunal of Alexandria in April, 1926, condemning him to a fine and to the payment of dues to the Municipality of Alexandria for the occupation of the public road. The appellant was an honorary consul, but claimed that he was entitled to the immunity given to diplomatic and consular officers in Egypt from the local law and the jurisdiction of the courts.

Held: On the question of jurisdiction, that the immunity from both civil and criminal jurisdiction applies, as regards all matters outside their official functions, only to diplomatic and consular officers who are of the class of "missi consules."[1] [Report: *Gazette des Tribunaux Mixtes d'Egypte*, 17th year, 1927, p. 279.]

E. MISCELLANEOUS

Case No. 270

Diplomatic and Consular Immunities and Privileges—Right of Other Persons to Privileges and Immunities—Officials of the United States Shipping Board.

H. E. W. R. LANDAHL *v.* SWEDISH GOVERNMENT.

Supreme Administrative Court of Sweden. 9 December, 1927.

THE FACTS.—The Swedish income-tax law grants exemption from tax, except on certain income, to persons belonging to a foreign Legation or Consulate with their servants.

A United States citizen, resident in Sweden, who was assessed for income-tax by the local commissioners, appealed against their decision on the ground that he was an official of the United States Shipping Board which is a State Department of the United States to be assimilated to a United States Legation or Consulate.

Held: That the appeal should be dismissed. [Report: *Regeringsrättens årsbok*, 1927. *Not. Fi*, No. 1155.]

NOTE.—On the position of the United States Shipping Board, (i) before English courts, see *Compañia Mercantil Argentina* v. *United States Shipping Board* (1920), 40 T.L.R. 601; 18 Lloyd's List Law Reports 369; and (ii) before Portuguese courts, see *Annual Digest*, 1925-1926, Case No. 133.—[Ed.]

---

[1] That is, *consuls de carrière*: see Fauchille, § 742.

PART VIII

TREATIES

II.—Forms of International Agreement and Methods by which they are Concluded

i.—Treaties. Conventions. Governmental Agreements. Exchanges of Notes

Treaties—*Pactum de Contrahendo*—How far Controlled by the First Treaty—Article 349 of the Treaty of Versailles and the Definitive Statute of the Danube.

See Case No. 304 (*Jurisdiction of the European Commission of the Danube between Galatz and Braila*).

IV.—Conditions of Validity of Treaties. Registration of Treaties

Conditions of Validity of Treaties—Registration of Treaties—Conditions of Registration—Treaties Concluded between a State Member and a State not Member of the League of Nations—Proof of Registration—Effect of Non-Registration—Conditions of Application of Article 18 of the Covenant. **Case No. 271**

PABLO NÁJERA (OF THE LEBANON) CASE.

France and Mexico: Mixed Claims Commission.
19 *October*, 1928.
(VERZIJL, President.)

THE FACTS.—In connection with the claims of Syrian and Lebanese protected persons, the Mexican Government unexpectedly asserted the non-fulfilment by France of its duty under Article 18 of the Covenant of the League of Nations with regard to the French-Mexican Claims Convention of 25 September, 1924, in order to challenge the binding force of that Convention, which it had not attacked before with regard to claims of French citizens.

Held: (*a*) With respect to the general meaning of Article 18, that its provisions do not impair the binding force as between the parties, Members of the League of Nations, of a duly ratified treaty, so that, in spite of the neglect of registra-

Case No. 271 ***contd.***

tion, the parties can not withdraw from it or conclude with third Powers treaties contrary to it ; that, however, the Article precludes the parties from invoking the treaty as obligatory, not only before the Assembly and the Council of the League of Nations but also before the Permanent Court of International Justice and any other international tribunal.

(*b*) With respect to the proof of registration, that, on the one hand, an international tribunal is not bound, in each case, to enquire *ex officio* if registration has taken place, but that, on the other, the contracting States cannot, even by mutual consent and in order to circumvent Article 18, prevent such tribunal from making such enquiry ; that, therefore, an intermediate solution recommends itself, consisting in leaving to the discretion of the tribunal to decide in each particular case whether or not the contentions or the silence of the parties with regard to registration require an investigation in Geneva.

(*c*) With respect to the applicability of the Article to treaties concluded between a State Member and a State not a Member of the League, that, on the one hand, the State Member is bound by the Article towards its fellow-Members and the League and would not therefore be entitled to invoke the treaty either in the Assembly or in the Council of the League without previous registration ; that, on the other hand, the Article is an innovation in international law and therefore does not bind the State not Member, who is entitled to invoke the treaty in every international tribunal, notwithstanding the lack of registration ; that, however, this inequality of treatment between States Members and States not Members of the League, though fully justifiable with regard to the League itself and its organs, ceases to be so when the treaty is in discussion in an international tribunal unconnected with the League, so as to compel such tribunal to apply it, Article 18 notwithstanding ; and that, at all events, and according to the principle *pacta tertiis nec nocent nec prosunt*, the State not Member is not entitled to invoke the fact of neglect of registration in its favour in order to avoid its international obligations.

[Till now unreported.]

V.—Parties to Treaties. Right to Conclude Treaties. Composite and Dependent States and Territories

Treaties—Parties to—With Native Chiefs and Princes.

See Case No. 70 (*Island of Palmas Arbitration Case*).

VIII.—Ratification of Treaties. Entrance into Force

Treaties of Peace—Measures taken between Signature and Ratification—Seizure of a Bank Safe—Burden of Proof as to Objects Contained therein. **Case No. 272**

A. A. MEGALIDIS *v.* TURKEY.

Turkish-Greek Mixed Arbitral Tribunal. 26 *July*, 1928.

(Baron DE NORDENSKJOELD, AHMED RECHID, KYRIACOPOULOS.)

THE FACTS.—On 14 August, 1923, the Turkish authorities in Smyrna seized and opened, in the Bank Credit Lyonnais, a safe hired by the plaintiff and containing jewellery, coins, paper money and negotiable documents. Together with the contents of the safe they seized the original of a list of objects contained therein, a list which Turkey failed to produce before the Tribunal. The Treaty of Lausanne was signed by Turkey on 24 July, 1923.

Turkey relied on Article 67 of the Treaty of Lausanne and contended that the coins, paper money and shares were exempted from the duty of restitution.

Held: (*a*) That the Turkish contention was unfounded. The presumption was that Turkey was still in possession of these objects. For the seizure cannot be deemed to have been made with the view to appropriating the objects in question in view of the fact that from the time of the signature of the Treaty and before its entry into force the contracting parties were under the duty to do nothing which might impair the operation of its clauses.[1] Neither has Turkey proved that at any time after the signature of the Treaty the objects in question ceased to be in her possession. Accordingly, Turkey was bound to restore the objects seized.

(*b*) As Turkey did not produce and did not attempt to produce the original of the list of objects deposited in the safe, the presumption was that the copy of the list produced by the claimant was correct.[2] Accordingly, the restitution was to be effected in accordance with the copy produced by the claimant. [Report: *Recueil*, VIII, p. 390.]

[1] The Tribunal referred here to Fauchille, vol. I, part III, p. 320.

[2] In addition to this very natural presumption arising from the failure of Turkey to produce the original, it is perhaps permissible to refer to the maxim *omnia praesumuntur contra spoliatorem*, for which in English law see the notes to *Armory* v. *Delamirie* in Smith's *Leading Cases*, vol. I (13th ed., 1929), pp. 393-405.

Case No. 273

Treaties—Entry into Force—Effect of Provisions Fixing No Date for the Commencement of their Operation.

JULES BARANYAI *v.* YUGOSLAVIA.

Hungarian-Yugoslav Mixed Arbitral Tribunal.
15 *September*, 1927.

(VAN SLOOTEN, ZOLTAN, ARANDJELOVITCH.)

THE FACTS.—(See also Case No. 359.) In this action the claimant asked for the restitution of his property taken away by the Yugoslav State contrary to the provisions of Article 250 of the Treaty of Trianon which prohibited measures of retention and liquidation of the private property of Hungarian subjects. It was contended on behalf of Yugoslavia that as the Treaty provided for no date within which restitution of property should take place, Yugoslavia was not bound to restore the property before a judgment of the Mixed Arbitral Tribunal to that effect had been given.

Held: That the fact that the Treaty provided no date for restitution of property meant that restitution was due on the day of the entry into force of the Treaty. [Report: *Recueil*, VII, p. 858.]

Case No. 274

Treaties—Ratification—Entrance into Force—Operation and Enforcement—Operative Effect of the Date of Signature for Reasons of Equity—Retroactive Effect of Treaties Dealing with Public Law.

SCHRAGER *v.* WORKMEN'S ACCIDENT INSURANCE INSTITUTE FOR MORAVIA AND SILESIA.

Supreme Court of Poland, Third Division. 2 *March*, 1927.

THE FACTS.—After the war, both the Austrian currency maintained in Czechoslovakia and the Austrian and German currencies (subsequently unified into the Polish mark system) temporarily maintained in Poland depreciated considerably. In 1924 a currency reform was carried out in Poland, a new unit (zloty) was introduced, and, in connection with that reform, a Decree of May, 1924, enacted *inter alia*:

(1) (s. 40) that payment of a debt would be complete if the sum due, or a sum valorised under the rules

of that Decree, were deposited with a public trustee Office;

(2) (s. 43) that a foreigner could take advantage of the Decree only if his State treats Polish citizens in this respect on equal terms with his own citizens;

(3) (s. 47) that valorisation would be admissible (with certain exceptions) in the course and at every stage of every judicial process (including appeal stages).

Plaintiff was owner of certain real estate in Polish (formerly Austrian) Silesia. Defendant is a Czechoslovak (formerly Austrian) institution. Plaintiff had obtained from defendant in 1913 a loan secured on plaintiff's real estate, the mortgage being duly entered in the land registry. Under the terms of the agreement, plaintiff in 1921 gave notice of his desire to repay the loan and deposited with the competent public authorities a sum of Polish marks calculated on the original Polish rate of 10 Austrian crowns to 7 Polish marks, without taking into consideration the depreciation of both crowns and marks.

In 1925 plaintiff brought the present action to obtain a declaration that the mortgage had been repaid and that, consequently, the charge should be struck off the registry.

In the course of the proceedings before the court of first instance (the District Court of Cieszyn) the Court obtained from the Ministry of Justice the information (25 June 1925) that in Czechoslovakia the law differentiated between creditors in the matter of debts which had arisen before 26 February, 1919, the criterion being the place of residence (at home or abroad) of such creditors, so that residents in foreign countries who had not obtained payment before that date could not sue for it in Czechoslovakia or could obtain it only in Austrian crowns (unstamped) which had lost all value.

In the meantime, *i.e.* on 23 April, 1925, a Treaty had been signed between Poland and Czechoslovakia regulating legal and financial matters: it stipulated, *inter alia*, that the Polish laws concerning valorisation would be fully applied to creditors possessing Czechoslovak citizenship, " so that each one of the aforesaid creditors " shall be treated on terms of equality with Polish

Case No. 274 ***contd.***

" creditors " (with a certain exception which is immaterial in the present case). A Polish statute of 30 July, 1925, authorised the President to ratify the Treaty. The statute was published in the Journal of Laws on 1 September, 1925. The exchange of ratifications took place on 14 April, 1926, and the Treaty itself was published in the Journal of Laws on 1 May, 1926, accompanied by the declaration of the Polish Government that the Treaty entered into force on 29 April, 1926.

On 9 July, 1925, the District Court of Cieszyn, basing its decision on the reciprocity stipulation of s. 43 of the Decree of 1924 (see 2 above), granted to plaintiff the declaration asked for, because, as appeared from the certificate of the Ministry of Justice, the reciprocity requirement had not been fulfilled and, consequently, defendant could not take advantage of the Decree of 1924. On appeal,

Held: On 4 March, 1926, by the Court of Appeal at Katowice:

(1) That it was not proved that the Czechoslovak courts persisted in recognising, or had the legal duty to recognise, payments in settlement of debts due to Polish creditors in Polish marks, at a rate of exchange which corresponded to that preceding the depreciation of the Polish mark.

(2) That s. 43 of the Decree of 1924 was intended only to make retorsion possible.

(3) That, since the issue of that Decree, a change had come about owing to the fact of negotiations between Poland and Czechoslovakia which could not fail to influence the interpretation of s. 47, these negotiations having resulted in the signing of the Treaty of 23 April, 1925, as well as in the publication in Poland of the statute authorising the ratification of that Treaty, it being generally known that the Treaty was under discussion in the Czechoslovak Parliament and would doubtless soon be ratified, especially since exchange of ratifications had already taken place as to a number of conventions negotiated between the two countries at the same time, one of these conventions guaranteeing to the citizens of each party equal treatment with the citizens of the other party in civil cases.

(4) That, consequently, " although it must be admitted that " the convention now in question had not as a matter of fact " been put into force because exchange of ratifications had not

" taken place, it would . . . be contrary to the principles of
" equity if at the present stage a Czechoslovak citizen were
" denied the right of taking advantage of the stipulations of
" valorisation decrees and if the stipulations of which retorsion
" was the object were applied to him. . . ."

On appeal to the Supreme Court,

Held: (1) That the Court of Appeal was right in deciding that in view of the statute of 30 July, 1925, which authorised the Government to ratify the Treaty, " it would not be in accord-" ance with the principles of equity if a Czechoslovak, in the " period during which only the exchange of ratifications is " being awaited, were denied the advantage of the valorisation " stipulations under the rules of the Convention," and were thus compelled to accept a sum of 153 zloty for a debt worth about 80,000 zloty.

(2) That the appeal was unjustified since the Treaty had in the meantime been ratified and put into effect as of 29 April, 1926.

(3) That since the Treaty is in character one falling under public law, its stipulations are retroactive in effect and should be applied to all actions which are not yet determined.[1] [Report: P.P.A., 1927, pp. 295-296.]

[1] See also *Bank Gospodarstwa Krajowego* (*State Development Bank*) v. *Czyzewicz*, decided by the Supreme Court of Poland, Third Division, on 20 June, 1928.

In this case the defendant, having appealed unsuccessfully to the Court of Appeal of Lwów, now appealed to the Supreme Court, claiming, *inter alia*, that the Peace Treaty of St. Germain could not be regarded as the peace treaty which was to have been concluded at the termination of the war by the Austro-Hungarian Monarchy and from the conclusion of which a term of years was to have elapsed before the debt fell due. He also pleaded that the term to elapse after the conclusion of the peace must be counted not from the day of the signature of the treaty but from that of the ratification, and, in particular, of the ratification by Poland (which, under a law of 1924, took place in that year).

It was held that the appeal must be dismissed on the following grounds:

1. That the Peace Treaty of St. Germain of 10 September, 1919, recognises the Austrian Republic to be the successor of the former Austro-Hungarian Monarchy, taking over the rights and duties of that Monarchy, and, more particularly, those of the so-called Austrian part of the Monarchy: " this is established by the Preamble of the Treaty and by stipulations con-" tained in a number of Articles such as Articles 36, 86, 203, 208, 209 and others; " that, therefore, that Treaty is the one referred to in the bond as actually " concluding the war in the territory of the former Austro-Hungarian Mon-" archy, excepting the lands of the Hungarian Crown."

2. That this conclusion was not weakened by the fact that the Peace Treaty was concluded in conditions and circumstances other than those which may have been anticipated at the moment of the conclusion of the loan agreement, and that there was no foundation for the supposition, which, moreover, was not in harmony with the text of the bond, that the Monarchy had

Case No. 274 *contd.*

NOTE.—The "principles of equity" referred to in the judgments of the two higher courts are, clearly, not principles of equity in the technical English sense, but those of what has been described as "natural "justice" so far as the subject's interests go, and of "good faith" in the field of the rules of international law concerning treaties. These two judgments furnish, indeed, a most important example of the correct way of answering the much-discussed question "*ex tunc* or *ex nunc*?" with regard to the effect of treaties, the answer depending in each case on the circumstances of the case, according to the principle of good faith. For the whole problem, see Oppenheim, *International Law*, vol I (4th ed., 1928), § 518; Moore, *Digest*, vol. V, 762. The Permanent Court of International Justice recognised the applicability of the principle of good faith in this question in its Judgment No. 7 (Case concerning certain German interests in Polish Upper Silesia), p. 30.

Case No. 275

Treaties—Coming into Force in Municipal Law—Relevance of Exchange of Ratification.

KUHELJ *v.* GROM.

Italian Court of Cassation. 25 *May*, 1927.

THE FACTS.—On 17 December, 1925, a judgment by consent was given by the district judge of Lubiana (Yugoslavia) between Carlo Kuhelj and Francesco Grom. An action for the execution of the judgment having been brought before the Court of Appeal at Trieste, the defendant lodged an objection to the jurisdiction of that Court on the ground that according to Article 4 of the Convention between Italy and Yugoslavia signed at Rome on 6 April, 1922, and promulgated in Italy by a Royal Decree of 13 December, 1923, jurisdiction in the matter of enforcing rights pertaining to foreign land belonged to the civil tribunal of the place stipulated for their execution. The defendant maintained that the Convention did not apply on the ground that it had not

stipulated repayment of the loan only in case it suffered no loss of territory in the war;

3. That, in the circumstances, the lapse of time should be counted as from the year of the signature of the Treaty and not from that of its subsequent confirmation by the legislative body;

4. That, even should the later contention be admitted, the date of ratification would be that of that by the Austrian Republic, being the State which stepped into the place of the former Austro-Hungarian Monarchy. [Report: P.P.A., 1928, pp. 497, 498.]

The Supreme Court uses a misleading expression in speaking of ratification as "subsequent confirmation by the legislative body." Ratification is an act of the President of the Republic, though it requires, in certain cases, the previous assent of the House of Deputies or of the whole legislature. (See Note to Case No. 9 (*Polish*) *State Treasury* v. *Wlodzimierz* (*City of*).)

yet acquired legal force, since the exchange of ratifications had not so far taken place. The Court of Appeal at Trieste upheld this objection.

Held : That Italian courts had jurisdiction, and that the decision of the Court of Appeal of Trieste must be quashed. By the Royal Decree of 13 December, 1923, the Convention had been given full and absolute executive effects. Accordingly, it acquired full and absolute legal effects within the Kingdom quite independently of the fact whether or not the exchange of the ratifications had taken place. The exchange of ratifications is an act of an international character unknown to the internal laws, which do not provide for it or make its publication necessary. As the exchange of ratifications is an act of which neither a private person nor a judge is bound to know, it cannot constitute an objective element in considering the question as to the coming into force of the Convention. The judge would, otherwise, be compelled, in order to establish the coming into force of a law, to consult sources outside the objective sources of the law. The Decree which gives the Convention its legal force is unconditional and does not mention any reservation with regard to the exchange of ratifications. It is, therefore, binding on the judge. It would be contrary to common sense to connect the application of a provision of the law duly published with a future and uncertain event the knowledge of which cannot be acquired from that law and which is not binding either on the citizens or the judge. [Reports : *Foro delle nuove provincie*, 1928, pp. 120-122 ; *Rivista di diritto internazionale*, 1929, pp. 412 ff., with a critical note by T. Perassi.]

NOTE.—This decision, which lays down the rule that international conventions come into force by virtue of a law giving them full executive effects, but quite independently of the exchange of ratifications, constitutes a departure. In previous judgments the Court of Cassation had applied the opposite principle. In the judgment of 11 February, 1925 (see *Annual Digest*, 1925-1926, Case No. 256), the Court held that the rules derived from the Treaty of St. Germain relative to the conferring of Italian nationality upon the inhabitants of the territory annexed by Italy came into force at the date of ratification of the Treaty (16 July, 1920), though the Treaty had been given executive effects by a Royal Decree (*decreto-legge*) of 6 October, 1919. See also the Penal Court of Cassation, which held by judgment of 17 September, 1926 (see *Procedura penale italiana*, 1927, p. 318), that the convention between Italy and Austria for the extradition of offenders, signed at Rome on 6 April, 1922, was not yet applicable as the exchange of ratifications had not yet taken place, though it had already acquired executive effects by the Royal Decree of 13 November, 1923.

Case No. 276 **Powers of Ceding State to Dispose of Property in the Period between the Signature of the Treaty and its Entrance into Force.**

RENTENGUTSVERTRAG (DANZIG) CASE.

High Court (Obergericht) of Danzig. 7 March, 1928.

THE FACTS.—The plaintiff had been the lessee of landed property in former West Prussia, now forming part of Poland. The property in question was held by him before the war on the basis of a *Rentengutsvertrag* (a kind of lease), the Prussian State being the owner and the lessor of the property.[1] In August, 1919, the Prussian State ceded to the defendant, an agrarian bank, its residuary rights to this and other properties similarly held. The plaintiff thereupon purchased from the defendant bank the full, that is, the reversionary, right of property in the land. In December he was registered as the owner of the property. Subsequently, by virtue of certain legislation passed by Poland and refusing to recognise transfers of property effected by Germany after the armistice, the plaintiff's name was expunged from the registry[2] and the Polish Treasury substituted for it.

The plaintiff now claims from the defendant bank the return of the sums paid to it on the ground, *inter alia*, that, in view of the Armistice Agreement of 11 November, 1918, of the Spa Protocol of 1 December, 1918, and of the signature of the Treaty of Versailles on 28 June, 1919, Germany had no right to dispose of the *Rentengut*; that the alienation of the property, as being contrary to these agreements, was null and void; that it was effected with the intention to deprive the Polish State of its rights as the successor of Germany; that the defendant bank was aware that Poland would not recognise the transaction; and that it withheld fraudulently—or at least negligently—this fact from the plaintiff.

Held: That the action must be dismissed. In its Sixth

[1] The meaning of *Rentengutsverträge* is discussed in detail in the Sixth Advisory Opinion of the Permanent Court of International Justice, Series B, No. 6, pp. 29-34.

[2] It is not clear whether the effect of this act was that the plaintiff lost everything or that he merely reverted to the position of a leaseholder.

Advisory Opinion of 10 September, 1923, and its Seventh Judgment of 25 May, 1926, the Permanent Court of International Justice adopted the view that the international agreements in question did not prevent Germany from disposing, between the armistice and the ratification of the Treaty, of her fiscal property "in the course of the normal "administration of the country." The present Court fully adopted that view. There was no evidence to show that the alienation of the property in which the plaintiff had an interest was outside the normal course of fiscal administration. [Reports: *Danziger Juristische Monatschrift*, 1928, p. 108; *Z. für ö. R. und V.*, I (2) (1929), p. 175.]

NOTE.—See Permanent Court of International Justice, Judgment No. 7, *Annual Digest*, 1925-1926, Case No. 79.

Ratification—Exchange of Ratifications—Relevance in the Sphere of Municipal Law.

See Case No. 275 (*Kuhelj* v. *Grom*).

Preliminary Occupation under Armistice Agreement—Sovereignty over Ceded Territory in the Period between the Armistice Agreement and the Entry into Force of the Treaty.

See Case No. 374 (*A. Kemeny* v. *Yugoslav State*).

IX.—Operation and Enforcement of Treaties. Necessity of Municipal Legislation

[See also Part I, INTERNATIONAL LAW IN GENERAL: IV. *Relation to Municipal Law*; and Part VI, THE INDIVIDUAL IN INTERNATIONAL LAW: (*A*) *General*, Cases Nos. 187, 188.]

Treaties—Operation of—Private Rights under Treaty—Renunciation of Rights prior to the Conclusion of the Treaty. **Case No. 277**

LA HOUVE *v.* GERMANY.

Franco-German Mixed Arbitral Tribunal.
30 *November*, 1927.

(ASSER, GANDOLPHE, FROELICH.)

THE FACTS.—This was a claim arising out of certain requisitions made by the German Government in 1917.

Case No. 277 *contd*

It was pointed out by Germany that the claim could not be entertained, on the ground, *inter alia*, that on 23 August, 1917, the claimant company signed an agreement with German authorities in which it renounced all claims to indemnity on the ground of requisitions.

Held: That the renunciation of the right to an indemnity at a time prior to the entry of the Treaty into force could not deprive the claimant of the right to compensation. That right was established by the Treaty, and as such it did not exist at the time of the waiver. [Report; *Recueil*, VIII, p. 100.)

NOTE.—*Marqua* v. *Germany, Recueil*, I, p. 104, followed.

Case No. 278

Treaties—Relation to Municipal Law—Provisions of German Law Inconsistent with the Treaty of Versailles.

HOWSE MEAD AND SONS LTD. *v.* MAX MOSESMANN.

Anglo-German Mixed Arbitral Tribunal. 1 *March*, 1928.

(HEECKEREN, HART, JOHANNES.)

See the above case for a statement by the Tribunal that any provision of the law prevailing in the country of any party to the Treaty of Versailles which proceeds upon a ground inconsistent with the dissolution of the contract as laid down in Article 299 (*a*) of the Treaty is overridden by the Treaty. The statement was made in answer to the contention of the German Government that an agreement of compromise concluded before the war between the claimants and defendants was still valid by virtue of sections 169 and 674 of the German Civil Code. [Report: *Recueil*, VIII, p. 6.]

Case No. 279

Treaties—Operation and Enforcement of—Transformation into Municipal Law—Implied Transformation into Municipal Law of Subsequent Agreements Made by virtue of the Treaty—The London Protocol of 1924 and the Coblenz Agreement of 1925.

LONDON PROTOCOL (COBLENZ AGREEMENT) CASE.

German Reichsgericht. 17 *May*, 1927.

THE FACTS.—In paragraph 6 of the London Final Protocol of 16 August, 1924, which regulated in a general manner, *inter alia*, certain matters arising out of the occupation of the Ruhr in 1923, it was laid down that the regulation of specific points and questions as to the technical execution of the Protocol should be reserved for future negotiations and agreements. In pursuance of that paragraph an agreement was arrived at on 10 February, 1925, in Coblenz, to the effect, *inter alia*, that property confiscated before 31 August, 1924, or sums paid before 21 October, 1924, as customs dues in respect of such property returned to the owners, shall be regarded as having definitely passed into the ownership of the respective Allied authorities. By a German Law of 30 August, 1924, the London Protocol was incorporated into German municipal law.

In November, 1923, the plaintiff handed over to the defendant certain goods to be forwarded from the Ruhr to Glasgow. The goods were then confiscated at the frontier by the Belgian authorities on the ground that they were not accompanied by an export licence. The defendant subsequently bought these goods back from the Belgian authorities. The plaintiff contended before the Court that, as the confiscation of the goods by the Belgian authorities was illegal, he never lost the title in them, and asked that the defendant should hand over the goods to him without payment.

Held: That the claim must be rejected. Although the confiscation was originally illegal, it had become validated by the Coblenz Agreement. It was true that that Agreement had never been expressly incorporated into German law. However, the London Protocol which referred to future agreements calculated to put it into effect was part of German law, and the agreements concluded in execution of it must therefore equally be regarded as forming part of German law. Accordingly, the plaintiff must be regarded as having lost his title in the goods. [Report: *Z. für a. ö. R. und V.*, I (2) (1929), p. 190.]

NOTE.—See also *ibid.*, p. 192, for the decision of the *Reichsgericht* of 29 November, 1927, which also deals with the question of the Final Protocol of the London Conference of 1924 as forming part of German municipal law.

Case No. 280

Treaties—Enforcement and Operation of—Necessity of Municipal Legislation—Self-Executing Provisions—Direct Conferment of Rights upon the Subjects of the State Undertaking an Obligation—Article 365 of the Treaty of Versailles.

GERMAN RAILWAYS (MOST-FAVOURED TREATMENT) CASE.

German Reichsgericht. 29 *March,* 1928.

THE FACTS.—Article 365 of the Treaty of Versailles provided as follows:

"Goods coming from the teıritories of the "Allied and Associated Powers, and going to "Germany, or in transit through Germany from or "to the territories of the Allied and Associated "Powers, shall enjoy on the German railways as "regards charges to be collected (rebates and draw-"backs being taken into account), facilities and all "other matters, the most favourable treatment "applied to goods of the same kind carried on any "German lines, either in internal traffic, or for "export, import or in transit, under similar con-"ditions of transport, for example as regards length "of route. The same rule shall be applied, on the "request of one or more of the Allied and Associated "Powers, to goods specially designated by such "Power or Powers coming from Germany and going "to their territories. . . ."

The present action was brought by a German subject against the German Federal Railways Company. In his capacity as the assignee of the sender he asked for the refund of part of the freight paid for the transport, in May, 1924, of a number of cattle from Denmark through Germany to Czechoslovakia. The freight paid was the ordinary freight charged by the Company. However, at that time the Company announced a reduced freight, from 15 February to 31 May, for cattle to be used in Germany. The plaintiff contended before the Court that according to Article 365 of the Treaty of Versailles goods in transit to Czechoslovakia were entitled to an equally favourable treatment. The Court dismissed the action. On appeal,

Held: That the plaintiff acquired a direct right under

Article 365 of the Treaty of Versailles to most-favoured treatment. The Treaty of Versailles has become part of German municipal law, and its provisions may be invoked by every one in so far as, having regard to their content, purpose and wording, they are calculated to have effect in the sphere of private law without the necessity of further measures in the sphere of international or public law. This is the case in regard to Article 365, in particular in view of the fact that that Article contains the expression "*de plein droit*" [1] (*von Rechtswegen*).

The economic purpose of this Article was to secure the most favourable treatment possible not only for individual subjects of the former enemy countries, but also for their territories conceived as an economic unit. This meant that it could be invoked not only by the subjects of those States, but also by German subjects. [Reports: *Entscheidungen des Reichsgerichts in Zivilsachen*, vol. 117, p. 284; *Z. für a. ö. R. und V.*, II (2) (1930), p. 81.]

NOTE.—(*a*) The appeal was, however, dismissed on the ground that the cattle were not in fact transit goods covered by Article 365 of the Treaty. The Court found that the cattle were conveyed in the first instance to Flensburg-Weiche in Germany, that there was no "through" freight contract, and that the sender was in a position to dispose of the cattle in Germany had he so wished.

(*b*) It will be noted that the opinion of the Court was partly based on the expression "*von Rechtswegen*," which is a translation of the words "*de plein droit*" in the French text of the Treaty. The English text contains no reference at all to any automatic effect to be given to Article 365. See on the subject of the translation of "*de plein droit*" as "*von Rechtswegen*," Bruns in *Z. für a. ö. R. und V.*, II (2) (1930), p. 83, who doubts the correctness of the German translation and draws attention to the fact that only the French and English texts are authoritative. He suggests that "*de plein droit*" means "*ipso facto*" or "*ipso jure*," *i.e.* that no further *international* act is necessary, whereas "*von Rechtswegen*" may convey that no further municipal act is necessary. He denies the latter alternative. However, as mentioned, in the English text the equivalent of the words "*de plein droit*" does not appear at all.

(*c*) See Bruns, *ibid.*, p. 84, who criticises the opinion on the ground that even if the Treaty intended to confer rights directly upon individuals—which in his opinion is doubtful—it could only refer to rights of foreign subjects against Germany, but it could in no case be interpreted as conferring upon German subjects rights against their own State.

(*d*) Contrast this case with Case No. 281.

---

[1] In the French text of the Treaty the words "shall enjoy" appear as "*bénéficient de plein droit.*"

Case No. 281 **Treaties—Enforcement and Operation of—How far Conferring upon Individuals Direct Right of Action—Self-Executory Provisions—Liquidation of Property of German Subjects in France—Germany's Obligation to Compensate.**

LIQUIDATION OF GERMAN PROPERTY (TREATY OF VERSAILLES) CASE.

German Reichsgericht. 29 *March*, 1928.

THE FACTS.—This was a claim by a German national against the German State. He resided before and during the war in Colmar, in Alsace-Lorraine. He left the country before it was occupied by French troops and settled in Germany. His property in Alsace-Lorraine was then liquidated by the French authorities. He received from Germany only a fraction of that sum. He put forward a claim for the balance, and based his claim, *inter alia*, on Articles 74 and 297 of the Treaty of Versailles.

Article 74 of that Treaty provided that the French Government reserves the right to retain and liquidate all the property, rights and interests which German nationals or societies controlled by Germans possessed in certain territories ceded to France, and that Germany will directly compensate her nationals who may have been dispossessed by these liquidations.

In Article 297 (*i*) of the Treaty Germany undertook to compensate her nationals in respect of the sale of their rights or interests in Allied or Associated States.

Held: That the claim must be dismissed.

The persons affected by measures of liquidation do not derive from Articles 74 and 297 (*i*) of the Treaty of Versailles any direct rights against the *Reich*. The Treaty of Versailles is an international treaty and creates in the first instance rights and duties only between the contracting parties. It is true that by the Federal Law of 16 July, 1919, the Treaty of Versailles acquired the force of a municipal law. However, the individual can derive rights from it only in so far as, having regard to the nature and object of the provision in question, it is clear beyond doubt that it is self-executory, namely, that it has a direct effect in the sphere of private law without the necessity of further international or municipal regulation.[1]

[1] See Case No. 280.

Instances of such provisions are Articles 299 and 300 (relating to private contracts between enemies), and 365 of the Treaty of Versailles. But Articles 74 (2) and 297 (*i*) do not have direct effect in the sphere of private law. They constitute a general agreement between France and Germany to the effect that the latter shall compensate her own subjects. They do not say what is to be the form and the amount of the compensation. It was a matter of indifference to the Allied Powers in what manner Germany fulfilled that obligation.[1] Accordingly, the Articles in question bound only the contracting parties; they did not confer upon individuals any direct rights against Germany.

The Court also rejected the view that the Articles in question constituted a *pactum in favorem tertii* for the benefit of the individuals affected by measures of liquidation.[2] [Reports: *Entscheidungen des Reichsgerichts in Zivilsachen*, vol. 121, p. 7; *Z. für a. ö. R. und V.*, II (1930), p. 84.]

Treaties—Relation to Municipal Law—Operation and Enforcement—Possible Conflict with Municipal Legislative Acts—Competence of Municipal Tribunals. **Case No. 282**

VATERLÄNDISCHER FRAUENVEREIN IN ODOLANÓW *v.* EVANGELICAL PARISH IN ODOLANÓW.

Supreme Court of Poland, Fifth Division. 28 *October*, 1927.

THE FACTS.—Before the restoration of Poland, Odolanów was situated in the Prussian part of Poland. The plaintiff was an official institution there. In 1908 the plaintiff lent to the defendant 10,000 German marks and obtained the right of perpetual user of certain land belonging to defendant, for the purpose of establishing there a German Evangelical children's home. The loan was to be repaid immediately, should the defendants withdraw the user of the land, or sell, lease or otherwise dispose of the land without the permission of the chief administrative official of the district (*Regierungspräsident*). The agreement was duly approved by the Royal Consistory and the chief administrative official of the

[1] The Court referred here to the French Note to Germany of 26 July, 1922, in which France intimated that Germany might postpone or slow up the execution of Article 297 (*i*) for so long as she may deem fit.

[2] The Court referred here, among others, to Schücking in *Z.V.*, IX (1920), p. 548, as supporting the theory of *pactum in favorem tertii*, and to Isay, *Die privaten Rechte und Interessen im Friedensvertrage*, 3rd ed., § 33.

Case No. 282 *contd.*

province (*Oberpräsident*), and was entered in the land registry. After the armistice of 11 November, 1918, it being clear that Odolanów would return to Poland, the defendant obtained the striking of the mortgage off the land registry. A Polish statute of 14 July, 1920, provides, however, that where since 11 November, 1918, real estate rights (incorporeal hereditaments) entered in the land registry in favour, *inter alia*, of institutions of the German *Reich* or of the States have, at the request or with the consent of such institutions, been alienated, or struck off, or have undergone any change, the courts will restore the entries in the land registry to the state in which they would have been had such institutions not made the request or granted the consent in question. Thereupon the entry in favour of the plaintiff was restored. The plaintiff brought the present action to recover from the defendant the user of the land. Defendant pleaded, *inter alia*, that plaintiff was now a Polish institution, whereas the original grant had been made in favour of a German institution. The first and second courts decided for the plaintiff; the Supreme Court, while holding that the legal personality of plaintiff had undergone a change, quashed the judgment of the Court of Appeal at Poznan and directed it to establish certain additional facts. The latter Court again gave judgment for the plaintiff, and defendant appealed to the Supreme Court, on the ground, *inter alia*, that the restitution of the entry under the Law of 14 July, 1920, was inadmissible, that Law being, in the opinion of the defendant, inconsistent with the so-called Minorities Treaty of 28 June, 1919.

Held: Dismissing the appeal, that under Article 81 of the Constitution the Courts have no right to enquire into the validity of a statute: "in particular, a court has no power to destroy "the binding force of a statute on the ground of its alleged "inconsistency with an international treaty: for such inconsistency would only oblige the State, in the international field, "to withdraw such statute, but it would never authorise "courts to refuse to apply such a statute, because of its possible inconsistency with an international obligation contracted by the State."[1] [Report: O.S.P., VII, No. 22.]

[1] See also *Polski Bank Przemyslowy we Lwowie (Polish Industrial Bank in*

Treaties—In General—Relation to Municipal Law—Interpretation by Courts—Respective Positions of Courts and Parliaments—Conformity with Municipal Law. **Case No. 283**

COLOMBIAN MINING & EXPLORATION CO. LTD. CASE.

Supreme Court of Colombia. 16 *December*, 1926.

THE FACTS.—This was a petition to declare Law No. 38, of 1926, unconstitutional.

Held: That, although the Law approving a public treaty is subject, as to its enactment, to the ordinary requirements

Lwów) v. (*Polish*) *Ministry of Finance*, decided by the Polish Supreme Administrative Court on 30 April, 1928.

The facts of this case were as follows: In 1924, Poland concluded with Danzig an agreement to prevent double taxation, notably in the field of direct taxes. The agreement was published in the official Journal of the Polish Ministry of Finance (but not in the Journal of Laws) and in the Journal of Laws for the Free City of Danzig. As between the two contracting parties the agreement went into effect on 19 July, 1925.

The plaintiff, a bank domiciled since its foundation in Poland, but having a branch office in Danzig, was assessed in Poland with capital levy in respect, *inter alia*, of its property situated in Danzig in connection with the Danzig branch. It claimed exemption on the basis of the Polish-Danzig agreement and brought the present action.

Under a Polish law of 1919 there must be published in the Journal of Laws, *inter alia*, "international agreements ratified by the Diet," and "declarations of the Government which, under the prevailing rules, should be "published in the Journal of Laws." Since the creation of the Free City of Danzig in 1920 and the conclusion of the (so-called Paris) Polish-Danzig Convention of the same year (in pursuance of Article 104 of the Peace Treaty of Versailles), a Presidential decree (having the force of law by statutory authorisation) prescribed that there shall be published in the Journal of Laws, *inter alia*, "international agreements concluded in pursuance of "Article 49 of the Constitution as well as agreements of the Republic of the "Free City of Danzig approved by the Legislature or concluded by legislative "authorisation."

It was held (1) That the plaintiff, being a corporation domiciled in Poland, is subject exclusively to Polish law;

(2) That, the assessment being in accordance with the law concerning the capital levy, the plaintiff could not claim exemption from the law on the basis of a Polish-Danzig agreement which had not yet been published in the Polish Journal of Laws. [Report: Zb. W.N.T.A. (1928), No. 1446.]

And see the case *Dębiccy* (*The Dębicki Family*) v. (*Polish*) *Treasury*, decided by the Supreme Court of Poland, Third Division, on 4 October, 1927.

In this case the appellants contended before the Supreme Court that the Court of Appeal (*i.e.* the Court appealed from) ought, if it had doubts as to the existence of a treaty pleaded by the appellants and alleged by them to have deprived the Austrian Government of the right to recover loans granted in 1914-1918 in connection with war losses, to have addressed itself *ex officio* to the Ministry of Foreign Affairs in order to obtain information on the subject. It was held that it would have been inadmissible for a court to enquire whether there exists some vaguely described treaty referred to by the appellants, and that it would have been inadmissible to address an enquiry to that effect to the Ministry of Foreign Affairs, since the treaties in force must, under Polish law, be published in the Journal of Laws. [Report: P.P.A., 1929, pp. 85, 86.]

Case No. 283 *contd.*

which precede the issuing of common legislative acts, it cannot be declared null and void on account of a doubt whether or not in other aspects it differs substantially from the ordinary Laws. The latter are unilateral acts, the expression of the will of the sovereign which commands, prohibits or permits, and which is complied with only by the requirement of his sanction and promulgation. The former is part of a complex juridical act ; it is the form in which one of the High Contracting Parties manifests its consent to the stipulations of an international synallagmatic compact ; it does not establish of itself legal relations, and its efficacy depends on the consent of the other contracting nation, if the latter on its part ratifies the provisions agreed to by its negotiators. The Law which approves a public contract has, therefore, a special character. " The " part played by Parliament in the matter of treaties," says the eminent French professor, Mérignhac, " does not resemble " the part it plays in legislative matters."

Notwithstanding that, as has been said before, the Law becomes a necessary element in the treaty, the compact cannot, on that account, logically be confused with the Law that approves it. The former contains the reciprocal stipulations of the parties, the obligations undertaken by each and the rights acquired, and it does not attain juridical life until the supreme contracting powers have ratified it, and the ratifications have been exchanged. The latter, that is, the Law, is only the act in virtue of which one of the two negotiating States accepts the stipulations agreed upon, when, according to its institutions, the intervention of the legislative power is required for the adoption of public treaties.

As the bases of the suit initiated in this Court all tend to show that there is a conflict between some of the clauses of the Treaty of 6 April and various provisions of our Constitution, it is evident that the matter subjected to the decision of the Court is the Treaty itself. This Court does not, according to the Constitution, possess any power to enquire whether or not the stipulations agreed upon ought to be upheld, since it is not charged with the cognisance of public treaties. [Report : 33 *Gaceta Judicial*, 66.]

Treaties—Operation and Enforcement—Self-Executing Treaties. **Case No. 284**

ROBERTSON *v.* GENERAL ELECTRIC CO.

United States District Court, D. Maryland. United States Circuit Court of Appeals, Fourth Circuit. 13 July, 1927. 9 April, 1929.

THE FACTS.—This was a suit by a German inventor and his assignee against the United States Commissioner of Patents claiming that letters patent of the United States should be issued. The application for a German patent was made on 11 October, 1915, and the German patent was issued on 20 October, 1919. The application for a United States patent was made on 10 May, 1922. The latter application was barred under United States Revised Statutes, § 4887, since it was not filed within twelve months after the application for a foreign patent, made on 11 October, 1915. It was barred under the Nolan Act of 1921 (41 U.S. Stat. L. 1313), since it was not filed within six months after March 3, 1921. It was contended by plaintiffs, however, that the Treaty of Berlin between Germany and the United States (42 U.S. Stat. L. 1939) extended the time for filing a German patent in the United States for six months after 11 November, 1921, the date the Treaty took effect. The Treaty of Berlin provided that the United States should have all rights and privileges stipulated for its benefit in the Treaty of Versailles. The Treaty of Versailles (Articles 306, 307, 308) restored the International Convention of Paris of 1883, as revised at Washington in 1911, and provided (Article 308) that rights of priority stipulated by the Convention of Paris for the filing of applications for patents, which had arisen during the war or would have arisen but for the war, should be " extended . . . for a period of six " months after the coming into force of the present " treaty." On motion to dismiss the bill of complaint,

Held: That the motion should be denied. The matter of patents is within the scope of the treaty-making power in the United States. The Treaty of Berlin was self-executing. Affirmed, upon final hearing, in 25 F. (2nd) 146. On appeal,

Held by the Circuit Court of Appeals: That the judgment

Case No. 284 *contd.*

of the District Court should be reversed. The Treaty of Berlin is not to be construed as providing that " the priority rights of " German and American inventors should be again extended for " a six months' period, in view of the fact that their rights had " already been protected in accordance with the provisions of " Section 308 of the Versailles Treaty by the Nolan Act and " the reciprocal decree of Germany." (32 F. (2nd) 495, 498.)

Delivering the opinion of the Court, Judge Parker said: " We think that Section 308 of the Treaty of Versailles is one of " those which had accomplished its purpose and become obso- " lete at the time of the negotiation of the Treaty of Berlin, and " that, therefore, it is not to be construed as imposing additional " obligations or conferring additional rights upon either the " United States or Germany because of that Treaty." (32 F. (2nd) 495, 498.)

Even if the Treaty of Berlin were construed as plaintiffs contended, Article 308 of the Treaty of Versailles was not self-executing. While a treaty affecting patent rights may be so drawn as to be self-executing, Article 308 could not reasonably be so construed. The fact that the *Reichsgericht* had arrived at a similar conclusion (114 *Entscheidungen des Reichsgerichts in Zivilsachen*, 252) was " highly persuasive." [Reports: 21 F. (2nd) 214; 25 F. (2nd) 146; 32 F. (2nd) 495.]

Case No. 285

Treaties—Operation of—Effect on Private Individuals.

S. PAPADOPOULOS, OF PÉRA (CONSTANTINOPLE) (appellant) *v.* (1) N. V. KONINKLIJKE NEDERLANDSCHE STOOMBOOT-MAATSCHAPPIJ, OF AMSTERDAM (respondent); (2) J. W. WHITTAL AND CO. LTD., OF CONSTANTINOPLE (interveners).

Court of Appeal, Amsterdam. 13 *March*, 1928.

(Appeal from judgment of District Court of Amsterdam, 17 April, 1925: for which see *Annual Digest*, 1925-1926, Case No. 19.)

THE FACTS.—(See *Annual Digest*, 1925-1926, Case No. 19, pp. 27 and 28). The respondents invoked Article 137 [1]

[1] Article 137 provides as follows:

" Subject to any agreements concluded between the High Contracting " Parties, the decisions taken and orders issued since the 30th October, 1918, " until the coming into force of the present Treaty, by or in agreement with " the authorities of the Powers who have occupied Constantinople, and con- " cerning the property, rights and interests of their nationals, of foreigners " or of Turkish nationals, and the relations of such persons with the authori- " ties of Turkey, shall be regarded as definitive and shall give rise to no claim " against these Powers or their authorities.

" All other claims arising from injury suffered in consequence of any such " decisions or orders shall be submitted to the Mixed Arbitral Tribunal."

of the Treaty of Lausanne in order to contend that the appellant was precluded by that Article from attacking in the Dutch courts the legality of certain measures taken by the G.O.C. of the Allied troops at Constantinople.

Held, dismissing the appeal: That the Treaty of Lausanne not only binds the Governments of the contracting States in the exercise of their sovereign rights, but also directly concerns the rights and interests of their subjects, so that the Treaty forms part of the law of the States concerned; that Article 137 of the Treaty obviously tends to accept the decisions and orders of the occupying Powers as definitively clothed with legal effect, and that, therefore, the subjects of the contracting States are equally bound to respect the legal situation thus created. [Reports: *Weekblad van het Recht*, 31 May, 1928, No. 11816.]

Treaties—Rights of Individuals under.

See Case No. 363 (*McCandless* v. *United States*).

Treaties—Enforcement and Operation of—Change of Treaty Provision in Consequence of New Treaties.

See Case No. 8 and on p. 445, n. 1 (*Hardt* v. *Governor of Poznan*).

Treaties—Operation and Enforcement of—Retroactive Effect of Treaties Bearing upon Public Law.

See Case No. 274 (*Schrager* v. *Workmen's Accident Insurance Institute for Moravia and Silesia*).

Treaties—Operation of—Whether Conferring Rights Directly upon Individuals.

See Case No. 36 (*E. L. Wirbelauer, of Paris*, v. *de Handelsvennootschap onder de firma Lippmann Rosenthal en Co., of Amsterdam*).

Treaties—Operation of—Whether Conferring Rights Directly upon Individuals.

See Case No. 187 (*Jurisdiction of the Courts of Danzig*).

Treaties—Operation and Enforcement of—Interpretation by Courts.

See Case No. 266 (*Princess Zizianoff* v. *Kahn and Bigelow*).

Effects of Treaties of Peace—Treaty of Versailles, Article 257 —Transfer of Private Property of German Emperor and "Other Royal Personages"—Trust Property Administered by German Emperor in Trust as Head of Royal Family.

See Case No. 16 (*Das Königlich Preussisch-Brandenburgische Hausfideikommiss* v. *The Administration of South-West Africa and the Registrar of Deeds*).

X.—Effect of Treaties on Third Parties

Case No. 286

PERMANENT COURT OF INTERNATIONAL JUSTICE.

JUDGMENT No. 13.

Treaties—Effect upon Third Parties—Poland and the Armistice Convention of 1918.

GERMANY *v.* POLAND.

CASE CONCERNING THE FACTORY AT CHORZÓW.

(CLAIM FOR INDEMNITY. MERITS.)

13 *September*, 1928.

THE FACTS.—(See Case No. 177.) In this case Poland (in the alternative) asked the Permanent Court provisionally to suspend its decision on the claim for indemnity for the damage sustained by the company in question. As one of the reasons of this request Poland relied on the Armistice Convention of November, 1918, and on Article 248 of the Treaty of Versailles. The latter provided that,

"Subject to such exceptions as the Reparation Commission may approve, a first charge upon all the assets and revenues of the German Empire and its constituent States shall be the cost of reparation and all other costs arising under the present Treaty or any treaties or agreements supplementary thereto or under arrangements concluded between Germany and the Allied and Associated Powers during the armistice or its extensions . . ."

Poland admitted that in Judgment No. 7, the Court had held that Poland, not being a party to the Armistice Convention, was not entitled to avail herself of that instrument, nor, for other reasons, of the above-quoted Article of the Treaty of Versailles, in order to establish the invalidity of certain transactions concerning the factories in question.[1] In the present case, however, Poland contended that a suspension of the decision of the Court was justified as the Armistice Convention gave the parties to it the right to oppose the sale of the factory, and also as the Reparation Commission, in particular in view of the right reserved to it under Article 248, had the right to ensure the discharge of the reparation debt, and that, therefore, Poland's obligation to pay to Germany an indemnity in regard to the factories in question was dependent on the previous approval of these States and of the Reparation Commission.

Held: That the request for suspension of the Court's decision must be rejected. Poland invoked the Armistice Convention in order to reserve the possibility of having the sale of the factory declared invalid by means of an action brought for that purpose by the signatories. "As, however, the Court, in Judg-"ment No. 7, has held that Poland cannot avail itself "of the provisions of the said Convention to which she "is not a party, the Court cannot without incon-"sistency admit that country's right to invoke the "Convention in order to delay making reparation for "the damage resulting from her adoption of an attitude "not in conformity with her obligations under the Geneva Convention" (at p. 45). Neither can Poland rely on her own account on the provision of Article 248 of the Treaty of Versailles. [Report: Series A, No. 17, pp. 43-46.[2]]

[1] See *Annual Digest*, 1925-1926, Case No. 46.
[2] See also Series E, No. 5, pp. 183-195.

Case No. 287

Effect of Treaties upon Third Parties—*Pacta tertiis nec nocent nec prosunt*—Rights Conferred upon Subjects of a State not Party to a Treaty.

STEINER AND GROSS *v.* POLISH STATE.

Upper Silesian Arbitral Tribunal. 30 *March*, 1928.

THE FACTS.—(See Case No. 188.) One of the claimants being a Czechoslovak subject, Poland contended that the Tribunal had no jurisdiction. She contended that the expression "*l'ayant droit*" used in the Treaty and referring to claimants before the Arbitral Tribunal could not be interpreted as including a Czechoslovak seeing that Czechoslovakia was not a party to the Convention; that such an interpretation would be prejudicial to Czechoslovakia seeing that it would compel its subjects to appear before a tribunal in the creation and composition of which it did not participate; and that that interpretation would be contrary to the rule of international law according to which individuals are not subjects of international law.

Held: That that contention must be rejected, and that the Tribunal had jurisdiction. There was no reason to depart from the literal interpretation of the expression "*l'ayant droit.*" It was difficult to see how such an interpretation could be prejudicial to the interests of a third State. The grant to subjects of a third State of a legal remedy can only be regarded as an advantage conferred upon that State. (The Tribunal referred also to the principles of respect of private rights and of economic unity of the country (see Case No. 188 *in fine*) as militating in favour of the interpretation adopted by it.) [Report: *Decisions of the Upper Silesian Arbitral Tribunal*, vol. I, Nos. 1/2 (in German and Polish), pp. 2-36.]

Case No. 288

Treaties—Effect upon Third Parties—Communication of a Treaty to a Third Party—Effect of Silence of Third Party—Communication to Holland of the Treaty of Paris of 1898 between the United States and Spain.

ISLAND OF PALMAS ARBITRATION CASE.

United States and Holland: Permanent Court of Arbitration. 4 *April*, 1928.

(HUBER, Arbitrator.)

THE FACTS.—(See Cases Nos. 1, 68, 70.) It was contended by the United States that as Article 3 of the

Treaty of Paris of 1898 must be considered as an affirmation of sovereignty on the part of Spain, and that as the United States communicated that Treaty to Holland and no reservations were made by the latter in respect of that part of the Treaty, Holland was precluded from questioning the sovereignty of the United States over the island.

Held: That the contention of the United States must be rejected. "The question whether the silence of a third Power, "in regard to a treaty notified to it, can exercise any influence "on the right of this Power, or on those of the Powers signa-"tories of the treaty, is a question the answer to which may "depend on the nature of such rights. Whilst it is conceivable "that a conventional delimitation duly notified to third Powers "and left without contestation on their part may have some "bearing on an inchoate title not supported by any actual "display of sovereignty, it would be entirely contrary to the "principles laid down above as to territorial sovereignty to "suppose that such sovereignty could be affected by the mere "silence of the territorial sovereign as regards a treaty which "has been notified to him and which seems to dispose of a part "of his territory." [Reports: *Permanent Court of Arbitration, Arbitral Award rendered in conformity with the Special Agreement concluded on 23 January, 1925, between the United States of America and the Netherlands*, p. 23; *A.J.*, XXII (1928), p. 880.]

Treaties—Effect on Third Parties—Termination as the Result of War—Rights of Indian Nations under the Jay Treaty.

See Case No. 363 (*McCandless* v. *United States*).

Treaties—*Pacta tertiis nec nocent nec prosunt*—Effect of the Treaty of Versailles on Turkey—Extent of the Recognition of the Treaty of Versailles in the Treaty of Lausanne.

See Case No. 298 (*Eastern Bank Ltd.* v. *Turkish Government*).

Treaties—*Pacta tertiis nec nocent nec prosunt*—Effect of Article 18 on Non-Members of the League of Nations.

See Case No. 271 (*Pablo Nájera (of the Lebanon) Case*).

XI.—Termination of Treaties

i.—By Operation of Law

(c) OUTBREAK OF WAR

[See Part XI, WAR AND NEUTRALITY.]

(d) THE *CLAUSULA REBUS SIC STANTIBUS*

Case No. 289 ***Clausula rebus sic stantibus* as Applied to State Servitudes—State Servitude between Swiss Cantons.**

CANTON OF THURGAU *v.* CANTON OF ST. GALLEN.

Swiss Federal Court. 10 *February*, 1928.

THE FACTS.—In the border district between the Cantons of Thurgau and of St. Gallen, the Catholic parishes of Thurgau have ever since 1669 included a village lying within the territory of St. Gallen, namely, within the political district of Kirchberg, and a number of households, including the household of Lampertswil. On 8 October, 1868, after several disputes about the payment of dues, the Cantonal Governments of Thurgau and St. Gallen agreed that all Catholics living within these parts of St. Gallen should be treated as belonging to the parish of Rickenbach in Thurgau and should pay school and church rates according to the tax laws of that Canton. Disputes arose over the treatment of new households in these territories, and a new agreement was reached on 27 March, 1883. It was agreed that the members of new households must buy their place in the church and school system of Thurgau along with their purchase of the homestead. This provision provoked the opposition of the ecclesiastical authorities of St. Gallen, and on 14 December, 1891, two new agreements were reached, covering church and school questions respectively, to settle the rating and frontier difficulties in the parish of Rickenbach in Thurgau. The school agreement was for ten years; after that period either side was to be free to renounce upon due notice. The church agreement contained neither time limit nor a renunciation clause. In the year 1923, the authorities of St. Gallen informed those of Thurgau that the occupant of the Lampertswil homestead was seeking membership in the ecclesiastical community of Kirchberg, and that his request had been acceded to. The authorities of Thurgau refused to permit such an alteration of the terms of the agreement, and in consequence in 1925 St. Gallen denounced the church agreement. Thurgau denied the validity of this denunciation, and maintained that there were no reasons which could justify the action of St. Gallen on the ground of the *clausula rebus sic stantibus*. St. Gallen meanwhile informed Thurgau that as from 1 July, 1926, they would treat the agreement, so far as it affected Lampertswil, as non-existent.

The Canton of Thurgau thereupon brought an action against the Canton of St. Gallen on the constitutional question, and asked for a declaration that the agreement of 1891 cannot be denounced, that it cannot be varied or terminated except by agreement between the parties, and that the existing relations do not justify the transfer of Lampertswil to the jurisdiction of the Parish Council of Kirchberg and to the authorities of St. Gallen solely on the unilateral request of the occupant. St. Gallen opposed the request.

Held: The agreements of 1868, of 1883 and of 1891 did not have the effect of allotting St. Gallen territory to the ecclesiastical authorities of Thurgau for the first time. This connection dates from long before the creation of the two Cantons of Thurgau and of St. Gallen in 1803. It is only the consequences flowing from this state of the law which are governed by the agreements in question, in particular, the application to inhabitants of St. Gallen territory of the rating system in use in a district of Thurgau. It is laid down in these agreements that the inhabitants of the territory in question shall not be subjected to heavier rating burdens than are imposed upon those enjoying an equal income in the territory subject to the Thurgau authorities. The connection of Lampertswil for church purposes with the parish of Rickenbach is unaffected by the denunciation of the agreement, since the legal origin of this connection is not to be drawn from the agreement, but is there assumed and recognised as already existing.

The situation with which the Court has to deal is substantially one of a so-called international or State servitude, by virtue of which the Canton of St. Gallen is bound to refrain within some part of her territory from exercising certain powers

Case No. 289 *contd.*

of a public law character flowing from its territorial sovereignty, and, on the other hand, to permit a corresponding assumption of these powers by a public authority of Thurgau. The possibility and permissibility of such a relationship and of the partial abandonment of sovereignty which it implies, are recognised by the doctrines of international law. Accordingly, in the present case, the relations between the Cantons are to be treated precisely as those between independent States, as was said in the judgment rendered by the Federal Court on 17 February, 1882, in the case between Lucerne and Aargau.[1] Agreements between States of a legal nature which, as in the case of the creation of a servitude, contemplate an objective legal tie involving subjective rights and duties, must remain binding in the absence of a provision for renunciation contained in the original agreement or otherwise recognised as sufficient by law. The present relation between the Cantons has lasted for a long time, and was adopted from the foregoing period without alteration at the time of the creation of the two Cantons in 1803. This is an additional reason for holding that it is neither a temporary relation, nor one terminable at the will of one party. Even a change in the internal legislation, or in the constitution of the servient Canton, cannot suffice to justify the repudiation of an agreement of this type. The only question to be considered is whether St. Gallen is entitled to release herself from this agreement under the doctrine of *rebus sic stantibus* on the ground of a change in the material circumstances. "The Federal Court, in the often quoted judgment in the "case between Lucerne and Aargau, conceded the right of "denunciation on such grounds, not merely because the con-"tinuation of the servitude was incompatible with the existence "of the servient Canton as an independent State, or that it had "become meaningless, but also because there had been a change "in those circumstances which, having regard to the declared "intentions of the parties at the time the servitude was created, "must be regarded as having constituted the tacit condition "of the agreement. We may leave the question open whether "this does not in reality go a little too far—in the case then "before the Court the power of repudiation had to be "denied even from this point of view—but even if this view "were to be accepted, it is still essential that if such a change "of circumstances is to be invoked as a reason for denunciation, "the party interested must invoke it within a certain defined "interval from the moment when the change was first clearly

[1] *Entscheidungen des schweizerischen Bundesgerichts*, vol. 8 (1882), p. 57.

" perceived. But if the servient Canton nevertheless permits " the relationship to continue for decades, her conduct shows " that these changed circumstances were not present to her " mind as the tacit condition of the agreement. Hence, according to the principle of good faith which must obtain in interstate matters as elsewhere, the change cannot later on be " invoked by her in order to obtain a release from the " obligation."

In any case, the circumstances which St. Gallen now invokes as " new " are only trifling. A desire on the part of St. Gallen, and of the occupant of the land in question, to incorporate Lampertswil in Kirchberg for church purposes does not afford this Canton the right to proceed to a unilateral repudiation of an existing international obligation, to which she agreed and which she took over, at the time of her creation, from the régime previously existing in the territory.

For these reasons the Court allows the claim of Thurgau. [Report: *Entscheidungen des schweizerischen Bundesgerichts*, vol. 54, I, 188.]

Clausula rebus sic stantibus.

See Case No. 56 (*Land Tax Immunities Case, Note* (2)).

ii.—By Act of Party

(*c*) UNILATERAL DENUNCIATION. RESULT OF NON-PERFORMANCE BY THE OTHER PARTY

Treaties—Termination—Unilateral Denunciation of—Denunciation of Capitulations by Turkey.

See Case No. 126 (*Syrian Capitulations* (*Denunciation by Turkey*) *Case*).

iii.—Effect of Termination upon Acquired Rights

Treaty—Alleged Subsequent Renunciation of Treaty Rights by Delegate not Duly Authorised thereto—Effect on Liability of Individuals. **Case No. 290**

(POLISH) STATE TREASURY *v.* SKIBNIEWSKA.

Supreme Court of Poland, Third Division. 24 January, 1928.

THE FACTS.—(See Case No. 48.) The defendant pleaded, *inter alia*, that a delegate of the Polish Government had declared at a meeting of the Reparation Com-

Case No. 290 *contd.*

mission that the Polish Government would not (under Article 208 of the Treaty of St. Germain transferring to it claims belonging to the Austrian Government) try to recover at law sums spent to facilitate the economic reconstruction of the territory formerly known as Galicia. On appeal,

Held: That an alleged declaration of a delegate of the Polish Government before the Reparation Commission could not form the subject of judicial evidence in this case, since the plaintiff's claim against the defendant could not be waived or released by such a delegate, who had not the statutory authority to do so. [Report: P.P.A., 1928, p. 284.]

Suspension of Treaties—Effect of Rupture of Diplomatic Relations—Capitulations.

See Case No. 40 (*Hergenstein* v. *Public Prosecutor of the Native Courts*).

XII.—Interpretation of Treaties

i.—Construction in Accordance with the Intention of the Parties

Case No. 291

Treaties—Interpretation—Consideration of the Intention of the Parties—The Purpose of the Treaty—Inadmissible Consequences of a Literal Interpretation.

SARROPOULOS *v.* BULGARIAN STATE.

Greco-Bulgarian Mixed Arbitral Tribunal. 14 *February*, 1927.

(DE LA BARRA, YOUPIS, PAPAZOFF.)

THE FACTS.—(See Case No. 173.) This was a claim for compensation put forward by a Greek subject resident in Bulgaria who suffered damage in the course of riots directed against Greek subjects. The claim was put forward by virtue of Article 179 of the Treaty of Neuilly which provided as follows:

"Diplomatic or consular claims made before "the war by the Representatives or Agents of "the Allied and Associated Powers with regard to "the private property, rights or interests of nationals "of those Powers shall, on the application of the "Power concerned, be submitted to the Mixed "Arbitral Tribunal provided for in Section VI."

It was contended that the Treaty did not contemplate claims other than those directly or indirectly connected with the war, and that the Tribunal therefore had no jurisdiction.

Held: That the Tribunal had no jurisdiction. Article 179 was couched in very general terms; it did not contain any qualifications either in respect of the nature of the private rights to which it referred or of the form or date of the diplomatic action relating thereto. If the Tribunal were to interpret that provision literally, it would be competent to adjudicate in respect of any claim, without limitation of time, in regard to which diplomatic or consular action was taken by any of the Allied and Associated Powers. This was an inadmissible interpretation. It was contrary to the generally accepted rules of interpretation according to which the intention of the parties and the spirit of the Treaty had precedence over the wording of any of its individual provisions.[1]

The Mixed Arbitral Tribunals created by the Peace Treaties were tribunals of an exceptional character. This fact imposed upon them the duty of special restraint. Any disregard of that duty involved the grave risks of excess of jurisdiction.

The parties to the Treaty of Neuilly had no intention of conferring upon the Mixed Arbitral Tribunal jurisdiction in regard to all diplomatic claims which might have arisen between them at any time before or even after the entrance into force of the Treaty. They must certainly have intended to limit the jurisdiction of the Tribunal either to claims connected with the war, or to claims which although not arising out of the war could not have been brought forward or examined on account of the war. An indirect or direct connection of these claims with the war of 1914-1918 was necessary in order to invest the Tribunal with jurisdiction. The Tribunal could not disregard the fact that claims of the nature of the one raised in the present case were entirely disregarded both in the Greek-Bulgarian Treaty of Alliance of 1912 which was intended to establish the relations between the two countries on a permanent basis, and in the Peace Treaty of Bucarest of 1913 in which Greece, as the victorious State, could have imposed,

[1] The Tribunal referred here to Heffter, No. 95; Rivier, II, p. 157; Hall, p. 344 (8th ed., 1924, p. 393); and Fauchille, II, p. 1036—the last-named to the effect that "treaties of peace are conventions in which compulsion is "permitted, but which are in principle governed by the general rules relating "to treaties."

Case No. 291 contd.

had she so wished, the recognition of these claims by Bulgaria. [Report : *Recueil*, VII, p. 47.]

NOTE.—The case *Prewlocki* v. *Bulgarian State, Recueil*, II, p. 935, followed.

Case No. 292

Treaties—Interpretation—Intention of the Parties—Consideration of Preparatory Diplomatic Negotiations—Tacit Reference to General Principles of International Law—Reasonable Interpretation of Scope of the Convention—Inadmissibility of Interpretation Depriving Clause of its Practical Application.

GEORGES PINSON CASE, § 50.

France and Mexico : Mixed Claims Commission.
19 *October*, 1928.

(VERZIJL, President.)

In view of the contradictory contentions of the Agents of the parties concerning the real scope of the main provisions of the French-Mexican Claims Convention (reparation of damages originating in the Mexican revolutions from 1910 to 1920), and of the difference of opinion between his fellow-Commissioners, the President formulated the following general rules of interpretation (§ 50 of the Award) :

" (i) Inasmuch as the text of the Convention is clear in " itself, there is no reason to appeal to alleged contrary inten- " tions of its authors unless both parties concerned agree that " the text does not cover their common intention ;

" (ii) In so far as the text is not sufficiently clear, it is " allowable to have recourse to the intentions of the parties " concerned. If, in this case, the intentions are clear and " unanimous, they must prevail over every other possible in- " terpretation. If, on the contrary, they diverge or are not " clear, that meaning must be sought which, within the context, " best gives either a reasonable solution of the controversy, or " the impression which the offer of the party which took the " initiative must reasonably and in good faith have made on " the mind of the other party ;

" (iii) In order to determine the true sense of the text, or the " intention of the parties, the diplomatic negotiations which led " up to the conclusion of the convention may be taken into " account, unless the parties have finally adopted a text which is " incompatible with the original scope of the negotiations, or " have consciously waived their right to invoke the elements of " interpretation which those negotiations might furnish ;

"(iv) Every international convention must be deemed "tacitly to refer to general principles of international law for all "questions which it does not itself resolve in express terms and "in a different way;

"(v) In case of doubt as to the true scope of a treaty "stipulation it should be understood in a sense that assures the "possibility of its application, whereas in the case of absolute "impossibility of ascertaining the exact meaning it should be "interpreted in favour of the party which pledges itself by "the stipulation."

See for the application of these rules, *inter alia*, Cases Nos. 159, 206, 318.

[Till now unreported.]

Treaties—Interpretation—Intention of the Parties—Effectiveness of Treaty Provisions.

See Case No. 177 (*Case concerning the Factory at Chorzów*) (*b*).

ii. Restrictive Interpretation

(*a*) Restrictions of Sovereignty

Treaties—Interpretation—Restrictive Interpretation on account of Limitation of Sovereignty.

Case No. 293

PERMANENT COURT OF INTERNATIONAL JUSTICE.

ADVISORY OPINION No. 14.

Jurisdiction of the European Commission of the Danube between Galatz and Braila.

8 *December*, 1927.

The Facts.—See Case No. 303. It was contended by Roumania that as the Treaty of London of 1883 had not been adhered to by her, the extension, under that Treaty, of the powers of the European Commission from Galatz to Braila constituted a violation of her sovereign rights.

Held: That the contention must be rejected. "As "the Court has had occasion to state in previous "judgments and opinions, restrictions on the exercise "of sovereign rights accepted by treaty by the State "concerned cannot be considered as an infringement "of sovereignty." [Report: Series B, No. 14, p. 36.]

(*b*) Interpretation against the Party Responsible for the Drafting

Treaties—Interpretation—Ambiguous Clause to be Construed against Party Responsible for it.

See Case No. 369 (*Goldenberg and Sons* v. *Germany*).

iii.—Bilingual Treaties

Case No. 294

Treaties — Interpretation — Bilingual Treaties — Treaty of Versailles, Article 311—Reference to Text in which Clause was originally Drafted.

Société Audiffren-Singrun *v.* Liquidation Morlang, Binger et Société Atlas.

Civil Tribunal of Strasbourg (First Chamber). 21 July, 1927.

The Facts.—Article 311, paragraph 2, of the Treaty of Versailles reads:

" Rights of industrial, literary and artistic " property which are in force in territories separated " from Germany under the present Treaty at the " moment of the separation of these territories from " Germany . . . shall be recognised by the State to " which the said territory is transferred and shall " remain in force in that territory for the same " period of time given them under the German law."

The patent of the plaintiff company was still valid in Germany as a result of two prolongations granted after the armistice. The plaintiff contended that the effect of these prolongations in Germany was to produce automatically similar prolongations of the duration of its patent in Alsace-Lorraine, and it brought an action for violation of patent rights involved in the construction of machines similar to those protected by the patent.

The dispute centred around the word " *sera*," in the French text of Article 311 : " *pour la durée qui leur* " *sera accordée suivant la législation allemande*."

Held: That the action must be dismissed. The word " *sera* " by itself would not be a sufficient basis for a decision. " The examination of the English text, the language in which " the chapter involving these rights of property was drafted in " the course of the preparatory discussions, provides an in-

"valuable guide to the intentions of the draftsmen of the "Treaty of Versailles." The German translation gave a similar meaning. Moreover, "it would be illogical and "opposed to all ideas of equity to recognise the right of an "enemy nation to alter the character of a patent by sub-"sequent legislation."[1] [Report: 55 *Clunet* (1928), p. 733.]

NOTE.—The plaintiff company's contention appears in effect to have been that the word "*sera*" necessarily implied futurity.—[Ed.]

Treaties—Language of—Translation of the Authentic Texts.

See Case No. 280 (*German Railways (Most-Favoured Treatment) Case, Note (b)*.)

Treaties—Interpretation—French Words as Having a Meaning ordinarily Attaching to them in French Law.

See Case No. 241 (*Rights of Minorities in Upper Silesia*) (*in fine*).

iv.—Consideration of Preparatory Work

Treaties — Interpretation — Preparatory Work — When the Meaning of the Treaty is Clear—Confidential Records—Admissibility of—Interpretative Protocol of the Danube Commission—Power of International Commissions to Abandon Functions Entrusted to them by International Treaties.

Case No. 295

PERMANENT COURT OF INTERNATIONAL JUSTICE. ADVISORY OPINION No. 14.

JURISDICTION OF THE EUROPEAN COMMISSION OF THE DANUBE BETWEEN GALATZ AND BRAILA.

8 *December*, 1927.

THE FACTS.—(See Cases Nos. 85, 303.) As Roumania had refused to recognise the validity of the Treaty of London of 1883, she maintained that the words "under the same conditions as

[1] See also the case (*Polish*) *State Treasury* v. *Paduchowa and Others* decided by the Supreme Court of Poland, Third Division, on 20 March, 1927. In this case (see also Case No. 307), the question having arisen whether the expression "*biens et propriétés*" in Article 208 of the Treaty of St. Germain ("all property and possessions" in the English text) includes incorporeal hereditaments (claims against a debtor of the Austrian Government), and the Court of Appeal of Lwów having held, *inter alia*, that the Treaty had in view only corporeal (tangible) objects, such as notably real estate, and having referred to the English text, it was held, on appeal, that a reference to the English text, which, moreover, does not support the contention of the Court of Appeal, is superfluous in view of the clause which provides that, the Treaty being in French, in English, and in Italian, in case of divergence the French text shall prevail. [Report: P.P.A., 1927, p. 310.]

Case No. 295 ***contd.***

"before, and without any modification of its "existing limits" used in Article 6 of the Definitive Statute of the Danube ought to be interpreted as meaning that the powers exercised by the Danube Commission from Galatz to Braila were merely "technical "powers," *i.e.* the power of maintaining the river in a condition suitable for navigation, but not juridical powers, *i.e.* especially the power of enforcing regulations. In support of her contention Roumania adduced, *inter alia*, (*a*) the history of the drafting of Article 6 of the Statute and of the relevant Articles of the Treaty of Versailles, and (*b*) the so-called *Protocole interprétatif* to the Definitive Statute signed by the delegates to the European Commission who were invited to the Danube Conference in an advisory capacity.

Held: (*a*) In regard to preparatory work: "The "Court adheres to the rule applied in its previous "decisions that there is no occasion to have regard to "the protocols of the conference at which a convention "was negotiated in order to construe a text which is "sufficiently clear in itself" (at p. 28). The Court, however, then proceeded to consider in detail the Roumanian contention with regard to the proceedings of the Conference, and came to the conclusion that they did not bear out the Roumanian contention. As to the history of the relevant articles of the Treaty of Versailles, the Court held that "the record of the "work preparatory to the adoption of these Articles "being confidential and not having been placed before "the Court by, or with the consent of, the competent "authority, the Court is not called upon to consider "to what extent it might have been possible for it to "take this preparatory work into account" (at p. 32).

(*b*) As to the *Protocole interprétatif*: The Court rejected the view that it could be regarded as an authoritative interpretation of the Statute. The Protocol was signed by the delegates to the Danube Commission; it purported to be drawn up at the request of the Conference. However, it appeared from the record that both the States interested and the members of the Commission disagreed as to its meaning. It could not be regarded as an international agreement between the Parties to the Definitive Statute; it was neither annexed to it nor mentioned in it. It could not, therefore, be regarded as part of the Statute. As it was given by the Commission when attending the Conference in an advisory and expert capacity, it could not be regarded as a decision of the European Commission modifying the terms of the Definitive Statute. In any case the Commission had no power to decide to abandon functions with which it was entrusted under existing international treaties. [Report: Series B, No. 14, pp. 28-35.[1]]

Treaties—Interpretation—Preparatory Work—Drafts of the Lausanne Convention.

Case No. 296

PERMANENT COURT OF INTERNATIONAL JUSTICE.

JUDGMENT No. 9.

FRANCE *v.* TURKEY.

THE CASE OF THE S.S. *LOTUS*.

7 September, 1927.

THE FACTS.—(See Case No. 98.) It was contended on behalf of the French Government that the expression "principles of international law," in accordance with which Turkey undertook in Article 15 to exercise her jurisdiction, should be read in the light of the evolution of the Convention. Thus, it was pointed out on behalf of France that in the course of the preparatory work an attempt was made by Turkey to amend the relevant Article so as to enable Turkey to exercise jurisdiction in respect of crimes committed outside Turkish territory,

[1] See also Series E, No. 4, pp. 201-212. And see on this case Vallotton, *Le régime juridique du Danube maritime devant la Cour permanente de Justice internationale*, 1928; Hajnal, *Le droit du Danube international*, 1929, pp. 316-323, and the same in *R.I.*, 3rd ser., vol. IX (1928), pp. 588-645; Ravard, *Le Danube maritime et le port de Galatz*, 1929, pp. 107-129; Krieg in *Z.V.*, XV (1929), pp. 215-244.

Case No. 296 ***contd.***

but that, after Italy and France made reservations to the amendment and after Great Britain rejected it altogether, the drafting committee evolved a draft, which was eventually adopted, according to which jurisdiction might be exercised in accordance with international law. This, it was contended, showed that the assumption by Turkey of jurisdiction over a French subject for an offence committed on the high seas was contrary to the intention of those who drafted the Convention.

Held : That the argument based on preparatory work must be rejected. "The Court must recall in "this connection what it has said in some of its pre-"ceding judgments and opinions, namely, that there "is no occasion to have regard to preparatory work if "the text of a convention is sufficiently clear in itself." The words "principles of international law," as ordinarily used, could only mean international law as applied between all nations belonging to the community of States. This interpretation was also borne out by the context of the Article and by other Articles of the Convention like the Preamble of the Convention which referred to the High Contracting Parties as desirous of affecting a settlement in accordance with "modern international law." [Report : Series A, No. 10, pp. 16, 17.]

NOTE.—It should, however, be noted that, after having refused to consider preparatory work in view of the fact that the text was sufficiently clear, the Court discussed the merits of the French contention as to the preparatory work. The Court found that the preparatory work did not bear out the French contention. Thus it attached importance to the fact that the reasons for the French and Italian reservations to the original draft and for the omission from the draft of any reference to jurisdiction over offences committed abroad were unknown, and might have been unconnected with the reasons advanced by France before the Court. The Court also pointed out that the original draft which limited the jurisdiction of Turkey to crimes committed within Turkish territory was equally discarded, and that "this circumstance "might with equal justification give the impression that the intention "of the framers of the Convention was not to limit this jurisdiction "in any way" (p. 17).

Treaties—Interpretation—Historical Interpretation—Consideration of Preparatory Work.

Case No. 297

ROUMANIAN MINISTER OF WAR *v.* TURKISH GOVERNMENT.

Roumanian-Turkish Mixed Arbitral Tribunal. 26 *April,* 1928.

(Baron DE NORDENSKJOELD, AHMED RECHID, JONESCU, MOUZAFFER SABRI, LYCURG MANU.)

THE FACTS.—(See Case No. 14.) It was contended by Turkey that Article 65 of the Treaty of Lausanne under which this action for restitution was brought, applied only to certain categories of goods, which did not include those claimed by Roumania. In support of her contention, Turkey adduced the preparatory work of the Lausanne Conference relating to Articles 65 and 67 of the Treaty.

Held : (*a*) In regard to the relevance of preparatory work in general: the text of a law is the principal guide of interpretation, and caution ought to be exercised in order not to disregard the text under the plea of giving effect to the spirit of the law. It is only when the text is obscure, doubtful or contrary to the principles elsewhere expressed by the legislator, that the judge may search for the true meaning of the text and avail himself of the generally recognised rules of interpretation. It is true that recourse to preparatory work is undoubtedly one of the means of ascertaining the true intention of the legislator. However, it is equally generally recognised that the value of the arguments drawn from preparatory work is very limited, and that extreme caution is required in order not to allow them to modify the clear and precise provisions of the law. If this is the case in regard to municipal law, which as a rule is the result of laborious and careful preparation, then these reasons apply with special force to international treaties, the preparation of which may necessarily have been a hasty one. Very frequently, it is only in the final clauses as actually adopted that the common intention of the parties reveals itself. In addition, it must not be forgotten that a treaty is not a statute, but only a synallagmatic convention, and that consequently preparatory work, if it is to be of material use for the purpose of interpretation, must establish the *common* intention of the contracting parties. It is only then that the preparatory work may be used with the view to modifying the clear wording of a treaty.

Case No. 297 ***contd.***

(*b*) The Tribunal then examined at great length, in the light of these principles, the Turkish submissions as to the various phases of the preparatory work relating to Articles 65 and 67, and found that they did not justify any departure from the text of Article 65, which made no distinction between various categories of property subjected to the duty of restitution. [Report : *Recueil*, VII, p. 993.]

NOTE.—See also for further examples of an exhaustive treatment of preparatory work the following cases :

Karl Toth v. *Yugoslav State*, decided on 2 April, 1927, by the Hungarian-Yugoslavian Mixed Arbitral Tribunal (*Recueil*, VII, p. 850). In this case, the claimant asked for compensation for damages done to his property, situated in the part of Hungary which was occupied by Yugoslav troops, in contravention of the armistice agreement, but which subsequently was restored to Hungary. He contended that Article 250 of the Trianon Treaty was applicable to these territories. The Tribunal rejected this contention and based itself mainly on the preparatory work relating to certain Articles *in pari materia*, namely, 49 and 267 of the Treaty of St. Germain, including the original drafts of these Articles, the notes of the Austrian delegates and the letters of the President of the Peace Conference;

Schreiber & Co. v. *Czechoslovak State*, decided on 29 July, 1927, by the Hungarian-Czechoslovak Mixed Arbitral Tribunal (*ibid.*, p. 897) on the same question;

Abbas Hilmi Pasha v. *Great Britain*, decided on 29 June, 1927, by the Anglo-Turkish Mixed Arbitral Tribunal (*ibid.*, p. 909), in which the claimant, the former Khedive of Egypt, claimed certain sums alleged to be due on account of the liquidation of his property situated in Egypt. The claimant invoked the preparatory work relating to Articles 60 and 65 in support of his contention that these Articles applied to property situated in Egypt. In particular, he relied on the declaration of the Turkish delegate in which the latter refused to accept the declaration of the British delegate excluding the claims of the Khedive from the purview of Articles 60 and 65. The Tribunal pointed out that the Turkish declaration was followed by a further British statement reiterating the British position, and that in any case the Turkish reservations were not incorporated in the Treaty as finally signed.

Ekrem Bey v. *Italy*, decided on 5 November, 1927, by the Turkish-Italian Mixed Arbitral Tribunal (*ibid.*, p. 965). In this case the claimant contended that Lybia was detached from Turkey by virtue of Article 22 of the Treaty of Lausanne of 1923. The Tribunal stated that that contention was refuted, *inter alia*, by the preparatory work relating thereto.

Banque d'Orient v. *Greece*, decided on 9 February, 1928, by the Greco-Turkish Mixed Arbitral Tribunal (*ibid.*, p. 967), relating to the interpretation of Articles 65 and 67 of the Treaty of Lausanne.

Treaties — Interpretation — Preparatory Work — Treaty of Lausanne—Recognition of the Treaty of Versailles by the Treaty of Lausanne—Interpretation of the Latter by Reference to the Provisions of the Former.

Case No. 298

EASTERN BANK LTD. *v.* TURKISH GOVERNMENT.

Anglo-Turkish Mixed Arbitral Tribunal. 28 *December*, 1927.

(HAMMERICH, MEMDOUH, GRIMSTON.)

THE FACTS.—In Article 58 of the Treaty of Lausanne the contracting parties mutually renounced all claims for loss and damage suffered by their nationals " as the " result of acts of war, or measures of requisition, " sequestration, disposal or confiscation." On the other hand, Articles 65 and 66 imposed upon the contracting parties the duty to restore property which was still in existence and capable of being identified, or its proceeds if it had been liquidated.

In the present action the claimant asked for the restoration of certain negotiable instruments taken away by Turkish officials in November, 1914. He contended that the action was one covered by Articles 65 and 66 of the Treaty. In support of his contention he invoked Article 297 (*h*) of the Treaty of Versailles which provided for the restitution of " all cash assets of " enemies," on the ground that Article 25 of the Treaty of Lausanne had incorporated that Article into its own provisions.

Held : That the Tribunal had no jurisdiction.

(*a*) The measure complained of constituted in reality a war measure within the meaning of Article 58 of the Treaty. It was of special importance to draw a clear line of demarcation between the provisions of Article 58 and those of Articles 65 and 66 in view of the fact that the mutual renunciation of damages for war measures constituted one of the fundamental features of the Treaty of Lausanne, as shown by the *travaux préparatoires* in which that mutual renunciation of claims was described as the *conditio sine qua non* of reopening negotiations between the parties at Lausanne.

(*b*) The recognition by Turkey of the Treaty of Versailles was merely intended as a recognition of the fact that certain Peace Treaties, concluded prior to the Treaty of Lausanne, had put an end to the state of war between the former allies of

Case No. 298 *contd.*

Turkey and the Western Powers. It could not be regarded as an authorisation to apply directly, as against Turkey, the dispositions of the Treaty of Versailles. Even any indirect application of the latter Treaty for the purposes of interpreting the Treaty of Lausanne could be permitted only in so far as the respective provisions were analogous or were in conformity with one another. This was not the case in regard to Article 297 of the Treaty of Versailles. There existed in this respect a fundamental difference between the two Treaties. [Report: *Recueil*, VIII, p. 188.]

Case No. 299

Treaties—Interpretation of—Preparatory Work—Consideration of Preparatory Work and of the Circumstances of the Conclusion of the Treaty rather than of the Letter of the Treaty—The Treaty of Lausanne.

POLYXENE PLESSA *v.* TURKISH GOVERNMENT.

Greco-Turkish Mixed Arbitral Tribunal. 9 *February*, 1928.

(Baron DE NORDENSKJOELD, AHMED RECHID, KYRIACOPOULOS.)

THE FACTS.—This was a claim for loss of rent and damage to and destruction of furniture arising out of requisitions on the part of Turkish military authorities.

Article 58 of the Treaty of Lausanne provides as follows:

" Turkey, on the one hand, and the other contracting Powers (except Greece) on the other hand, reciprocally renounce all pecuniary claims for the loss and damage suffered respectively by Turkey and the said Powers and by their nationals (including juridical persons) between the 1st August, 1914, and the coming into force of the present Treaty, as the result of acts of war, or measures of requisition, sequestration, disposal or confiscation. . . ."

Article 59 of the same Treaty provides as follows:

" Greece recognises her obligation to make reparation for the damage caused in Anatolia by the acts of the Greek army or administration which were contrary to the laws of war.

" On the other hand, Turkey, in consideration of the financial situation of Greece resulting from the prolongation of the war and from its consequences, finally renounces all claims for reparation against the Greek Government."

The Treaty did not contain any such renunciation on the part of Greece.

Held: That Greece was not entitled to put forward claims for reparation in respect of such war measures as were in conformity with the laws of war.

The Tribunal was prepared to admit, in particular having regard to the interpretation put on that provision by the chief of the Turkish delegation at the Lausanne Conference, that the renunciation of reparation for acts *contrary to* the laws of war was mutual. On the other hand, the literal reading of the Treaty showed that there was no renunciation on either side of claims for acts *in conformity with* the laws of war, including requisitions. However, the Tribunal was of the opinion that this was a case in which the text of the Treaty did not reproduce with necessary precision the intention of the parties, and that the Treaty must be read as containing a mutual waiver of claims for reparation also in respect of measures in conformity with the laws of war.

Turkey remained victorious in the war with Greece. It was improbable that the victor should have undertaken to indemnify the vanquished for any war measures whatsoever. If that had been the intention of the parties they would have declared that expressly. It was true that it was customary for the victor to relieve himself formally, in the treaties concluded by him, of any responsibility under this head, but the circumstances in which the Treaty of Lausanne was concluded nevertheless justify the conclusion that the intention of the parties was that Greek subjects should possess no rights of compensation for war damages.

The *procès-verbal* of the meetings, both private and public, at the Lausanne Conference showed that it was Turkey who first put forward demands for compensation under this head. Similar demands on the part of Greece were put forward later, apparently in order to obtain a solution by way of a compromise. It was true that, apart from the meeting of 28 May, 1923, the discussions between the parties related only to war damages proper as dealt with in Article 59. But this omission shows that there was no intention on the part of the Greek delegates to raise the question. When at the above-mentioned meeting the Turkish delegate declared that the regulation of compensation for illegal war measures did not settle the question of compensation for requisitions and confiscations for which the Greek army was responsible, the Greek delegate,

Case No. 299 *contd.*

while protesting that Greece was unable on account of her economic situation to accept any obligation under this head, in no way made it known that Greece would press for such compensation in her favour.

It was true that preparatory work should be used only with utmost caution for the purpose of interpreting and supplementing a treaty, but in view of the accompanying circumstances the Tribunal felt justified in having recourse to preparatory work in order to fill a gap in the provisions of the Treaty relating to compensation for acts in conformity with rules of warfare. In doing so [1] the Tribunal in no way modified the Treaty seeing that it contained no provisions on the subject.

An interpretation contrary to that adopted by the Tribunal would mean that subjects of the Allied Powers would, as against Turkey, be in a worse position than Greek subjects, although at the end of the war the Allied Powers were in a better position *vis-à-vis* Turkey than Greece.

It followed that, notwithstanding the formal elimination of Greece from the operation of paragraph 1 of Article 58, its provisions actually applied to Greek subjects. The exception in favour of Greece was calculated not so much to regulate legal interests as to take into account certain sentimental considerations. [Report: *Recueil*, VIII, p. 224.]

NOTE.—It was thought desirable to give a detailed digest of this case in view of the prominent part allotted by the Tribunal to the *travaux préparatoires*. [No opinion is expressed by the editors on the question how far the weight thus attached by the Tribunal to the *travaux préparatoires* has resulted in an alteration of the provisions of the Treaty.]

Case No. 300

Treaties—Interpretation—Preparatory Work—Arrangement Made during the Negotiations—Merger in the Treaty—Treaty of Lausanne—Interpretation *a contrario*.

G. KAUROKLIS *v.* TURKEY.

Turko-Greek Arbitral Tribunal. 14 *June*, 1928.

(Baron DE NORDENSKJOELD, AHMED RECHID, KYRIACOPOULOS.)

THE FACTS.—This was a claim for the restoration of certain vessels seized by Turkey in 1922. Turkey objected to the claim on the ground that the question of the restitution of seized vessels was the subject of a

[1] The Tribunal referred here to other documents issued during the Lausanne Conference. See *loc. cit.*, p. 228.

special arrangement, made during the negotiations for the Treaty of Lausanne between the Turkish and Greek delegations, which exempted Turkey from any obligation to restore such vessels. Greece contended that the arrangement, not having been incorporated in the Treaty, was of no legal value.

Held: That the claim must be rejected. Article 140 (3) of the Treaty of Lausanne, without mentioning Greek ships seized by Turkey, provided that vessels under the Turkish flag seized by the Greek forces after 30 October, 1918, should be restored to Turkey. *A contrario*, one was justified in assuming that no such restitution was intended in favour of Greece. This interpretation was corroborated by a letter addressed on 8 July, 1923, by the chiefs of both delegations to the President of the Conference at Lausanne to the effect that Turkish ships seized after the armistice should be restored without reciprocity. [Report: *Recueil*, VIII, p. 398.]

Treaties—Interpretation—Effect of Undertaking Given in Course of Negotiations Preceding the Conclusion of a Treaty—Validity of Australian Vesting Orders. **Case No. 301**

A. HARTRODT *v.* HENRY OLSEN & CO.

Anglo-German Mixed Arbitral Tribunal. 18 *June*, 1928.

(KLAESTAD, HART, JOHANNES.)

THE FACTS.—The claim in this case was resisted on the ground that during the war the debt in question was vested in the Public Trustee of the Commonwealth of Australia. On 25 June, 1919, an order was made pursuant to the Australian Trading with the Enemy Act, 1914-1916, vesting in the Public Trustee all property, real or personal, belonging to the claimant, an enemy subject.

It was contended by the German Government that the vesting order must be deemed to be invalid on the ground, *inter alia*, that it was contrary to the spirit and to certain provisions of the Treaty of Versailles. The German Government referred to the negotiations which preceded the Treaty, and contended that a general vesting in the Public Trustee of German debts in Australia (on 25 June, 1919, three thousand orders were signed) was a violation of the undertaking contained in

Case No. 301 *contd.*

the Reply of the Allied and Associated Powers of 16 June, 1919, that there should be full reciprocity with regard to the "Clearing Procedure."

Held: In respect of the above contention, that the vesting order was valid. The Treaty contained no express provision forbidding the making of vesting orders after the armistice of 11 November, 1918. [Report: *Recueil*, VIII, p. 26.]

Treaties — Interpretation of — Consideration of Preparatory Work.

See Case No. 292 (*Georges Pinson Case*, § 50).

Treaties — Interpretation — Preparatory Work — Diplomatic Notes Preceding the Arbitration Agreement.

See Case No. 54 (*in fine*) (*Tripartite Claims Commission*).

Treaties—Interpretation—Preparatory Work—Recourse to for the Purpose of Corroborating Conclusions Reached by a Logical Interpretation of the Treaty.

See *A. A. Megalidis* v. *Turkey* (Case No. 272) at p. 396 of the *Recueil*.

Treaties—Interpretation—Provisions and Negotiations of a Previous Treaty as Basis of Interpretation.

See Case No. 325 (*C. E. Blair Case*).

Treaties—Interpretation—Preparatory Work.

See Case No. 59 (*Kulin, Emeric* v. *Roumanian State*) in which the Tribunal based its decision, *inter alia*, on the preparatory work relating to Article 250 of the Treaty of Trianon and Article 267 of the Treaty of St. Germain.

Treaties—Interpretation—Interpretation by Reference to Admissions Made during Negotiations for the Settlement of a Dispute after the Entry into Force of the Treaty.

See Case No. 337 (*Kulin, Emeric* v. *Roumanian State*).

Negotiations—Admissions and Declarations Made in the Course of Abortive Negotiations.

See Case No. 353 (*Case concerning the Factory at Chorzów: The question of set-off*).

Negotiations—Offers of Compensation during Abortive Negotiations—Binding Force of.

See Case No. 177 (*Case concerning the Factory at Chorzów, Note* (*d*)).

v.—Various other Rules of Interpretation

Treaties—Interpretation of—Interpretation in accordance with Requirements of Certainty and Stability.

Case No. 303[1]

PERMANENT COURT OF INTERNATIONAL JUSTICE.

ADVISORY OPINION No. 14.

JURISDICTION OF THE EUROPEAN COMMISSION OF THE DANUBE BETWEEN GALATZ AND BRAILA.

8 *December*, 1927.

THE FACTS.—Article 5 of the Definitive Statute of the Danube of 1921 provided as follows:

"The European Commission retains the "powers which it possessed before the war. "No alteration is made in the rights, pre- "rogatives and privileges which it possesses "in virtue of the treaties, conventions, "international acts and agreements relative "to the Danube and its mouths."

Article 6 of the same instrument provided as follows:

"The authority of the European Com- "mission extends, under the same conditions "as before, and without any modification "of its existing limits, over the maritime "Danube, that is to say, from the mouths "of the river to the point where the "authority of the International Commission "commences."

The last international treaty, prior to the Definitive Statute, relating to the internationalisation of the Danube was the Treaty signed at London, on 10 March, 1883, which, *inter alia*, extended the jurisdiction of the European Danube Commission from Galatz to Braila. Roumania, who was refused admission to the Conference and who did not sign the Treaty, refused to recognise its validity.

[1] Case No. 302 has been omitted.—[Ed.].

Case No. 303 *contd.*

However, the Commission actually extended its jurisdiction from Galatz to Braila and exercised it until the outbreak of the war of 1914-1918.

It was contended on behalf of Roumania that the passages " retains the powers which it " possessed before the war " and " under the " same conditions as before " were intended to perpetuate the divergence of views which had arisen under the Treaty of London between the States represented on the European Commission.

Held : That that contention must be rejected. If accepted it would amount to the maintenance over the Danube of an uncertain and precarious situation. The passages in question referred to conditions which existed in fact before the war in the disputed sector of the Danube. Their effect was " to maintain and " confirm these conditions, thus putting an end to the " questions which had arisen under Article 1 of the " Treaty of London." As the divergence of opinion concerning the validity of the Treaty of London had not prevented the European Commission from accomplishing its task, and as no one denied that it exercised some powers on the sector from Galatz to Braila, regardless of the legal nature of the powers thus exercised, the confirmation of the jurisdiction of the Commission as it was exercised before the war " might " easily have appeared to be the best possible solution " of the difficulty." [Report: Series B, No. 14, pp. 24-28.]

Case No. 304

PERMANENT COURT OF INTERNATIONAL JUSTICE.

ADVISORY OPINION No. 14.

Treaty—Interpretation—Not Controlled by Clause in Previous Treaty between same Parties Providing for Conclusion of Treaty in Question.

JURISDICTION OF THE EUROPEAN COMMISSION OF THE DANUBE BETWEEN GALATZ AND BRAILA.

8 *December*, 1927.

THE FACTS.—Article 349 of the Treaty of Versailles provided that the régime for the Danube should be laid down by a conference of the Powers nominated by the Allied and Associated Powers. The Conference met at Paris in 1920, and the result of its deliberations was the Definitive Statute of the Danube signed on 23 July, 1921. Among its signatories were all the States parties to the dispute with which the Court dealt in the present Advisory Opinion. In the course of the argument before the Court the question was raised whether the Conference which resulted in the Definitive Statute had authority to modify the provisions of the Treaty of Versailles in regard to the Danube, and also whether the meaning and scope of the relevant provisions of the two Treaties were the same or not.

Held: That "as all the Governments concerned "in the present dispute have signed and ratified both "the Treaty of Versailles and the Definitive Statute, "they cannot, as between themselves, contend that "some of its (*i.e.* the latter's) provisions are void as "being outside the mandate given to the Danube "Conference under Article 349 of the Treaty of "Versailles." [Report: Series B, No. 14, p. 23.]

Treaties—Interpretation—Reasonable Construction by Reference to other Treaty Provisions—Articles 248 and 231 of the Treaties of St. Germain and Trianon Respectively. **Case No. 305**

HENRY NEUGASS *v.* AUSTRIA AND HUNGARY.

Tripartite Claims Commission (*United States, Austria and Hungary*). *January*, 1928.

(PARKER, Commissioner.)

THE FACTS.—This was a claim for the amount of interest due upon the coupons attached to bonds issued by the Austrian Empire in 1868. Some time after 1868 the Kingdom of Hungary, in a convention concluded with the Austrian Empire, agreed to contribute to the service of the debts of the Austrian Empire to the

Case No. 305 *contd.*

extent of 28·652 per cent. These debts subsequently came to be known as the "unsecured unified public "debt."

The Treaty of St. Germain provided that each Succession State, including Austria, shall be liable for a portion, to be fixed by the Reparation Commission, of the unsecured bonded debt of the Austrian Empire, such liability to begin from the coming into force of the Treaty. The Treaty also provided that the "Austrian "Government shall be solely responsible for all the "liabilities of the former Austrian Government in-"curred prior to July 28, 1914" unless otherwise provided by the Treaty. The Treaty of Trianon contained analogous provisions. In Article 248 [231] of Section III of Part X of the Treaty of St. Germain [Trianon], dealing with and defining "debts" falling within that Section, it is provided:

> "In the case of interest or capital sums payable in "respect of securities issued or taken over by the "former Austro-Hungarian Government the amount "to be credited and paid by Austria [Hungary] will "be the interest or capital in respect only of the "debt for which Austria [Hungary] is liable in "accordance with Part IX (Financial Clauses) of "the present Treaty, and the principles laid down "by the Reparation Commission."

The questions before the Commission were:

1. To what extent, if at all, is Hungary liable upon the coupons here presented? and

2. When did the liability of Austria and/or Hungary for the payment of the said coupons terminate and the liability of the Succession or Cessionary States (including Austria and Hungary), resulting from the dismemberment of the former Austrian Empire and the former Kingdom of Hungary, attach?

Held: That the Austrian Republic was liable for all interest which became due on or prior to 16 July, 1920 (the day of the entry into force of the Treaty of St. Germain) in respect of the pre-war "Austrian unsecured debt," and that the bondholders must look to the new obligations issued by the Succession States for interest accruing subsequent to that date. The same applied to Hungary in respect of her share (28·652 per cent.) and as from 2 July, 1921 (the day of the entry into force of the Treaty of Trianon).

It was true that Article 248 [Trianon 231] referred to "securities issued or taken over by the former Austro-Hungarian Government," but the only securities answering to the substance, although not the letter, of this description were the unsecured unified public debt. "As each provision of the "Treaty must be given such reasonable construction in connection with every other provision as to give effect to all of "them, the Commissioner holds that the phrase 'securities "'issued or taken over by the former Austro-Hungarian "'Government' found in these paragraphs refers to the unsecured unified public debt, the liability for which, for all of "the purposes of the Treaties, has been apportioned as to "71·348 per cent. of the total and no more to Austria, to be "treated as a part of 'the Austrian unsecured debt,' and as to "28·652 per cent. of the total and no more to Hungary, to be "treated as part of the 'Hungarian unsecured debt.'"[1] [Report: *A.J.*, XXII (1928), p. 693.]

NOTE.—So far as State Succession is concerned the decision is based on the interpretation of relevant treaty provisions, and it does not raise any general point of State Succession. But the question of interpretation appears to be of sufficient importance to justify the inclusion of the case.

---

[1] See, for another instance of the interpretation of a treaty by reference to the provisions of another treaty, *Hardt* v. *Governor of Poznan*, decided by the Supreme Administrative Court of Poland, on 21 December, 1927. In this case the plaintiff claimed, *inter alia*, that Article 91 of the Peace Treaty of Versailles and Article 4 of the Treaty of the same date between the Allied and Associated Powers and Poland, which attribute Polish nationality *ipso facto* to German nationals habitually resident in territories returned to Poland, etc., should be understood to refer to "residence" in the sense of the laws prevailing in those territories, *i.e.* in that of the German Civil Code. The plaintiff complained that the defendant had interpreted the Vienna Convention as introducing an entirely new conception of residence.

It was held (1) That, the Treaty of Versailles not having defined the nature of "residence" to which they referred, this gap was filled by Article 4 of the Vienna Convention, by establishing criteria which were not those of residence in the sense either of the German Civil Code or in the sense of other German laws which, each for its own purpose, define residence in various ways differing from those of the Civil Code.

(2) That, consequently, various decisions taken previous to the Treaty of Versailles by German authorities on the basis of those various German laws could not prejudice the result of the application of the Treaty of Versailles and of the Vienna Convention. [Report: P.P.A., 1928, pp. 378-395.] See also Case No. 8.

Case No. 306

Treaties—Interpretation—Interpretation by Analogy with other Provisions of the same Treaty.

TYPOGRAPHIE "HERTZ" *v.* SOCIÉTÉ ANONYME "TUDOR."

Roumano-Hungarian Mixed Arbitral Tribunal.
27 *December*, 1927.

(CEDERKRANTZ, ANTONIADE, SZEKACZ.)

THE FACTS.—In this case the claimant company was Roumanian and the defendant company Hungarian. The latter contended that Article 239 (*b*) of the Treaty of Trianon, which conferred upon the Mixed Arbitral Tribunal jurisdiction in regard to contracts concluded before the entry of the Treaty into force between nationals of the Allied and Associated Powers and Hungarian nationals, did not apply to persons, formerly Hungarian nationals, who acquired the nationality of one of the Allied and Associated Powers as the result of the Treaty. As the claimant company was such a person, it was contended that the Tribunal had no jurisdiction.

Held: That the Tribunal had jurisdiction. If it had been intended to exclude former Hungarian nationals from the operation of Article 239 (*b*) of the Treaty, that would have been expressly stated. When in paragraph (*d*) of Article 234 of the same Treaty it was decided to exclude certain former Hungarian nationals from the operation of its provisions, an express provision was inserted to that effect. [Report: *Recueil*, VII, p. 845.]

Case No. 307

Treaties—Literal Interpretation—Meaning of Words and Expressions—Use of Dictionaries—Legal Expressions in French Interpreted by Reference to French Civil Code.

(POLISH) STATE TREASURY *v.* PADUCHOWA AND OTHERS.

Supreme Court of Poland, Third Division. 20 *March*, 1927.

(See Case No. 49.) In this case the Court had to interpret the expression "*biens et propriétés*" in Article 208 of the Peace Treaty of St. Germain, and for that purpose used Larousse, *Dictionnaire complet*, to establish the meaning of "*biens*," and that of "*disposer*" in

Article 201 of the Treaty. The Court also quoted the following Articles of the French Civil Code in order to support its interpretation by the "entirely clear" French legal usage: 516 for the expression "*biens*," 529 to prove that "movables" may include obligations and choses in action, and 543 and 544 to support its interpretation of "*propriétés*." [Report: P.P.A., 1927, p. 310.]

Treaties—Interpretation—Liberal Interpretation—Treaty of 1911 between Japan and the United States. **Case No. 308**

JORDAN *v.* TASHIRO.

United States Supreme Court. 19 *November*, 1928.

THE FACTS.—This was a petition for a mandamus by Japanese subjects residing in California to compel the issuing of a certificate of incorporation for the "Japanese Hospital of Los Angeles." Petitioners desired to incorporate, to lease land, and to erect and maintain a hospital thereon. The California Secretary of State refused to issue the certificate on the ground that it was forbidden by the State's Alien Land Law. The Law prohibited the ownership of lands by aliens ineligible to citizenship, but expressly authorised whatever any treaty in force might prescribe. The Treaty of 1911 between Japan and the United States, Article 1, provided: "The citizens or subjects of each of the "High Contracting Parties shall have liberty to enter, "travel and reside in the territories of the other to "carry on trade, wholesale and retail, to own or lease "and occupy houses, manufactories, warehouses and "shops, to employ agents of their choice, to lease land "for residential and commercial purposes, and gener-"ally to do anything incident to or necessary for trade "upon the same terms as native citizens or subjects, "submitting themselves to the laws and regulations "there established." (37 U.S. Stat. L. 1504.) The State Supreme Court held that the petitioners were entitled to the certificate. (201 Calif. 236.) On certiorari,

Held: That the judgment of the State Supreme Court should be affirmed. Treaties should be liberally construed.

Case No. 308 *contd.*

Delivering the Opinion of the Court, Mr. Justice Stone said: "The principle of liberal construction of treaties would be "nullified if a grant of enumerated privileges were held not to "include the use of the usual methods and instrumentalities "of their exercise. Especially would this be the case where "the granted privileges relate to trade and commerce and the "use of land for commercial purposes. It would be difficult "to select any single agency of more universal use or more "generally recognized as a usual and appropriate means of "carrying on commerce and trade than the business corpora-"tion." (278 U.S. 123, 130.) [Report: 278 U.S. 123.]

Case No. 309

Treaties—Interpretation—Alleged Inconsistency with *ordre public*—Superior Obligation of Treaty.

Banca Commerciale Italiana (Yugoslavia) Case.

Yugoslav Court of Cassation. 1 October, 1928.

The Facts.—The Banca Commerciale Italiana of Milan bought at public auction a mill and some adjacent land in the suburb of Bitoli (Monastir) not far from the Greco-Yugoslav frontier. The purchase was contested on the ground that a foreigner cannot acquire immovable property in a frontier zone.

Held: (*a*) By the tribunal of first instance of Bitoli: That the purchase was invalid. Article 324 of the Finance Act of 1927/1928 lays down that aliens may not acquire immovable property within 50 kilometres of the frontier except by virtue of a special authorisation of the Minister of War and of the Minister of the Interior. This provision is one relating to public policy (*ordre public*).

(*b*) By the Court of Cassation: That the judgment of the Court below must be reversed. The legal provisions which the Court was bound to apply in this case are those contained in the Convention concluded on 28 October, 1879, between Italy and Serbia. That Convention was extended to the whole of the territory of Yugoslavia by a Law of 19 June, 1920, which is still in force. According to Article 3 of that Convention Italians have the same rights as nationals in regard to acquisition of property. A law, even if it is one of *ordre public*, cannot derogate from a binding international treaty. [Report: Decision of the Supreme Court, 1928, No. 9869.]

Treaties—Rights of Consuls in regard to Navigation and Commerce of their Fellow-Nationals—Scope of these Rights. **Case No. 310**

ESTATE OF CLAUSEN CASE.

Supreme Court of California. 10 *October,* 1927.

THE FACTS.—This was a petition by the consul of Denmark asking that the executor of a Danish subject who had died testate in California be ordered to pay the distributive shares of Danish heirs to the consul to be remitted through the Danish Government to the proper distributees. Petitioner relied upon the Treaty of 1826 between Denmark and the United States, Article 8, which provided as follows: "To make more "effectual the protection which the United States and "his Danish Majesty shall afford in future, to the "navigation and commerce of their respective citizens "and subjects, they agree mutually to receive and "admit Consuls and Vice Consuls in all the ports open "to foreign commerce, who shall enjoy in them all "the rights, privileges, and immunities of the Consuls "and Vice Consuls of the most favoured nation, each "contracting party, however, remaining at liberty to "except those ports and places in which the admission "and residence of such Consuls may not seem con-"venient." (8 U.S. Stat. L. 340, 342.) The Treaty of 1923 with Germany had authorised consuls to give receipts for and remit distributive shares in behalf of their non-resident countrymen. (44 U.S. Stat. L. 2132.) The petition was denied. On appeal,

Held: That the judgment denying the petition should be affirmed. The rights, privileges and immunities which the Treaty assured to consuls were in general those which relate to navigation and commerce. The right asserted by appellant was not a right, privilege or immunity of this class, but obviously something more. Delivering the opinion of the Court, Judge Seawell said: "Applying the well-recognized rule that "treaties are subject to the same rules of interpretation as "other documents, and aided by the further consideration that "those nations which have deemed it wise to change the rule "of transmitting property acquired from estates in foreign "lands to their subjects to whom distribution is ordered have "done so by express treaty provisions, we conclude that inas-

Case No. 310 *contd.* " much as the treaty made between the United States and the " King of Denmark contains no such provision or article, the " appellant is without authority to maintain this proceeding." (202 Calif. 267, 272.) [Report: 202 Calif. 267.]

Treaties—Interpretation of—Provisions Fixing Date for the Commencement of their Operation.

See Case No. 273 (*Jules Baranyai* v. *Yugoslavia*).

Treaties—Interpretation—Recognition of one Treaty by another—Interpretation of one Treaty by the Provisions of another.

See Case No. 298 (*Eastern Bank Ltd.* v. *Turkish Government*).

Treaties—Interpretation of—Reference to Provisions of other Treaties.

See Case No. 345 (*Case concerning the Factory at Chorzów*) (*d*).

Treaties—Interpretation of—Logical Interpretation—Argument *a Majore ad Minus*.

See Case No. 345 (*Case concerning the Factory at Chorzów*) (*c*).

XIII.—Special Kinds of Treaties

(*a*) COMMERCIAL TREATIES. MOST-FAVOURED-NATION CLAUSE.

Case No. 311

Treaties—Commercial Treaties—Interpretation—Expression " Reciprocal Liberty of Commerce."

CLARKE *v.* DECKEBACH.

United States Supreme Court. 16 *May*, 1927.

THE FACTS.—This was a petition for mandamus to compel the Auditor of Cincinnati to issue a licence for a billiard and pool room to a British subject. A city ordinance prohibited the issuing of such a licence to an alien. The Treaty of 1815 between Great Britain and the United States, Article 1, stipulated for " a reciprocal " liberty of commerce." (8 U.S. Stat. L. 228.) The

Supreme Court of Ohio dismissed the petition. On writ of error,

Held : That the judgment should be affirmed. There was a reasonable basis for discrimination. The Treaty did not apply. *Asakura* v. *Seattle*, 265 U.S. 332, was distinguished upon the ground that the treaty with Japan invoked in that case secured to Japanese citizens the right to " enter, travel and reside " in the United States and to " carry on trade, wholesale and retail . . . " and generally to do anything incident to or necessary for " trade." [1] The language of the Japanese treaty was plainly broader than the language of the British treaty. [Report: 274 U.S. 392.]

Most-Favoured-Nation Clause—Application in Municipal Law—Takes Precedence over Clauses Guaranteeing Reciprocal Treatment Envisaged by Internal Legislation—French-Belgian Treaty of 1927—Belgian-Italian Treaty of 1882. **Case No. 312**

TROSSY *v.* DUMORTIER.

Brussels Civil Court (*Chamber of Rent Restriction Appeals*). 31 *May*, 1928.

THE FACTS.—The special legislation regulating the duration of tenancies (consolidated by the Royal Decree of 1 February, 1926) renders nationals of countries which were either neutral or allied to Belgium during the Great War eligible to share in its benefits, on condition of reciprocal treatment. (Article 29.)

The claimant complains that the privilege of the legal extension of her tenancy, contemplated in Article 1 and following Articles of the above-mentioned legislation, has been denied her because of her French nationality and of the lack of reciprocal treatment of Belgian nationals in France.[2]

Held for the claimant: The Franco-Belgian Convention of 27 October, 1927, stipulates that the nationals of each of the High Contracting Parties shall enjoy on the territory of each other most-favoured-nation treatment in all questions of residence and establishment, as also in the carrying on of trade,

[1] For the full text of Article 1 of the Treaty with Japan see Case No. 308.

[2] See Justice de Paix d'Ixelles, 9 February, 1928, *Journal des Juges de Paix*, 1928, p. 116, with critical note.

Case No. 312 *contd.* industry and the professions (Article 1). This privilege is extended to cover the possession, acquisition and leasing of real or personal property (Article 2).

The Treaty concluded between Belgium and Italy on 2 December, 1882, provides in its Article 3 that "The nationals "of each of the High Contracting Parties shall enjoy within "each other's territory full civil rights on an equal footing."

"It follows, then, that by virtue of the most-favoured-"nation clause, French nationals in Belgium are completely "assimilated to Belgian nationals for the purposes of their civil "rights, and consequently share in the legislation regulating "rents. It is immaterial whether these treaties precede or "succeed the legislation in question. . . .

"The Franco-Belgian Treaty of 6 October, 1927, was con-"cluded by the Belgian Government in the hope of securing for "its nationals in France the benefit of all legislation affecting "tenancies and commercial property, in order that the nationals "of each country should be treated on an equal footing. . . .

"The claimant, as a French national, is therefore entitled to "claim a legal extension of her tenancy of the premises by "virtue of the Treaty of 6 October, 1927." [Reports: 56 *Clunet* (1929), p. 203 ff.; *Belgique judiciare*, 1929, cols. 60-61.]

NOTE.—This judgment passes over in silence the important fact that the Belgian Landlord and Tenant legislation admits foreign nationals to its benefits "only if their respective national legislation upon tenancies "is applicable to Belgian nationals" (Article 29). The interest of the decision lies in the fact that by it the treaty provisions rank above the reciprocity conditions imposed by the municipal legislation. The converse principle finds expression in French decisions, based sometimes upon the fact that the French Rent legislation is earlier in point of time than the Treaty (Tribunal Civil de la Seine, 21 February, 1928, 56 *Clunet* (1929), p. 81), sometimes upon the exceptional nature of this legislation. (Commission supérieure de Cassation, 19 May, 1928, 23 June, 1928, *ibid.*, p. 87 ff.) See also for this view: J. Perroud, *La Législation des loyers d'habitation et les étrangers*, 54 *Clunet* (1927), p. 295 ff. This interpretation, which has already received doctrinal criticism (Niboyet, *Manuel*, 2ème éd., p. 246; Lapradelle-Niboyet, *Répertoire de Droit International*, III, p. 495), has also been formally condemned in a Circular of the Guardian of the Seals, dated 22 July, 1929 (56 *Clunet* (1929), p. 1223). Since this, the French courts have followed the Belgian decisions in giving precedence to the most-favoured-nation clause. (Commission supérieure de Cassation, 11 November, 1929, 57 *Clunet* (1930), p. 149, with a note by J. Perroud.)

Most-Favoured-Nation Clause—Franco-Greek Convention of 8 September, 1926—Franco-Danish Convention of 9 February, 1910—Interpretation of a French Law subsequent to the Treaty—Privileges of Foreigners Dependent upon Reciprocity. **Case No. 313**

BETSOU *v.* VOLZENLOGEL.

Civil Tribunal of the Seine. 23 *December*, 1927.

Court of Appeal of Paris (*First Chamber*). 24 *December*, 1928.

THE FACTS.—The brothers Betsou, Greek subjects, in 1917 leased certain premises in Paris for commercial use. The lease expired in 1926. The lessors refused to renew the lease, whereupon the plaintiffs claimed 200,000 francs as damages for eviction. Their claim was based on the provisions of the Law of 30 June, 1926, which grants certain privileges to those engaged in business activities. In support of their claim to the privileges of this Law in spite of their foreign nationality, they cited the Franco-Greek Convention of 8 September, 1926, and, through the operation of the most-favoured-nation clause, the Franco-Danish Convention of 9 February, 1910, Denmark being in this regard the most-favoured nation. Article 19 of the Law of 1926 provided that aliens shall be entitled to its privileges only subject to reciprocity.

Held by the Civil Tribunal of the Seine for the plaintiffs. Through the operation of the most-favoured-nation clause, Greek subjects in France enjoyed the same privileges in commerce and industry as Danish subjects. The Franco-Danish Convention stipulated that in the exercise of their commercial activities Danes enjoyed all the privileges granted to French nationals by subsequent legislation. The Law of 30 June, 1926, undoubtedly confers privileges upon those who were engaged in commerce. Although the terms of Article 19 of the Convention required reciprocity in legislation as an absolute and imperative rule, and although there was no legislation on commercial property in Denmark, the French law should be interpreted in accordance with the Franco-Danish Convention. Danish subjects could not be deprived of their rights and privileges by subsequent French legislation. " A convention between nations, " as a contract between private persons, is a reciprocal engage- " ment which should be observed by both parties so long as the

Case No. 313 *contd.* " treaty is not denounced or replaced by a new treaty which " restricts the effects of the original contract." [Report: 55 *Clunet* (1928), p. 999.]

Held by the Court of Appeal of Paris, reversing the decision of the Court below: That the brothers Betsou could not claim a right to the renewal of their lease. The Law of 30 June, 1926, clearly showed that it construed the right of commercial property as " *un droit civil stricto sensu*," that is to say, as a right subject to the provision of Article 11 of the Civil Code which made the enjoyment of rights by foreigners dependent upon the reciprocal treatment of French subjects abroad. In the Franco-Danish Treaty it had been carefully stated that the nationals of the two States would only enjoy the rights and privileges stipulated in so far as those rights and privileges were compatible with the existing legislation of the two States, and Danish legislation did not recognise the rights of foreigners to hold commercial property in Denmark. [Report: 56 *Clunet* (1929), p. 1269.]

NOTE.—In French law a lease of business premises is comprised within the term " *la propriété commerciale*."

Treaties—Treaties of Commerce—Interpretation of—The Text of the Treaty and Intention of the Parties—Literal Interpretation.

See Case No. 225 (*Reparations Levy* (*Aliens in Germany*) *Case*).

Most-Favoured-Nation Clause—Interpretation of—Protection of Property of Aliens.

See Case No. 230 (*Valorisation in Germany Case*).

Most-Favoured-Nation Treaties—Interpretation of—Position of Consuls.

See Case No. 310 (*Estate of Clausen Case*).

PART IX

INTERNATIONAL ORGANISATION AND ADMINISTRATION

A. LEAGUE OF NATIONS

III.—The Council

League of Nations—Council—Jurisdiction—Alleged Conflict of Jurisdiction with the Permanent Court of International Justice.

See Case No. 343 (*Rights of Minorities in Upper Silesia*).

IV.—Interpretation of the Covenant of the League

League of Nations—Article 18 of the Covenant (Registration of Treaties)—Validity of Unregistered Treaty.

See Case No. 271 (*Pablo Nájera (of the Lebanon) Case*).

League of Nations—Economic Sanctions—Blockade—Effectiveness of—New Developments in Maritime Warfare.

See Case No. 361 (*The Oriental Navigation Company Case*).[1]

V.—The League and Non-Member States

League of Nations—Effect of Covenant on Non-Members—Article 18 of the Covenant (Registration of Treaties).

See Case No. 271 (*Pablo Nájera (of the Lebanon) Case*).

C. OTHER ORGANS OF INTERNATIONAL ADMINISTRATION

[See also Part II B (*Territories under Joint or International Government*), and Part III B (*Functions and Competence of International Commissions on International Rivers*).]

International Commissions—Danube Commission—Power to Abandon Functions Entrusted to them by Treaties.

See Case No. 295 (*Jurisdiction of the European Commission of the Danube between Galatz and Braila*).

[1] A reference to the above topics will be found in *Opinions of the Commissioners*, 1929, p. 23.

D. MISCELLANEOUS

Case No. 314 **International Red Cross—National Branches—Position of—Russian Red Cross.**

LATVIAN MINISTRY FOR HOME AFFAIRS *v.* FORMER RUSSIAN RED CROSS ASSOCIATION.

Senate of Latvia. 28 *April*, 1927.

THE FACTS.—The Latvian Ministry for Home Affairs, acting on behalf of the State of Latvia, asked to be recognised as proprietor and successor to the property of the former Russian Red Cross (apparently the defendant), there being no other successor to the said property. The Court of Justice having granted the request, the defendant appealed to the Senate.

Held by the Senate: That the decision of the Court of Justice should be affirmed. " Red Cross Associations are of " public character and should be considered persons of public " law. The Russian Red Cross constituted a person of public " law of the Russian State of the Tsarist period, and it un- " doubtedly lost its legal basis after the Russian Empire had " suffered dismemberment. The Russian Red Cross could " only have conserved its legal basis if it could be proved that " it became in due time an international institution, such as " the Latvian Red Cross is, in view of its statutes of 1919 and " 1927 and of the adherence [1] of Latvia to the Geneva and " Hague Conventions for the Amelioration of the Condition of " the Wounded and Sick in Armies and Navies.

" As the Court of Justice did not establish that the Russian " Red Cross, or the Association of the Russian Red Cross, have " the character of an institution of international law, it could " not attribute to it an international existence." [Report: F. Konradi un A. Valters, *Izvilkumi no Latvijas senata civila kasacijas departamenta spriedumiem*, 1927, p. 111.]

[1] On 8 April, 1923.

PART X

DISPUTES

A. ARBITRATION

I.—Arbitration in General

i.—Conception and Function of Arbitration

Arbitration—Term of—Characteristics of Arbitration properly so-called.

Case No. 315

PERMANENT COURT OF INTERNATIONAL JUSTICE.

ADVISORY OPINION No. 16.

INTERPRETATION OF THE GRECO-TURKISH AGREEMENT OF 1 DECEMBER, 1926.

28 *August*, 1928.

THE FACTS.—(See Case No. 320.) It was contended by Greece that as the concluding passage of Article IV of the Final Protocol annexed to the Agreement provided for reference to arbitration by the President of the Greco-Turkish Mixed Arbitral Tribunal of " any question of principle " of importance which may arise in the Mixed " Commission," that provision constituted an arbitration clause ; this, she contended, implied that, unless expressly provided otherwise, only States might refer a matter to the tribunal which had jurisdiction, and that they alone might appear as parties before that tribunal.

Held : That that contention must be rejected. The Court could not attribute any special importance to the use of the word " arbitration " in the Article ; it considered it " not a very happy way of expressing " the idea underlying the Article." There could be here no question of arbitration except in the broadest sense of the expression, as the characteristics of arbitration properly so-called were not present in this case. First, as the Mixed Commission was composed of individual members and not of delegations representing the contracting States, there were no parties able to

Case No. 315 *contd.*

bring a dispute for an arbitral decision. Secondly, Article IV provided for reference to the arbitrator not only of differences of opinion between the members of the Commission but also of questions of principle of general importance. It was not inconceivable that a question might be submitted to the arbitrator in regard to which members of the Commission were agreed among themselves. Accordingly, Article IV could not be regarded as an arbitration clause. [Report : Series B, No. 16, pp. 22-24.]

Case No. 316

Relation between International Claims Convention and National Claims Regulations—Recourse to International Mixed Commissions against Decisions of National Claims Commission—Juridical Character of the Recourse: Appeal or Revision.

GEORGES PINSON CASE, §§ 4-9, 45.

France and Mexico : Mixed Claims Commission.
19 *October*, 1928.

(VERZIJL, President.)

THE FACTS.—Shortly after the outbreak (in February, 1913) of the Constitutionalist Revolution against the equally revolutionary Government of President Victoriano Huerta, its leader, Venustiano Carranza, constitutional Governor of the Mexican State of Coahuila, acting in his capacity of First Commander-in-Chief of the Constitutionalist Army, and designated by the Plan of Guadalupe of 26 March, 1913, as interim President of the Republic, issued the so-called Decree of Monclova, dated 10 May, 1913, pursuant to which (Articles 1-3) definite rights of indemnification were granted to Mexican citizens and, to a greater extent, to foreigners, on account of damages which they had suffered during and since the revolution of Francisco Madero of 1910, or which they still might suffer during the new revolution, up to the restoration of constitutional order; and by Articles 4 and 5 a National Claims Commission and various Mixed Commissions would be set up to examine the claims. Identical promises were made at the same time by the Huerta Government in Mexico City. After the success of the Constitutionalist Revolution the necessary steps were taken to call the Claims Commissions into existence and to elaborate the outlines of the Decree of Monclova, which gradually underwent, in the meantime, certain changes and evolution. On 24 November, 1917, the Carranza Government enacted a Law which specified the rights of indemnity of nationals and foreigners, established a National Claims Commission and announced once more the creation of Mixed Commissions, this time under neutral Presidents, either *ad hoc* for the examination of isolated cases, or for the trial of all claims of citizens of a definite country, in which latter case the Commission would be created by means of a regular international convention with the State concerned. In spite of this Law, the definitive settlement of the matter was put off again and again.

At length, in 1921, the new Government of President Obregón decided to give way to foreign pressure and to enter into serious negotiations with the Governments concerned, always on the old basis of the Decree of Monclova and the Mexican Claims Law of 1917 (afterwards modified by a new Law of 1919), in order to institute the Mixed Commissions as planned. According to the express terms of the letter of invitation of the Mexican Government of 12 July, 1921, the Commissions were intended for two different groups of cases, viz. (*a*) those in which the claimants would already have submitted their claim to the previous decision of the National Claims Commission; (*b*) those in which the claimants preferred to call directly upon the international Commission; in the former group of cases, the Commission would decide as a tribunal of appeal or of second instance. Like the analogous conventions, the French-Mexican Claims Convention of 1924 did not deal with the point in express terms, but even after that Convention came into force the Mexican Claims Laws remained unaltered and the National Claims Commission continued to mention in its decisions concerning the claims of foreigners their right of recourse to the Mixed Commissions. Moreover, the subsequent German-Mexican Claims Convention of 16 March, 1925, nevertheless provided *expressis verbis* (Article 12) for the confirmation, modification or revocation of the awards of the National Commission by the Mixed Commission.

Case No. 316 ***contd.***

On the strength of the facts summarised above, the French Agent sustained the contention that in the group of cases mentioned under (*a*) the Commission performed the duties of a genuine Court of Appeal under Mexican law, that is to say, that the Commission was only authorised in conformity with Article 424 of the Federal Mexican Code of Civil Procedure to enter into a re-examination of those points on which the claimant had formally appealed to the Commission, all other points being thenceforth considered as juridically unassailable.

Against this contention, the Mexican Agent argued that in that event Mexico would find herself in a very inferior position in the litigation, and he therefore urged the Commission to ignore completely the activity of the National Commission and the existence of previous decisions, and to submit the cases to an unprejudiced new trial.

The controversy was still more complicated by the attitude of the Mexican Commissioner, who defended a third system which amounted to the following, namely, that awards of the National Claims Commission should be considered as real judgments and, as such, vested with the international authority of regular judicial decisions ; the only case in which it could be lawful to reverse the same would be that of clearly established denial of justice ; in all other cases the awards ought to be considered by the Commission as incapable of attack.

Held by the President : That he could not subscribe to any of the three contentions :

(*a*) Not to that of the French Agent, since, *inter alia*, it is not permissible to apply to international proceedings particular provisions of municipal law, the term " appeal " having never been understood, in the diplomatic correspondence, in its strict technical meaning under Mexican civil law, and since the admission of this contention would, indeed, place the defendant party in an unreasonably inferior position ;

(*b*) Not to that of the Mexican Agent, since, *inter alia*, it was impossible, in the light of the genesis of the Convention, of the explicit clause of the corresponding German-Mexican Claims Convention of 16 March, 1925 (Article 12), of the clear terms of the National Claims Regulations and of the practice of the National Commission and the Mexican Government themselves, to deny every juridical connection between the activity of the two Commissions ;

(*c*) Not to that of the Mexican Commissioner, since, *inter alia*, the whole scope and economy of this particular Claims Convention were opposed to confining its effect, in case of the existence of previous awards of the National Commission, to the consideration of the same from the exclusive point of view of denial of justice, although, *in abstracto*, the matter could have been arranged by the Convention in this way.

Held, therefore : That in the case of existing awards of the National Commission the Mixed Commission could not refuse, and was prepared, to take cognisance of the same in its capacity of a tribunal of revision (in a non-technical sense) ; that, however, it was in no respect bound by the considerations and *dicta* therein contained ; that it preserved its full freedom of action and judgment, particularly with regard to the juridical appreciation of the cases submitted to its trial (questions of nationality, classification of the military forces whose acts engaged the responsibility of the Mexican Federation, limits of that responsibility, admissibility of claims of shareholders in Mexican companies, etc.) ; that, however, the results of the accurate investigations of the National Commission and its organs into matters of fact would, from the nature of things, have a considerable weight as evidence for the Mixed Commission, especially when those enquiries had already confirmed the correctness of the statements of the claimant. For the rest, the Mixed Commission was governed by the substantial provisions of its own paramount constitution, viz. the Claims Convention, and therefore the substantial provisions of the National Mexican Claims Regulations possessed as a rule no direct importance for the said Commission, but merely subsidiary or interpretative force in case the Convention should be silent, especially in view of the principle of international law according to which a State is generally bound to award to foreigners at least the same indemnities that it awards to its own citizens.

[Till now unreported.]

Arbitral Tribunals—Independent as Distinguished from Mixed —Law Applicable by.

See Case No. 369 (*Goldenberg & Sons* v. *Germany*).

ii.—The Law Applied by Arbitral Tribunals. Arbitration and Judicial Settlement

Case No. 317

International Arbitration—In General—The Law Applied by International Tribunals—The Analogy of Article 38 of the Statute of the Permanent Court—Filling of Gaps—Principles of Equity.

PORTUGAL *v.* GERMANY.

(THE MAZIUA AND NAULILAA CASES.)

Special Arbitral Tribunal. 31 *July*, 1928.

(MEURON, FAZY, GUEX.)

THE FACTS.—(See Case No. 360.) This was an arbitral tribunal constituted by virtue of paragraph 4 of the Annex to Articles 297 and 298 of the Treaty of Versailles which dealt, *inter alia*, with claims arising out of acts committed by the German Government or by any German authorities since 31 July, 1914, and before Portugal entered into the war. The same Article provided that the arbitrator entrusted with the assessing of the amount of the claim shall be nominated by M. Gustave Ador. At the suggestion of the arbitrator thus nominated, Germany and Portugal agreed to enlarge the Tribunal by the addition of two other neutral arbitrators. A question having arisen as to the law applicable, the Tribunal

Held: That the decision must be governed by general rules of international law as distinguished from any particular treaty provisions. The question was one of State responsibility, and as such must be determined by general international law. The designation of a purely neutral tribunal and the use of the term "acts committed"—a term taken from the terminology of international law—showed that there was no intention to substitute a special *jus tractatus* for general international law.

The fact that the Treaty did not expressly lay down the rules of law to be applied by the Tribunal could be interpreted only as meaning that the Tribunal should apply international law.[1] This being so, the law applicable by the Tribunal will

[1] The Tribunal referred here to the case of *H. Chatterton* v. *Germany*, decided on 8 November, 1923, by the Anglo-German Mixed Arbitral Tribunal (*Recueil*, VII, p. 21), and to Judgment No. 3 of the Permanent Court of International Justice in which the expression "acts committed" is stated to contemplate "acts contrary to the law of nations and involving an obligation "to make reparation." (Series A, No. 3, p. 8.)

be that laid down in the first four paragraphs of Article 38 of the Statute of the Permanent Court of International Justice. In cases where there is no rule of international law applicable to the case the arbitrators will fill the gap by applying principles of equity. In doing so they will remain within the orbit of international law applied by analogy and having regard to its evolution.[1] [Report: *Recueil*, VIII, p. 408, and pp. 412, 413.]

Disputes—Law Applied by Mixed Claims Commission—Meaning and Scope of the Phrase "to decide according to the "Principles of Equity"—Relation between the Principles of Equity and Positive International Law—Effects of the Clause upon the Application of the Convention in respect of Interest, Damages, Evidence. **Case No. 318**

GEORGES PINSON CASE, §§ 10-12, 43, 44, 56, 67, 69.

France and Mexico: Mixed Claims Commission.
19 *October*, 1928.
(VERZIJL, President.)

THE FACTS.—The French-Mexican Claims Convention of 25 September, 1924 (Article 2), instituted a Mixed Claims Commission in order to examine carefully all claims presented to it for decision by French subjects and protected persons on account of loss and damage suffered by them or by their properties during the revolutions and disturbed conditions which existed in Mexico from 1910 to 1920, and which were due to the acts of certain definite categories of military forces, etc., and to "decide the same impartially, in accordance with the "principles of equity, since Mexico wished to repair "'*gracieusement*' the damage and not to have her "responsibility fixed according to the general principles of international law." Therefore, in case it should be established that the alleged damage was sustained and was due to any of the causes enumerated in Article 3 of the Convention, Mexico declared herself *ex gratia* prepared to make indemnification. On the strength of these clauses the Mexican Government argued before the Commission that the Convention itself recognised implicitly the principle of absolute

[1] The Tribunal referred here to Lammasch, *Die Lehre von der Schiedsgerichtsbarkeit*, pp. 178-181.

Case No. 318 ***contd.***

irresponsibility of the State under positive international law for all damage whatsoever suffered by foreigners during revolutions and civil wars, and that therefore it should constantly be interpreted as strictly as possible.

Held by the President of the Commission: That the Mexican contention was unfounded. Far from rejecting absolutely the principle of responsibility of the State for revolutionary damage, the Convention seems on the contrary to admit to a certain extent the possibility of such responsibility but without expressing itself as to its exact limits. The context of the Treaty provisions and the origins of the Claims Convention place it beyond doubt that the scope of the clause quoted above was clearly to extend the financial responsibility of Mexico under the Convention beyond the limits of her strict juridical responsibility under positive international law, and that therefore the Commission was bound to allow indemnification in case of mere fulfilment of the conditions fixed by the terms of Articles 2 and 3, even when no responsibility could be recognised under the general principles of international law (as, for instance, for acts of military defence, for wrongful acts of unsuccessful revolutionaries, etc.). The Commission had, therefore, in general, no reason to enter, so far as the main point was concerned, into an express and general examination of the limits of State responsibility for damage suffered by foreigners in revolutionary periods from wrongful or other acts of governmental or revolutionary forces, etc. The necessity for such examination could, however, be revealed in the course of the proceedings, in connection with incidental questions; thus it reappeared, in effect, with regard to the question of indebtedness for interest: in this respect the President was of the opinion that he was not entitled to award interest in cases other than those where the responsibility of Mexico was founded equally in positive international law. (See also Case No. 181.)

For the rest, the express reference to the principles of equity, with formal exclusion of the application of the general principles of international law, did not extend beyond the central question of State responsibility. In all other respects positive international law remained paramount in the application and interpretation of the Convention. Therefore international law alone and not the indefinite principles of equity must govern the solution of all other doubtful points of law that might arise in the course of the proceedings, such as admissibility of claims, admissibility of evidence, questions of nationality, extent of the rights of shareholders in the assets of their companies, etc. For the same reason, the principles of equity referred to in Articles 2 and 3 of the Convention are themselves constantly to be interpreted in accordance with the principles of international law; thus, whenever a doubt arises as to the true meaning of a legal term therein used, or the real scope of those Articles, the Commission must have recourse to the general customary law, pursuant to which, *inter alia*, a State is generally bound to award to foreigners the same damages as it awards to its own subjects, and its responsibility is not confined to wrongful acts committed by the highest military commanders within the limits of their authority, but extends beyond, etc.

This interpretation of the fundamental clause of the Convention does not encroach in the least upon the natural rôle of equity in the appreciation of evidence and damages, nor upon its subsidiary function as a supplementary source of law, or as a corrective in exceptional cases, where the application of strict law would lead to inconvenient consequences.

[Till now unreported.]

II.—Procedure

i.—Procedure before the Tribunal (Oral and Written Arguments)

Arbitral Procedure—Rôle of the Agents—Mouthpiece of their Government—Article 62 of the Hague Convention No. 1, 1907—Invocation by Agent of Anti-Constitutional Character of National Legislation—Estoppel. **Case No. 319**

GEORGES PINSON CASE, § 12bis.

France and Mexico : Mixed Claims Commission.
19 *October*, 1928.
(VERZIJL, President.)

THE FACTS.—In the course of the oral proceedings, the Mexican Agent repeatedly advanced contentions contradictory to Mexican legislation, or to the opinion of his own Government as evidenced by official documents, criticised presidential decrees, imputed anti-constitutional character to national Mexican legislation, etc. Interrogated on many occasions as to whether he pro-

Case No. 319 *contd.*

pounded personal opinions or the official point of view of the Mexican Government, he failed to give positive answer. In order to avoid further misunderstanding,

Held : That the Agents were to be considered as the official representatives of their Government (reference was here made to Article 62 of the Hague Convention No. 1 of 1907) and not merely as unofficial barristers free to put forward before the Commission all kinds of personal contentions, juridical and political, even contradictory to the official point of view of their Government. Thus, *inter alia*, the charge brought by the Mexican Agent against the constitutionality of the Mexican Nationality Law of 1886 could not be admitted as a merely personal opinion of the Agent, but only as an official argument of the Mexican Government, against which the Commission would be fully justified in holding that Mexico was estopped from invoking this argument before an international tribunal, since the successive Mexican Governments themselves had for more than forty years failed absolutely to obtain a judicial decision on the matter from their own High Court of Justice, or to propose to Congress the repeal of the law concerned.

[Till now unreported.]

ii.—Competence. Competence to Determine Jurisdiction

Case No. 320

PERMANENT COURT OF INTERNATIONAL JUSTICE.

ADVISORY OPINION No. 16.

International Arbitration—Right of Jurisdictional Bodies to Determine the Extent of their Jurisdiction.

INTERPRETATION OF THE GRECO-TURKISH AGREEMENT OF 1 DECEMBER, 1926.

28 *August* 1928.

THE FACTS.—Article IV of the Final Protocol of the Agreement of 1 December, 1926, between Greece and Turkey concerning the Exchange of Greek and Turkish populations provided as follows:

" Any questions of principle of importance " which may arise in the Mixed Commission " in connection with the new duties entrusted " to it by the Agreement signed this day and " which, when that Agreement was concluded, " it was not already discharging in virtue of "previous instruments defining its powers, "shall be submitted for arbitration to the "President of the Greco-Turkish Arbitral "Tribunal sitting at Constantinople. The "arbitrator's awards shall be binding."

A dispute having arisen between Greece and Turkey as to who is to decide whether "a "question of principle of importance" has arisen and by whom this matter may be submitted to arbitration,

Held: That from the very silence of the Article on this point it was possible and natural to deduce that the power to refer a matter to the arbitrator rested with the Mixed Commission itself. As there was no doubt that only questions arising in the course of the deliberations of the Commission were contemplated, it was clear—"having regard amongst other things to the "principle that, as a general rule, anybody possessing "jurisdictional powers has the right in the first place "itself to determine the extent of its jurisdiction—that "questions affecting the extent of the jurisdiction of the "Mixed Commission must be settled by the Commission "itself without action by any other body being "necessary." [Report: Series B, No. 16, pp. 19-21.[1]]

NOTE.—The Court also pointed out that "to accord to individual "members of an organisation constituted as a corporate body any "right to take action of any kind outside the sphere of proceedings "within that organisation, would be clearly contrary to an accepted "principle of law" (at p. 25).

International Arbitration—In General—Recourse to International Tribunals after Unsuccessful Recourse to Municipal Tribunals. **Case No. 321**

KULIN, EMERIC *v.* ROUMANIAN STATE.

Roumanian-Hungarian Mixed Arbitral Tribunal.

10 *January*, 1927.

(CEDERKRANTZ, SZEKACZ.)

THE FACTS.—(See Case No. 59.) It was contended on behalf of Roumania that the claimant was precluded

[1] See also Series E, No. 5, pp. 227-235. And see Michel de Grotte in *R.I.*, 3rd ser., vol. X (1929), pp. 424-430.

Case No. 321 *contd.*

from bringing his claim before the Mixed Arbitral Tribunal, as he had previously appeared before Roumanian courts without invoking Article 250 of the Treaty of Trianon, and had there pleaded to the merits, and thus recognised that the measure complained of constituted an "expropriation,"[1] so that he was precluded from now asserting that it was a "liquidation" within the terms of Article 250.

Held: That that contention must be rejected. It was a generally recognised principle in international jurisprudence that there is nothing to prevent a person from exhausting first the means of redress offered by national law before resorting to an international tribunal. The fact that the claimant invoked only municipal law before Roumanian tribunals could not deprive him of his right to invoke the provisions of the Treaty before the Mixed Arbitral Tribunal. [Report: *Recueil*, VII, pp. 138, 150.]

Case No. 322

International Arbitration—Recourse to—Necessity of Exhaustion of Legal Remedies Excluded by Convention.

STEINER AND GROSS *v.* POLISH STATE.

Upper Silesian Arbitral Tribunal. 30 *March*, 1928.

THE FACTS.—(See Case No. 188.) Poland contended that the Tribunal had no jurisdiction as the claimant made no attempt to obtain justice through Polish courts. Article 5 of the Geneva Convention of 15 May, 1922, relating to the jurisdiction of the Tribunal, provided as follows: "La question de savoir si et dans quelle "mesure une indemnité pour la suppression ou la dimi-"nution de droits acquis doit être payée par l'Etat, "sera directement tranchée par le Tribunal Arbitral "sur plainte de l'ayant droit."

Poland contended that the expression "directe-"ment" was merely intended to emphasise the innovation which the Convention introduced by giving to individuals, who are not subjects of international law, the right to bring actions before the Tribunal, but that it was not intended to oust the well-recognised rule of international law that local remedies must be exhausted before recourse is had to an international tribunal.

[1] That is to say, presumably, an expropriation in pursuance of domestic policy and for reasons of public welfare.

Held: That the Tribunal had jurisdiction. The expression "directement" must be interpreted as conferring upon the claimants the right to have recourse to the international tribunal without previous recourse to local courts and authorities. [Report: *Decisions of the Upper Silesian Arbitral Tribunal*, vol. I, Nos. 1/2 (in German and Polish), pp. 30-34.]

International Arbitration—In General—Recourse to—Concurrent Jurisdiction of International and Municipal Courts. **Case No. 323**

E. THALHEIMER *v.* YUGOSLAV STATE.

Hungarian-Yugoslav Mixed Arbitral Tribunal.
6 *September*, 1928.

(VAN SLOOTEN, ZOLTAN, ARANDJELOVITCH.)

THE FACTS.—This was a claim put forward by virtue of Article 250 of the Treaty of Trianon, for damages for measures of sequestration taken after the war by Yugoslav authorities in respect of the property of the Hungarian claimant. Article 250 of the Treaty of Trianon provided for the jurisdiction of the Mixed Arbitral Tribunal in regard to claims of Hungarian nationals arising out of retention, liquidation, other measures of transfer, or compulsory administration or sequestration, of their property, rights and interests.

On the part of Yugoslavia it was contended that the Tribunal had no jurisdiction, seeing that there were remedies open to the claimant before the competent Yugoslav authorities and that there was therefore no necessity for him to carry the matter before the Mixed Arbitral Tribunal.

Held: That the objection must be overruled. The possibility of obtaining compensation by way of recourse to the administrative authorities of Yugoslavia could not deprive the claimant of the right to avail herself of international remedies provided for by the Treaty. Should the Tribunal arrive at the conclusion that the action was brought in spite of the readiness of the Yugoslav authorities to redress the wrong, then it will take this circumstance into consideration when dealing with the question of costs. [Report: *Recueil*, VIII, p. 579.]

Case No. 324

Arbitral Tribunals—Competence—Interpretation of National Laws Independently of Government Statements—Criticism of Alleged Anti-Constitutional Character of National Legislation—Enquiry into Compatibility of National Legislation with International Law.

GEORGES PINSON CASE, §§ 29, 30 ff., 34 ff.

France and Mexico: Mixed Claims Commission.
19 *October*, 1928.

(VERZIJL, President.)

THE FACTS.—In the course of the oral proceedings, the Mexican Agent communicated from time to time to the Commission official statements of his Government concerning the interpretation of doubtful legal provisions discussed before the Commission, particularly with respect to nationality laws, to the Decree of President Obregón of July, 1924, relating to the classification of certain military forces as "revolutionary" (see Case No. 159), etc., evidently in order to have them admitted as authentic interpretations of the provisions at issue. On the contrary, on other occasions, he attacked the national legislation as being contrary to the Mexican Constitution, in regard to which point the Commission itself hesitated whether it should embark upon a criticism or not. Finally, he denied the right of the Commission to examine the provisions of the Mexican Constitution from the point of view of their compatibility with customary international law.

Held (*a*) (by implication): That the Commission was entitled to enter into an independent enquiry into the meaning of national legal provisions, the more so when they had never been interpreted by the national Courts of Justice. The statements of the interested Government could not be accepted as authoritative;

(*b*) That, although the Commission considered itself to be fully justified in refraining from entering into the question (see Case No. 319), it preferred to examine the charge of unconstitutionality brought against the Mexican legislation by the Mexican Agent, since the same or germane questions had already been discussed in the American-Mexican Claims Commission of 1868 (*in re Anderson and Thompson*, arbiters Dr. Lieber and Thornton, Moore, *International Arbitrations*, III, pp. 2480, 2482), and the controversies presented a more general interest from the point of view of constitutional as well as international law; and that at all events the competence of the Commission to enter into this enquiry could not be denied, since the Mexican Government themselves had raised the point;

(c) "That every international tribunal is bound and en-"titled, from the very nature of its functions, to examine "municipal legislation in the light of the Law of Nations." (Reference was made here to the 7th Award of the Permanent Court of International Justice, *Publications of the Permanent Court*, Series A, No. 7, p. 19.) In this respect no difference exists between provisions of ordinary laws and those of the Constitution of the State. See also Case No. 4.

[Till now unreported.]

Arbitration—Jurisdiction—Jurisdiction Excepting Matters "Arising out of Recent Revolutions"—Meaning of the Phrase—Interpretation of a Treaty by having Recourse to a Preceding Treaty. **Case No. 325**

C. E. BLAIR CASE.

United States and Mexico: General Claims Commission.
18 *October*, 1928.
(SINDBALLE, MACGREGOR, NIELSEN.)

THE FACTS.—This was a claim for compensation on account of an alleged denial of justice arising out of the alleged failure of Mexico to punish a certain Gutierrez guilty of assault on an American subject. Gutierrez was arrested by the Mexican authorities and confined in prison at Cosamaloapan. Before he was brought to trial, however, the town was occupied by one of the leaders of the Madero revolution who released all the prisoners. Gutierrez then joined the revolutionary forces and was killed in battle.

Article 1 of the General Claims Convention of 8 September, 1923, exempted from the jurisdiction of the Commission claims "arising from acts incident to "the recent revolutions." On 10 September, 1923, another convention was concluded, which set up a Special Claims Commission to deal with claims of this description.

It was contended on behalf of Mexico that as Gutierrez was released during the revolution the present Commission had no jurisdiction.

Held (Nielsen, the American Commissioner, dissenting): That as the claim was based on an alleged denial of justice in

Case No. 325 *contd.*

consequence of the failure to punish the offender, who was released by the revolutionary forces, the Commission had no jurisdiction. [Report: *Opinions of Commissioners*, 1929, p. 107.]

NOTE.—The American Commissioner dissented on the ground that the physical injuries and loss of property upon which the claim was based occurred during the administration of President Diaz, and therefore the claim was not excluded by the terms of the General Claims Convention. In the course of his Opinion he considered the question whether in order to interpret the provisions of the Convention of 8 September, 1923, recourse might not be had to the provisions of the Convention of 10 September, 1923. He said (at p. 105):

"While the Commission obviously has no power to decide that "a claim is within the jurisdiction of some other Commission, it "may be proper for this Commission, in construing the Convention "of 8 September, 1923, to consider provisions of the Convention "of 10 September, 1923, as the Commission previously has done. "See the Opinion in the *Home Insurance Company* case, Docket "No. 73. When there is need of interpretation of a treaty it is "proper to consider provisions of earlier or later treaties in relation "to subjects similar to those treated in the treaty under considera-"tion. Pradier-Fodéré, *Traité de Droit International Public*, "vol. II, Sec. 1188, p. 895. And it is permissible to consider "negotiations leading to the conclusions (*sic*) of a treaty. Crandall, "*Treaties, Their Making and Enforcement*, 2nd ed., pp. 377-386. "This principle is one that may sometimes be given important "application."

He then referred to the cases *Jacob Kaiser*, Docket No. 1166, *Bond Coleman*, Docket No. 209, and *Pomeroy's El Paso Transfer Company*, Docket No. 218, as throwing light on the meaning of the phrase "in-"cident to the recent revolution."

The dissenting Opinion contains a discussion and references to a number of cases bearing upon the subject of the jurisdiction of international tribunals. Jurisdiction is defined as "the power of a tribunal "to determine a case conformably to the law creating the tribunal or "other law defining its jurisdiction." The Opinion is expressed that when a point of jurisdiction is raised the Commission must look "to "the averments of a complainant's pleading to determine the nature of "the case" and that "matters pleaded in defense with respect to the "merits of the case are not relevant to the question of jurisdiction."

Case No. 326

Arbitration—Mixed Arbitral Tribunal Instituted by Peace Treaties—Multiplicity of Suits—Competence of Municipal Court in Suit between Parties already Litigating before the Arbitral Tribunal.

LANDWIRTSCHAFTLICHER ZENTRALVERBAND IN POLEN *v.* LIQUIDATING COMMITTEE IN POZNAN.

Supreme Administrative Court of Poland. 17 *November*, 1927.

THE FACTS. — The defendant, being the competent authority, had ordered in 1925 the liquidation of real estate belonging to the plaintiff. The latter brought the present action to quash the order. The defendant pleaded, *inter alia*, that, arising out of the same order, an action brought by the plaintiff was already pending before the German-Polish Mixed Arbitral Tribunal, and that that Tribunal had issued an injunction to the defendant to prevent the disposal of the plaintiff's property.

Held: That this plea could not prevent the Supreme Administrative Court of Poland from hearing and determining the action which had been brought before it. The organisation of the Mixed Arbitral Tribunal being based on Articles 304 and 305 of the Treaty of Versailles, and its jurisdiction in the present case arising out of Articles 297 (*b*) and (*h*) and 305 of the Treaty, "it follows clearly that there is legally no conflict "between the jurisdiction of the Mixed Arbitral Tribunal and "that of the Supreme Administrative Court, since the fields of "the jurisdiction of both Courts are different." [Reports: Z.W.N.T.A., 1927, No. 1310; O.S.P., VII, p. 160; R.P.E.S., 1928, p. 473.]

NOTE.—See *Annual Digest*, 1925-1926, Case No. 324.

International Arbitration—Competence—Distinction between Plea to Jurisdiction and the Question of Substance—Articles 232, 239 and 250 of the Treaty of Trianon.

See Case No. 59 (*Kulin, Emeric* v. *Roumanian State*).

International Arbitration—Excess of Jurisdiction.

See Case No. 291 (*Sarropoulos* v. *Bulgarian State*) for reference to the limited jurisdiction of a Mixed Arbitral Tribunal and to risks involved in a possible excess of jurisdiction.

Arbitration—Jurisdiction of Arbitral Tribunals—Jurisdiction in Matters of Reparation.

See Case No. 345 (*Case concerning the Factory at Chorzów*).

iii.—Intervention

Case No. 327

International Arbitration—Intervention—Meaning of the Term "Legitimate Interest."

UNGARISCHE LANDES-CENTRAL-SPARKASSA ET AL. *v.* CZECHOSLOVAK STATE ET AL.

Hungarian-Czechoslovak Mixed Arbitral Tribunal. 22 *February*, 1927.

(SCHREIBER, SZLADITS, HORA.)

THE FACTS.—This was a question of intervention in a case pending before the above Tribunal and involving a request that the Tribunal should annul the decision of the Minister for Slovakia refusing to recognise a concession previously granted to the intervening party. It was objected, against the party asking for permission to intervene, that Article 29 of the Rules of Procedure of the Tribunal relating to intervention spoke of a "legitimate interest," which implied an interest justified both in law and morals.

Held: That intervention must be permitted. A juridical interest was quite sufficient; no other justification was necessary. [Report: *Recueil*, VII, p. 59.]

iv.—Counter-Claim and Set-Off

Case No. 328

International Arbitration—Procedure—Set-Off.

THE BEELY WOOD STEEL CO. LTD. *v.* FRANZ AND MASSMANN.

Anglo-German Mixed Arbitral Tribunal. Interim Decision of 26 *October*, 1928.

(SANDSTROEM, ROBINSON, WENDRINER.)

THE FACTS.—In this case a German purchaser claimed the right to set-off, against the claim of a British seller for the balance of the price of steel supplied in pursuance of several orders given during the years 1911 to 1913, a claim for damages on account of defects in the steel supplied in 1912 and 1913.[1] The German purchaser

[1] The exact periods of time to which the claim for the price and the set-off respectively refer are not stated in the report.

contended that the several orders formed a series to be considered, by reason of their connection, as one transaction.

Held : That the set-off must be allowed. It was immaterial that the damages were unliquidated. The relevant consideration was that the set-off arose out of several of the series of contracts upon which the British seller's claim was based, and that the series must be considered as forming one transaction. [Report : *Recueil*, VIII, p. 289.]

NOTE.—See Ralston, No. 376, on counter-claims and set-off before international tribunals.

vii.—Injunctions and Interlocutory Orders

Interlocutory Judgments—Rate of Exchange and Interest Applicable to.

See Act of the Commissioner of the Tripartite Claims Commission (United States, Austria and Hungary), taken in pursuance of " Settlement of War Claims Act of 1928 " fixing the Rate of Exchange and of Interest and the Period during which Interest shall run with respect to Interlocutory Judgments entered by the Commissioner, dated 9 April, 1928. [Report : *A.J.*, XXIII (1929), p. 179.]

III.—Rules of Evidence. Burden of Proof

[As to Consideration of Preparatory Work in the Interpretation of Treaties, see Part VIII, TREATIES : XII. *Interpretation of Treaties.*]

International Arbitration—Evidence—Formal Rules of Evidence in International Arbitration—Allegations not Supported by Evidence—Evidence Produced at Later Stages of Procedure—Articles 51, 63, 67, 68 and 69 of the Hague Convention for the Pacific Settlement of International Disputes. **Case No. 329**

ISLAND OF PALMAS ARBITRATION CASE.

United States and Holland : Permanent Court of Arbitration.
4 *April*, 1928.

(HUBER, Arbitrator.)

THE FACTS.—(See Cases Nos. 1, 68, 70.) In respect of some of the evidence produced by Holland, the

Case No. 329 ***contd.***

United States contended that " statements without " evidence to support them could not be taken into " consideration by an international tribunal, and that " evidence is not only to be referred to but is to be laid " before the tribunal."

It was also contended on the part of the United States that any evidence in support of the statements made in the original Memorandum laid before the tribunal should have been produced in the Memorandum and not at the subsequent stages of the procedure.

On the part of Holland it was contended, first, that no formal rules of evidence existed in international arbitration, and secondly, that statements made by a Government in regard to its own acts were evidence in themselves and were in no need of supplementary corroboration.

Held : That the contentions of the United States must be rejected. " However desirable it may be that evidence should " be produced as complete and at as early a stage as possible, " it would seem to be contrary to the broad principles applied " in international arbitrations to exclude (*a limine*), except " under the explicit terms of a conventional rule, every allega-" tion made by a party as irrelevant, if it is not supported by " evidence, and to exclude evidence relating to such allegations " from being produced at a later stage of the procedure." In accordance with the provisions of Article 51 of the Hague Convention of 1907 for the Pacific Settlement of International Disputes, its provisions should be applied when necessary as a subsidiary law in regard to the procedure of the tribunal. Articles 67, 68 and 69 admitted the production of documents, with the consent or at the request of the tribunal, other than those mentioned in Article 63 and relating to the filing of cases, counter-cases and replies.

Article 3 of the Special Agreement conferred upon the arbitrator the power to ask the parties for further written explanations. His powers in this respect would be unduly limited if such explanations could not extend to any allegations already made and could not consist of evidence which included documents and maps. It was for the arbitrator to decide whether allegations of the parties were in need of evidence to support them, and whether the evidence produced was sufficient or not.

In the absence of explicit provisions to the contrary, the arbitral tribunal must have complete freedom to gauge the value of assertions made by the parties. " It is entirely free " to appreciate the value of assertions made during proceed- " ings at law by a government in regard to its own acts. Such " assertions are not, properly speaking, legal instruments as " would be declarations creating rights ; they are statements " concerning historical facts. The value and the weight of " any assertion can only be estimated in the light of all the " evidence and all the assertions made on either side, and " of facts which are notorious for the tribunal." [Reports : *Permanent Court of Arbitration, Arbitral Award rendered in conformity with the Special Agreement concluded on* 23 *January*, 1925, *between the United States of America and the Netherlands*, pp. 19-21 ; *A.J.*, XXII (1928), pp. 877-879.]

Evidence—Admissibility of—Freedom of Admission and Appreciation of Evidence—Freedom of Obligation to Follow the *Lex Loci*. **Case No. 330**

GEORGES PINSON CASE, §§ 43-46.

France and Mexico : Mixed Claims Commission.
19 *October*, 1928.

(VERZIJL, President.)

THE FACTS.—The Mexican Agent having urged the Commission to refuse all evidence as to the existence, the causes and the extent of damages not allowed by the general Mexican law of civil procedure, and the French Agent having advocated the application of the special Mexican Claims Laws,

Held : That the Commission had perfect freedom to admit any evidence which it considered necessary, without being bound by any provisions of the *lex loci*, either of the Federation or of a particular Member State, and either of a general or of a special character, and to appreciate its intrinsic value. Consequently, the Commission declined to enter into an examination of the bearing of the Mexican laws of procedure upon the documentary evidence submitted to it.

[Till now unreported.]

Case No. 331

Rules of Evidence—Duty of Both Parties to Co-operate in Placing All Material Facts before the Tribunal.

GEORGES PINSON CASE, § 44.

France and Mexico: Mixed Claims Commission.
19 *October*, 1928.

(VERZIJL, President.)

THE FACTS.—In this and in many other cases the Mexican Agent confined himself to what appeared to the Commission to be a purely negative attitude in face of documents presented by the French Agent in support of the claim, and which adduced at least a *prima facie* evidence of rights or facts. The Commission felt obliged, in its first award, to disapprove of this attitude, and expressly to declare that it shared in this respect the opinion of the General American-Mexican Claims Commission with regard to the duty of parties in an international procedure to co-operate in finding out and presenting all facts throwing light on the merits of the claim presented. Reference was made to the *William A. Parker* case, 1926 (see *Annual Digest*, 1925-1926, Case No. 315).

[Till now unreported.]

See also Cases Nos. 194 and 196 in this *Digest*.

Case No. 332

International Arbitration—Evidence—Exclusion of Evidence in respect of Events Taking Place after the Beginning of the Dispute.

ISLAND OF PALMAS ARBITRATION CASE.

United States and Holland: Permanent Court of Arbitration.
4 *April*, 1928.

(HUBER, Arbitrator.)

THE FACTS.—(See Cases Nos. 1, 68, 70.) The dispute between the United States and Holland in regard to the Island of Palmas on the ground of conflicting claims to sovereignty over the island arose in 1906.

Held (the point not being in dispute [1]): That events subsequent to 1906 must, in accordance with the general principles

[1] The Arbitrator referred here to an exchange of Notes between the two Governments adopting that view (see p. 55 of the Award).

of arbitral procedure, be excluded for the purpose of evidence as to the legal position of the disputed territory. [Reports: *Permanent Court of Arbitration, Arbitral Award rendered in conformity with the Special Agreement concluded on* 23 *January*, 1925, *between the United States of America and the Netherlands*, p. 55; *A.J.*, XXII (1928), p. 906.]

Evidence—Burden of Counter-Proof—Failure of the Defendant to Produce Proof which he could have Produced. **Case No. 333**

MARY ANN TURNER CASE.

United States and Mexico: General Claims Commission.
23 *July*, 1927.
(VAN VOLLENHOVEN, NIELSEN, MACGREGOR.)

THE FACTS.—(See Case No. 152.) Mexico pleaded that it was impossible to produce evidence in rebuttal of the charge of undue and illegal delay of court proceedings in the District Court of Vera Cruz because of the court records having been destroyed by American naval forces in April, 1914.

Held: That the plea failed. The evidence before the Commission showed that the court records in question, if not in Vera Cruz, might be in the archives of certain other courts, and that they apparently had been mislaid or destroyed by Mexican officials. Mexico could not possibly invoke in its favour, or as an excuse, this lack of counter-proof. [Reports: *Opinions of Commissioners*, 1927, p. 416; *A.J.*, XXII (1928), p. 663.]

NOTE.—The *Faulkner* case [1] distinguished.

International Arbitration—Evidence—Proof of Nationality—Importance of Affidavits—Nationality of Claims—Double Nationality. **Case No. 334**

G. L. SOLIS CASE.

United States and Mexico: General Claims Commission.
3 *October*, 1928.
(SINDBALLE, NIELSEN, MACGREGOR.)

THE FACTS.—This was a claim to obtain compensation for cattle said to have been taken from the claimant's

[1] *Opinions of Commissioners*, 1927, p. 86.

Case No. 334 ***contd.***

ranch by Mexican soldiers. The claim consisted of two items. One related to cattle taken by the Huerta revolutionary forces; the other to cattle taken by Mexican Federal forces. There was no birth certificate to prove the American nationality of the claimant, but only a certificate of baptism and a number of affidavits. It was contended by Mexico that the American nationality of the claimant was not sufficiently proven. In particular, objection was taken to one of the affidavits on the ground that "it is wanting "in probatory force, inasmuch as it is *ex parte*." It was also contended that the Commission had no jurisdiction owing to the possibility of the claimant possessing both Mexican and American nationality.

Held by Nielsen, the American Commissioner, for the Commission:

(*a*) As to the proof of nationality, that the Commission cannot reject the claim on the ground of inadequate proof of nationality, or on the theory that the United States is espousing a claim of a person possessing Mexican as well as American nationality.

In principle the same evidence may be offered before international courts as before national tribunals: thus testimony of witnesses may be offered, subject to cross-examination, but, for obvious reasons, in international arbitrations this procedure is seldom practicable. It is true that affidavits may contain false statements, but this does not justify the presumption that all testimony thus obtained is false, and that a form of evidence sanctioned by the arbitral agreement and by international practice cannot be used profitably. The use of an affidavit in an arbitration is to some extent a substitute for evidence given before domestic tribunals with the prescribed sanctions of judicial procedure. The parties are free, if they wish, to question the value of a particular affidavit and to analyse its statements. "The affidavits could not, more "particularly, be disregarded in the present case seeing that "affidavits are used extensively in the United States by "administrative and by judicial officials," and that "citizen-"ship is a domestic matter in no way governed by international "law, although multiplications of nationality frequently result "in international difficulties." The statement that, since obviously the nationality of a claimant must be determined in the light of the law of the claimant Government, proof adequate to establish citizenship under that law must be considered sufficient for an international tribunal, may require some qualification. It is clear that an international tribunal could not ignore local law and practices with regard to proof of nationality.

It is true that a certificate of baptism is of smaller evidential value than a birth certificate, seeing that the claimant might have been born in one country and as an infant taken into another country and baptized there, but in view of the accompanying evidence the Commission cannot assume this to be a fact. It is not immaterial that birth certificates are often not available among official records in the United States.

(*b*) As to dual nationality. There was no evidence to show that the claimant was of Mexican nationality. The fact that claimant's name appears to be of Spanish origin is not decisive in view of the prevalence of Spanish names in territories of the United States bordering on Mexico, and of the fact that a century ago Texas was Spanish, and within a somewhat less period Mexican, territory. [Reports: *Opinions of Commissioners*, 1929, p. 48; *A.J.*, XXIII (1929), p. 454.]

NOTE.—No point of law seems to be involved in the part of the decision relating to double nationality. It is included in the *Digest* as pointing to the possible effect of double nationality on the question of nationality of claims.

International Arbitration—Evidence—Nationality of Claims—Jurisdiction of a Claims Commission—Receipts as Evidence—Requisitions—Conformity of Requisition Receipts with Requirements of Domestic Law—Burden of Proof.

Case No. 335

EDGAR A. HATTON CASE.

United States and Mexico: General Claims Commission.
26 *September*, 1928.

(SINDBALLE, NIELSEN, MACGREGOR.)

THE FACTS.—This was a claim for the value of two mules and five saddle horses alleged to have been requisitioned by a commanding general of the Mexican Federal troops. Mexico contested the claim on the grounds: (*a*) that the American citizenship of the claimant was not adequately proved (this objection was not put forward until the oral argument); (*b*) that the receipt for the goods requisitioned was not "authenticated" according to Mexican law; (*c*) that the receipt did not mention the claimant as the person from whom the animals were requisitioned.

Case No. 335 *contd.*

Held: That the claim succeeded.

By Nielsen, American Commissioner, for the Commission: (*a*) The nationality of claimants is the justification in international law for the intervention of a Government of one country to protect its subjects and their property abroad. According to Articles I and VII of the Convention of 8 September, 1923, relating to jurisdiction, each Government is restricted to the presentation of claims in behalf of its own nationals. Convincing proof of nationality is necessary not only from the standpoint of international law, but as a jurisdictional requirement. It is true that, as stated in the oral argument for the United States, had the nationality of the claimant been challenged in the Mexican Answer, the United States would have been in a position to amplify the proof of nationality. This circumstance, however, cannot be regarded as the decisive consideration. " In refusing, as it does, to " sustain the contention made in oral argument that the claim " should be rejected (the Commission) should not be understood " to concede that admissions of the respondent government of " the nationality of claimants could in all cases take the place " of adequate proof of nationality. Such admissions do not " appear to be analogous to a waiver before a domestic court of " a question of personal jurisdiction. The jurisdictional pro- " visions of the Convention of 8 September, 1923, are concerned " with certain specified claims. Having in mind that the ad- " mission in the Mexican Answer relates to the nationality of a " person resident in Mexico and owning property in that " country; that under the arbitral agreement the Commission " must take cognisance of all documents placed before it; and " that nothing has been adduced to throw any doubt on the " assertions of the claimant, who swears that he was born in the " United States, or on the sworn statement of persons who, in " addition to their statement respecting the claimant's citizen- " ship, state that they have known the claimant all their lives, " it is believed that the claim should not be rejected on the " ground of unsatisfactory proof of nationality."

(*b*) The Commission cannot properly disregard the evidential value of that receipt on the ground that it had not been " authenticated " as required by Mexican law. The validity and evidential value of such receipts are not wholly a matter of national law. Military requisitions are a matter frequently regulated in international law and practice as may be seen from the Convention of The Hague of 1907 respecting the Law and Customs of War on Land which contains provisions with regard to receipts for military requisitions and contributions. An alien in the situation of the claimant is entitled under international law to compensation for requisitioned property, and no formalities required by domestic law as to the form of authentication of a receipt for requisitioned property, or the failure of a military commander to comply with those formalities, could deprive the receipt of evidential value before the Commission.

There was no evidence adduced to show that the receipt had been altered fraudulently.

(*c*) The fact that the receipt does not mention the claimant as the person from whom the property was requisitioned could not be regarded as decisive. If the claimant were not the owner of the ranch, Mexico would have been in a position to show that fact. "And while it is not the function of the respondent government to make a case for a claimant government, it is believed that, in view of the fact that the claimant is in possession of the receipt, and in view of the further fact that Mexico has adduced nothing to show that the claimant was not the owner of the ranch at the time of the requisition, the Commission should accept without question the claimant's allegation that the property requisitioned from the ranch belonged to him. The justification for drawing inferences from the non-production of available evidence has often been discussed by domestic courts. See, for examples, *Kirby* v. *Tallmadge*, 160 U.S. 379; *Bilokumski* v. *Tod*, 263 U.S. 149." [Report: *Opinions of Commissioners*, 1929, p. 6.]

International Arbitration—Evidence—Maps.

Case No. 336

ISLAND OF PALMAS ARBITRATION CASE.

United States and Holland: Permanent Court of Arbitration. 4 *April*, 1928.

(HUBER, Arbitrator.)

Among the proofs produced by the United States of the existence in law—as distinguished from exercise—of the sovereignty over the Island of Palmas was evidence from maps. In dealing with the question of admissibility of maps as evidence the arbitrator pointed out that the information supplied by the two parties showed that account could only be taken of maps with the greatest caution in deciding the question of sovereignty over a disputed territory. The arbitrator must be satisfied that the cartographer has not merely referred to maps already existing, but that he has based his decision on information

Case No. 336 ***contd.***

carefully collected for that purpose.[1] If the arbitrator has satisfied himself that there exist legal relevant facts which refute the statements of cartographers, whose sources of information are not revealed, he is precluded from attaching weight to the maps, however numerous and generally valid they may be. [Reports: *Permanent Court of Arbitration, Arbitral Award rendered in conformity with the Special Agreement concluded on 23 January*, 1925, *between the United States of America and the Netherlands*, pp. 36, 37, 39; *A.J.*, XXII (1928), p. 891.]

Evidence—Admissibility of Opinion of University Faculty of Law as to Status of a National Corporation—Royal Prussian Brandenburger Family Trust.

See Case No. 16 (*Das Königlich Preussisch-Brandenburgische Hausfideikommiss* v. *The Administration of South-West Africa and the Registrar of Deeds*).

International Arbitration—Evidence—Admissibility of Sworn Statements by Interested Parties.

See Case No. 157 (*Daniel Dillon Case, Note*).

Evidence—Burden of Proof—Loss of Nationality—Proof of Residence Abroad.

See Case No. 208 (*India and Far East Company* v. *Schaefer and German Office*).

Arbitration—Evidence—Admissions in the Course of Negotiations for the Settlement of the Dispute.

See Case No. 337 (*Kulin, Emeric* v. *Roumanian State*).

Evidence—Proof of Quality of Protected Person.

See Case No. 204 (*N. N. Berouti* v. *Turkish Government*).

Evidence—Burden of Proof—Presumption against the Party Failing to Produce the Proof.

See Case No. 272 (*A. A. Megalidis* v. *Turkey*).

[1] It appeared from the explanations filed by the Dutch Government that the authors of the map did not rely on new and authentic information but reproduced older maps.

International Arbitration—Evidence—Estoppel—Recourse to Municipal Courts—Whether Barring Subsequent Recourse to International Tribunals.

See Case No. 321 (*Kulin, Emeric* v. *Roumanian State*).

Arbitration—Evidence—Burden of Proof in the Matter of Nationality.

See Case No. 198 (*Ruinart Père & Sons* v. *Franzmann*).

IV.—Admission of Liability. Waiver. Estoppel

Admissions—Admissions made in the Course of Negotiations for the Settlement of a Dispute—Value of. **Case No. 337**

KULIN, EMERIC *v.* ROUMANIAN STATE.

Roumanian-Hungarian Mixed Arbitral Tribunal.
10 *January*, 1927.

(CEDERKRANTZ, SZEKACZ.)

THE FACTS.—(See also Case No. 321.) It was contended on behalf of Roumania, in the course of the oral proceedings before the Tribunal, that Hungary was precluded from maintaining that the Roumanian measures of expropriation were contrary to Article 250 of the Treaty of Trianon, on the ground that in the course of negotiations which took place between the two Governments in May, 1923, in Brussels, the Hungarian delegate admitted that the Treaty of Trianon did not forbid the expropriation of the property of optants for reasons of public welfare, including the agrarian reform.

Held : That the contention must be rejected. It was not admissible to detail an isolated statement made in the course of abortive negotiations, and to treat it as an official admission by the Hungarian Government binding the Hungarian State. The record showed that the statement in question was a conciliatory declaration made in the desire to facilitate an understanding which was not in fact reached. The records of the proceedings did not show from whom the declaration emanated. In any case, it was clear from the record that the statement was not intended as an admission that the expropriation was justified without actual compensation. [Report : *Recueil*, VII, p. 138.]

Arbitral Procedure—Estoppel—Estoppel against Pleading Unconstitutionality of Municipal Laws.

See Case No. 319 (*Georges Pinson Case,* § 12[bis]).

Estoppel—Refusal to Recognise as a Subject—Effect on Future Diplomatic Protection.

See Case No. 168 (*H. Rothmann* v. *Austria and Hungary*).

V.—The Award[1]

ii.—*Res Judicata*

Case No. 338

Arbitral Procedure—Admissibility of Interpretative Decisions of a General Character—Juridical Force of Such Decisions —*Res Judicata*.

Georges Pinson Case, § 3.

France and Mexico : Mixed Claims Commission.
19 *October*, 1928.

(Verzijl, President.)

The Facts.—In order to obtain from the outset and once for all authoritative interpretations by the Commission of the scope and principal provisions of the French-Mexican Claims Convention of 25 September, 1924, in view of the various fundamental differences of opinion between the Mexican Agent and himself, the French Agent urged the Commission to formulate in its first award its opinion on the questions concerned, in the form of general interpretative decisions. The Mexican Agent firmly opposed this demand, which he considered to be outside the competence of the Commission.

Held : That the Commission was undoubtedly entitled to proceed in the way advocated by the French Agent (reference was here made to various " administrative decisions " of the American-German Mixed Claims Commission of 1922), in order to ensure from the beginning a regular and constant application of the Convention according to certain fundamental principles of interpretation ; that such preliminary decisions of a general character would, however, necessarily partake of the binding force of arbitral awards and of *res judicata* ; and that,

[1] For sub-title i. (Scope and Binding Force of the Award) see pp. 492-494.

therefore, and with a view to the great variety of the claims submitted for adjudication, the Commission preferred to lay down its fundamental interpretations in the form of ample statements of reasons in the first test case, which would be a guide for the Agents, without hampering the Commission too much in revising and adapting the same to special circumstances.

[Till now unreported.]

iii.—Appeal and Revision

International Arbitration—Award—Revision—Discovery of New Facts—Distinction between Appeal and Revision. **Case No. 339**

BARON DE NEUFLIZE *v.* DISKONTOGESELLSCHAFT ET AL.

Franco-German Mixed Arbitral Tribunal. 29 *July*, 1927.

(BOTELLA, HOENE, SERRUYS.)

THE FACTS.—Paragraph 79 of the Rules of Procedure of the Franco-German Mixed Arbitral Tribunal provided for the revision of a judgment rendered by the Mixed Arbitral Tribunal in case of discovery of a new fact which was unknown when the judgment was given and which is of such a nature as to exercise decisive influence on the judgment.[1]

In October, 1924, the Franco-German Mixed Arbitral Tribunal rendered in the above case[2] a judgment in which there occurred the following sentence: "Considering that the damage of which "the bondholders complain is merely a hypothetical "one since it will only actually take place if Turkey "does not fulfil her obligations to the bondholders . . ."

It was contended on the part of the applicant for revision that in April, 1925, a judgment was given by Professor Borel in the Ottoman Debt Arbitration as the result of which the damage described in the judgment of 1924 as a mere possibility had now become a fact, and that this circumstance warranted a revision of the judgment in accordance with paragraph 79 of the Rules of Procedure.

Held: That the application must be rejected. The reason

[1] See to the same effect Article 61 of the Statute of the Permanent Court of International Justice.

[2] *Recueil*, IV, p. 794.

Case No. 339 *contd.*

expressed in the sentence quoted above was in no way decisive for the judgment given. Even if the judgment of 1924 had been based on a mistaken appreciation of a fact, that would not in itself justify the revision of a judgment. Revision ought not to be confused with appeal. In order to justify revision it is not enough that there has taken place an error on a point of law or in the appreciation of a fact, or in both. It is only lack of knowledge, on the part of the judge *and* of one of the parties, of a material and decisive fact, which may in law give rise to the revision of a judgment. [Report : *Recueil*, VII, p. 629.]

NOTE.—It has not been thought necessary to give a detailed account of the facts underlying this judgment, but in view of the scarcity of precedent in the matter of revision a digest of this decision appears to be appropriate.

i.—Scope and Binding Force of the Award

Case No. 340

International Arbitration—Award—The Duty of the Arbitrator to Give a Decision—Question of *Non Liquet*—Relative Strength of Titles Involved—Assuring the Coexistence of Conflicting Interests Worthy of Legal Protection.

ISLAND OF PALMAS ARBITRATION CASE.

United States and Holland : Permanent Court of Arbitration. 4 April, 1928.

(HUBER, Arbitrator.)

THE FACTS.—See Cases Nos. 1, 68, 70, 72, 75.

Having arrived at the conclusion that Holland had proved her title to the Island of Palmas acquired by continuous and peaceful display of State authority, the arbitrator pointed out that he would have reached a similar conclusion even if the evidence laid before the Tribunal did not suffice to establish such continuous and peaceful display of sovereignty by the Netherlands over the disputed island. " In this case no party " would have established its claims to sovereignty over the " island, and the decision of the arbitrator would have to be " founded on the relative strength of the titles invoked by each " party." As in the Arbitration Agreement the parties referred to their wish to " terminate " the dispute, it was evident that they intended the Arbitral Award not to conclude by a *non liquet* but to decide in any case that the island formed part of the territory of one or the other of the parties to the dispute. This was also to be inferred from the terms of the Arbitration Agreement, which presupposed that the Island of Palmas could belong only to one or to the other party to the dispute and must form in its entirety a part of the territory of one of the disputants. It was to be foreseen that the evidence produced in support of the acts of sovereignty over the island might not prove to be sufficient for a clear determination of the exclusive rights of sovereignty, and that the arbitrator would therefore have to found his decision on the relative strength of the titles invoked on either side.

At least some acts of exercise of sovereignty have been proved conclusively on the part of Holland, whereas no such conclusive evidence had been produced on the part of Spain. These proved acts of exercise of sovereignty created an inchoate title in favour of Holland which had precedence over any inchoate title invoked by the United States by virtue of mere discovery by Spain. "International law, like law in general, "has the object of assuring the coexistence of different interests "which are worthy of legal protection. If, as in the present "instance, only one of two conflicting interests is to prevail, "because sovereignty can be attributed to but one of the "parties, the interest which involves the maintenance of a "state of things having offered at the critical time to the "inhabitants of the disputed territory and to other States a "certain guarantee for the respect of their rights ought, in "doubt, to prevail over an interest which—supposing it to be "recognised in international law—has not yet received any "concrete form of development." [Reports: *Permanent Court of Arbitration, Arbitral Award rendered in conformity with the Special Agreement concluded on* 23 *January*, 1925, *between the United States of America and the Netherlands*, pp. 60-62; *A.J.*, XXII (1928), pp. 910, 911.]

International Arbitration—In General—Effect of Arbitral Awards on Decisions of National Court—Decision of German Court contrary to the Treaty of Versailles. **Case No. 341**

MECCANO LIMITED *v.* MAERKLIN BROTHERS & CO.

Anglo-German Mixed Arbitral Tribunal.
Decision of 6 *November*, 1928.

(HEECKEREN, HART, ZACHARIAS.)

See the above case for an instance of the application of Article 305 of the Treaty of Versailles which provides for an appeal before the Mixed Arbitral Tribunal against a decision of a German court deemed to be inconsistent with the provisions

Case No. 341 *contd.*

of the Treaty of Versailles. In the present case a British company asked for the removal from the Register of a trade mark standing in the name of the purchaser and acquired as the result of the liquidation of a Germany company owned by the claimant British company. The German courts, holding that the liquidation proceedings were confirmed by Article 297 (*d*) of the Treaty, refused to remove the name of the purchaser from the Register. The Tribunal held that the attitude of the German courts was inconsistent with other provisions of the Treaty, and that the redress should take the form of an order that the defendants should assent to the removal of their name as proprietors of the trade mark from the Register of the Imperial Patent Office. [Report: *Recueil*, VIII, p. 293.]

International Arbitration—Award—Fixing the Rate of Exchange in Monetary Awards.

See Case No. 137 (*George W. Cook* (*No.* 2) *Case*).

International Arbitration — Awards — Enforcement of — Enforcement of Awards of Mixed Arbitral Tribunals by National Courts: (a) against Individuals; (b) against Foreign States; (c) against the State in Question.

See Case No. 111 (*Enforcement of International Awards* (*Czechoslovakia*) *Case*).

International Arbitration—Awards—Relation to Judgments of Municipal Courts.

See Case No. 356 (*Case concerning the Factory at Chorzów*).

B. PERMANENT COURT OF INTERNATIONAL JUSTICE

I.—Organisation of the Court

Permanent Court of International Justice—Advisory Opinions —National Judges—Renunciation of the Right to Appoint.

See Advisory Opinion, No. 16 (Interpretation of the Greco-Turkish Agreement of 1 December, 1926), Series B, No. 16, p. 8, for an instance of a waiver by both parties to the dispute of their right to appoint a national judge by virtue of Article 31 of the Statute and of Article 71 [1] of the Rules of the Court.

Permanent Court of International Justice—Organisation—National Judges—Whether Required in regard to Measures of Interim Protection.

See Case No. 352 (*Case concerning the Factory at Chorzów (Indemnity), Note*).

III.—Contentious Jurisdiction

i.—Competence

Permanent Court of International Justice—Jurisdiction—In General — Presumption of Restricted Jurisdiction — Limits of.

Case No. 342

PERMANENT COURT OF INTERNATIONAL JUSTICE.

JUDGMENT No. 8.

GERMANY *v.* POLAND.

CASE CONCERNING THE FACTORY AT CHORZÓW.

(CLAIM FOR INDEMNITY. JURISDICTION.)

26 *July*, 1927.

THE FACTS.—It was contended on the part of Poland that in the present case (see Cases Nos. 345 and 346) the jurisdiction of the Court was in doubt, and that in case of doubt the Court should decline jurisdiction.

Held: That the above contention must be rejected. It was true that the Court's jurisdiction was always a limited one, that is to say, that it existed only in so far as States have accepted it. Accordingly, in case of objections being raised, the Court will affirm its jurisdiction only "provided that the force of the arguments "militating in favour of it is preponderant." However, the mere fact that weighty arguments can be advanced against the jurisdiction of the Court does not in itself constitute a doubt sufficient to eliminate jurisdiction. It is in each case the proven intention of the parties that is decisive. [Report: Series A, No. 9, p. 32.]

[1] As amended on 7 September, 1927.

Case No. 343
PERMANENT COURT OF INTERNATIONAL JUSTICE.
JUDGMENT No. 12.

Permanent Court of International Justice—Jurisdiction of—Implied Acceptance of the Jurisdiction of the Court—Article 38 of the Rules of the Court—Distinction between the Jurisdiction of International and of Municipal Tribunals—Exception in case of Conflict of Jurisdiction—Requirement of Form—Concurrent Jurisdiction of the Council of the League.

GERMANY *v.* POLAND.

RIGHTS OF MINORITIES IN UPPER SILESIA.

(Minority Schools.)

26 *April*, 1928.

THE FACTS.—(See Case No. 241.) In its Counter-Case submitted in reply to the German application, the Polish Government asked the Court either to dismiss the claim, or to give judgment in accordance with the Polish view on the merits of the dispute (see Case No. 241). In the Rejoinder, however, the Polish Government, although stating that it did not raise the objection as a preliminary objection but intended it to be taken with the merits, submitted that the Court should decline jurisdiction.

This submission was also maintained in the oral proceedings on the ground, as stated in the Rejoinder, that the Geneva Convention provided for the jurisdiction of the Court only in regard to provisions preceding Article 72 of the Convention, but not in regard to those following that Article. It was also contended by Poland that the Court had no jurisdiction as the matter had already been settled by the Council of the League of Nations.

Article 38 of the Rules of the Court provides, *inter alia*, that when proceedings are begun by means of an application, any preliminary objection shall be filed after the filing of the Case by the applicant and within the time fixed for the filing of the Counter-Case.[1]

[1] See p. 22 of the Judgment for a more detailed summary of the relevant provisions of that Article.

Held: That the plea to the jurisdiction must be overruled. The Polish Government has impliedly accepted the jurisdiction of the Court to give judgment on the merits in respect of all the claims of the German Government, and the objection to the jurisdiction made in the Rejoinder cannot invalidate the acceptance which existed at the time of the submission of the Counter-Case.

A. *Limitations upon the Competence of the Court.*

The will of the parties determines the jurisdiction of the Court, and there is no dispute which States entitled to appear before the Court cannot refer to it. This principle, clearly expressed in the first paragraph of Article 36 of the Statute, becomes inoperative only in those exceptional cases in which the dispute falls within the exclusive jurisdiction reserved to some other authority. This exception does not arise in the present case, since the jurisdiction possessed by the Council of the League of Nations under Articles 147 and 149 of the Geneva Convention is one relating to deciding upon individual or collective petitions, whereas the jurisdiction of the Court relates to hearing and determining disputes between States.

B. *Jurisdiction of the Court Contrasted with the Jurisdiction of Municipal Tribunals.*

" The Court's position, in regard to jurisdiction, " cannot be compared to the position of municipal " courts, amongst which jurisdiction is apportioned by " the State, either *ratione materiae* or in accordance with " a hierarchial system. This division of jurisdiction is, " generally speaking, binding upon the Parties and " implies an obligation on the part of the Courts *ex* " *officio* to ensure its observance. Since in such cases the " raising of an objection by one Party merely draws the " attention of the Court to an objection to the jurisdic- " tion which it must *ex officio* consider, a Party may take " this step at any stage of the proceedings " (at p. 23).

C. *Requirement of Form.*

Under the Statute of the Court, submission to the

Case No. 343 *contd.*

Court's jurisdiction is not dependent upon the observance of certain forms. Thus the previous conclusion of a special agreement is not essential. " There seems " to be no doubt that the consent of a State to the sub- " mission of a dispute to the Court may not only result " from an express declaration, but may also be inferred " from acts conclusively establishing it. It seems hard " to deny that the submission of arguments on the " merits, without making reservations in regard to the " question of jurisdiction, must be regarded as an un- " equivocal indication of the desire of a State to obtain " a decision on the merits of the suit " (at p. 24). The submission of the Counter-Case aims at a decision on the merits. (The Court referred here to Judgment No. 5, in which it accepted as sufficient for the purpose of establishing its jurisdiction a mere declaration made by the respondent in the course of the proceedings agreeing that the Court should decide a point which, in the Court's opinion, would not otherwise have come within its jurisdiction.)

D. *Extent of Implied Submission.*

Such implied submission may take place even if, as in the present case, the suit was originally brought on the basis of a clause conferring compulsory jurisdiction, while the implied submission relates to a matter not falling within the category of those in respect of which compulsory jurisdiction is established. The Court referred here to Judgment No. 5, in which such an extension of jurisdiction had taken place by virtue of an express declaration. However, the Court saw no reason to treat differently an implied submission and an express declaration. Once the respondent has, in either way, indicated his desire to obtain a decision on the merits and his intention to abstain from raising the question of jurisdiction, it seems clear that he cannot, later on in the proceedings, go back upon that declaration. The fact that the respondent asked the Court to "dismiss" ("*débouter*") the action must be regarded as another indication of his submitting to the jurisdiction of the Court on the matter. For the word "*dé-*" *bouter*" must be taken as possessing the meaning ordinarily attached to it in French law. [Report: Series A, No. 15, pp. 17-29.[1]]

NOTE.—See also pp. 29, 30, for another plea to the jurisdiction of the Court on the ground that the matter had already been settled by a resolution of the Council of the League of Nations. The Court overruled the plea on the ground that the two jurisdictions were different in character, namely, that the Council did not wish to settle the question of law which was now being submitted to the Court.

Permanent Court of International Justice—Jurisdiction of —Forms of Acceptance of the Jurisdiction of the Court— The Treaty of Locarno—Counter-Claims.

Case No. 344

PERMANENT COURT OF INTERNATIONAL JUSTICE.

JUDGMENT No. 13.

GERMANY *v.* POLAND.

CASE CONCERNING THE FACTORY AT CHORZÓW.

(CLAIM FOR INDEMNITY. MERITS.)

13 *September*, 1928.

THE FACTS.—(See also Case No. 177.) In the course of the consideration of the question of damages to be awarded to Germany in consequence of the dispossession of the Oberschlesische Stickstoffwerke Company (see Case No. 177), it was contended on behalf of Poland that the company has not suffered damage, on the ground that the company, by virtue of its articles of association and of certain transactions with the German *Reich*, was not the lawful owner, the property of the company being in fact the property of the *Reich* which passed to Poland under Article 256 of the Treaty of Versailles.[2] In answer to this con-

[1] See also Series E, No. 4, pp. 191-199.

[2] Paragraphs 1 and 2 of that Article provided as follows:

"Powers to which German territory is ceded shall acquire all property "and possessions situated therein belonging to the German Empire or to the "German States, and the value of such acquisitions shall be fixed by the "Reparation Commission, and paid by the State acquiring the territory to "the Reparation Commission for the credit of the German Government on "account of the sums due for reparation.

"For the purposes of this Article the property and possessions of the "German Empire and States shall be deemed to include all the property of "the Crown, the Empire or the States, and the private property of the former "German Emperor and other Royal personages."

Case No. 344 ***contd.***

tention, Germany pointed out that the Polish submission, without referring to any instrument conferring upon the Court jurisdiction in this matter, raised in fact the question of the jurisdiction of the Court under Article 256 of the Treaty of Versailles.

However, in her Reply, Germany said: "The German Government does not know "whether the Polish Government has in mind "the general treaty of arbitration signed at "Locarno according to which any dispute of a "legal nature must be submitted to arbitra-"tion, and, unless some special arbitral tribunal "is agreed upon, to the Permanent Court of "International Justice. But, however that "may be, the German Government, being "animated by a wish to ensure that full scope "shall be given to the Treaty of Locarno, "without pausing to debate questions as to "the procedure therein provided for, and also "to see the Chorzów case settled once and for "all, abstains from undertaking a detailed "examination of the questions of lack of "jurisdiction."

Germany also referred to the possibility of the Court exercising jurisdiction under Article 40 of the Rules of the Court, which states that the conclusions of the parties in their Counter-Cases may also include counter-claims in so far as the latter come within the jurisdiction of the Court. She agreed to the Court exercising jurisdiction under this head.

Held: That the Court had jurisdiction to decide on the matter of the applicability of Article 256 of the Treaty of Versailles to the question in dispute. Although Poland had subsequently made no statement on the question of jurisdiction, she had not withdrawn her claim, and it could therefore be assumed that she wished the Court to decide on the matter. Thus it appeared that both parties agreed to submit to the

Court the question raised in the submission. "As the "Court has said in Judgment No. 12, concerning certain "rights of minorities in Upper Silesia, Article 36 of "the Statute establishes the principle that the Court's "jurisdiction depends on the will of the parties; the "Court therefore is always competent once the latter "have accepted its jurisdiction, since there is no "dispute which States entitled to appear before the "Court cannot refer to it, save in exceptional cases "where a dispute may be within the exclusive juris-"diction of some other body. But this is not the case "as regards the submission in question" (at p. 37). [Report: Series A, No. 17, pp. 31-40.[1]]

NOTE.—The Court then considered the Polish submission on its merits, and found, for reasons which raise no question of general international law, that the Polish contention was not well founded. In particular, it found that the company was not legally identified with the *Reich*.

Permanent Court of International Justice—Jurisdiction of—Jurisdiction in the Matter of the Interpretation and Application of Treaties—Whether Implying Jurisdiction on the Matter of Reparation—Reparation for Damages and Obligatory Arbitration—Article 13 of the Covenant.

Case No. 345

PERMANENT COURT OF INTERNATIONAL JUSTICE.

JUDGMENT No. 8.

GERMANY *v.* POLAND.

CASE CONCERNING THE FACTORY AT CHORZÓW.

(CLAIM FOR INDEMNITY. JURISDICTION.)

26 *July*, 1927.

THE FACTS.—(See also Case No. 346 and *Annual Digest*, 1925-1926, Case No. 60.) In Judgment No. 7 the Court held that the action of the Polish Government in dispossessing certain German companies, in consequence of judgments of Polish courts given in pursuance of certain Polish laws, was contrary to her international obligations. The Court gave this judgment under Article 23 (paragraph 1) of the Geneva Convention of 15 May, 1922, between Germany and Poland, which conferred upon the

[1] See also Series E, No. 5, pp. 183-195.

Case No. 345 *contd.*

Permanent Court jurisdiction in regard to differences of opinion resulting from the interpretation and the application of Articles 6 to 22 of the Convention. After the judgment was given, the parties engaged in negotiations calculated to establish a situation conforming to the judgment of the Court. These negotiations led to no result.[1]

Germany then, relying on Article 23 of the Convention, brought the present action, asking the Court: (*a*) to declare that, in consequence of the judgment previously given by the Court, the Polish Government was under an obligation to make good the injury sustained by the companies in question; (*b*) to fix the amount of the indemnity and the method and time of payment.

Poland objected to the jurisdiction of the Court on the ground that paragraph 1 of Article 23, which gave the Court jurisdiction in the matter of "differences of opinion resulting from the interpretation and application of Articles 6 to 22," did not contemplate differences in regard to reparations claimed for the violation of these Articles, and also that Article 23 covered only the question whether in a given case the application of Articles 6 to 22 was correct or not.

Held: That the Court had jurisdiction.

(*a*) "It is a principle of international law that the breach of an engagement involves an obligation to make reparation in an adequate form. Reparation therefore is the indispensable complement of a failure to apply a convention, and there is no necessity for this to be stated in the convention itself. Differences relating to reparations, which may be due by reason

[1] The main reason of the failure of the negotiations was the fact that Poland, although willing to pay part of the indemnity in respect of one of the dispossessed companies, claimed the right to set-off, as against the claims of the other company, certain claims of her own against Germany in regard to Social Insurance in Upper Silesia. See Case No. 353.

" of failure to apply a convention, are consequently " differences relating to its application." [1]

The history of reservations to arbitration agreements showed that although it had been found necessary to include reservations of various kinds in regard to general questions of legal right and obligation, it had been found possible to omit reservations in arbitration agreements submitting pecuniary claims for judicial settlement. To say, therefore, that an arbitration clause providing generally for judicial settlement questions of the rights and obligations of a treaty was intended to exclude claims for pecuniary reparation would be contrary to the principal tendencies of the movement in favour of general arbitration.

(*b*) In interpreting Article 23 of the Geneva Convention, the Court must take account, not only of the history of arbitration treaties, and the grammatical and logical meaning of the words used, " but also and more " especially of the function which, in the intention of " the contracting parties, is to be attributed to this " provision." The object of that Article, as well as of other Articles providing for other means of redress, was to remove the possibility of persistent differences of opinion between the parties concerning the interpretation and the application of the Convention. " An " interpretation which would confine the Court simply " to recording that the convention had been incorrectly " applied or that it had not been applied, without being " able to lay down the conditions for the re-establish- " ment of the treaty rights affected, would be contrary " to what would, *prima facie*, be the natural object " of the clause ; for a jurisdiction of this kind, instead " of settling a dispute once and for all, would leave open " the possibility of further disputes."

(*c*) The classification of international disputes adopted in Article 13 of the Covenant of the League and

[1] The Court referred here to Judgments Nos. 6 and 7 in which it recognised that under Article 23 it had jurisdiction not only in regard to differences relating to the question whether the application of a provision has or has not been correct, but also in regard to the applicability of these Articles, *i.e.* in regard to any act or omission creating a situation contrary to these Articles.

Case No. 345 ***contd.***

in Article 36 of the Statute of the Court militated in favour of the view that the Court's jurisdiction in "differences of opinion resulting from the interpretation and application" of the Geneva Convention included also questions of reparation. It was true that the Covenant mentioned separately "disputes as to the "interpretation of a treaty" and those relating to "the "nature or extent of the reparation." However, the Covenant also mentioned separately disputes as to "the existence of any fact which, if established, would "constitute a breach of an international obligation," and the Court had established in Judgments Nos. 6 and 7 that it had jurisdiction to decide whether a breach of the Geneva Convention had taken place. "The "decision whether there has been a breach of an engagement involves no doubt a more important jurisdiction "than a decision as to the nature or extent of reparation due for a breach of an international engagement "the existence of which is already established. If "Article 23, paragraph 1, covers the disputes mentioned "in the first and third categories by the two provisions "above mentioned, it would be difficult to understand "why—failing an express provision to that effect—it "should not cover the less important disputes mentioned in the fourth category."

(*d*) No decisive importance could be attached to the fact that in a Convention concluded in 1921 between Poland, "acting also in the name of the Free City of "Danzig," and Germany, the parties had deemed it necessary, in addition to the clause conferring upon the arbitral tribunal jurisdiction in regard to the interpretation or the application of the Convention, to confer upon it jurisdiction as to reparation; "the fact that a "convention explicitly confirms the conception generally "adopted in regard to arbitration clauses, cannot be "construed to mean that the same parties, when employing in another convention the wording ordinarily "used in conventions of this kind, have, by so doing, "given evidence of an intention contrary to that which "is to be presumed when interpreting an arbitration

" clause in a convention." [Report: Series A, No. 9, pp. 20-25.[1]]

Permanent Court of International Justice—Jurisdiction—Litispendence—Concurrent Jurisdiction of Other Tribunals—Deprivation of the Interested Party of the Recourse to the Proper Tribunal by a Wrongful Action of the State.

Case No. 346

PERMANENT COURT OF INTERNATIONAL JUSTICE.

JUDGMENT No. 8.

GERMANY *v.* POLAND.

CASE CONCERNING THE FACTORY AT CHORZÓW.

(CLAIM FOR INDEMNITY. JURISDICTION.)

26 *July*, 1927.

THE FACTS.—(See Case No. 345.) Article 305 of the Treaty of Versailles provided that whenever a competent municipal court had given a decision inconsistent with the provisions of Sections III, IV, V or VII of the Treaty, the party who is prejudiced by the decision shall be entitled to obtain redress which shall be fixed by the Mixed Arbitral Tribunal. It appeared that one of the companies (the Oberschlesische), the dispossession of which gave rise to the present action, brought an action before the Germano-Polish Mixed Arbitral Tribunal in a matter substantially the same as the one pending before the Court. In regard to the question of a conflict of jurisdiction, the Court

Held: (*a*) In general, " the Court, when it has to " define its jurisdiction in relation to that of another " tribunal, cannot allow its own competency to give " way unless confronted with a clause which it considers " sufficiently clear to prevent the possibility of a nega- " tive conflict of jurisdiction involving the danger of a " denial of justice."

(*b*) The fact that dispossession had already taken place and that, therefore, the Mixed Arbitral Tribunal would seem to have jurisdiction under Article 305 was not material. That Tribunal would have had no

[1] See also Series E, No. 4, pp. 155-162.

Case No. 346 *contd.*

jurisdiction but for the fact that Poland disregarded the Geneva Convention of 15 May, 1922, one of the fundamental principles of which was that no dispossession may take place without previous notice to the interested party, affording him the opportunity of having recourse to the competent tribunal. Accordingly, the Polish Government could not expect the interested parties to have recourse to tribunals which might have been open to them if the Convention had been applied. After the illegal dispossession had thus taken place, the utmost that the interested parties could obtain from the Mixed Arbitral Tribunal would be reparation for the wrong committed, whereas, if the procedure laid down in the Convention had been followed, the wrong would perhaps not have occurred at all. It was " a principle generally accepted in the juris-" prudence of international arbitration, as well as by " municipal courts, that one party cannot avail himself " of the fact that the other has not fulfilled some " obligation or has not had recourse to some means of " redress, if the former party has, by some illegal act, " prevented the latter from fulfilling the obligation in " question, or from having recourse to the tribunal " which would have been open to him." [Report: Series A, No. 9, pp. 31, 32.[1]]

Case No. 347

PERMANENT COURT OF INTERNATIONAL JUSTICE.

JUDGMENT No. 11.

Permanent Court of International Justice—Procedure—Interpretation of the Judgments of the Court—Article 60 of the Statute—Meaning of the Term " Dispute "—Previous Negotiations—Operative Part of the Judgment—*Res Judicata*—Declaratory Judgments—Article 59 of the Statute.

GERMANY *v.* POLAND.

INTERPRETATION OF JUDGMENTS NOS. 7 AND 8.

(The Chorzów Factory.)

16 *December*, 1927.

THE FACTS.—(See Cases Nos. 345, 346.) Article 60 of the Statute of the Court provides as follows:

[1] See on this aspect of the case Michel de Grotte in *R.I.*, 3rd ser., vol. X (1929), pp. 246-248, who sees in the decision of the Court an implied acceptance of the English doctrine of estoppel.

"The judgment is final and without "appeal. In the event of dispute as to the "meaning or scope of the judgment, the "Court shall construe it upon the request of "any party."

In the course of Judgment No. 7, in which the Court held that the attitude of the Polish Government in regard to the Oberschlesische Company was not in conformity with the international obligations of Poland, the Court dealt with the Polish contention that the German Government was not entitled to alienate the Chorzów factory, and also that the said company had not validly acquired the right of ownership of the factory. The Court rejected these contentions. In the course of the relevant part of the judgment the Court said:

"If Poland wishes to dispute the validity "of this entry, it can, in any case, only be "annulled in pursuance of a decision given "by the competent tribunal; this follows "from the principle of respect for vested "rights . . ."

In the course of Judgment No. 8, the Court said:

". . . it follows that once dispossession "has taken place without previous investiga-"tion of the right of ownership, the possible "undertaking of this investigation in order "to justify such dispossession after it has "taken place cannot undo the fact that a "breach of the Geneva Convention has "already taken place, or affect the Court's "jurisdiction."

Relying upon the passage quoted from paragraph 7 of Judgment No. 7, the Polish Government brought an action against the said company before a Polish court with the view to annulling the entry of the company in the land register. Germany thereupon requested the Court to

Case No. 347 ***contd.***

declare, by way of interpretation of Judgments Nos. 7 and 8 in accordance with Article 60 of the Statute, that the contention that in Judgment No. 7 the Court reserved to the Polish Government the right to annul by process of law the entry of the company in the land register, and the action actually brought by Poland before a Polish court with that object in view, were not in accordance with the true construction of Judgments Nos. 7 and 8.

Held: That by Judgment No. 7 the Court did not reserve to the Polish Government the right of asking by process of law before its courts that the entry of the Oberschlesische Stickstoffwerke in the land register was null and void, and that by the above Judgment the Court meant to recognise the right of ownership of the above company under municipal law.

A. *Question of Jurisdiction.*

(i) In regard to the Polish contention that there was no " dispute " between the parties as no negotiations had taken place: " according to the tenor of " Article 60 of the Statute, the manifestation of the " existence of the dispute in a specific manner, as for " instance by diplomatic negotiations, is not required. " It would no doubt be desirable that a State should " not proceed to take as serious a step as summoning " another State to appear before the Court without " having previously, within reasonable limits, en- " deavoured to make it quite clear that a difference of " views is in question which has not been capable of " being otherwise overcome. But in view of the word- " ing of the article, the Court considers that it cannot " require that the dispute should have manifested itself " in a formal way; according to the Court's view, it " should be sufficient if the two Governments have in " fact shown themselves as holding opposite views in " regard to the meaning or scope of a judgment of the " Court " (at p. 10). The Court referred here to the same view expressed by it in Judgment No. 6 (see *Annual Digest*, 1925-1926, Case No. 326).

(ii) In regard to the Polish contention that the German application did not refer to interpretation of the "meaning or scope of the judgment": that that contention must be rejected. "In order that a difference of opinion should become the subject of a request for an interpretation under Article 60 of the Statute, there must therefore exist a difference of opinion between the parties as to those points in the judgment in question which have been decided with binding force. That does not imply that it must be beyond dispute that the point the meaning of which is questioned is related to a part of the judgment having binding force. A difference of opinion as to whether a particular point has or has not been decided with binding force also constitutes a case which comes within the terms of the provision in question, and the Court cannot avoid the duty incumbent upon it of interpreting the judgment in so far as necessary, in order to adjudicate upon such a difference of opinion" (at p. 11). As the German Government contended that Judgment No. 7 finally decided the question of ownership possessed by the company over the factory at Chorzów also under municipal law, and as the Polish Government relied on certain passages of the judgment in support of the contrary view, there was a true dispute as to the meaning and scope of Judgment No. 7.

(iii) In regard to the Polish contention that the request does not relate to the operative part of the judgment: that that contention must be rejected. It was true that the operative part of the judgment did not directly refer to the question raised in the application, but "the fact that the grounds for the judgment contain a passage which one of the parties construes as a reservation (the effect of which would be to restrict the binding force of Judgment No. 7), or as affirming a right inconsistent with the situation at law which the other party considers as established with binding force, allows of the Court's being validly

Case No. 347 *contd.*

"requested to give an interpretation fixing the true "meaning and scope of the judgment in question" (at p. 14).

B. *Merits.*

(*a*) The operative part of Judgment No. 7, namely, that the attitude of the Polish Government was not in conformity with the provisions of the Geneva Convention, was based, *inter alia,* on the finding that from the standpoint of municipal law the Oberschlesische Company had validly acquired the right of ownership to the factory. This finding constituted an essential condition of the Court's decision, which has now acquired the force of *res judicata.* Accordingly, that finding was included amongst the points decided in Judgment No. 7, and possessed binding force in accordance with Article 59 of the Statute.

(*b*) Judgment No. 7 was in the nature of a declaratory judgment, "the intention of which is to "ensure recognition of a situation at law, once and for "all and with binding force as between the parties; "so that the legal position thus established cannot "again be called in question in so far as the legal "effects ensuing therefrom are concerned." There was nothing in Article 59 to prevent the Court from giving purely declaratory judgments. The object of that Article was merely to prevent legal principles accepted by the Court in a particular case from being binding also upon other States or in other disputes.

(*c*) In regard to the above-quoted passage from Judgment No. 7 relied upon by Poland: Although from the fact that the Court used the present tense ("If Poland wishes to dispute the validity of this "entry, it can, in any case, only be annulled in pur-"suance of a decision given by the competent tribunal"), it could be concluded that the Court envisaged the possibility of institution by Poland in the future of proceedings before the Polish courts with the view to obtaining the annulment of the entry; it would be contrary to the whole of the Court's reasoning to interpret it as making the actual effect of the judgment of the Permanent Court dependent upon the results of any future proceedings before municipal courts. Such a reservation would deprive the operative part of the judgment of its logical and necessary foundation, and give to it the character of a merely provisional decision. [Report: Series A, No. 13, pp. 9-21.[1]]

NOTE.—(*a*) The above case has been digested in some detail for the reason, *inter alia*, that it bears closely upon the important subjects of *res judicata*, declaratory judgments and the meaning of Article 59 of the Statute.

(*b*) The student will note in this case the combination of the decision on the merits with the decision on jurisdiction.

(*c*) See, however, the dissenting decision of Judge Anzilotti to the effect that the subject-matter of the interpretative judgment of the Court was not *res judicata*.

Permanent Court of International Justice—Jurisdiction under Optional Clause (Article 36).

See Case No. 351 (*Denunciation of the Treaty of November 2, 1865, between China and Belgium*).

Permanent Court of International Justice—Jurisdiction—How far Dependent upon Previous Negotiations.

See Case No. 347 (*Interpretation of Judgments Nos. 7 and 8—The Chorzów Factory*).

ii.—Procedure

Permanent Court of International Justice—Procedure—Defects of Form in the Documents Submitted to the Court.

Case No. 348

PERMANENT COURT OF INTERNATIONAL JUSTICE.

JUDGMENT No. 11.

GERMANY *v.* POLAND.

INTERPRETATION OF JUDGMENTS NOS. 7 AND 8.

(The Chorzów Factory.)

16 *December*, 1927.

See Case No. 377. Before dealing with the merits of the German application for an interpretative judgment, the Court pointed out that the form of the application was not in conformity with the Rules of

[1] See also Series E, No. 4, pp. 184-190. See also Michel de Grotte in *R.I.*, 3rd ser., vol. X (1929), pp. 248-254.

Case No. 348 *contd.*

the Court, in particular with Article 66, "which "was intended by the Court to furnish information "indispensable in regard to proceedings for inter-"pretation." However, the Court pointed out that, within reasonable limits, it may disregard the defects of form of documents placed before it. The Court "does not consider itself as bound simply to reply "'yes' or 'no' to the propositions formulated in the "submissions of the German Application. It adopts "this attitude because, for the purpose of the inter-"pretation of a judgment, it cannot be bound by "formulae chosen by the Parties concerned, but must "be able to take an unhampered decision." [Report: Series A, No. 13, pp. 15, 16.]

Case No. 349

PERMANENT COURT OF INTERNATIONAL JUSTICE.

JUDGMENT No. 13.

Permanent Court of International Justice—Procedure—Fresh Claims put forward in Addition to the Original Submissions.

GERMANY *v.* POLAND.

CASE CONCERNING THE FACTORY AT CHORZÓW.

(CLAIM FOR INDEMNITY. MERITS.)

13 *September*, 1928.

After setting forth the points of divergence between Germany and Poland as appearing from the original submissions, the Court pointed out that the parties have in the course of the written and oral proceedings formulated other claims, but that, inasmuch as these claims do not constitute developments of the original submissions or alternatives to them, the Court could regard them only as "subsidiary arguments" or as mere suggestions as to procedure. Although there was no occasion for the Court to decide on these requests, it could take them into account, when discussing the arguments submitted by the parties, for the purpose of stating the reasons of the judgment. [Report: Series A, No. 17, p. 18.]

Permanent Court of International Justice—Procedure—Provisional Measures—Orders—Revocability of at the Instance of the Parties.

Case No. 350

PERMANENT COURT OF INTERNATIONAL JUSTICE.

Order in the Case between Belgium and China, 15 February, 1927.

DENUNCIATION OF THE TREATY OF 2 NOVEMBER, 1865, BETWEEN CHINA AND BELGIUM.

Order of 15 *February*, 1927.

THE FACTS.—(See Case No. 351.) It appeared that after the Court indicated on 7 January, 1927, certain provisional measures calculated to safeguard certain Belgian interests in China pending the judgment of the Court in the matter of the denunciation by China of the Treaty of 1865, the two parties arrived at an agreement in regard to the establishing of a provisional régime according a specified treatment to Belgian nationals. Thereupon the Belgian Government requested the Court to revoke the Order indicating the provisional measures. The Court

Declared: That the Order of 8 January, 1927, should cease to be operative. The Court considered itself justified in revoking the Order in view of the fact that the action was brought by way of unilateral application; that, as the time allowed for filing the Counter-Case had not expired, the Chinese Government had had no opportunity of indicating whether it accepted the Court's jurisdiction; and that there was, therefore, nothing to prevent Belgium, subject to the decision of the Court, from modifying her original submissions, including the request for provisional measures. There were in the present case no other circumstances independent of the legal situation created by the parties, resulting either from agreements concluded between them or from unilateral declarations in regard to matters concerning which they may use their discretion, which would point to the indication of measures of protection in the interests of the procedure alone. However, as the application of provisional measures

Case No. 350 *contd.*

of protection could not be dependent upon the position of the negotiations in progress between the parties, the Order must be revoked finally and in its entirety. [Report : Series A, No. 8, pp. 9-11.]

Case No. 351

PERMANENT COURT OF INTERNATIONAL JUSTICE.

Order in the Case between Belgium and China, 8 January, 1927.

Permanent Court of International Justice—Procedure—Provisional Measures—Article 41 of the Statute.

DENUNCIATION OF THE TREATY OF NOVEMBER 2, 1865, BETWEEN CHINA AND BELGIUM.

Order of 8 *January*, 1927.

THE FACTS.—Although Article 46 of the Treaty of 2 November, 1865, between China and Belgium contained provisions for the modification and renewal of the Treaty only on the initiative of the Belgian Government, the Chinese Government claimed the right to denounce the Treaty. In April, 1926, the Chinese Government informed the Belgian Government that it regarded the Treaty as ceasing to operate as from October, 1926. In November, 1926, a Chinese Presidential Order was issued granting protection to the Belgian Legation and Consulates and to Belgian nationals, property and ships in China in accordance with the rules of international law and usage.

Belgium refused to recognise that the Treaty gave China the right of unilateral denunciation, and, after China had refused to have the matter brought before the Court by special agreement, Belgium brought the dispute before the Court by way of an application, relying on the fact that both parties had previously adhered to the Optional Clause of Article 36, paragraph 2, of the Statute of the Court. In her application, Belgium asked the Court, *inter alia*, to indicate, pending judgment, " any provisional measures to be taken for " the preservation of rights which may subse- " quently be recognised as belonging to Belgium "or her nationals." The application was dated 25 November, 1926.[1]

Ordered: That the application for provisional measures must be granted. Such provisional measures were necessary, as in the event of an infraction "of "certain of the rights, which Belgium or her nationals "would possess in China, if the Treaty of 2 November, "1865, were recognised as still operative, such in-"fraction could not be made good simply by the "payment of an indemnity or by compensation or "restitution in some other material form." The object of the measures of interim protection was to prevent any rights of this nature from being prejudiced.

The Court then indicated provisionally that pending the final decision of the Court the protection of Belgian interests in accordance with international law and usage granted in the above-mentioned Presidential Decree should include a number of rights and safeguards provided in the Treaty of 1865 and also other safeguards.[2] [Report: Series A, No. 8, pp. 6-11.[3]]

Permanent Court of International Justice—Procedure—Provisional Measures—Article 41—Request for Payment of Part of the Sum Claimed—*Res Judicata*.

Case No. 352

PERMANENT COURT OF INTERNATIONAL JUSTICE.

Order concerning the Factory at Chorzów.

GERMANY *v.* POLAND.

CASE CONCERNING THE FACTORY AT CHORZÓW.

(INDEMNITY.)

21 *November*, 1927.

THE FACTS.—(See Cases Nos. 177, 178.) This was a request by the German Government that the Court should indicate, by virtue of Article 41 of the Statute, that Poland must pay to the German Government as a provisional

[1] The Belgian case, in which the demand for indication of *interim* measures of protection was substantiated, was not filed until 3 January, 1927.

[2] Paragraph 1 of Article 41 of the Statute of the Court provides as follows: "The Court shall have the power to indicate, if it considers that circumstances "so require, any provisional measures which ought to be taken to reserve the "respective rights of either party."

[3] See also Series E, No. 3, pp. 125-130, and No. 5, pp. 203, 204. See also Michel de Grotte in *R.I.*, 3rd ser., vol. X (1929), pp. 265-270, and Schücking in *Festgabe der juristischen Fakultäten zum 50-jährigen Bestehen des Reichsgerichts*, 1929, vol. I, pp. 72-121.

Case No. 352 *contd.*

measure the sum of thirty million Reichsmark. The request was made after the Court held (in Judgment No. 7) that the action of Poland in regard to the factory at Chorzów was contrary to her international obligations, and that (in Judgment No. 8) it had jurisdiction to entertain a claim for indemnity.

It was contended on behalf of Germany that not only the amount of compensation was essential but also the date of payment, and that if it were necessary to wait for the final judgment of the Court, the opportunities for the economic reconstruction of the factory which had arisen could not be made use of. Reference was made to the work of the Committee of Jurists who in 1920 drafted the Statute in support of the view that Article 41 of the Statute envisaged as the subject of measures of protection not only an omission by the parties, but also definite acts.

Held: That effect could not be given to the request of Germany. The request could not be regarded as relating to the indication of measures of interim protection, but as calculated to obtain an interim judgment in favour of a part of the claim. [Report : Series A, No. 12, p. 10.[1]]

NOTE.—It was pointed out in the Order that in regard to provisional measures of interim protection the Court was entitled to take the necessary steps in its normal composition, without specially obtaining the assistance of national judges.

Case No. 353

PERMANENT COURT OF INTERNATIONAL JUSTICE.

JUDGMENT No. 13.

Counter-Claims—Set-Off—Admissibility under International Law—Jurisdiction of International Tribunals to Pronounce upon—Effectiveness of the Judgment of the Court.

GERMANY *v.* POLAND.

CASE CONCERNING THE FACTORY AT CHORZÓW.

(CLAIM FOR INDEMNITY. MERITS.)

13 *September*, 1928.

THE FACTS.—(See Case No. 177.) One of the requests contained in the German application

[1] See also Series E, No. 4, pp. 163-165.

was that the Court, in awarding an indemnity for damages, should declare that the Polish Government is not entitled to set off, against the German claim for indemnity, either the Polish claim in respect of social insurances in Upper Silesia [1] or any other claim, or, in the alternative, that set-off is permissible only in respect of a debt recognised by Germany or established by a judgment given between the two Governments. Poland asked for the rejection of the request, and it appeared from the argument advanced on her behalf that she denied the jurisdiction of the Court to entertain the request.

Held: That the Court had no jurisdiction to entertain the German request.

(*a*) The question whether, and under what conditions, international law allows claims to be set off against each other is outside the jurisdiction of the Court as derived from Article 23 of the Geneva Convention of 15 May, 1922, which conferred upon the Court jurisdiction in regard to the interpretation and application of the provisions of that Treaty. The Court's jurisdiction under that Article could be relied upon only if Poland had raised the plea of set-off. But Poland had not done it. It was true that this claim was put forward by Poland in the course of the negotiations following upon Judgment No. 7. However, the Court could not take into account declarations, admissions or proposals which the parties may have made during direct negotiations among them, which were intended to lead to a compromise and which led to no result. There was no reason to assume that Poland would now put forward the same claim against the final judgment of the Court. As already stated in Judgment No. 1, the Court "neither can nor should contemplate the contingency of the judgment not being

[1] The above claim was put forward by Poland in the course of the negotiations following upon Judgment No. 7, and it appeared that this claim was responsible for the failure of the negotiations.

Case No. 353 *contd.*

"complied with at the expiration of the time fixed for "compliance."

(*b*) These reasons contained also an answer to the German contention that the Court had jurisdiction under Article 23 of the Geneva Convention to deal with the German request on the ground that it related to one aspect of the payment to be made by Poland. As stated in Judgment No. 8 (see Case No. 345), the Court had jurisdiction to decide on the forms and methods of reparation, for instance, the time and place of payment, the question of costs, etc. "But this "principle would be quite unjustifiably extended if it "were taken as meaning that the Court might have "cognisance of any question whatever of international "law even quite foreign to the convention under con-"sideration, for the sole reason that the manner in "which such question is decided may have an influence "on the effectiveness of the reparation asked for. Such "an argument seems hardly reconcilable with the "fundamental principles of the Court's jurisdiction, "which is limited to cases specially provided for in "treaties and conventions in force" (at p. 61). [Report: Series A, No. 17, pp. 60-63.[1]]

Case No. 354 PERMANENT COURT OF INTERNATIONAL JUSTICE. JUDGMENT No. 9.

Evidence—Acquiescence—Absence of Protest.

FRANCE *v.* TURKEY.

THE CASE OF THE S.S. *LOTUS*.

7 September, 1927.

THE FACTS.—See Case No. 98.

Referring to the several instances, quoted in argument, of criminal proceedings in respect of collision cases before the courts of a country other than that the flag of which was flown, the Court stressed the fact that in these cases the States affected refrained from protesting. This fact was directly opposed to the alleged existence of a tacit consent on the part of States to the exclusive jurisdiction of the State whose flag was flown. It seemed hardly probable and it

[1] See also Series E, No. 5, pp. 183-195.

would not be in accordance with international practice that in such cases the States affected would have omitted to protest against the assumption of jurisdiction by the other States if they had really thought that this was a violation of international law. [Report : Series A, No. 10, p. 29.]

NOTE.—See also *ibid.*, p. 23, where the Court attached importance to the circumstance that States had omitted to protest against the fact that the criminal law of another State contained provisions asserting jurisdiction over foreigners for acts committed abroad and injuring the nationals of the State assuming jurisdiction.

Permanent Court of International Justice—Counter-Claims.

See Case No. 353 (*Case concerning the Factory at Chorzów*).

International Arbitration—Evidence—Burden of Proof—Onus of Proof upon the State Alleging a Restriction of Independence.

See Case No. 98 (*The Case of the S.S. Lotus (A)*).

iv.—Judgment

Permanent Court of International Justice—Binding Force of the Court's own Judgments—Citability.

Case No. 355 PERMANENT COURT OF INTERNATIONAL JUSTICE.

Judgment No. 8 (Series A, No. 9) refers on p. 23 to Judgments Nos. 6 and 7 (given in the same matter).

Judgment No. 8 refers on p. 24 to Judgment No. 5, referred to by Counsel, in order to show that that judgment cannot be cited in favour of a restricted interpretation of the word " application " as suggested.

Judgment No. 9, p. 16 (Series A, No. 10), refers generally to previous judgments and opinions on the question of preparatory work.

Judgment No. 11, p. 11 (Series A, No. 13), refers to Judgment No. 6 to the effect that, in the absence of an express provision, previous negotiations are not essential for the jurisdiction of the Court.

Judgment No. 11, p. 16 (Series A, No. 13), refers generally to previous judgments on the effect of defects of form of documents placed before the Court.

Judgment No. 11, p. 20 (Series A, No. 13), refers to Judgment No. 7 on the question of declaratory judgment and their relation to Article 59 of the Statute.

Judgment No. 12, pp. 23 and 24 (Series A, No. 15),

Case No. 355 *contd.*

refers to Judgment No. 5 on the question of the extension or acceptance of the Court's jurisdiction in the course of the proceedings.

Judgment No. 13, pp. 22-28, 31-34, 44-46, 61 (Series A, No. 17), refers frequently to Judgments Nos. 6, 7 and 8. All these judgments related to various aspects of the same case, *i.e.* to certain German interests in Polish Upper Silesia, and the citations appear, therefore, to be well within the frame of Article 59 of the Statute. On the other hand, some of them show the unwillingness of the Court to depart, in the judgment on the merits, from the reasoning adopted in the former judgments on the matter of jurisdiction.

Judgment No. 13, p. 37, refers to Judgment No. 12 concerning the different forms of submission to the jurisdiction of the Court.

Judgment No. 13, p. 63, refers to Judgment No. 1 on the matter of the execution of the Court's judgments.

In Advisory Opinion No. 14, p. 28, the Court adhered " to the rule applied in its previous decisions " as to the admissibility of preparatory work in the interpretation of treaties.

In the same Opinion, on p. 36, the Court referred generally to its previous judgments and advisory opinions to the effect that restrictions on the exercise of sovereign rights accepted by treaty do not imply limitation of sovereignty.

In Advisory Opinion No. 16, p. 15, the Court, " following the precedent afforded by its Advisory Opinion " No. 3," formulated and, in part, changed the terms of the question on which its opinion was being sought.

Case No. 356

PERMANENT COURT OF INTERNATIONAL JUSTICE. JUDGMENT No. 13.

Permanent Court of International Justice—Judgments of—How far Affected by Judgments of Municipal Courts.

GERMANY *v.* POLAND.

CASE CONCERNING THE FACTORY AT CHORZÓW.

(CLAIM FOR INDEMNITY. MERITS.)

13 *September*, 1928.

THE FACTS.—(See also Case No. 177.) In the course of the consideration of the question of damages to be awarded to Germany in consequence of the liquidation of the property of the Oberschlesische Stickstoffwerke Company (see Case No. 177) by the Polish authorities, it was contended on behalf of Poland that no damages ought to be awarded as the company had suffered no loss as the result of its dispossession because it was not the lawful owner. This, it was contended, was so on the ground, *inter alia*, that on 12 November, 1927, a Polish court at Katowice had given judgment to the effect that the company had not become the lawful owner of the landed property at Chorzów, that the entry in the land register made in its favour in 1922 was not valid, and that the ownership of the landed property in question fell to the Polish Treasury.

This judgment was given subsequently to Judgment No. 7 (see *Annual Digest*, 1925-1926, Cases Nos. 60 and 150), in which the Permanent Court declared that the dispossession of the company in consequence of certain Polish laws passed in 1920 and 1922 was contrary to the international obligations of Poland. It was contended by Poland that the judgment of the Polish Court in 1927 was given on grounds other than those two laws, and that the Permanent Court should therefore consider this new fact.

Held: That that contention must be rejected. Judgment No. 7 was based on the fact that the dispossession of the company was unlawful. The matter was in so far *res judicata*.[1] As the present application for damages was based on that judgment, it was impossible that the rights of the company should be looked upon differently for the purpose of Judgment No. 7, and in relation to the claim for reparation based on the same judgment. The terms of the judgment of the Polish Court of 1927, which was given by

[1] But see here the dissenting opinion of Professor Ehrlich, p. 76.

Case No. 356 ***contd.***

default as regards the Oberschlesische Company, did not state the reasons for which the company's ownership was declared null and void, but it appeared from the terms of the submissions made by the Polish Treasury to that Court that the reasons underlying the Polish judgment of 1927 were substantially those which the Permanent Court in Judgment No. 7 declared to be insufficient to show that the company was not protected by the Geneva Convention. "If the Court "were to deny the existence of a damage on the "ground that the factory did not belong to the Ober-"schlesische, it would be contradicting one of the "reasons on which it based its Judgment No. 7, and "it would be attributing to a judgment of a municipal "court power indirectly to invalidate a judgment of an "international court, which is impossible. Whatever "the effect of the judgment of the Tribunal of Katowice "of November 12th, 1927, may be at municipal law, "this judgment can neither render inexistent [*i.e.* non-"existent] the violation of the Geneva Convention "recognised by the Court in Judgment No. 7 to have "taken place, nor destroy one of the grounds on which "that judgment is based" (at p. 33). [Report: Series A, No. 17, pp. 31-34.[1]]

NOTE.—See on the question of the relation of judgments of international courts to those of municipal courts, Lammasch, *Die Rechtskraft der internationalen Schiedssprüche*, 1913, pp. 113-118.

Case No. 357

PERMANENT COURT OF INTERNATIONAL JUSTICE.

JUDGMENT No. 13 AND ORDER.

Permanent Court of International Justice—Judgment—Appointment of Experts—Articles 48 and 50 of the Statute.

GERMANY *v.* POLAND.

CASE CONCERNING THE FACTORY AT CHORZÓW.

(INDEMNITY.)

13 *September*, 1928.

See Case No. 177. In Judgment No. 13 the Court, after having decided on the principle governing the award of the indemnity to Germany, reserved the

[1] See also Series E, No. 5, pp. 183-195.

fixing of the amount of the indemnity for a future judgment to be given after receiving the report of experts to be appointed by the Court " for the purpose " of enlightening it " on a number of specified questions (see Case No. 177, Note (*e*)). The Court issued, simultaneously with the judgment, an Order setting forth the constitution and the procedure of the Committee of Experts composed of three members appointed by the President, the parties having the right to appoint one assessor each in an advisory capacity. The Order provided, *inter alia*, for a solemn declaration to be made by the experts and assessors (paragraph 4), the evidence and documents to be communicated to the experts (paragraphs 7 and 8), the fees of the experts, and the amounts to be contributed by the parties for this purpose. [Reports: Series A, No. 17, p. 64, and Order, pp. 99-103.]

Permanent Court of International Justice—Judgments—Presumption as to the Effectiveness of.

See Case No. 353 (*Case concerning the Factory at Chorzów*).

Permanent Court of International Justice—*Res Judicata*—Whether Covering Grounds of Decision.

See Case No. 347 (*Interpretation of Judgments Nos. 7 and 8—The Chorzów Factory*).

Permanent Court of International Justice—Judgments—Declaratory Judgments—How far in Accordance with Article 59.

See Case No. 347 (*Interpretation of Judgments Nos. 7 and 8—The Chorzów Factory*).

Permanent Court of International Justice—Effect of Decisions of.

See Case No. 94 (*Czechoslovak Agrarian Reform (Swiss Subjects) Case*).

Permanent Court of International Justice—Appointment of Experts—Article 60 of the Statute.

See Case No. 357 (*Case concerning the Factory at Chorzów*).

IV.—The Advisory Opinion

i.—Competence

Case No. 358

PERMANENT COURT OF INTERNATIONAL JUSTICE. ADVISORY OPINION No. 16.

Permanent Court of International Justice—Advisory Opinions—Form of Request for—Power of the Court to Alter the Terms of the Question put to it.

INTERPRETATION OF THE GRECO-TURKISH AGREEMENT OF 1 DECEMBER, 1926.

28 *August*, 1928.

In this case (as to the Facts see Case No. 320), the request of the Council of the League of Nations for an Advisory Opinion did not formulate the question submitted to the Court, but merely referred to a letter addressed by the President of the Mixed Commission for the Exchange of Greek and Turkish Populations to the Secretary-General with a view to obtaining an Advisory Opinion of the Court upon the interpretation of a disputed clause of an agreement existing between the two parties. The Court referred to Article 72, paragraph 2, of the Rules of the Court, which lays down that " the request shall contain an exact statement of the " question upon which an opinion is sought." The Court then pointed out that " as the letter referred " to above does not exactly state the question upon " which its opinion was sought, it is essential that [the " Court] should itself determine what this question is " and formulate an exact statement of it, in order " more particularly to avoid dealing with points of law " upon which it was not the intention of the Council " or of the Commission to obtain its opinion." The Court observed that although, " owing to the re-" latively simple nature of the present case," it was able to perform this task, this " may not always be so." After examining the documents submitted to it and the written and oral arguments, the Court arrived at the conclusion that the differences of opinion between the parties referred not, as stated in the letter of the Commission, " to the question as to what are the conditions

" to which the submission of a question by the Com- " mission to an arbitrator is subject, but to the question " for whom it is to decide whether these conditions are " fulfilled and by whom a question may be referred " to him." In view of this conclusion and " following " the precedent afforded by its Advisory Opinion " No. 3," the Court proceeded to formulate the question in regard to which it considered its opinion was sought. [Report: Series B, No. 16, pp. 14-17.]

D. UNILATERAL MEANS OF REDRESS SHORT OF WAR

i.—Retorsion

Retorsion—How far Admissible in Derogation of Treaty Provision. **Case No. 359**

JULES BARANYAI *v.* YUGOSLAVIA.

Hungarian-Yugoslav Mixed Arbitral Tribunal.
15 *September*, 1927.

(VAN SLOOTEN, ZOLTAN, ARANDJELOVITCH.)

THE FACTS.—(See also Case No. 273.) The plaintiff asked for restitution and damages for having been deprived of his property contrary to the provisions of Article 250 of the Treaty of Trianon, which prohibited the retention and liquidation of private property. One of the defences put forward by the defendant Government was that the property of Hungarian nationals was retained as a measure of retorsion.

Held: That this particular defence must be rejected. Retorsion, in so far as it involves the disregard of a provision of a treaty, cannot be regarded otherwise than as a simple manifestation of the unilateral will of the State not to fulfil its international obligations. If the defendant State were in the position to invoke the plea of retorsion each time it resorted to measures of sequestration and liquidation, the provisions of Article 250 would remain illusory. [Report: *Recueil*, VII, p. 858.]

NOTE.—Retorsion (*rétorsion*) seems to be used here as equivalent to " reprisals," and not in the sense advocated by Oppenheim, II (4th ed., 1928), § 29.

ii.—Reprisals

Case No. 360

Reprisals—Nature of—Question of Justification of Reprisals—Necessity of Previous Attempts to Secure Redress—Relation between Reprisals and the Injurious Act—Question of Proportionality.

PORTUGAL *v.* GERMANY.

(THE NAULILAA CASE.)

Special Arbitral Tribunal. 31 *July*, 1928.

(MEURON, FAZY, GUEX.)

THE FACTS.—On 19 October, 1914,[1] a German official and two German officers of German South-West Africa were killed by members of a Portuguese frontier post at Naulilaa. Two other Germans were wounded and interned. As a measure of reprisals, and at the order of the Governor of German South-West Africa, German forces attacked and destroyed a number of forts and posts in the frontier region of Portuguese territory. In addition, the German Governor sent a military expedition in the direction of the fort of Naulilaa, whose garrison offered resistance but was finally forced to give up the fort and to retire. The retreat continued well into Portuguese territory, although the German troops withdrew, after the engagement, into the German colony. As the result of the Portuguese retreat the evacuated regions were subjected to looting and pillage on the part of the native population.

The claim was put forward by Portugal in accordance with paragraph 4 of the Annex to Article 297 of the Treaty of Versailles (see Case No. 369) before a tribunal of three neutral arbitrators. Portugal contended that the reprisals were unjustified, and that Germany was responsible for the damage caused by the invasion. (See Case No. 179.)

After examining the circumstances accompanying the death of the three Germans on 19 October, 1914, the Commission found that the incident was entirely due to a misunderstanding caused largely by the fact that the Germans did not speak Portuguese and that the Portuguese officer who gave the order to fire believed himself to be in danger.

[1] War between Germany and Portugal did not begin until March, 1916.

Held : That Germany was responsible.

(*a*) *Justification of Reprisals.* A necessary condition for the legitimate exercise of the right of reprisals is the violation of a rule of international law by the State against which the reprisals are directed. There was no such violation in the present case, seeing that the death of the German officers was due to an accident caused by a misunderstanding. Neither could the internment of the two surviving Germans be regarded as an act contrary to the law of nations. A neutral State is entitled to disarm and intern members of belligerent forces which come into its territory.

(*b*) *Necessity of Request to Redress the Injury.*—Reprisals are illegal if they are not preceded by a request to remedy the alleged wrong. There is no justification for using force except in cases of necessity. It was true that this principle was not denied by Germany, who pleaded that the German Governor informed all German posts by wireless of the assassination of German officers, and this notice, which must have reached the Portuguese authorities, should have been sufficient warning. Germany also pleaded that the Governor refrained from sending a party with a flag of truce because he feared that the members of the party might be put to death or imprisoned. However, the Tribunal was not prepared to regard these reasons as sufficient.

(*c*) *Question of Proportionality.*—Reprisals which are altogether out of proportion with the act which prompted them, are excessive and therefore illegal. This is so even if it is not admitted that international law requires that reprisals should be approximately of the same degree as the injury to which they are meant as an answer. In addition, Germany did not, in the pleadings, deny the requirement of proportionality. There was an obvious lack of proportion between the incident of Naulilaa and the reprisals which followed the incident. [Report : *Recueil*, VIII, pp. 409, 422-425.]

NOTE.—In regard to the modern tendencies of international law in the matter of proportionality the Tribunal remarked that there is a tendency to restrict the notion of legitimate reprisals and to prohibit any excess in their use (p. 423).

Reprisals—Application by Courts against a Foreign State—Exclusive Competence of the Sovereign Power.

See Case No. 110 (*The National Navigation Company of Egypt* v. *Tavoularidis*).

PART XI

WAR AND NEUTRALITY[1]

[1] As it is at present not intended to go back further than the beginning of the year 1919, and not to digest decisions of Prize Courts save in so far as they raise questions of general international law, War and Neutrality are only dealt with in this Classification in very general terms.

A. WAR IN GENERAL

I.—Definition and Technical Meaning of War. Insurgency

Insurgency—Closing of Ports Occupied by Insurgents.

Case No. 361

THE ORIENTAL NAVIGATION COMPANY CASE.

United States and Mexico : General Claims Commission. 3 *October*, 1928.

(SINDBALLE, NIELSEN, MACGREGOR.)

THE FACTS.—In April, 1924, the port of Frontera and some other Mexican ports were in the hands of insurgents. The Government of Mexico declared these ports to be closed to international trade, and had officially informed the Government of the United States to this effect. The Government of the United States, however, assumed the position that, as, in its opinion, according to international law a port in the hands of insurgents can be closed only by an effective blockade, it was its duty to advise American citizens that they were entitled to engage in commerce with persons in control of the ports thus closed.

On April 15, 1924, the steamship *Gaston*, operated by the Oriental Navigation Company, an American corporation, cleared from the port of New Orleans with a cargo of general merchandise consigned to Frontera, but without obtaining clearance from the Mexican consul at New Orleans. When this cargo was unloaded, the vessel was to load a cargo of bananas, which had been purchased by agents of the Oriental Navigation Company and was to be transported from Frontera to New Orleans. When the *Gaston* arrived at Frontera and began unloading her cargo, a Mexican gunboat, *Agua Prieta*, which cruised in the offing, ordered the *Gaston* to put to sea. The order was subsequently repeated and accompanied by some random shots. The *Gaston* after having unloaded only part of her cargo, and with-

Case No. 361 *contd.*

out having loaded any part of the cargo of bananas, was obliged to put to sea. The cargo of bananas became a total loss.

The United States claimed before the Commission that Mexico should indemnify the company for the loss suffered by it from the action of the *Agua Prieta*. The loss was alleged to amount to $15,400.91, which sum was claimed with the allowance of interest thereon. Mexico contended that as the belligerency of the insurgents had not been recognised by any foreign Power, and that as the Federal Government of Mexico was vested with full sovereignty over all Mexican territory, the question whether the Mexican Government was entitled to order the closure of the ports was a question solely dependent upon domestic Mexican law.

Held by Sindballe, the Presiding Commissioner, for the Commission, Nielsen, the American Commissioner, dissenting: While not admitting that the question was one governed solely by Mexican law,[1] that the claim must be rejected.

The Federal Mexican authorities were not obliged to permit the unloading and the subsequent loading of a neutral vessel trading to an insurgent port without such clearance documents as are prescribed by Mexican law. It could not properly be said that the port of Frontera was in the hands of insurgents at the time of the unloading of the *Gaston*. "It was in fact partly "commanded by the *Agua Prieta*." Accordingly, her action in forcing off the *Gaston* can hardly be considered as a violation of international law as it obtained before the World War. It did not matter that the commercial relations of the *Gaston* with the port of Frontera were otherwise perfectly lawful and not liable to punishment or interference, and that a Mexican warship would have no right to interfere if it met the *Gaston* bound for the port in the hands of insurgents. [Reports: *Opinions of Commissioners*, 1929, p. 23; *A.J.*, XXIII (1929), p. 434.]

NOTE.—Attention should be drawn to the learned dissenting opinion of Nielsen, the American Commissioner, in which there are discussed precedents bearing upon the case before the Commission, the

[1] The Commission said: "In time of peace, it no doubt would be a question of domestic law only. But in time of civil war, when the control of a "port has passed into the hands of insurgents, it is held, nearly unanimously, "by a long series of authorities, that international law will apply, and that "neutral trade is protected by rules similar to those obtaining in case of war. "It is clear, also, that if this principle be not adopted, the conditions of neutral "commerce will be worse in case of civil war than in case of war."

position of insurgents and some questions of blockade, in particular with reference to the new developments of maritime warfare, including the so-called economic sanctions under Article 16 of the League of Nations. It will be noted that the Presiding Commissioner's opinion is principally based on the view that the port was in fact partly controlled by the Federal gunboat. This point is dealt with by the American Commissioner at p. 43 of the *Opinions*, where he expressed the opinion that the presence of the gunboat in the vicinity of the port was in the nature of a casual visit. He said : " I do not believe that a single, " brief visit of a war vessel in the vicinity of a port occupied by in- " surgents is tantamount to a control or command of the port that would " relieve a government of the obligation to maintain a blockade as " required by international law for the purpose of effecting a closure of " the port." And see, for an analysis of this case, the article in *A.J.*, XXIV (1930), pp. 69-78, by Dickinson, who seems to approve of the decision of the Commission.

Belligerency—Occupation of Enemy Territory—Recognition of Belligerency—Article 43 of the Regulations Attached to the Fourth Hague Convention of 1907. **Case No. 362**

GUGLEWICZOWA *v.* MAZUR.

Supreme Court of Poland, Third Division. 25 January, 1927.

THE FACTS.—The Fourth Hague Convention of 1907 had been published in the Austrian Journal of Laws in 1913, and was undoubtedly binding on the Austrian courts as part of Austrian law ; it subsequently remained in force in that part of Poland which had at one time formed part of the Austrian State. After the downfall of Austria in 1918, during a few months of the subsequent chaos in what was called Eastern Galicia, a body calling itself the Government of the Western Ukrainian Republic established its officials in various parts of the territory to govern various territorial units. This body never received any recognition of belligerency from the Polish Government. After the re-establishment [1] of Polish authority, the plaintiff in the present action sued the defendant, who had been a Ukrainian official, for damages for torts committed while in the exercise of his functions. Defendant demurred on the ground that he had been a State official and, as such, exempt from actions for wrongs committed in the exercise of his duties, by virtue of an Imperial Austrian Decree of 1806. On appeal,

[1] This term refers to the re-establishment of the former Polish State. See the case *Kulakowski and Others* v. *Szumkowski*, Case No. 375.

Case No 362 ***contd.***

Held: That Article 43 of the Hague Land Warfare Regulations "refers only to the occupation of a territory by a "belligerent State, and cannot be applied to the Ukrainians' "invasion since there cannot be attributed to them the char-"acter of a belligerent State," so that their officials are responsible under the Civil Code and by way of an ordinary action. [Report: P.P.A., 1927, p. 196.]

II.—Commencement of War

War—Declaration of—Decision of Egyptian Government to Treat Enemies of Great Britain as Enemies of Egypt Equivalent to Declaration of War—Great Britain in Egypt during the World War.

See Case No. 25 (*Heinrich Finck* v. *Egyptian Government*).

V.—Effects of Outbreak of War

ii.—On Treaties

(*a*) During the War

Effects of Outbreak of War on Treaties—Capitulations.

See Case No. 126 (*Syrian Capitulations* (*Denunciation by Turkey*) *Case*) (though in that case it was the effect of Turkey's unilateral denunciation of the capitulations and not the automatic effect of the outbreak of war upon them that was in question. However, the Court held that the capitulations survived the outbreak of war).—[Ed.]

Effects of Outbreak of War—Suspension of Treaties—German Capitulatory Rights in Egypt.

See Case No. 25 (*Heinrich Finck* v. *Egyptian Government*) (in which it was held by the Cairo Court of First Instance that the effect of the beginning of a state of war between Egypt and Germany was to suspend the capitulations *vis-à-vis* German nationals. The Court of Appeal, however, declared that, since the Mixed Courts were never closed to German subjects even during hostilities, the Court of First Instance ought to have dealt with the case on purely juridical and non-political grounds and to have recognised the equality of all persons before the law. Having regard, however, to paragraph 2 of their judgment (see Case No. 25), it was unnecessary to examine the effect of Germany's retrospective renunciation of the capitulations by Article 147 of the Treaty of Versailles).

(*b*) After the War

Effects of War upon Treaties—Abrogation of Article 3 of the Jay Treaty by the War of 1812—Rights of Third Parties. **Case No. 363**

McCandless *v.* United States.

United States Circuit Court of Appeals, Third Circuit.
9 *March*, 1928.

The Facts.—This was a petition for habeas corpus. Relator was a full-blooded Indian of the Iroquois tribe of the Six Nations. He was born on a reservation of that tribe in Canada. He was employed as a structural iron worker in the United States. He was arrested for entering the United States without complying with the immigration laws. The Jay Treaty of 1794, Article 3, provided in part: " It is agreed that it shall at all " times be free to His Majesty's subjects, and to the " citizens of the United States, and also to the Indians " dwelling on either side of the said boundary line, " freely to pass and repass by land or inland navigation, " into the respective territories and countries of the two " parties, on the continent of America (the country " within the limits of the Hudson's Bay Company only " excepted), and to navigate all the lakes, rivers and " waters thereof, and freely to carry on trade and " commerce with each other." The writ was granted and relator discharged. On appeal,

Held: That the judgment granting the writ should be affirmed. The Treaty was not abrogated by the War of 1812. Delivering the opinion of the Court, Judge Buffington said: " It will be observed that we are not here dealing with the " rights and obligations of the two signatories to that treaty to " and from each other, but with the rights of a third party " created by the joint action of the signatories. While it may " be contended that in the nature of things treaties and treaty " rights end by war, and if they are to again exist it must be by " a new treaty, this reasoning does not apply to these Indians.

Case No. 363 *contd.*

"If through the War of 1812 the Six Nations remained neutral, "as they had through the Revolutionary War, there was no "reason why either of the contending nations in 1812 should "desire to change the status of the Six Nations and thereby "anger and drive them into hostilities. They had contended, "when the Jay Treaty was being negotiated, that they should "have free access to all parts of their tribal territory by consent "of both nations. And there was no reason why this right "should come to an end because the two nations became in-"volved in war, while they remained neutral." (25 F. (2nd) 71, 72.) [Report: 25 F. (2nd) 71.]

NOTE.—So far as the termination of treaties by the outbreak of war is concerned, this decision would seem by implication to be overruled by the decision in *Karnuth* v. *United States* (Case No. 364), though the editors venture to prefer the decision in *McCandless'* case. The decision in *McCandless'* case is also relevant on the Rights of Third Parties under Treaties, and the position of private individuals in international law.—[Ed.]

Case No. 364

Effects of War upon Treaties—Article 3 of the Jay Treaty and the War of 1812.

KARNUTH *v.* UNITED STATES.

United States Circuit Court of Appeals, Second Circuit. United States Supreme Court. 5 *March*, 1928. 8 *April*, 1929.

THE FACTS.—This was a petition for habeas corpus. Relators were British subjects residing in Canada. One entered the United States to engage in employment at Niagara Falls, the other to seek employment. Both were arrested and ordered to be excluded by United States immigration authorities because they did not have the visas required of immigrants by the Immigration Act of 1924. The Act provided that the term "immigrant" should include "any alien depart-"ing from any place outside of the United States "destined for the United States except . . . an alien "visiting the United States temporarily for busi-"ness or pleasure." Regulations promulgated under the Act classified as immigrants "aliens residing in "foreign contiguous countries and entering the United "States to engage in existing employment or to secure "employment." Relators invoked Article 3 of the

Jay Treaty of 1794, which is quoted in the preceding case, No. 363. (8 U.S. Stat. L. 116, 117.) The District Court denied the writs. On appeal,

Held: That the judgment of the District Court denying the writs should be reversed. Article 3 of the Jay Treaty was not terminated by the War of 1812. The Immigration Act should be construed in harmony with the prior treaty if possible. On certiorari to the Supreme Court,

Held: That the judgment of the Circuit Court of Appeals should be reversed. Article 3 of the Jay Treaty was abrogated by the War of 1812. After referring to Article 9, held unaffected by the War of 1812 in *Society for the Propagation of the Gospel* v. *New Haven* (1823), 8 Wheaton 464,[1] Mr. Justice Sutherland, delivering the Opinion of the Court, continued: " Article IX and Article III relate to fundamentally different " things. Article IX aims at perpetuity and deals with " existing rights, vested and permanent in character, in respect " of which, by express provision, neither the owners nor their " heirs or assigns are to be regarded as aliens. These are " rights which, by their very nature, are fixed and continuing, " regardless of war or peace. But the privilege accorded by " Article III is one created by the treaty, having no obligatory " existence apart from that instrument, dictated by considera- " tions of mutual trust and confidence, and resting upon the " presumption that the privilege will not be exercised to un- " neighborly ends. It is, in no sense, a vested right. It is " not permanent in its nature. It is wholly promissory and " prospective and necessarily ceases to operate in a state of " war, since the passing and repassing of citizens or subjects " of one sovereignty into the territory of another is incon- " sistent with a condition of hostility. See 7 Moore's *Digest* " *of International Law*, § 1135; 2 Hyde, *International Law*, " § 606. The reasons for the conclusion are obvious—among " them, that otherwise the door would be open for treasonable " intercourse. And it is easy to see that such freedom of " intercourse also may be incompatible with conditions follow- " ing the termination of the war. Disturbance of peaceful " relations between countries occasioned by war is often so " profound that the accompanying bitterness, distrust and " hate indefinitely survive the coming of peace. The causes, " conduct or result of the war may be such as to render a " revival of the privilege inconsistent with a new or altered

[1] Hudson, *Cases*, p. 964.

Case No. 364 *contd.*

"state of affairs. The grant of the privilege connotes the "existence of normal peaceful relations. When these are "broken by war, it is wholly problematic whether the ensuing "peace will be of such character as to justify the neighborly "freedom of intercourse which prevailed before the rupture. "It follows that the provision belongs to the class of treaties "which does not survive war between the high contracting "parties. . . ." (279 U.S. 231, 239.) The departmental regulation was in harmony with and justified by the Immigration Act. [Reports: 24 F. (2nd) 649; 279 U.S. 231; and Hudson, *Cases*, p. 977.]

(See Editor's Note to preceding case, No. 363.)

iii.—On Private Contracts

Case No. 365

Effects of Outbreak of War on Private Contracts—Distinction between Executed and Executory Parts of a Contract—Lawfulness of Performance of Term not Involving Intercourse between Nationals of Opposing States.

OTTOMAN BANK (appellants) *v.* JEBARA (respondent).

House of Lords on Appeal from the English Court of Appeal.
1 *May*, 1928.

THE FACTS.—The defendants (appellants), the Ottoman Bank, were incorporated in Turkey, and in 1914 there were branches in Manchester, England, and in Beyrout in Syria, which was then part of the Turkish dominions. (Whether these branches had legal personality independently of the headquarters bank does not appear.) The plaintiff (respondent) was a British subject domiciled and carrying on business as a merchant in Manchester. Before war was declared between Great Britain and Turkey on 5 November, 1914, he had bought goods in England and shipped them to Syria for purchasers there. In accordance with his usual practice he drew bills of exchange (expressed in pounds sterling) upon the Syrian purchasers of the goods and handed the bills of exchange and the bills of lading covering the goods to the defendants' Manchester branch for transmission to their Beyrout branch. On the date of the declaration of war several consignments of goods had arrived in Beyrout and the relevant bills of exchange and the bills of lading were still in the hands of the defendants' Beyrout branch. The Syrian purchasers thereupon came forward and met the bills of exchange by paying to the defendants the number of Turkish piastres estimated to be required to produce in sterling in London on the respective days of payment the sums expressed in the bills. Thereupon the purchasers obtained possession of the goods. It being then impossible (and presumably illegal) to remit funds from Beyrout to England, the defendants retained the proceeds of the bills of exchange, and no payment was ever made to the plaintiff. In 1922 he instituted proceedings in England against the defendants to recover the sterling equivalent of the amount received by them on his behalf calculated as at the date of the receipt, or alternatively the value of the goods or damages for their conversion. The defendants contended that, the right of their Beyrout branch to deal with the goods depending on the mandate given by the plaintiff to their Manchester branch, this mandate was, like a contract, terminated by the outbreak of war, and that the defendants were therefore only liable after the conclusion of the war to remit to the plaintiff the number of piastres which they had actually received on his account and had been unable to remit to him. The value of the piastre had meanwhile depreciated heavily and the defendants contended that the plaintiff must bear the loss.

Rowlatt, J., in the King's Bench Division gave judgment in favour of the plaintiff for the full amount claimed. The Court of Appeal (Bankes, Scrutton and Atkin, L.JJ.) varied his judgment by holding that the defendants, by parting with the goods after their mandate to deal with them had been terminated by the outbreak of war, had committed a conversion of them and were therefore liable to the plaintiff in damages which in default of agreement must be assessed.

Held on appeal to the House of Lords (Viscount Dunedin, Lords Shaw, Phillimore, Carson and Blanesburgh): That the outbreak of war did not affect the legality of the subsidiary contract between Turkish nationals, namely, the defendants' Beyrout branch and the Syrian purchasers, to the effect that on payment of the bills the shipping documents should be

Case No. 365 *contd.*

handed over; accordingly, the defendants upon receiving these payments constituted themselves debtors in sterling in pursuance of the original contract and must pay the sterling equivalent at the time of the payments. The claim in conversion failed; the defendants could not carry out the whole of the plaintiff's mandate by remitting to him the proceeds of the goods, but he could not complain that his mandate was carried out so far as was legally possible, namely, by handing over the shipping documents and receiving payment for the goods. Accordingly the judgment of Rowlatt, J., was restored.

Per Viscount Dunedin (at p. 276): " It is not every contract that is abrogated by war; it is only a contract which is still executory and which for its execution requires intercourse between the English subject and the enemy."

(Argument also took place on the construction and effect of Article 84 of the Treaty of Lausanne of 1923, but this point is not considered to require treatment in this *Digest.*)

[Reports: L.R. [1927] 2 K.B. 254; [1928] A.C. 269.]

Case No. 366

Effects upon Contracts—Fire Insurance.

EXCESS INSURANCE COMPANY LIMITED (plaintiffs) *v.* MATHEWS (defendant).

English High Court of Justice (King's Bench Division). 2 *November*, 1925.

(MR. JUSTICE BRANSON.)

In this case, which does not require a detailed digest, it was common ground between the parties, and was assumed by the learned judge, that a pre-war contract of fire insurance between a British insurance company and the owners of a Hungarian corn mill (which was destroyed by fire during the currency of the policy and during the war) would have been abrogated by the outbreak of war, so that the loss would not be recoverable but for the provisions of the Treaty of Trianon contained in Article 234 (*a*) and Clauses 8 and 9 of the Annex to the Treaty of Peace (Hungary) Act, 1921, and the Order in Council made thereunder. These provisions gave the policy retrospective validity " as if the enactment had been in existence at all material times," and the amount of the loss was recoverable. [Reports: 31 Commercial Cases, p. 43; 23 Lloyd's List Law Reports, p. 71.]

iv.—On Enemy Subjects with regard to

(*b*) THEIR PROPERTY AND OTHER RIGHTS

War in General—Effects of Outbreak of War on Property of Enemy Subjects in Belligerent Territory—Sequestration of Property of Enemy Subjects. **Case No. 367**

UNITED STATES *v.* S. S. WHITE DENTAL MANUFACTURING CO.

United States Supreme Court. 16 *May*, 1927.

THE FACTS.—This was a suit to recover income-tax. The plaintiff was a Pennsylvania corporation which owned prior to 1918 the stock in a German corporation. The German sequestrator took over the property of this German corporation from 1918 to 1920. During his administration the value of the assets of the corporation was almost completely destroyed. Plaintiff filed a claim with the Mixed Claims Commission, and in 1924 was awarded $70,000. In 1918 plaintiff charged off as a loss its entire German investment and deducted this amount from its gross income. The deduction was disallowed on the ground that the loss was not evidenced by a closed and completed transaction in 1918. The tax was paid under protest and this suit followed. The Court of Claims allowed recovery. On certiorari,

Held: That the judgment allowing recovery should be affirmed. Delivering the Opinion of the Court, Mr. Justice Stone said: "The sequestration of enemy property was within "the rights of the German Government as a belligerent Power "and when effected left the corporation without right to "demand its release or compensation for its seizure, at least "until the declaration of peace. See *Littlejohn & Co.* v. "*United States*, 270 U.S. 215; *White* v. *Mechanics Securities* "*Corp.*, 269 U.S. 283, 300, 301; *Swiss Insurance Co.* v. *Miller*, "267 U.S. 42; *Stoehr* v. *Wallace*, 255 U.S. 239, 242-244; "*Central Trust Co.* v. *Garvan*, 254 U.S. 554; *Brown* v. *United* "*States*, 8 Cranch. 110, 122. What would ultimately come "back to it, as the event proved, might be secured not as a "matter of right, but as a matter either of grace to the van-"quished or exaction by the victor. In any case the amount "realized would be dependent upon the hazards of the war "then in progress." (274 U.S. 398, 402.) [Report: 274 U.S. 398.]

v.—On Enemy Merchant Ships in Port

Case No. 368

War—Effects of—Enemy Merchant Vessels in Port at the Outbreak of Hostilities.

PATENT CLAIMS (TRIPARTITE COMMISSION) CASE.

See an *obiter dictum* of the War Claims Arbiter (Edwin B. Parker) functioning under the Settlement of War Claims Act of 1928, in his Administrative Decision No. 2, Dealing with Bases of Determining Fair Compensation in Patent Claims, to the effect that enemy merchant vessels could " under " recognised international law . . . be detained or requisitioned " if found on the outbreak of the war within the territorial " waters of the United States." (Decision of 12 December, 1928, *A.J.*, XXIII (1929), p. 661.)[1]

vi.—On Neutral Persons and Property. Embargo. The Right of Angary

Case No. 369

Requisitions of Neutral Property—Duty of Compensation—Section 4 of the Annex to Articles 297 and 298 of the Treaty of Versailles—Article 52 of the Fourth Hague Convention —Meaning of the Term " Acts Committed "—Meaning of the Term " Acts Contrary to International Law "—The Law Applicable by Arbitral Tribunals.

ROUMANIA *v.* GERMANY (GOLDENBERG & SONS *v.* GERMANY).

Special Arbitral Tribunal. 27 *September*, 1928.

(FAZY, Arbitrator.)

THE FACTS.—The present case, which arose out of a requisition of the property of a Roumanian subject

[1] The above is one of the series of decisions given by the Arbiter under the Settlement of War Claims Act of 1928. These decisions, which are printed in a separate volume—*Decisions and Opinions of the War Claims Arbiter*—do not as a rule raise questions of international law, and it is therefore not necessary to digest them here. (The decision of 9 March, 1929, construing and applying the term " merchant vessel " as used in the Act will be digested in the volume for 1929-1930.) See also for some of the decisions, *A.J.*, XXIII (1929), pp. 193, 428, 659.

The Settlement of War Claims Act of 1928 (*A.J.*, XXII (1928), Suppl., p. 40) made provision for the ascertainment and payment of the claims of German, Austrian, and Hungarian nationals against the United States arising out of the taking over by the United States, under war legislation, of certain classes of German property like vessels, patents and use of inventions belonging to the nationals of these States. These were obligations voluntarily assumed *before* the entry of Roumania into war, came, by virtue of paragraph 4 of the Annex to Articles 297 and 298 of the Treaty of Versailles, before a single arbitrator designated by M. Gustave Ador.

The plaintiffs, who were merchants in Roumania, bought, in July, 1914, a quantity of tin from a German firm. The goods, which were paid for in advance, were forwarded to Antwerp to be shipped to Roumania. Owing to the outbreak of war, they remained in Antwerp, where they were requisitioned by the German authorities on 11 September, 1915. In 1921 the plaintiffs received from the German authorities compensation representing about one-sixth of the amount paid by them for the goods. They claimed the difference.

The claim was put forward on the basis of paragraph 4 of the Annex to Articles 297 and 298 of the Treaty of Versailles, which provided as follows:

"All property, rights and interests of German "nationals within the territory of any Allied or "Associated Power and the net proceeds of their "sale, liquidation or other dealing therewith may "be charged by that Allied or Associated Power "in the first place with payment of amounts due "in respect of claims by the nationals of that Allied "or Associated Power with regard to their property, "rights and interests, including companies and "associations in which they are interested, in "German territory, or debts owing to them by "German nationals, and with payment of claims "growing out of acts committed by the German "Government or by any German authorities since "31 July, 1914, and before that Allied or Associated

by the United States. On the other hand, the claims against Germany were based on the Treaty of Berlin of 25 August, 1921, and were submitted to the jurisdiction of a Mixed Claims Commission established under the Agreement of 10 August, 1922 (*A.J.*, XVI (1922), Suppl., p. 171), and the claims against Austria and Hungary were based on the Treaty of Vienna of 24 August, 1921, and on the Treaty of Budapest of 21 August, 1921, and were submitted to a Tripartite Commission established by the United States, Austria, and Hungary under an Agreement of 26 November, 1924 (*A.J.*, XX (1926), p. 51). Such of the decisions of these two Commissions as are of general interest are digested in the volumes of the *Annual Digest*. For a lucid statement of the United States' war claims settlements see Anderson in *A.J.*, XXIII (1929), p. 383. See also on the Settlement of War Claims Act of 1928, Borchard, *ibid.*, XXII (1928), p. 373, and, on certain decisions of the Tripartite Commission, *ibid.*, p. 142.

Case No. 369 ***contd.***

" Power entered into the war. The amount of such " claims may be assessed by an arbitrator appointed " by M. Gustave Ador, if he is willing, or, if no such " appointment is made by him, by an arbitrator " appointed by the Mixed Arbitral Tribunal provided " for in Section VI. . . ."

It was contended on behalf of Roumania that the expression " acts committed " signified any injurious act. The German contention was that the expression referred only to acts contrary to international law, and that as both customary international law and Article 52 of the Fourth Hague Convention allowed requisition, subject to compensation, the action must be dismissed.

Held: (*a*) *Meaning of the Term " acts committed."*—In accordance with the interpretation adopted by the Permanent Court of International Justice [1] and by a number of arbitral tribunals,[2] the term " *acts committed* " must be interpreted as meaning acts contrary to international law. As the clause was imposed upon Germany, and as it gave rise to doubts, it could not be interpreted extensively. Ambiguous clauses must in case of doubt be interpreted against the party responsible for their drafting.

Further, in contradistinction to the claims dealt with under Article 297 (*e*) of the Treaty, referring to damages suffered during the war, and entrusted to the jurisdiction of Mixed Arbitral Tribunals whose law is largely determined by the provisions of the Treaty, the damages suffered during the period of neutrality by non-enemies were the subject of proceedings before independent tribunals, like the present one, deciding in accordance with international law. For such tribunals the words " acts committed " must necessarily connote acts contrary to international law.

(*b*) *The Law Applicable.*—As to what constituted international law applicable by the Tribunal, the arbitrator was of the opinion that by instituting the arbitral tribunal the contracting parties wished it to follow the practice of international arbitral tribunals and to apply not only rules of conventional international law but also international custom, general principles recognised by civilised States and, as a subsidiary

[1] Judgment No. 3, Series A, No. 3, p. 80.

[2] The arbitrator referred here, *inter alia*, to the case *Karmatzucas* v. *Germany*, *Annual Digest*, 1925-1926, Case No. 291, and to the award in the Germano-Portuguese arbitration, *ibid.*, 1927-1928, Case No. 360.

means, judicial decisions.[1] Accordingly, an act contrary to international law was an act which if submitted before the World War to an arbitral tribunal would have involved the duty of reparation.

(*c*) *Requisitions and Respect of Private Rights.*—Respect of private property and of acquired rights of aliens constitutes undoubtedly one of the general principles recognised by international law. Military requisitions are a form of expropriation for the public benefit. As such they are not prohibited by international law. On the contrary, they are sanctioned by Article 52 of the Fourth Hague Convention. However, they are permitted only subject to the duty of compensation. This being so, the requisition of the plaintiffs' property did not originally constitute an act contrary to international law. But it became an act contrary to international law when, after a reasonable time, the plaintiffs did not obtain full compensation. The compensation given to them amounted only to one-sixth of the value of the property. Accordingly, the requisition constituted an "act contrary to international law" and Germany was liable to compensate the plaintiffs. [Report: *Z. für a. ö. R. und V.*, I (2) (1929), p. 87.]

NOTE.—The decision is criticised by Schmid, *ibid.*, pp. 96, 97, on the ground, *inter alia*, that there is no rule of international law which lays down that full compensation has to be paid for requisitioned property. The alien owner, he suggests, is merely entitled to the same treatment as is accorded to nationals.

Military Requisitions in Time of Revolutionary Disturbances —Lawful Act or International Delinquency? **Case No. 370**

GEORGES PINSON CASE, § 70.

France and Mexico: Mixed Claims Commission.
19 *October*, 1928.

(VERZIJL, President.)

THE FACTS.—See Case No. 159.

Held: That military requisitions at the expense of subjects of a foreign State in times of revolution are not in themselves illegal, according to the general principles of international law. Even in case of the existence of a revolt or civil war with regard to which the foreign Government concerned has not granted recognition of belligerency to the insurgents, the

[1] The arbitrator referred here to Article 38 of the Statute of the Court.

Case No. 370 *contd.*

authorities of the State suffering from a revolution may as a rule lawfully exact requisitions from foreigners, on the same footing as from the nationals of the State, but only on condition that they make full compensation. The legality of requisitions in time of civil war may only be questioned under particular treaty relations, when an express exemption from "réquisitions ou contributions de guerre" is stipulated, as in the case of the French-Mexican Treaty of 27 November, 1886 (Article 7). Their legal or illegal character is, however, not of particular importance in regard to the question of damages under the later French-Mexican (Revolutionary) Claims Convention of 25 September, 1924 (see Case No. 318), and to the question of interest (see Case No. 181).

[Till now unreported.]

NOTE.—The President quoted and rejected the opinion of A. Rougier, *Les guerres civiles et le droit des gens*, p. 476, as to illegality of military requisitions in civil wars.

VI.—Enemy Character

i.—Of Individuals

Case No. 371

Enemy Character—Application for Reacquisition of Nationality of Origin.

CHARLES MAYR *v.* EGYPTIAN GOVERNMENT.

Egyptian Mixed Court of Appeal. 13 *December*, 1927.

THE FACTS.—The appellant in this case was an official of the Egyptian Government at the outbreak of the Great War. He was born a German subject, but had lost his German nationality under the German law which deprived a German of his national character if he remained abroad for more than ten years. After the German Nationality Law of 1913 was passed, he made application for the reacquisition of his nationality of origin, but at the outbreak of the war had not yet been readmitted. In September, 1914, however, he made a declaration that he was of Bavarian origin; but that, having refused to do his military service, he was provisionally an Egyptian subject until he reacquired his German nationality. In accordance with the Decree of the Egyptian Government issued after the outbreak of the war, which provided for the discharge of all enemy subjects from the Government service, the appellant was discharged, but was re-engaged in 1917 after he had obtained the protection of another foreign State. He subsequently brought an action against the Egyptian Government claiming to be restored to the post from which he was originally discharged, and for damages representing the difference between his salary in the new post and that in the original post.

Held: (1) The military authorities were entitled to treat a person who was born a German and who during the war openly declared himself an applicant for the reacquisition of his nationality of origin as an enemy subject; and the Egyptian Government had therefore acted in good faith in treating him as such.

(2) Whether or not the appellant was to be regarded as a stateless person at the date of the outbreak of the war, his discharge by the Egyptian Government was made in purported application of the powers of the military authority acting under martial law, and was covered by the Bill of Indemnity of 5 July, 1923. [Reports: *Gazette des Tribunaux Mixtes d'Egypte*, 18th year, p. 245; 55 *Clunet* (1928), p. 1263.]

iv.—Of Goods

Enemy Property—Meaning of "Alien Enemy" in Treaty of Peace—Involuntary Residence in Enemy Territory. **Case No. 372**

LEO W. M. BAUMFELDER *v.* SECRETARY OF STATE FOR CANADA.

Exchequer Court of Canada. 18 *and* 25 *February*, 1927.

THE FACTS.—This was a petition for a declaration that the petitioner was not an "enemy" within the meaning of the Treaty of Peace (Germany) Order, 1920, and that he was entitled to certain funds in the hands of the Custodian of Enemy Property.

The petitioner was born of German parents in Germany in 1897 and was a German national. In 1910, with his parents, he went to England and took up his permanent residence there. At the age of eighteen, he was interned until 1919. In that year he and his father were deported to Germany, followed voluntarily by his mother and half-sister. In 1922, on the death of his mother, petitioner came to Canada, where he has remained ever since. The petitioner has an interest in

Case No. 372 *contd.*

a family trust estate which, it is suggested, belongs to the Custodian on account of the nationality of the petitioner.

Held by the President, Mr. Justice Maclean: The operation of the Treaty of Peace (Germany) Order, 1920, is confined to the property of "alien enemies." This expression is defined by Clause 32 of the Order, of which section (*a*) (the only material section) runs:

"Enemy" means:

"(*a*) A German national who during the war resided or "carried on business within the territory of a "Power at war with His Majesty."

The petitioner's residence in Germany immediately after his deportation to that country in 1919 does not bring him within this definition. The conception of "residence" implies a voluntary presence within the State in question. The petitioner's sojourn was neither permanent nor voluntary in nature. He was unable to leave before 1922 owing to poverty, and to the difficulty in obtaining a visa from the Allied and Associated Powers. Hence the petitioner and his property are outside the operation of the Order.

Declaration that the petitioner owns the property in question, with costs to the petitioner. [Report: Canada Law Reports [1927] Exch., p. 86.]

VII.—The Binding Force of the Laws of War

Rules of Warfare—Binding Force—Absence of Redress of Private Persons against the Belligerent—Effect on the Binding Force of the Rules in Question.

See Case No. 379 (*The Commune of Contich* v. *The State Commissioner at Brussels*).

IX.—Prisoners of War

Case No. 373

Prisoners of War—Position of—Non-Contractual Character of their Employment.

DANIELS *v.* GERMANY.

Germano-French Mixed Arbitral Tribunal. 7 *May*, 1928.

(GUEX, FAUQUEL, HOENE.)

THE FACTS.—The claimant, a French national, asked, *inter alia*, for compensation for work performed by him, when a prisoner of war, on certain German agricultural estates in the years 1915 and 1916. He alleged that his work was insufficiently paid. The claim was based, *inter alia*, on the second paragraph of Article 304 (*b*) of the Treaty of Versailles, which provided for the jurisdiction of Mixed Arbitral Tribunals in questions relating to contracts concluded before the coming into force of the Treaty between nationals of the Allied and Associated Powers and German nationals.[1]

Held: That the claim must be rejected. The second paragraph of Article 304 (*b*) applied only to contracts. It was not by virtue of a contract that the plaintiff was employed as a worker on the agricultural estates during his captivity in Germany. [Report: *Z. für a. ö. R. und V.*, II (1930), p. 57.]

NOTE.—This case illustrates the fact that the relation between the prisoner of war and the belligerent is one of public law, even in cases when the former performs work for private persons. The conditions of such work were not laid down in a contractual agreement between the private owner and the prisoner of war; they were determined "in "conjunction with the military authorities." Paragraph 3 of Article 6 of the relevant Hague Regulations lays down that the prisoner of war is entitled to remuneration for his work. The above decision shows that such remuneration lacks a contractual basis. See the note of von Elbe, *ibid.*, pp. 58, 59. See *Polyxene Plessa* v. *Turkish Government*, below, Case No. 382.

X.—Non-Hostile Relations between Belligerents, Especially Armistices

Preliminary Occupation under Armistice Agreement—Sovereignty over Ceded Territory in the Period between the Armistice Agreement and the Entry into Force of the Treaty—Administrative Measures of the Occupant. **Case No. 374**

A. KEMENÝ *v.* YUGOSLAV STATE.

Hungarian-Yugoslav Mixed Arbitral Tribunal.
13 *September*, 1928.

(VAN SLOOTEN, ZOLTAN, ARANDJELOVITCH.)

THE FACTS.—The claimant applied on 28 October, 1918, and was granted on 6 November, 1918, by the central

[1] It will be noted that the Mixed Arbitral Tribunals in their previous decisions—see *Annual Digest*, 1925-1926, Case No. 12—interpreted the term "nationals" in paragraph 2 of Article 304 as meaning not only private persons but also the German State acting in the capacity of a private person.

Case No. 374 ***contd.***

authorities in Budapest certain rights of prospecting and digging in some districts of the territories transferred by the Treaty of Trianon from Hungary to Yugoslavia. The Armistice Agreement by virtue of which these territories were occupied by Yugoslav forces was concluded on 3 November, 1918. The Treaty of Trianon entered into force on 26 July, 1921.

On 20 March, 1920, the Yugoslav authorities issued a Decree intended to ensure continuity in the administration of mining rights, and requiring, *inter alia*, that the holders of any mining rights should register them with the Yugoslav authorities within a period of thirty days. The claimant, who was at that time in Budapest, did not comply with the requirements of the Decree. The mining rights in question were subsequently conferred upon a third party. The present claim was brought by virtue of Article 250 of the Treaty of Trianon.[1]

Held: That the claimant was entitled, in part, to compensation.

(*a*) The Hungarian authorities were entitled to grant to the claimant the mining rights in question. The Armistice Agreement did not have the effect of transferring sovereignty to the Yugoslav Government over the occupied territories. The Hungarian authorities in question, *i.e.* the Department of Mines in Budapest, continued, until the entry into force of the Treaty, to exercise the relevant rights of sovereignty over these territories.

(*b*) On the other hand, according to a generally recognised rule of international law, the Yugoslav Government was authorised to replace the Hungarian authorities in the occupied territory by its own officials, and even to create new organs in so far as this was necessary for safeguarding public order and the economic well-being of the territory. The Decree of 20 March, 1920, could well be considered as such a measure.

(*c*) However, as that Decree provided for no penalty in case of non-compliance with the time limits fixed therein; as the claimant had no knowledge of the Decree and could not therefore comply with its time limits; and as in any case there was no imperative necessity for transferring the rights in question to a third person, Yugoslavia was bound to indemnify the claimant. [Report: *Recueil*, VIII, p. 588.]

[1] For the text of this Article see p. 88.

Armistice—Rights of Sovereignty over Territory of One Party Occupied by Another Party by Virtue of an Armistice Agreement.

See Case No. 374 (*A. Kemeny* v. *Yugoslav State*).

XII.—Effects of Treaties of Peace

i.—In General

War—*Jus Postliminii*[1]—Polish View of Continuity of Pre-Partition Polish State. **Case No. 375**

KULAKOWSKI AND OTHERS (appellants) *v.* SZUMKOWSKI (respondent).

Supreme Court of Poland, First Division (Plenary Session). 12 *May*, 1928.

THE FACTS.—Upon the defeat of the Polish insurrection of 1863, respondent's father, who had taken part in the insurrection, was exiled to Siberia, and his property, which included real property (about 800 acres), was declared to be forfeited. The order was confirmed by the Governor-General of Wilno, Muraviev, in 1872, and, by permission of the Emperor, irrespective of an administrative procedure which was still pending at the instance of a co-owner of the estate (the exile's brother), the estate was sold in 1874 on behalf of the Russian Treasury to the chief clerk to the Governor-General, Rubtsov, at a nominal price (approximately £350 payable in twenty yearly instalments of approximately £17, 10s.). Upon the recovery of independence by Poland, the respondent brought suit against the children and grandchildren of Rubtsov to recover the estate. The Circuit Court of Białystok, and (on appeal) the Court of Appeal of Warsaw, both declared the plaintiff to be the owner (as the rightful heir to his father) and directed that the estate be restored to him, taking as *terminus a quo* the year 1874.

Held by the Court of Appeal of Warsaw, *inter alia*: That the defendants could not plead that their ancestor, Rubtsov,

[1] The editors have labelled this case as one of *Jus Postliminii* in deference to what they understand to be the view adopted by Polish courts and jurists of the continuity of the pre-partition State. Otherwise it would have been classified as a case of Succession of States and Respect of Private Rights.

Case No. 375 ***contd.***

was purchaser in good faith, since he could not have failed to know that the vendor, *i.e.* the Russian State, had no good title, the confiscation having taken place without any legal basis, since the ministerial decree confirming the confiscation in 1874 was contrary to the amnesty law of 1873 and to the fundamental laws of the Russian Empire. To maintain the present status of the confiscated estates would mean to continue the reprisals directed against those who had fought to bring about the restoration of Poland and not to recognise the legal consequences of the restoration to the Polish State of its independent existence.

Held by the Supreme Court: That the appeal must fail. The defendants are the direct descendants and heirs of Rubtsov, whose acquisition of the property in question was not good in law, and could give them no good title. All legislative and executive acts of the Russian Government which were based on such public law rules as could not be recognised by the Polish State or Nation as lawful bases of property in Poland (among such acts being the confiscation of the property in question) must be considered not as legal acts, but as instances of simple violence. Property conditions (under private law) created by such violence could last only while there was the power able to enforce the conditions based on such violence. Once, however, the organisation which was enforcing that state of affairs had disappeared, and Poland had regained her independence, there must disappear automatically such illegal property conditions as were irreconcilable with the state of public and private law henceforth prevailing; the rights and titles of the lawful owners of confiscated estates must be considered to revive in so far as they had not been lost in the meantime in accordance with rules prevailing in Poland, that is, in so far as the purchaser cannot put forward a good title. It would require a Polish statute to abolish altogether, or in certain cases, the possibility of recovering property lost in the above conditions and remaining in the hands of the unlawful purchasers. The fact that no Russian court could have restored the property to the respondent created the legal impossibility, based on the public law of the time, of raising the claim before Poland regained her independence. This operates against the plea of prescription. [Reports: Z.O.S.N.C., 1928, No. 98; O.S.P., VIII, No. 1; digested in R.P.E.S., 1929, 210-213.]

NOTE.—The decision of the Supreme Court in this case views the titles of plaintiff and defendants respectively as based on two sets of legal rules, one set (private law in its ordinary aspects) based on a system which could and does exist in modern Poland as in any other civilised State, the other set (the régime which made possible the confiscation) based merely on violence and more particularly aiming at preventing all further attempts to bring about the independence of Poland which is the logical condition of the existence of Polish law and of Polish courts. The Supreme Court takes the view that the latter set cannot be enforced if a title based on it is in conflict with a title based on the former set, since Poland cannot enforce laws of which the main or sole purpose was to prevent the independence of Poland, and, consequently, the possibility for Poland to enforce any laws at all.

The Supreme Court admits *obiter* that its attitude would be different if the title opposed to that based on the first set of rules were itself based on the same set, *e.g.* if a purchaser *bona fide* had stepped into the place of the one (or of the direct heirs of the one) who obtained the property on exceptionally and unreasonably easy terms from the Treasury, which had deprived the legitimate owner of that property.

The general view that the Polish State is a continuation of the pre-partition State, that the laws introduced by the partitioning Powers remain only in so far as they are not in contradiction with the independence of Poland, and that from the point of view of public law the period of the partitions was only a *de facto* condition, is based on views, to which some expression was given by the Supreme Court in the earlier cases of *Pantol*, *Girsa* and *Glinski*.

This view, now more explicitly developed in the *Kulakowski* v. *Szumkowski* case, amounts to the recognition of a *jus postliminii* so far as the Polish State goes, entailing, *inter alia*, the destruction of conditions created as a result of acts directed against the resurrection of Poland. Clearly all *bona fide* purchasers must be protected. Conversely, the Treasury itself would be liable to restore to the descendants of the rightful owners such property as had been taken from the latter by the Russian State and had been taken over by the Polish Treasury since 1918. The Courts of Poland, fully realising this consequence, have so decided in a series of actions against the Polish Treasury (test judgment of the Supreme Court, 21 March, 1930). The judgment in *Kulakowski* v. *Szumkowski* has been followed not only in that case, but also by lower courts in other cases where property confiscated by Russia and taken over by the Polish Treasury was claimed by heirs of the owners.

ii.—Amnesty

Amnesty—Lausanne Declaration VIII concerning Amnesties —An Amnesty Takes Effect Only for Acts which Precede it in Date. **Case No. 376**

AMNESTY (GREECE) CASE.

Areopagus. 1925, *No.* 435.

THE FACTS.—A judgment of the Court at Salonica, dated 11 November, 1924, condemned two persons to death. The condemned appealed to the amnesty provided for by Declaration VIII of the Treaty of Lausanne of 24 July, 1923.

Case No. 376 contd.

Held: That the Amnesty Declaration of Lausanne is not applicable to acts taking place after the date when it came into effect (6 August, 1924). [Report: Themis, vol. 37, p. 149.]

iv.—Miscellaneous

Case No. 377

War—Effects of Treaties of Peace—Nature of Charge Imposed by Treaties of Peace at Conclusion of World War upon Private Enemy Property—Article 249 of the Treaty of St. Germain.

JOSEF INVALD AKTIEN GESELLSCHAFT *v.* PFEIFFER AND ANOTHER.

House of Lords on appeal from the English Court of Appeal. 6 *March*, 1928.

THE FACTS.—In July, 1914, the defendant, Pfeiffer, a Norwegian subject living in England, owed to the plaintiffs, a company incorporated under the laws of the former Austrian Empire, the sum of £494, the price of goods sold and delivered. In November, 1926, the plaintiffs commenced an action in the King's Bench Division of the English High Court of Justice to recover this sum, and joined the Administrator of Austrian Property as a defendant in respect of any interest which he might have by way of charge upon the said debt. The defendant Pfeiffer contended that as the result of the Treaty of Peace between the Allied and Associated Powers and Austria, of the Treaties of Peace (Austria and Bulgaria) Act, 1920, and of the Treaty of Peace (Austria) Order, 1920, which gave effect in the United Kingdom to the Treaty of Peace between the Allied and Associated Powers and Austria, the debt was charged in favour of the Administrator of Austrian Property, and that he alone was entitled to sue for it. It was admitted by the plaintiffs that the debt was the "property, right or interest" of an Austrian national in England and came under the charge created by Article 249 (*b*) and paragraph 4 of the Annex to Section IV of Part X of the Treaty of St. Germain, and that consequently any sum recovered by them would be subject to the Treaty of Peace and the charge thereby created and become the property of the Administrator, but the plaintiffs argued that their right to sue for it was not taken away by the Order in Council.

The Master in Chambers made an order striking out the plaintiffs' claim. His decision was affirmed by Shearman, J. The plaintiffs appealed. The Court of Appeal (per Lord Hanworth, M.R., Scrutton, L.J., dissenting[1]) dismissed the appeal on the ground that although the claim was against a neutral subject, yet, as section 7 of the Treaty of Peace Order made the debt payable to the Administrator and transferred to him all the rights of the creditors, the plaintiffs had no right to bring the action. On appeal,

Held (by Lords Sumner, Warrington and Atkin): That, for the reasons above mentioned, the debt had been transferred to the said Administrator (including the right to sue) in such a way that for the time being it was a debt due to him and to him alone. The peculiarly English doctrine of an equity of redemption outstanding in the mortgagor (or in this case, by analogy, in the plaintiffs) could not be said to have been within the contemplation of the framers of the Treaty. Accordingly, the plaintiffs could not sue and the writ must be struck out. [Reports: 43 T.L.R., p. 399; 44 T.L.R., p. 352.[2]]

NOTE.—(*a*) The "charge" created by the Treaties of Peace thus is something more than a charge in the English legal sense.

(*b*) The point that the Treaty, the Act of Parliament, and the Order in Council did not bind a Norwegian subject, Norway not being a party to the Treaty, was not mentioned and was not arguable, for (i) the debtor was living in England when the debt was incurred, and (ii) the debt was locally situated in England.

(*c*) If the plaintiffs had succeeded in the action and had recovered the amount claimed, it would have passed to the Administrator of Austrian Property, leaving them with a right of recoupment against the Austrian Government under paragraph (*j*) of Article 249, which is as follows: "Austria undertakes to compensate her nationals in "respect of the sale or retention of their property, rights or interests "in Allied or Associated States."

---

[1] Lord Justice Scrutton did not agree with the Master of the Rolls, but he did not formally dissent.

[2] See also *B.Y.*, 1928, pp. 168 and 176, and *ibid.*, 1929, p. 244, n.

B. WARFARE ON LAND

III.—Occupation of Enemy Territory

ii.—Legislative, Judicial and Administrative Functions of the Occupant

Case No. 378 **Laws in Force in the Territory of the Occupant do not Extend Automatically by the Fact of Occupation to the Occupied Territory—Territorial Limits of the Application of Municipal Legislation — Austro-Hungarian Occupation of Montenegro—The Operation of the Austrian Law concerning War Services.**

WAR SERVICES LAW (CZECHOSLOVAKIA) CASE.

Supreme Administrative Court of Czechoslovakia.
29 *December*, 1928. *No.* 23.573.

THE FACTS.—After the territory of Montenegro had been occupied in 1916 by the Austro-Hungarian forces, the Austrian military administration seized the property of the plaintiff (a former Austrian, now Czechoslovak, firm), consisting of motor cars by which he, in accordance with a contract concluded in 1908 with the Montenegro Government, carried on the postal traffic in Montenegro. The plaintiff claimed an indemnity according to the former Austrian, now Czechoslovak, Law of 26 December, 1912, No. 236, regarding war services (of personal and material nature) rendered by the civil population. The Commission appointed to deal with the claims made in accordance with the Law No. 236 declared itself, however, not to be competent [1] in the matter, holding that the seizure of the motor cars took place outside the territory to which the Law No. 236/1912 applied, and that, therefore, the seizure was not an act governed by that Law, but a requisition under the general provisions of international law.

Held upon appeal, by the Supreme Administrative Court: That the appeal must be dismissed. ". . . The point at " issue is whether the Austrian Municipal Law of 26 December, " 1912, No. 236, at the time when the seizure of the motor cars

[1] The question of State Succession between the Austrian State and the Czechoslovak State, being a question of merits, was therefore not involved in the case.

" was effected, *i.e.* in 1916, was to be applied to all Austrian " citizens without distinction, whether they reside on Austrian " territory or outside it, and to their property without regard to " the place where it was situated. This question is to be con- " sidered in the first place from the general point of view, and " then from the point of view whether and, if so, to what extent " the fact that the seizure of the motor cars took place at a time " when the territory concerned was under occupation by the " Austrian military forces was relevant to the question of the " territorial scope of the application of the law concerned."

(i) " It appears from the nature of a municipal law as an " emanation of the sovereignty over a certain territory that its " application is limited, as a rule, to the territory of the State " concerned. This principle was also expressly enunciated as " to the former Austrian State by paragraph 3 of the Law of " 10 June, 1869, No. 113, according to which all legal provisions " contained in the Collection of Laws applied, if not otherwise " provided, to the whole Austrian territory. Accordingly, if a " law was to be applied in a larger sphere, an express provision " was necessary for this purpose. . . . It is, therefore, necessary " to examine whether there is a provision according to which the " application of the Law No. 236/1912 was extended beyond the " limits of the Austrian territory." Such a provision, however, can be found neither in the Law No. 236 itself nor in other legal provisions. " Consequently the application of the Law No. " 236/1912 as such was limited to the Austrian territory."

(ii) " It remains, therefore, to deal with the question whether " the fact of military occupation had any influence on the " application of the law in question. It is to be noted that in " the matter before the Court there is a question only of a " transitory occupation of enemy territory by belligerent forces " and not of a permanent annexation, or incorporation of that " territory into the own State, *i.e.* of extension of sovereignty " over it. . . . According to the unanimous opinion of the " authors of treatises upon international law the occupant is not " entitled to introduce in the occupied territory changes in " legislation and administration, except those which are tempo- " rarily required by the necessity of maintaining and safe- " guarding the army and of the prosecution of the war. On the " contrary, it is his obligation to administer the occupied terri- " tory in conformity with the existing laws and administrative " rules. This principle means that the application of the laws " of the occupying State do not by the fact of the occupation " extend automatically to the occupied territory. Should the

Case No. 378 *contd.*

"occupant consider it necessary from the point of view of his "interests in maintaining and safeguarding his army or in "the prosecution of the war to extend the application of a certain law in force in his own territory to the occupied territory, "he must do it expressly. The Court, however, is not aware, "nor does the plaintiff contend, that such a measure was taken "with regard to the Law No. 236/1912 during the occupation "of Montenegro exercised by the Austrian forces in the Great "War. The Law No. 236/1912 did not apply to the territory "of Montenegro at the time of the seizure of the motor cars in "question," and the Commission concerned was not competent to deal with the matter. [Report: Boh. 7661 adm.]

Case No. 379

Illegality of Establishment of Special Courts in Occupied Territory—Continuance of Laws in Force—German Occupation of Belgium—Article 43 of the Fourth Hague Convention of 1907.

THE COMMUNE OF CONTICH *v.* THE STATE COMMISSIONER AT BRUSSELS.[1]

Belgian Court of Cassation. 18 *May*, 1928.

THE FACTS.—The Commune of Contich claims, in the Brussels Court of War Damages, compensation for war damages on two grounds. First, for non-payment for goods requisitioned by the occupying Power; secondly, for the amount of a penalty inflicted by the special courts of the occupying Power on account of the destruction of certain goods in the occupied territory belonging to German nationals. The Brussels Court of War Damages dismissed the claim under both headings, on 18 March, 1927, and said of the second claim that "the penalty imposed upon the claimant Commune "followed simply from the judicial organisation established by Germany in the territories occupied by her "in favour of her own nationals." (For the award in the first claim see Case No. 385.)

The Commune appealed from this decree to the Court of Cassation.

Held: That the judgment of the Court below must be reversed. On the question of compensation for the penalty laid on the claimant Commune:

[1] The State Commissioner represents the interests of the Belgian State in regard to its liability for compensation for war damage.

" Since the rights of German nationals continued throughout the war to enjoy the protection afforded them by Belgian legislation, the new rules adopted by the occupying Power to afford them further guarantees, and the special courts created to apply these rules, must be considered illegal." The appearance of the claimant Commune before these German courts " was designed solely to soften the harshness of the penalties with which it was threatened " and " should not be construed as in any way a renunciation of the right to claim in the national courts compensation for the impositions illegally laid upon it."

" It lay within the province of the court of first instance to consider whether, in imposing a penalty upon the whole Commune for the culpable acts of a few private persons, the occupying Power had not acted in excess of its powers, and whether, since it had injured the material estate of the claimant Commune, it was not properly liable to pay the compensation asked." As this question had been ignored in the Court below, " the judgment in that Court was without legal basis." [Report : *Pasicrisie Belge*, 1928, I, p. 160.]

NOTE.—(1) In general, the Belgian legislature has considered itself free to avoid or confirm the acts of the occupying Power (Cassation, 19 March, 1925, *Pasicrisie Belge*, 1925, I, p. 184). It follows that the State whose territory is occupied is free to disregard even those acts of the occupying Power which may be capable of justification under Article 43 of the Rules annexed to the Hague Convention IV of 1907. This is in accordance with the principle that the *occupatio bellica*, from the point of view of the State whose territory is occupied, constitutes a situation whose significance is solely factual. In the silence of the legislature, the courts have always assumed this power of revision, and tested the validity of the acts of the occupying Power by the criterion of Article 43 to which reference is made above. (See, for example, Cour d'Appel de Bruxelles, 25 June, 1925 ; Tribunal Arbitral Germano-Belge, 19 October, 1925. *Annual Digest*, 1925-1926, Cases Nos. 361, 362.) Since the courts lack the power to transform a mere factual into a legal situation, it seems to follow from these precedents that only those acts of the occupying Power capable of being justified in international law have a valid legal effect internally. There seems a certain contradiction here which is scarcely avoidable in the absence of a legislative regulation of all the acts of the occupying Power.

(2) " Acts in excess of its powers " should be understood in the sense of " acts involving payments of compensation." It is not necessary that such acts should be wrongful by the standards of international law for them to entail payment of compensation under the legislation governing payment for war damages.

Case No. 380 **Occupation of Enemy Territory—Change of Law by Actual Sovereign—Effect in Occupied Territory.**

STASIUK AND JAGNYCZ *v.* KLEWEC.

Supreme Court of Poland, Third Division. 11 *May*, 1927.

THE FACTS.—A strip of the then Austrian part of Poland had been occupied immediately after the outbreak of the war by Russian troops, who remained in possession until 1917. In October, 1914, an Imperial Austrian decree changed certain provisions of the Austrian Civil Code of 1811, abolishing, *inter alia*, the inability of women to be witnesses of an oral will. The Civil Code provides that an oral will must be witnessed by three persons (until October 1914 three men), at least two of whom must in the course of probate proceedings on their oath confirm the identity of the deceased and the will expressed by him. The brother of the plaintiffs had died in 1916, and, before his death, had, in the presence of three men (two of whom could not be traced for purposes of probate) and of one woman, bequeathed his entire estate to his father (who died later leaving his estate to the two plaintiffs). In 1923 in the original probate proceedings the will was disregarded, and one-half of the estate fell to the defendant, who was the widow of the deceased (the balance fell to the plaintiffs, partly in their own right and partly as inherited through their father). The present action was then brought to establish that, under the will, the plaintiffs were entitled to the whole estate. The local court at Tluste gave judgment for the plaintiffs; on appeal, the District Court at Czortków gave judgment for the defendant. The latter

Held: That since under the Austrian Law of 1869 statutes and decrees published in the Austrian Journal of Laws were considered to be published as from the date of the appearance and distribution of the German copy of the issue of the Journal containing the statute or decree in question, and since, therefore, the intention must have been to bring the Law to the knowledge of the citizens, the Law could not be applied to facts which had arisen in territory occupied by enemy troops before the Journal of Laws had reached that territory.

On appeal to the Supreme Court,

Held: Allowing the appeal, that, since the Law of 1869

contains no provision making the binding force of a law dependent on its reaching the locality in question, the fact of enemy occupation has no importance for the consideration of the binding force of the law which had been duly promulgated in Austrian territory and had entered into force there. [Report: O.S.P., VI, No. 442.]

NOTE.—The above decision, while demonstrating the inconvenience of a strict application of the principle of mere promulgation in the capital, is interesting to students of international law as presenting one more difficulty of the present law of occupation in war: Article 43 of the Hague Rules (1907) prescribes that the occupant "shall respect, "unless absolutely prevented, the laws in force in the country," but there is no provision permitting peaceful and innocent intercourse with the unoccupied territory, for instance to the extent of obtaining official information about the development of law. In the case digested above, the occupant was clearly not entitled to change the rules of testamentary succession, while the then legitimate authority either had to resort to an obvious fiction (such as that applied by the Supreme Court in the present case) or it also was debarred from changing the law in the territory in question.

Warfare on Land—Occupation of Enemy Territory—Legislative and Administrative Functions of the Occupant—Sale of Private Property—Articles 43 and 46 of the Regulations Annexed to the Fourth Hague Convention of 1907—German Occupation of Poland. **Case No. 381**

TENCER AND OTHERS (defendants and appellants) *v.* MINING AND INDUSTRIAL CORPORATION "HRABIA RENARD" (plaintiff and respondent).

Supreme Court of Poland, First Division. 12 *May*, 1927.

THE FACTS.—The German Eastern High Command issued in 1915 a decree authorising the German authorities in the occupied parts of (the then Russian part of) Poland to subject to compulsory administration businesses conducted or supervised from foreign enemy countries. The plaintiff was a corporation consisting of 1000 shares, of which 17 were owned by German citizens and 983 by French citizens or French companies. An administrator was appointed for the plaintiff by the German civil occupying authorities, and he called a meeting of the German shareholders, who elected a representative of the company. The latter sold to the defendants certain property belonging to the plaintiff. In 1922 the plaintiff brought action against the defendants, claiming a declaration that the sale was void, being a liquidation of the property of French citizens,

Case No. 381 *contd.*

which, under the Treaty of Versailles, was declared void. The courts below gave judgment for the plaintiffs. The defendants appealed.

Held: (1) That the transaction was void under section 1 of the Annex to Articles 297 and 298 of the Treaty of Versailles;

(2) That acts which resulted from exceptional war measures, aiming at compulsory liquidation of the property of enemy subjects, could not be compared to acts of a person who voluntarily undertakes the care of another's interests for the latter's benefit;

(3) That, " by virtue of rules in the matter of the powers of " war authorities in occupied territory, such authorities could " undertake measures aiming at the administration of the " plaintiff's property if this were necessary in order to insure " order and revive social activities, but that such authorities " had no right to take measures directed against private pro- " perty (Articles 43 and 46 of the Hague Rules) ";

(4) That, consequently, the courts below had no duty to enquire either into the question whether the transaction was beneficial to the plaintiff or into the good faith of the purchase by the defendants. [Reports: Zb. O.S.N., 1927, No. 57; R.P.E.S., 1927, p. 868.]

iii.—Respect of Private Property. The Public Property of the Enemy State. Requisitions and Contributions

Case No. 382

Requisitions—Legal Nature of Requisitions—Unilateral and Not Contractual.

POLYXENE PLESSA *v.* TURKISH GOVERNMENT.

Greco-Turkish Mixed Arbitral Tribunal. 9 *February*, 1928.

(Baron DE NORDENSKJOELD, AHMED RECHID, KYRIACOPOULOS.)

THE FACTS.—(See Case No. 299.) It was contended by Greece that the requisitions in question should be considered as forced contracts and thus be brought within the provision of Article 73 (*f*) of the Treaty of Lausanne, which provided for the continuance of contracts concluded between individuals or companies and the State, provinces, municipalities or other similar juridical persons charged with administrative functions.

Held: That this contention must be rejected. Requisitions are manifestations of the unilateral will of the authorities fulfilling the function of mobilising the resources of the country for the purpose of military defence. They are sufficiently justified by the necessities engendered by the war. A construction such as that suggested by Greece is artificial and contrary to the legal nature of the act of requisition. The latter undoubtedly created a right in favour of the individual concerned, but that right was not of a contractual nature. [Report: *Recueil*, VIII, p. 224.]

NOTE.—See *Daniels* v. *Germany*, above, Case No. 373.

War on Land—Occupation—Respect for the Property of the Occupied State—Forests Belonging to Occupied State—Exploitation—Rule of Usufruct—Article 55 of the Fourth Hague Convention of 1907. **Case No. 383**

ADMINISTRATION OF WATERS AND FORESTS *v.* FALK.

French Court of Cassation, Criminal Chamber.
11 *February*, 1927.

THE FACTS.—See *Annual Digest*, 1925-1926, Case No. 367. An appeal had been lodged with the Court of Cassation against the judgment of the Court of Nancy by the Administration of Waters and Forests.

Held by the Court of Cassation: That the judgment of the Court of Nancy must be quashed. "In accordance with "Article 55 of the Hague Convention of 18 October, 1907, relating to the laws and customs of war, the occupying State is "only entitled to the rights of administration and usufruct of "the real property, including the forests, of the enemy State. "It should protect the substance of such property and administer it in accordance with the rules of usufruct." An individual, therefore, who had not observed the régime applied to forests, but felled trees contrary to the provisions of the Forest Code, could not invoke contracts for the exploitation of the forest made with the occupying military authorities. Neither can an individual, who is not an agent of the German Government but a private person acting for speculative purposes, escape civil and criminal responsibility by invoking international conventions which impose upon Germany an obligation to make reparation for the damage caused by the occupation of French territory. [Report: Sirey, 1928, Part I, p. 369, with a note by M. J. A. Roux.]

NOTE.—For a French case arising out of the felling of trees in French State forests by a German contractor during the Franco-Prussian war, see Oppenheim, vol. II (4th ed., 1926), § 282 (note).

Case No. 384 **Occupation of Enemy Territory—Respect of Private Property—Property of Private Persons Absent from Occupied Territory—Article 47 of the Hague Regulations.**

MAZZONI *v.* MINISTRY OF FINANCE.

Court of Venice. 8 *January*, 1927.

THE FACTS.—In consequence of the invasion of Venetian territory in October, 1917, by Austro-Hungarian troops, the sisters Mazzoni had to leave Sacile, where they resided. They had to abandon bonds of the National Debt and shares in local companies which were deposited with a bank in Pordenone. These bonds and shares were subsequently seized by the occupying authorities and taken outside Italy. In accordance with and in execution of Articles 184 and 185 of the Treaty of Peace of St. Germain, the Austrian Government restored these bonds and shares. A dispute arose between the sisters Mazzoni and the Italian Ministry of Finance with regard to the restitution of some of the bonds, and the Court of Venice had to examine, in this connection, certain questions relating also to the general principles of international law. In particular, it was contended on behalf of the Ministry of Finance that the plaintiffs' title to the bonds and shares was extinguished.

Held : The Court cannot admit the objection that, the title to the bonds and shares in question *de quo* having been acquired by the enemy as war booty, they must be considered as definitely lost to the former owners. The argument that the property of citizens absent from occupied territory is to be considered *res nullius* or war booty cannot be admitted. On the contrary, such private property must be treated according to the rules of the Hague Regulations of 1907, which lay down that movable or immovable private property must be respected in land warfare. Exceptions to these rules are only admitted as to money contributions, requisitions in kind and services, and sequestration for the needs of the army. The juridical notion of war booty does not include everything seized by the occupying army. According to the principles of international law, war booty is solely the appropriation of things left by the other belligerent and capable of being used for war purposes. The conception of booty cannot consequently be extended to include pillage, which is expressly forbidden (see Hague Regulations, Article 47). " The principle based upon the Roman law according to which property seized during a war is put on an equal " footing with the property seized in the air, in the sea or in the " earth, and which in a similar way becomes the property of " the captor—since the right of war constitutes a just cause of " acquisition—may be applicable to things liable or apt to be " used for the needs of the army and belonging to the other " belligerent. But it cannot be applied to private property " which, if it has not become the object of requisition or " sequestration, must be restored or compensated. The objects " involved in the present case are private property which had " not been requisitioned or sequestrated as it could not be used " for the needs of the army. Their seizure must therefore be " considered as having been effected by pillage." Consequently, the title of the private citizen is not extinguished, provided that he has not alienated or otherwise parted with it. [Report : *Foro italiano*, 1927, pp. 960-967, with a critical note by M. Udina.]

Requisitions—Default in Payment—Absence of Sanctions for Article 52 of the Rules Annexed to the Fourth Convention of The Hague of 1907—The German Occupation of Belgium. **Case No. 385**

THE COMMUNE OF CONTICH *v.* THE STATE COMMISSIONER AT BRUSSELS.

Belgian Court of Cassation. 18 *May*, 1928.

THE FACTS.—(See also Case No. 379.) Article 52 of the Rules annexed to the Fourth Hague Convention of 1907 provides :

" Contributions in kind shall, as far as possible, " be paid for in cash ; if not, a receipt shall be given " and the payment of the amount due shall be made " as soon as possible."

The Commune of Contich made a claim before the Brussels Court of War Damages for non-payment in respect of requisitions made by the occupying Power. This Court disallowed the claim, on the sole ground that the rule embodied in the said Article 52 is " without sanction." (18 March, 1927.)

Held for the claimant Commune : That the decision of the Court below must be reversed.

Case No. 385 *contd.*

It is true that the provisions of Article 52 concerning payment for requisitions "amount only to a rule to which no "sanction is attached, and one, moreover, which the enemy "has not hesitated to repudiate, in spite of his previous ad- "hesion to it," but "the Belgians have been the sufferers from "its breach, and the terms of this Article cannot preclude them "from seeking, through another channel, compensation for the "damage done them." In the decision here challenged, the Court below did not pass upon the substantive nature of the wrong done the claimant Commune; "hence it failed to base "its decree upon any legal ground." [Report: *Pasicrisie Belge*, 1928, p. 160 *et seq.*]

NOTE.—In declaring that the rule laid down in Article 52 of the Rules annexed to the Convention is "without sanction," the Court appears to have had in mind only the absence of any direct redress in the hands of the parties against the Power in occupation. The Court cannot well have overlooked the existence of the international sanction provided for in Article 3 of the same Convention. In other quarters, the obligatory character of the rule does not seem to have been called into question. (See Fauchille, t. II, § 1216; Oppenheim, vol. II, § 147.)

Case No. 386

Occupation of Enemy Territory—Requisitions and Contributions—Articles 46, 47, 48, 49, 50 and 52 of the Regulations Annexed to the Hague Convention IV of 1907—Validity of Title Acquired by Purchase of Articles Seized by the Occupying Forces.

I. VÉTEK *v.* N. DÜRNBACHER & CO.

Supreme Court of Hungary.
30 *September*, 1927. (*No. P. VI*, 7067/1926.)

THE FACTS.—In accordance with the terms of the Armistice Agreement of November, 1918, the major part of the Hungarian district of Baranya was occupied by Serb troops which remained there until August, 1921. In the summer of 1919 the civil authorities of the occupying Power seized certain property belonging to the plaintiff and consisting of horses, sheep and machines and a quantity of wheat and wine, and sold it by compulsory auction. The auction was conducted under the supervision of a judge of the Serb Lower Court and was announced in the Press the day before. (It appears that the seizure and public auction of the property took place in the execution of a fine imposed upon the plaintiff.)

The present action is brought by the plaintiff against the purchasers of these objects on the ground that the compulsory auction was arbitrary and illegal and that, accordingly, the purchasers could not acquire any property in them.

Held by the Supreme Court of Hungary that the action must be dismissed: "According to Article 52 of the "Regulations of the Fourth Hague Convention, requisitions "for the requirements of the army of occupation from munici- "palities and inhabitants cannot take place in the manner in "which the plaintiff has been deprived of his property. In "addition, the fact that he has been deprived of all his property "shows that there was no question of requisitions in kind in "accordance with the above-mentioned paragraph, that is to "say, that the plaintiff was dispossessed not by virtue of a general "levy, but only as the result of procedure directed specifically "against him and his property. This goes beyond the con- "ception of requisition as generally understood.

"However, the fact that there had taken place no proper "requisition does not necessarily mean that the plaintiff has "been deprived of his property as the result of deprivation of "property or pillage prohibited in Articles 46 and 47 of the "Convention. For according to Article 48 the occupying Power "is entitled to levy contributions and dues; according to "Article 49 he may impose other burdens; and it follows from "Article 50 that the occupying Power may impose upon in- "dividual persons fines as punishment for offences committed "by them. It follows that the occupying Power has the right "to seize the property of the debtor thus fined and to sell it "for the purpose of paying the fine. No evidence has been "adduced to show that the compulsory auction was mani- "festly illegal." [Report: *Magánjogi Döntvénytár*, XXI, No. 11.]

War on Land—Requisitions—Provisions of Hague Convention of 1907—Applicability to Requisitions in Time of Peace.

See Case No. 335 (*Edgar A. Hatton Case*).

C. WARFARE AT SEA

II.—Visit, Search, Capture, and Destruction

(*b*) Of Neutral Merchantmen

Case No 387 **Warfare at Sea—Visit and Search—Convoy—Neutral Merchantmen under Convoy of Enemy Men-of-War.**

Nicolas G. Kyriakides *v.* Germany.

Greco-German Mixed Arbitral Tribunal. 8 *November*, 1928.

(Asser, Froelich, Youpis.)

The Facts.—This was a claim for the sinking without warning by a German submarine of a Greek vessel during the period of Greek neutrality in 1917. The vessel was under the convoy of Allied maritime forces. The claim was based on paragraph 4 of the Annex to Articles 297 and 298 of the Treaty of Versailles providing, *inter alia*, for the payment of claims arising out of acts committed by Germany since 31 July, 1914.

Held: That the claim must be rejected. The fact that a merchantman has put itself under the protection of enemy naval forces and that it is accompanied by one or more men-of-war is sufficient to assimilate it to an enemy man-of-war. A neutral merchantman who in order to secure that protection exposes itself to the danger of direct and continuous proximity of the convoying vessels is not entitled to expect the other belligerent to make a special effort to spare a vessel under convoy while attacking the enemy convoy. The other belligerent is entitled to assume that a merchantman accompanying an enemy squadron is directly engaged in the military operations of that squadron.

As to the argument of the claimant that the necessity of a convoy was imposed on them by the German order of 31 January, 1917, authorising German submarines to sink neutral merchantmen at sight and without warning, the Tribunal pointed out that a request for a convoy should have been made on behalf of such neutral merchantmen to their Government in conformity with Article 61 of the Declaration of London, and that, if such convoy had been granted, neutral merchant vessels, protected by neutral warships, would not have exposed themselves to the risks connected with the proximity of enemy vessels. [Report: *Recueil*, VIII, p. 349.]

NOTE.—This case seems to be of special interest in view of the scarcity of modern judicial precedent in this matter. See Oppenheim, vol. II, § 424.

Warfare at Sea—Destruction of Enemy Merchantmen—Destruction of a Greek Ship Chartered by the French Government. **Case No. 388**

D. P. AND C. MAROULI (Banque Marouli Brothers) *v.* GERMANY.

Greco-German Mixed Arbitral Tribunal. 4 *October*, 1928.

(ASSER, FROELICH, YOUPIS.)

THE FACTS.—This was a claim put forward by certain Greek shipowners by reason of the torpedoing, during the period of Greek neutrality in 1917, of the *Kyma*, a Greek steamer temporarily chartered by the French Government. The ship was sunk while laden with a cargo of rifles and ammunition, on a voyage undertaken in execution of the contract. The claim was put forward on the basis of paragraph 4 of the Annex to Articles 297 and 298 of the Treaty of Versailles, which provided, *inter alia*, for the payment of claims arising out of acts committed by Germany since 31 July, 1914.

Held: That the destruction of the *Kyma* did not fall within the conception of "acts committed" in the above-mentioned Article of the Treaty, that is, acts contrary to international law,[1] and that the claim must therefore be rejected.

According to a generally recognised rule, confirmed by Article 46 of the Declaration of London, neutral merchantmen chartered by a belligerent may be treated like enemy merchantmen. Accordingly, Germany was entitled to treat the *Kyma* as an enemy merchantman. There was general agreement that enemy merchantmen can be destroyed if they cannot be conducted to port without compromising the safety of the capturing man-of-war and if, prior to destruction, all persons on board the merchantmen have been removed to a position of safety. The extract from the log showed that in view of the weather

[1] See on the meaning of the term "acts committed," *Annual Digest*, 1925-1926, Cases Nos. 291, 348.

Case No. 388 *contd.*

conditions and of her position the submarine could not bring the ship into port without compromising her safety. It also appeared that the crew of the vessel was put into lifeboats, and that no member of the crew was lost. [Report: *Recueil*, VIII, p. 345.]

D. AIR WARFARE

Case No. 389

Aerial Bombardment—Analogy with Land Bombardment—Article 26 of the Hague Regulations concerning the Laws and Customs of War on Land—Bombardment of Salonica by German Air Forces prior to the Entrance of Greece into War—Greek Territory as a Region of War—Military Operations against Occupied Neutral Territory.

COENCA BROTHERS *v.* GERMANY.

Greco-German Mixed Arbitral Tribunal. 1 *December*, 1927.

(ASSER, FROELICH, YOUPIS.)

THE FACTS.—This was a claim against Germany for compensation on account of damage suffered as the result of the bombardment of Salonica by German air forces in January, 1916, before Greece entered the war. In consequence of the bombardment certain stores of coffee belonging to the claimants were destroyed by fire. It was contended by the plaintiffs that as at the time of the occurrence Greece was not a belligerent, the bombardment constituted an "act committed" by Germany within the meaning of paragraph 4 of the Annex to Articles 297 and 298 of the Treaty of Versailles, and that in consequence Germany was responsible for the damage caused.

It was contended on behalf of Germany that as the result of the occupation of Salonica by Allied Powers that city had ceased to be neutral territory, and that according to the Hague Convention the bombardment of enemy positions was contemplated by the laws of war and was not contrary to international law. It appeared that the bombardment had been carried out during the night, from a height of about 3000 metres and without warning.

Held: That Germany was responsible.

(*a*) The expression "acts committed" used in Articles 297 and 298 of the Treaty of Versailles was—as was decided in the case of *Karmatzucas* v. *Germany*[1]—meant to refer to acts contrary to international law. The bombardment of Salonica, which was responsible for the damage caused to the plaintiffs, was contrary to international law, and the claim came therefore within the jurisdiction of the Mixed Arbitral Tribunal.

(*b*) In general, Germany was entitled to conduct military operations against neutral Greek territory occupied by Allied troops. The occupation of Salonica by the Allies in the autumn of 1915 constituted a violation of Greek neutrality. The question whether the Greek Government protested against the occupation or whether the occupation had taken place with its express or tacit consent was irrelevant. In any case the occupation constituted an unlawful act so far as Germany was concerned, and it justified the latter in conducting on Greek territory the necessary measures of warfare.

(*c*) However, the fact that Germany had the right to defend herself against the occupation of Greek territory by the Allies did not absolve her from the duty of observing the established rules of international law in the matter of bombardment. It was one of the generally recognised principles of international law that the belligerent ought to respect, so far as possible, the life and the property of the civilian population. Article 26 of the Hague Regulations Respecting the Laws and Customs of War on Land (Convention IV) provided that " the officer in " command of an attacking force must, before commencing a " bombardment, except in cases of assault, do all in his power " to warn the authorities." The intention of this Article was to enable the authorities of the town thus threatened either to evade bombardment by offering capitulation or to order the evacuation of the population. It was true that Article 26 envisaged only land bombardment. However, it was generally recognised that there was no reason why the rules as to land bombardment should not apply to bombardment from the air. The argument of the defendant State that bombardment from the air must necessarily be a surprise attack may be correct from the military point of view, but this does not imply that bombardment without warning ought to be permitted. On the contrary, the implication would be that such bombardment is generally inadmissible. In conse-

[1] See *Annual Digest*, 1925-1926, Case No. 291. For a confirmation of the interpretation of this term as applied in the case of *Karmatzucas* v. *Germany*, see the cases of *Angélique Franghiskou* v. *Germany*, *Recueil*, VIII, p. 815; *Sofia M. Harsoula* v. *Germany*, *ibid.*, p. 820; *Anastase F. Alexandrato* v. *Germany*, *ibid.*, p. 823; *Frères G. and N. Sumbassacu* v. *Germany*, *ibid.*, p. 825.

Case No. 389 contd.

quence, as the bombardment of Salonica, in the circumstances described, was contrary to international law, Germany was liable for the damage caused by the bombardment. [Report: *Recueil*, VII, p. 683.]

E. NEUTRALITY IN GENERAL

II.—Neutral and Military and Naval Operations and Preparations

Neutrality—Prohibition of Passage of Munitions—Claims of Private Individuals for Losses Caused by.

See Case No. 12 (*The Egyptian Government* v. *The British India S.S. Navigation Co.*)

Neutrality—Services to Belligerents—Unneutral Service—Neutral Vessels Chartered by Belligerent—Assimilation to Enemy Merchantmen.

See Case No. 388 (*D. P. and C. Marouli Brothers* v. *Germany*).

Occupation of Neutral Territory—Right of the Other Belligerent in respect of the Territory thus Occupied—Occupation of Salonica by the Allied Troops in 1915.

See Case No. 389 (*Coenca Brothers* v. *Germany*).

G. BLOCKADE

I.—Establishment of Blockade, Conditions of Validity

Blockade—Effectiveness—Closure of Ports—New Developments in Maritime Warfare.

See Case No. 361 (*The Oriental Navigation Company Case*).[1]

[1] A discussion of the above topics will be found in *Opinions of Commissioners*, 1929, p. 23.

INDEX

D

F

G

J

R

T